Advance Comments

❝ This multifaceted study richly details the complex interactions between urban economy, municipal finance, religious confessionalization, and the changing character of charity in a preindustrial German city. Emphasizing the dynamic linkages between nascent capitalism and public assistance, Thomas Safley shows how continuity in charitable purposes, premises, and practices both masked and molded important institutional innovation. Firmly grounded in archival sources and recent theorizations, *Charity and Economy in the Orphanages of Early Modern Augsburg* makes a signal contribution to debates about the 'Great Confinement' of the poor and the emergence of a new economic order. ❞

                  Robert S. DuPlessis, Professor of History, Swarthmore College

❝ Professor Safley's contribution presents a variety of astounding results. . . . This book is . . . more than a fresh contribution to the study of early modern charity and poor relief. It throws new light on the origins of capitalism, not actuated by abstract ideas or proceeded from entrepreneurial psychology but, rather, by a steady refinement of experience that originated in the application of appropriately motivated practices. ❞

                  Professor Wolfgang Weber, University of Augsburg

❝ In this wide-ranging, solidly documented, and closely argued book Safley makes a major contribution to our understanding of the economics of confessionalism. In selecting Augsburg for his study, he has chosen a city that was formally bi-confessional, with legally separate spheres for Catholic and Lutheran populations. And in selecting the administration of orphanages, he has chosen institutions that turn out to play an integral and exemplary role in the economy of this city. . . . All of this Safley demonstrates with an impressive mastery of the relevant archival resources and a considerable sophistication in the methods of economic analysis. His book provides enormous illumination to our understanding of the role of charity in early modern European society. ❞

                  Robert M. Kingdon, Hilldale Professor of History,
Institute for Research in the Humanities, University of Wisconsin–Madison

Charity and Economy in the Orphanages of Early Modern Augsburg

STUDIES IN CENTRAL EUROPEAN HISTORIES

GENERAL EDITORS

Thomas A. Brady Jr.
University of California, Berkeley

Roger Chickering
Georgetown University

BOARD OF EDITORS

Jan de Vries
University of California, Berkeley

Charles Ingrao
Purdue University

Susan Karant-Nunn
Portland State University

Jonathan Sperber
University of Missouri

H. C. Erik Midelfort
University of Virginia

Atina Grossmann
Columbia University

David Sabean
University of California, Los Angeles

Peter Hayes
Northwestern University

Charity and Economy in the Orphanages of Early Modern Augsburg

Thomas Max Safley

HUMANITIES PRESS, INC.
BOSTON

First published in 1997 by Humanities Press International, Inc.

©1997 by Thomas Max Safley

Library of Congress Cataloging-in-Publication Data
Safley, Thomas Max.
    Charity and economy in the orphanages of early modern Augsburg / Thomas Max Safley.
        p.   cm.—(Studies in Central European histories)
    Includes bibliographical references and index.
    ISBN 0-391-03983-0
    1. Orphanages—Economic aspects—German—Augsburg. 2. Poor—Services for—Germany—Augsburg—History. 3. Charities—Germany—Augsburg—History. I. Title. II. Series.
HV1180.A95S24 1996
362.7'32'0943375—dc20   96–3380
                                          CIP

All rights reserved. No part of this publication may be reproduced or transmitted, in any form or by any means, without written permission.

Printed in the United States of America

Humanities Press, Inc. is a subsidiary of Brill Academic Publishers—Boston, Leiden, Cologne.

Humanities Press, Inc.
112 Water Street
Suite 400
Boston, MA 02109
U.S.A

Contents

	List of Illustrations	vi
	Note on Money	viii
	Preface	x
	Introduction: The Orphanages of Early Modern Augsburg and the Limits of Theory	1
1.	A Brief History of Poverty and Charity in Late Medieval and Early Modern Augsburg	19
2.	Capitalistic Practices and Pre-Capitalistic Organizations: Land, Calculation, and Administration in the Orphanages	58
3.	Subventions, Donations, and Earnings: Paying for Poor Relief	79
4.	Charity and Capital in the Orphanages	113
5.	Provisioning Augsburg: Buying and Selling Commodities in an Early Modern City	151
6.	Charity and Consumption in the Orphanages	178
7.	Labor and Industry	209
8.	Welfare and Work in the Orphanages	243
	Conclusion: Toward a New Organizational History	279
	Appendix I: Figures of Receipts, Expenditures and Consumption	291
	Appendix II: Documents from the Orphanages	313
	Bibliography	318
	Index	341

List of Illustrations

Maps

1. Central European Political Boundaries circa 1648   18
2. Trade Routes around Augsburg circa 1600   21
3. Early Modern Augsburg   24

Illustrations

1. Münster Sketch of 1550   4
2. Seld Plan of 1521   22
3. Killian Plan of 1626   25
4. Orphanage Meadow circa 1750   70

Tables

2.1 Land-Related Expenses of the City Orphanage, 1575–90   67
2.2 Land-Related Income of the City Orphanage, 1575–90   68
3.1 Index of Fiscal Disparities between Orphanages, 1704–21   91
3.2 Operating Resources of Augsburg's Orphanages   98
4.1 Debts Payable to the Alms Office   125
4.2 Capital of the Catholic Orphanage, 1784–87   130
5.1 Cash and Commodities Distributed by the Alms Office   164
5.2 Average Price per Schaff of Rye   167
5.3 Average Price per Pfund of Lard   169

List of Illustrations

6.1	Approximate Calculation of What an Orphanage, in Which 200 Children Might be Supported, Might Cost Yearly	181
6.2	Comparison of Expenses for Private and Public Households	193
7.1	Guild Masters in the Artisanal Economy of Augsburg	225
7.2	Master Craftsmen in the Clothing Trade of Augsburg	232
7.3	Orphan Apprentices in the Clothing Trade of Augsburg	233
7.4	Orphan Apprentices in the Artisanal Economy of Augsburg	234
7.5	Fates of Augsburg's Orphans	235
8.1	Persistent Reliance of Orphans on Orphanages	260
8.2	Types of Assistance Requested by Out-Placed Orphans	261

Note on Money

Money is no simple matter in early modern Augsburg. As might be expected in an important manufacturing and mercantile center, coins of many realms circulated. The Imperial *Taler*, Bohemian *Groschen*, and Munich *Schilling* are probably the best, most frequently encountered, but by no means the only, examples. Moreover, periodic minting reforms in Augsburg itself introduced new coins and altered established equivalencies. During the fifteenth century, the city relied on the *Pfund, Schilling, Pfennig*, and *Heller*, in which the pfund contained 20 schilling, 60 pfennigen, or 120 heller.[1] In 1539, the pfund disappeared from accounts—though not from circulation—to be replaced by *Gulden, Kreutzer, Pfennig*. Augsburg refined its coinage once again, in 1546, replacing the pfennig with the heller. The gulden, kreutzer, and heller were the most frequently used coins of account and exchange from the founding of Augsburg's orphanage in 1572 to the city's loss of independence in 1806.

In nearly all accounts rendered by the orphanages and Alms Office, sums of money were recorded in gulden, abbreviated "fl." Its commonly coined subdivisions, again taken from accounts and receipts, were the kreutzer, abbreviated "kr.," and the heller, abbreviated "hl." Yet, donors and orphans brought a variety of capital in a variety of forms, all of which had to be specifically recorded in accounts. The following equivalencies apply as a general rule:

1 gulden (fl.) = 60 kreutzer (kr.) = 420 heller (hl.)
1 kreutzer = 7 heller
1 gulden = 15 batzen = 60 kreutzer
1 batzen = 4 kreutzer
1 gulden = 60 kreutzer = 210 pfennigen
1 kreutzer = 3.5 pfennigen
1 gulden = 30 schilling (ß) = 360 heller
1 schilling = 12 heller.

Some exceptions deserve particular notice. During the inflation years of 1621 and 1622, Augsburg minted small coins, the so-called *Kippermünzen*, of 30, 15, and 6 kreutzer. Because no accounts survive from that catastrophic period, neither these coins nor the inflation to which they contributed affect the analysis. At some point in the late seventeenth century, Augsburg devalued its pfennig from 3.5 to 4 in the kreutzer, raising the content of the gulden from 210 to 240 pfennigen. This alteration, too, seems to have had little effect on orphanage accounting, which continued to record values according to the old equivalencies.

Unless noted, all money values have been rendered in gulden and kreutzer just as the orphanages' monthly and annual accounts were kept. For the reader's ease, these are usually rounded to the nearest gulden in the text.

Note

1. Elsas, Umris, 118.

Preface

This economic history of Augsburg's orphanages is actually a book within a book within a book. My original and enduring scholarly interest is the political economy of early modern urban families, their various transactions in the marketplace and over the lifecycle, and the underlying material strategies that guided them. Examining these strategies yields insights into their values concerning work, property, and wealth. Yet, transactions, strategies, and values vary between the strata of society, and the archives of Europe do not preserve equally the experience of all early modern people. Only the broad middle strata, comprising families from the status of common artisan to that of elite merchant, come regularly to the fore. The extremes must be sought elsewhere, in the private papers of patrician and aristocratic dynasties and in the communal records of criminality and charity. Attempts to reconstruct the histories of humble families—their transactions, their strategies, their values—led to the orphanages of Augsburg.

Thus, an organizational history of poor relief takes its place in an extended economic, social, and cultural study of family life, a single project in four parts. A comparison of the domestic economies of urban families from eight free imperial cities in the region of Swabia in southern Germany will eventually reveal the economic activities of these groups but fail to account adequately for the richest and the poorest, families that respectively shaped those societies and economies and were victimized by them. A close study of the estates and businesses of the Hörmann von und zu Gutenberg, factors in the Fugger enterprises and landed aristocrats in their own right, will remedy the one failing; a study of south German linen weavers caught in the toils of deindustrialization and *Children at the Edge: Expectation and Experience among the Orphans of Early Modern Augsburg*, a prosopography of Augsburg orphans and their families, will redress the other.

As I began to study the orphanages and their dependents, however, it soon became clear that the material experiences and expectations of those needy folk had been altered radically by exposure to the organization. A political economy of poor, marginal, or truncated families would make little sense without an exact understanding of the orphanages, their function and their effects. Furthermore, the orphanages were organized along the lines of domestic units, large communal households whose economic activities and transactions could provide an interesting benchmark for those of private families. An attempt to reconcile the apparently contradictory notions of charity and capital, therefore, grew logically out of my continuing studies of domestic economies in German cities and of poor families in Augsburg. Taken together, the present volume and its forthcoming companion, *Children at the Edge*, form a single part of the envisioned quartet of studies on the history of the family.

In the course of shaping this series of projects, I have incurred a larger than usual number of debts to the organizations that have supported my work and to the colleagues who have shaped my understanding. The enterprise began when I was appointed the Byron K. Trippet Assistant Professor of History at Wabash College. That chair provided travel and research funds for two summers, during which I explored archives across Germany, looking for collections that might serve my interests. Professor Paul McKinney was the Dean of the College at that time, and I thank him for his steadfast support at an early but critical stage. Also, my colleagues in the History Department, Professors James Barnes, George Davis, and Peter Fredericks, offered constant encouragement, even when it took me away from the college and the classroom. Most of the archival research for these studies, including the one that follows, was done during a two-year period as a fellow of the Alexander von Humboldt Foundation. The administrators of that organization may never know—but the fellows past and present will immediately recognize—the extraordinary debt I owe them. While in Germany, I was fortunate to have as my sponsor Professor Wolfgang Reinhard. He and his assistants and students at the University of Augsburg took a lively interest in my work, encouraging it at every step and guiding it with their profound knowledge of early modern Augsburg. The staffs of that city's Stadtarchiv, Staatsarchiv, and Stadt- und Staatsbibliothek facilitated my researches by locating obscure materials, correcting many errors, and generally introducing a neophyte to the fascination of Augsburg's history. Particularly deserving of mention are Professor Wolfram Baer and Dr. Wolfgang Wüst of the Stadtarchiv, whose intimate knowledge of the city and its archives helped me to find the orphanages and their orphans in the first place. Professors Rolf Kießling of the University of Augsburg and Paul Münch of the University of Essen became good friends during my stay; the superb economic and institutional histories of late medieval Swabia and Augsburg by the former and the profound reflections on the development of early modern culture and bourgeois values by the latter inspired my thinking and humbled my aspirations. When I returned to the United States and a new position at the University of Pennsylvania, I again found a circle of colleagues who took an active interest in the work. Professors Thomas Childers, James Davis, Lynn Hunt, Michael Katz, Alan Kors, Lynn Lees, Walter Licht,

Edward Peters, Maureen Quilligan, and Peter Stallybrass listened to my ideas or read portions of my text and vastly improved the content of both with comments and criticisms that were unsparingly honest and unfailingly sympathetic. The graduate students of the departments of History, Religious Studies, and English were no less acute and collegial as an audience for ideas even at the earliest stages of development. As this book neared completion, the University of Pennsylvania Research Foundation came to my assistance with funds to return to the archives and libraries of Augsburg and search out the answers to a few final questions.

A number of colleagues read the entire manuscript and improved it with many observations and suggestions. Professors Christopher Johnson of Wayne State University, Susan C. Karant-Nunn of Portland State University, Robert Kingdon of the University of Wisconsin at Madison, and Philip Kintner of Grinnell College contributed greatly to the completion of the project.

Mr. Earnest A. Tremblay, II, also gave the manuscript a most thorough reading. An accomplished author and editor in his own right, he very unselfishly shared his knowledge and sense of style with me and made the text far more readable than I ever could.

Several maps were created especially for this book. My thanks to Mr. Eric Olsen, who designed them, to Ms. Jamie Powell, Ms. Mindy Richens, and Mr. Tom Anderson, who prepared the cartographic data, and to Ms. Christy Calvin, who composed the data on computer.

Particular thanks are due Professors Thomas A. Brady, Jr., of the University of California at Berkeley and Roger Chickering of Georgetown University, the editors of the series, Studies in Central European Histories, of Humanities Press. They proved to be masters of their craft, encouraging and challenging me with their own vision of what this book could and should become.

Of all the many friends who have had a hand in this project, Professor Leonard N. Rosenband of Utah State University must be remembered last and above all. He alone followed this project from the very beginning, listened to my first dawning ideas, read and reread every part of the text, stimulated the slowly emerging vision, and never doubted the importance of the work. My gratitude to him surpasses my ability to express it; he knows the part he played and the debt I owe him.

The only people more steadfast and long suffering were my own family. Michele, Rebecca, and Michael inspire my interest and my stake in the history of the family. To them and all who contributed along the way I offer my deepest thanks. Theirs in large measure is the credit for any virtues this book may have. I remain only too aware of my responsibility for its vices.

My father, Max West Safley, did not live to see the completion of this book, though he, unlike his son, never doubted it would one day appear. His passing gave me some sense of the desolation that must have been the lot of Augsburg's orphans and, so, deepened my interest in them and in the house that sheltered them. Ever alert to the big picture or grand theory, he reserved a special fascination during his life for the way things really worked and the effects they actually had. Something of him is in the pages that follow; they are dedicated to his memory.

Havertown, Pennsylvania

Introduction: The Orphanages of Early Modern Augsburg and the Limits of Theory

On 2 October 1572 the City Council of the Free Imperial City of Augsburg decreed the founding of a City Orphanage, one of the earliest in Europe and the first in Germany.[1] It happened in the midst of disaster but without fanfare. In the dry language of officialdom, too many poor people burdened the city with the support of their children.[2] A poet captured the tragedy of that time.

> Many were driven from the city,
> Leaving wife and child in necessity.
> Time and again they set aside
> All their commerce and their trade.[3]

In some 70 pages of verse he described the speculation and exploitation, the unemployment and homelessness, the hunger and disease, and the hopelessness and desperation that accompanied one of the worst periods of catastrophic inflation in Augsburg's history, 1571–72.[4] Unable to find work to earn a living or even to afford the necessities when they did, many parents abandoned their children and fled the city. Some probably acted with complete disregard for the young they left behind; others must have hoped to find sustenance of some sort and either return to or send for their families eventually; but all trusted their neighbors and the city to assume the burden of care in the interim.

By 1572, the number of orphaned or abandoned children had spiralled to ruinous levels. Authorities had responded by placing 280 of them in 164 foster homes; the annual cost to the city stood at approximately 3,680 fl.[5] The number of children still living on the streets could not be estimated, but the magistrates in charge of poor relief admitted that it grew every day. To control the expenses associated with the care of these orphans, the city fathers proposed the creation of a central orphanage that would house needy children under a single roof, draw income from a number of public and private sources, and spend it in the city's marketplaces to purchase necessary goods and services. Such an orphanage would support 200 young people at a cost to Augsburg of 3,237 fl. annually, a slight increase in the expenditure per orphan—from 13.14 fl. to 13.18 fl.—that promised a couple of important advantages.[6] It would prevent the misuse of funds, thought to be common among households that took in foster children to supplement their incomes. It would also systematize the rearing of orphans, believed to be too often abused, exploited, or ignored by mercenary guardians. Convinced by this argument from efficiency, the City Council ordered that an suitable dwelling be purchased and readied for the purpose.

The council authorized a payment of 4,000 fl. to the Alms Office (*Almosenamt*) for the purchase of a house and garden in a side street near the Imperial Abbey, Sts. Ulrich and Afra, in the vicinity of the city's south gate.[7] The council also approved the solicitation of donations to furnish the building and provide for its inhabitants. From Augsburg's congregations and citizens came 3,319 fl. in cash and an untold amount in used furniture, clothing, and housewares. This was the orphanage's initial capital, but it was by no means all. The Alms Office provided for the maintenance and sustenance of the orphanage from its annual budget, money acquired from a complex of sources that included indirect taxes, private donations, and communal subsidies. Yet, the orphanage did not rely solely on state revenues for its income, a fact that would enable it to avoid the pessimism, dependence, and conservatism that limited so many centralized welfare organizations in the early modern period.[8] Augsburg's elite continued to donate capital, forming an endowment that paid interest throughout the institution's history. The orphans themselves contributed, too, by transferring to the orphanage any property they might have inherited before or received during their residency. In consequence, Augsburg's orphanage commanded considerable independent resources, cobbled together from public and private sources.

These the orphanage administered with little interference, a practice that continued even after the City Orphanage was divided into two confessionally specific orphanages in 1649. Tension between Catholics and Protestants as well as the institution of parity to regulate it affected competition for resources and aspects of management but not this essential independence. Despite the fact that the orphan father (*Waisenvater*) was hired and fired by the alms lords (*Almosenherren*) and was bound to observe their direction while in office, making regular reports and rendering monthly and annual accounts, he was lord and master within the walls of the orphanage. Its domestic economy was his responsibility; daily disbursements and daily operations were in his hands. It was a considerable responsibility. In a projection of costs, drawn up by Alms Lord Johannes Stöcklin in 1572, over 70 percent of the 3,237 fl. needed each year to run an orphanage would be spent on foodstuffs, especially grains.[9] A further 13 percent would be devoted to clothing and linens, and 7 percent would be absorbed by labor costs. Not mentioned in Stöcklin's hypothetical budget were expenses associated with apprenticeship fees and other forms of extramural training and education that would also burden real accounts. Most important, the orphan father would purchase or contract all the necessities of this material and moral regime in the marketplaces of Augsburg. The organization he administered became one of the largest consumers in the city.

THE UNIQUE CASE OF AUGSBURG

The decision to organize an orphanage occurred in response to increasing demands on resources and should be understood as an attempt to make poor relief more efficient, that is, to minimize its costs by limiting it to specific persons and using it for specific purposes. However straightforward the decision, its consequences provoke a number of questions about the changing nature of charity in the early modern period and its historical interpretation. Taking their lead from Hans Scherpner, Robert Jütte and others have described the general pattern of poor relief from the sixteenth century onward in terms of a number of broad processes: the centralization of financial resources in a community chest; the communalization of poor relief administration in the hands of civic magistrates; the registration and examination of the poor by competent officials; and the displacement of begging by a work ethic.[10] As useful as these concepts may be, they are not adequate to the more complex history of the Augsburg orphanage.

The replacement in 1572 of a system of fostering in private households with a "total institution," that is, an enclosed establishment that offers its residents a complete environment separate from society, at the initiative and under the direction of the state, seems to correspond to scholarly notions of centralization and communalization.[11] The correspondence, however, is superficial and problematic. While it drew some support from the city's treasury and occupied a specific place in the city's administration, Augsburg's orphanage depended totally on neither.

The founding of an orphanage had nothing to do with the secularization and transfer of ecclesiastical properties and foundations, an epiphenomenon of the Reformation that never occurred in biconfessional Augsburg. Its resources had to be garnered over time from a multitude of subsidies, donations, and transfers. This and the coexistence of substantial Catholic and Protestant communities, both laying exclusive claim to the largesse of their own members and demanding equal access to state funds, created a uniquely competitive situation. What emerged in fact was a capitalistic organization, possessing its own fixed and working capital, maneuvering to expand income and limit costs, delivering an essential service, and relying on local markets and marketplaces.[12]

That the orphan father was subject to the alms lords and, thus, the City Council must not be confused with a genuine communalization of function

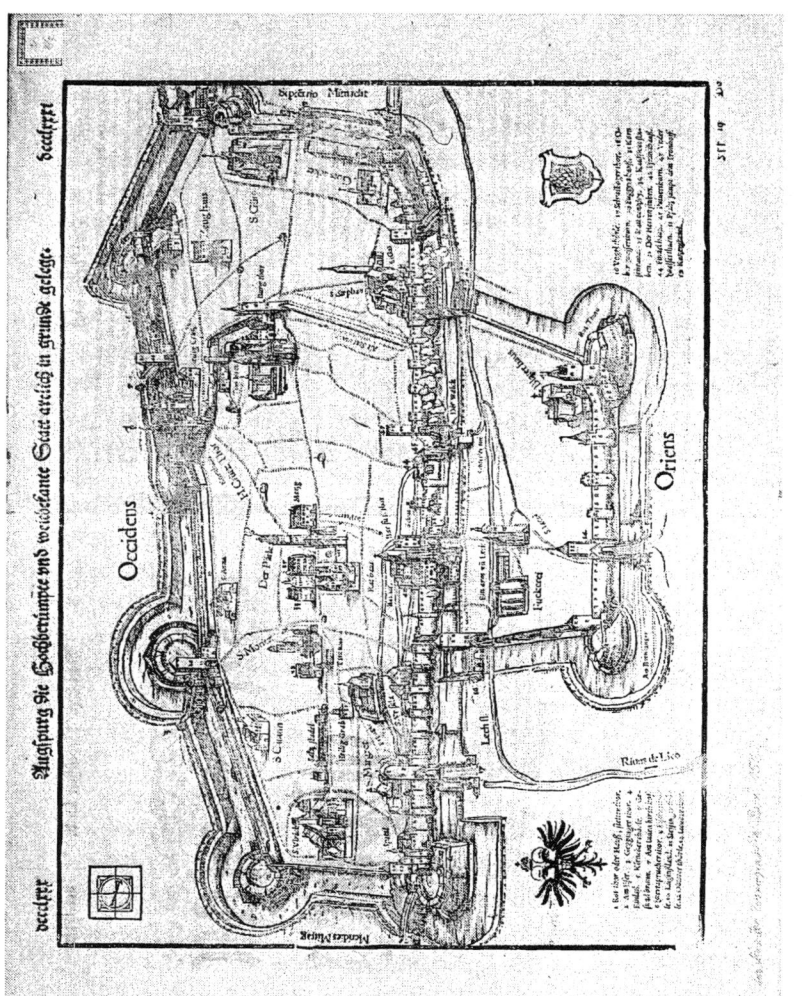

ILLUSTRATION 1 Sketch of Augsburg from the east, limited to principal landmarks, from the Cosmographia of Sebastian Münster, 1550. Courtesy of the Stadtarchiv Augsburg, Plansammlung 0742.

in the hands of state authorities. Unlike his superiors, no orphan father was ever a member of the urban patriciate or rose to higher office within the magistracy. Drawn from the broad strata of petty professionals, local merchants, and artisanal masters, he certainly depended upon the approval of the city fathers but, surprisingly, was independent within his office. Once appointed the orphan father was not easily dismissed, and the oversight and regulation of the alms lords were imperfect at best. Indeed, the relationship between the Alms Office and the orphanages of Augsburg until the early nineteenth century is best characterized by the constant efforts of the former to control and curtail the activities of the latter. In many respects, the orphan father was an independent agent and the orphanage an independent organization.

Augsburg had required the examination, visitation, and registration of its poor since 1541, well before the founding of its orphanage. To receive alms had ceased to be a universal prerogative of all the needy and had become a privilege awarded only to certain individuals. Magistrates tried to direct assistance to those they distinguished as most deserving and to adjust the amount and type of relief according to individual needs.[13] They examined the backgrounds of many needy children but registered and admitted only a few to the orphanage.[14] Augsburg's "orphanage" was for the exclusive benefit of Augsburg's "orphans." The term applied to father- and motherless children, a formula readily familiar but possessing a deeper meaning. Apparently many abandoned or neglected children were described as orphans despite the fact that either or both of their parents were living. The new orphanage sought with increasing determination to exclude these and others from its shelter. Abandoned or neglected children were returned to parents or relatives whenever possible. Infants and invalids were transferred to the Foundling Home or the *Pilgerhaus* (Augsburg's hospice for the chronically diseased or disabled) respectively because these institutions were dedicated to their care. The offspring of foreigners and noncitizens had no claim on the city's generosity and were banished from Augsburg altogether.

The orphan father determined who would enjoy the shelter of the orphanage, but this minor functionary was subject to a number of pressures. The limited resources at his disposal and his responsibility for their proper use must have encouraged him to exclude every orphan whose title to admission was the least questionable. Real human suffering, however, seldom fell on deaf ears; the orphanages sheltered many neglected or abandoned young people regardless of the parents' status. Moreover, the alms lords could overrule his decisions, and the influence of patrician patrons opened doors for any number of needy, but not necessarily orphaned, children. Examination, therefore, hardly expresses the reality of access to early modern poor relief.

To register and examine the poor signalled the intention of magistrates to differentiate among them and offer assistance based on individual circumstances. Nevertheless, individualization and differentiation violate the principle of a centralized system or a central organization, especially those omni-competent hospitals, asylums, and workhouses that appeared in the seventeenth century. They applied with greater force and accuracy to specialized establishments, but even in such cases the fit was imperfect. The efficacy and efficiency of Augsburg's orphanages rested on a high degree of regimentation and uniformity, practices that suppressed the individual in favor of the group and were spelled out in great detail early in the its history.[15] Although orphans received a degree of individualized treatment—personal records were carefully kept, work was assigned on the basis of individual capacities, and boys could choose a craft or trade according to their own preferences and abilities—daily routine and regulation stressed conformity and subservience. The tension between individuality and uniformity, between the orphan as a specific person to be nurtured and trained and the poor as an undifferentiated mass to be controlled and disciplined, remained unresolved throughout the early history of Augsburg's orphanages and contributed to their particular character.

Group indoctrination and routinization characterized much of the attempt to displace begging with a work imperative. The orphanage's purpose was not only to care for certain needy children but also and above all to "teach them the fear of God as well as work and other virtues."[16] Once in the orphanage they were accustomed to a life of labor, that is, they engaged in directed, productive activities throughout the day and were raised in such values of discipline, obedience, and industry as encouraged work.

This simple observation begs the question of a mechanism. It remains far from clear how any organization translated social ideals into economic realities. How, for example, did Augsburg's City Orphanage mediate the requirements of preindustrial artisanal production and the restrictions of guild regulation—the need for a labor surplus and the concomitant mandate for a labor shortage—to place needy people in the city's labor force?[17] Because they were raised in an orphanage, orphans absorbed a work discipline abstracted from its social setting. That is to say, they learned to labor without exposure to the social relations of production. Although the orphanage later placed these children in artisanal workshops, where they were taught much more than work techniques, it offered initial training that inclined orphans to view themselves as laborers rather than artisans and to view their labor power as a commodity rather than a craft. This may have had implications for the emergence of labor not as a social but rather as an economic and, therefore, marketable factor of production.[18] In an age of well-documented friction between journeymen and masters as well as between urban masters and rural craftsmen, there was a steady demand for disciplined, obedient, and industrious hands. Yet, in a age when guild restrictions on the employment of foreign, unqualified, or dishonorable individuals became more extreme, Augsburg's masters were not open to admitting into their ranks people whose resources were limited and whose antecedents were questionable. A new work ethic, which many historians have posited, is far removed from creating a new workforce. The connection between elite perceptions and common experience is found in the quotidian efforts of institutions like the orphanages to discipline the needy and put them to work.

THE PERSPECTIVE OF HISTORY AND THE LIMITS OF THEORY

The creation of a central orphanage suggests a growing preference for institutionalized care that finds its historiographic place in Gerhard Oestreich's theory of social discipline (*Sozialdisziplinierung*) and Michel Foucault's image of a great enclosure (*grande renfermement*).[19] But these models imply a desperate, crisis-driven break with the past and a marginalization of the needy that Augsburg's orphanage did not share in 1572. Rather, the orphanage demonstrated notable continuity with civic traditions, especially with the ecclesiastical and private institutions that served as its models.[20] It also followed a more integrative approach toward the poor, one that exercised a genuine concern for people in need and emphasized self-sufficiency through work.[21] Sweeping metaphors, such as communalization and centralization or social discipline and great enclosure, may characterize the general process and intention of early modern poor relief, but they fail to capture the mundane choices and transactions that amounted to their realization.

Most traditional scholarship has taken the intention of charity as its subject, by relying on a broad array of prescriptive literature. Some of the earliest examples focused on decree, legislation, and regulation, especially the alms ordinances (*Almosenordnungen*) themselves, to capture the changing structure of charity and its political and social purposes.[22] The results described first efforts at poor relief as the product of magisterial ambitions and concerns, as attempts to extend the purview and power of the state and to police the extreme effects of poverty.

Other studies have built upon this literature, placing regulation in the context of a larger intellectual history.[23] By probing the treatises of religious and social reformers, these works associated the transformation of charity with the ebb and flow of intellectual currents, especially the changing value ascribed to good works as tangible evidence of Christian love. The reform of charity coincided to a certain degree with the reformation of religion. In their pursuit of an ideal Christian community, Protestants and some Catholics saw the relief of poverty as both a duty and a necessity that could not be left to the chance of private largesse.[24]

While taking their cue from theologians and moralists, recent champions of this traditional perspective have abandoned ideas in favor of values. In the process, the poor have become a symbol and charity has been reduced to ritual.[25] It cannot be denied that a substantial symbolic element persisted in charity and, indeed, in much of urban life into the eighteenth century. In the eyes of many Protestants and Catholics the poor remained emblematic of Christ and his call for Christian love, and charity took advantage of this association to quicken the generosity of benefactors. But what of it?

The conclusion many intellectual and cultural historians have drawn casts the entire issue in benign, otherworldly terms. Charity was an act at once transcendental and self-annihilating because it neither derived from any calculation of personal need or desire nor enhanced available material resources or advantages; poverty was an essential component of early modern society precisely because it created opportunities for ceremonial acts of solidarity.

Charity may, indeed, have been one of the sinews binding early modern society against the centrifugal forces of scarcity and inequity. This conclusion ignores, however, a darker, less altruistic, but no less actual function. The rich gave alms for complex reasons, not least among which were the necessities of maintaining dependence and enforcing deference. Lacking the armed force daily to coerce the masses of needy people who swept along public streets and lodged in private doorways, Augsburg's merchants and patricians turned to more subtle means of deflecting their hostility. Like mercy in the theater of law, charity disguised a rigid social hierarchy with a mask of paternal solidarity.[26] More disturbing than the over-simplification of the motives behind charity, however, are the implications of an argument that posits the necessity of poverty as a source of community. Simply put, it legitimizes a positive social evil as a putative social good. The daily transactions of Augsburg's orphanage contradict such romantic notions of need and assistance in bygone times and distant places. Charity was both selfish and selfless: poverty was not to be prolonged with the aid of alms but rather to be rooted out with the spade of self-sufficiency.

Recent scholarship has devoted more attention to social institutions in their social contexts. According to these interpretations, the changing face of poor relief reflected the changing face of early modern European society. Chronic price inflation accompanied by declining real income caused widespread impoverishment during the sixteenth century. Periodic crop failures, as in 1570–72, promoted economic, social, and political instability through dearth and disease. Frequent warfare and banditry deprived people of their livelihoods if not their lives. Degenerating social conditions bred a marginal, immiserated subpopulation. Confronting this crisis with insufficient resources, states sought to limit the extent of poor relief both by discriminating more effectively between the deserving and undeserving and by disciplining the needy in order to promote their eventual self-sufficiency. Most modern social histories recognize an explicit desire to reform the mode of assistance in such a way that the poor would cease to burden their betters.[27] They are equally unanimous that these efforts at reform failed either to relieve suffering or to reduce costs. Few of them, however, agree on the reasons why.

Like intellectual and cultural histories of poverty and poor relief, these studies fall into a number of rough and ready categories. One set of studies—what might be called an Anglo-American school, working primarily on France and England—concludes that the sheer magnitude of the problem overwhelmed all attempts at assistance.[28] Another group of scholars, mostly French working on France, portrays poverty as the product of profound, largely unchanging, metahistorical forces—population, lifecycle, climate, communication, hierarchy—all of which contributed to its ubiquity in the Old Regime. Under these circumstance, poor relief was not so much defeated as doomed, a futile gesture toward an insurmountable problem.[29] Central European studies, especially those devoted to the problem in the city-states of the Holy Roman Empire and the Italian peninsula, eschew crisis and collapse altogether. They adopt instead tradition and continuity as their leitmotives.[30] Regardless of social or political pressures, poor relief developed within parameters set by the larger institutional histories of the communities in which it occurred. Judging by the scant attention paid to the consequences of this development, they are either understood or uninteresting.

Nonetheless, it is the consequences of the founding of Augsburg's orphanage in 1572 that set it apart. The Catholic and Lutheran orphanages that replaced the City Orphanage in 1649 persist as central organizations to the present. The institution of parity transformed the distribution of power and resources in Augsburg and forced both confessionally distinct orphanages to contend with new material realities. Far from collapsing for lack of resources, however, they developed the ways and means to shelter thousands of orphans, the majority of whom lived to adulthood and reentered society. Though modeled upon traditional charitable and religious foundations, they operated in ways that enabled them to survive and ultimately to succeed. The received social history of charity has made poor relief a vector of inhuman forces. While there is some truth in this perspective, it fails to explain satisfactorily the historical process of change. Not only the social context of Augsburg's orphanages but also the accumulation of practical knowledge determined their history.[31] In other words, the development, transmission, and preservation of managerial experience in the city's markets by alms lords and orphan fathers shaped the city's orphanages over time.

What has recently been described as "a hard core of theorists still under the spell of Marx and Foucault" also concentrates on a larger context, although in this case poor relief becomes a means by which "the rich tranquillize the poor."[32] Marxist studies interpret poverty as a consequence of the social relations of production that elites wish to preserve and control rather than ameliorate or eradicate. Capitalist enterprises require state-sponsored support in order to police a reserve of labor and maintain its availability at the lowest possible price.[33] Rather than relieve poverty, assistance renders the lower strata of society dependent by shaping their activities in conformity with the established requirements of the economy and by curbing their aspirations in opposition to it. The total institutions that emerged in the seventeenth century seem ideally suited to these disciplinary ambitions.[34] Workhouses, prisons, and hospitals placed the marginal in a minutely scrutinized regime based on industry and regularity, authority and obedience, in order to encourage economic dependence and social deference. Regardless of the form that it took, however, charity articulated the power of the elite by coercing and oppressing the poor.

Neither the orphanages of Augsburg nor any other such organization ever foreswore regimentation and routine as the best long-term responses to the problems posed by poverty. And all of these methods retained a degree of coercion, the fact that some poor people consented to them notwithstanding. Yet, this focus on political objectives, motivated by the emergence of capitalism and expressed in a movement to immurement, has obscured or obviated the historical reality. Given that charity in every age served to maintain the social order and promote the interests of a social elite, the methods by which, and thus the more exact ends toward which, it operated still remained open to question. Augsburg's orphanages did not create an industrial proletariat. They did, however, help to educate, train, and discipline an artisanal workforce and place it in the city's preindustrial labor market.

The several differences that distinguish schools of recent historiography on poverty and poor relief are less remarkable than the single characteristic that unites them: they examine motive rather than behavior and have yet to analyze how poor relief actually operated in early modern Europe. They have refused to test empirically the grand hypotheses, based on the expressed intentions of elites, that have informed their explorations for the past thirty years. Content with a limited description of charitable finance and administration, most histories continue to rely on prescriptive literature, quickened by a series of anecdotes, to yield an inert image of the past. Charity as a dynamic enterprise, relying on daily economic practice to create by process of accretion a body of capitalist expertise, constantly adjusting to changing circumstances and so becoming a force for change itself, remains an uncharted country. The orphanages of Augsburg provide an opportunity for a broad revision.

CHARITY AND CAPITAL IN THE ORPHANAGES

The history of charity in Augsburg presupposes the dominance of capital and the presence of capitalism from the fifteenth century. These terms must be defined for the purposes of this study and applied to the specific case of Augsburg's orphanages.

Capital is most precisely understood as money or goods used to set in motion the process of generating further capital for the purpose of private gain.[35] Augsburg's orphanages were not capitalist in the strict sense. Not engaged in exchange or production for profit, they nonetheless relied on the stimulative power of capital in financial matters. Donations from their benefactors, subventions from the state, and interest from their endowments provided income to maintain operations. Administrators worried openly that waste or scandal might alienate donors, increase the burden upon the state, and ultimately reduce available resources. Capital formation relied on the degree to which the orphanages were perceived to be meeting their stated objective of caring adequately for the city's orphans at the least possible cost. In this context, capital was understood to be self-perpetuating so long as its purpose remained efficiently charitable. This was charity with a catch. The complex link between it and capital is a focus of this study.

The emphasis on a process of generation suggests that practices and values are fundamental to the definition of capitalism. Capitalistic practices are simply those procedures, whatever they may be, required to operate successfully in a market-driven economy. They might be reduced to two simple principles: maximize resources and minimize risks of any sort. The orphanages drew their administrators from the ranks of Augsburg's merchant capitalists. These men consistently attempted to expand the capital and maintain the status of their organizations through managerial practices, such as accounting, budgeting, supervising, and contracting, that were born of their experience in the marketplace. They understood their assets in the markets and at play in the markets, and they used this liquid capital not to build an estate but to regenerate itself. Capitalistic values, above all a utilitarian approach to the maximization of resources, rationalized those market-oriented procedures. The capitalism that these organizations reflect is, therefore, not rooted in a particular mode of production.[36] It existed before the advent of the factory and mechanization. Capitalism is not triggered by the simple existence of markets.[37] Markets are necessary but not sufficient; many transactions are simple exchanges that do not involve capital formation. Capitalism is not actuated by abstract ideas.[38] Abstraction does not precede but follows the systematic application of procedures. Capitalism does not proceed from the psychology of the entrepreneur.[39] Neither risk-aversity nor risk-avidity adequately characterizes the capitalist mentality. Rather, capitalism is defined according to appropriately motivated practices that are themselves products of a steady refinement of experience.

Empiricism characterized the capitalism of early modern Augsburg and of Augsburg's orphanages. Capitalistic practices and values were learned through experience in the marketplace and transmitted through the tutelage of practitioners. This applied to orphan fathers and alms lords no less than merchants and masters. Although theoretical discussions were not unknown at the time—handbooks and commentaries were available—they had as yet little bearing on the practice of day-to-day fiscal management.

The systematic application of capitalistic practices, however, does not demonstrate the existence of capitalism. Capitalistic attitudes, objectives, and methods were present in early modern Augsburg. They were discussed in the writings of scholastic and legal commentators on political economy; they were revealed by the behavior of merchant capitalists.[40] They were also found in non-capitalistic organizations, like the orphanages. But Augsburg's orphanages, like Augsburg's society, were not capitalist. Organizations cannot be understood apart from their environments.[41] The political, social, and economic institutions that support the domination of capital, such as property rights or social mobility, were either absent or nascent in early modern German society. What follows is a study in their emergence.

In order to care for the city's needy children in an age when the demands on poor relief consistently outran the resources available to meet them, Augsburg's orphanages acted in capitalistic ways. The administrators calculated and innovated in order to marshall resources. They systematically planned the acquisition of goods and services, carefully reckoned the relative cost and benefit of particular transactions, and constantly tinkered with the structure and function of supposedly traditional communal institutions. The houses entered and affected local markets: the market for capital, where they derived part of their income; the market for commodities, where they acquired the necessities of life; and the market for labor, where they placed self-sufficient workers. In doing so, they transmitted capitalistic practices and values to an emergent market society.

The organization of this study follows these activities self-consciously. The orphan fathers were aware of their manipulation of capital, goods, and labor as discrete activities within a single enterprise. They frequently listed circulating capital, purchased goods, and labor costs as separate sections of their monthly and yearly accounts. That organizing principle has been adopted here, with chapters 3 and 4 devoted to capital, chapters 5 and 6 to commodities, and chapters 7 and 8 to labor. This tripartite structure does more than slavishly reflect the style and substance of early modern management. It captures a particular vision of the orphanages as economic units and economic agents, simultaneously subject to the constraints and opportunities of a larger system of exchange and sovereign in their capacities to forge the system's "rules of play."[42] It also permits examination of institutions as a hitherto unappreciated vehicles of social and economic change.

CONCLUSION

What follows, therefore, is an organizational history in a new key. It is an examination of state rather than social discipline. However desirable a population submissive to the ruler's will, the end of the discipline portrayed here was a state apparatus sensitive to the dictates of the market. It is a study of the actual relief of poverty, of piecemeal empirical choices rather than sweeping heuristic metaphors. Capitalistic practices slowly shaped Augsburg's orphanages, transforming traditional charitable organizations into innovative market-oriented enterprises. It is finally an exploration of the ambiguity of change in early modern cities. Though Augsburg's economic, political, and confessional circumstances varied sometimes radically from the sixteenth to the eighteenth century, the means and ends of charity did not. Responding steadily to official directives, social needs, and market imperatives, the orphanages altered themselves and the contexts within which they functioned, thus making possible a process that resembled economic involution.[43] Change occurred through the unchanging pursuit of unchanging ends.

Though profound, the resemblance is not perfectly accurate. Orphanage administrators altered managerial practice little over the first two and one-half centuries. Nonetheless, they tinkered with their methods within the range of possibilities set by the nature of their resources, the goals of their organization, and the limits of contemporary institutions. The unchanging pursuit of unchanging ends permitted a certain cautious refinement of ways.

This is the story of that pursuit as told in the accounts of Augsburg's orphanages, in the daily buying and selling of goods and services, in the hurly-burly of the city's marketplaces, and in the sharp-eyed calculation of advantage. Poor relief was what it has always been and remains today: a transfer of material resources undertaken for social and economic ends. What emerges from the telling is nothing less than a metaphor for the economic function and development of early modern cities.

Notes

1. A distinction is made here between orphanages and foundling homes, the latter dedicated to the care of abandoned and often illegitimate children whose parentage may be suspected but is not known with certainty. By contrast, an orphanage—at least in the early modern understanding of the term—cares for parentless, legitimate children only. Omnicompetent institutions that sheltered orphans and foundlings, as well as other needy souls, had existed since the early Middle Ages. Likewise, foundling homes that housed both foundlings and orphans are known to have existed since the fifteenth century in some Italian and German cities. Though it appeared in a period when others were coming into being, Augsburg's orphanage is the first, to my knowledge, dedicated strictly to the care of orphans. Among recent studies of foundling homes, see Gavitt, *Charity and Children in Renaissance Florence*; Hunecke, *Die Findelkinder von Mailand*.
2. StAA, W A1. Supplicatio der gemainen Außthailer des Allmuesens alhie jn Augspurg.
3. StAA, EWA 48, Poetische Beschreibung der Teuerung, 1571–72: "Wie hab ich mit ungedult/ Offt forderen sehen ainer shuldt/ Dem Reichen vonn ainem armen Mann/ Der doch mit nott sein brott gewan/ Vill worden aus der statt getriben/ Ist weib und kind im seckhel bliben/ Es legen sonst auch hin und wider/ Alle gewerb und handel nider."
4. The crisis was by no means limited to Augsburg. Poor harvests swept the agricultural economy of Europe from Britain to Russia between 1570 and 1572, bringing dearth, inflation, and starvation in their train. I wish to thank Philip Kintner, who has explored in detail the effects on the imperial city of Memmingen, for the reference. See Kintner, "Die Teuerung von 1570–72 in Memmingen." Cf. Abel, *Massenarmut und Hungerkrisen*; Cipolla, *Europe before the Industrial Revolution*.
5. StAA, W A1, Die Errichtung, Abtheilung, und paritaetische Gleichstellung der beeden Wayßenhäußer vom Jahr 1571–1795.
6. StAA, W 10, Ain ungeferlicher Uberschlag was ain Waisenhaus darinnen 200 Kinder erhalten mochten werden jerlich kosten möcht, 1572.
7. The property belonged to one Bartholme Scheurle and was located in the Bakers' Alley (Bäckergasse). StAA, Alms, Jahresrechnungen, 1570–1579.
8. Cf. Fairchilds, *Poverty and Charity in Aix-en-Provence*; Forrest, *The French Revolution and the Poor*; Gutton, *La société et les pauvres* and *L'état et la mendicité*; Jones, *Charity and Bienfaisance*.
9. StAA, W 10. Ain ungeferlicher Uberschlag was ain Waisenhauß darinnen 200 Kinder erhalten mochten werden jerlich kosten möcht, 1572.
10. Scherpner, *Theorie der Fürsorge*. Cf. Jütte, *Obrigkeitliche Armenfürsorge*, 359–62; Isenmann, *Die deutsche Stadt im Spätmittelalter*, 187–90; Sachße, Tennstedt, *Geschichte der Armenfürsorge in Deutschland*, 30.
11. The term "total institution," developed from sociological research and was first used by Erving Goffman. He saw the consequences of such enclosure as negative, at least for those within, a perspective that historians have ignored until recently. See Goffman, *Asylums*, xiii.
12. For an exploration of the distinction between market and marketplace, see Kaplan, *Provisioning Paris*, 23–40.
13. They refused assistance not only to the able-bodied but also to the drunken or

rebellious. Again, this development was not limited to Augsburg. See Jütte, *Obrigkeitliche Armenfürsorge*, 334–37.
14. No ordinance specifically defined an orphan until some fifty years after the organization's founding. StAA, EW 1. Ordnung und Beshaffenheit der Waisenkinder so sich im Waisenhauß befinden alhier in Augspurg, 21 January 1638.
15. StAA, EW 1, Ordnung auß dem Waissenhauß jn Augspurg, 1599.
16. StAA, W 10, Ain ungeferlicher Uberschlag was ain Waisenhauß darinnen 200 Kinder erhalten mochten werden jerlich kosten möcht, 1572: "...weliche die kinder zu der forcht gottes, dem gepett, auch zur arbaitt, und allen gueten thugeten trewlich underwisen unnd leerten...." For a more general discussion of *Pädagogisierung* see Jütte, *Obrigkeitliche Armenfürsorge*, 364–67; Sachße, Tennstedt, *Geschicht der Armenfürsorge*, 30.
17. Werner Sombart's conundrum of simultaneous labor shortages and labor surpluses in preindustrial urban economies, that is, the perception of a dearth of qualified craftsmen accompanied by the surfeit of illegal competition, suggested the full complexity of this issue. Sidney Pollard later adopted this notion and applied it to the process whereby labor was disciplined and trained for new productive techniques during the emergence of machine industry. See Pollard, *The Genesis of Modern Management*; Sombart, *Der moderne Kapitalismus*, I, 788.
18. Polanyi, *The Great Transformation*, 68–76.
19. Foucault, *Madness and Civilization* and *Discipline and Punish*; Oestreich, "Strukturprobleme des europäischen Absolutismus," 329–47, and "Policey und Prudentia civilis in der barocken Gesellschaft von Stadt und Staat," 367–79.
20. Among these many institutions, the Foundling Home was the one most closely associated with the orphanage. Established in 1533 in an abandoned cloister, it not only shared the orphanage's mission to care for needy children but also served as a model for the new orphanage's administration and organization. StAA, W A1, Supplicatio der gemainen Außthailer des Allmuessens alhie jn Augspurg, 1572: "dise arme khinder zusamen verordnet unnd wie jnn dem Findel underhalten wurden...." Neither was the 1572 orphanage singular in this regard. Sherrill Cohen has pointed to a noteworthy institutional continuity marking refuges for women in late medieval and early modern Italy and modern women's shelters. Cohen, *The Evolution of Women's Asylums since 1500*, 4–6.
21. Among the scholars attending to the history of early modern poor relief, Sherrill Cohen has pointed directly to this inadequacy of received theory. Social discipline and great enclosure emphasize only the coercive and repressive elements in the approach to poverty that was adopted with increasing frequency from the seventeenth century onward. They overlook the truly charitable and humanitarian aspects that were also and equally present. One of the problems confronting historians of this issue is to recognize that these polarities could and did coexist in the workhouses, asylums, and orphanages of early modern Europe. Cohen, *The Evolution of Women's Asylums since 1500*, passim.
22. Barge, "Die älteste evangelische Armenordnungen"; Feuchtwanger, "Geschichte der sozialen Politik"; Förstl, *Das Almosen*; Pischel, "Die erste Armenordnungen der Reformationszeit"; Winckelmann, "Die Armenordnungen."
23. Pullan, "Catholics and the Poor in Early Modern Europe"; Chrisman, "Urban Poor in the Sixteenth Century"; Davis, "Poor Relief, Humanism, and Heresy"; Ehrle, *Beiträge zur Reform der Armenpflege*; Fischer, *Städtische Armut und Armenfürsorge*; Grimm, "Luther's Contribution to Sixteenth-Century Organization of Poor Relief"; Kingdon, "Social Welfare in Calvin's Geneva"; Lindberg, "There

Should Be No Beggars among Christians" and *Beyond Charity*; McKee, *John Calvin on the Diaconate*; Ratzinger, *Geschichte der kirchlichen Armenpflege*.

24. Scholars have long understood that the reform of charity was an impulse not limited to Protestants but shared by many Catholics, especially those inspired by humanist treatises on the topic. It is worth noting, however, that those initiatives that placed charity under the administration of the state were still likely to be labelled Lutheran and heretical by conservative Catholic prelates. See especially Davis, "Poor Relief, Humanism and Heresy"; Gavitt, *Charity and Children in Renaissance Florence*; Martz, *Poverty and Welfare in Habsburg Spain*; Pullan, *Rich and Poor in Renaissance Venice*.

25. To be sure, the liturgical and ceremonial functions of charity have long been recognized, especially in studies of Italian confraternities. See, for example Pullan, *Rich and Poor in Renaissance Venice*; Trexler, *Public Life in Florence*; Weissman, *Ritual Brotherhood in Renaissance Florence*. More recent monographs, however, have tended to extend the ceremonial elements of charity to color the early modern response as a whole to the problem of poverty and marginality. Cf. Flynn, *Sacred Charity*; Schneider, *Public Life in Toulouse*; Wandel, *Always among Us*.

26. Cf. Hay, et al., *Albion's Fatal Tree*; Linebaugh, *The London Hanged*.

27. The scholarly interest in a history of discipline may have a number of sources, but two merit particular notice. The first is the work of Gerhard Oestreich, who saw the development of police policy as an effort on the part of rising absolute states to discipline their subjects to an omnipresent and omnicompetent political authority. The second derives from E. P. Thompson's work on labor history, which understood early attempts to remake the poor as efforts to discipline and subjugate the lower orders of society. See: Gerhard Oestreich, "Strukturprobleme des europäischen Absolutismus" and "Policey und Prudentia civilis in der barocken Gesellschaft von Stadt und Staat"; E. P. Thompson, *The Making of the English Working Class* and "Time, Work-Discipline, and Industrial Capitalism." A more recent study of England in the eighteenth century combines elements of social and labor discipline by interpreting the connection between charity and discipline in terms of a shifting elite consciousness of the national condition and national needs. Andrew, *Philanthropy and Police*.

28. Fairchilds, *Poverty and Charity in Aix-en-Provence*; Forrest, *The French Revolution and the Poor*; Hufton, *The Poor of Eighteenth-Century France*; Jones, *Charity and Bienfaisance* and *The Charitable Imperative*; Martz, *Poverty and Welfare in Habsburg Spain*; Norberg, *Rich and Poor in Grenoble*; Snell, *Annals of the Laboring Poor*.

29. Above all, these notions of poverty as a unknowable and structural element of early modern society and of charity as a hopeless enterprise come to the fore in annaliste studies. See especially Gutton, *La société et les pauvres* and *L'état et la mendicité*.

30. The localized charities of smaller polities may have been better suited to respond to the exigencies of early modern poverty than the institutions of emergent nation states. This argument in certainly implicit in Mack Walker's classical study of German home towns and is born out in much of the literature on charity in Germany and Italy. See Bisle, *Die öffentliche Armenpflege der Reichsstadt Augsburg*; Fischer, *Städtische Armut und Armenfürsorge im 15. und 16 Jahrhundert*; Gavitt, *Charity and Children in Renaissance Florence*; Jütte, *Obrigkeitlichen Armenfürsorge*; Pullan, *Rich and Poor in Renaissance Venice*; Moritz, *Die bürgerlichen Fürsorgeanstalten der Reichsstadt Frankfurt am Main*; Sachße, Tennstedt, *Geschichte*

der Armenfürsorge; Walker, *German Home Towns*.
31. In many ways the history of Augsburg's orphanages presages the development of the firm. Cf. Chandler, *The Invisible Hand*; Penrose, *A Theory of the Organization of the Firm*.
32. Prochaska, "Charitable Motives," 27.
33. See especially Lis, Soly, *Poverty and Capitalism in Pre-Industrial Europe*.
34. Cohen, *The Evolution of Women's Asylums since 1500*; DeLacy, *Prison Reform in Lancashire*; Foucault, *Madness and Civilization* and *Discipline and Punish*; Ignatieff, *A Just Measure of Pain* and *The Prison*; Rothman, *The Discovery of the Asylum*.
35. Heilbronner, *The Nature and Logic of Capitalism*, 33–52; Marx, *Capital*, I, 247–57; Safley, Rosenband, *The Workplace before the Factory*, 2–5; Tilly, *The Contentious French*, 5.
36. Marx, *Capital*, I, 283–92; Weber, *Economy and Society*, 154–56, *General Economic History*, 275–78, 341–43, and *The Protestant Ethic and the Spirit of Capitalism*, 17–27.
37. Abu-Lughod, *Before European Hegemony*, 8–20; Braudel, *Civilization and Capitalism*, 91–92; Heilbronner, *The Logic and Nature of Capitalism*, 87, and *the Making of Economic Society*, 42–66; Wallerstein, *The Modern World System*, 16–18.
38. See the discussion of Sombart and Weber in Marshall, *In Search of the Spirit of Capitalism*, 36–45; Sombart, *Moderne Kapitalismus*, passim; Weber, *The Protestant Ethic and the Spirit of Capitalism*, passim.
39. Eisenstadt (ed.), *Max Weber on Charisma and Institution Building*; Schumpeter, "The Instability of Capitalism," 361–86, and *Capitalism, Socialism and Democracy*, passim; Weber, *The Protestant Ethic and the Spirit of Capitalism*, 56–58. Weber and Schumpeter see the force of genius, be it charisma or innovation, as the efficient means of change, and the capture of genius in any institutional sphere as a loss of vitality. In the realm of economics particularly, Weber understood that force of genius to be conservative, calculating for gain rather than gambling for a windfall. Cf. Marshall, *In Search of the Spirit of Capitalism*, 41–45.
40. Hutchison, *Before Adam Smith*, 4–6.
41. North, *Institutions, Institutional Change and Economic Performance*, 3–10, Supplement. *Commercial Crisis and Change in England*, 1–20; Tawney, "A History of Capitalism," 311, and *Religion and the Rise of Capitalism*, passim.
42. North, *Institutions, Institutional Change and Economic Performance*, 3–10 and passim. North's theory of economic change and development points to some terminological obscurities that plague historical research especially. Those entities usually identified as institutions are, according to North, better understood as organizations, that is, groups of individuals bound by a common purpose. Organizations exist in response to the opportunities and constraints that any society constructs to direct human interaction and exchange. These rules of the game, as he puts it—the larger social, political, and economic contexts in which organizations function—are institutions proper. In this North varies little from the traditional definitions put forward by Max Weber. Weber understood organizations as associations devoted to continuous purposeful activity, and institutions as the social spheres in which organizations and symbols attempt to capture and preserve the transforming genius of charisma. See, especially Weber, *Theory of Social and Economic Organization*; Eisenstadt (ed.), *Max Weber on Charisma and Institution Building*.
43. Geertz, *Agricultural Involution*, 32ff.

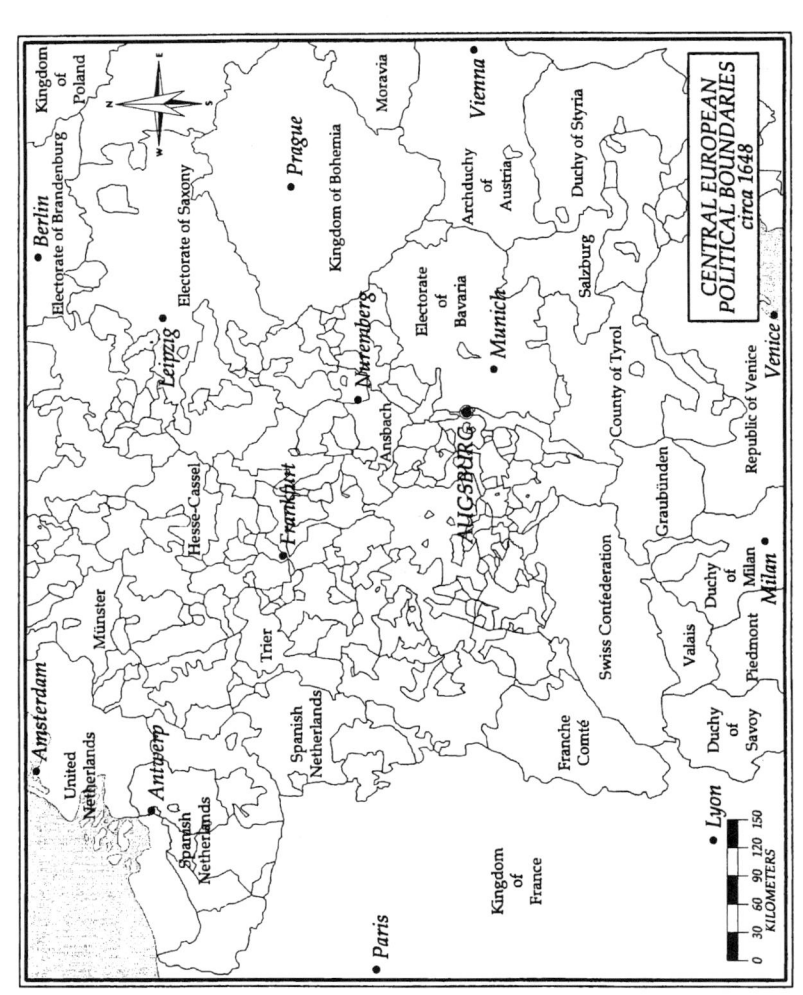

MAP 1

1

A Brief History of Poverty and Charity in Late Medieval and Early Modern Augsburg

Histories of poverty and charity draw heavily upon the themes of crisis and change. Distinct turning points, usually marked by bureaucratic innovation, accompany the movement from pious alms to poor relief to social welfare. This emphasis is not entirely misplaced. Real crises occurred; real poverty existed; real measures were taken. A perceived increase in need in 1521 inspired the creation of a public Alms Office in Augsburg. Catastrophic inflation in 1572 caused the founding of the City Orphanage. Violent religious strife inspired the institution of parity and the establishment of confessionally specific orphanages in 1649. Yet, no less important than change is the continuity of economic and social contexts. Singularity is easily exaggerated. What follows, therefore, is an abbreviated history of poor relief and the orphanages of Augsburg, a sketch of change and changelessness over time.

Though the intensity of suffering in the 1570s gave rise to horrified contemporary comment in Augsburg and elsewhere, dearth and inflation were recurring events in the history of all economies during the sixteenth century. Primitive markets that lacked efficient means of communication and transportation regularly fell victim to sudden changes in the supply of raw materials—above all, foodstuffs—or in the demand for finished products.[1] Inflation haunted states and cities, rich and poor, confronting all with the possibility of sudden ruin and indigence. The poet had seen it: "One gulden purchased so little [wool yarn for weaving] that many [weavers] fell into debt and, overburdened with poverty, abandoned their craft altogether."[2] Even in the best of times pre-mechanized industries that relied on the strength and skill of human hands experienced low labor productivity and consequently generated low wages relative to prices, a situation further aggravated in the sixteenth century by the chronic inflation known as the Price Revolution.[3] Local and regional economies supported large populations of wage-dependent households, capable of eking out a self-sufficient living only under circumstances of stable prices and available work.[4] A combination of chronic volatility and marginality resulted; the structure of the premodern economy continuously generated widespread poverty.

Continuity rather than crisis defined the nature of early modern charity, too. Not the continuity of traditions and institutions, though this played a part as well, but that of social structure determined the form and circumscribed the function of poor relief. Most cities, including Augsburg, experienced a widening material gap between the top and the bottom of the social hierarchy from the late fourteenth century onward. A radical distribution of property, that is, the concentration of wealth in the hands of a few and the concomitant marginalization of the many, was an essential prerequisite for economic growth. Investment capital and employable labor made possible export industries, commercial ventures, and international finance to say nothing of the more extravagant forms of art patronage, conspicuous consumption, and public piety. The concentration of wealth was also an essential prerequisite for the development of charity. While the process of accumulation spurred impoverishment by appropriating part of the value created by the labors of the population, concentrated capital succored the poor through private donations and public subsidies.[5] Yet, the link between nascent capitalism and poor relief extended beyond resources to means and ends. Charity adopted the methods and served the needs of capital.[6] That much of this occurred with state sponsorship rather than through private initiative emphasizes the proximity of political and economic ends. This was a matter of state support not state intervention. It comes as no surprise that Augsburg's golden age of power and influence was also its golden age of poverty and charity.

THE CITY OF AUGSBURG

From its beginnings, Augsburg possessed all the necessary conditions for that golden age of magnificence and marginality that occurred in the fifteenth and sixteenth centuries. Situated on high ground at the confluence of the Lech and Wertach rivers, it was a defensible location, a fact that recommended itself to the Romans, who established a town in the first century and later a provincial capital, Augusta Vindelicum, on the site. Both rivers supplied power for industrial production, but only the Lech was navigable. More important for commerce were the ancient overland routes that converged on the city and linked it to important trading partners: the salt highway from Salzburg of old via Pfaffenhofen and Gauting and later via Munich; a connection from Lake Constance via Lindau and Memmingen

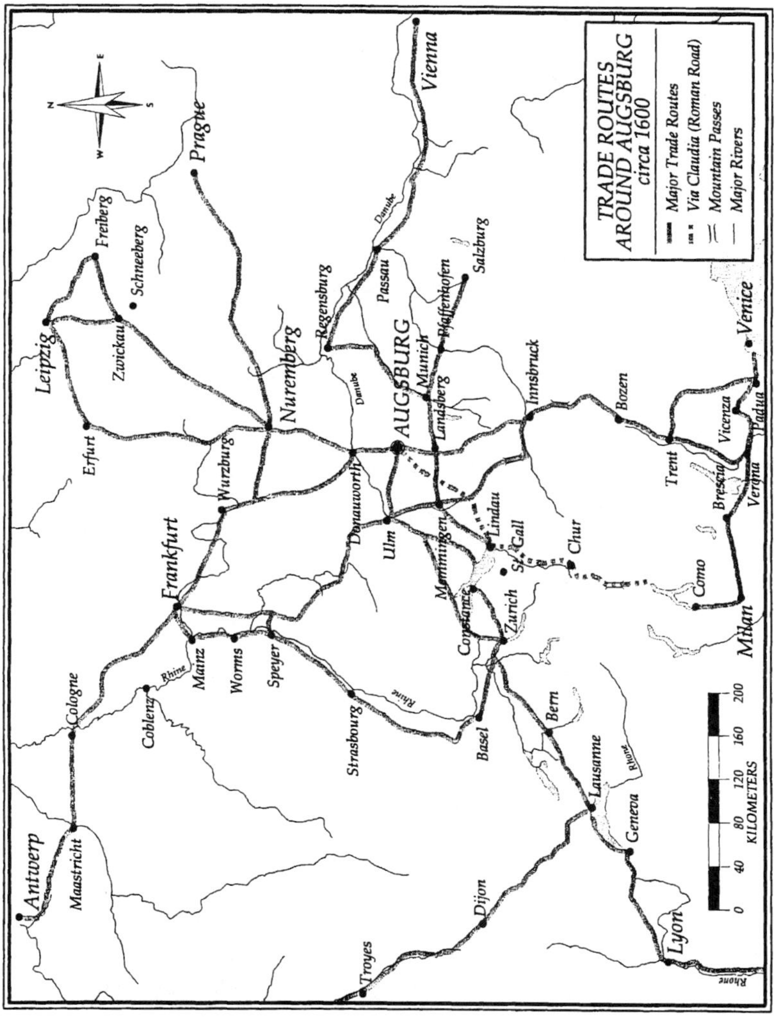

A Brief History of Poverty and Charity 21

MAP 2

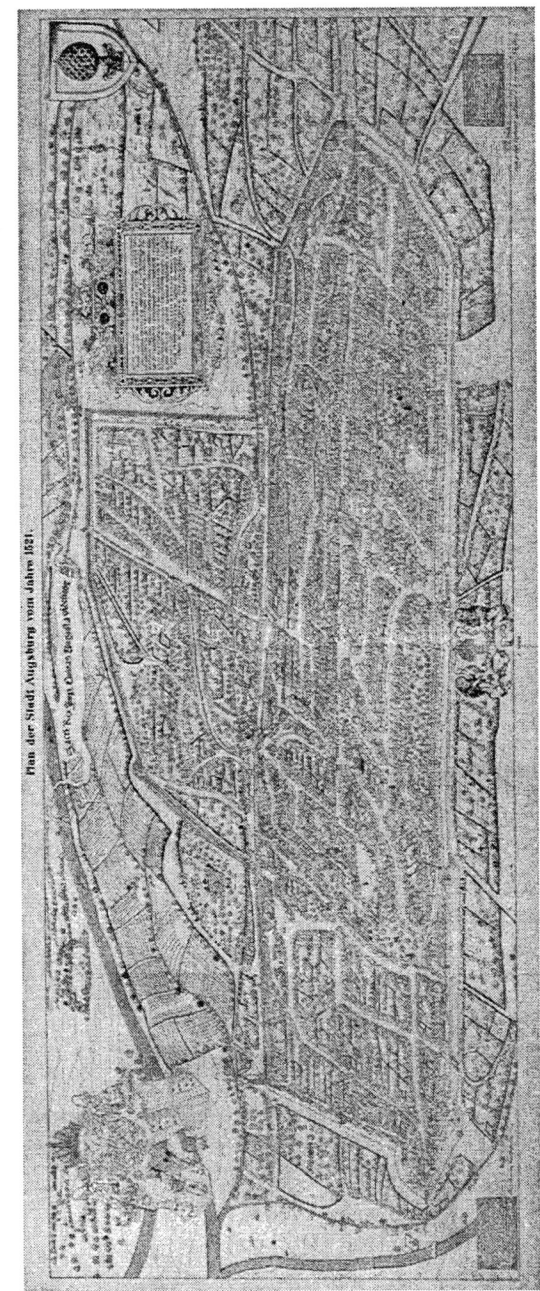

ILLUSTRATION 2 The only plan of Augsburg to view the city from the west, by the Augsburg goldsmith Georg Seld, 1521. Courtesy of the Stadtarchiv Augsburg, Plansammlung 0592.

and the Roman road, the *Via Claudia Augusta,* that traversed the Alps. Of more symbolic meaning was its situation on the cultural border between Swabia to the west and Bavaria to the east, suggesting Augsburg's future not only as an entrepôt but also as a battlefield for more powerful neighbors.

By the late fifteenth century, these geographic realities had left traces in the physical appearance of Augsburg. Approaching from Ulm to the west, a wandering journeyman might have left the rolling wooded hills of the Stauden by the village of Steppach and looked across the Wertach-drained lowlands to one of the largest cities of the Holy Roman Empire. He would have been struck first by the vast expanse of the city wall, strengthened at points by more than 100 turrets and towers. Among the many belfries rising above these—Augsburg was home to no fewer than 17 ecclesiastical establishments—two might have caught his eye particularly, the double spires of the cathedral of the Diocese of Augsburg and the belltower of an Imperial foundation (*Reichsstift*), the Benedictine Abbey of Sts. Ulrich and Afra. These two formed the historical termini between which the city had grown: the cathedral in the so-called bishop's city located at the northern extreme on the site of the Roman settlement, Augsburg's ancient and medieval center; the abbey and its precincts built on their own ground independent of the bishop and to the south of his see. The worldly city of burghers and their affairs, marked by a tower of its own, the *Perlach* by the city hall, had grown up in the middle of these two great ecclesiastical foundations.

Continuing on his way, the journeyman would have made for the Wertach Bridge Gate (*Wertachbruckertor*) on the northwestern corner of the city, and entering would have found himself eventually on the thoroughfare connecting cathedral and abbey. It had become the city's main commercial artery and marketplace. Daily and weekly markets occurred along its entire length: the bread market from the city hall south to the Weavers' Hall and the Collegiate Church of St. Moritz; the wood market adjoining it; the wine market further south in the abbey's shadow. Patrician palaces and commercial counting houses lined either side. Here also stood the guildhalls, the first stop of any journeyman in his search for work and shelter.

Down the narrow side streets and alleys, barely visible behind these most striking symbols of the city's economic vitality, were the artisanal and industrial districts. The journeyman might have settled to work in any of Augsburg's four quarters. Every type of craft and every degree of wealth could be found in every part of the city.[7] Yet, though rich and poor lived as neighbors in Augsburg, they were not equally distributed throughout it. Most densely populated was the Lech Quarter (*Lechviertel*), east of the main thoroughfare and south of the city hall, home to one-third of the city's taxpayers and most of its industries. Other, less sturdily prosperous workers' neighborhoods were the James' Suburb (*Jakobervorstadt*), east from the city

24 A BRIEF HISTORY OF POVERTY AND CHARITY

MAP 3

ILLUSTRATION 3 Most famous of all plans of Augsburg, by Wolfgang Killian, 1626, shows the city from the traditional eastern perspective with the James Suburb in the foreground. Courtesy of the Stadtarchiv Augsburg, Plansammlung 1046.

center to the Lech, the poorest section of Augsburg with the highest percentage of propertiless residents, and the Lady Suburb (*Frauenvorstadt*), north of the cathedral, where nearly half the city's textile workers lived and labored. Of more interest, perhaps, but less promise to a journeyman would have been Augsburg's wealthiest quarter, the Upper City (*Oberstadt*), west of the main thoroughfare, home to nearly 60 percent of the patrician and mercantile elite but less than 4 percent of the artisanal population.

Urban topography reflected urban society. Both were hierarchical in late medieval and early modern Augsburg. The most powerful inhabitants lived along the main street and in the Upper City; geographic distance from these locations signalled a social distance from the elite. In general, hierarchical societies resolved themselves into strata defined by legal status, economic function, and political power. Birthright or sanction determined an individual's place in the hierarchy, a place that brought with it specific behavioral expectations and limitations.[8] Described thus briefly, the social structure of the past appeared static, with each member assigned more or less permanently to a given stratum and with little or no possibility of vertical social mobility. Yet, the society of Augsburg was more dynamic than its topography. Each level manifested substantial internal distinctions according to wealth and status. Prescriptive literature of that time usually discussed the social hierarchy in terms of three ideal strata: those who fight; those who pray; and those who work. A 1683 police ordinance (*Policey-Ordnung*) for Augsburg acknowledged a more diverse reality by organizing the city into no less than five levels: political leadership, mercantile elite, independent masters, dependent masters, and urban poor. In 1713, a similar ordinance for Württemberg recorded no less than nine strata, similarly based on a combination of prestige and function.[9] Furthermore, despite the limits of hierarchy, the society of early modern Augsburg demonstrated considerable opportunity for horizontal and vertical mobility. That this was so had to do with the forces of social transformation.

THE RISE OF CAPITAL AND ITS CONSEQUENCES

The late medieval period in Augsburg was one of institutional transition, during which services traditionally offered by the Church were expanded, duplicated, and finally replaced by state initiatives.[10] A profound economic transformation—expansion interrupted by temporary contractions—during the fifteenth century alternately drove and drew countryfolk to the cities. Many of these immigrants found a place, however modest, in burgeoning urban industry, but the unabated stream of migration also fed a marginal subpopulation that had no real prospect of securing a regular livelihood. These people sank into wretchedness and subsisted through mendicancy and criminality. Their presence in what seemed to be ever growing numbers exceeded the resources of traditional, medieval charity, threatening and challenging the social order.

Beginning in the early fifteenth century, Augsburg entered a period of economic growth, based on the protoindustrial production of fustian, a cloth woven from linen and cotton. Commerce and manufacturing flourished; capital accumulated.[11] Between 1396 and 1492, the city's population rose from 12,000 to 19,000 as newcomers sought their fortunes in the shops and mills of Augsburg's burgeoning textile industry.[12] New mercantile companies appeared, such as those of the Fugger, Meuting, Rehlinger, and Welser families, who would eventually join the ranks of the Augsburg patriciate. These parvenus traded in cloth and reinvested the profits in mining and banking. At the same time, they laboriously climbed the social ladder, a struggle Burkhard Zink and Lucas Rem captured in their autobiographies.[13] Expanding size and wealth etched itself on the face of Augsburg. The city absorbed the James' Suburb and extended the stone fortifications to enclose it. It raised the Perlach tower first to 100 and later to 200 feet. The newly rich built urban palaces throughout the Upper City. The numerous poor crowded into less exalted quarters. Augsburg entered the centuries-long transition toward a capitalistic society. This meant an attenuation of the social hierarchy, an increased distance between elites and commons, and an increased concentration of wealth in the hands of a few.

Augsburg's early economic development has been divided into three phases: a period of rapid expansion until about 1440; a contraction from 1444 to 1466; and a period of renewed growth from 1466 to the end of the century.[14] According to city tax registers, 2.4 percent of the population controlled 49 percent of the taxable wealth on the eve of the transition in 1396. By the end of the century, in 1492, the concentration of wealth was no less extreme with 80 percent of taxable property in the hands of 4.7 percent of the taxpayers. Only 22 people, each of whom held property assessed at more than 10,000 fl., controlled 30 percent of all wealth in Augsburg. Crisis helped to concentrate capital in fewer and fewer hands. During the period 1444–66, Augsburg's fledgling industry was shaken by dearth, inflation, and plague, culminating in a conflict with Bavaria that cut trading connections and closed markets. During these hard times as many as 4,200 poor people depended on charity for their survival.[15] A writer from 1475 alleged 107 foreign beggars were within the walls.[16] Of all taxpayers at that time, 60 percent were reckoned have-nothings (*Habnitse*) and paid the minimum rate.[17] The proportion of Augsburg's population that owned little or no property expanded dramatically. In 1408, 78 percent of the population possessed only 10 percent of all taxable wealth. The disparity rose to 85 percent of all taxpayers with 6 percent in 1462, and settled at 83 percent owning 3 percent of all wealth in 1492. In both relative and absolute terms, the number of rich in Augsburg increased after the crisis years. Their share of all wealth grew from 50 percent in 1396 to more than 80 percent in 1516, accelerated by crises that forced marginal firms and poor families into the hands of creditors.

Many early modern cities, for which social structures can be reconstructed, evinced similarly unequal distributions of wealth and high levels of impoverishment. Not all of Augsburg's poorest were poverty stricken, but most lived on the margin and survived at least occasionally through begging, crime, or by-employment. Foreign vagrants belonged to the penumbra of early modern society; magistrates rarely bothered to count them. Yet, none doubted that their numbers were increasing too. Beginning in the late Middle Ages and continuing throughout the early modern period, the rising tide of poverty overwhelmed traditional alms, provided by the Church, the guilds, and the wealthy, and forced burghers and the state to respond.

The earliest providers of charity as well as hospitality—the two could not be separated because both were based on the Christian's duty to clothe, feed, and shelter such needy persons as travelers and pilgrims, not to mention the sick and poor—were ecclesiastical foundations such as religious houses and collegial chapters. Beginning sometime in the twelfth century, however, charitable and sacerdotal functions began to separate with the establishment of hospitals (*Spitäler*) devoted solely to the care of the sick, the elderly, and the needy.[18] The Hospital of the Holy Spirit (*Heilig-Geist-Spital*) in Augsburg was founded in 968 by Ulrich, bishop and patron saint of the city.[19] The first clear archival reference from 1150 placed it under the direction of the Augustian Canons of the Church of the Holy Cross. As a rule, communal hospitals did not emerge until the thirteenth century. By 1245, a lay confraternity had assumed direction of Augsburg's hospital, ostensibly because of ecclesiastical neglect, and the organization had moved from its original location near the cathedral to a site in the city near the Imperial Abbey of Sts. Ulrich and Afra. Two council-appointed trustees appeared in records from 1288. From the thirteenth through the fifteenth century, hospital property grew steadily, until the institution could rely on financial support from widespread holdings in Augsburg proper and in the countryside to the west.

With the appearance of hospitals began a basic shift away from universal charity toward more differentiated forms. Augsburg's hospital provided care for the aged as did the first purely civil foundation in the city, the Hospital of St. James, established in 1348.[20] The chronically ill looked for assistance from any of three sanitaria (*Siechenhäuser*): St. Servatius, founded in 1264; St Sebastien, founded in 1448; and St. Wolfgang, also founded in 1448. The first of these, a corporation without a fixed location until a bequest from the Langenmantel family provided a house with eight beds in 1288, served as a leprosarium outside the walls of the city.[21] The other two were founded by the city: St. Sebastien outside the James' Gate (*Jakobertor*) to the east and St. Wolfgang outside the Wertach Bridge Gate to the northwest. Because they were frequently underwritten and governed by local burghers, these communal organizations soon began to prefer needy residents of the city. Strangers and the physically able still had to beg.

Like institutionalized charity, alms-giving depended on the generosity of princes and people, the result of their desire to aid the poor, to achieve salvation, and to maintain social status. Charity in this form involved donors in direct personal exchanges with paupers, who requitted beneficence with prayers for their benefactors' souls. So great was the need for assistance and so strong the fear of damnation that alms-giving flourished in most German cities and towns in the fourteenth and fifteenth centuries.

Many scholars have argued that until the sixteenth century charity gave little evidence that donors understood poverty to be anything other than a natural state, a condition created by God that must be accepted and ameliorated rather than resisted and cured.[22] If this argument is accepted, then donors may have exchanged alms for prayers but must have viewed their largesse as a gift for which no material benefit could be expected. The charitable imperative was traditionally religious. Alms-giving was the responsibility of a Christian and worked to the eventual salvation of a Christian soul, but it was far from an "unthinking reflex."[23] Alms-giving helped to fix social rank and identity in an age increasingly open to change. Charity involved, therefore, the calculation of benefits to the giver that, if intangible, were not necessarily transcendental. Max Weber described the rise of capitalist society as a shift from status based on consumption to status based on production.[24] Consumption remained, however, an important visible index of status and public charity a visible form of consumption.

A closer examination offers some limited evidence either that late medieval foundations were not altogether altruistic or that altruism and a cleareyed practicality could co-exist. First, the foundations differed from traditional, medieval charity in that they were not anonymous; they usually bore the names of their donors. In an age in which status required appropriate display, charity had to be conspicuous. Indeed, these private charities are identified by family names to this day, immortalizing the public spirit and private resources of their creators. Second, they usually made specific provision for the care of family members through the inclusion of some form of pension or life annuity. The foundation was required to provide an income or accommodation for any member of the donor's family who wished it. Even the alienation of family property for charitable purposes could not interfere with the material solidarity of the family itself. Third, charity signalled the family's commitment to the social order. In a hierarchical society of orders, the wealthy bore an immediate responsibility for the poor. Their station required that they make some provision for the less fortunate. Expressing status, generosity worked to preserve it by eliciting deference from the lower orders and palliating the worst consequences of an unbalanced distribution of wealth. Not unlike gift-giving in some respects, charity was an exchange that promised social and economic returns beyond the things given.

In Augsburg, individuals and families of every status, from middling artisans and shopkeepers to elite merchants and patricians, provided eleemosynary bequests and created charitable foundations that in sheer numbers may be unique in the history of late medieval and early modern poor relief.[25] Private charities, named for the families who founded them, offered food to the hungry, dowries to maidens, apprenticeships to youths, and stipends to scholars. The more modest provided festive meals (Gottberate) at regular intervals to the inhabitants of the city's hospitals and sanitaria or gave small amounts of cash (Almosenstiftungen) to those honorable poor unable or unwilling to beg. These endowments, small or large depending on the property donated, provided regular assistance to the non-institutionalized poor. Others offered institutionalization itself. The practice of purchasing living space and sustenance as a form of old-age insurance or pension, the Pfründsystem, came to dominate hospital activity after the fourteenth century. Many bequests, therefore, furnished the deserving recipient with a residence (Seelgeräte and Pfründe) in a specified foundation. Altogether more ambitious were those that established the foundation itself to meet the physical and spiritual needs of certain elderly or infirm persons. Unmarried or widowed women, unable to provide for themselves and at risk of falling into sexual or social deviance, found shelter in small enclosed communities (Seelhäuser) established by well-to-do burghers. Before 1500, Augsburg claimed no less than seven of these, housing at least 70 residents. Similar to small monasteries or hospitals, these foundations possessed their own buildings, chapels, and staffs to house and serve the needy and substantial incomes to provide their financial support.

Despite individual differences, the earliest private foundations corresponded to tried-and-true ecclesiastical charity in the importance attached to the relationship between succor and sanctity.[26] Each required that the poor requite material assistance with prayers for the soul of the donor. Most included regular worship as part of the daily routine of their beneficiaries and even provided a chapel and the services of a chaplain for the purpose.

By the late fourteenth century urban magistrates felt compelled to coordinate these private initiatives and make them more effective and more efficient.[27] From these first attempts at magisterial oversight emerged the public Alms Offices and begging ordinances, the earliest of which were established in Nuremberg in the 1380s. Despite the presence of a growing public apparatus during the sixteenth century, private initiatives continued to provide assistance across the entire spectrum of charity.

What materialized during the late Middle Ages in Augsburg and elsewhere was a bazaar of charities that provided many opportunities for benefactors and beneficiaries alike.[28] The well-to-do confronted a bewildering assortment of foundations, institutions, and programs, through which they might exercise their generosity. The poor, too, probably moved from one source of support to another or enjoyed several simultaneously. Unlike a bazaar, however, not all forms of philanthropy were temporary or voluntary. Regulations bound most charities to a limited group among the many poor. Neither did the appearance of opportunity, associated with all markets regardless of structure, guarantee greater freedom for the needy. None of the many pious foundations addressed the social and economic causes of poverty or relieved the misery or insecurity of the majority of Augsburgers. Still, variety and opportunity existed largely as a result of the initiative of wealthy citizens.

Augsburg's Tarnished Golden Age

Since the end of the nineteenth century, historians have recognized the social forces at work in early modern Augsburg. "A slowly progressing proletarianization seems to have gone hand-in-hand with the substantial economic expansion based on the development of concentrated capital."[29] A more recent attempt to emphasize positive aspects of this golden age by references to "a gradual trickle down of well-being from the upper classes to the lower" and to "the general development of the urban economy toward the end of the century" shifted the attention rather than altered the conclusion.[30] Augsburg built upon the social and economic foundations laid in the fifteenth century. Capital accumulation continued, despite occasional recessions, throughout the "long sixteenth century," sharpening the images both real and imagined of the city as an economic colossus. Immigration continued to meet the demand for labor and to fill the lower strata of society, broadening the already considerable gap between rich and poor. The greater needs of poverty and the expanded resources of charity would challenge the city to assist its poor directly.

Augsburg had become one of the largest mercantile and manufacturing centers in the Holy Roman Empire if not in all of Europe. Though crafts and trades that met demand in local marketplaces employed the majority of residents, long-distance commerce and export-oriented industries, especially fustian production and metalworking, set the pace of economic life. As a result the city was home to a flourishing community of wealthy merchants and entrepreneurs and a growing population of impoverished, wage-dependent laborers. Total population doubled from about 20,000 at the beginning of the century to more than 40,000 in the early decades of the seventeenth.[31] Wealth tripled even more quickly: taxable property rose from between 2.58 and 5.16 million fl. in 1498 to between 8.46 and 16.9 million fl. in 1554.[32] Buildings and monuments grew as well. Fortifications were expanded and improved. Mills of every sort were constructed inside and outside the walls. Arcades of shops were added to the Franciscan Church and the Collegiate Church of St. Moritz. New municipal edifices appeared: a city customs house (1605), a city armory (1607), a city butchery (1609), and a city hall (1624). Housing filled the empty spaces in the James Suburb. In Augsburg, however, the frenzy of monumental building came several decades after the period of peak prosperity, when the economy was stagnant. Fiscal discipline—the retirement of debt and the accumulation of reserves—rather than private fortunes made these projects possible.[33] With the economy producing less wealth, architectural brilliance masked dreary social realities.

The poor were everywhere, and the common ground between them and the rich eroded psychologically and socially in the sixteenth century. Fustian weavers constituted by far the largest and the poorest artisanal craft in Augsburg. Their dependence on merchants to supply materials and purchase products gave rise to economic hardship and social tension that found tongue in the poet's repeated diatribes against the stockpiling and price-gouging of a heartless, self-serving elite.[34] He spoke not only of the consciousness of exploitation but also of a sense of limitation, a loss not only of the possibility of self-sufficiency but also of the prospect of prosperity.

The lower classes experienced less upward mobility because of declining real wages. Despite the complications of distinguishing real and nominal incomes in the sixteenth century, some studies conclude that wages rose for most occupational groups. The rapid increase in population, however, brought an increase in prices for essential commodities with the result that "in the entire sixteenth and early seventeenth centuries wages hobbled behind."[35] Thus, between 1498 and 1554 the middling strata of Augsburg, those who rendered less than 10 fl. in tax, grew only 17.3 percent while the number of have-naughts grew 88 percent and the number of rich, those who paid more than 100 fl. in tax, grew 94 percent.[36] Though the proportion of propertiless Augsburgers relative to the total population slipped from 65 to 53 percent, the radical distribution of property continued into the seventeenth century. According to tax returns from 1610, the number of have-naughts had declined to 39 percent of all taxpayers, but wealth was no less concentrated in the hands of a few.[37] Only 7.5 percent of the city's taxpayers controlled 86 percent of its taxable property, while nearly three-quarters of the population struggled along with less than 3 percent. In Augsburg the rich got richer and the poor got poorer.

So unequal a distribution of wealth bore a threefold consequence for poor relief. First, the overwhelming numbers of needy and potentially needy persons made charitable donations from the wealthy absolutely essential. Simply put, the spread of wage labor under the aegis of capitalism increased the population at risk of poverty. Second, the wealthy possessed the resources necessary to make charitable donations. Like poverty, charity existed long before the advent of capitalist forms of commerce and industry; concentrated capital merely accelerated the shift from occasional, haphazard, to regular, fixed forms of assistance. Third, within organizations of poor relief a commonsense tradition of maximizing resources merged with a new capitalist notion of manipulating assets to secure the liquidity and longevity of poor relief itself. Traces of this process are visible in the endowments and foundations of individual merchant-capitalists as early as the fifteenth century. When the state began to assist the poor and manage charity it did little more than confirm and co-opt structures and functions already present.

The passage from private to public charity and from charity to relief began in Augsburg as elsewhere with the state's direct involvement during the fifteenth and sixteenth centuries. In part, urban magistrates responded to the threat to the social order posed by increased vagrancy, poverty, and beggary. In part, they attempted to bring order to the welter of private and ecclesiastical charities that had emerged over time.[38] In part, they sought simply to expand their authority into all areas of public life, a process clearly identifiable in many facets of church-state relations. The results were an expanded state competence and increased state expenditures by the 1500s.

Early policies were prophylactic rather than charitable. Instead of making more resources available for the needy, the magistrates of Augsburg sought to limit the needy themselves. They neither expanded nor rationalized charity. In 1459, the city promulgated its earliest recorded ordinance controlling begging and policing the poor.[39] Foreign beggars could remain in the city for three days; those without a permanent abode were to be expelled immediately. Once recognized by the city, in the form of a lead insignia to be worn at all times, the poor could seek alms only at certain places and on certain days; begging door-to-door or in the churches was illegal. In Augsburg, these police ordinances were renewed in 1491, 1512, and again in 1519, evidence that they neither prevented mendicancy nor limited poverty.

The earliest begging ordinances prescribed the behavior of the poor but did nothing to provide for them. Not until 1522 did the city take the first positive step toward addressing poverty by creating a state Alms Office to relieve and discipline the poor.[40] As originally conceived, the alms ordinance of that year became a model for other cities and remained essentially unchanged until the end of the eighteenth century.[41] To rationalize resources it gathered most of the non-ecclesiastical, social foundations of medieval Augsburg under its loose supervision. The ordinance further divided the city into thirds and assigned to each district two alms lords. These officials were usually chosen from the members of the council or their close associates and relatives, men of the patrician and mercantile corporations, the elite *Herrenstube* and *Kaufleutestube* respectively, who possessed administrative experience and commercial skills essential to operate a large relief agency. Assisted by a number of alms servants (*Almosenknechte*), they visited and examined the poor at home, collected and distributed such alms as the law allowed, and reported and accounted to the City Council. Augsburg's Alms Office directed the flow of charity throughout the city.

From this central agency came funds and goods for a variety of charitable enterprises. It distributed cash, food, fuel, and clothing directly to honorable local poor people (*Hausarme*) in their own dwellings. The Alms Office also saw to the needs of those poor who could not maintain independent households; it administered several public institutions for these needy souls, most notably but not exclusively Augsburg's three sanataria. As early as 1471, the city signalled its concern for foundlings and illegitimate orphans with the decision to devote the proceeds from fines and penalties to the eventual purchase of a foundling home (*Findelhaus*).[42] These efforts concluded in 1533 with the purchase by the Alms Office of the former Cloister of St. Clara on the Horbruck.[43] Another medieval initiative, the travelers' hostel—or pilgrim house (*Pilgerhaus*) as it was known—used a 1440 endowment from the merchant couple Konrad and Afra Hirn to provide temporary shelter for four pilgrims. The Alms Office took it over in 1552, expanding and transforming it into a hospital for ill citizens. Finally, the Alms Office maintained two institutions for those poor who were neither domestic nor deserving: a hospital, known as the need house (*Nothaus*), for diseased foreigners and an alms house (*Almosenhaus*) for institutionalized beggars. Despite the range of its engagements, the Alms Office initially did nothing more than uphold medieval notions and administer existing forms of charity.

If poverty was dynamic, charity could not remain static. The inflationary growth of the economy, steady migration from the countryside, the closing of guilds, and the easy availability of alms, attracted needy people to Augsburg throughout the sixteenth century.[44] The Alms Office recorded 1,066 persons in 455 households receiving alms in 1550.[45] By 1624 the number had risen to 3,400 exclusive of beggars.[46] Among those most directly affected were independent craftsmen of limited means, dependent wage-laborers, members of dishonorable trades, and the traditional poor, such as widows, orphans and invalids.[47] As the numbers of marginal or dependent persons and families grew, they put intolerable pressure on the city's resources and citizens' patience and made further reform of poor relief necessary. Limited earlier, public begging was prohibited in 1541.[48] The City Council mandated further that the Alms Office assist the poor in kind—in food, fuel, and clothing—rather than in cash and that this assistance be limited to specific, controllable places. To make these provisions more efficient the ordinance ordered the creation of storehouses (*Kapelle*) in which to keep grain and other commodities and from which to distribute them to the needy in each third of the city. Only the deserving poor—those truly unable to support themselves—were permitted to receive relief, and only in their own neighborhoods, where they and their situations were best known. The undeserving and the foreign poor had to find some kind of work and support themselves. Although disciplinary in intent, the ordinance of 1541 bore economic consequences. The Alms Office had established itself as the intermediary of charity and connected the privilege of receiving alms to an appropriately modest or "honorable" lifestyle. Now it became a conduit, directing funds to specific ends independent of the donors' wishes. No longer content to encourage private or ecclesiastical charity, the city became the most important provider of relief and patron of the poor through the organization of the Alms Office.

In 1563 yet another set of regulations sharpened and restricted the distinctions between deserving and undeserving poor that had appeared two decades earlier.[49] Henceforth only the very young and the very old, orphaned children and sick people without any means of self-support, received alms. Measures of this sort did not so much eliminate poverty as limit eligibility.

The events of 1571 and 1572 overwhelmed all such efforts. The number of needy and dependent people, which had been rising steadily throughout the century, now leaped upward as starving peasants poured into the city and joined unemployed weavers in their quest for alms. According to one source, starvation and malnutrition more than doubled the mortality rate of Augsburg in a single year.[50] The magistrates earned the poet's praise as they tried to keep pace with the problem: "God reward the authorities who did well by giving the burghers bread every week at great expense."[51] Not only the resources of the Alms Office but also the city's commodity reserves, which were purchased and stored by the Provisions Office (*Proviantamt*) against such an eventuality, were distributed at low cost or dumped on the market to control prices. The more charity the city provided, the more poor people appeared to need it. "Every day there were more of them; no one knew from where they came."[52] The alms lords, however, had no such doubts. They were convinced that "in these hard times people would rather enjoy alms and live on them."[53] And, indeed, "because one was generous they came in great numbers and men, women, and children went from house to house until the city was full of poor people."[54] The authorities had no choice but to shut the gates and attempt to deal with the city's inhabitants first.

The founding of Augsburg's orphanage occurred in these conditions of increased suffering and strained resources. That city and citizens donated substantial capital to create a new organization demonstrates that suffering was not universal and resources were available.[55] The scale of orphanage operations quickly exceeded anything communal authorities had estimated or imagined. When it opened its doors in 1573, the orphanage admitted 320 needy children. Though this number fell to 275 with the easing of inflation at the end of the year, the institution consistently saw to the care of far more souls than the 200 that had been intended. According to one source, it regularily housed between 300 and 400 orphans until the 1620s.[56] This is probably an exaggeration because many older orphans continued to be listed as resident even after they had been placed out of the house and no longer lived there. The orphanage's costs were far higher than planned, too. First, the orphanage employed a much larger staff; by the 1590s the services of 9 schoolmasters and mistresses and 6 or more artisans supplemented those of an in-house staff of 14.[57] Second, the feeding and clothing of all these dependents absorbed more resources; by 1595, though exact expenditures are impossible to calculate, both the unit costs and total volumes of such basic commodities as bread, meat, and fuel had exceeded projections.[58] The quick growth of the orphanage over its first fifty years seemed to confirm elite suspicions that charity itself induced poverty.

The city scrambled to meet these expenses by dedicating certain taxes and duties to the support of the orphanage and by increasing the subsidies provided by the Alms Office. The orphanage took steps of its own as well. It became involved in various capital transactions, purchasing annuities and extending credit to increase its income. It tried to control costs by contracting long-term fixed rates for the delivery of goods and services. And it shortened the period of in-house residency—thus reducing the dependence of residents on orphanage support—by placing orphans in service and apprenticeships at a younger age. Until the crisis years in the middle of the seventeenth century, when inflation, pestilence, and warfare stalked Augsburg, the orphanage remained a remarkably robust institution, mediating between the city and its markets to care for large numbers of needy children.

THE REFORMATION AND CHARITY IN AUGSBURG

Augsburg's public charity, "introduced in 1522 at the time of the Reformation's first successes in Augsburg," drew no particular inspiration from the introduction of Protestant religion.[59] "Its [the alms ordinance] original impetus was civic rather than evangelical, and it was paralleled by many other Poor Laws introduced throughout European towns in the first decades of the century." The shifting balance between means and ends—the requirement to maintain order in a hierarchical society—weighed far heavier in the balance of poor relief than did moral or theological considerations. Yet, mounting confessional tensions between Augsburg's Protestant majority and its Catholic minority posed a challenge to charity as intractable, in fact, as the immiseration caused by worsening political and economic conditions.[60] By the middle of the seventeenth century, religious strife transformed the city's entire system of poor relief, including the orphanage, and altered its relationship to state and market.

Lutherans, Zwinglians, Schwenckfeldians, and Catholics had coexisted in Augsburg since the 1520s.[61] A minority, Augsburg's Catholics were protected by the divisions among their Protestant opponents, the proximity of powerful political and military allies, and the coalition of patrician families within their ranks. In the first half of the sixteenth century, most of Augsburg's Protestants were Zwinglians, who harbored a profound distrust of the Lutherans, who controlled the City Council. These hostilities affected the course of reform in the city but no more so than the fact that Augsburg was surrounded by powerful Catholic neighbors: the Wittelsbach Duchy of Bavaria to the east, the Habsburg County of Burgau to the west, and the ecclesiastical and political territories of the Bishop of Augsburg to the north and south. As these powers offered unstinting support to the city's Catholic community and leadership, Lutheran authorities had to handle them—and all other religious groups for that matter—with extreme deliberation.

The 1547 defeat of Protestant forces in the Schmalkaldic War altered the balance of power, if not the composition of Augsburg's confessional communities. First, the Imperial victory placed the city under pressure to accept the Augsburg Interim. That pressure was all the greater because Augsburg was a visible center of reform and one of the principal free cities of the Empire. The lack of support from Augsburg's Protestant allies, the threatened loss of Imperial freedom, and the determined resistance of the city's Catholic minority also encouraged acceptance.[62] The Zwinglian majority bitterly resisted the Interim because it recognized only the Lutheranism of the Augsburg Confession; their opposition eventually forced the City Council to replace incumbent pastors, custodians (*Zechpfleger*), and schoolmasters with more conciliatory Lutherans. As a result, most of the Zwinglians converted or emigrated, and Augsburg became largely a Lutheran city from 1548 until the 1700s, when immigration finally created a Catholic majority. Second and more important, the constitutional reforms imposed by Emperor Charles V in 1548 banned guilds from direct participation in city government and placed political authority in the hands of a patrician oligarchy dominated by Catholics. According to tax registers, Catholics constituted less than 20 percent of the city's population but they held a majority of seats in the Small Council, the highest legislative body in Augsburg. Thus, the minority could dominate the majority.

It failed to do so because of the political realities that continued to shape

Augsburg's history. If a Catholic minority wielded political power in the city, the Lutheran majority carried the greater economic and demographic weight. The majority of the wealthiest burghers, the ones whose resources paid taxes, provided credit, and generated patronage, were Lutherans. Though marooned in a Catholic sea, this population was large enough to make any direct confrontation risky. The Religious Peace of Augsburg in 1555 stabilized this tenuous balance between political and social powers. It preserved the non-religious civil rights of all burghers in accordance with a rule of strict equality, and it regulated religious expression and religious property according to precedent. This made difficult any change in the confessional status quo and enforced a sort of toleration.

Yet, confessional tensions left their mark on charity in Augsburg. During the sixteenth century, well-to-do Augsburgers contributed 303,457 fl. in 56 separate donations to various foundations and organizations.[63] More than half of these were confessionally specific: 14 of these donations, valued at 50,505 fl., were limited to needy Lutherans; 15 donations, valued at 172,750 fl., were specifically dedicated to Catholics. And the proportion rose steadily. From 1555 to 1586, from the Religious Peace to the Calendar Conflict, 61 percent of all charity was specifically reserved for the benefit of a single confession. Between 1584 and 1650, 91 percent of all charity was confession-specific, a consequence of the religious tensions further strained by the Calendar Conflict and the Thirty Years' War.[64] Only after the cessation of open hostilities in the peace of exhaustion did confession become a somewhat less urgent consideration. Between 1651 and 1699 only 55 percent of all charity specified confession.

The preponderance of Catholic wealth among the private charities of this period was the result of the patronage of the Fugger family. In six different donations to Catholic charities, they contributed 153,950 fl., over 89 percent of all funds between 1532 and 1599. In 1548 and 1560, they donated 20,000 fl. and 28,000 fl. respectively for the construction of the so-called *Holzhäuser* for the care of the sick. After 1579 the foundation of the Jesuit college of St. Salvador in Augsburg became their favorite project, to which they gave 30,000 fl. in 1579, 19,950 fl. in 1580, 16,000 fl. in 1586, and 40,000 fl. in 1598. Had Fugger money been removed from the total of Catholic charity in the sixteenth century, the Lutherans would have emerged as generally more active in private charity by 50,505 fl. to 18,000 fl. The relative weakness of Catholic charity, to which Lutheran administrators pointed in the seventeenth and eighteenth centuries, is very much in evidence a century earlier.

Public charity generally and the orphanage specifically long escaped the confessionalization that characterized the history of Augsburg in the sixteenth and seventeenth centuries. The Alms Office remained in the hands of Lutheran officials after 1548 despite a Catholic majority in the City Council.[65] The most important sources of financial support remained communal subventions and private contributions, most of which came from Lutheran donors. As noted, neither the Alms Office nor the orphanage ever benefitted from the secularization of Catholic ecclesiastical properties, although many private donations stipulated memorial masses and other Catholic observances. Not surprisingly, therefore, the early inspiration and direction of the orphanage came from the Lutheran community. Johannes Stöcklin, a Lutheran merchant and alms lord, is generally recognized as the founder of the organization. The first orphan fathers, Hanns Oswaldt, Hanns Limm, and Heinrich Fischer, were Lutherans too.

It is difficult to imagine continued Lutheran control of charity had it been used for partisan purposes. In fact, life inside the orphanage seems to have escaped most of the confessional tensions that plagued the city in other respects. When the council dismissed Augsburg's Lutheran ministers on 15 July 1586 for their opposition to the introduction of the Gregorian calendar, the city continued to provide assistance to its poor inhabitants regardless of confession. Under uninterrupted Lutheran administration, the orphanage admitted, raised, and placed Catholic and Lutheran orphans alike. Catholic children were occasionally denied admission, but whether by reason of their confession, their citizenship, or their legitimacy was debated.[66] Regardless, the weight of evidence indicates that Catholic children in need usually found a home in the orphanage. A decree of 1609 warned the alms lords to ensure that all Catholic children admitted to the orphanage were raised in the religious faith of their parents.[67] According to a list of orphans, drawn in 1629, 7 Catholics resided in the orphanage among 59 Lutherans.[68] Thus, the orphanage served, albeit hesitantly at times, the needs of the entire community. In the age of the Reformation, charity in Augsburg transcended confession.

THE CONFESSIONALIZATION OF CHARITY

That this did not continue to be the case may be attributed to the confrontational politics and deteriorating economy that characterized much of Europe in the middle of the 1600s. Bernd Roeck demonstrates exhaustively that warfare and inflation "neither initiated a previously unestablished decline nor destroyed a blooming prosperity."[69] That is not to say that crisis left unchanged the orphanage and the society and economy of which it was part.

The accommodation between Augsburg's Catholics and Lutherans after 1555 did not survive the renewal of armed hostilities in 1618. Although the city was spared violence until the 1630s, the policies and practices of the Thirty Years' War affected it nonetheless. Emboldened by the defeat of his Protestant enemies, Emperor Ferdinand issued the Edict of Restitution on 3 March 1629 and restored to the Catholic Church all ecclesiastical property seized after 1622. When Augsburg's Lutheran pastors and magistrates refused to comply, they were dismissed en masse. By 1631 no non-Catholics sat on the City Council.[70] The Alms Office became a Catholic relief agency, providing alms only to those needy people willing to attend Catholic worship services.[71] The orphan father at the time, Heinrich Fischer, was dismissed; orphans were given a choice of conversion to Catholicism or banishment from the orphanage.[72] Many chose the latter and faced an uncertain fate. In a single stunning moment, the character and operation of Augsburg's orphanage changed radically. With the occupation of the city by Swedish forces on 20 April 1632, City Council, Alms Office, and City Orphanage returned to Lutheran hands. Yet, Protestant forces did not hold Augsburg for long. Imperial and Bavarian troops laid ruinous siege to the city in 1634, finally capturing it in 1635. The Leonberger Accord that arranged the surrender reversed Swedish policy, banishing all Lutherans from public office and returning all ecclesiastical properties without exception to the Catholic Church. As a result, the orphanage came once again under the aegis of a Catholic administration and remained there until 1648. Between 1629 and 1648, therefore, the orphanage became what it had never been, the victim of a confessional struggle, deprived not only of its spiritual solidarity but also of its material support.

Economic collapse complicated confessional relations.[73] It suffices here to say only that this catastrophe in 1622–23 heralded a series of disasters, including the epidemic of 1627–28 and the siege of 1634–35, that decimated the population, ruined the economy, and restructured the society of Augsburg.[74]

The series of calamities that marked the history of Augsburg between 1622 and 1635 ended the city's golden age. By the close of the Thirty Years' War, Augsburg no longer possessed even a pale shadow of its former greatness. The population of 40,000 at the beginning of hostilities in 1618 had fallen to less than 17,000 by the end of the siege.[75] The leading export industry collapsed: annual fustian production declined from a robust 400,000 pieces, from the looms of more than 2,000 masters before the war, to barely 60,000 pieces from about 500 weavers in 1662.[76] More than 2,216 buildings stood damaged or abandoned.[77] Neither were the resources at hand to rebuild the wreckage, estimated by the City Council at 9,330,248 fl.[78] The total wealth of the population, calculated on the basis of tax returns, had fallen over 75 percent, and the public debt had risen from 200,000 fl. in 1648 to over 1,800,000 fl. by 1650.[79] Even the means to create wealth had been destroyed. Augsburg's most prominent families, those whose capital had turned the wheels of commerce and industry, had lost over 90 percent of their property.[80]

Great as the loss and destruction in Augsburg were, a study of the city's property taxes indicates that they had a limited effect on the social structure.[81] Over the course of the war the total wealth of the city declined: the average property assessment fell from 6 fl. 34 kr. in 1618 to 3 fl. 16 kr. in 1646. Though less taxable property existed, still its distribution remained largely unchanged. The proportion of have-naughts fell from 48.5 percent in 1618 to 37.2 percent in 1646, but the proportion of taxpayers rendering 1 fl. or less stood at 75 percent in both years. Changes within this group—the relative decrease in those paying 15 kr. or less and the relative increase in those paying between 16 and 60 kr.—have been explained in terms of the possibility that Augsburg tax officials increased assessments, sparing only the truly propertiless, in a desperate attempt to increase public revenue.[82] The broad middle strata, those charged between 1 and 100 fl, in property taxes, remained stable too. In 1618 these groups comprised 23.1 percent of the total taxable population; in 1646 they had grown to 23.7 percent. In comparison, the wealthiest groups in Augsburg shrank during the crisis years. Propertyholders taxed in excess of 100 fl. decreased from 1.4 percent of all taxpayers in 1618 to 0.5 percent in 1646. At the beginning of the war 10 residents of Augsburg boasted a tax assessment greater than 500 fl. By the end none remained. The rich were, indeed, less rich; the distribution of wealth was somewhat less radical. Yet, the changes should not be overstated. If the top decile of Augsburg's tax-paying population controlled 92 percent of the city's wealth in 1618, it still held 85 percent in 1646. Augsburg was still a hierarchical society, and the distance between base and pinnacle remained vast.

The persistent concentration of capital explains the persistence of Augsburg charity in two ways. First, it permitted the city to raise tax revenues, part of which flowed into the Alms Office and the orphanage, to relieve the suffering of the poor. Bernd Roeck calculated average poor-relief expenditures that demonstrate the extraordinary costs of charity to the Alms Office during the decades of crisis.[83] These rose from 24,984 fl. annually during the 1610s to 38,183 fl. per year in the 1620s, before declining to 17,819 fl. in the 1630s and 9.978 fl. in the 1640s.[84] The gradual collapse of the Alms Office's capital (*Hauptgut*) throughout the period, from 130,329 fl. in 1606–7 to nothing in 1649, complicated the expense of poverty.[85] Proceeds from these investments, based on interest and annuities from various kinds of credit and property transactions, had freed the Alms Office from strict reliance on the state; their decline forced the city to take a more direct role in poor relief. A variety of measures, including new indirect taxes and the sale of real property, failed to secure the finances of public charity and forced the city to provide annual subventions, a practice that began in 1618 and endured into the modern period.[86] Second, concentrated capital enabled the more fortunate to continue to support the poor despite hard times. In the seventeenth century, the number of pious foundations established by Augsburgers rose to 70 while the total value declined to 168,239 fl. The Lutheran community made 33 donations worth 105,765 fl., while the Catholic community created 15 donations equalling 26,314 fl.[87] The changing socioeconomic composition of the city in the wake of the steady migration of poor Catholics from country to city and the declining aggregate and per capita wealth of the Catholic population reduced the total private resources available to meet their needs. The fact that donations in church collection plates and public collection boxes declined steadily at the same time that private foundations and endowments remained robust demonstrates amply the particular connection between capital and charity. Augsburg's radically unequal distribution of property enabled the Alms Office and orphanage to continue operations throughout the worst years of the 1600s.

Augsburg's orphanage weathered the storms of the seventeenth century but not the peace that followed. It became one of the spoils of war, an object of contention and negotiation to be divided among the warring parties.

The Peace of Westphalia ended conflict, if not hostilities, in 1648. Article 5, sections 4 through 10, applied to the situation in biconfessional Augsburg particularly. It established as a constitutional principle the numerical parity of offices between Catholics and Lutherans.[88] The city's seven chief executives (*Geheime*) were divided between four Catholics and three Lutherans, and the Small Council was split between 23 Catholics and 22 Lutherans.[89] All other communal offices were divided evenly—either simultaneously or consecutively.[90] Thus, Lutheran and Catholic officials would each have exclusive responsibility for the religious affairs of their own confession, an urban adaptation of the principle *itio in partes* that applied to the Imperial Diet.[91]

Of particular concern was the further disposition of church property. A special sub-delegation, mandated by the agreement governing implementation of the peace (*Friedens-Executions-Receß*) and charged with the resolution of disputes arising from the Instrument of Peace, set the year 1624 as the benchmark for all matters "in Ecclesiasticis."[92] All church-related affairs, including control over church property, educational institutions, and social foundations, would return to the status quo of 1624. Since 1635 Lutherans had been deprived of the benefits of social services and forced to worship outdoors because the Catholic Church controlled all church property and church-related functions. For them, the sub-delegation's decision marked a return to a more normal communal life. Many churches and schools were returned to Lutheran administration. And the orphanage, which had been operated strictly by Lutherans and housed no Catholic orphans in 1624, passed finally to the direction of a Lutheran orphan father.

From 1648 onward, the orphanage would serve the Lutheran community solely, and other arrangements would have to be made for the Catholics.[93] First, the building with all of its contents (*cum omnibus appertinentiis*) reverted to Augsburg's Lutherans. Second, in accordance with a broad interpretation of parity between confessions, the sub-delegation ordered the city to provide another "healthy and comfortable dwelling" to house a Catholic orphanage and to supply it with "support, clothing, and other things" in the same manner as the Lutheran. Third, Lutheran orphans currently in Catholic hands would have to be surrendered to an Imperial notary for eventual transfer to their families or the Lutheran authorities. From a single communal orphanage, separate but equal confessional orphanages had emerged.

Catholic and Lutheran authorities struggled every step of the way. After much searching they located a suitable house near the cathedral that the owner agreed to sell for 3,500 fl.[94] Lutherans opposed the sale as too expensive, and, indeed, the city's treasury could not afford in 1649 the sum it had provided in 1572. In the end, the Catholics had to settle for a loan of 950 fl. at interest, enough to cover a downpayment and fees. Neither were private resources available to furnish the new Catholic Orphanage. Catholics demanded that half of all movable property in the Lutheran Orphanage be placed at their disposal.[95] The Lutherans refused, interpreting narrowly the ruling that house and contents were their's alone, but had to yield in the end to the force of material necessity. The confessions could not even agree which orphans belonged properly in which orphanages. It would take years before both houses settled their differences and settled down to work.

The peace of 1648 introduced a degree of economic irrationality into the administration of poor relief. In this respect, it may well be considered the defining moment in the history of charity in Augsburg. The task of providing the best possible care at the lowest possible cost had been effectively compromised by political considerations embodied in the principle of parity. Creating two separate but equal confessional orphanages sacrificed the efficiencies and economies of scale that had been the rationale for establishing a single organization in the first place. The fixed costs for two houses would be greater than for one, and an orphanage that housed far fewer than the originally projected 200 orphans would be less economical. Moreover, the new arrangement forced both orphanages to compete for scarce resources, a conflict that endured until the end of the eighteenth century. Parity changed the role of the orphanage as an agency of the state operating more or less independently within the economy. No longer charged simply with the efficient care of needy children, the two confessional orphanages had to incorporate a new set of political and social imperatives—above all the separation of Catholic and Lutheran communities and the maintenance of discipline within each—that had economic implications. Agencies and organizations involved in poor relief had always been forced to mediate between the government and the market, but now the rules of the game had changed. Managerial practices, however, remained constant despite the institutional transformation. From 1650 until 1780, the Catholic and Lutheran orphanages struggled with the tensions implicit in the simultaneous pursuit of parity and efficiency.

OLD REGIME AND NEW REALITIES

During that period, Augsburg's economy stabilized and slowly began to grow again. The process was not without setbacks, such as the food shortage of 1693–95 and the siege and occupation by French and Bavarian troops in 1703–4, and the city never regained its former economic stature. Yet, the accomplishments and prosperity were no less real. By 1670, Augsburg had recovered from many of the direct economic effects of the Thirty Years' War. The City Council had managed to retire the public debt and to repurchase much of the property it had alienated.[96] This singular achievement must be attributed both to a tough-minded fiscal policy that limited interest payments and stopped the loss of city resources and to the renewal of trade that accompanied the end of hostilities and increased customs revenues.

From 1650 onward Augsburg's economy rested on three forms of enterprise: finance and banking, gold- and silversmithing, and mill-based calico printing.[97] All of these relied fundamentally on connections to international markets that were renewed as soon as military hostilities ended in 1648. Augsburger merchants returned to Europe's major commercial fairs, provided market access to Augsburger artisans, and encouraged exchange activities. As a result, industry and banking flourished from the second half of the seventeenth century to the end of the 1700s, despite occasional political hostilities and growing foreign competition. Not until the crop failures of 1770–71 did Augsburg again confront acute economic crisis.

Social change accompanied economic recovery. Anxious to increase the number of taxpayers and provide Augsburg with needed skills, communal authorities encouraged immigration by lowering financial requirements and granting citizenship liberally after 1648.[98] Catholics and Lutherans alike wandered to Augsburg, the former coming from the neighboring Catholic hinterlands, the latter traveling from distant Protestant cities and territories.[99] Immigration gradually altered the demographic relationship between confessions.[100] Around 1750, two centuries of Protestant domination ended, and a Catholic majority emerged.

Despite economic renewal and demographic change, Augsburg remained a hierarchical society with property unequally distributed among the strata. The 1688 property tax assessed 5,186 taxpayers, of whom 24.3 percent paid the rate of have-naughts and 4.0 percent rendered taxes of 100 fl. or more.[101] By 1712 the number of taxpayers had risen to 5,474, and the proportions of poor and rich had increased to 27.3 and 4.1 percent respectively. Change occurred at the expense of the broad middle strata. Those who paid between 1 and 100 fl. declined from 71.8 to 68.3 percent of all taxpayers, but the distribution within their ranks tended to be somewhat less weighted toward the bottom. Payers of 1 to 6 fl. in tax declined more precipitously, from 59.2 to 48.2 percent, while other levels increased. Augsburg still felt the consequences of crisis and war. Wealth remained capped, as Roeck put it; the number of rich Augsburgers decreased as did their proportion of the city's total wealth. A social pyramid persisted albeit somewhat lower and broader.

If changing fortunes tended to blunt certain socioeconomic distinctions, immigration sharpened others. Typically seeking employment as day-laborers, mill workers, or domestic servants, unskilled rural Catholics tended to fill the lower strata of Augsburg's society. Trained and educated urban Lutherans, on the other hand, entered the city's professions, trades, and crafts. Thus, in the late seventeenth and eighteenth centuries, a disproportionate number of Catholics were trapped at the bottom of the social hierarchy while Lutherans occupied positions at or near the top.[102] The former absorbed a growing proportion of poor relief; the latter provided the lion's share of charitable donations. In the last decades before Augsburg surrendered its independence for a place in the Kingdom of Bavaria, between 1785 and 1806, over 74 percent of the city's poor were Catholic.[103] Similar findings in other cities, notably Kaufbeuren and Colmar, suggest that material inequalities may have chilled already cool relations between confessions or delayed a reconciliation between them in seventeenth- and eighteenth-century Germany.[104] Such disparities of faith, wealth, and station had characterized urban society and complicated poor relief throughout the early modern period.

Apart from their gradual increase in size and number, the agencies and organizations charged with assisting the needy changed little between 1522 and 1806. The city remained committed to the assistance of its needy citizens and residents. The number of persons dependent on poor relief—the Alms Office listed 1,074 in 1711–12, 1,033 in 1757, and an average of 1,227 in the 1790s—remained relatively stable.[105] Those poor people not reflected in these figures turned to the many other sources of assistance that had characterized Augsburg's charitable regime since the fifteenth century. Like the city as a whole, these had experienced crisis and recovery. Between 1600 and 1619, 89,420 fl. were given to private charitable initiatives. In the most difficult period, between 1620 and 1650, donations dropped to 20,400 fl., only to rise again in the second half of the century to 59,419 fl. In an age when donations to the Alms Office all but disappeared and the city was forced to assume a direct role in the relief of poverty, charity survived remarkably well as a private endeavor. Those who relied on the Alms

Office received support despite a steadily worsening economy. According to the terms of parity, three Catholic and three Lutheran alms lords drew upon the same mixture of private contributions and public subventions that had been the rule since 1618 to provide relief to the poor. The ability and willingness to give signalled both the prosperity of a certain part of the city's population—the concentration of capital that made large-scale charity possible—and a general sense of communal responsibility for those in need. Yet, that sense was not limited to the community but extended, despite repeated proscriptions to the contrary, to foreign vagrants. The Alms Office succored 7,533 beggars in 1712, 5,190 in 1714, and 2,461 in 1725.[106] Most of these vagabonds passed through Augsburg; those who attempted to stay were quickly expelled from the city or compelled to work.

The recourse to labor as an adjunct or alternative to relief marked the single most important innovation in Augsburg's charity after the introduction of parity in 1648.[107] The city founded a poor house (*Armen- und Almosenanstalt*) in 1711 and a workhouse (*Zucht- und Arbeitshaus*) in 1755 to control the poor, make them productive, and limit their support. Yet, this was no great enclosure of the marginal and deviant. The experiment never supplanted open-air charity and never spread to other institutions, especially not to the orphanages. Neither the poor house nor the workhouse provided goods and services or earned profits because of the general variation of skill among their inhabitants, the coercive nature of the enterprise, and the high costs of institutionalization. The latter contributed as well to the steadily rising costs of poor relief. Workhouse expenses alone rose from 2,615 fl. per year in the 1760s to 4,606 fl. per year in the 1790s.[108] With the two orphanages, it contributed to an annual budget of about 15,000 fl. for the Alms Office by the 1790s.

After the crisis of the seventeenth century, private charity also became more purposefully utilitarian, wasting no money sustaining the poor but contributing the means to a productive and, above all, normative existence. Donors stipulated with increasing frequency that charity be used to provide such advantages as might secure a self-sufficient livelihood within the community. Lutherans in particular distributed scholarships, apprenticeships, and dowries, their favored form being stipends for education at the local College of St. Anna. The entailed estate (*fideicommissum familiae*) of Lucas Stenglin is a case in point.[109] He created a legacy that provided 12 fl. annually as a dowry for an orphan in the Lutheran Orphanage but remained the property of his family. Catholics gave to the same ends but spent proportionally more on liturgical observances. Reichsgraf Anton Joseph Fugger established a legacy in his testament of 1 June 1689, according to which the annual proceeds from a trust fund of 150 fl. (7.5 fl. reckoned at 5 percent annually) were to be distributed among the orphans of the Catholic

Orphanage on the day of his death every year in perpetuity.[110] In return for this generosity, the children were commanded to pray for the donor's soul. Those who gave understood utility in confessional terms: Lutherans quickened the education and socialization that were the mainstays of their observance; Catholics strengthened the traditional piety that was the essence of post-tridentine Catholicism. In general, however, private donors determined to help the needy up and left to the city the task of helping them out.

Though Augsburg's orphanages never experimented with work regimes to supplement income or discipline poverty, both experienced the steadily rising costs and falling resources that beset eighteenth-century poor relief. As was the case in 1571, natural disasters finally forced the authorities to rethink administration and finance. When dearth and famine struck in 1771 and 1772, the Catholic community suffered disproportionately because of the large number of wage-dependent laborers and petty producers within its ranks. The costs of provisioning its starving inhabitants, coupled with a series of defaults on loans held by the city, drove Augsburg some 400,000 fl. into debt. To meet these obligations, the City Council began to borrow money and continued to do so until the public debt and its costs were out of control.[111] The result was a quickening fiscal scandal that revealed widespread malaversation of communal funds and led ultimately to the dissolution of Augsburg's constitution and the loss of its independence. Over the short term, however, the crisis fostered the paradox of a reform of alms and orphanage administration within the context of confessional tensions that had marked Augsburg since the Reformation.

In December of 1784, concerned about the worsening condition of the fisc and a bitter controversy between Catholic and Lutheran authorities, the City Council ordered an investigation into the finances of the Alms Office and specifically into the maintenance it provided the city's two orphanages.[112] A report indicated that the problem had existed for more than fifty years, stemming from wasteful management and a lack of cost controls in the 1720s.[113] One chronicler attributed the rising costs of the orphanages and of poor relief generally to the quartering of troops and the harboring of refugees during the War of the Spanish Succession in 1704.[114] No one knew exactly when or how the deficit had arisen, but all agreed that it placed an intolerable burden on city finances.

As early as 1722, Catholic and Lutheran elders of the Alms Office (Ältere, successors of the alms lords) had debated finances. In a wide ranging attempt to improve the economy and parity of poor relief, Catholic authorities demanded that subventions for both orphanages be increased to reflect the rising costs of their operations and made equal in accordance with parity.[115] Their Lutheran colleagues promptly and energetically rejected these proposals, justifying the status quo with the arguments that the Lutheran

Orphanage housed 15 to 20 more needy children than the Catholic Orphanage and that the Lutheran community gave specifically to support its own orphanage.[116] At stake was the real interpretation of parity in Augsburg. Assuming that the orphanages were to be maintained on a separate but equal basis, the Catholic elders stressed the equality that was implicit in parity and essential for harmony, while the Lutherans emphasized the separate status of the two houses and, indeed, of the two confessions that was explicit in the execution of the peace.

Inequities persisted until 1741, when the elders took steps, if not to restore parity, then at least to control the spiralling costs of the orphanages. Since the City Orphanage came into existence, the orphan fathers had been solely responsible for its administration. They had purchased all the necessary goods and services, rendering monthly accounts that the Alms Office paid. The Alms Office also provided basic commodities, such as grain, bread, lard, and wool, from its own stores in response to orders placed by the orphan father. No mechanism limited the amounts of money an orphan father could spend. As a result, the orphanage became the single most expensive item in the budget of the Alms Office by the middle of the seventeenth century. Beginning in 1741, fixed monthly subventions (*Monatsgelder*) replaced monthly accountings.[117] Commodity distributions continued too. For the moment, however, the Lutheran Orphanage had the better of the argument; it received more of every sort of subvention, whether in cash or kind. Between 1741 and 1784, the city paid 13,259 fl. more to the Lutheran Orphanage than to the supposedly equal Catholic Orphanage, a fact attributed years later to the "all too great tractability of the Catholic deputies toward their colleagues of the Augsburg Confession."[118] The deepening crisis of the 1780s made such concessions impossible.

Over fifty years the terms of the debate changed very little. Lutheran authorities argued consistently for the discrete, separate status of each orphanage, and Catholic elders insisted on absolute equality between the orphanages. Because it supported larger numbers of orphans—so the Lutherans—their orphanage required greater support from the Alms Office. Moreover, donations that the Lutheran community contributed to its orphanage, more generously than the Catholics did to theirs, were not communal property to be transferred by the state but rather private largesse given by individuals for particular purposes. Theirs was an argument for the complete separation of confessions and the rational distribution of resources based on a per capita interpretation of parity. They may have viewed any alms, but especially those given to Catholics, as wasteful and any regulation, but certainly those disruptive of the unrestricted flow of goods, as uneconomical. The Catholics never denied the truth of the Lutheran claims. Placed thus at a disadvantage, they shifted the ground of the argument.

Calculations based on relative poverty or relative charity—so the Catholics—violated both the religious duty of every Christian to give alms and the constitutional guarantee of the state to maintain separate but equal institutions. Though by no means anxious to associate with or depend on Lutherans, they argued for what amounted to an ancient tradition of solidarity: a communal approach to poor relief and an absolutely equal division of resources. That one confession argued from the marketplace while the other argued from the monastery is only a slight caricature.

Yet, by 1788, after two years of hard, often acrimonious negotiation, Catholics and Lutherans reached a compromise.[119] The Alms Office instituted absolute equality between the two orphanages: all subventions of whatever sort would be paid equally to both houses; all subventions in kind would be replaced by cash payments; a ceiling of 1,500 fl. per year would be imposed on total subventions. The traditional notion of universal access to assistance for all the deserving poor apparently emerged victorious, but the Lutheran authorities had managed to make two significant points. First, they obtained a commitment from the Catholic side to increase their contributions to the Alms Office. With the equal status of both orphanages came the responsibility for their equal support. Second, both orphanages would henceforth operate directly and independently within the city's markets.

Parity had fixed the ground between Catholic and Lutheran and shifted the ground between state and market. The principle of separate but equal organizations had been resoundingly confirmed and sharpened. The flexibility that had permitted a more generous support in response to greater needs had been replaced by an iron rule of equity. Now the burden shifted to the orphan fathers. Like any householders, they took limited funds into the marketplace and extended them to meet the needs of their houses. The rules of the game—the institutional framework of poor relief in Augsburg—had changed again, but the administrative and managerial practices of alms lords and orphan fathers remained the same.

Conclusion

The history of poverty and charity in Augsburg exhibits continuity interrupted by few moments of change. Yet, those few moments deserve particular attention.

First among them was the emergence of concentrated capital and a radically unequal distribution of property in the fifteenth century. The result of commercial and industrial expansion, it shaped the contours of social structure and social assistance into the nineteenth century. A radical distribution of wealth, based on new forms of expropriation, such as wage labor, increased the population at risk and made large-scale, secular charity necessary. Accumulated resources in the hands of a few endowed the many private and public foundations of the early modern period, making large-scale, secular charity possible.

The expansion of Augsburg's economy in the fifteenth century created a social problem that endured through the end of the Old Regime. To solve it, the elite adapted practices and values that reflected their engagements and interests, a utilitarian program born of experience in the marketplace.

Contrary to the emphasis of most modern scholarship, state intervention immediately altered neither the structure nor the function of charity, because charity drew its inspiration from social and economic realities rather than political or ideological impulses. The desire to maximize resources, limit expenses, and regulate uses preceded the state's involvement; these ends are visible in the administration of private foundations as early as the fifteenth century. In other words, rationalization, specialization, and bureaucratization derived from the concern of capitalist benefactors rather than civil magistrates. That the state assumed responsibility for poor relief as and when it did remains, therefore, difficult to explain. It is probably best understood as the result of no single factor but rather as part of the general trend toward expanded secular authority. Certainly in Augsburg the modest incentives of City Council and Alms Office, beginning in 1522, intended neither to reform charity nor to eradicate poverty. Instead, they disciplined both along established lines to limit the risks of poverty and expand the efficiency of charity.

If the rise of concentrated capital was the first critical juncture in the history of charity in Augsburg, then the introduction of parity after 1649 was surely the second. Though not intended to affect poor relief, this political principle compromised it by introducing confessional considerations. From the orphanage's beginnings, the authorities stressed the need for a more efficient use of resources. Indeed, efficiency was the genius that had inspired the founding as it had inspired other facets of public charity. Parity weakened the pursuit of simple efficiency—the best possible care at the least possible expense—as the purpose of Augsburg's orphanages.

The creation of capitalistic methods and a capitalist mentality occurred during the late Middle Ages. By powerfully reviving the public significance of religion, especially through the institution of parity, the Reformation and the Counter-Reformation constrained, but did not hinder, their advance.

The crisis of the seventeenth century, of which 1648 and parity marked the end in Augsburg, merely intensified processes already present. Public and private funds had long been committed to the relief of charity; donations and subsidies became more regular thereafter. Efficiency had always been the goal; rationalizing methods and specializing operations escalated in later years. Intensification had, however, as much to do with the accumulated experience of capital—a sharpening of memory, an improving of methods, a changing of engagements—as with changed political circumstance. Over time and without ever abandoning the principle or the practices used to achieve it, the magistrates utterly transformed the meaning of efficiency. No longer limited to the containment of cost, it acquired political and social aspects by the 1780s that were muted or missing in the 1570s: the discipline of the state apparatus through market forces; the rational distribution of resources to provide for needy children; and the commitment to a broader notion of social utility.

Notes

1. Of particular note for the connection between period price instability and impoverishment in Central Europe are the works of Wilhelm Abel. These include *Agrarkrisen und Agrarkonjunktur*, and *Massenarmut und Hungerkrisen*.
2. StAA, EWA 48, Poetische Beschreibung der Teuerung, 1571–72: "Offt kaum 6 Vierling fur ain gulden/ Das kamen sie zue grossen shulden/ Unnd jnn armuett über die massen/ Vill mueßten gar vom handtwerchk laßen."
3. Concise introductions to the structure of early modern economies, with particular attention to market conditions and factors of production, can be found in Cipola, *Before the Industrial Revolution*; Davis, *The Rise of the Atlantic Economies*; de Vries, *The Economy of Europe in an Age of Crisis*.
4. The historical problems of marginality and its consequences have been ably treated in a number of recent studies, such as Geremek, *The Poor in Late Medieval France*; Hufton, *The Poor of Eighteenth-Century France*; Snell, *Annals of the Labouring Poor*.
5. For a discussion of the relationship between profits and wages, see Heilbronner, *The Nature and Logic of Capitalism*, 65–77; Marx, *Capital*, I, 675–82; Mill, *Principles of Political Economy*, 13; Smith, *The Wealth of Nations*, 66.
6. Lis and Soly insist correctly that poor relief assumed a dual function in the preindustrial economy: first, it maintained a supply of cheap labor; second, it preserved social equilibrium. See Lis, Soly, *Poverty and Capitalism in Pre-Industrial Europe*, 24, passim.
7. The distribution of population according to wealth and occupation is based on an analysis of tax records from 1610. See Clasen, "Arm und Reich in Augsburg."
8. This definition of a hierarchical society is developed at some length in Schulze, "Die ständische Gesellschaft des 16./17. Jahrhunderts." See also Kocka, "Stand, Klasse, Organization."
9. As cited in Münch, *Lebensformen in der frühen Neuzeit*, 102–03.
10. Kießling, *Bürgerliche Gesellschaft und Kirche*, 215.
11. Jahn, "Die Augsburger Sozialstruktur in 15. Jahrhundert." See also Dirlmeier, *Untersuchungen zu Einkommensverhältnissen und Lebenshaltungskosten*; Geffcken, *Soziale Schichtung in Augsburg, 1396 bis 1521*.
12. Jahn, "Die Augsburger Sozialstruktur im 15. Jahrhundert," 188.
13. Greiff, "Tagebuch des Lucas Rem"; Zink, *Bourkard Zink et sa chronique*.
14. Geffcken, *Soziale Schichtung in Augsburg*, passim; Jahn, "Die Augsburger Sozialstruktur im 15. Jahrhundert," passim.

15. *Die Chroniken der deutschen Städte vom 14. bis ins 16. Jahrhundert*, V, 127, as cited in Jahn, "Die Augsburger Sozialstruktur im 15. Jahrhundert," 188.
16. Kießling, *Bürgerliche Gesellschaft und Kirche*, 217.
17. Kießling set the proportion of have-nothings in Augsburg between 45 and 65 percent from the late fourteenth to the mid-sixteenth century. See Kießling, *Bürgerliche Gesellschaft und Kirche*, 216.
18. On the history of German hospitals and their function, see Jetter, *Geschichte des Hospitals*, I; Merzbacher, "Das Spital im kanonischen Recht bis zum Tridentinum"; Reicke, *Das deutsche Spital und sein Recht im Mittelalter*; von Steynitz, *Mittelalterliche Hospitäler*.
19. Hörmann, "Zur Geschichte des Heilig-Geist-Spitals in Augsburg"; Lengle, "Spitäler, Stiftungen und Bruderschaften."
20. Werner, *Die örtlichen Stiftungen*, passim.
21. Lengle, "Spitäler, Stiftungen und Bruderschaften," 203.
22. Kießling, *Bürgerliche Gesellschaft und Kirche*, 224.
23. Jones, *Charity and Bienfaisance*, 76.
24. Weber, *Economy and Society*, II, 937.
25. Cf. Kießling, *Bürgerliche Gesellschaft und Kirche*, 215–189; Lengle, "Spitäler, Stiftungen und Bruderschaften," 202–7; Clasen, "Armenfürsorge im 16. Jahrhundert," 337–42; Stark, "Die christliche Wohltätigkeit"; Werner, *Die örtliche Stiftungen*; Bisle, *Die öffentliche Armenpflege der Reichstadt Augsburg*.
26. Kießling, *Bürgerliche Gesellschaft und Kirche*, 236.
27. The history of communal poor relief and social welfare systems in late medieval and early modern cities has become a small field onto itself. Some of the more recent and representative studies for Germany include Fischer, *Städtische Armut und Armenfürsorge im 15. und 16. Jahrhundert*; Fischer, *Armut in der Geschichte*; Jütte, *Obrigkeitliche Armenfürsorge in deutschen Reichsstädten der frühen Neuzeit*; Sachße, Tennstedt, *Geschichte der Armenfürsorge in Deutschland*; Scherpner, *Theorie der Fürsorge*.
28. Sonenscher, *Work and Wages*, 22–29. In describing the world of work in eighteenth-century France, Sonenscher evoked the bazaar, a world of "short-term arrangements, fleeting opportunities, and brief associations...." (p. 23). Though difficult to demonstrate conclusively, the world of charity in early modern Augsburg probably demonstrated many of the same characteristics. Donors and recipients may well have picked and chosen among the many foundations that spread their charitable wares in the city.
29. Hartung, "Die augsburgische Vermögenssteuer," 178: "So scheint in dem Augsburg des 16. Jahrhunderts mit dem bedeutenden auf der Entwicklung des Großkapitals beruhenden wirtschaftlichen Aufschwung eine langsam fortschreitende Proletarisierung der Bürgerschaft Hand in Hand gegangen zu sein, die dahin führte, daß um die Mitte des Jahrhunderts Besitzlose schon wieder mehr als die Hälfte der letzteren ausmachten, während sie zu Beginn dieser Periode nur 42,6 Prozent derselben gebildet hatten."
30. Kellenbenz, "Wirtschaftsleben der Blütezeit," 291.
31. Rajkay, "Die Bevölkerungsentwicklung von 1500 bis 1648," 252–58.
32. Kellenbenz, "Wirtschaftsleben der Blütezeit," 290. The differing assessment rates for movable and real property necessitates the use of ranges rather than specific valuations.
33. Roeck, "Wirtschaftliche und soziale Voraussetzungen der Augsburger Baukunst"; *Elias Holl: Architekt eine europäischen Stadt*, 83–88, 172–85; and *Eine Stadt in*

Krieg und Frieden, I, 193–200. Cf. Goldthwaite, *The Building of Renaissance Florence*, 29–112.
34. StAA, EWA 48, Poetische Beschreibung der Teuerung, 1571–72. "Die Kauffleutt hielten sie so cluegl/ Gaben jnn dann echt nit genueg/ Das mueßten sie groß Saumnus han/ Sehr lang offt umb die woll anston. Dann mueßt spinnen offt mann weib und kindt/ Kundten nit furderen das gesindt/ Mueßten derhalb mit großern haufen/ Spueler mägde und knappen laßen laufen. Darann hernach gar vill verdorben/ erfroren und gar hunger sturben."
35. Kellenbenz, "Wirtschaftsleben der Blütezeit," 295–97.
36. Ibid., 270.
37. Clasen, *Die Augsburger Steuerbücher um 1600*, 15–16.
38. The economic and political pressures on states to provide social services, first in conjunction and ultimately in place of churches, is nowhere more competently examined than in Kießling, *Bürgerliche Gesellschaft und Kirche*.
39. Clasen, "Armenfürsorge im 16. Jahrhundert," 337.
40. Ibid. 337–43; Kießling, *Bürgerliche Gesellschaft und Kirche*, 234.
41. Roeck, *Eine Stadt in Krieg und Frieden*, 607.
42. von Stetten, *Geschichte der Heiligen Römischen Reichs Freyen Stadt Augspurg*, 208: "... das Straff-Geld solle aufbehalten, und zu Erkauffung eines besonderen Hauses vor Waysen und Findel-Kinder, so bishero an unterschiedlichen Orten durch besondere Zieh-Mutter erzogen worden, angewendet werden."
43. Obermeier, "Findel- und Waisenkinder."
44. These conditions—and the problems they caused—were not limited to Augsburg. See, among others, Fischer, *Städtische Armut und Armenfürsorge im 15. und 16. Jahrhundert*, 162ff.
45. Kießling, *Bürgerliche Gesellschaft und Kirche*, 217.
46. Clasen, "Armenfürsorge in Augsburg," 70.
47. Sachße, Tennstedt, *Geschichte der Armenfürsorge in Deutschland*, 28.
48. Clasen, "Armenfürsorge im 16. Jahrhundert," 337–38.
49. Ibid., 338.
50. StAA, Reichsstadt Akten, Statistik, Geburts-, Hochzeits-, und Sterbens-Register. The number of deaths recorded in Augsburg rose from 1,640 in 1570 to 3,071 in 1571 and 3,306 in 1572, before falling to 1,371 in 1573.
51. StAA, EWA 48, Poetische Beschreibung der Teuerung, 1571–72: "Die obrigkeit Gott geb jr lonn/ Am armen volck hat woll gethon/ Den burgeren alle wochen geben/ Umb zimblich geltt das brott zum leben."
52. Ibid.: "Und wurden jrn täglich mehr/ Niemandt wußt wo sie kamen her."
53. StAA, W A1, Supplicatio der gemainen Außtheiler des Allmuesens alhie jn Augspurg: "... dann bey disen geshwinden leuffen unnd theuren zeiten will jedermann jr geniessen unnd mit jnen essen...."
54. StAA, EWA 48, Poetische Beschreibung der Teuerung, 1571–72: "Das man da so barmherzig war/ Da liefen sie mit haufen dar/ Man weib und kindt jnn grosser Sum/ Hausierten jnn der Statt herumb/ Das wurdt die statt erst armer voll/ Gefiell der obrigkeit nit woll/ Damit mann kein des jamers ab/ Ordtnung under die Thor man gab/ Kainn frembden mann ein lassen soll/ Der in der Statt nur betlen woll."
55. Recall that at the height of the inflation the city apportioned 4,000 fl. to acquire a suitable building, and citizens donated over 3,300 fl. in cash and far more in movable property to furnish it.
56. StAA, EW 9, "Notizen über die Geschichte des evangelischen Waisenhauses,"

Intelligentz-Blatt und wochentlicher Anzeiger von Augsburg 132 (1833), 618.
57. StAA, W 10, Monatsrechnungen, 1595.
58. Ibid.
59. Roper, *The Holy Household*, 58.
60. Confessional relations in Augsburg, especially during the period between the founding of the orphanage and the crisis of the Thirty Years' War, have been the subject of a number of recent studies. See Fassl, *Konfession, Wirtschaft, und Politik*; François, *Die unsichtbare Grenze*; Roeck, *Eine Stadt in Krieg und Frieden*; Warmbrunn, *Zwei Konfessionen in einer Stadt*.
61. Warmbrunn's term, biconfessional, though apt in the period after 1548, hardly captures the vibrant and varied confessional life of Augsburg in the first decades of the Reformation. The same may very well be said of most south German cities in which the standard of religious reform was raised.
62. Immenkötter, "Kirche zwischen Reformation und Parität," 401.
63. The statistics for this discussion are derived from materials published by Werner, *Die örtlichen Stiftungen*.
64. Again, the exhaustive and authoritative treatment of this period in the history of Augsburg is Roeck's *Eine Stadt in Krieg und Frieden*, 604–53.
65. Warmbrunn, *Zwei Konfessionen in einer Stadt*, 307.
66. Catholics and Lutherans hotly debated the cases of Rosina Heichelerin and Salome Hefelerin, in 1649, as each group tried to determine whether or not the orphanage had always been reserved strictly for the use of its own coreligionists. StAA, W A1, Die Errichtung, Abtheilung, und paritätische Gleichstellung der beiden Waisenhäuser, 1571–1795, Bericht vom hiesigen Waisenhaus, 6 July 1743.
67. StAA, KW 13, Decretum in senatum secret., 6 June 1609: " . . . denen Almosenherren anzuzeigen, daß sie die Kinder ihrer Verwaltung dero Eltern der alten catholischen Religion zugethan gewesen oder noch seyn bey derselben auferziehen sollen. . . ."
68. StAA, W A1, Verzeichnis der Waisenkinder, 1629.
69. Roeck, *Eine Stadt in Krieg und Frieden*, 981: "Anscheinend jedoch trifft für Augsburg keine der beiden von Rabb genannten Möglichkeiten zu, was die Auswirkungen des Dreißigjährigen Krieges betrifft: Weder setzt mit ihm ein vorher nicht zu konstatierender Niedergang ein, noch zerstörte er eine blühende Prosperität."
70. Warmbrunn, *Zwei Konfessionen in einer Stadt*, 162ff.
71. Ibid., 308
72. StA Augsburg. Reichsstadt Akten. Almosenamt. Waisenhäuser, A1. Extract aus Herrn Diakon Kaspar Krez 1750 des 8. Novembris gehaltenen Jubelrede in dem neuen evangelischen Waysenhaus.
73. The immediate effects of an extended period of hyper-inflation in 1622–23, the so-called *Kipper- und Wipperzeit*, have been described elsewhere in some detail. Most recently and excellently for Augsburg is Roeck, *Eine Stadt in Krieg und Frieden*, 527–603.
74. Ibid., 553–603.
75. StAA, EWA 448/II; Clasen, *Die Augsburger Weber*, 21; Fassl, "Wirtschaft, Handel und Sozialstructur, 1648–1806," 468; Zorn, *Augsburg*, 40.
76. Clasen, *Die Augsburger Weber*, 20ff., 437; Fassl, "Wirtschaft, Handel und Sozialstruktur," 468–69.
77. StAA, EWA 448/II.
78. StAA, Bestand des historischen Vereins für Schwaben, 98.
79. Fassl, "Wirtschaft, Handel und Sozialstruktur," 468.

A Brief History of Poverty and Charity

80. Ibid.
81. Roeck, *Eine Stadt in Krieg und Frieden*, 905–09.
82. Ibid., 907: "Ein Steuervermögen, das 1618 15 kr. Leistungen erforderte, wurde später erheblich höher bewertet; und man wird auch sonst vermuten können, daß die Finanzschwierigkeiten, in welchen die Stadt steckte, die Steuerherren zu einer rigiden Politik zwangen."
83. Ibid., 616.
84. Roeck calculated that the Alms Office supported 3,500 people from its three chapels in 1624, at the height of its activities.
85. StAA, Alms, Jahresrechnungen, 1600–70.
86. Roeck, *Eine Stadt in Krieg und Frieden*, 623.
87. Warmbrunn, *Zwei Konfessionen in einer Stadt*, 314–16. Cf. Kießling, *Bürgerliche Gesellschaft und Kirche*; Seida und Landsberg, *Historisch-statistische Beschreibung*; Werner, *Die örtlichen Stiftungen*, passim.
88. Muller, ed., *Instrumenta pacis Westphalicae*, 26. Instrumenta pacis osnabrugense (hereafter IPW), Art. V, §1. "In religuis autem inter utriusque Religionis Electores, Principes, Status, omnes et singulos, sit aequalitas exacta mutuaque, quatenus formae reipublicae, constitutionibus Imperii et praesenti conventioni conformis est, ita ut quod uni parti iustum est, alteri quoque sit iustum."
89. Ibid., 26–8. IPW, Art. V, §4: "In specie autem quoad civitatem Augustam sint septem Senatores Consilii secretioris ex familiis patriciis delecti, ex his desumpti republicae Praesides duo, vulgo Stadtpfleger dicit, unus sit Catholicus, alter Augustanae Confessionis, ex reliquis quinque tres Catholicae Religioni et duo Augustanae Confessioni addicti. Senatores reliqui senatus, ut vocant, minoris, nec non Syndicii, Assessores Iudicii Urbani aliique Officiales omnes sint aequali numero utriusque Religionis...." Though a minority in the upper councils, Augsburg's Lutherans retained the right to claim a Catholic seat in specific instances, when deliberations and votes were believed to be prejudiced.
90. Ibid., 26–28. IPW, Art. V, §5: "... si uno anno duo officia (veluti quaestura et cura annonae vel aedelitii muneris) penes duos Catholicos et unum Augustanae Confessionis sint, eodem anno duo alia officia (veluti Praefectura rei tormentariae et collectarum) duobus ex Augustana Confessioni et uno Catholico commitantur; sequenti autem anno circa haec officia duobus Catholicis, duo Angustanae Confessioni addicti et uno Catholico, unus Augustanae Confessionis surrogetur."
91. Warmbrunn, *Zwei Konfessionen in einer Stadt*, 181.
92. Ibid., 183.
93. StAA, W A1, Notamina, Friedens-Executions-Receß, 24 March/3 April 1649: "Wenn sich auch befunden daß das Waysenhaus A. C. verwandte allein in possession und keine als A. C. verwandte darin gehabt, als ist es dahin gestellt worden, daß ermeldtes Waysenhaus ihnen A. C. verwandte wieder solle eingeraumet darinnen nicht allein alle Waysenkinder sondern auch die beammte und dienstbothen so der A. C. zugethon seyn hergegen denen Cathol. Waysenkinder eine andere gesunde und bequeme Aufenthalt... gerichtet und eingeräumnet auch ihnen gleich den A. C. verwandten Waysenkinder der Unterhalt, Kleider, und anderes von dem Allmosen gereichet und so es beyderseits ermanglen sollte, aus dem aerario beygetragen werden.
94. StAA, W A3, Akta im Sachen Friedens-Execution, 1648–1650, Bericht der Ältern des heiligen Allmosens, 13 April 1649. The building "auf dem Kreutz" is still in use though much renovated.
95. StAA, W A1, Notamina 18. Jhdt, Akta die Abteilung der Fahrnisse in den Waisenhäuser betr., April-November 1649.

96. Bátori, "Reichsstädtisches Regiment, Finanzen, und bürgerliche Opposition," 457–60.
97. Fassl, "Wirtschaft, Handel und Sozialstruktur," 469.
98. Fassl, Konfession, Wirtschaft und Politik, 20.
99. Ibid., 470.
100. François, Die unsichtbare Grenze, 45.
101. Fassl, Konfession, Wirtschaft und Politik, 95.
102. Historians of Augsburg have long noted and debated the shift in distribution of wealth during the eighteenth century to the advantage of a Lutheran minority, a development that reversed the traditional social and ecomonic composition of the city. See Bátori, "Reichsstädtisches Regiment, Finanzen und bürgerliche Opposition," 459–60; Fassl, Konfession, Wirtschaft und Politik, 95–106; François, Die unsichtbare Grenze, 73–110; Hartung, "Die direkten Steuern und die Vermögensentwicklung in Augsburg," 1256–97; Mayr, Die großen Augsburger Vermögen, 115–23.
103. Fassl, Konfession, Wirtschaft und Politik, 102.
104. Junginger, Geschichte der Reichsstadt Kaufbeuren, 160; Wallace, Communities and Conflict, 163–76. The intervention of French royal officials after 1673 complicated the confessional relations in Colmar.
105. Fassl, Konfession, Wirtschaft und Politik, 100.
106. Ibid., 97.
107. Roeck, Eine Stadt in Krieg und Frieden, 976.
108. Fassl, Konfession, Wirtschaft und Politik, 98.
109. StAA, W A1, Die Errichtung, Abtheilung und paritätische Gleichstellung der beiden Waisenhäuser, 1571–1795: ". . . zu ihrer Verheurath- und Aussteuerung oder wo keine der Zeit vorhanden für andere arme Waysen. . . ."
110. StAA, KW 25, Obligation für den Kultus wegen der Fugger'schen Jahrtagsstiftung im katholischen Waisenhaus, 1701.
111. Bátori, "Reichsstädtisches Regiment, Finanzen und bürgerliche Opposition," 463. That this situation was not quickly corrected when dearth and inflation ended had to do with the nature of communal finance in early modern Augsburg. Decentralized accounting was a commonplace of early modern states that permitted individual offices of government to borrow and lend against their own capital and to disburse funds with little or no check on their activity. Its signal advantage lay in the fact that these agencies could develop independently a buffer against economic conditions and government policies. The converse was also true: they could overspend communal funds and drive the state as a whole into default. Lacking an effective central administration to control the fisc, Augsburg lacked also the motivation to install one. Communal government was oligarchic. The Caroline Constitution had effectively limited participation in Augsburg's city council to a few patrician families, and the introduction of parity in 1649 had done nothing to loosen their hold on it. Over time, Augsburg's council and magistracy had become a closed company of sorts, a collection of sinecures (Bátori used the term Versorgungsinstitut) that passed among the members of the same Catholic and Lutheran families and provided them with livelihoods without interference from the broader citizenry.
112. StAA, W 5, Beylage zur Cassa-Rechnung des älteren Almosenamts, 10 December 1784.
113. StAA, W A1, Notamina, 18. Jhdt.

114. StAA, EW 9, "Notizen über die Geschichte des evangelischen Waisenhauses," *Intelligenz-Blat und wochentlicher Anzeiger von Augsburg* 132 (1833), 630–31.
115. StAA, KW 2, Punkte die Schulden des catho. Waysenhauses betr., 28 January 1722.
116. StAA, W A1, Notamina, 18. Jhdt. To support their claims, the Lutheran elders cited extracts from the annual accounts of the Alms Office, which indicated that the Lutheran Orphanage had received 4,700 fl. more but that Lutheran burghers had given 12,000 fl. more than their Catholic counterparts.
117. StAA, W 5, Beylage zur Cassa-Rechnung des älteren Almosenamts, 10 December 1784.
118. Ibid: "... allzugrossen Nachgiebigkeit der damahligen katholischen Herren Deputierten zum älteren Allmosen gegen ihre Herren Collegen Augustanae Confessionis...."
119. StAA, KW 13, Decretum in senatum secretioris, 17 February 1788.

2

Capitalistic Practices and Pre-Capitalistic Organizations: Land, Calculation, and Administration in the Orphanages

Land, understood here as real property beyond the city's walls, played almost no role in the funding of Augsburg's civic charities. Unlike ecclesiastical foundations, including many charitable endowments and hospitals, which accumulated vast landed estates, the Alms Office and the orphanages rarely received endowments of land, and land provided an insignificant part of their support.[1]

Since land was the basis of most wealth in early modern Europe, however, it stands to reason that the lack of landed resources made the orphanages particularly subject to market conditions. Under these circumstances, even modest land holdings assumed a disproportionate significance in the domestic economy. They gave some protection against price instability either through direct production or added income, thus providing the marginal gain necessary to survive hard times. The ways in which orphanage administrators understood and exploited even small amounts of land serve, therefore, as benchmarks of their economic calculations and capitalistic practices.

CAPITALISTIC PRACTICES

To locate economic calculations and capitalistic practices in what are traditionally understood to be non-capitalistic organizations violates certain earnestly held and passionately defended scholarly categories. It suggests, for example, that the boundaries between capitalistic and pre-capitalistic societies or between market and moral economies are less distinct than is usually assumed. Within the period of study, from the fifteenth to the early nineteenth century, no "great transformation" occurred in Germany.[2] Neither machine technology, nor consumer demand, nor overseas markets, nor economic ideologies radically altered the pace of economic life or the forms of economic organization. Rather, these were determined by a radical empiricism. Capitalistic practices and values were not subject to theoretical abstraction and exposition but were acquired by hands-on experience and word-of-mouth teaching. Early modern capitalism developed and changed over time through accumulated experience in the marketplace and the refinement of hard-won wisdom.

Premodern entrepreneurs, managers, and capitalists adopted practices that were rudimentary but flexible. They had to be changeable, subject to experience, and applicable under different circumstances. These methods served two straightforward ends: maximize gain and minimize risk. Though such practices were by no means new in the sixteenth century, being the bedrock of all economic practice since exchange began, still the end to which they were put, that is, a ceaseless cycle of capital formation and private profit, were not universal in the sixteenth century.

One way to maximize resources was to contain costs. Premodern capitalists sought to economize expenses wherever possible, frequently buying cheap materials, employing non-guild labor, and fixing high prices, all in violation of local ordinances. Beyond an elementary exercise in thrift, they constantly strove to add value to their enterprises by increasing income. In place of the modern distinction between accounts payable and accounts receivable, they reckoned debits and credits on the basis of whether or not they generated income and, accordingly, referred to them as passive or active credit. Masters, merchants, and managers also carefully assessed the risks and rewards, the costs and benefits of alternative business engagements. They were, for example, familiar with economies of scale and weighed these carefully when considering an expansion of their undertakings. Costing, therefore, joined notions of economy and value in the armory of capitalistic practices. What is more, they kept careful account of their transactions, of all income and expenditure, a process that itself made possible notions of profit and capital.[3]

Associated with methods to increase resources were those intended to prevent their loss. Costly externalities that most concerned early capitalists were price and labor instability. The period from the fifteenth through the eighteenth century was notorious for steady, long-term price increases interrupted by violent, periodic fluctuations. Merchants and administrators frequently adopted contracting as a means of deflecting the worst effects of chronic inflation. This practice fixed prices for certain commodities and maintained relations with suppliers in a way that not only limited unforeseen expenses but permitted planning. No less pernicious, from the employers' perspective, was the independence of labor. Almost constant conflict between masters and hands over control of the relations of production punctuated the history of work relations in this period. Many strategies sought to reduce labor to a status of dependence by exercising the power of capital to determine the process of production. In the orphanages, for example, these strategies revolved around a reduced reliance on seasonal, part-time, extra-mural workers, a decrease in the size of the regular, full-time, in-house staff, and a more precise definition of their tasks and duties. A disciplinary regime that stressed industry and obedience among orphans worked to the same end. Though simple, such methods had several virtues for early modern capitalists: they regulated some of the imponderable elements of the economy, and they expanded the power of capital to control the distribution of resources and the production of goods. In other words, these methods enabled capitalism to realize its fullest potential under the circumstances of the premodern economy.

Early modern charity demonstrated all of the same qualities and methods. Apart from its social consequences and their connection to impoverishment, concentrated capital provided the resources without which large-scale organized charity would have been unthinkable. Yet, capitalism and charity shared ways as well as means. Orphanage administrators engaged in all the managerial practices typical of their day: calculating costs and benefits, pursuing economies, increasing value, controlling prices, and disciplining labor belonged to their daily routine. They maximized resources and manipulated assets with an eye toward organizational longevity and liquidity rather than private gain. Theirs was an empirical capitalism that sought advantage under changing circumstances and pursued flexible strategies according to their success or failure. Such practices could only occur in and through markets. As their manipulation of land demonstrated, caritas and capitalism were inseparable.

THE ROLE OF LAND IN THE ECONOMY OF AUGSBURG

The minor role of land in the finances of Augsburg's orphanages, and possibly in the city's economy as a whole, may be attributed to two factors. First, Augsburg's geopolitical situation prevented the development of a dependent territory beyond its walls. This, in turn, may have complicated the acquisition of estates by individuals or organizations and reduced their desirability as capital investments. Second, the commercial orientation of Augsburg's elite, from whose ranks the administrators of charity were drawn, may have discouraged or at least deemphasized the accumulation of estates. Given their pursuit of profit and their need for liquidity—so long as their interests remained commercial—merchants may not have found land an ideal repository for their wealth. The urban market offered far better opportunities for these individuals and the organizations they managed.

Unlike many free Imperial cities, Augsburg never established political control over a region beyond its walls. It remained tightly hedged by territorial polities that were not always friendly and frequently fearful or envious of the economic vitality of the city and its inhabitants. Augsburg's repeated attempts to develop a consolidated territory along its southern trade route, the so-called *Straßvogtei*, have been well documented.[4] Yet, the city's neighbors proved ever able to frustrate these ambitions.

It seems reasonable to assume that political tensions and divided jurisdictions made the accumulation of estates by Augsburgers a slow and complicated affair. The degree to which state politics really frustrated investment in land, however, cannot yet be determined with certainty. Few scholarly studies have explored in detail the role of land in the economy of early modern Augsburg.[5]

Beginning in the fourteenth and accelerating in the fifteenth century, the accumulation of real property and the development of consolidated holdings tightened the relationship between town and country, capital and land.[6] By purchasing real property, urban elites pursued two connected goals: they sought to imitate the manner and acquire the status of landed aristocrats, and they wished to secure their wealth for future generations.[7] Beyond prestige and security, acquisition of land brought other advantages: regular income in the form of taxes, rents, and fees; credit secured by mortgages; potential profit as a result of speculation.[8] The apparent stability and immutability of the land made it an appealing social and economic investment.

The late fourteenth and fifteenth centuries were years of expansion for the Augsburg economy and probably corresponded to the period of greatest interest in rural investment. Though the amount of land, calculated either in numbers of estates or monetary worth as a percentage of total wealth, cannot be reconstructed, Augsburgers in this period acquired rights to 150 holdings in the territories of the Bishop of Augsburg, a very unprepossessing number.[9] If this signifies great interest in the land, then the volume of investment from the late sixteenth to the early eighteenth century, characterized as a period in which "external land holdings played no very great role in the constitution of Augsburg property," must have been considerably smaller.[10] Seen this way, the market for land in Augsburg was modest at best.

The Reformation of the sixteenth century may have influenced the appeal of land as an object of investment. Increasing tensions between the Protestant city and the staunchly Catholic hinterland may have made the risks seem greater than the rewards. Were this the case, Catholic and Protestant elites as well as Catholic and Protestant organizations would have developed different economic commitments to the land.

Religious affiliation may have correlated to the proportion of landed wealth owned by a given family, but economic activity, social ambition, and total wealth were certainly more important factors in the calculus. At one extreme, the Fugger transferred most of their wealth to the land and accumulated estates in the late sixteenth century, comprising over 100 villages, covering an area of some 230,250 square kilometers, and carrying a value estimated at 2,000,000 fl.[11] The vast majority of Augsburgers, including the very wealthy, maintained greater diversity and liquidity. The few estate inventories and tax declarations from patrician families of the early modern period indicate that most large capital holdings were relatively land-poor.[12] The majority of their real property concentrated within the city walls.[13] The 1581 testament of the elder Hieronymus Imhof listed a series of such holdings.[14] The marriage portion of his wife, Maria Welserin, had included a house in the town of Bobingen and a house, garden, and bathhouse in Augsburg, as well as cash and silver, all valued at over 10,000 fl. Imhof himself possessed holdings in Blintheim in the Oberpfalz, which were fiefs (*Lehen*) of the Bishop of Augsburg, as well as scattered fields and interests in numerous villages south and west of the city. The testament makes very clear that the combined value of these scattered properties was but a modest part of the entire estate. In 1729 silver merchant Balthasar von Schnurbein left an estate valued at 122,993 fl., of which 40.9 percent was in urban and rural real property as opposed to 44.5 percent in cash and capital.[15] The estate of City Senator Paul von Stetten contained 45,289 fl., of which real property formed 17.7 percent and cash and capital 53.2 percent. Finally, Wolfgang Jakob von Sulzer, also a city councillor, left an estate worth 85,192 fl. in 1734, with 37.6 percent of its worth in land and buildings as compared to 51.0 percent in money and money instruments. On the basis of these few examples, the wealthy purchased land but made it an important, not predominant, element of their wealth.

Scholars assume, probably with good reason, that land was both key to and emblematic of a conservative economic strategy, a means of securing rather than accumulating capital and translating economic accomplishments into social status. Whether land contributed directly to the generation of urban wealth is another, more open question. Such evidence as exists for Augsburg is fragmentary and conflicting. For example, the geography of urban land-holdings may have been the result of mercantile calculation. Estates owned by Augsburg merchants tended to concentrate along trade routes, the most important of which was the overland route that approached the city gates from the Alpine passes to the south. Merchant estate-building along this axis laid the foundation for the city's abortive expansionist policy.[16] Away from the highways, land holdings clustered within the area that was subject to the city's market regulations (*Zihl*), or the distance that was accessible in a day's ride from the city, roughly 10 to 20 kilometers. This corresponded to a line formed west of the city by the Zusam River, along or within which the estates of Augsburg's elites notably concentrated.[17] Such geographic distribution suggests at least the possibility that merchants chose their estates with an eye to their integration into a larger framework of commercial activity and profitability.

Few merchants or patricians openly stated their economic goals or explicitly recorded the calculations behind a given transaction. The reasoning must be inferred from its consequences. So, the creation of a small territorial state *ex nihilo* by the Fugger was less a capitalistic than a social and political enterprise, a flight from the risks of the market to the security of status. On the other hand, merchant entrepreneurs may have used their rights over land and peasants to organize industrial production of goods, such as linen and woolen thread, needed for urban markets. Neither had the Fugger abandoned all commercial interests. As territorial lords, they made a concerted effort during the 1580s to transform Babenhausen, a local market town and the center of one of their counties, into a regional center for the production and sale of linens.[18] Christian von Münch purchased the villages of Aystetten and Neusäß, near Augsburg, in 1729 as part of an experiment in textile production.[19] He acquired these holdings from the Langenmantel family for 42,000 fl. in order to establish a silk plantation. Providing the capital necessary, he planted groves of mulberry trees, imported workers and masters from Italy, and constructed a factory for the production of finished silk cloth. Though the enterprise did not survive his death, it represents one of the clearest examples of capital investment in land and the integration of land into industrial and commercial enterprise in early modern Augsburg.

THE USES OF LAND IN AN URBAN ECONOMY

In fact, land might serve the interests of urban wealth in many ways, as revealed by a description of the Mill Meadow (*Muhlanger*), written by its owner, Johann Paulus Amman, in the early eighteenth century.[20] Named for a grain mill, which stood on it before the Thirty Years' War, this pasture bore the marks of Augsburg's recent history. Located east of the city walls, just beyond the James Gate (*Jakobertor*), the mill had been destroyed by Imperial troops who fled Augsburg when the city fell into Swedish hands in 1624. Thereafter, the field lay in waste, producing no crops and rendering no taxes, until 1648. The city finally assumed ownership. At what point and at what price Amman purchased it is not known. In 1719, he traded it to the Lutheran Orphanage and wrote the document in question.

What determined the value of the Mill Meadow, or presumably any parcel of land, were opportunity costs, a flexible combination of physical qualities, potential production, and multiple uses. For merchants like Amman and the administrators of the Lutheran Orphanage, land was a commodity, whose value depended on its marketability, that is, the degree to which its qualities could be assigned an economic value and exchanged.

The document he wrote around 1719 carefully listed the many advantages of his field for a prospective user.[21] Most fundamental among these were its physical condition and location. The meadow measured 70,823 *Quadratschuhe*, or roughly the area an individual could mow in one and three-quarter days (*Tagwerk*). On two sides ran streams, the Lech and the Herrenbach. Along the two landward borders ran high hedges and a ditch. Though bounded and protected by these natural features, it was still accessible, being close to the city gate and highway. These features made the meadow a valuable and desirable property.

It lacked the diseconomies that burdened so many of the landholdings around Augsburg. First and foremost among these, the feature listed by Amman before all others, was its freedom from financial obligations of any sort. The field carried full proprietary rights and rendered no dues (*Grundzins*) or rent whatever. Second, it would require very little maintenance, given its location and features. Lying between two streams, the Mill Meadow was "at all times damp and in the event of heat waves and dry summers, because of its good, moist situation, nonetheless gives much good soil and long grass, even when it fails in other places and especially if it is well fertilized."[22] The hedges protected young grasses from wind damage in the spring and provided a natural fertilizer in the form of falling leaves in the fall.[23] The same hedges were so large and overgrown that they relieved the owner of any need to invest in fences; they served as a functional barrier against humans and beasts. Third, the field bore little risk of damage or loss for many of the same reasons. The natural fertility and moisture ensured good crops. The hedges prevented unnatural damage. If the hedges proved insufficient, the owner benefitted from the field's location across the Herrenbach from the bleaching fields of the Widow Greifin. The dogs and guards, who were on duty there night and day to protect the great pieces of textile as they bleached white in the sun, would intimidate any "evil people" who tried to get at the Mill Meadow.[24] Open but undeveloped, having no buildings on or near it, the field was immune to certain forms of damage due to human carelessness, including damage by fire and the quartering of troops.[25] Because it was isolated, its owner was spared the necessity of negotiating with neighbors over fences, gateways, right-of-ways, and access.[26] One did not have to arrange the use of the field to suit a neighbor's convenience and thereby avoided a variety of legal unpleasantries. All of these qualities promised their owner ease and profit.

If the condition and location of the field assured the potential buyer that it had no hidden diseconomies, they assured its intrinsic economies as well. It "had a choice, fertile ground and earth containing neither sand nor stones, which hinder the growth of grass or make it less and thinner."[27] As noted, the soil was naturally watered and composted. Furthermore, the debris-filled ditch could be cleared, the contents spread over the field as compost, and the ditch itself used to irrigate and fertilize the ground further.[28] Clearly, Amman thought the meadow well suited to some form of capital-intensive development.

It was, in fact, suited to a variety of uses. Currently a pasture to grow fodder for livestock, it could be transformed into a garden because it possessed the "garden-right."[29] In other words, its produce could be taken to the city's vegetable market and sold at profit. With the Widow Greifin and her bleaching field in mind, one might "rent the place to the calico-makers etc. or use it for that purpose oneself."[30] As bleaching was both capital- and labor-intensive, especially before the invention of chemical reagents, the establishment of a bleaching enterprise would be a large, daring investment. Were the owner not directly interested in production, the meadow could be a ready source of cash. Amman related his conviction that it could yield 40 fl. annually in rent—this fact alone justified a sale price of 1,000 fl.— because he had been offered 36 fl. by numerous interested parties without any solicitation on his part.[31] Moreover, and this was Amman's final and most important point, the field constituted a capital investment of 1,000 fl. at 4 percent that would "richly interest any artisans seeking their own utility."[32] It could be let to a butcher, who would presumably graze livestock on it before slaughter, fertilize it with their manure, and so improve it without cost or effort to the owner. Then, in "better and happier years and times it would be sought not merely by artisans, who use such useful property for their support, but also by other citizens, especially capitalists [rentiers] and foundations, who wish to invest their wealth well and securely."[33] The value of this field lay not in its price alone but in its potential. This potential was protean, constantly changing with the times and the circumstances. Yet, at any time it offered its owner a wide range of opportunities for profit.

Amman's description testifies extraordinarily to the enterprising spirit awake in the Empire and its cities during the early modern period. This spirit was not limited to the few merchants and patricians but, as Amman noted, extended to artisans, capitalists, and rentiers of every station and even to the administrators of the Lutheran Orphanage, for whom Amman was specifically writing. It suggests not a moral economy but rather a market economy.[34] Organizations as well as individuals pursued not merely security. At every level of society and in every conceivable way, they strove to maximize their resources.

Evidence of this sort seems to support the argument that Augsburg's economic redevelopment after the crisis of the seventeenth century was a result of aggressive enterprise and productive investment rather than cautious accumulation and tight-fisted hoarding.[35] Under such actively market-oriented circumstances, land would be expected to play a subordinate role, unless purchased for its potential profitability. Whatever the interest in land among individual investors—as a low-risk means of capital preservation or as a high-risk means of capital expansion—the involvement of Augsburg's elite, seen as a percentage of their total wealth in the land market, was probably never very great and certainly subject to change. This holds true for the orphanages of Augsburg as well. Like most private, individual investors, they possessed only limited holdings in land.

Land Use and the Orphanages

It is not possible to reconstruct exactly how much land Augsburg's orphanages held at any one time. By 1719, the year of Amman's prospectus, the Lutheran Orphanage had acquired at least seven meadows of assorted sizes and in assorted places outside the city walls.[36]

The motives for acquiring land varied. The meadows purchased in the 1570s were highly productive and correspondingly expensive. The alms lords probably intended some self-sufficient enterprise, but extraneous factors may have influenced the purchases as well. It is worth noting that David Haug, whose widow sold a meadow to the City Orphanage via the Alms Office in 1573, was one of the principals of the firm, David Linck, Hans Langnauer, Melchior Linck, and Associates (*Mitverwandte*), whose close ties to the Manlich Company drew them into bankruptcy when the latter ceased payments in 1574.[37] The Manlich also sold land to the city in 1577.[38] Cash shortages, which plagued many of Augsburg's great mercantile and banking houses in those years, may have forced Haugin and Manlich to sell their property at a fraction of its real worth. All the holdings acquired later seem to have been the result of chance. Some settled debts owed for the support of children in the orphanage; some were attractive financial opportunities.[39] Apart from the possibility that the magistrates wished to secure a certain proportion of the orphanages' capital in real property, the gradual accumulation of these fields resulted from no explicit economic strategy.

Financial accounts from the first decades of the City Orphanage captured in practice the kind of calculating and manipulating that Amman described more than a century later. Between 1572 and 1600, the orphanage used its fields solely to grow fodder for livestock kept at the house in the city. A herd of dairy cows, varying between 14 and 18 head, and a small number of goats provided milk for the orphans of Augsburg.[40] Beginning in the 1580s and ending sometime after 1595, the house gradually abandoned direct production and rented its land, a change which exposed without explaining

TABLE 2.1
Land-Related Expenses (Gulden: Kreutzer) of the City Orphanage, 1575–1590.

Expense	1575	1580	1585	1590
Rents and fees	70:31	84:08	74:53	74:38
Hay transport costs		80:00	5:24	9:00
Hay purchased		18:00	10:54	
Straw purchased	20:58	35:38	20:42	14:26
Grains purchased	16:36	9:15	5:15	15:25
Salt purchased	3:34	1:25	1:36	2:30
Cows, calves purchased		31:32	11:56	23:31
Manure purchased			4:48	
Herders' wages	9:03	9:16	7:31	6:51
Harvesters' wages	105:37	29:23	19:30	29:18
Total Land Expenses	225:14	298:37	164:29	96:38
Total Household Expenses	2170:00	1873:44	2316:43	3694:09
Number of Orphans in House	144–68	126–79	166–208	262–310

the shifting strategies of orphanage administrators (See Table 2.1).[41]

They apparently hoped to make the orphanage independent of the marketplace, at least in a few essential commodities. Guided by the long tradition of medieval foundations that drew sustenance from their own vast estates, orphanage administrators put their few land-holdings to productive use. Yet the experiment was quickly abandoned. Dairy farming proved to be a complex and expensive enterprise, perhaps more than the alms lords and orphan father anticipated.

Producing fodder for livestock was seasonal work, for which the orphanage hired day laborers from town and country. Though not complicated, it was subject to the elements. The harvest was a race against time because hay would rot if allowed to become wet. Ripe grass had to be mowed into hay, cut hay had to be raked and dried as fodder, and dried fodder had to be loaded and carted from the fields to the stalls at the orphanage. Damp weather at any point in this process could spoil the entire crop and force the administrators to support their livestock on the market.

But hay was only a single factor in the maintenance of livestock and the production of milk. Beyond pasturage, cows and goats required straw for bedding. Salt, grain, and foliage rounded their diets. Herders tended them while pastured during the summer. Three servants, from a staff of 12, devoted their time exclusively to the care of cows rather than orphans.[42] Deaths within the herd occasionally made the purchase of new livestock necessary. Milk production was much more complicated than the simple possession of fields.

TABLE 2.2
Land-Related Income (Gulden: Kreutzer) of the
City Orphanage, 1575–1590

Source	1575	1580	1585	1590
Sale: cows and goats	2:30	56:00	23:21	8:00
Sale: calves and kids	8:28	25:49	26:30	26:46
Sale: rearing calves	4:30	3:00	4:00	
Sale: milk, eggs, lard	19:00	34:33	17:46	7:00
Sale: goat's milk	1:20	1:20	0:40	
Milk to Poor House	20:48	26:00	26:00	
Lard produced	120:00	96:26	43:00	
Total Land Income	176:36	250:08	141:17	41:46
Total Land Expenses	225:14	298:37	164:29	96:38
Net from Land	–48:38	–48:29	–23:12	–54:52

It was labor intensive as well and, therefore, much more expensive. From 1575 to 1590, the City Orphanage rarely paid its field hands less than 100 fl. annually.[43] The labor costs of working land consumed 11.9 percent of the total orphanage budget in 1580. In the same year, the gross cost of milk production absorbed 15.9 percent of total expenditures. That proportion, however, declined rapidly to 3.8 percent in 1590. The rapid increase in resident orphans and the associated increase in the cost of their care may help to explain the decline in land-related expenses as a proportion of total costs.

The productivity of the land may have played a role too. Whether through good fortune or good management, the orphanage's fields and herds yielded more than need required. As a result, receipts from the sales of cows, their hides, their milk, their meat, and their calves compensated for some of the expense of their maintenance. Like expenditures, however, this income fell from 250 fl. 8 kr. in 1580 to 41 fl. 46 kr. in 1590 (see Table 2.2). The fields and herds of the orphanage were never a profitable enterprise; they never managed to recover their costs.

Given the unprofitability of its land, measured in regular net losses, the City Orphanage abandoned dairy farming.[44] The annual and monthly accounts for 1612 indicate that the entire herd of cows and goats had been liquidated. Apart from a few pigs and chickens, the house kept no livestock. The orphanage hired no labor to tend fields or animals; the permanent staff of servants shrank from 12 to 7. It harvested no hay; the market supplied its meager needs. Though a precise indication of its use is not recorded, the land was probably rented to provide a cash income. Administrators contracted to purchase milk at a fixed price from two private vendors, Jörg Mausihler and Joachim Pfefferlin. With the number of orphans relatively stable, between 150 and 160, the house bought 840 liters of milk at a cost of 14 fl. every four weeks, or 182 fl. annually. The gross expense of milk purchased in the marketplace in 1612 was comparable to that produced in house in 1585 and far less than in earlier years.

The archival sources do not record the deliberations of the alms lords with regard to the early administration of the orphanage or, more specifically, its lands. They offer no direct indication of changing strategies. Financial records, however, permit the reconstruction of one possibility.[45] Compared to other years and relative to the number of orphans in residence, the total cost of dairy production was very high in the first years of the orphanage, between 1 fl. 20 kr. and 1 fl. 34 kr. per child in 1575, and between 1 fl. 40 kr. and 2 fl. 22 kr. in 1580. In the 1580s the number of orphans began to rise and continued to do so through the 1590s, by which time as many as 310 parentless children found shelter in Augsburg's orphanage. As the population increased, the per capita costs of dairy production declined until it reached a recorded minimum of 22 kr. Because the orphan father neither increased production nor purchased milk, per capita consumption probably declined, too. At the same time that per capita costs were decreasing, however, total land-related costs were falling steadily. The fact that the single largest component in this trend was reduced wages suggests that the orphanage was moving away from direct exploitation of its own land. Indeed, it had begun to do so before the increase in the population of orphans. By 1612, the subcontracting arrangement stabilized cost per capita between between 1 fl. 8 kr. and 1 fl. 12 kr., that is, between the extremes of the previous decades. Providing milk was more expensive than in the late 1580s or 90s but far less so than in the 1570s and early 80s. The high initial costs of dairy production and the gradual increase in the population of orphans confronted the orphanage with a serious fiscal challenge in its first decades. By 1612, the administrators responded decisively by reducing expenditures, renegotiating contracts, and pursuing new sources of income.

Experience inspired a shift in strategy. The entire process preceded in practice what Johann Paulus Amman later described in theory. In a period of price instability and spreading impoverishment, the orphan father and alms lords maximized resources wherever possible. An assessment of the opportunity costs of direct exploitation of the land took them out of the dairy business. They quickly abandoned their scheme of self-sufficiency but not in favor of a policy of cheese-paring. Orphans continued to receive milk as a regular part of their diet. To maintain the quality of orphanage life while reducing its expense, the administrators had to add value. Rather than sharpen regulations to limit the number of those eligible to receive charity, they lowered expenses and added income by ending production and

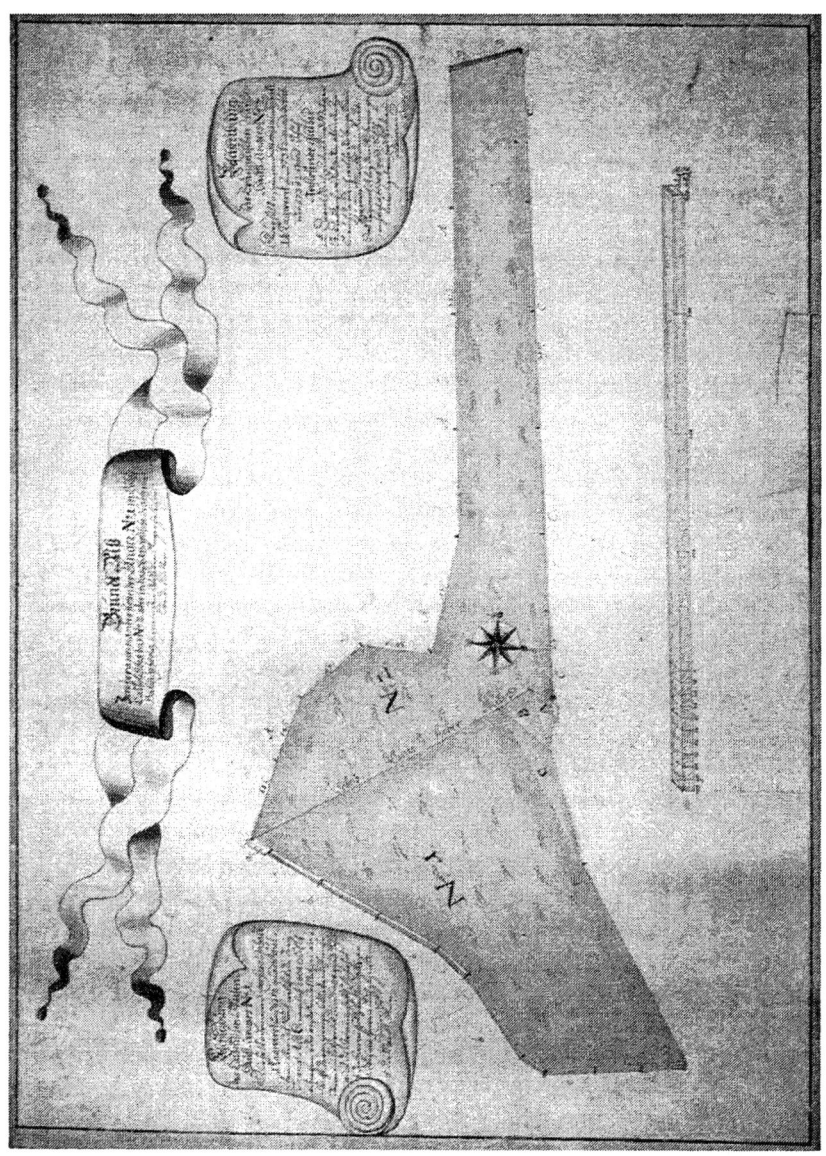

ILLUSTRATION 4 Sketch of a meadow divided between the Catholic and Lutheran orphanages, ca. 1750. Courtesy of the Stadtarchiv Augsburg, Plansammlung 0578.

renting fixed capital. They stabilized prices by contracting goods and services in periods of inflation. Their costing of dairy production indicates a habit of calculating relative advantage under changing conditions, an essential skill among early modern capitalists.

CONFESSION AND THE LAND

Yet, calculation was by no means mechanical. The same material conditions might prompt a variety of responses, depending on the circumstances of the particular organization or the attitudes of its administrators. This became clear as parity transformed charity in Augsburg.

When two confessionally specific orphanages were created out of the one state organization in 1649, all movable and real property was divided and apportioned to the new houses.[46] As was the case with the original orphanage building, its contents, and even its inhabitants, however, land holdings were easier to divide on paper than on the ground. Because equity could not be divorced from complex notions of value, these few pastures also became the object of an intense debate that extended into the eighteenth century.

The reapportionment, achieved in 1648–49, proved durable but unsatisfactory. Records made reference to a new survey of the boundaries in 1685, so disagreement and debate began almost immediately.[47] In their course, Catholic and Lutheran administrators demonstrated and advocated different bases for establishing material value, different attitudes toward productivity, and even different conceptions of land as an economic resource.

At some point after 1648, both Catholic and Lutheran orphanages returned to direct exploitation of their modest landholdings. This may have been a response to the fiscal crisis that beset the city at that time.[48] Rents were hard to collect, and the pressures for increased self-sufficiency were acute. Accounts from 1680 show both houses engaged in limited forms of agriculture, once again raising fodder for livestock kept in the city proper.[49] In August of that year the Catholic Orphanage paid 7 fl. 42 kr. to harvest hay and transport it into the city. One month later the Lutheran Orphanage worked its fields, paying 21 fl. 12 kr. Both accounts mention brood hens and beef cattle in passing, without revealing the exact number of animals. Although this return to the land in the seventeenth century is difficult to reconstruct, total expenditures alone reveal it to have been a far more modest enterprise than in the previous century.

The two orphanages gradually adopted quite different approaches to their land and its uses. The Catholic Orphanage engaged in direct exploitation along the lines of the City Orphanage in the sixteenth century. Its accounts from 1706 to 1708 show regular disbursements to transport hay and manure and to pay herders, mowers, and rakers.[50] The administrators made regular payments for milk, though these were so small as to suggest that regular household production supplemented rather than replaced the market. The Lutheran Orphanage never reentered direct production of dairy products or other foodstuffs.[51] Rather, Lutheran administrators rented the fields at their disposal to provide a regular cash income for their house.[52] Proceeds rose from 132 fl. in 1734 and 1735 to 172 fl. in 1778 and 1779.[53] Land provided considerable rent or interest income for the Lutheran Orphanage throughout the eighteenth century.

Variations in land use may have had something to do with relations to the countryside or to other foundations. That the hinterland remained true to the old religion may have made it easier for the Catholic Orphanage to engage in agricultural pursuits. Lutheran administrators might have seen more sense in allowing others to exploit the land and expropriating profits in the form of rent. By contrast, links to other Catholic foundations may have relieved the Catholic Orphanage of the need to exploit its land intensively. Lutheran magistrates suspected their Catholic colleagues of receiving fodder and other goods from the estates of monasteries, an advantage that violated the spirit and letter of parity. Augsburg's religious houses were exempt from all direct and indirect taxes within the city, with the result that all goods imported by these foundations were noticeably less expensive.[54] It is possible that the Catholic Orphanage used tax-free, and therefore less expensive, monastery-produced goods to expand its budget.[55] This would have been particularly galling in the context of repeated, ultimately successful Catholic demands that civic charity, which originated chiefly in Lutheran purses, be divided equally without regard to confession. The Lutheran Orphanage could balance any associated advantage, which the Catholic Orphanage enjoyed through its connection to wealthier Catholic foundations, only through the development and exploitation of its own estates. Unfortunately, its resources never extended beyond a few small holdings.

Not only opportunity costs but also economic attitudes determined practice. In 1722, during a broader discussion of parity and subventions for the two orphanages, Catholic Elders Leopold Ferdinand von Rehlingen and Caspar Balthus Gadner demanded the equal division of a disputed meadow.[56] The Lutheran Orphanage had apparently enjoyed sole use of it since 1685 in exchange for an annual fee (*Angerzins*) of 8 fl.[57] The Lutheran officials refused this demand, noting that the field was their property. Furthermore, they provided fodder for the Catholic Orphanage worth 12 fl.[58] As a result, the Catholics had enjoyed an advantage worth 20 fl. per year since 1685, roughly 720 fl. in total. The Catholics clearly saw the meadow as communal property to be divided equally; the Lutherans saw it as their private property subject to payment of rent.

These arguments implied certain assumptions. The Catholics seem to have understood the land as a finite commodity with a fixed value, perhaps equivalent to the purchase price. Thus the only equitable division was one in which the land itself, as a physical commodity, was divided perfectly in half. For their part, the Lutherans viewed land in more flexible terms. In addition to any value the land might have in itself, they reckoned a value for the productivity of its soil. The fact that such a calculation was made at all suggests a sensitivity to the market and the values it set that seems not to have entered into the reasoning of these particular Catholic officials. The dispute was finally resolved in 1734 when the field was divided equally between the two orphanages.

Another pasture became the bone of contention in 1753. This meadow had been divided equally between the Catholic and Lutheran orphanages when it was acquired in 1661. Yet, equal areas of ground did not mean equal crops of hay. The soil was not uniformly good; some parts were more moist and fertile than others.[59] "On the Lutheran Orphanage's portion grew many sour and marshy grasses," unsuitable for animal feed.[60] As a result of the poorer productivity of its share, the Lutheran Orphanage had received slightly more than half the total area in order to secure for each house an equal value in terms not of the quantity of land but rather of the land's productivity.

In 1753, a geometer named Wanner surveyed the field and renewed the boundary between Lutheran and Catholic shares.[61] Apparently there was some uncertainty regarding its overall extent and demarcation, resulting from the destruction of fences and boundary markers in the first decade of the century by military forces involved in the War of the Spanish Succession.[62] The lack of fixed points of reference had confused the property claims of many Augsburgers. Wanner's efforts did nothing to resolve these difficulties.

The new subdivision of the field awarded the Lutheran Orphanage an even larger area than had traditionally been its portion. The difference did not sit well with Catholic authorities, who maintained that it violated parity.[63] If each house were deprived of the total areas that had been their due, they still had to receive equal shares. Lutheran officials sought to deflect this claim as they did all others against their orphanage by attributing the loss of property to the destruction of markers.[64] Though willing to share the field equally with their Catholic colleagues, still the Lutherans complained that their house, too, had lost property through the new survey and did not have enough for its own purposes.[65] Worse, the condition of the Lutheran subdivision complicated the cultivation of fodder and effectively negated any advantage in size.[66] Again, using a notion of productivity rather than quantity, potential rather than actual value, they considered the Wanner survey equitable under the circumstances.

Evidently the worth of this or any pasture was a function of both the volume of crops that might be raised on it and the possible diseconomies due to location, topography, or other factors. Economic value, then, was an equation based on roughly reckoned probabilities that assumed risk, required calculation, and projected returns. Such reckoning would be alien to a world in which the worth of land derived from its physical possession rather than its potential productivity, and native to a market where money was the means and exchange the way.

Distinct, apparently confession-specific economic behavior may reflect fundamentally different orientations toward the marketplace and the land, but it may also derive from pressures that confronted the two orphanages in the eighteenth century. The Lutheran Orphanage benefitted from regular cash surpluses, the result of generous donations and dwindling admissions, and existed more fully in a cash nexus. The Catholic Orphanage struggled to manage swelling numbers of orphans and chronic cash shortages with help from monasteries and their exemptions. Price instability, which plagued the late eighteenth century no less than the late sixteenth, posed greater risks to individuals and organizations with limited resources. For reasons that are not clear, Catholic administrators did not rely to the same extent on the city's markets to ease their constraints. Unlike the administrators of the late sixteenth century, they found rental income less attractive than household production. Nonetheless, the practices of Catholic and Lutheran administrators remained more similar than different; they were little affected by religious or economic ideology. Given material support from those sources most accessible to them, they struggled to control costs and maximize resources.

By the late eighteenth and early nineteenth centuries, both orphanages apparently had turned away from the land; their accounts give no record of the costs of haying or stockkeeping.[67] They do, however, continue to list rents. The Catholic Orphanage possessed six fields worth 8,325 fl. These yielded 246 fl. 22 kr. in dues or rents, or 5.3 percent of its total returns from capital in 1803.[68] The Lutheran Orphanage earned 237 fl. from its fields that year, or roughly 7.4 percent of returns from capital.[69] Whether engaged in direct or indirect exploitation of the land, however, the administrators of each orphanage sought to extract the maximum value from the resources at their disposal.

Conclusion

Rented or worked, land served both orphanages in similar ways. The fields added a modest surplus value and helped maximize household resources. When worked, the fields produced hay to support livestock that produced commodities for consumption or sale. When rented, the fields generated a modest but not unimportant cash income. These shifting contributions underscore the fact that landholdings, though perhaps originally intended to

Capitalistic Practices and Pre-Capitalistic Organizations 75

make the orphanages self-sufficient, were put to more flexible uses. Experience dictated that direct exploitation could be too expensive. The early lesson in adaptable market engagements was well learned. Neither house ever acquired woodlands for fuel or gardens for vegetables; neither house ever raised enough livestock to supply all their meat and milk products. Land never constituted a major component in the finances of Augsburg's orphanages. Its changing role casts light on the empirical nature of managerial practice in Augsburg's charity, management that reckoned opportunity costs in accordance with the particular, confession-specific circumstances of the institution and the condition of the economy. The orphanage administrators calculated the use of land to reduce costs, maximize resources, and add value to their domestic economies, economies embedded in the Augsburg's markets. Insofar as these practices tended toward the longevity and liquidity of the orphanages themselves, they may be termed capitalistic. The process of involution, the ceaseless application of capitalistic practices toward unchanging capitalist ends, hollowed out non-capitalistic organizations. As will be seen, these practices and processes were apparent in other aspects of fiscal management: in capital, in commodities, and in labor.

Notes

1. One of the most striking examples in Swabia was the Hospital of the Holy Spirit in Lindau, which exploited and administered territories far greater than those of the city-state itself. See Zeller, *Das Heilig-Geist-Spital zu Lindau im Bodensee.*
2. Polanyi, *The Great Transformation,* passim.
3. Nussbaum, *The History of the Economic Institutions of Europe,* 160.
4. Kießling, *Bürgerliche Gesellschaft und Kirche,* 203–14.
5. The relationship of cities to the land has been closely treated in a magisterial work, Kießling, *Die Stadt und Ihr Land.* Unfortunately the author's excellent study does not directly address Augsburg.
6. Kießling, *Bürgerliche Gesellschaft und Kirche,* 198.
7. Ibid.
8. Lis, Soly, *Poverty and Capitalism in Pre-Industrial Europe,* 61.
9. Kießling, *Bürgerliche Gesellschaft und Kirche,* 198.
10. Mayr, *Die großen Augsburger Vermögen,* 7.
11. Lis, Soly, *Poverty and Capitalism in Pre-Industrial Europe,* 61.
12. Fassl, *Konfession, Wirtschaft und Politik,* 50.
13. This is a problem that besets any attempt to calculate the volume of real property held by Augsburgers or the vigor of a land market at a given time. Though many of the city's inhabitants, including modest artisans, possessed property or an interest in it, as indicated by estate inventories or tax declarations, the overwhelming majority of these holdings were in the city proper. In many instances, however, neither specific location nor monetary value is given.

14. StAA, Reichsstadt Akten, Stadtkanzlei, 242/5.2.
15. In these instances real estate in the city itself cannot be distinguished from real estate in the surrounding countryside. As will be seen, the market for urban real estate was much larger and more active, being intimately connected with the market for capital. The cases of Schnurbein, Stetten, and Sulzer suggest greater holdings inside than outside the walls.
16. Kießling, *Bürgerliche Gesellschaft und Kirche*, 199.
17. Ibid., Abb. 5.
18. StA Memmingen A475/7. Supplikation des Weberhandwerks, 15 July 1583.
19. Mayr, *Die großen Augsburger Vermögen*, 75.
20. StAA, EW 13, Beschreibung des Angers vor dem Jacober Thor bey der Lechhauser Brugg und dem Schiffplaz gelegen, s.d. s.a.
21. Ibid.
22. Ibid.: "... allezeit feucht und wenn die grose hitze und trokne Sommer seyn, dennoch wegen der guten und feuchten Situation, allezeit, wenn eß gleich anderer orthen fehlet, absonderlich wenn er wohl gedunget, viel und gutes Boden und landes Graß gibet...."
23. Ibid.: "Stehen von morgen her von seiten des Lechs lauter grose felber, welche im frühling die sharffe und rauhe Winde und Reifen abhalten ... im herbt aber die darvon abfallende Blätter dortherum viel zu einer bedungung helffen."
24. Ibid.: "Ist gerad vor hinüber über den Bach der frau Greifin Bleich, woselbst wegen des ausgelegten Tuchs zu Nacht stets Wächter und Hünde: Worbeÿ denn zubedenken, daß ... wegen böser Leuthe anlauf und einsteigen sicher und ruhig seyn könte, indeme man von dortherum Communication haben und bäldesten Hülfe und Beystand sich getrösten kan."
25. Ibid.: "12. worbey denn ferners wohl zu considerieren, daß er als ein frey liegendes Gut, nicht wie bey Häusern öffters, wie mancher mit seinem grosen Schaden erfahren, zugeshehen pflegt, durch heulose zinsleuth ruiniret und verderbet werden kan...."
26. Ibid.: "9. hat es nirgend von allen Seiten keinen Anstoß sonder gantz stehet es freÿ, allein und ohne alle Nachbarschafft, so daß man deßhalben wegen dillen, einshranken, außfahrt, zu gewiser Zeit zuheuen etc., wie sonsten bey derggleichen Gütern offt geshihet und beshwerliche Servitutes darauf liegen night die geringsten Händel, geshworenen Amts Augenschein, noch Processe zu besorgen noch vonnöthen hat."
27. Ibid.: "3. hat er einen treflichen guten fruchtbahren boden und Erde darinn weder kieß noch stein, welche das wachsen des Grases hindern oder weniger und dunner machen."
28. Ibid.: "8. wenn beliebt kan das Stük Graben ... wieder auslerhert ... werden ... und so das Wasser und das gantze Gut, zudessen grossen Nutzen geführet werden."
29. Ibid.: "2. hat er die Garten Gerechtigkeit, weßhalben er auch nach des Besitzers Belieben, zu einem Anger vor das Graß, oder zu einem Garten for Kräutel Wahr kan angelegt werden."
30. Ibid.: "... den Plaz entweder zu allerley gefärbten Cottuns etc. verleihen oder aber dessen sich selber darzu bedienen...."
31. Ibid.: "Ist demnach beshriebener Anger auß angeführten wahrhafften und andern Ursachen, sonderlich weil er auf fl. 40 Interesse zubringen, nicht zutheuer, wenn er vor An- und Leykauf zusammen pro fl. 1000 angeshlagen und kauflich überlassen würden."
32. Ibid.: "13. schließlich aber, welches wohl ein unwiedersprechliches Hauptpunct,

alß ein Capital von fl. 1000 á 4 procento welches bey dergleichen Gütern waß rahr und ungemeines, indeme sie sonsten nur á 3 procento auch; bißweilen darunter genuzet werden, sich ohne einige Muhe, Sorg, Gefahr und Conti allerley nur ihren eigenen Nutzen suchenden Handwercksleuthen reichlich verinteressire...."

33. Ibid.: "... besseren und glüklichen Jahren und Zeiten, weil dergleichen liegend nuzliche Güter nicht so wohl von Handwercksleuthen zu ihrer Nahrung, alß auch von andern Bürgern so ihr Vermögen sicher und wohl anlegen wollen, vornehmlich aber Capitalisten und Stifftungen aufgesucht werden."
34. Thompson, "The Moral Economy of the English Crowd," 76–136.
35. Mayr, *Die großen Augsburger Vermögen*, 109–11. Mayr understood that his findings contradicted the theory of economic development put forward by Werner Sombart in *Der moderne Kapitalismus*. His theme has been adopted and confirmed by more recent scholarship. Cf. Fassl, *Konfession, Wirtschaft und Politik*, 123–70.
36. In these parcels of land the orphanages possessed rights, ranging from proprietary to usufructuary. Four of the seven were owned by the Alms Office, which held them on behalf of the orphanages. Three others were donated directly to the Lutheran Orphanage after the introduction of parity and, so, were owned outright by it.
37. StAA, Alms, Schuldbuch, 1585–1590, 163v. See also StAA, EW 3, Aktenrepertorium, July 1719.
38. StAA, Alms, Schuldbuch, 1585–1590, 163r; Jahresrechnung, 1570–1579, 15 March 1579.
39. StAA, EW 3, Aktenrepertorium, July 1719.
40. StAA, EW 10, Monatsrechnungen des evangelischen Waisenhauses.
41. StAA, EW 14, Jahresrechnungen, 1575, 1580, 1585, 1590.
42. StAA, EW 10, Monatsrechnungen des evangelischen Waisenhauses, 1595. The accounts listed two stock maids and a stock-feed mistress, who were paid 6 fl. per annum, the same wage as a chamber maid and only slightly less than the cook, who received 8 fl. yearly. In other words, those servants charged with the care of livestock were among the best-paid employees of the orphanage.
43. StAA, EW, 14, Jahresrechnungen des evangelisches Waisenhauses, 1575, 1580, 1585, 1590.
44. StAA, EW 10, Monatsrechnungen, 1612.
45. StAA, EW 14, Jahresrechunungen des evangelischen Waisenhauses, 1575, 1580, 1585, 1590.
46. StAA, EW 3, Aktenrepertorium, July 1719.
47. Ibid., Kopia aus dem Grundriß, 9 October 1722.
48. Whether this "return to the land" held true for other individuals or organizations in Augsburg specifically or in other cities generally is difficult to ascertain. Though it bears some superficial resemblance to the flight from the sea of the Venetian elite, still the trend in Augsburg was substantially different, dictated by economic calculation rather than social conservatism.
49. StAA, Alms, Monatsrechnungen, 1680.
50. StAA, KW 10.
51. StAA, EW 18, Deputiertensitz im evangelischen Waisenhaus, 16 March 1723. One issue which occupied the deputies was the disposal of an old cow. Because it was too old and unhealthy to be slaughtered for meat, they decided to turn it over to the house butcher, Andreas Lutz, who would, in turn, arrange to sell

it to a foreign butcher. Although the possession of a cow raises the possibility that the Lutheran Orphanage was keeping livestock and producing milk, financial accounts for this period list none of the costs associated with such an operation.
52. Interestingly, neither orphanage alienated its land, even during the crisis years beginning around 1610. Cf. Roeck, *Eine Stadt in Krieg und Frieden*, 621–30.
53. StAA, EW 6, Jahresrechnungen, 1734–1735, 1778–1779, 1802.
54. Fassl, *Konfession, Wirtschaft und Politik*, 85. Fassl reports that the city lost 1500–1800 fl. in meat tolls per year between 1790 and 1802, and at least 12,000 fl. in beer tolls for the eighteenth century. Based on the amounts imported and the numbers of persons in Augsburg cloisters in that period, he believes that the foundations were importing more than they could consume and were selling the surplus below market rates to the laity.
55. StAA, W A1, Notamina, 18. Jhdt, Decretum in senatum secretioris, 7 November 1697. An inquiry into the finances of the Alms Office at the close of the seventeenth century revealed that several of Augsburg's cloister regularly provided material assistance to the city's poor inhabitants. The Dominican sisters of St. Catharina's delivered 100 one-pound loaves—later changed to 12 *Scnaf* of rye flour—to the Alms Office each week for distribution among the hungry. The Benedictines of St. Ulrich's also provided an undisclosed amount of bread weekly. The Augustinians of Heiliger Creutz offered aid too. In a period of extreme confessional tension and competition, it is highly unlikely that this food, produced by Catholic hands for the benefit of Catholic foundations, was allowed to assist heretics.
56. StAA, KW 2, Punkte den Schulden des catholischen Waisenhauses betr., 29 January 1722.
57. StAA, EW 3, Kopia aus dem Grundriß, 9 October 1722.
58. StAA, KW 2, Augustanae Confessionis Antwort auf Punkten den Schulden des catholischen Waisenhauses betr., s.d. 1722.
59. StAA, EW 3, Unmaßgebliche Notamina, 1753.
60. Ibid.: "... wie dann auf des evangelischen Waisenhauses Platz zimmlich viel Saur und Moßicht Graß wächst."
61. StAA, EW 3, Pro memoria, 1753.
62. Ibid., Unmaßgebliche Notamina, 1753.
63. Ibid.
64. Ibid.
65. Ibid., Bericht ad senatum secret., 1754.
66. Ibid., Pro memoria, 1754.
67. StAA, Alms, Monatsrechnungen, 1774.
68. StAA, KWA 16, Samlung Aus den katholishen Waisenhauß Akten über die bedeitendste Gegenstände.
69. StAA, EW 16, Jahresrechnungen, 1803, 1804.

3

Subventions, Donations, and Earnings: Paying for Poor Relief

Without estates of their own, Augsburg's orphanages and Alms Office could not be self-sufficient in the manner of medieval foundations; they could not produce commodities for their own consumption. With few exceptions— and these decreased over time— administrators sought regular incomes, which they exchanged in the marketplace for the goods and services needed by the children in their care. Consistently, the most important sources of cash were donations, subventions, and earnings, the three financial pillars of early modern charity.

Yet, these pillars shifted over time and forced poor relief to rest first on one, then on another. Alms from individuals and families were the traditional source of charity. From the sixteenth into the nineteenth century, many types of donations and legacies underwrote the Alms Office and the orphanages. As donations declined in response to the crisis of the seventeenth century, for example, the city replaced the loss from its own coffers and stores. Over the course of the seventeenth and eighteenth centuries, subventions grew to be the largest source of income for the Alms Office and, through it, for the orphanages as well. As private donations and public subventions ebbed and flowed with shifting mentalities and fortunes, returns from capital provided a degree of compensation. Earnings included rents from real property, interest from credit transactions, and annuities from long-term investments. Manipulating capital and a variety of incomes enabled the Alms Office and orphanages to respond flexibly to changing circumstances and maximize their income.

An examination of incomes illuminates the constraints that alms lords and orphan fathers confronted. What might be called the capitalization of charity, that is, the tendency among donors to view their donations both as capital that should bring some kind of tangible return and as property that remained somehow under their disposition, caused this resource to change direction and flow to different organizations. As administrators adapted to new economic and social realities, they explored new ways of providing poor relief. The result frequently resembled a process of trial and error. Yet, the discordance, between gifts and profits, between exchanges and transfers, between the orphanages as homes and the orphanages as banks, was more apparent than real. It was, in fact, an exercise in flexibility characteristic of that empirical capitalism, that slow accumulation of experience and refinement of expertise based on market practices, of which these men and their organizations were part.

THE THREE PILLARS OF PUBLIC CHARITY

Whatever the effects of bureaucratization and centralization elsewhere, the Alms Office in Augsburg enjoyed noteworthy financial independence. During its first hundred years, it drew almost all of its income from private donations and its own capital. In periods of extreme need, when these funds proved insufficient, the City Council opened the public purse to offer loans at interest to support charity.[1] Even in the first decades of the seventeenth century, the Alms Office still depended largely on private generosity (see Appendix I, Figure 1). Augsburgers remembered the poor by subsidizing state-sponsored relief through a variety of collections and contributions that changed little until the 1620s and 30s, when times were hard for all and contributions declined never to recover. Only the Alms Office's proprietary earnings—the returns from its capital—closely matched the pattern of change in total income, suggesting that the alms lords used this resource to balance the budget and redress the instability of other incomes.

Charity grew out of voluntary donations to assist those in need (see Appendix I, Figure 2). Small sums flowed constantly from burghers approached in their homes, from boxes attached to the entrances to public houses and churches, and from persons attending baptisms, marriages, and burials. Collections taken in church, however, constituted the largest source of public alms-giving in Augsburg by the seventeenth century and increased in the crisis years, especially 1626–27 and 1634–35, when famine and siege gave the burghers greater cause than usual to pray and give for their own salvation. Why the church proved so ideal a venue for gathering charity is not entirely clear but may have had to do with the setting, in which such generosity was most immediately apparent to the community and to God. No form of private generosity, however, withstood the test of hard times. The Alms Office derived 31.6 percent of its income from these sources in 1600 but only 17.7 percent in 1670. Churches, ever the most profitable places for gathering donations, yielded only 12.5 percent of all alms in 1670 as opposed to 26.3 percent in 1600. Testamentary legacies (*Stiftungen*), by which the alms lords meant capital donations to be invested at interest, and pious gifts (*Gottesgaben*) to be used for the immediate needs of the poor, also became smaller as economic conditions worsened (see Appendix I, Figure 3). None of these changes can be clearly explained. Though a year never passed without occasional income from contributions, collections, and legacies, still donations as a proportion of total income shrank from 32.9 percent in 1600 to a mere 2.2 percent in 1670.

A decline in total donations notwithstanding, individual offerings could provide very important infusions of cash. In 1600, for example, the Alms Office received a legacy from the estate of Leonhart Rehlinger in the form of an Imperial debt that yielded 1,667 fl.[2] Two years later, the Alms Office collected the remaining principal and interest—14,253 fl.—that constituted nearly half of the entire year's income. For an organization frequently pressed for funds such singular receipts could determine whether the needs of Augsburg's poor would be met from alms or would require earnings from capital and funds from the city.

As important as donations were to the Alms Office, they were too changeable to offer reliable support. Therefore, public charity looked to other resources to earn a regular income. It invested capital in ways that sought liquidity. In the first decade of the 1600s, the Alms Office commanded total capital reserves (*Hauptgut*) in excess of 130,000 fl (see Appendix I, Figure 4). These included roughly 17,000 fl. in commodity stores, 21,000 fl. in real estate, and 91,000 fl. in credit.[3] The largest and most profitable portion of this capital took the form of money loaned to persons and polities, usually at a fixed interest and secured through collateral (*Anligentgeld* or *Ewiggeld*). Greater reliance on annuities from liquid capital than on rents from fixed capital explains why the Alms Office was so slow to recover after the 1630s and 40s, and never achieved its former level of endowment. Its working capital had been irretrievably lost. Earnings retreated from 25 percent of all income in 1600 to 2.9 percent in 1670. The loss of other incomes, the increase of prices, and the difficulty of collecting debts created deficits in the 20s and 30s that forced poor relief to consume its own resources.

In hard times the Alms Office became a debtor as well as a creditor, a fact which complicated the evaluation of its capital and created idiosyncrasies in its accounting. Operating surpluses formed an especially problematical element of the Alms Office's income (see Appendix I, Figure 5). They grew in the late 1640s, while capital and earnings declined and cash was in short supply. Though the reason for the existence of a surplus in a period of extreme austerity cannot be determined, it suggests that the Alms Office liquified capital reserves and borrowed funds to meet operating expenses. Not only during crises but at all times, charitable foundations balanced debits and credits to capital. For example, the Alms Office regularly paid debt and maintained capital as part of its annual operating overhead (see Appendix I, Figure 10). Interest payments, including the servicing of loans and the amortization of losses, were a substantial expense. The amalgamation of certain penalties (*Zubüßgelder*) with conditional interest around 1630, and of conditional interest with the loss account (*Verlustkonto*) around 1670, encourages the speculation that these were connected with losses to capital. Single expenses in settlement of long-term capital transactions with individuals or families, such as the purchase of land or the repayment of loans, became increasingly common during the seventeenth and eighteenth centuries. In 1604, they absorbed over 700 fl. The range of these transactions testified to the dynamism of Augsburg's capital markets and the engagement of charity in them.

Augsburg's crisis of the mid-seventeenth century forced a fundamental restructuring of poor relief. That donations declined and low levels persisted into the period of recovery reflects changing mentalities. A new generation of merchants and patricians was less inclined to aid the poor from their own substance, and burghers generally shared this inclination, all of which speaks for a fundamental change in values. The existence of state-sponsored relief for the poor changed the nature of charity from exchanges between individuals to transfers among groups. Medieval charity had emphasized the personal and reciprocal nature of generosity: the donor offered aid to ease the distress of the needy, and the recipient responded with prayers for the benefactor's soul. After 1522, the state gradually broke that immediate connection between individuals.[4] The Alms Office used its funds to support numerous forms of relief; charity gradually lost the quality of an exchange between individuals and became a voluntary but regular transfer of wealth between social strata. As a result, the particular wishes of donors regarding the eventual uses of their charity or the prescribed responses of beneficiaries simply could not be considered. There were exceptions. In 1581 the alms lords received a legacy of 1,000 fl. from Simon Scheibenhardt, a canon of the Collegiate Church of St. Moritz.[5] The interest from half of this sum was intended to provide a dowry or stipend for an orphan; the remainder supported the Foundling Home. More often, however, the names of donors merely appeared in general lists of benefactors and their gifts quietly disappeared into the general fund of public assistance. Shifting opportunity costs may have encouraged the abandonment of the city's omni-competent charity in favor of foundations that pursued specific charitable ends, especially the ability to be self-supporting. It is telling, if inconclusive, evidence of that rejection of begging and charity in favor of work and self-sufficiency that would become increasingly characteristic of modern social welfare.

The shifts in private finance and public charity during the seventeenth century mark the capitalization of welfare. More donors abandoned the Alms Office in favor of private or independent foundations, through which they could stipulate the purpose of their generosity or, in the case of family foundations, maintain control over the donation itself. They did not so much give charity as invest capital where its support would contribute to the discipline and integration of the poor. Patterns of donations suggest that these were the donors' motives. Needy persons in whom such an investment offered little promise of immediate return, such as the aged, the infirm, and the deviant, were left to the state, which reacted more and more with policies of segregation. Funds for organizations—the Alms House and the orphanages—increased from 37.8 percent of the Alms Office's total budget in 1600 to 53.6 percent in 1670 (see Appendix I, Figure 12). Indeed, the decay of private donations and the commitment to enclosure forced the Alms Office to rely on other sources of income. It added particular urgency to its search for capital earnings. It also forced the state to subsidize charity directly and regularly through a conglomeration of subventions.

The decline of donations and the exhaustion of capital, coupled with significant increases in costs and commitments, jeopardized support for the needy. From the late sixteenth century, steadily rising costs outran the charity of citizens and the income from capital. Between 1550 and 1574, the Alms Office disbursed 257,500 fl., an average of 10,300 fl per year.[6] By the period 1600 to 1620, the average annual expenditure rose to 19,106 fl., before falling in the second half of the century[7] (see Appendix I, Figure 6). The pattern reflects increased need on the one hand and decreased population on the other.[8] In responding to periodic crises, early modern poor relief was subject to radical variation. During the catastrophes of 1627 and 1635, for example, expenditures rose to about 55,000 fl. and 30,000 fl. respectively.[9] This pattern of abrupt change defied rational planning or administration and forced an approach to resources that derived flexibility from a reliance on a number of sources. Such flexibility inspired calculation and became the hallmark of managerial practice in the Alms Office and the orphanages. Abrupt, unexpected changes in need also necessitated regular support from the state. In this crisis the City Council assumed direct financial support of charity, first by transferring certain indirect taxes to it and finally by subsidizing it from the treasury (see Appendix I, Figure 7). Unnecessary in 1600, public funds provided 46.3 percent of the Alms Office's annual income by 1670.

Various indirect taxes bolstered charity according to the principle that the primary beneficiaries should also be the primary benefactors. The first was a tariff on fustians, instituted in 1616 and continued throughout the seventeenth century.[10] Magistrates justified this duty with the thought that most weavers were themselves supported by the dole.[11] A tariff on meat (*Fleischaufschlag*) proved profitable for the Alms Office, yielding over 16,000 fl. in 1629 and again in 1630, not the best of years for Augsburg consumers.[12] Catholic authorities favored this tax in particular, possibly capitalizing on the Lutheran insistence that meat be eaten on Friday, an ironic twist to dedicated taxes.

Augsburg favored indirect taxes to support its public charity in the early seventeenth century. Tariffs and duties, however, were not ideally suited to the purpose because they fluctuated with consumption and were, therefore, likely to decrease in periods of high prices. In other words, receipts would fall at precisely those times when the demand for charity and the strain on public funds would be greatest, as occurred in 1634–45. Furthermore, by simply transferring taxes, the city surrendered part of its ability to manage its own moneys, shifting various incomes among many commitments. A more efficient means of supporting charity had to be found.

What signalled a fundamental change in the nature of charity and an intensification of its relationship to the state were direct payments from the treasury. For four months, beginning in November 1633, the Alms Office received its first subvention from the city's Incomes Office (*Einnehmeramt*), a sum of 200 fl. monthly for the support of the orphanage.[13] In 1642 the city transferred 50 fl. weekly for five weeks. This weekly assistance (*Wochenhilfe*) became a permanent feature the following year and grew from 2,600 fl. in 1643 to 8,015 fl. in 1650 before stabilizing at 5,200 fl. in 1654. It remained at that level until 1668, when it rose to 8,100 fl. and again to 9,100 fl. in 1669. The city would never again escape direct involvement in the finance and administration of public charity.

State support did not, however, mean renewed vitality for public charity. In 1661, the Alms Office had the opportunity to purchase a large supply of fuel, wood, and lard but lacked the cash.[14] A private individual agreed to lend 500 fl. at no interest for the purpose, the loan to be repaid in weekly installments of 10 fl. The City Council approved this arrangement with the proviso that its subsidy from the tax on meat be reduced from 50 fl. to 10 fl. weekly until the debt was paid. Though the obligation should have been discharged in less than a year, the council renewed the agreement in 1661, 1662, and 1663. Relying on donations, earnings, and subventions, the Alms Office still had to struggle to fulfill its duties. Far from guaranteeing adequate resources, the three financial pillars of charity required adaptability, the capacity to learn from experience and respond flexibly to changing conditions and occasional opportunities.

Parity and the Changing Fiscal Basis of Augsburg's Orphanages

The seventeenth century worked a sea change in the finances of charity. An economy in crisis forced administrators to exploit capital adroitly, shifting back and forth between donations, subventions, and earnings, in order to secure adequate incomes. During and after the Thirty Years' War, the orphanage entered a period of spiralling costs. Because it received subsidies on the basis of accounts payable with no fixed mechanism to control expense, the costs to the Alms Office soared. Most critical was the period 1626–49 (see Appendix I, Figure 13). In the early years of the seventeenth century, the City Orphanage regularly consumed between 20 and 30 percent of the Alms Office's budget. After 1629, however, when the numbers of deserving poor increased, charitable resources dwindled, and religious conflict escalated, the level of orphanage support rose to between 35 and 50 percent of the Alms Office's total expenses. In periods of acute dislocation, payments climbed: above 9,500 fl in 1628 and above 8,100 fl. in 1634.[15] Only in 1649, when parity divided the City Orphanage into two confessionally specific orphanages, did these subventions again increase so drastically.

No less invasive were confessional tensions that freighted the distribution of resources with non-economical considerations. To a certain extent, politics dictated orphan care in the 1630s and 1640s. Catholics expelled or converted Lutheran orphans in the aftermath of the Edict of Restitution in 1629. To provide separate care for non-Catholic orphans, the alms lords adopted two expedients: they opened the so-called New Orphanage, an extension of the city's central facility, of which no other record survives; and they returned to fostering Lutheran children with private families and providing only a weekly sum of money for their support. Lutherans responded in kind with the support of the Swedish occupation of 1634. When the fortunes of war turned once more, in 1635, Catholic children again occupied the orphanage. In each instance, the Alms Office provided little assistance for those excluded from alms by reason of religion. Though the numbers of Catholic and Lutheran orphans during the 1630s and 1640s is uncertain, the annual accounts of the Alms Office reveal plainly that those forced to subsist outside the orphanage received far less support per capita than those favored inside. The politicization of charity in this period constrained it in unexpected ways and compelled its administrators to seek new sources of income and adapt new economic strategies.

In the 1570s Johannes Stöcklin and others made the argument that caring for large numbers of orphans in a single institution would cost less than caring for them individually in many separate dwellings. By tying the delivery of poor relief to price rather than to need, institutionalized charity became truly market-oriented. These magistrates expected the advantages of an orphanage to extend beyond marginal economies of scale, however, to matters of social and political discipline, because both orphans and their care-givers would be subject to greater scrutiny and correction. Yet, economy and discipline were not always consistent or even concordant goals. The establishment of parity in 1649 proved this rule. The offices of Alms Lord were divided equally among Catholic and Lutheran magistrates, who, though bound to enforce an equal division of resources, relentlessly pursued the interests of their own confessions. To maintain two orphanages in place of one, however, raised real economic issues. Separate but equal organizations were essential to Augsburg's religious and social order, but absolute equality divided resources regardless of the shifting realities of economy or utility. The magistrates soon learned that parity altered the transactions and compromised the incomes upon which poor relief was based. It doomed the city to a fruitless competition for increasingly scarce charity.

Orphan care in Augsburg involved the same constellation of charitable resources as poor relief in general, a combination of donations, subventions, and earnings. In the orphanage, however, the three pillars of public charity created a system of unusual complexity and opportunity. When the house in the Bäckergasse was purchased, a coalition of supporters and resources had to be cobbled together. The City Council provided the capital needed to acquire the real property. Private donors contributed the furnishings. The Alms Office covered normal operating expenses, based on monthly accounts payable submitted by the orphan father. As donations and legacies continued, they formed a reserve in the hands of the house's administrators because they were unnecessary for the basic maintenance of the organization and its occupants. This income created the opportunity to accumulate and manipulate a capital endowment.

Transforming a state organization into separate, confessionally specific ones provoked an acrimonious debate over the division of resources that was never fully resolved. Within two years, Catholics and Lutherans agreed that capital had to be shared equally regardless of relative numbers of orphans or other sources of support. Once this fundamental issue had been resolved, the debate extended to subventions.[16] According to the logic of parity, each orphanage should have enjoyed equal support from the city. The funds provided by the Alms Office, however, were not subject to this sort of division.

Each orphanage continued to receive operating expenses in the tried and true manner. The Catholic and Lutheran orphan fathers submitted their monthly expenses as accounts payable to the Alms Office, but because their needs varied so did the funds they received. Under such circumstances, the magistrates could neither maintain equality nor control costs. The immediate results of parity, therefore, were an increase in the marginal costs of orphan care, a loss of planned economies of scale, and a dilution of each institution's capital base. Even as resources shrank, the price of providing care for orphans grew. Two houses were simply more expensive to maintain and operate than one. Though the City Orphanage had been well funded, neither the Catholic nor the Lutheran Orphanage started on the same firm footing.

Beyond the division of capital and subventions, parity destabilized the balance between resources and population. The division of Augsburg into separate but unequal communities altered the distribution of donations and charged social and political relations into the nineteenth century. Its consequences suggest at the very least that confessionalization cannot be reduced to a matter of confession.[17] Economic and social disparities and aspirations played a considerable role. General support for the needy both to private and to public foundations declined steadily and became above all confession-specific. This was true of Augsburg's economy in general: Catholics traded with Catholics and Lutherans with Lutherans.[18] "A Catholic did not readily buy his bread from a Protestant baker."[19] Nor did a Catholic readily give bread to a Protestant.

Charity was no longer seen as the responsibility of every Christian nor were the poor understood to be the burden of all. Rather, Lutheran alms succoured the Lutheran poor and Catholic alms the Catholic poor, each strengthening the solidarity and identity of its community. By dividing, and so reducing, resources, parity created constraints that gradually forced the Catholic and Lutheran orphanages to pursue more predictable incomes. Established to serve their confessions separately and independently, the new orphanages relied on the city to an ever greater extent.

Inequalities in the subventions provided by the Alms Office to the Catholic and Lutheran orphanages persisted from 1650 to the 1780s. The differences varied in the accustomed manner from a few gulden in 1659 to nearly 5,000 fl. annually during the mid-1660s. In those early years, the Catholic Orphanage received more funding from the Alms Office than did the Lutheran Orphanage. Forced to renovate and furnish a new facility and burdened with far more orphans, the new house arguably had the greater need. Yet, it was not always so. The Lutheran Orphanage enjoyed an inexplicably large edge in 1657, 1659, 1661, 1662, 1668, and 1669. Though no pattern of consistent advantage emerged until the early eighteenth century, when the Lutheran Orphanage regularly received greater subventions than its Catholic counterpart, still variations based on changing numbers of orphans and changing levels of need in each house created a situation in which conflict was likely. In the end, rising costs and persistent inequalities forced administrators to reconsider the nature of parity and the economics of charity.

Matters came to a head in the 1690s. On Christmas Eve, 1692, the Lutheran leadership of the city appealed to their coreligionists to assist the Alms Office and especially the Lutheran Orphanage.[20] The privations of war had reduced the state treasury to such an extent that it could no longer support the poor. The Lutheran Orphanage, according to magistrates, had been particularly affected by inflation, which made it nearly impossible to provide even minimal necessities. To meet the crisis, the magistrates announced their intention to go door-to-door and collect alms for the needy. Faced with the failure of state supervised poor relief, they relied on a tried and true method, one with a long tradition but unpracticed since the early years of public charity. Lutheran citizens were urged to offer "a charitable, sufficient, extraordinary contribution."[21]

War costs, contributions, and damages were common fiscal problems for early modern states. Yet, the shortage of funds that beset the Alms Office was more than a temporary economic disruption. In 1697, the City Council ordered the alms lords to submit their accounts to review in order to determine "how to aid the so greatly decayed alms."[22] Words and deeds suggest that the council suspected mismanagement if not malfeasance on the part of charity's administrators. The inquiry revealed that the Alms Office possessed capital worth approximately 30,000 fl., a sum insufficient to operate Augsburg's public charities.

Under-capitalized, the Alms Office had to borrow in order to maintain operations. This, too, was a tried and true method; long lists of credit, debt, and interest were regular features of the annual accounts.[23] Although its capital base had shrunk in the hyper-inflation of 1622–23, reliance on capital transactions to fund charity increased throughout the seventeenth century, at the same time that voluntary gifts and contributions decreased (see Appendix I, Figure 1). For Augsburg's Alms Office, credit supplemented donations, and poor relief approached a capitalistic enterprise.

Crisis followed crisis, and the economic woes of the city's charities deepened. The War of the Spanish Succession laid the city under siege and involved the quartering of Bavarian troops, both of which inflicted hardship on Augsburg and its needy. In 1714, the deputies (*Deputierten*) of the Lutheran Orphanage, those council members appointed to oversee its administration, complained about the ongoing decline in alms-giving.[24] In their opinion, the orphanage could no longer support itself. Despite the collections boxes permitted in 1694, the home had a deficit of over 255 fl. Debt plagued the orphanage just as it beset the Alms Office.

Apart from forcing a search for private support, the pressure on subventions emphasized the imperfections of parity and the inequality of the two orphanages. In 1720, Catholic magistrates complained that parity no longer existed between the two houses.[25] Certain expenditures were too high and rising constantly; controls were needed to preserve an already overburdened Alms Office. What was more, action had to be taken to restore equality between Catholic and Lutheran orphanages and to preserve the fabric of parity.

By 1722, this Catholic complaint had merged into a program for the thoroughgoing reform of state charity. On 28 January, Leopold Ferdinand von Rehlingen and Caspar Balthas Gadner, the Catholic elders (*Ältere*, who succeeded the alms lords) of the Alms Office, submitted a list of demands to improve economy and to reestablish parity.[26] These included a number of peripheral issues, but parity and its implications were at the heart of the matter. Subventions for both orphanages had to be increased and made equal.[27] The proposal constituted a turn to absolute parity between the orphanages regardless of need and a considerable expansion of the resources for each.

The Alms Office provided funds for the purchase of many commodities but occasionally supplied the commodities themselves. Everything from lard and meat to grains and bread to cloth and clothing to wood and fuel arrived in the orphanages by way of the Alms Office. The Catholic and Lutheran orphan fathers recorded all of it in their monthly and yearly accounts. While all expenditures had risen steadily in the late seventeenth and early eighteenth centuries, only three caused the Catholic elders particular concern. The subventions, or monthly moneys (*Monatsgelder*), provided on the basis of monthly accounts payable submitted by the orphanages should, they proposed, be raised from 100 fl. for the Lutheran Orphanage and 80 fl. for the Catholic to 120 fl. for each; the purchase account (*Einkaufskonto*) should be set at a maximum of 300 fl. per year for each orphanage; and the woolen weavers' account (*Lodweberkonto*) that provided money for the production of clothing should be fixed at 100 fl. for each annually. These three, perhaps because their vague definition encouraged a certain latitude, had risen faster than all others.

Rehling and Gadner advocated a hitherto unheard-of economy for Augsburg's public charity. Although it limited the assistance given to the independent honorable poor, the Alms Office always assisted foundations as needed. Accounts had never been fixed. The orphan fathers had enjoyed the enviable position of providing generously, even lavishly for themselves and their families to a degree beyond the means of their salaries. Fraud of this sort became a concern of the City Council and the Alms Office in the straitened circumstances of the early 1700s. Apart from the risks of malfeasance, the system of open accounts and accounts payable overburdened municipal resource. It was absolutely essential that public organizations practice economy, limit expenditures, and achieve self-sufficiency.

Whether Catholic officials were more concerned with economy or parity is impossible to know. The Lutheran response, however, focused attention on the relationship between confessions rather than the balance between ways and means.[28] Their arguments would be repeated throughout the century. Parity had not been violated; Catholic and Lutheran orphans individually received the same amount of care from the state. Larger subventions for the Lutheran Orphanage were justified because it cared for a larger number of orphans.[29] Moreover, Lutherans donated larger amounts of charity to the

Alms Office and to their orphanage. As such, they had a greater claim on the resources of state charity.

Whether because of the merit of the Lutheran position or for other reasons the City Council took no action on the Catholic proposal. Rehling renewed the petition on 6 February 1724.[30] Three points touched orphanage finance and administration directly. First, Rehling advocated the same fixed limits on accounts as in 1722 and added that each organization would reimburse the Alms Office for any excess spent. Such strict controls would force both orphanages to operate within their means. Second, he insisted that the orphan fathers record, maintain, and return the property of orphans in an orderly and timely manner. Many orphans entered the orphanage with property inherited from one or both of their parents or provided by a patron or relative. The administrators exercised usufruct over these so-called children's moneys, or savings (*Kindergelder* and *Sparhafen*), as long as their owners remained in the house. Thus, Rehling threatened to introduce municipal scrutiny of an important source of capital, in which the Lutheran Orphanage was particularly involved at the time.[31] Third and last, he proposed that certain commodities, especially wood, lard, and grain, be purchased on the open market. In this he mooted a means of achieving economies and extending resources that would be taken up by the Lutherans and adopted finally in the 1780s.

The Catholic reform was to be a conservative one. It intended to reduce the orphanages to complete dependence on subventions and to strip them and the Alms Office of most of their independent capital. The investment of such resources as remained, including the property held in trust for the needy, would be hindered. Indeed, as Rehling later admitted, his proposal would permit the orphan fathers to take no action of any sort without the advice and consent of the deputies or other superiors.[32] Rather than increase incomes, it attempted to cut costs. Even the apparently radical proposal to reorient commodity acquisition toward the marketplace was directed at certain items only and was born, at least in part, of frustration with their quality. Economic control rather than market freedom was the watchword.

The Lutheran officials—members of Augsburg's mercantile and financial elite—might have occupied a different world.[33] Well versed in the city's markets, they had no hesitation about entering them to purchase commodities and agreed readily to the third of Rehling's suggestions. They also agreed that the orphan fathers must manage the property of orphans honestly and carefully, but they insisted that such management was the responsibility of the specific orphanage and refused to render accounts to the biconfessional Alms Office. In all else, however, their response was unwavering. They refused fixed, equal subventions on the same grounds as they had two years earlier. The Lutherans supported more orphans and gave more charity.

TABLE 3.1
Index of Fiscal Disparities between Orphanages, 1704–21

Year	Monthly Accounts		Purchase Accounts		Alms Collections	
	Luth.	Cath.	Luth.	Cath.	Luth.	Cath.
1704	100	101	100	78	100	31
1705	98	94	113	120	105	42
1706	95	88	87	78	126	52
1707	91	84	90	88	138	55
1708	93	83	84	86	121	41
1709	92	84	95	81	107	39
1710	96	85	93	73	109	36
1711	101	82	95	78	122	51
1712	102	85	106	81	148	57
1713	105	85	106	85	118	48
1714	105	83	107	93	124	52
1715	108	87	119	127	139	56
1716	111	100	126	106	146	55
1717	119	103	176	105	140	46
1718	116	99	181	135	148	45
1719	119	96	177	111	157	56
1720	115	98	175	142	163	51
1721	104	102	148	139	160	51

Therefore, they deserved larger subventions from the Alms Office. The Lutheran position on charity, at least as inferred from their position regarding parity, contained an understanding of property and profit that was irreconcilable with more traditional notions of communal oversight.

To support their claims to both greater need and greater support, the Lutherans offered extracts of orphanage accounts from 1704 to 1721.[34] These records revealed that the Lutheran Orphanage had enjoyed a material advantage over the Catholic Orphanage, a fact which neither party contested. That advantage, however, was more than offset by the generosity of Lutheran alms.

The inequalities between the Catholic and Lutheran orphanages are best indicated by an indexed table (see Table 3.1). In each category—monthly accounts, purchase accounts, and alms collections—the annual sums for the Lutheran Orphanage in 1704 have been set as 100. The results show that the subventions to the Lutheran Orphanage were larger than those to the Catholic Orphanage, but less than expected. From 1704 to 1721, the purchase account revealed no striking inequities between Lutheran and Catholic. Over the entire period, the Lutheran Orphanage received 8,669 fl. compared to 7,114 fl., a difference of 1,555 fl. in total or 84 fl. per year. Beginning in 1705, the Lutherans had consistently received more monthly moneys, but less than Catholic rhetoric made them. Over the sampled 18 years, Lutheran orphans received a total of 37,845 fl., compared to 33,191 fl. for the Catholics, an average difference of roughly 258 fl. each year. Lutheran alms, however, far exceeded Catholic charity, and the disparity increased over the years. Whereas Catholic contributions changed little over the sample period, annual Lutheran giving increased by more than 50 percent. Between 1704 and 1721, they donated nearly three times the total Catholic charity, 18,850 fl. compared to 6,867 fl.[35] In sum, while the Lutheran Orphanage received about 5,000 fl. more in support, Lutheran donors gave 12,000 fl. more in alms.

This was a disagreement in principle that no facts could resolve. Catholic magistrates insisted that the economic problems of the Alms Office pressed hardest on the Catholic needy, and they believed the inability to compromise spoke of Lutheran stubbornness and a lack of public spirit.[36] Greater contributions in no way justified a greater share. Rather, such reasoning flew in the face of Augsburg's tradition and law. Lutherans did not donate more than Catholics when the charity of Catholic foundations, especially the mendicant orders, was considered. Augustinians and Dominicans had long contributed substantially to the support of the poor. Furthermore, unequal numbers of orphans had not prevented the peace agreement from mandating equality of means. In 1649, the Catholic Orphanage had supported many more parentless children than the Lutheran Orphanage. Nonetheless, the Lutherans had received support from the state equal to that given the Catholics. Parity specifically dictated equality of food, clothing, and other necessities for the children of both orphanages. Finally, Rehling charged that reductions in monthly moneys had been ordered as early as 1689 but had never been achieved by the Lutherans. Their orphanage should spend far less on its orphans; the "sumptuous care" they received was a shameful waste of alms and an affront to all citizens in times of scarcity.[37] Responsible for a debt of nearly 60,000 fl., the Lutheran leadership would eventually ruin both orphanages and the Alms Office.

The accusation of waste raised questions about management and expenditures that could not go unanswered. The Lutheran deputies compared the ways both orphanages disbursed their monthly moneys in 1724 and revealed interesting dissimilarities.[38] The Lutheran orphan father devoted his subvention, for example, to a limited range of essential, subcontracted services.[39] He paid for the labors of the cobbler and tailor who shod and clothed the orphans in his care. He compensated the artisans who bleached the orphanage's homespun. He reimbursed both the praeceptors who instructed the living and the servants who buried the dead. In contrast to these limited applications, the Catholic orphan father found much broader use for his subventions.[40] Most of them provided feasts on holidays: wine at Christmas, Easter, and Pentecost (*Pfingsten*); fish at New Year; meat and beer at

Shrove Tuesday (*Fasnacht*), church festivals, and the feasts of Sts. Jerome and Martin; eggs at Easter; bread, sausage, and beer at Corpus Christi (*Fronleichtnam*); sweets, nuts, and wax at the feast of St. Nicolas. They made possible work on the Catholic Orphanage building and in its fields. Chimneysweeps, joiners, coppersmiths, glaziers, carpenters, and masons appeared in the accounts. The peasants who harvested hay in the orphanage's pastures, transported fodder to the stables, and carted dung to the fields were paid from the monthly moneys. Finally, these funds made a degree of hygiene possible through bathing, barbering, and bleeding orphans, orphanage servants, and orphan parents alike. The subventions clearly had no set purpose.

The Lutheran elders saw the root of all excess in that lack of specificity. Catholic administrators were charging a wide range of expenses to the Alms Office that should have been paid properly, and perhaps more economically, from other house funds.[41] Moreover, the holiday celebrations with which the Catholic Orphanage burdened their accounts seemed frivolous when compared to the sober services provided in the Lutheran house. The Lutheran leadership claimed explicitly in 1728 that the limits on spending proposed by their Catholic colleagues had been calculated deliberately to include the many feasts and fasts of their own religious calendar, and to take no account of the number of Lutheran orphans or the requirements of Lutheran life.[42] Mutually distrustful, both sides refused to negotiate or to compromise.

Religious tensions must not, however, obscure the central point separating Catholics and Lutherans. At issue was the distribution of resources in accordance with the institution of parity. Lutherans upheld a relative interpretation in which each orphan received equal support and subventions were calculated on the basis of the number of orphans in each house. Catholics opposed this per capita reckoning and insisted on an absolute definition with each institution receiving exactly the same subvention from the state. They strove to establish equality, which was implicit in parity and necessary for social harmony. But the Lutherans insisted that any transfer of charity, donated by their own for their own, would violate both the efficient use of resources that reason mandated and the segregation of confessions that parity implied.

The Lutherans blurred the understanding of subvention with those of donations and earnings. Within their position were notions of charity as capital and property, that is, as an investment that earned a return and was subject to the donors' intentions. Lutheran magistrates insisted that donors provided charity for certain specific ends, an opinion that coincided broadly with trends already noted in the disposition of private donations. They understood those donations as a form of private property; that they were given for the common good did not negate the owners' rights. To ignore the donors' wishes or to use the donation as if it were communal property was a form of expropriation. Once given, donations became the property of the organization and as property acquired the qualities of capital. Unless set to some productive purpose, they were limited and finite. Therefore, properly managed donations had to be applied usefully under the most advantageous circumstances possible. Properly managed donations also sought social and economic returns in the form of poor relief and social discipline and in the form of interest income and greater self-reliance, if not profitability. Hence, the Lutheran magistrates were as concerned as their Catholic colleagues to control costs but not in ways that fixed income or limited options. They treated their income, regardless of its source, as capital to be allocated according to the circumstances of the house. Though self-interested, their arguments sought to limit an economically irrational use of resources. At issue, then, were not only the balance between orphanages and the social harmony of parity but also the nature of charity as a market-oriented operation.

As of 1725, attempts to reorganize the finances of the Alms Office had broken down. Catholics and Lutherans abandoned the bargaining table and settled into an internecine struggle of minor irritations. In 1727, the Catholic elders ordered their orphan father to increase his accounts unilaterally by any means necessary, to the point that the Catholic Orphanage received subventions as large as those of the Lutheran Orphanage.[43] They slowed all Alms Office business by making every action requiring the joint approval of Catholic and Lutheran elders contingent on equal subventions for the two orphanages. Annual accounts were left open for the same reason, making it increasingly difficult to transact business because deficits and surpluses could not be calculated and applied to the following year.[44] They harassed employees of the Lutheran Orphanage, as in January 1728, when Catholic Bürgermeister Bernhard Valentin Langenmantel seized and questioned two servants of the Lutheran Orphanage regarding the domestic economy of their organization, without permission of the Lutheran authorities.[45] All such efforts proved futile; the matter came no closer to resolution until the late 1730s.

Meanwhile orphanage costs and, with them, the burden of public charity continued to rise.[46] It was no longer possible to provide relief for the independent, honorable poor and to maintain specialized organizations on an ad hoc basis. The climbing costs of state charity had surpassed the resources of private generosity. In 1737, the City Council moved to support the Alms Office by a direct subvention from the treasury.[47] Hitherto the city had provided a weekly subsidy of 25 fl. from receipts of the city's indirect tax on meat. Henceforth these would be replaced by a weekly subvention of 100 fl. paid by the Incomes Office from the City Counting House (*Stadtkassa*).

The city increased its support for its Alms Office and shifted the source to control incomes and expenditures more flexibly. Yet, increased support and improved efficiency neither mended the material disparity between the orphanages nor controlled the steady increase in their expenses. Between 1730 and 1739, the expenditures of the Alms Office rose steadily, driven by the uncontrolled spending of the two orphanages. The magistrates noted that both houses artificially inflated their expenses by "accounting more costs than were actually paid."[48] The result had been a series of catastrophic increases in the Alms Office budget.[49] The rate of increase made renewed and expanded support from the state at once necessary and futile. No reasonable income would be sufficient without control of expenditures.

Four decades later, the controversy began anew.[50] In December 1784, the City Council launched a formal investigation into the persistent inequality of incomes between the orphanages. A report of that year traced the problem to a change in orphanage subventions in 1741, when the practice of rendering monthly accounts payable had ceased.[51] Instead, the Alms Office capped support for both orphanages: the Lutheran Orphanage received 100 fl. monthly; the Catholic Orphanage received 80 fl. Some subventions in kind continued to be provided; in each category the Lutheran Orphanage received more than its Catholic counterpart. Between 1741 and 1784, the Lutheran Orphanage enjoyed an advantage totalling more than 13,250 fl.[52] The creeping inequality had added up.

A City Council decree of 1 March 1785 ordered the Alms Office to meet with members of the council to hammer out a compromise.[53] Lutheran officials used the same arguments as in 1722 to reject the Catholic charge that parity had been violated. The Lutheran Orphanage housed more children, therefore it required more support. Fundamentally, they called for the rational distribution of resources based on a per capita application of parity. Furthermore, Lutherans consistently contributed more generously to charity, and alms were private property regardless of the fact that they flowed through the Alms Office. Lutheran representatives insisted that subventions, which were subject to parity, could not be separated from donations and earnings, which were not. As such, they sought to remove their orphanage from the regulatory mechanism of the city but without directly challenging the principle of separate but equal organizations. Catholic negotiators continued to argue, as they had since the 1720s, in favor of absolute equality between the orphanages.[54] Though they limited their reasoning to subventions and never mentioned the other facets of orphanage income, their contention suggested that parity might apply to all resources. They insisted that all public organizations remained subject to the institution of parity and the bureaucratic oversight that upheld it.

For reasons that are not clear, Lutheran officials unexpectedly conceded absolute parity in the orphanages to their Catholic counterparts on 31 August

1788 and, for the first time, proposed their own reform of charity finance.[55] All subventions in kind would cease, and the orphanages would immediately and directly enter the city's markets.[56] Each orphanage would receive a monthly allowance of 90 fl. to cover sundry necessities; each would receive a quarterly allowance of 200 fl. to purchase grain. Administrators could petition for temporary increases in case of inflation. They would receive fixed allowances to purchase other commodities and services on the open market too. To underwrite these allowances and guarantee that they would not overburden the treasury, Lutheran officials proposed two measures.[57] First, the Alms Office would set aside 1500 fl. annually for the two orphanages. This sum would serve as a ceiling for subventions. Second and more important, Catholic magistrates and clergy would take the measures necessary to increase donations from Catholic citizens. Beyond easing the state's involvement, increased private charity from the Catholic laity would justify increased state support for Catholic organizations. Reduced fiscal involvement would give the city less reason to regulate the orphanages.[58] The Alms Office would henceforth meet quarterly instead of monthly to review orphanage finances, and accounts would remain the internal documents of each orphanage. Opportunities for state interference in orphanage affairs would be reduced; each orphanage would be freer to pursue its own utility, to maximize the efficient use of its own resources.

In a counter-proposal of 21 February 1788, Catholics accepted the suggested limits on allowances and commodity expenditures that established absolute parity in communal subventions for the two orphanages.[59] They also embraced as fiscally responsible the proposed ceiling of 1500 fl. on state support. They rejected, however, the Lutheran initiative to emancipate orphanage administration from state control.[60] Catholic and Lutheran deputies had to meet monthly and render accounts to the Alms Office in order to monitor Lutheran prosperity and preserve organizational parity. Despite areas of disagreement, the basis for an agreement had been reached.

The final accord of 1788 was a compromise, which incorporated "the principle of a complete equality of both orphanages and the greatest possible stabilization and simplification of their subsidies which they have to enjoy from the most ancient and holy alms."[61] Lutheran negotiators yielded on the issue of absolute parity with the provision of fixed limits on municipal support. They yielded on the issue of municipal regulation. In fact, they surrendered every point save one. They gained a commitment to try to increase the giving of alms by Catholics.

The reform of 1788 changed the finances of charity superficially rather than substantially. Cash allowances and limited support placed the orphanages more fully in the market than had ever been the case, but the orphanages had always oriented themselves in the markets of Augsburg. Henceforth, market conditions would discipline the allocation of resources. Each orphanage received equal subventions regardless of need, but market prices rather than city coffers limited expenditures. This, too, had long been and would continue to be the case. Lutheran administrators reported on 20 October 1795 that their orphanage suffered from rapidly rising costs of grain and other commodities.[62] Having realized all possible economies, they requested a temporary increase in the grain subvention that would return to normal "by commencing cheaper prices" as allowed by the 1788 reform.[63] Catholic officials supported the proposal, noting that prices had risen "despite a right bountiful year to a very oppressive dearness for the most part only through human usury and as a result all victuals are increased quite extraordinarily in price."[64] In November 1795, the City Council agreed and raised the grain subventions for both houses from 200 fl. to 250 fl. quarterly.[65] Though the city was prepared to protect its orphanages from the worst effects of the market, Catholic and Lutheran administrators alike had to continue to react and adapt to market conditions.

The orphanage had always been engaged in market transactions, hiring and firing, buying and selling. Parity diminished orphanage capital, and created a situation in which each new house had to pursue more self-conscious economic strategies. Catholics and Lutherans kept a close watch on one another's expenditures to prevent their opponents from gaining any material advantage. Repeated conflicts over inequalities in subventions make this clear. They became more involved in capital markets as a way of exploiting and expanding scarce resources. They transferred and invested funds—their own, those of their orphans, and those of their neighbors—in a variety of ways. Each regarded the other as a competitor and maneuvered accordingly to limit the other's gain. A marketplace mentality, in which scarcity and competition were dominant elements, penetrated the internal affairs of the orphanages themselves. The City Orphanage had always struggled to discipline the needy young in ways useful to a manufacturing metropolis. Its confessional successors became increasingly aware of themselves not only as social organizations but also as guardians of a unique disciplinary regime. As will be seen, they educated and placed their orphans according to the demands of the labor market and their own confessional interests. As parity shaped the opportunities available to each house, administrators shaped their activities to exploit new conditions and to support new ends.

FISCAL MANAGEMENT IN THE ORPHANAGES

An examination of orphanage incomes sheds some light on the regular reaction to experience in the market and the slow accumulation of administrative knowledge[66] (see Table 3.2). Charity finances were more complicated than political debates indicated.

TABLE 3.2

Operating Resources (Gulden: Kreutzer) of Augsburg's Orphanages

Type	1580	1590	1725	1735	1780	1803	
	City	City	Cath.	Luth.	Luth.	Luth.	Cath.
Balance	—	0:00	0:00	1479:55	107:04	1322:02	—
Subventions	—	—	850:00	1400:00	1800:00	3076:00	3028:00
Purchase acct.	—	—	—	619:49	(abolished 1751)		
Sales	81:00	35:18	—	21:52	0:00	164:43	—
Kindergelder	179:44	443:39	311:53	0:00	228:42	28:24	5955:15
Sparhafen	0:00	0:00	—	740:53	390:32	366:41	—
Stores	376:00	291:03	—	—	—	—	—
Donations, etc.	2315:00	619:20	1945:00	82:00	162:00	1285:18	—
Collections	474:18	110:22	—	0:00	0:00	0:00	—
Collect. boxes	95:53	103:02	—	1806:43	864:43	586:09	—
Rents	—	0:00	0:00	211:29	272:49	370:53	442:22
Interest	—	0:00	595:30	11:30	1005:56	973:53	1094:07
Misc.	—	0:00	88:34	0:00	1288:46	0:00	—
Liturgy bequests	—	—	199:35	—	—	—	69:00
Total	3145:55	1601:24	3990:32	6581:12	6120:33	9013:21	10587:44

Prior to the Thirty Years' War, the City Orphanage drew funds from many sources, none of which was applied to meeting daily expenses. Because the Alms Office automatically met all operating expenses, donations of many kinds formed the backbone of the orphanage's capital. Collections taken before the doors of Augsburg's churches every Sunday and New Year's Day provided sums that, if less spectacular than those provided in testaments, were nonetheless substantial and regular. Collection boxes located at the orphanage itself and at the Church of the Holy Cross were another important source. The house supplemented these gifts with modest earnings from the sale of surplus foodstuffs, old clothing, and used housewares. Its stores of linen, grain, and lard were also accounted a part of its capital. Finally the orphans contributed from their own substance that they had inherited from parents or received from patrons, the property referred to as children's moneys. Taken together these sources could generate substantial values.

Inflation and economic decline, which characterized Augsburg from the late sixteenth to mid-seventeenth centuries, altered the distribution of incomes for the City Orphanage. Voluntary giving fell, while orphan wealth rose. All forms of donations declined steadily, from 73 percent of all income in 1580 to 38 percent in 1590. Children's moneys, on the other hand, grew steadily despite the looming crisis. They increased as a proportion of total income, from nearly 6 percent in 1580 to 27 percent in 1590. Over the entire early modern period, orphan wealth played an increasingly crucial role in orphanage finance, especially in the Catholic Orphanage where it assumed surprising proportions in light of the general poverty of Augsburg's Catholic population. By the eighteenth century, donations and collections had dwindled to the level of a minor source of support, far less important than capital earnings or state subventions. Though they were to remain an important occasional source of capital in the Lutheran Orphanage, donations and collections seldom figured greatly in Catholic accounts, a startling turn on the medieval notion of charity as a voluntary exchange between individuals.

Far from engaging in the deficit spending bemoaned by Catholic officials, the Lutheran Orphanage operated at an annual surplus of nearly 1,500 fl. between 1734 and 1736.[67] The most substantial sources of income were the now familiar subventions in the form of monthly moneys and purchase accounts, donations from collection boxes, and capital from children's moneys. The collection boxes generated the largest single source of income for the Lutheran Orphanage in the 1730s and very nearly matched the total of all state subventions. Small wonder that Catholic officials sought to gain a share of this largesse by insisting that donations to the Alms Office be treated as communal property. Small wonder, too, that Lutherans bitterly resisted this suggestion by insisting that donations remained private property. Monthly moneys had stabilized at 1,400 fl. per year, not indicative of runaway inflation. Likewise, the purchase account varied in a narrow range well below the catastrophic level alleged by Catholics. The private property of orphans gave the Lutheran Orphanage an income in excess of 820 fl. in 1734 and of 740 fl. in 1735, a substantial addition to working capital that would have been lacking had the administrators been content simply to hold it against the future.

More modest sources of income abounded, but all of these earnings barely exceeded 300 fl. in any year. By its own admission, the Lutheran Orphanage was far from prosperous in the 1730s. The most arresting aspect of these accounts, however is the annual surplus brought forward and applied as income in the following year. In 1734, the Lutheran Orphanage enjoyed a positive balance of 1,174 fl., created by operating surpluses from the three previous years: 395 fl. in 1729, 480 fl. in 1730, 299 fl. in 1731. The following year the balance had grown to 1,480 fl., and reached 1,668 fl. in 1736. The Lutheran Orphanage was earning more money than it was spending, but its accounts do not make clear how this was accomplished. No single source of income increased; no expenditures decreased. What the orphan father called "Saldo" were accounted as part of the orphanage's capital. The operating surplus may have been loans taken by the orphanage, as the Alms Office had done in the crisis years of the seventeenth century. In any event, these sums represented a combination of resources that suggest that the

Lutheran Orphanage was deeply involved in the city's capital markets than its own accounts reveal.

An account from the Catholic Orphanage in 1725 demonstrates a familiar financial stucture.[68] In most respects, it was comparable to the Lutheran.

The Catholic Orphanage's purchase account amounted to 850 fl. more than the Lutheran Orphanage's in 1721 or 1735. It also listed 1,855 fl. in total monthly expenditures for the year 1725.[69] Because the Alms Office assumed payment for these monthly accounts, they represented the same expenditures listed as monthly moneys by the Lutheran Orphanage. Again, the Catholic Orphanage in 1725 received slightly more than the Lutheran in 1735 but less than in 1721. The survival of records does not permit a more exact comparison, but the pattern of variation in subventions seems consistent.

The Catholic Orphanage enjoyed substantial income from earnings, 596 fl. from 17 separate obligations. This amounted to a capital of 14,300 fl., far more than the Lutheran Orphanage boasted a decade later. Like its Lutheran counterpart, the Catholic Orphanage was involved in local capital markets albeit, as will be seen, in significantly different ways.

Five orphans provided property worth 312 fl. to the Catholic Orphanage, far less than the 824 fl. in 1734 or 740 fl. in 1735 accounted by the Lutherans. This was probably the result of the relative size of the institutions as well as external factors, especially the numbers of orphans admitted to each and the wealth of Catholic and Lutheran populations in Augsburg.

The Catholic Orphanage operated with a budget surplus, but the balance in 1725 was so small as to be evanescent. Income exceeded expenditures by only 23 fl., and the orphanage just managed to break even without resort to credit.

That it had any surplus at all must be attributed to a single donation of 1,820 fl. from Councillor and Elder Caspar Balthus Gadner. The account described this sum as principal and interest (*anheim bezahlten Capitalien*) received by Gadner from Count Marquandt Fugger in payment for 260 pieces of marble, valued at 7 fl. each. Whether Gadner rendered payment of capital borrowed from the orphanage or donated the proceeds of a business transaction is not entirely clear. It may even have been a pious donation by Fugger through Augsburg channels, another instance of that family's capital underwriting Catholic charity in Augsburg. Coming in a period of intense debate over parity, Gadner's donation may have been intended to balance Lutheran advantages. Whatever the source or motive, this one payment prevented the Catholic Orphanage from operating at a large deficit.

Like the Lutheran Orphanage, the Catholic enjoyed a miscellany of funds. It received five modest legacies from commoners in 1725, the largest being 50 fl. The collection box set by the Catholic cemetery on Good Friday and Saturday generated 20 fl., a pittance compared to proceeds from the Lutheran collection boxes. A small foundation named for Christoph Peutinger paid 2 fl. 30 kr., probably the interest on a small principal, and the Lutheran Orphanage paid 8 fl. as rent for a pasture. The eight priests who served the Church of the Holy Cross each donated 16 fl. annually. What might be described as a confraternity, the Citizens' Confederation for the Bearing of Lights, paid 11 fl. for 66 candles over the year.[70] And finally, the Catholic Orphanage inherited the property of an orphan who died while resident in the home, a common practice of all Augsburg's charitable foundations.[71] Striking is less the assortment than the size of these incomes. They awaken the impression of charity-less charity, of a foundation totally dependent on subventions and capital.

In one other respect the Catholic Orphanage differed from the Lutheran. It was a focus for Catholic liturgy that received nearly 200 fl. to pay for worship services and prayers in its chapel in 1725. The Catholic laity ordered 16 worship services, including 8 memorial services (*Jahrtage*), 5 exegies (*Exequien*), and 3 other services dedicated to deceased persons. A further 11 persons ordered prayers for the good of their souls. It is not immediately clear whether the orphans or the priest serving their chapel did the praying. Commoners frequently ordered memorial services but very infrequently paid for prayers. These seem to have been a practice favored by elites and elite organizations, such as the Counts of Ettingen and Wöllenburg, the Countess of Wolfegg, the aristocratic ladies of the Imperial Foundation of St. Stephen's, and the noble Leopold Ferdinand von Rehlingen. Those few commoners who received the prayers of the orphanage were most frequently city officials or their families. In the Catholic Orphanage charity could not be separated from religiosity.

The persistence of liturgy in the context of charity emphasizes the ambiguity of the history of poor relief. The vectors of change frequently flow in opposite directions. Changing levels of private and state support, both of which began declining in the second half of the seventeenth century, drove foundations like the Catholic and Lutheran orphanages to a more aggressive exploitation of their own resources. Hence, they entered the local capital market and helped to shape those structures and practices recognizably indigenous to a modern capitalist economy and society. The orphanages engaged in early social welfare that involved impersonal transfers of resources made available to individuals only in exchange for their participation in disciplinary regimes designed to solidify the current economic order. At the same time, however, they remained the objects of traditional impulses, of which the Catholic practice of invoking the prayers of the needy was but one. Elements of a medieval *caritas*, which incorporated a highly personal and transcendental exchange between material and spiritual spheres, survived into the early modern and modern periods. Most social programs incorporate these contrary elements—call them medieval and modern, personal and impersonal, or charitable and disciplinary—to this day. Change results less from the triumph of one or the other, by which the vanquished disappears from the organizational calculus, than from their relative weights, which shift with the political and economic necessities of the moment.

Those necessities began to change more rapidly in the middle of the eighteenth century. The mounting costs of poor relief and the lack of parity between Catholics and Lutherans had not been resolved since they became the focus of discussion and debate in the 1720s. The City Council shifted the source of its financial support for the Alms Office in 1737 but did nothing until 1741 to control expenses or establish equality. In that year, the Alms Office abandoned its system of accounts payable in favor of fixed subventions in either cash or kind.[72] The result was not fully satisfactory. Subventions constrained expenses artificially insofar as they detached spending limits from the numbers of orphans dependent on them. Moreover, as adopted in 1741, subventions did not restore parity. The reform of orphanage finance neither fully capped spending nor adequately upheld parity, as Catholic complaints in the 1780s made clear.

Once again, however, accounts of orphanage incomes reveal a complex financial situation. Both orphanages enjoyed a wide and shifting range of incomes, but the relative weights had changed since the early 1700s. Lutheran Orphanage accounts from the 1770s and 1780s reveal that subventions and donations still supplied most of the organization's operating revenues.[73] It was far better capitalized and had more diverse sources of income than had been the case a half century earlier. Even as charity declined and support became fixed, the orphanage expanded other incomes and moved further into the city's capital market. Though managing to operate in the black, it saw its operating surplus shrink to less than 250 fl. The financial strength of the orphanage lay less in its economy—that is, in its capacity to control costs—than in its ability to generate income. Most of this came from those public subventions that had been fixed in 1741. The Lutheran Orphanage received 1,300 fl. per year in monthly moneys, 250 fl. for wood (*Holzgelder*), and 250 fl. for lard (*Schmalzgelder*). The purchase account, which had been a considerable source of discretionary income, had been dissolved in 1751.[74] Although each house supposedly received other subventions every year, including apprenticeship fees and cloth subventions, no other public funds appear in the Lutheran accounts. Private generosity in several forms continued to underwrite the Lutheran Orphanage. Collection boxes at Augsburg's Lutheran churches yielded about 850 fl. annually. As usual, other donations were always subject to wide annual variation. Insignificant in the 1730s, these contributions netted nearly 550 fl. in 1778 but less than 200 fl. in 1780.

As was the case earlier in the century, the property of orphans still generated an important income. It reached 228 fl. in new funds in 1780 for the Lutheran Orphanage. At the same time, invested children's moneys paid 87 fl. and 89 fl. in 1778 and 1780, indicative of a principal of approximately 2,250 fl. New children's property remained a stable source of capital, yielding between 300 and 400 fl. annually. It may not be too much to claim that the orphans helped to fund the Lutheran Orphanage in the late eighteenth century.

Fixed and operating capital still generated only a minor income. This property was needed for the care of orphans and could only be sold when it had outlived its usefulness. Hence, the sale of used housewares and clothing only occasionally earned small amounts. In 1778 such a sale brought in 119 fl. Gone were the days, as in the 1500s, when the sale of surplus food or clothing was a regular means of supplementing revenue. Rents and liens from various pieces of real property, most of which was located within the city's walls, paid regular returns as well. Although it rose to over 360 fl. in 1781, various forms of rents and dues from buildings and fields usually earned about 260 fl. annually for the Lutheran Orphanage.

Thus cursorily reviewed, the incomes of the Lutheran Orphanage leave the impression of an organization in which every conceivable source of income was utilized. About the only missing element was the exploitation of orphan labor. The Lutheran Orphanage was not a workhouse; it encouraged work as a form of discipline but did not compel it as an enterprise. It used child labor to reduce cost but never used it to increase income. By the eighteenth century, many of the older orphans assumed tasks that had earlier been the responsibility of paid servants. Still, very few opportunities to gain revenue were overlooked. Regular budget surpluses were but one consequence. Another, even more interesting, was the orphanage's large capital base.

In 1778, the Lutheran Orphanage earned 860 fl. in interest on a capital of 21,500 fl., a remarkable increase from the meager 100 fl. in capital reported in 1734 and 1735. By 1780 the orphanage's capital had grown to 22,900 fl. and earned 916 fl. By 1781 it stood at 23,350 fl. The Lutheran Orphanage invested most of its capital with the city's Incomes Office, where it fed the city government's then insatiable appetite for cash and credit.[75] The Lutheran Orphanage was very much a part of a larger network of capital and credit.

Lutheran Orphanage finances had assumed their final form, one that would endure until the dissolution of the Imperial city in 1806. An account from 1803 demonstrates the relative weights of subventions, donations, and capital, those three pillars of poor relief.[76] They remained the mainstays of charity from the early eighteenth into the nineteenth century. The Lutheran

Orphanage relied on all three. By contrast, the Catholic Orphanage listed no income from voluntary charity in 1803. Both houses, however, turned increasingly to fixed, reckonable resources, such as state subventions and returns from capital, as the basis of finance and administration.

Lutheran administrators enjoyed a positive balance of 1,322 fl., or 14 percent of its total income, during the fiscal year 1803 and carried an even larger surplus of 1,569 fl. into 1804. State subventions, now fixed by law, provided nearly 30 percent of the orphanage's annual revenues in 1803, a proportion thoroughly consistent with accounts from the 1770s and 1780s. Donations, too, remained stable as a percentage of total income, accounting for 25 percent of income in 1778, 15 percent in 1780, and 19 percent in 1803.

The sources had assumed different proportions among themselves. Whereas the proceeds from collection boxes had always been the greatest source of charity since the founding of the orphanage, these were supplanted by legacies, of which 918 fl. were given in 1803. Once again, this change may have indicated the worsening economic situation in the city generally; spontaneous donations are probably more subject to these sorts of pressures than testamentary legacies or even the large, public donations made by elites.

Earnings from capital had fallen behind the orphanage's operating budget. Rents on real property still amounted to 4 percent of income, but returns on capital had declined from 16 percent in 1778 to only 9 percent of total income, or 894 fl., in 1803. Although this interest suggests that total principal remained steady at around 22,000 fl., other revenues—especially the budget surplus—had assumed greater importance. The stability of interest and capital confirm that these funds were invested on a long-term basis, probably with the city. Yet, a portion surely found its way into other pockets because of the cash shortage and attendant high interest rates of the early 1800s. The orphanage placed its own surplus as well as orphans' property and citizens' donations in Augsburg's capital market as credit and investment transactions.

In the late eighteenth century, the orphans generated between 7 and 10 percent of all income for the Lutheran Orphanage. By the early nineteenth century, their importance had declined. The orphanage received healthy returns on children's moneys—366 fl. or 4 percent of total revenues—but new principal in this category had become negligible at a paltry 28 fl. Interest on these funds reached nearly 60 fl., implying total children's moneys worth approximately 1500 fl., again considerably less than several decades earlier. Because these resources were a product of private generosity and orphan property, they too reflect hard times for Augsburg.

The shifting of subventions, donations, and earnings, especially in eighteenth-century orphanage accounts, indicates at once the flexibility offered by multiple incomes and the necessity of adapting to changing circumstances. In their capacity to exploit resources and maximize incomes, Catholic and Lutheran administrators differed little, certainly less than their rhetoric suggested. Yet, differences there were of organizational affiliation and, perhaps, of economic orientation. These coalesced around the interpretation of parity. That alms lords and orphan fathers employed the same strategies to similar ends while espousing different mentalities manifests the fundamental empiricism of early capitalism.

CONCLUSION

The lessons learned applied in political as well as economic realms. The interpenetration of subventions, donations, and capital on a city-wide basis played a role both in Augsburg's loss of independence and in the orphanages' survival and transformation.

Augsburg's economic recovery from the catastrophes of the Thirty Years' War was slow but steady. An enormous public debt, caused by damages, requisitions, and reparations, gradually disappeared, while private wealth slowly accumulated. Growth reached its peak around 1769 only to be undercut abruptly by runaway inflation in the years 1770 and 1771.

This abruptly reversed the course of public finance. Although annual income exceeded payments, according to the accounts of the Incomes Office, the public debt grew sharply from 668,388 fl. in 1769, to 1,808,346 fl. in 1793, to 3,113,383 fl. by 1806. Interest payments followed in step from 27,001 fl., to 69,045 fl., to 124,535 fl. in 1806.[77] Given regular budget surpluses, the deficit resulted from borrowing. Between 1768 and 1794, the city acquired debts of 1,771,739 fl., far in excess of the amount needed to balance the books.[78] While recording the course of debt, these accounts reveal no reason for it.

Paul von Stetten attributed the need for credit to the requirements of "private citizens, civic foundations, and youthful dependents."[79] The orphanages, for example, held funds in trust, lending them as opportunity dictated and disbursing them as need required. Many of these resources, however, existed in the accounting of the orphanages but resided in actuality elsewhere. Thus, disbursal required that these funds be collected first or that credit be acquired to cover them. Not the amount of capital and interest but the lack of a centrally organized and controlled system was the problem. An accurate accounting became almost impossible.

The burgeoning public debt fueled a reform movement in the 1790s, led by Augsburg's largely Lutheran merchant community. Business interests called for an administrative and fiscal reform that would break the patrician monopoly of political power and prevent the looming bankruptcy. They were joined by enlightened thinkers—also Lutherans, for the most part—in urging annexation by the Kingdom of Bavaria as key to the introduction of rational economic and social policy in the city. Political pressure for reform were crowned with success, paradoxically, when the Battle of Austerlitz and Treaty of Pressburg finally brought an end to Augsburg's status as a free Imperial city in 1806.

Bavarian control of city finance had immediate consequences for the incomes of Augsburg's orphanages. The royal administration refused to continue the annual subvention on which both houses relied for the largest part of their regular income. Instead it thoroughly reorganized the city's poor relief and social services. A series of edicts and ordinances between 1806 and 1811 divided foundations and their property into seven coherent groups: Catholic liturgical, Lutheran liturgical, Lutheran educational, parity-based, Catholic charitable, and Lutheran charitable.[80] Although the medieval welter of private foundations was thus rationalized and "each foundation retained its own capital, competence, and thus its individuality," the fact remains that the Bavarian administration drastically altered both the finance and the character of the orphanages.[81] By 1808, all public assistance had ceased, and the orphanages faced an immediate cessation of services.

The Catholic Orphanage apparently found its salvation in the Foundling Home, with which it was united and whose resources it absorbed in 1811. The move made historical sense insofar as the Foundling Home had been closely associated with the Catholic Church and community at least since the introduction of parity in 1649. Lutheran foundlings were usually fostered for lack of a similarly dedicated house. It made administrative and fiscal sense as well because of the relative capital strength of the Foundling Home Foundation (*Findelhausstiftung*) and the few infants in its care. The foundation had long enjoyed the generous support of Augsburgers and continued to do so well into the nineteenth century.[82] In 1811 there were only 12 children in the Foundling Home, and they could easily be accommodated in the orphanage.[83] Annexation, then, changed little in the Catholic Orphanage, joining it to another Catholic foundation for the care of needy children and allowing it to continue its work.

In some respects, the Lutheran Orphanage fared less well. No single Lutheran foundation provided it with the ready reserves needed to weather the change. Rather, an ad hoc infusion of capital and donations prevented its collapse.[84] Collections at the city's Lutheran churches raised 1,298 fl. while adminstrators secured a credit of 6,000 fl. with the orphanage itself as collateral. The Klauk Foundation (*Klauk'sche Stiftung*), a private endowment, contributed 27,000 fl. to keep the doors of the orphanage open. Without subventions, capital and donations kept the house operating for a further 15 years. Finally in 1823 a royal decree provided 3,000 fl. annually for the support of the orphanage, to be paid from the Lutheran Beneficent Foundation

(*Wohltätigkeitsstiftung*) until a new subvention from the municipal budget could be arranged.[85] A new patron appeared at about the same time. The city's finance councillor (*Finanzrat*) and banker, Johann Lorenz Freiherr von Schäzler, prevented the proposed consolidation of the two confessional orphanages into a single municipal house, provided 2,500 fl. for the renovation of the Lutheran Orphanage, donated a further 25,000 fl. for the support of six to eight orphans, and worked to improve aspects of orphan training, especially the "industrial by-employment of the children."[86] Troubled as its transition into the modern era was, the Lutheran Orphanage continued to rely as it always had on the three pillars of public charity: subventions, capital, and donations.

This was the triumph not of tradition over change but rather of involution over revolution. Managerial practices remained stable despite institutional change. Once the institutional framework tipped, the orphanages slid in the given directions. Freed from state involvement, they ceased to be state organizations. Ties to other Catholic foundations strengthened, and the Catholic Orphanage was drawn into the orbit of Catholic schools and services. Dependent on private resources, the Lutheran Orphanage responded to private interests and came to resemble an industrial workhouse. Even as the orphanages helped to shape a capitalistic society, so they were shaped by their changing involvements in it.

The Alms Office and orphanages enjoyed a fundamental financial independence. This was a function, in part, of the lack of oversight by higher state authorities. It was a function as well, of the three pillars that comprised their incomes. Augsburg's public charity utilized state subventions, private donations, and capital earnings to provide poor relief and to weather the changing conditions of their day. As inflation and parity reduced certain incomes, administrators relied more on others. This process of calculating and manuevering were constant in the administration of the Alms Office and the orphanages; the methods did not emerge as the result of particular moments in their history. Capitalistic organizations always responded to institutional changes of this sort to maximize their utility and to avoid risk. Theirs was neither a blind pursuit of profit nor an equally blind aversion to loss, but rather a conservative approach that involved a slow accumulation of experience. That experience and the sense the administrators of Augsburg's orphanages made of it are revealed in their manipulation of capital.

Notes

1. Classen, "Armenfürsorge im 16. Jahrhundert," 340.
2. StAA, Alms, Beschluß des h. Allmosen Jahrs Rechung von Anno 1600 bis 1609.
3. Roeck, *Eine Stadt in Krieg und Frieden*, 615.
4. Though coincident with the introduction of Protestantism, as Lyndal Roper has noted, the reform of charity had nothing to do with the reform of religion in Augsburg. Rather than draw inspiration from the teachings of Luther or Zwingli, who could do little more than seek to legitimize the actions of civic magistrates, the Alms Ordinance of 1522 looked to structures and initiatives that had been present since the Middle Ages. Cf. Lindberg, *Beyond Charity*, passim; Roper, *The Holy Household*, 7–55.
5. StAA, W A1, Die Errichtung, Abtheilung und paritätische Gleichstellung der beiden Waisenhäuser, 1571–1795, Bericht vom hiesigen Waisenhaus, 6 July 1743.
6. Clasen, "Armenfürsorge im 16. Jahrhundert," 340.
7. Ibid., 341.
8. The most radical yet convincing estimate of Augsburg's demography during the Thirty Years' War sets the losses due to famine disease and violence at 65 percent, a decrease from approximately 45,000 souls in 1600 to 17,000 by 1635: Roeck, *Brot, Bäcker und Getreide in Augsburg*, 66–71. The surmise seems reasonable that, though these disasters probably struck the poor hardest, they did little to relieve the misery or poverty of the survivors in general and damaged the financial basis of charity in the city.
9. StAA, Alms, Beschluß des h. Allmosen Jahrs Rechnung, 1600–1670.
10. Clasen, "Armenfürsorge in 16. Jahrhundert," 340. There is some unclarity as to the date from which indirect taxes were dedicated to the assistance of the needy. Though generally given as 1616, the first year may have been earlier still. An eighteenth-century transcription records a Senate Decree of 1615 in which the *Herren ob dem Weberhaus* were informed that the *Barchentumgeld* collected for the support of the Alms Office would be altered from 4 pf. per piece of cloth to "von jedem Stk. gefärbten rohen und weisen barchet 2 kr. einzuziehen...." This information suggests that transfers of public funds for poor relief may have begun prior to 1615 and been inspired less by a sense of crisis than by a desire for sound fiscal management.
11. Clasen, "Armenfursörge in 16 Jahrhundert," 338. Clasen asserts that three-quarters were donated to the public charity between 1616 and 1628. On the other hand, the annual accounts of the Alms Office record annual receipts from the tax on fustians until the end of the century.
12. StAA, Alms, Beschluß des h. Allmosen Jahr Rechung von Anno 1620 bis 1629, Summa alles Einnemmens. Cf. StAA, W A1, Notamina, 18. Jhdt.
13. StAA, W A1, Notamina, 18. Jhdt.
14. Ibid.
15. StAA, Alms, Jahresrechnungen, 1628. These extraordinary figures defy simple explanation. The accounts for 1628 show a subsidy of 7,753 fl. for the orphanage and a further 1,777 fl. for an institution called the "Neues Waisenhaus am Eser." This may have been a temporary arrangement for Protestant orphans during the first period of Catholic control of the Alms Office. Unfortunately, no reference to such a development appears elsewhere.
16. Ibid.

17. François, *Die unsichtbare Grenze*, passim.
18. Fassl, *Konfession, Wirtschaft und Politik*, 120. "Die Konfession war eine öffentliche Angelegenheit, noch nicht Privatsache. Zünfte und Innungen hatten katholische und protestantische Herbergen. Man verkehrte im privaten und gesellschaftlichen Leben mit Leuten fleichen Glaubens und gleicher Gesinnung...."
19. Nicolai, *Beschreibung einer Reise durch Deutschland*, 8, 80–81: "ein Katholik ... nicht leicht seyn Brot bey einem protestantischen Bäcker [kaufte]...."
20. StAA, EW 13, Apellation, 24 December 1692. The date for this open appeal may well have been chosen to remind Christians of their responsibility to succor the poor. In any case, it was prompted by the War of the League of Augsburg, also known as the Nine Years' War, 1689–97, which pitted Louis XIV and his allies against a coalition of the Emperor Leopold, the Electorates of the Palatinate, Bavaria, and Saxony, the United Provinces, Spain, Sweden, and England. A nominal neutrality did not saved the city.
21. Ibid: "eine milde zuelängliche extraordinari beysteur...."
22. StAA, W A1, Notamina, 18. Jhdt., Decretume in senatum secretioris, 7 November 1697: "wie dem in so grosse decadenz gekommen Allmosen wieder aufzuhelfen...."
23. StAA, Alms, Beschluß des heil. Allmosen Jahrs Rechnungen, 1609, 1635, 1665.
24. StAA, EW 4, Supplikation der Deputierten des evangelischen Waisenhauses, ca. 1714.
25. StAA, W A1, Notamina, 18. Jhdt., Zettel, 1720.
26. StAA, KW 2, Punkte die Schulden des cathl. Waysenhauses betr., 28 January 1722.
27. StAA, W A1, Notamina, 18. Jhdt.
28. StAA, KW 2, Augustanae Confessionis Antwort auf Punkte der Schulden des catholischen Waysenhauses betr., 28 January 1722.
29. StAA, W A1, Notamina, 18. Jhdt. Lutheran authorities declared that their orphanage supported 15 to 20 more orphans on average than did the Catholic Orphanage.
30. StAA, EW 4.
31. Ibid. Rehling noted that the Lutherans failed to account for orphan property with the same care as the Catholics. This may have had to do with the fact that Lutherans placed a higher proportion of these funds in the market and so had less immediate control over them.
32. StAA, EW 4, Katholischer Antwort..., 1724.
33. Ibid., Antwort auf den catholischen..., 1724.
34. StAA, W A1, Notamina, 18. Jhdt., Rechnungen der beiden Waisenhäuser, 1704–21.

Fiscal Disparities (Gulden: Kreutzer) Between Orphanages, 1704–21

Year	Monthly Accounts		Purchase Accounts		Alms Collections	
	Luth.	Cath.	Luth.	Cath.	Luth.	Cath.
1704	2022:45	2047:08	398:01	311:42	794:40	243:51
1705	1978:31	1893:15	447:34	476:32	834:45	333:54
1706	1924:39	1776:06	348:23	311:58	997:42	413:43
1707	1840:04	1690:36	357:55	351:18	1098:42	434:10
1708	1871:35	1677:40	333:48	261:22	961:29	327:07

(continued on page 110)

Fiscal Disparities (continued)

YEAR	MONTHLY ACCOUNTS		PURCHASE ACCOUNTS		ALMS COLLECTIONS	
	LUTH.	CATH.	LUTH.	CATH.	LUTH.	CATH.
1709	1854:51	1696:35	376:30	323:02	853:54	314:26
1710	1933:32	1722:37	370:00	291:19	863:11	283:38
1711	2038:37	1648:55	379:51	310:42	969:27	401:57
1712	2072:28	1713:26	421:05	322:42	1176:08	454:46
1713	2126:49	1717:42	423:18	338:00	938:06	384:45
1714	2121:32	1685:57	427:22	368:59	985:22	415:52
1715	2186:30	1764:39	471:55	506:31	1104:32	441:36
1716	2246:44	2032:01	501:08	420:39	1161:34	434:00
1717	2410:42	2086:04	701:28	418:19	1110:54	362:56
1718	2339:52	2008:26	721:34	539:13	1179:04	356:55
1719	2410:49	1946:59	703:16	441:56	1248:56	449:24
1720	2323:46	1979:04	695:08	567:14	1299:27	406:31
1721	2111:31	2067:24	590:33	553:01	1271:40	407:02
Total	37845:31	33190:34	8668:55	7114:19	18849:43	6866:33

35. StAA KW, 2, Antwort auf den Punkten a parte cathol..., 21 June 1724.
36. StAA, EW 4, Katholischer Antwort..., 1724.
37. Ibid.: "... villmehr beederzeits burgershafft eine grosse ombrage nemmen werde wann sye wissen wird, dz durch der gleichen sumptuese verpflegung nit nur die milde steuer, als von einem abgrundt gleichsamb ehr sye zum Allmosen kombt, shon absorbiert ja noch über 50 in 60,000 fl. schulden auf dem buchl vorhanden...."
38. The Lutheran leadership was clearly interested both in presenting the administration of their orphanage in the best possible light and in casting doubt on the probity of Catholic claims. This alone might explain the extraordinary difference in Lutheran and Catholic accounts. Yet, the records of both homes were public, kept by the biconfessional Alms Office. Therefore, it seems unlikely that the matter could have been deliberately misconstrued for the sake of temporary advantage. The *Monatsrechnungen* of 1725 probably reflect the ways of each house accurately.
39. StAA, W A1, Notamina, 18. Jhdt., Verzeichnis deß jenigen so in den 13 Monatrechnungen dem Waysenvatter ausgestellt worden, 1724.
40. Ibid.
41. StAA, W A1, Notamina, 18. Jhdt., Zettel, 1725.
42. StAA W A1. Notamina, 18. Jhdt. Notizen, 1728: "... zuo haushaltung bey denen jährlich einfallenden so vielen fasttagen in dem kathl. Waysenhs. ohngefehr gebraucht...."
43. StAA, W A1, Notizen, 1727.
44. StAA, W A1, Notamina, 18. Jhdt., Almosenamtsprotokolle, 11 June 1727.
45. Ibid., 1728.
46. StAA, W A1, Notamina, 18. Jhdt., Anzeige der kathl. Allmosenherren die Verpflegung der Waysenhäuser betr. an den kathl. Gehm. Rath, 1727.
47. StAA, KW 2, Decretum in senatum secretioris, 26 February 1737.

48. StAA, W A1, Notamina, 18. Jhdt. "monatlich mehr berechnete Kosten als wirklich bezahlt worden."
49. Ibid. Changes in total expenditures were calculated on the basis of Alms Office annual accounts from 1730 to 1339. The following net increases occurred:

1730	1,474 fl. 26 kr.
1731	1,344 fl. 5 kr
1732	1,246 fl. 58 kr.
1733	1,242 fl. 39 kr. 4 hl.
1734	1,358 fl. 20 kr.
1735	1,284 fl. 27 kr.
1736	1,367 fl. 23 kr.
1737	1,374 fl. 41 kr.
1738	1,451 fl. 45 kr.
1739	1,361 fl. 22 kr. 4 hl.
Total	13,506 fl. 7 kr. 1 hl.

50. StAA, W 5, Decretum in senat. secret. cath., 5 February 1782.
51. StAA, W 5, Beylage zur Cassa-Rechnug des älteren Almosenamts, 10 December 1784.
52. StAA, W 5, Beylage zur Cassa-Rechnung des älteren Almosenamts, 10 December 1784: ". . . allzugrosen Nachgiebigkeit der damahligen katholischen Herren Deputierten zum älteren Allmosen gegen ihre Herren Collegen Augustanae Confessionis. . . ."
53. StAA, W 5, Decretum in sen. secret., 1 March 1785. The first commission apparently failed to resolve the controversy. A new commission of council members was appointed on 11 February 1786 to mediate the claims of Catholics and Lutherans. Cf. StAA, W 5, Decretum in sen. secret., 11 February 1786. Its membership carefully maintained parity between the parties. Johann Baptist von Rehlingen, member of the *Geheimer Rat*, and the jurist, Fleiner, were the Catholic members; Albrecht von Stetten, member of the *Kleiner Rat*, and the pastor, Dr. Prieser, represented the Lutheran community.
54. StAA, W 5, Actum in curia, 13 July 1786. The Catholic officers of the Alms Office suggested a compromise according to which all current donations to the orphanages would be divided equally. Thus, both houses would receive 90 fl. *Monatgelder* and so forth. This became the benchmark for the final agreement.
55. Ibid, Gegenerklärung der Deputierten Confessionis Augustanae, 31 August 1786.
56. Interestingly Catholic officials suggested in 1724 the economic advantages of obtaining certain commodities, such as grain, wood, and lard, on the open market. Though the Lutherans agreed readily, the proposal languished in council with all other reform measures until 1788.
57. StAA, W 5, Gegenerklärung der Deputierten Confessionis Augustanae, 31 August 1786.
58. Ibid.
59. Ibid., Finalerklärung der Deputierten Religionis Catholicae, 21 February 1788. Source materials offer no explanation for the apparent two-year hiatus in negotiation. Whereas the *Weberunruhe* of 1784–85 initially may have distracted the authorities from naming a commission to resolve the orphanage dispute, the delay in the commission's activities remains somewhat obscure.
60. StAA, KW 13, Decretum in senat. secret., 17 April 1788.

61. Ibid. Secretum in senat. secret., 17 February 1788: "... auf den Grundsatz einer vollkommenen Gleichstellung der beyden Waisenhauser und möglichster Fixir- und Simplificirung ihrer aus dem älteren heiligen Allmosen zu genießen habenden Zuflüssen...."
62. StAA, W 5, Supplikation der Vorsteher des evangelischen Waisenhaus, 20 October 1795.
63. Ibid., Supplikation der Deputierten des evangelischen Waisenhaus, 23 October 1795: "bey eintrettend wohlfeilern Preyßen."
64. Ibid., Supplikation der Deputierten des katholischen Waisenhaus, 4 November 1795: "... ohnerachtet eines recht Segenreichen Jahrgangs, meistens nur durch Menschen Wucher auf eine sehr druckende Theuerung, sondern darmit auch alle Venalien ganz außerordentlich im Preiß gestiegen seyn."
65. Ibid., Decretum in senat. secret., 10 November 1795.
66. Statistics and table are based on accounts rendered to the Alms Office by the orphan fathers of the Lutheran and Catholic orphanages. See StAA, EW 6, EW 14, KW 14; KWA 16.
67. StAA, EW 6, Jahresrechnungen des evangelischen Waisenhauses, 1734-36.
68. StAA, KW 14, Jahresrechnung, 1725.
69. Ibid., Jahresrechnung des katholischen Waisenhaus, 1725.
70. Ibid.: "... aus der bürgerliche Bündnuß für dz Lichter tragen per 66 Lichter à 10 kr...."
71. Ibid.: "... für Johann Michael Karg seel. catholischen Waysensohn seine betreffente Erbs Portion von dem vorhandenen Vermögen empfangen fl. 30:39:—...."
72. StAA, W 5, Beylage zur Cassa-Rechnung des älteren Allmosenamts, 10 December 1784.
73. StAA, EW 6, Jahresrechnungen, 1778-80.
74. Ibid., Jahresrechnungen, 1778.
75. By the 1780s, the city was feeling the first signs of the crisis of payments that would shake its financial standing in Europe and create a party among the burghers that ultimately welcomed the loss of political independence and mediatization into Bavaria. Still, much was in the hands of private persons and foundations. See Fassl, *Konfession, Wirtschaft und Politik*, passim.
76. StAA, EW 16, Jahresrechnung, 1803.
77. Fassl, *Konfession, Wirtschaft und Politik*, 172.
78. Ibid., 173.
79. Cited in Fassl, *Konfession, Wirtschaft und Politik*, 173: "... bey weitem beträchtlichste Theil der aufgenommenen Capitalien von Bürgern, bürgerlichen Stiftungen und Pupillen...." *Pupillen* refers not only to orphans but also to wards, that is the practice of the city to administer the property and provide for the needs of dependent young people through its various social institutions and its Superior Assistance Office.
80. Obermeier, "Findel- und Waisenkinder," 146.
81. Werner, *Die örtlichen Stiftungen*, 68: "... fast jeder Stiftung ihr Vermögen, ihr Wirkungskreis und sohin ihre Individualität erhalten."
82. von Seida, *Historisch-statistische Beschreibung aller Kirchen-, Schul-, Erziehungs- und Wohltätigkeitsanstalten in Augsburg*, 2, 573-74.
83. Obermeier, "Findel- und Waisenkinder," 146.
84. StAA, EW 9, "Notizen über die Geschichte des evangelischen Waisenhauses," *Intelligenz-Blatt und wochentlicher Anzeiger von Augsburg* 132, (1833), 634.
85. Ibid. In 1833, the municipal budget was still a matter of debate.
86. Ibid.

4

Charity and Capital in the Orphanages

Subventions, donations, and earnings—the three financial pillars of public charity—permitted flexible responses to changing circumstances. When hard times or modern mentalities drove donations down, alms lords and orphan fathers relied more heavily on subventions and earnings to maintain their orphanages. When parity redefined subventions, administrators turned to private donations and their own capital to provide for needy children. This kind of adaptation within fixed parameters to changing circumstances is the essence of early modern capitalism, but it becomes truly empirical only when lessons learned in the marketplace are somehow incorporated into patterns of knowing and behaving. It is not sufficient simply to demonstrate the shifting of orphanage incomes.

As the administrators contended with constraints and opportunities, they engaged in continuous negotiation and transaction. These individual exchanges gave evidence of a practical knowledge of business and administrative affairs. That hard-won wisdom worked both inward and outward. It shaped single transactions and welded them into consistent strategies. And it provided the basis, however fragmentary and erratic at this early stage, of a more systematically capitalistic behavior and discipline. Process, wisdom, and system became most clearly visible in the manipulation of the orphanages' own capital, the only resource over which the administrators had unencumbered control and, therefore, the only resource that clearly reflected their intentions.

Infusions of cash from the city and its citizens not only supplied the orphanages' operating budgets but also constituted the basis for these capital operations. The orphanages engaged in a wide range of money transactions. They held and transferred the property of orphans and citizens. They borrowed and loaned money at interest to Augsburgers and foreigners alike. They sought secure capital investments—rarely in buildings and land, occasionally in commerce and industry, frequently with the city and its churches—to provide a regular, predictable cash income. In short, the orphanages served God and Mammon by caring for the needy and banking with the rest.

The orphanages did not keep full, accurate records of all their financial dealings. The City Council knew that its orphan fathers regularly inflated their accounts with fictive expenditures.[1] In 1741 they had to insist on practices that should have been commonplace: administrators were required to account for "nothing other than what they really take in or give out." Many incomes and expenses were either not recorded or recorded inaccurately. Beyond official malfeasance, historical mischance further reduced the volume of useful data. Many accounts were lost or destroyed over time. Nonetheless, occasional records indicate the scope of their involvement in capital transactions. The pattern of these exchanges reflects qualities similar to those evident in individual transactions: the mobilization of resources in the capital market; the avoidance of risk through a diverse but characteristic range of obligations; the pursuit of advantage not only through hard-nosed negotiation but also through flexible calculation and manipulation.

Financial records reveal a network of investment and dividend, credit and interest, debt and payment that bound together the entire society of Augsburg and extended beyond the city walls. Public and private organizations as well as rich and poor citizens all participated. Like patronage and deference or family and status, capitalistic behavior seems to have been one means of assuring the coherence and cohesion of early modern urban society.

AUGSBURG'S ORPHANAGES IN THE CAPITAL MARKET

Even a cursory review of orphanage records discloses myriad capital transactions. Those few that became matters of discussion or debate and were, therefore, preserved in greater detail capture the process of exchange and the function of Augsburg's capital market. They reveal as well the determined pursuit of advantage and the mobilization of resources by the administrators of charity, strategies that wink through the many individual transactions and exchanges in which each orphanage engaged.

In a conflict that extended over nearly twenty years, the Alms Office and the Catholic Orphanage pursued settlement of debt with a Catholic patrician, Johann Georg Anton Langenmantel von Westheim. Langenmantel was an ancient and revered name in Augsburg, and the head of the family was not only a Catholic aristocrat but also the city's tax master (*Steuermeister*).

As members of the city's Catholic elite, the Langenmantel family had long been patrons of the Catholic Orphanage. Their name appeared frequently among the list of benefactors who donated funds and received prayers. In hard times, the family also turned to it for assistance of a more material sort. Johann Georg borrowed 1,200 fl. from the Catholic Orphanage and failed to repay it; that he offered no collateral implies his intimate relations with the Catholic elite and that Catholic organization.

In 1756 the deputies of the Alms Office presented the problem to the Small Council.[2] Langenmantel was a powerful figure in Augsburg and could not be treated like any debtor in default. He had not, however, adequately secured his loan from the Catholic Orphanage, and the administrators feared the loss of their capital. The Small Council ordered Langenmantel to repay the principal immediately. A year later the deputies put the matter before the council again.[3] In the intervening period, Langenmantel had neither offered sufficient collateral nor repaid the debt. In addition, he now owed 156 fl. more for three years' arrears in interest. The Small Council futilely ordered a full settlement within 14 days. By 1761, the debt was still outstanding.[4] Langenmantel had managed to pay some of the interest due on his loan, but he was now four years behind and had otherwise failed to meet the council's demands. Confronted with the disobedience of one of its own, the Small Council gave Langenmantel four weeks to explain himself and settle his obligations or face executive action.

His hand forced, Langenmantel appeared before the Small Council and explained a very complex and dubious piece of finance.[5] His first wife had incurred the original debt with the Income Office of the city.[6] When she died, her obligation passed to him as her heir; likewise, the Income Office transferred to the Catholic Orphanage the right to collect principal and interest. Thus, neither he nor the orphanage were parties to the original contract.

By 1762 the administrators returned to the Small Council to plead for protection of their interests.[7] Langenmantel was clearly in default. At the request of the overseer (*Pfleger*) of the Catholic Orphanage, Johann Christoph Ignatz Maria Ilsung, the city brought suit against Langenmantel for nonpayment of debt.

The suit failed to resolve the conflict, and the city referred the matter to the highest Imperial official in Augsburg, the *Reichsstadtvogt*, in 1763.[8] The action aimed at collecting principal and interest owed by Langenmantel as well as recovering the mounting expense of the dispute. Council records do not reveal what actions the Imperial official took or whether they succeeded. By 1764, however, Langenmantel's debt had been reduced to 216 fl. in interest.[9] Whether the principal was repaid, renegotiated, or forgiven is unclear. Of the remaining amount, Langenmantel disposed of half by offering to transfer to the orphanage a lien on a house (*Hauszins*). Evidently, he hoped to discharge 108 fl. He promised the balance in four weeks. Not surprisingly, he failed.

In 1774, Langenmantel's widow, Maria Josepha Antonia von Rehlingen, the daughter of another of Augsburg's ancient Catholic families, asked that her late husband's debt to the Catholic Orphanage finally be forgiven.[10] Merely 54 fl. remained, but it was beyond her means. This must have been well known. The Small Council granted the petition on grounds of "notorious" inability to pay.[11]

The dispute over Langenmantel's debt sheds light on the capital market and exposes some of its more sophisticated aspects. Instruments and securities of many sorts were traded within it. Debt as well as credit flowed in it. Rights in property were exchanged too. These transactions were further complicated by subsidiary transfers between testatrix and heir or between state and agency. Within this intricate market the administrators of charity assumed a dual role: ministers to the needy on the one hand, and capitalist entrepreneurs on the other.

Dealing with Langenmantel, the Catholic administrators appeared to be particularly cautious. The possibility of setting a precedent or an example made it dangerous to proceed with the full force of the law to collect debts from the patriciate. Unmentioned throughout the entire proceeding was Langenmantel's profiteering through the office of tax master.[12] What was used against one might be turned on any and have the unforeseen consequence of discouraging support. Parity made powerful Catholic families like the Langenmantel the logical patrons and partners of all Catholic foundations that were cut off from the support of wealthy Lutherans. They provided political protection and material assistance, and the foundations returned the favor at need. It was a mutual relationship—if not born of, then certainly sustained by parity—that a bitter financial struggle might rupture. Reckoning the probability of gain and loss, administrators realized the risks implicit in changing relations of power.

Because parity created confessional subeconomies within Augsburg, in which Lutheran traded with Lutheran and Catholic with Catholic, it caused capital to flow within confessionally drawn boundaries. Organizations and individuals sought capital from and offered it to organizations and individuals of the same confession. Parity might, for example, have been expected to reduce the considerable risks associated with default, since capital flowed along lines defined by mutual interest and confessional solidarity. In fact, such was not always the case. The divergence of economic interests within contrasted frequently with the unity of political interests without.

As a rule, Catholic administrators unflinchingly demanded payment of what was owed them by their Catholic brethren. For example, the testament of Anna Catharina Seyfridin created a legacy of 200 fl. for the Catholic Orphanage in 1768.[13] Perhaps because the estate was burdened with debt, the heirs were unable to honor the legacy and pleaded with the orphanage "for merciful consideration." The deputies of the Alms Office, however, could not afford to let such a sum slip through their fingers. They petitioned the Small Council to enforce the will, and the council accommodated them. In another instance, a Major von Rehlingen, acting as trustee for the orphaned Gröninger children, offered a schedule for the payment of principal and interest owed by the children to the Catholic Orphanage.[14] Payment in full was disadvantageous to Rehling; his own capital and that of his wards were combined in the trust. It was not uncommon for trustees to make use of the resource placed in their care in a manner like that of the orphanages. They were responsible for the safe maintenance of properties and interests. Many fulfilled this charge by investing the capital where they had the greatest control over it, namely, in their own enterprises. So converged self-interest and common interest. As a result, it took time to sort the interests without loss to either party. The Alms Office pursued the debt, and Rehling avoided payment.[15] In 1773, he promised to sell a pasture for 1,775 fl., of which 1,205 fl. would redeem principal and interest owed by the Gröninger estate. Like any enterprise, charity required persistence to collect debts and often resorted to legal intervention by the city.

In 1781 the Small Council arbitrated a dispute between the Imperial Abbey of Sts. Ulrich and Afra and the Catholic Orphanage.[16] The orphanage had demanded repayment of 3,000 fl. capital invested in the abbey (an increase from the 2,000 fl. listed in 1725), and the abbey had refused to comply. Very likely it had reinvested the money and lacked sufficient liquidity to meet the demand. The dispute lasted some time until the orphanage administrators proposed a compromise. They suggested that the abbey repay 75 percent of the obligation (2,250 fl.), in return for which it would keep the remaining 25 percent (750 fl.) for five years at no interest. The abbot, an Imperial Prelate (*Reichsprälat*), refused this arrangement, and the matter passed to the Small Council for adjudication. Somewhat unexpectedly, given the longstanding tensions between the city and church in Augsburg, the council ruled in favor of the abbey. Neither the foundation nor its head could be compelled in this matter. The capital remained in the hands of the abbey, and the prelate was free to accept or reject the proposed compromise.

A similar problem arose a few years later with regard to orphanage capital held by the Cathedral Chapter of Augsburg.[17] Deputies of the Alms Office complained to the Small Council in 1787 that the Catholic Orphanage had received 82 fl. less interest than was due on capital invested with the chapter.[18] Rather than intercede on behalf of the confessionally bound but state-sponsored organization and the entire Alms Office, the magistrates insisted that the deputies themselves request clarification from the responsible authorities within the Cathedral Chapter, in this case a part of the Cathedral Chapter Administration Office (*Domkapitalisches Administrationsamt*), the Hospital Office (*Spitalamt*) of the town of Dinkelscherben. They probably realized the difficulty of approaching so powerful an organization in a matter made delicate by large sums of money. In 1788, the Small Council noted with displeasure that the deputies had not begun the mandated inquiry.[19] They took no further action, and the matter passed from the record.

Again, conflict made clear the sophistication of the early modern capital market. Capital took many forms and flowed in many directions. Orphanage resources combined proceeds from donations and subventions with the property of orphans and the house. It circulated as credit, debt, rentes, and fees beyond the city throughout the region of Swabia in a multitude of individual exchanges that brought buyer and seller or debtor and creditor face to face. Not fixed in a single marketplace, where transactions could be monitored and values established, the market for capital was decentralized and unregulated and required, therefore, nerve and knowledge from those who operated within it. Yet, those capitalists were not high-stakes gamblers but rather risk-averse investors. For this reason, orphanage administrators negotiated the complexities of parity.

As noted, parity constrained capital but did not prevent conflict. Catholics invested with Catholics—and Lutherans with Lutherans—because the institution of parity raised the social and economic costs of other possibilities. Exchanges between coreligionists were simpler and safer. Even so, their interests occasionally clashed. In those disputes, the administrators of charity proved hardnosed, determinedly pursuing their own advantage and using all of the resources at their disposal, including the legal and political weight of the city, to support them. Rather than banishing risk, parity shifted it.

The probability of loss required not only the relentless pursuit of advantage but also the mobilization of capital. Indeed, orphan fathers occasionally used their own resources to augment those of the organizations they administered. A case in point involved Franz Graf of the Catholic Orphanage, who contributed 1,000 fl. "to the aid and use of poor orphan children" during the 1690s.[20] The contemporaneous Lutheran orphan father, Tobias Groß, also used his own capital to provide funds for his orphanage.[21] These were debts that had to be paid but only after long haggling. Lacking the means to meet their commitments fully, the alms lords agreed in 1709 to provide annuities for the widows of Graf and Groß.[22]

Because of these commitments and obligations, therefore, a persistent, paradoxical sense of impotence ran throughout orphanage records. It emerged from the administrators' nearly constant efforts to limit new admissions to the orphanage and their equally constant pleas to increase subventions from the city. Reflecting on the merits of an orphan father, a superior magistrate specifically noted that he "had not made himself particularly meritorious in his service and the returns of the orphanage [were] for the most part uncertain and increased and decreased according to the number of donors while the number of orphans steadily grew."²³ His chief preoccupation and principal responsibility was to maximize resources. This in turn consisted of two basic activities: reduce the costs associated with larger numbers of orphans; expand the income derived from the orphanage's various sources of support. In the face of widespread family dissolution and impoverishment, the authorities could only argue for a strict application of the regulations that limited admissions. By the same token, the orphan fathers and all administrators of state charities could only petition the state to expand its subventions or encourage their coreligionists to make more generous donations. Yet, orphan fathers could completely control neither.

Powerless to affect either the supply of charity or the demand for it, they seized every possible source of capital and used it to generate earnings. Orphanage administrators overlooked nothing.

They rented empty space in their houses. Administrators of the Lutheran Orphanage made the attic available to third parties who paid increasing sums throughout the eighteenth century to store grain there. Administrators did not permit the organization's primary function as an orphanage to limit their efforts to generate income.

They sold living space to the elderly. Given an opportunity, orphanage administrators did not shy from providing a *Pfrund* within their walls to an adult.²⁴ Maria Jacobina Beckhin was no orphan but rather an elderly spinster. Still, in 1762 she found a place in the Catholic Orphanage through terms arranged in the will of a wealthy widow, Maria Renata Widemann.²⁵ The legacy provided a capital of 500 fl. in return for admission of Beckhin as an orphanage servant. She would work as a sick nurse but was excused from all heavy labor because of her weak physical condition and allowed to pursue her own business outside the walls as a by-employment. She would have an unheated room in the orphanage to herself and receive fuel, food, clothing, and care at the house's expense. Moreover, she would receive an annual stipend of 40 fl. until age fifty and 50 fl. thereafter. When she died, her entire property of 850 fl. as well as the 500 fl. from the Widemann estate would pass to the orphanage. It was an arrangement more reminiscent of an early modern hospital than of an orphanage and speaks to the necessary omnicompetence of organizations driven by their need for resources.

Administrators provided annuities to the well-to-do. In 1784, shopkeeper Franz Lehmann transferred his Augsburg house "auf dem Creutz" and a capital of 900 fl., invested in the tavern "zur Eggen," to the Catholic Orphanage.²⁶ In return, the Alms Office agreed to provide Lehmann with an annuity of 100 fl. annually for the rest of his and his daughter's days. It also promised to admit a parentless nephew to residence in the orphanage as soon as he reached the minimum age.

Administrators seized the property of dead orphans. Endowment pennies

(*Dotenpfennige*) were small, decorative items—often a silver object or religious book—given as keepsakes to Lutheran children by their godparents at baptism or their sponsors at communion.[27] When children entered the orphanage, these items accompanied them as witnesses to relationships in the larger community.[28] When orphans died, however, the orphanage inherited these remembrances along with the rest of their property. In 1739, Lutheran Orphan Father Johann Sturm converted to cash "the endowment pennies that have been inherited from deceased orphans over many years and melted down for the benefit of this house."[29] All of the fine metals in this unclaimed property were melted and assayed by the master of the city's mint, who then purchased the silver and gold for 420 fl. Orphan Father Mathias Pratsch recorded a similar transaction worth 378 fl. in 1762.[30] Again, in 1775, Matthäus Kunzelbach sold 399 fl. in endowment pennies.[31] Though irregular as a source of income, the endowment pennies generated resources comparable in given years to the proceeds of donations. It was a source of capital not to be despised.

And, of course, orphanage administrators invested the property of living. On 17 May 1645, the elders of the Alms Office ordered that Tobias Schuester be admitted to the orphanage and that his inheritance be inventoried by three alms servants (*Säckelknechte*).[32] As the authorities were careful to note, his mother had converted to Lutheranism when she married her first husband. Her second husband, Schuester, had been Lutheran as well, and his son, the orphan Tobias, had been born into that faith. Her third husband, Tobias' first step-father, was Catholic, and the mother and her son reconverted to the faith in which she had been born. Once in the orphanage, Tobias' rearing made itself plain; he could not recite the basic Catholic liturgy satisfactorily.[33] As the son of a Lutheran father, Tobias was apprenticed to a Lutheran master and his fortune was entrusted to two Lutheran trustees.[34] These were probably provisions of the father's will because they ran contrary to the mother's and step-father's conviction.

Perhaps the religious dimensions of this particular admission spurred the authorities to greater than usual care. Many orphans, however, possessed property in diverse forms and distant parts that required extra effort on the part of the Alms Office. The fate of Tobias' inheritance differs not in the basic manner in which it is handled but rather in the care and detail with which the handling is recorded.

The authorities began with the house that had belonged to the mother and now belonged to the son. They described it and its contents with care. It had a living room, two sleeping or storage rooms, and a kitchen on the ground floor and another room upstairs. Outside were a storage shed, a small garden, and a fishpond. Passing inside, the recording officials gave the number and condition of every piece of furniture, article of clothing, and item of houseware. They found 14 old Latin books in quarto and octavo editions, including copies of a Lutheran Bible in Latin and a book of prayers and sermons (*Hauspostill*).[35] Though well provided with clothing, bedding, and housewares, the dwelling contained little furniture apart from an old table and stool, two beds, and several chests. Foodstuffs in the form of ground dinkel (*Kern*), and fuel in the form of chopped birch wood rounded out the basic household necessities.

Movable and real property created storage and maintenance problems. In most cases, the authorities sold everything but the smallest, most valuable, or most useful items and invested the proceeds on behalf of the owner. Andreas Buechhofer purchased the Schuester house for 150 fl., 100 of which remained invested in the house as capital of Augsburg's association of herb growers and sellers (*Kräutler*). Buechhofer agreed to pay the balance in quarterly installments of 5 fl. at no interest. Though it generated no immediate cash or income, the sale eventually realized Tobias 50 fl. The Alms Office also sold housewares, clothing, and linen for a total of 65 fl. The late mother's sister, resident in a town southwest of Augsburg, received 12 fl. from the proceeds of the sale, netting Tobias about 53 fl. from the movable property.

As was strict legal practice at the time, Tobias' paternal inheritance was held apart from his mother's property. When one parent died and the other remarried, the inheritances of any surviving children were inventoried and placed in trust. Parties to such a trusteeship often agreed to allow usufruct of the children's inheritance by the surviving parent and step-parent in return for certain considerations, but the property was no less frequently held and managed separately.[36] Tobias' trustees controlled his paternal inheritance of 109 fl.

The value, therefore, of the maternal real estate and movable property and the paternal inheritance totalled just over 212 fl. From this amount the three alms servants settled obligations against the estate. Their fees amounted to 21 fl. The guardians charged the estate 20 fl. for expenses incurred during Tobias' wardship. Finally, upon entering the orphanage Tobias required 2 fl. worth of clothing, which had to be paid out of his own funds, all of which were part of the estate. Total expenses of 43 fl. left a cash balance of 169 fl., still a very considerable sum for a "poor" orphan.[37]

Tobias also inherited his parents' capital, that is, a series of wide-ranging, small-scale credit and capital transactions, which now fell to the alms servants to collect and administer for the boy. Georg Strohmayr owed 30 fl., and Jacob Mair, the butcher at the public house known as the "Peasant Dance" (*Bauerntanz*), paid 3 fl. Yet, against a total of 33 fl. in easily collected debts were 57 fl. in debts outstanding. Marx, a miller in the neighboring town of Derching, owed 10 fl., and Jacob Negelin owed 7 fl. Andreas Leixel of Lechhausen and Georg Prenberger rendered interest on loans of 10 and

30 fl. respectively. Finally the inventory listed several bad debts, acknowledged to be uncollectable either because of the debtors' insolvency or intransigence.

Modest shopkeepers and artisans, such as the parents of Tobias Schuester, invested a surprising proportion of their wealth in capital transactions. These obligations tended to be small-scale, individual loans for the purpose of consumption. Furthermore, their credit was not concentrated in Augsburg but rather distributed over villages and towns across Swabia. Petty shopkeepers and producers, far from being limited to local capital and commodity markets, made their presence felt regionally. The posture of the Tobias estate suggests attitudes toward capital that were generative rather than distributional and oriented toward growth rather than conservation.

Most orphans possessed less than Tobias. Thousands entered the orphanages accompanied only by the orphan father's terse notation, "Has nothing" (*Hat nix*). In 1592 orphan father Hans Limm admitted Maria Diettrichin, who "had nothing but poverty and misery and many lice."[38] Some children inherited liabilities from their parents. Jonas Holl, the seven-year-old son of a bleacher, entered the City Orphanage in 1634 with little more than the clothes on his back.[39] As the orphan father noted, "there are many debts . . . and one cannot yet tell whether something will be left the boy from his father."[40] In the midst of capital transactions and financial calculations, the administrators of the orphanage continually confronted the suffering and need of children who owned no worldly goods and depended on the kindness of strangers.

Like Tobias, however, some possessed property in the form of inheritances that passed to the orphanages and contributed, for a time at least, to their capital. Values ranged from mere pittances to stately expectations. Regina Böshin entered the City Orphanage in 1590 with 20 fl. in cash and miscellaneous linen and bedding, a considerable fortune for the daughter of one of Augsburg's weavers.[41] Three sisters, Sybilla, Maria, and Veronika Leschin, shared a house in the James' Suburb.[42] The house served as security for a 200 fl. debt held by their late mother's step-brother and brother-in-law, proof of the interconnections between family and capital even among the humbler members of urban society. The son of a miller, Hans Jerg Newmayr brought an interest in a field by the village of Lechhausen, just outside the walls of Augsburg.[43] Unfortunately for the Catholic Orphanage, where he was admitted in 1679, he shared that interest with his eight siblings. More useful was the sum of 15 fl. inherited by the three-year-old Theresia Braunin from her father.[44] The orphan father used the money to paint one of the rooms in the Catholic Orphanage. Accounts indicate that larger sums were not allowed to lie inactive but were invested as quickly as possible. Maria Theresia Schaumännin inherited 132 fl. and a silver belt from her mother.[45]

The money passed directly into the fund of children's moneys and thence into the capital market; the belt was wrapped in paper and set aside against the day its owner would reenter the world.

Orphanage administrators worked hard to maintain the property of their charges. Goods and money might be scattered over several households or communities, thus involving the city and its charity in the tedious and complex processes of probating, collecting, and tranporting. Out of motives both disinterested and self-interested, they kept meticulous account of this wealth and strove to protect the orphans from possible exploitation and loss. Such property as the children possessed was often the first and best guarantor of their eventual self-sufficiency, which was the constant, mandated goal of the organization. As a potential dowry, it attracted a more prosperous suitor; as part of an apprenticeship fee, it assured acceptance into the household of one of Augsburg's more skilled master craftsmen. Their property was also important capital for the orphanages to be used for general purposes, to offset the extraordinary expenses of childcare, or to generate added income. Much of this capital, however, was held in usufruct only and remained the property of the orphans. When they needed it or asked for it, the administrators had to surrender it.

These unique conditions called for forms of investment that were both secure and liquid. In 1733 the City Council prohibited the administrators of all charitable organizations from lending capital in foreign jurisdictions because such loans were infinitely more difficult to collect.[46] The edict further limited the size of all loans to no more than two-thirds the purchase price of the offered collateral. In 1750, the council repeated its warning that they "invest [such funds] at interest in a foundation within the city's territory and jurisdiction."[47] In 1788 the Small Council specifically refused to invest 1,000 fl. on behalf of the Catholic Orphanage, noting that the deputies must "locate another secure opportunity for the investment of the available money as prescribed by law."[48] Magistrates apparently shared a concern for the security of the property that belonged to the city's orphans. The administrators observed these regulations in the breach only; the need for income made such limits impractical.

Forced to rely on declining donations and shrinking subventions, orphanage administrators located supplementary sources of income. Their need to plan expenditures and realize economies as well as the unpredictability of financial support gave earnings from capital an importance beyond their value. A variety of resources, in themselves irregular and unpredictable became regular, predictable incomes in the capital market. Yet, investment and speculation were not hallmarks of early modern capitalists, whether organizational administrators or mercantile entrepreneurs. Though capable of calculating risk, they were fundamentally risk-averse and sought secure incomes wherever possible.[48] The nature of the economy—its lack of fixed institutions, common procedures, or uniform regulations—introduced an unavoidable element of chance. As a result, orphanage administrators maximized their resources wherever possible and pursued their economic advantage singlemindedly. They also diversified their obligations and interests in ways that were a direct expression and consequence of charity in the market.

Sources of Capital and Their Value

The City Orphanage owned diverse kinds of capital from its very beginning. Though modest, its endowments grew during the sixteenth century as a result of the steady circulation of capital in Augsburg as a whole. In 1535, for example, the alms lords accounted for orphanage capital worth more than 30,000 fl.[50] The Helena Streissin Business (*Geschäft*) held 1,000 fl. of this sum. As instructed in her testament, trustees managed the capital and paid an annual interest of 50 fl. to the orphanage. Similarly, the Martin Zobel Foundation (*Stiftung*) paid proceeds of 15 fl. annually on 300 fl. capital. A further 5,400 fl. took the form of real estate: two buildings and three fields at the time. Most interesting of all, the orphanage possessed 25,456 fl. in invested (*anligende*) capital. Placed on account with various local organization and individuals, these sums produced a regular interest income. The City Council was the orphanage's most important debtor, holding 17,700 fl at 5 percent and a further 3,000 fl. at 4 percent annually.[51] Five others were important figures in Augsburg's mercantile and artisanal communities: the patrician merchant Jacob Hochstetter owed 800 fl.; bakers Hans Schwertfurn and Hans Scheffler owed 800 fl. and 300 fl. respectively; and weaver Jacob Geiger, Peter Kraus, and Hans Hafner owed 500, 400, and 300 fl. respectively. Minors' accounts, including orphan property and smaller donations, constituted the balance.

Donations, subventions, and earnings provided a ready resource to which credit-hungry Augsburgers turned at need, giving orphanage administrators regular opportunity to convert cash reserves into investment capital. Whether growth continued or how orphanage endowments changed, especially during the dramatic first half of the seventeenth century, cannot be determined. Surviving accounts from that period preserved only the daily and monthly transactions in commodities and labor, the stuff of daily life. Records for the Alms Office as a whole followed the influence of changing times on the capital market.

In 1600, for example, 86 individuals, groups, or organizations paid simple interest ranging from 4 to 5 percent per annum on obligations owed to, that is, money invested by, the Alms Office[52] (see Table 4.1). A total capital of 77,468 fl. yielded an income of 2,973 fl. As was the case with the City Orphanage, state agencies were the largest consumers of charity's capital.

TABLE 4.1
Debts (Total Value in Gulden) Payable to the Alms Office

Category of Debtor	No.	1600	No.	1627	No.	1649	No.	1675
Men	65	(31,681 fl.)	24	(13,796 fl.)	54	(9,460 fl.)	13	(2,082 fl.)
Women	5	(1,786 fl.)	1	(800 fl.)	4	(1,175 fl.)	2	(400 fl.)
Families	1	(50 fl.)	0		2	(235 fl.)	0	
Estates	2	(849 fl.)	3	(1,525 fl.)	7	(6,420 fl.)	2	(1,250 fl.)
Foundations	7	(6,431 fl.)	0		1	(300 fl.)	0	
Guilds	4	(447 fl.)	0		1	(230 fl.)	2	(272 fl.)
City	2	(35,900 fl.)	1	(4,000 fl.)	5	(4,565 fl.)	4	(13,117 fl.)
Princes	0		1	(1,723 fl.)	2	(6,246 fl.)	3	(1,260 fl.)
Total	86	(77,468 fl.)	34	(23,748 fl.)	79	(28,329 fl.)	28	(18,402 fl.)

The City Council and Incomes Office held debts totalling 35,900 fl. Guilds owed a further 447 fl. Almost as valuable as the debts held by city agencies was credit to individuals. Sixty-five men borrowed 31,381 fl. from the Alms Office; five women owed a further 1,786 fl. A single family enterprise borrowed 50 fl. Estates and foundations managed over 7,000 fl. in assets the paid regular dividends to support Augsburg's civic charity.

The crisis that gripped Augsburg in the 1620s, and did not relent until 1649 and the recovery that extended at least into the 1670s, altered the structure of the Alms Office's capital. Around 1600 the city stood at or near its productive capacity.[53] Total capital in 1600, viewed both in number of obligations and their total value, reflected the wealth of the city as a whole. These reserves flowed in the first place from the property of orphans and the donations of benefactors. By 1627, with the city in the grip of famine and plague, the Alms Office's capital had shrunk to one-third its previous value, with the flight of individual and public borrowers leading the decline. Dearth-induced inflation ordinarily fueled demand for credit, but it forced state charity to consume rather than invest its resources, probably collecting its economic obligations to meet its social ones. Demand for small-scale credit by individuals, possibly to assist in rebuilding personal fortunes, fueled the modest recovery of 1649. Fifty-eight men and women borrowed about 10,500 fl., less than 200 fl. on average and far less than the sums acquired in earlier years. Despite or possibly due to the dual constraints of public debt and a depressed economy, the Alms Office reestablished itself in the capital markets of Augsburg as a source of credit. In 1665, it listed a total capital of 62,663 fl. that included real property valued in excess of 25,000 fl. and at least 36,696 fl. in debts receivable. By 1675, however, individual borrowers had abandoned the Alms Office, and, though the city again offered some opportunities for investment, the capital of charity had reached its nadir.

As noted, declining endowments forced public charity into the fiscal arms of the state. As the seventeenth century ended, Augsburg bore an increasing share of the costs of social assistance. The orphanages, however, occupied a different place in this connection. They had never depended entirely upon their own resources, enjoying also the regular support of subventions and donations, and, so, never consumed their own resources.

Accounts from the eighteenth century continued to record the capital transactions of Augsburg's two orphanages. It is reasonable to assume, despite the lack of supporting evidence, that they always engaged in credit and investment. What changed in the late seventeenth and eighteenth centuries was the scope and form of their involvement. As the sources of their income shifted, as subventions became limited and donations declined, earnings assumed a new meaning. Capital had to expand to meet rising costs. Since the state and individuals no longer guaranteed operating revenues, the orphanages had to draw on their own resources. Capital had to become more liquid. Nothing so marks the gradual shift to market enterprise as the changing nature of these financial dealings. The result was an expansion of banking activities that brought the orphanages into greater contact with state agencies, charitable foundations, business enterprises, and the common folk.

In 1725 the Catholic Orphanage held 17 debts, a total of 14,300 fl, invested at 4.5 percent and yielding 596 fl.[54] This capital reveals a unique structure of Catholic investment that was institutional rather than individual and ecclesiastical rather than secular.

Catholic administrators seem to have preferred institutional investment. They loaned relatively little to the city government despite an interest rate of 5 percent, higher than they actually earned. The Catholic Orphanage loaned 660 fl. to the city's Superior Trust Office (*Oberpflegamt*) and 2,000 fl. to the Incomes Office.[55] Local Catholic foundations, on the other hand, benefitted from a far larger share, just under half of the orphanage's total capital. The Imperial Abbey of Sts. Ulrich and Afra held 2,000 fl., half of which belonged to the orphanage and was invested at 5 percent, half of which belonged to the orphans and was invested at 4 percent. The monastery at Closterholz paid 4 percent on a capital of 1,000 fl., which belonged to the Catholic Orphanage. The Cathedral Chapter of Augsburg held more of the orphanage's capital than any other single individual or institution, 4,000 fl., which it invested at 4 percent in the Hospital Office of the town of Dinkelscherben. Though some of these obligations would become bones of contention later in the century, the concentration of orphanage capital in ecclesiastical foundations may have reflected the traditional Catholic view that charity was a religious responsibility. In eighteenth-century Languedoc, bishops blocked or minimized state involvement through political initiatives.[56] In eighteenth-century Augsburg, the Church checked state control through the manipulation of financial interests.

Private individuals held the balance of the Catholic Orphanage's capital, 6,640 fl. Of this total, 3,900 fl. was reinvested by those individuals in the public debt (*Statt Capital*). Johann Franz Sembler held the principal but donated the interest to the orphanage. The remaining 2,740 fl. was private capital in the strict sense. All but 150 fl. of this total belonged to the orphans, for whom the admininstrators invested by lending funds to individuals in amounts ranging from 50 to 1,000 fl. The orphanage loaned Michael Baur's 70 fl. at 5 percent to Joseph Schuester; Maria Ruffin's 70 fl. to Melchior Ott; the Hofel children's 400 fl. to Joseph Hofler; and the Schwab children's 250 fl. to Martin Trefler. Such loans were not always local: Afra Schempin, the wife of a brewer in the town of Mertingen, borrowed a capital of 1,000 fl., and Joseph Schuester, a brewer and publican from Rottenberg borrowed 800 fl., all of which belonged to children in the orphanage. The remaining 150 fl., which was the organization's own, also found its way into the hands of private borrowers.

The presence of small-scale borrowers is, perhaps, the most interesting aspect of the house's engagement in capital transactions. These modest loans served a range of needs from business investments to family consumption. Borrowers were not limited to Augsburg but came from other parts of Swabia, and the Catholic Orphanage accommodated the needs of all these consumers. It did not insist on one-to-one relationships between the owner and the borrower. Rather, it created consortia at need, using its own resources, those of one or more orphans, or a combination. Such flexibility reveals an awareness of market conditions, both on the part of the administrators and their borrowers large and small, as well as an ability to calculate the probability of gain and the risk of loss.

An inventory of Lutheran Orphanage contracts from the mid-eighteenth century reveals a similar variety of transactions and interests.[57] It also exposes the different strategies of the two confessional orphanages.

Unlike the Catholic Orphanage, which listed no transactions involving real property, the Lutheran Orphanage earned a modest but constant income from dues or rents on pastures, houses, lofts, and other properties. Meadows rents (*Angerzins*) grew from 132 fl. in 1734 to 177 fl. in 1780, to 237 fl. in 1803.[58] Rents (*Bodenzins*) from the attic (*Dachboden*) of the orphanage also grew from 18 fl. in 1734 to 44 fl. in 1780, to 54 fl. in 1803.

Fees or liens (*Grundzins*), collected on property held by a third party, derived from feudal rents in which the occupier of a piece of land paid a certain sum of money to the lord who possessed the land. The right to collect these fees eventually became alienable, and the orphanage acquired them as a source of income. By 1709, for example, it had purchased the rights to collect income on as many as 22 buildings and 3 gardens in and around Augsburg, an investment worth thousands of Gulden. This source of income grew also, though not as dramatically as others. From about 61 fl. in 1734, these fees eventually totalled nearly 80 fl. in 1803.

Unlike the Catholic Orphanage, the Lutheran Orphanage rarely offered credit to small-scale borrowers. Rather, it engaged in a series of transactions—financial and industrial—that involved uniformly large amounts of capital and usually well-to-do members of the city's Lutheran community. Some transactions involved business interests. In the eighteenth century the patrician Wolfgang Jacob Sulzer donated 7,200 fl. to the orphanage. A capital of 3,000 fl. was invested at 4.5 percent in an Augsburg beer brewery. The remaining 4,200 fl. was invested in an Augsburg printing and publishing enterprise. Another document referred to a 4,303 fl. interest in mining operations, donated to the orphanage by Daniel Philipp Widholz, another of Augsburg's Lutheran merchants.[59] Other transactions involved credit. In March 1718 the merchant Peter Laire turned to the orphanage for a loan of 4,600 fl. at 4.5 percent. Credit transactions required some form of collateral, usually in the form of real estate, but Laire's reputation exempted him from this precaution. Unlike the Catholic Orphanage and its loan to Langenmantel, however, the Lutheran Orphanage collected the Laire debt on time in 1726. The weaver Matthäus Hindermayr borrowed 1,200 fl. from the orphanage in 1735 and secured it with a mortgage on his house. He paid the debt off within three years. Likewise, baker Johannes Kornmann and wife Rosina Kagin borrowed 2,000 fl. against their house. The size of these transactions implies considerable resources on the part of the borrowers. It also demonstrates the willingness of the administrators to tie Lutheran economic interests to the orphanage's finance through credit operations.

Like the Catholic Orphanage, the Lutheran one invested a certain proportion of its capital with foundations and organizations. Its engagements, however, were mostly secular. Between 1735 and 1736 the orphanage invested 3,000 fl. with the city. In 1747 it transferred 1,000 fl. to the city's pawn shop (*Pfand- und Leihhaus*). This constituted a relatively secure means of holding money and generating an income, certainly safer than private loans or investments.

Both Catholic and Lutheran orphanages possessed sizable "portfolios" of diverse commitments and obligations, but they pursued their interests in distinct ways. Lutherans invested capital locally where Catholics exchanged capital regionally. Most Lutheran transactions involved individuals, as opposed to the Catholic predeliction for foundations. Whereas Lutheran money remained in secular hands, Catholic capital flowed through ecclesiastical organizations. Lutheran transactions tended to be large-scale and intended for production, while Catholic investments were small-scale for consumption. Finance, therefore, seemed to follow patterns that were confession-specific.

Between 1783 and 1789 the administrators of the Catholic Orphanage reviewed the capital investments of their organization.[60] They divided all obligations into so-called active capital (*aktiven Kapitalien*) and passive capital (*passiven Kapitalien*), that is, into accounts receivable, or all moneys owed to the orphanage, and accounts payable, or all moneys owed by the orphanage. In 1783 the Catholic Orphanage possessed active capital valued at 22,405 fl. This included all moneys loaned by and therefore owed to the house. It also included all payments promised or committed to it, such as legacies provided in private testaments and support from charitable or social foundations. Against this total were listed the various passive capital, which amounted to 11,666 fl. The orphanage owed 4,600 fl., that is, debts in the strict sense. Children's moneys constituted a further 7,066 fl. because they were a financial obligation on the part of the house. Though it might invest this capital and enjoy an interim usufruct, the orphanage did not strictly possess these moneys and would eventually have to pay them to their owners. The net balance of all capital transactions for 1783 was a healthy 10,739 fl. Yet, the total value rather than the balance of all transactions for that year, 34,071 fl., more accurately reflected the orphanage's involvement.

By 1789 the Catholic Orphanage was no less committed. Adding passive and active capital as well as petty cash, the total value of all capital transactions had risen to 41,188 fl., an increase of 19 percent. Total active capital amounted to 31,605 fl., as opposed to 9,055 fl in passive capital. Once again, these obligations included 5,555 fl. in children's moneys. The net at year's end was an even more striking balance of 23,078 fl.

The Catholic Orphanage was active in the capital market, but most of its transactions were modest[61] (see Table 4.2). In the years leading up to 1788, when the City Council imposed firm limits on orphanage spending and on the administrators' discretion, nearly all categories of incomes and expenditures declined (Table 4.2,A). The value of income from invested capital rose briefly then fell precipitously over the period (Table 4.2,B). In 1785, however, the amount was sufficiently high to suggest that a good proportion of the orphanage's capital was invested in short-term credit transactions, the sort that had to be paid regularly. As times worsened toward the end of the century, these debts would have become increasingly difficult to collect, reinforcing the decline of active capital. The Catholic Orphanage slowly withdrew from the capital market between 1784 and 1787; capital transactions declined in comparison with all other expenditures (Table 4.2,D,C). On the other hand, the net value to the orphanage of capital transactions, that is, obligations collected and paid, rose in 1787 (Table 4.2,F). Because of a tightening domestic economy and the debate concerning the costs of orphan care, reliance on earnings from capital increased and administrators continued to exchange money in Augsburg's capital market.

TABLE 4.2
Capital (Gulden:Kreutzer) of the Catholic Orphanage, 1784–87

INCOMES	1784	1785	1786	1787
(A) Total income *less* all invested capital (*Aktiva*)	13374:53	6462:01	6672:37	5545:09
(B) Total income *from* all invested capital	0:00	1800:00	600:00	100:00
(C) Total expenditures *less* invested capital and paid debt (*Passiva*)	5593:50	5295:09	4672:37	4676:57
(D) Total of all invested capital and paid debt	7425:00	2800:00	2600:00	500:00
(E) Balance less invested capital and paid debt	7781:03	1166:52	2000:00	868:12
(F) Balance of invested capital and paid debt	356:02	166:52	0:00	468:12

The Lutheran Orphanage was highly involved too. Its account of 1780, for example, listed dues and rents from real estate at 219 fl., and active capital worth 23,350 fl. invested at 4 percent with the city's Incomes Office and various, unspecified citizens.[62] Most of the orphanage's partners in exchange were members of Augsburg's aristocratic and merchant elite.[63] Yet also commoners participated regularly. The account does not, however, offer detailed descriptions of the orphanage's investment and obligations in 1780.

Also recorded were passive capital. The interest from children's moneys implied a principal of 1,766 fl. The account listed 3,877 fl. in new capital, not just the property of orphans but also donations from private foundations and individual benefactors. The orphanage received over 1,200 fl. from nine private foundations, all endowed by the individuals or families for whom they were named: Baron von Garb, Christoph von Rad, Ferdinand Renz, the Walter family, Gerhard Greiff, Andreas Bohm, Anna Regina Zobel, and Lucas Stenglin. These were all members of Augsburg's first families; a private foundation required capital backing beyond the means of humbler sorts. The sole commoner to contribute substantially to the Lutheran Orphanage was the orphanage's apothecary, Johann Christoph Michel, who donated a capital of 3 kr. for each orphan. The well-to-do also provided eight legacies, valued in excess of 3,500 fl., that generated an income of 190 fl. The persons behind these were: Gerhard Greiff, Johann Georg Hillerbrand, Johann Thomas Rauner, Lorenz Sigmund Welser, and Sabina Neuhoferin. The Lutheran elite were powerful supporters of the Lutheran Orphanage. Certainly, donations helped to build the total capital value of 29,212 fl.

Whatever the imperfections of a comparison between accounts from different years, the differences cannot be dismissed lightly. Changing economic conditions or financial regimes altered some of the contours of orphanage capital. By 1784, the Catholic Orphanage had expanded its endowment to a level quite similar to that of the Lutheran Orphanage. Yet, internal differences remained. Though the sums involved changed from year to year, the characteristics of investment remained remarkably stable.

The Catholics exploited a much broader territory in their use of capital. One reason was the geography of confession. Catholics dominated the towns and countryside around Augsburg politically, socially, and economically. Another was the organizational matrix created by the Catholic Church. Because of its religious affiliation, the Catholic orphanage maintained ties to Catholic Bavaria and the Catholic Diocese of Augsburg, to Catholic polities and Catholic foundations, that eased and encouraged financial transactions.

That the Lutheran Orphanage did not have economic interests in Lutheran Imperial cities, such as Nördlingen, Ulm, Lindau, Memmingen, or Kempten, is puzzling but may reflect the essential strength of Augsburg as a financial center in the eighteenth century. The house found enough opportunities at home. Lutheran capital depended more on individual investment than was the case with the Catholic Orphanage in the eighteenth century: 75 percent compared to 46 percent.

Insofar as Lutheran capital may be characterized as individual and Catholic capital as institutional, it seems that the former may also be justly described as particularly entrepreneurial. The Lutheran Orphanage drew a large portion of its resources from the property of families and individuals. Much of this capital returned to private entities in the form of investment and credit. None of these transactions was worth less than 1,000 fl., an indication that they were used not for consumption but rather for reinvestment in a business or household. By contrast, the Catholic Orphanage placed its funds in the hands of ecclesiastical foundations, such as monasteries or hospitals, that had liturgical as well as charitable functions. What little found its way into the hands of individuals frequently assumed the form of smaller sums— 100 fl. or less—reminiscent of the modest loans frequently needed by poor or marginal families to provide for daily expenses and survival. There were exceptions. Catholic administrators did not give where Lutherans invested.

As a single example, they agreed in 1749 to lend the gardner Johann Henrici 1,000 fl. and accepted his gardens as collateral.[64] They warned him, however, to do nothing that might damage or devalue the property, in which case they would immediately call the debt. As a rule, however, the Lutheran Orphanage pursued financial strategies that were oriented more to market and profit. The Catholic Orphanage contented itself to a far larger extent with incomes from a diverse array of secure foundations and consumer loans. There is an element of speculation in the larger credit transactions and financial interests of the Lutherans that corresponded more closely to classical notions of capitalistic behavior and that seems to be absent from the rentier activities of the Catholics. The difference is less a matter of economic orientation than of organizational affiliation. Individual accounts and transactions tell a tale of calculation by the administrators of both institutions that was usually market-oriented or economically rational but never purely so.

Certainly the finances of both orphanages were embedded in the capital market of the city and region. Neither home could afford dormant resources; they needed to generate income through recourse to earnings. An anonymous report on the economic status of the Lutheran Orphanage in 1780 noted a need for strict economy in the sense of reducing costs and, even more so, in terms of living within its means.[65] The orphanages had to draw on the profits of their own capital. The situation made clear "how absolutely necessary it is to manage well in all possible things."[66] The term *menagiren* implied more than simply good management; it suggested also a capitalistic discipline born of the need not merely to balance incomes and expenditures but essentially to calculate risk, pursue advantage, and maximize resources. Both Catholic and Lutheran orphanages met these goals by selecting from myriad possibilities and opportunities determined by their circumstances and experience.

THE DISCIPLINE OF CAPITAL: OPPORTUNITIES AND CONSTRAINTS

The administrators of charity were early capitalists. They controlled resources for purposes or organizational longevity if not private profit and deployed these resources within the markets. Doing so, alms lords and orphan fathers displayed characteristic wisdom. They maximized resources as a hedge against the unpredictability and uncontrollability of market forces. They were fundamentally risk averse but able to calculate risk in an environment that offered no certainty. They pursued their own advantage under circumstances in which no other surety existed. Individual transactions and organizational investment reflected this practical knowledge. Not systematic in the sense that they were formulated in abstract theory, the rules of the game were learned and applied under actual circumstances. Yet, at the same time, they were more than just circumstantial. Administrators applied economic wisdom beyond the marketplace, and so began the long process of transforming capitalistic behavior into a more thorough standard for perceiving, understanding and shaping the world. Only fragments of an emergent system of capitalism are visible, but they deserve attention.

Opportunity and discipline assumed distinctly capitalistic features. Within the microcosm of the orphanage, an ordered society of ranks metamorphosed into a society of ability. Discipline based on the honor intrinsic to one's station evolved into a discipline based on the authority derived from the control of capital.

The orphanages never maintained separate accounts for their various categories of incomes. All resources—donations, subventions, and earnings—constituted a single fund. An orphan's property could pay for general household expenses provided that the child had access to and ultimately received the equivalent value. When an orphanage or an orphan had a particular need, the value rather than the specific property had to be at hand.

Exercising the paternalism intrinsic to their positions, the orphan fathers disbursed capital on behalf of the orphans to meet a wide variety of their needs. It might have been applied toward the daily costs of health care. It might have defrayed the costs of education or apprenticeship. It might have provided a dowry to help assure the marriage of an orphaned young woman. It might have assisted adults at their request long after they had left the orphanage. Using the resources of the needy to care for the needy was a logical means of maximizing resource.

In many instances this common capital enabled administrators to provide more than threadbare maintenance. Many children received advantages no less than those they could have expected from their own families, but others obtained training and positions beyond their expectations. Though not all orphans were equal, the orphanages had a levelling influence. All of their children were wards of the organizations; all received the same basic care. Such differences as persisted resulted from wealth rather than rank. This fact contrasts strikingly with the historical stereotype of uniform wretchedness and suggests the need to revise accepted notions of social assistance and social discipline.

The administrators assessed the property of orphans not just as a resource to help meet mundane, childrearing expenses but even as a standard for admission. What emerged often resembled a pay-as-you-go system. Children with the means to contribute to their own care usually found a place in the orphanages. On the other hand, the administrators frequently resisted admitting the neediest orphans and tried instead to force other members of their families to assume the material and moral burdens of their support.

Regulations required, in fact, that financially capable persons assume the support and rearing of orphans to whom they were related by blood to the fourth degree.[67] So concerned were administrators to avoid the unnecessary costs associated with the support of needy children—and, so, extend the organization's means—that they further stipulated that more distant relatives might be forced to assume the burden were the closer ones too poor.

This led to calculation on all sides. The dyer (*Färber*) Georg Vogel had abandoned his sons Thomas and Jörg, aged twelve and seven years respectively, in an Augsburg tavern before fleeing the city to avoid his creditors.[68] On 21 May 1586, the authorities requested that the father's brother, Dr. Thomas Vogel, a counsellor of the Bishop of Augsburg, assume the care and support of his nephews. Vogel responded that he would take custody of Thomas, provided that he received usufruct of the boy's maternal inheritance of 150 fl. The younger son, Jörg, was physically handicapped and would pose too great a burden for a man with five children of his own. Evidently the problem was serious because the boys' trustees replied that Jörg could not be supported on the interest from his inheritance alone. They suggested that Vogel take custody of both boys and their entire maternal inheritance of 300 fl., or one boy and no inheritance.

Compromise proved impossible. As a result, Thomas and Jörg were admitted to the City Orphanage by express order of the City Council on 20 July 1586.[69] The records indicate that their mother had been dead a number of years and that their father had returned to Augsburg and died destitute in the *Spital*. Despite these sober beginnings, the boys had several advantages. They possessed a birthright to apprentice and practice the trade of locksmith (*Schlosserzunft*). Moreover, they had a considerable capital in their maternal inheritance, property that had already been transferred to the Alms Office.

This capital, held in account by the orphanage over twenty years, provided opportunities quite beyond the expectations of most orphans. Though reasonably well off, the boys eventually entered careers that might well have been impossible but for the financial activities of the orphanage.

For example, in 1591, at the age of seventeen, Thomas was released from the orphanage into the custody of Peter Wolff, a merchant and citizen of Nuremberg. Wolff agreed to train the orphan as a secretary, a position of considerable trust in which a young man of energy and ability might go very far in a merchant enterprise. The Alms Office recorded only that 100 fl. had been paid to him. The orphanage provided the assistance of a bank and trust, holding funds and disbursing them at the proper times.

The younger brother Jörg fared no less well despite his handicap. In 1597, at about sixteen years of age, the authorities apprenticed him to his relative Hanns Taigeler to learn the dyer's craft. The period of apprenticeship was set at three years, during which time Jörg would pay nothing but be boarded at the orphanage and provide his own clothing. Taigeler would see to the boy's training and food. By 1600, Jörg had completed his apprenticeship honorably but, instead of pursuing his craft, had taken residence under the roof of another relative, Hanns Vogel, who was a secretary to the Count of Sigmaringen. There he intended to learn the skills necessary to become a secretary in aristocratic service, another position with considerable potential for upward mobility. No further notice appeared until 1606, when he married Anna Maria Kellerin, the daughter of a goldsmith in Ensisheim in Upper Alsace. Jörg formally requested the release of all his property and forwarded legal proof of his marriage. The Alms Office noted that he would receive 78 fl. because he had been given a total of 22 fl. on three separate occasions to meet miscellaneous needs.[70]

For both brothers, the orphanage held and managed their property for at least twenty years, well beyond their period of residence. Nearly 100 fl. had been spent on their care and training while in the house. The remaining capital had enabled them to enter profitable service and conclude an advantageous marriage.

The fees for education or apprenticeship constituted one of the biggest single expenses in childrearing and one of the biggest hurdles to self-sufficiency. The orphanage commonly paid all or part of these expenses for its charges, calculating its own involvement on the basis of the orphans' resources.

Those who had nothing depended particularly on the organization's capital. Hans Vogelmair, who entered the City Orphanage as a have-naught in 1580, received a two-year apprenticeship with master weaver Leinhart Miller.[71] The orphanage's investment of 4 fl. was apparently well spent; in 1598 Vogelmair left Augsburg as a journeyman and wandered toward Nuremberg "to support himself with his craft." Those who could pay, on the other hand, did so. Hans Vetter also entered the City Orphanage in 1580 but possessed 15 fl.[72] In 1589, the orphan father used the sum to pay for the boy's apprenticeship with master tailor Bartelme Wangner. Vetter inherited a further 100 fl. from certain members of his family in 1593 and 1594. Despite the fact that he had completed his training and no longer lived in the orphanage, the authorities kept his capital and disbursed it for him to pay, among other things, 12 fl. for clothing. Regardless of a dissimilarity of means, orphans experienced quite similar, if not entirely equal, possibilities of apprenticeship.

The orphanage's capital gave orphans a latitude not available to many young people. For example, Bartholome Seitz became an apprentice at age thirteen to Matheus Fischer, a braid- and lacemaker (*Bortenwirker*).[73] His training was to last for four years at a cost of 14 fl. After two years, however, he fled his master. The orphanage administrators had to pay Fischer half the arranged fee; as Seitz had no money of his own, the house absorbed the loss. The orphan father arranged a new apprenticeship with a different craftsman, but Seitz fled again, after only eight days. Finally, he was apprenticed "out of mercy" to Hans Heffele for a fee of 6 fl. Seitz could not have afforded the first position on his own; he would never have received a second or third chance. A similar experience befell Hans Jerg Widenmann, who entered the Catholic Orphanage in 1689.[74] He bounced from an apprenticeship with a weaponsmith (*Schwertfeger*) to one with a combmaker (*Strelmacher*), completing neither. Finally in 1692 his uncle agreed to care for him because he was "fit for no handicraft."[75] Of a total estate worth 52 fl., more than 30 fl. had been lost compensating the injured master craftsmen. Again, in terms of the opportunities provided, access to orphanage capital, to which those orphans who had property contributed and from which those who had nothing benefitted, had a levelling influence.

By the late seventeenth century and increasingly in the eighteenth century, the orphanages limited payment of apprenticeship fees. Initially they paid in installments. The practice developed because of the rising costs of apprenticeship, the occasional fecklessness of apprentices, and the pressing need to maximize resources and limit expenditures. Hans Georg Probst, the penniless orphan of a member of Augsburg's garrison, apprenticed to a tailor in 1693 for three years at 20 fl.[76] The administrators of the Catholic Orphanage promised to render payment in two installments. Seven years later his younger brother apprenticed to an engraver.[77] In this case, the 25 fl. fee followed in three parts over the six-year indenture. Installments remained the rule among orphaned apprentices, a means of protecting the interests of all parties. More than anything, however, they guaranteed the orphanage tighter control of the resources of orphan property in an age of falling incomes and rising expenses. By the eighteenth century, material pressures had risen to such an extent that the authorities began to limit the assistance available for orphan apprenticeships. Jacob Reischle was apprenticed to a turner (*Drexler*) for three years at 60 fl.—20 fl. at the end of each year. The Catholic Orphanage paid 25 fl., and the apprentice provided 35 fl.[78] By 1713 he had completed his training and become a journeyman. Over the next four years the orphanage paid him 67 fl. for various purposes. When he died in Venice in 1717, the house claimed the remainder of his estate, an "inheritance" of 133 fl. As early as 1728 the Alms Office and its orphanages refused to pay more than 30 fl. toward the cost of an orphan's training. Ignatius Eberth received a position at a tailor's table for a fee of 45 fl.[79] The Alms Office paid 30 fl. and Eberth supplied the balance. Unfortunately, the boy did not last a year in the craft; his master returned him to the Catholic Orphanage with the remark that "he did not have enough brains to learn a craft." By 1788 a formal ordinance limited apprenticeship stipends to 30 fl.[80] Expenses in excess of this had to be met by the orphans.

Limits on apprenticeship stipends placed orphans in a dilemma. If their own resources proved insufficient, consortia of patrons, relatives, and donors had to be mobilized on behalf of the aspiring artisan. This could be a complex business, especially if they had no surviving friends or family in Augsburg. Christian Philipp Lindemann sought an apprenticeship with a copper-engraver.[81] The price was set at 180 fl., far beyond the boy's means and the legal limit. It was arranged finally that a relative would pay 100 fl., Lindemann 50 fl., and the Lutheran Orphanage 30 fl. In a similar instance, Christian Durschner entered the factory of calico printer Franz Genoux (Jean François Gignoux) to learn to cut the forms used to print calico cloth (*Modelschneiden*).[82] In the early eighteenth century this was a highly skilled and prized craft that paid well.[83] Since the boy lacked any property of his own, a patron promised to pay all the apprenticeship fees if the Lutheran Orphanage would supply adequate clothing and linen. Organizing cooperative efforts of this sort exceeded the resources and abilities of most orphans. Without the capital and offices of the orphanages, such arrangements would have been impossible.

When young people left the orphanage, having completed their apprenticeships or received placement as domestic servants, they had to be clothed and equipped to assume their roles as self-sufficient laborers. Weaver's apprentice Johann Polier requested assistance from the Lutheran Orphanage because he lacked the means to purchase a suit of clothing worn by a journeyman weaver (*Gesellenkleid*).[84] The deputies granted him 14 fl. for the necessary purchases. The way out of the orphanages for girls passed through household service rather than craft apprenticeship. Though a contract of service rarely cost the orphan anything, it required adequate clothing at the very least. Placed in the household of a silver engraver, Anna Maria Hungerin received 10 fl. from her savings to purchase attire fitting for a servant.[85] Once trained and placed, adult orphans depended on their own and the orphanages' resources to maintain their positions, another instance in which access to that common capital eased disparities of economic means and social station.

Marriage awaited many orphans, and here, too, orphanage capital was instrumental. In early modern Europe, marriage was a material as well as an emotional union. Finding a spouse and establishing a household required property of some sort. Orphanage administrators provided for their charges from a capital forged of private and public resources in common. The City Orphanage sent the balance of Jörg Vogel's inheritance to Alsace as his marriage portion. Susanna Beckhin neither traveled as far nor possessed as much. A penniless orphan occupied as a household servant, she married an Augsburg tinsmith (*Spengler*) in 1600 and received a dowry of 10 fl. "out of mercy" from the City Orphanage.[86] In 1771, Anna Barbara Lippin entered the Catholic Orphanage with the stately fortune of 1,025 fl. in cash. Five years later, the orphan father placed her as a servant in the household of Anton Hieber. After six months' satisfactory service, she received an unspecified portion of her property to provide the necessities for a life of "independent" employment (*Ausfertigung*). Between 1779 and 1783, Lippin asked for and was granted a further 27 fl. for such essentials as clothing. Finally, in 1784 she married with a dowry of 50 fl. The balance of her estate—still hundreds of Gulden—was paid to her only after she and her husband had taken up housekeeping. For some orphans, paternalism created opportunities that might not have existed otherwise. While not overcoming all the differences of wealth and station that orphans brought with them into the orphanages—that was never the intention—the organization's accumulated capital provided a common basis from which to pursue a self-sufficient existence.

The administrators of charity shaped their capital transactions to accord with the needs of orphans. Yet, they also shaped them to accord with conditions in the capital market. In 1785 former orphan Jacob Lipp requested the transfer of his estate, property valued at 900 fl., from the Catholic Orphanage in Augsburg to Munich, where he worked as a beerkeg-tapper (*Bierzäpfer*).[87] The Small Council ordered the house to comply but prohibited it from seeking credit as a means of paying Lipp his due. As they noted, "for one thing it is not at all proper or useful to the foundation to borrow money in order to release passive capital and deposits and on the other hand to lend capital again."[88] The comment acknowledged that the orphanage had long engaged in profitable transactions with the orphans' property, placing it in circulation through credit and investment. When the passive capital in question (an orphan's property) had to be returned to its owner, the administrators preferred to borrow at a low rate, discharge the obligation, and then lend the balance as a second loan, possibly at a higher rate. The property of the poor became the medium of the rich; inheritances and expectations enhanced venture and speculation.

Through involvement in the capital market, administrators of charity created opportunities for the poor. That a society of ranks metamorphosed, therefore, into a society of ability within the walls of the orphanages overstates the case. Augsburg's orphanages were no hothouses of social mobility or egalitarianism. Yet, a common regimen of care and training did tend to flatten the social hierarchy. Moreover, access to capital in the form of social assistance made possible a degree of advancement and security within the world of ranks. Whether this altered the experiences and expectations of the orphans is the tale of a forthcoming volume.[89] It was, however, the expressed intention of orphanage administrators to use the capital of charity to reforge and reinforce authority and deference.

The disposition of capital had disciplinary as well as economic aspects. Although it by no means supplanted the social relations of patronage that stemmed from birthright, the capitalistic activities of the orphanages introduced social relations of production that responded to market forces.

In 1793, the pastor and superintendent (*Vorsteher*) of the Lutheran Orphanage, Johann Jakob Wasser, wrote about the limits on apprenticeship stipends.[90] He noted that orphans were hard pressed to pay fees and expenses in excess of 30 fl. from their own property, forcing them in many instances to select a craft not on the basis of inclination or ability but on the basis of affordability. Constrained by lack of means, they sought less qualified masters, who were willing to accept less money. Because of their poor training, their capacity for economic self-sufficiency was limited.

Though restricted to apprenticeship, still his observations were valid for the entire range of lifecycle expenditures. Whether providing attire and equipment for the newly employed, dowries and property for the newly married, or arranging obsequies and burial for the newly deceased, arbitrary limits on social assistance might hamper all the efforts of orphanage teachers and administrators to discipline the young to a life of work and self-sufficiency. The danger was particularly acute in the last decade of the eighteenth century, when worsening social and economic conditions in connection with the war against revolutionary France straitened circumstances for Augsburg's marginal workers. Here was the classic conundrum: accepting assistance constituted dependence; refusing assistance constituted independence; but limiting assistance increased dependence. Wasser apparently recognized the paradox; he offered no suggestions regarding the objectionable limits.

In fact, discipline and capital were closely interconnected in the minds of the administrators of charity. The purpose of the orphanage had disciplinary elements from its very beginnings. Given this strong orientation toward shaping the values and actions of the young, the orphan fathers used whatever means were placed at their disposal—pedagogical, allegorical, physical, or financial—to accomplish it. Control over property, placed in the common capital fund of each organization, gave them a means of controlling behavior that they hardly forbore to use.

Capital promoted three kinds of discipline, all distinct but interrelated. First, the administrators used capital to modify directly the behavior of orphans through rewards and punishments. In this case, they granted access to capital as a means of encouraging moral conduct or right religion. Second, the existence of a network of capital transactions that penetrated all levels of society modified behavior indirectly by means of the common interests and shared values on which these transactions were based. In this case, discipline was less a matter of compulsion applied to an individual than of preference for certain types of transactions. Third, participation in the market required both an awareness of risk and an ability to calculate the probability of loss or profit, which were themselves a form of discipline. Neither compulsion nor preference, this discipline constituted a basic consciousness of economic activity. In fact, all three types of discipline permeated the orphanages and shaped their approaches to capital.

The orphan fathers and deputies did not hesitate to exercise that first sort of discipline, to consider comportment when deciding whether to pay or not to pay, whether or not to grant access to the organization's common capital. In responding to the petition of master braid- and lacemaker Hartmann Lorenz Wenzer that his apprentice, Hieronymus Schaumann, be supported in the Lutheran Orphanage for the final three years of his training, the deputies based their consent on the boy's good behavior and reputation.[91] Likewise, Maria Margaretha Barbara Mullerin's request that the orphanage supply her with linen, stockings, and shoes for a third year of service was "granted because of her good behavior and good references."[92] Their language suggests that the administrators understood assistance as a reward for conduct consistent with the standards of the house.

The connection between discipline, support, and capital, however, was neither direct nor simple. Sometimes the dictates of paternalism and need overcame other considerations. Wallburga Schillerin was no model of comportment.[93] She left the City Orphanage for household service at the age of eighteen. Claiming financial need in order to move with her master's family to Austria in 1594, she received 36 kr. for the road. Instead of pursuing her service she took to a vagabond existence in and around Augsburg, finally attached herself to a Fugger servant, and became pregnant by him. Though the authorities described her as a "loose person," still they gave her 12 fl. in alms to purchase desperately needed clothing. Sometimes demonstrated desire to conform and reform were rewarded despite infractions. Franz Xavieri Caspar abandoned his master's service for no adequate reason and took the clothing his master had provided.[94] For two years he tramped about Hungary before returning to Augsburg to complete training in a craft. At first he had no luck, but with persistence he finally obtained a position as apprentice. The Catholic Orphanage overlooked the earlier deviance and paid the fees. Neither were repentance and forgiveness strictly Catholic virtues. When Thomas Schmid was fined 25 fl. for impregnating a young woman, he appealed to the Lutheran Orphanage for assistance with the claim that he intended to marry her.[95] The deputies recommended that the orphanage pay the fine on Schmid's behalf because he was, as they said, repentant and industrious. Still, defiance could cut the tie between need and charity. When Bernhard Winterholer fled the Lutheran Orphanage in 1653 and took up residence with a Catholic priest in Bavaria, he acted in disregard of his religion, the magistrates' authority, and the state's charity. The authorities abruptly refused his petition for readmission.[96] Confessional conformity proved less flexible than other rules.

The fact that an orphanage's capital was composed in part of orphans' private property made the connection between discipline and assistance more complicated still. The question whether the deputies, superintendents, or orphan fathers might refuse to remit property to orphans who were ill-behaved or immoral arose in the late eighteenth century.[97] The superior authorities argued that the orphans' shares of orphanage capital belonged to the orphans themselves without regard to their character or comportment and had to be paid when they demanded it. The administrators of the Lutheran Orphanage, who were closer to the daily affairs of the organization, countered that its capital consisted not only of the property of individual children but also of the donations of benefactors.[98] As such, it represented a covenant between recipient and donor. By observing their faith and exhibiting moral conduct, orphans fulfilled the covenant and received material support. If they abjured or sinned, they broke the convenant and forfeited any claim to assistance.

A covenant binding charity to confession and capital to discipline was an interesting and problematical notion. On the one hand, it corresponded directly to the situation created by parity. Where charity and capital flowed within bounds prescribed by confession, any violation of confessional interests might interdict that flow. On the other hand, the notion of a covenant violated the orphans' rights in property and compromised their future in society. In early modern Europe, a child's inheritance established a material link with the interests and enterprises of the past generation and determined ways and means for the future. It provided the resources necessary for that child to learn a craft, establish a household, and assume a full place in the community. In the final analysis, the debate over capital and discipline derived from an irreconcilable conflict between the group's need to conserve its resources and the orphan's prerogative to dispose of his or her own. It grew from the contradictory imperatives of public and private property as well as social and religious discipline.

The superior magistrates addressed these issues directly.[99] They argued that access to the children's moneys—part of an orphan's rights in property—could not be tied to their conduct. First, the dictates of social discipline did not extend to matters of confessional loyalty or religious affiliation. Imperial law expressly forbade any prohibition regarding an individual's faith, and municipal law prohibited any regulation or statute that appeared to derive from religious antagonism. A person could not be punished merely for converting to another confession. Second, the difference between public and private resources, when applied to children's moneys, made any restraint impossible. The specific disposition of private property required the specific direction of the owner. It could not, therefore, be assumed that donors intended charity for the orphans of one confession alone merely on the basis of a their religous affiliation. That would have to be proven on a case-by-case basis. Furthermore, the administrators were prohibited from imputing a pact or covenant controlling the property of a third party without the consent of the City Council. For these reasons no Lutheran orphan could be denied access to his or her property held by the Lutheran Orphanage, simply because he or she converted to Catholicism. The administrators of charity could not simply treat the property of orphans as an undifferentiated public resource, as common capital.

This stricture had little effect because of the nature of organizational finance. Orphanage incomes combined state subventions that covered operating expenses, private donations that generated a capital base, and earned income that constituted an independently controllable resource. Thus obtained, the funds covered many expenses from household to childcare to capital. The Alms Office and the orphanages obtained credit for themselves and provided it to others by access to capital resources of various sorts. These transactions formed part of a network that carried not only capital but also its discipline—an abstract sense of value, a familiarity with and openness to certain forms of exchange, especially those involving such intangibles as credit, and an orientation toward markets—to Augsburg society at large.

One reason that poor relief in Augsburg merged into the city's marketplace, participating in it and shaping it at the same time, may simply have been that the capital market lacked as yet a fixed, physical location, where entrepreneurs and resources could concentrate. There were places where trading occurred more frequently, such as the quarters of the merchants' association (*Kaufleutestube*), but no single point of trade or regulation commanded this activity in the manner of an exchange or bourse. Rather, capitalistic enterprise was ubiquitous, occurring everywhere, from marketplaces to public houses, from pawnshops to counting houses, from profitable businesses to charitable organizations, from ecclesiastical foundations to state agencies.

The flow of capital and capitalistic practices, perhaps for this very reason, involved a much broader spectrum of Augsburg's society than is usually assumed. The great and the small borrowed and lent, placing their property in circulation, generating further wealth, if not for themselves then for the system as a whole. Augsburg's orphanages worked to integrate the city's lower orders into this emergent economic system, connecting and binding them to it with ties of dependence and obligation no less strong or crucial than those of patronage, citizenship, or relationship. The orphanages were the loci not only of social discipline but also of economic integration.

The traces are visible in their records. Their many transactions created bonds of association and interest that gave Augsburg and all early modern cities a coherence and cohesion as yet little appreciated. Certainly participation in the capital market strengthened the solidarity of Augsburg's elite. The orphanages participated in a system of exchange, through which the dominant strata of society borrowed and loaned capital. When a Langenmantel or a Laire obtained unsecured loans from the Catholic or Lutheran Orphanage, they profitted not only from their position as members of the elite but also from the position of the orphanages in the capital market. Similarly, when a Vogel or a Schuester received assistance from the orphanages, they benefitted from its ability to mobilize capital on their behalf. Elites and commons shared a stake in the availability of capital.

Whether these ties were vertical as well as horizontal is less apparent but highly probable. The houses themselves strengthened connections between the social strata without necessarily bringing them into more direct contact with one another. Orphanages placed the resources of the city and its leadership at the disposal of the needy. Paradoxically they used their position *in loco parentis* to gather the property of Augsburg's lower strata and place it at the disposal of the elite. Each orphanage acted as a capital nexus that created ties of financial dependency among the social orders.

Orientation toward and participation in markets required yet another form of discipline, that is, an awareness of the forces that dominated them. The poor were always conscious of the rudimentary value of commodities and the fluctuation of prices. They learned to calculate risk.

Calculation had always been a part of economic life. The inelasticity of local markets and domestic economies, their inability to respond efficiently to abrupt changes in supply, created a so-called elasticity of the margin.[100] Changing circumstances shifted the margin of subsistence suddenly and required a degree of flexibility or opportunism from those who existed on it.

The Lorentz family provides one example among many. Before Georg Lorentz and his wife joined a regiment and left Augsburg to go to war, they placed their three-year old daughter in the care of Georg's father, Ulrich, a hosteler.[101] In this case the calculation miscarried. Ulrich, though well-to-do, as indicated by the fact that he held letters of credit valued at over 5,600 fl., had eight children of his own. The fatal combination of a large family, bad loans, and extended illnesses conspired to shatter the foster family. Ulrich fled Augsburg to avoid his creditors, leaving an aged wife in charge of nine children, including "his four mentally deficient children who cannot earn their keep or serve any upstanding householder."[102] Ulrich's brothers and brothers-in-law, justifiably afraid that they might be forced to assume the burden of care for their nieces and nephews, requested that all of them or at least the foster child be placed in the orphanage. Arguing that members of the family were financially able to support these children and that the four handicapped children would never be self-sufficient, the authorities refused to admit any of Lorentz's children to the orphanage.

The availability of organizational support transformed these maneuvers from blind avoidance of loss to shrewd calculations of risk. Before the supposed consumer revolution of the eighteenth century, control of property by such organizations as Augsburg's orphanages created a material security for orphans that freed them from the cycle of feast and famine that was the lot of people on the margins of society.[103] With the supply of life's necessities ensured—their property administered, their support guaranteed, their self-sufficiency encouraged—they began to behave in new ways. They found themselves in a position to reckon the probabilities of loss and gain, that is, to calculate risk.

This is a speculation based on no direct evidence. The orphans' motives remain obscure. For example, Hanns Spinner entered the City Orphanage a have-naught in 1580. He was apprenticed to master shoemaker Leonhart Kammerer for three years at a cost of 20 fl. to the organization.[104] As a journeyman cobbler, a position he attained with the assistence of the orphanage, Spinner possessed at least the potential to earn a living and maintain a household. When he married a cobbler's daughter in a distant town, the orphanage specifically refused to provide him with a marriage portion. It assumed, however, the cost of sending him the official documents establishing his status as a free man and a properly trained cobbler (*Geburts-* and *Lernbrief*). Spinner's story, told thus briefly by a third party, offered no indication of the orphan's motives or rationale. Yet, it seems unlikely that Spinner could have passed through the orphanage, experiencing its daily routines, witnessing its management, and enjoying its assistance, without becoming aware of the calculation that guided it all.

Conclusion

Early modern organizations developed their own resources out of an amalgamation of public subventions, private donations, and their own capital. Changing circumstances determined the exact composition of this structure, whether public or private resources would dominate or how large a portion returns from capital would provide. When one or the other resource declined, as was the case with subventions and donations from the middle of the seventeenth century, organizations could rely on the support of institutional capitalism and the returns on their own property to cover expenses. When subventions froze in the late eighteenth century, earnings experienced a modest growth that guaranteed both the care of orphans and the discretion of their governors. Both orphanages compensated for a shifting balance of private charity and public subsidy with economies and investments. Clearly, then, the three pillars required a constant calculation and manipulation to balance and meet exigencies. Though circumstances and resources shifted, the practice of their management remained stable.

The process of calculation and manipulation, of which a conglomeration of transactions and commitments were the result, yielded practical knowledge. Beset by economic uncertainties, orphanage administrators learned consistently to pursue advantage, to avoid risk, and to maximize resources. These imperatives found systematic application in the disposition of orphanage capital. Both organizations maintained diverse obligations with local and foreign institutions and individuals. Yet, though the wisdom of the marketplace was the same for Catholics and Lutherans alike, their strategies varied according to their particular ties to the wider world, the former bound more closely to ecclesiastical foundations, the latter leaning more heavily on mercantile associations. These relationships conformed to the dictates of a hierarchical, confessional society. Rank and parity constrained the flow of capital. Within the orphanages, however, new practices that were less consistent with the traditional order and more congruent with the mandate of capital began to appear. Access to capital provided orphans with greater opportunities for advancement and mobility and disciplined them to a life of exchange and calculation. Ultimately, it may have altered attitudes toward capital and the economy itself, evidence that the emergence of capitalism and capitalistic society was less a function of an historical moment than of the slow accumulation of experience within traditional structures and organizations. Through involution, therefore, these traditional organizations were hollowed out and made to serve non-traditional ends.

The flexibility of variegated finance that encouraged calculation and capitalistic practices permitted Augsburg's orphanages to withstand economic crises remarkably well. Resources drawn from various sources equipped the orphanages to practice charity surprisingly free of frustrations and pressures. There was, as will be seen, little recourse to balancing budgets on the backs of the orphans. This is not to say that the need to maximize resources and control expenditures did not exist; it was a constant of all early modern economic life even at the highest levels. Through careful management, Augsburg's orphanages avoided the dark hopelessness suggested by recent scholarship; they did not immure the young in disease and depravity for lack of funds.[105] If the orphanages were not at all times institutions of plenty or humanity, neither were they places to be avoided except in great necessity. Administrators carried the lessons of an empirical capitalism from the capital market into the markets for more tangible commodities.

Notes

1. StAA, KW 2, Notamina, 1740–1741.
2. StAA, KW 13, Sammlung der Ratsdekreten, 1572–90, Decretum in senatum secretioris catholicum, 16 November 1756.
3. Ibid., Decretum in senatum secretioris catholicum, 22 December 1757.
4. Ibid., Decretum in senatum secretioris catholicum, 23 July 1761.
5. Ibid., Decretum in senatum secretioris catholicum, 10 October 1761.
6. As Langenmantel was tax master and head of the Income Office, a conflict of interest seems possible and even probable.
7. StAA, KW 13, Sammlung der Ratsdekreten, 1572–90, Decretum in senatum secretioris catholicum, 6 April 1762.
8. Ibid., Decretum in senatum secretioris catholicum, 19 February 1763.
9. Ibid., Decretum in senatum secretioris catholicum, 10 March 1764.
10. Ibid., Decretum in senatum secretioris catholicum, 12 November 1774.
11. Ibid.: "... bey notorischer Zahlungsunvermögenheit...."
12. Cf. Bátori, *Die Reichsstadt Augsburg*, 69–70.
13. StAA, KW 13, Sammlung der Ratsdekreten, 1572–90, Decretum in senatum secretioris catholicum, 28 May 1768.
14. Ibid., Decretum in senatum secretioris catholicum, 2 June 1767.
15. Ibid., Decretum in senatum secretioris catholicum, 16 October 1773.
16. Ibid., Secretum in senatum secretioris catholicum, 16 January 1781.
17. Ibid., Decretum in senatum secretioris catholicum, 26 April 1787.
18. Ibid., Decretum in senatum secretioris catholicum, 27 November 1787.
19. Ibid., Decretum in senatum secretioris catholicum, 16 February 1788.
20. StAA, KW 8: "zu behuelff und nuzen der armen Wasienkünder...."
21. StAA, KW 9, Decretum in senatum secretioris, 2 November 1709.
22. StA Augsburg. Waisenhäuser, A1. Notamina, 18. Jhdt. Zettel, s.d. s.a.: "In den 30gen Jahren had die cath. verwittibte Waysenmutter Gräffin von ihres Mannes todt an von dem gemainen Alt. Allmosen alle halb Jahr 15 fl. zu ihren benothigten lebens Unterhalt genoßen u. eben so viel auch die evangel. Waysenmutter Regina Größin."
23. StAA, EW 4, Gnadegeld des Tobias Groß evangelischen Waisenvater, 1720: "... sich seines dienstes eben nicht sonderlich meritirt gemacht auch die *reditus* des Waisenhauses meist ungewiß und nach der Zahl der Gutthäter zu und abnehmen hingegen der *numerus* der Waisenkinder immer mehrers anwächst."
24. The ancient practice among hospitals and other welfare organizations known as a *Pfrund* is similar to the modern agreement for entering a nursing home. The person to be admitted agrees to pay a sum of money or to transfer a quantity of property, either of which varied according to the elaborateness of the accommodation to be provided. The organization committed itself to provide for the person for the rest of his or her life. That provision might be as meager as space in a common dormitory and a place at the common table or as elaborate as a private suite of rooms and individual cuisine.
25. StAA, KW 28, Waisenbuch, 1653–1785, Maria Jacobina Beckhin, 27 November 1762.
26. StAA, KW 13, Sammlung der Ratsdekreten, 1572–90, Decretum in senatum secretioris, 4 November 1784.
27. There is no evidence of Catholic orphans receiving *Dotenpfennige*. At least,

Charity and Capital in the Orphanages 147

the Catholic Orphanage made no special effort to record such property.
28. StAA, EW 18. The Lutheran Orphanage kept two inventories that recorded the *Dotenpfennige* of orphans during the second half of the eighteenth century. A typical listing included the orphan's name, a list of the various items comprising the *Dotenpfennig*, the date on which these items were placed in the orphanage's keeping, and the date or dates on which they were returned to the orphan. As was the case with other forms of property, some orphans possessed modest *Dotenpfennige* while others received very elaborate and ornate ones. Quality probably varied with the status and wealth of the orphan's family and friends. It is interesting to note, however, that no orphans of that period came from such humble origins that they had no such property.
29. Ibid. Dotenpfennige, Band A, 11 February 1739: "Aus denen von vielen Jahren hero verstorbenen Waysenkinder ererbten und zum Nutzen diese haußes verschmeltzten dotenpfennige sind vermög einer von den Johann Christian Holeisen Muntz Meister unter 11 Febr. 1739 übergebenen Beschreibung Vierhundert sechs gulden, sieben kreutzer erlösst worden."
30. Ibid., 25 September 1762.
31. Ibid., 23 August 1775.
32. StAA, Alms, Pilgerhaus, Waisenhaus, Zuchthaus, Heiliger Almosen 6, Actum Augsburg den 17. May Anno 1645.
33. Ibid.: ". . . welliches sich nun also gründtlich befunden, daß er im Waißenhauß nit mer auf Catholishe weiß das Vatter Unser und Ave Maria recht betten khönnden dahero demselben zuversorgen. . . ."
34. Ibid. ". . . derowegen mit ihme und dessen Erbschaft nit allerdings rechthergeen möchte. . . ."
35. The Lutheran Bible in Latin was not more carefully described. It may, in fact, have been a copy of the Vulgate or an Erasmus translation with an introduction written by a Lutheran pastor.
36. The step-parent usually had to swear formally to regard the step-children as his or her own. This meant that the step-parent would treat the children as befitted a parent and would assume the responsibilities and costs of childrearing. Moreover, it committed that step-parent to deliver the full value of the inheritance enjoyed in usufruct at the proper time.
37. It is worth noting that only 128 fl. were ever collected. The Lutheran trustees insisted on a final 2 fl. in fees due them that Catholic authorities had not allowed. It is further evidence, if any is needed, of the care, born of distrust, that marked confessional relations in the mid-seventeenth century. It is also, however, evidence of careful planning. The alms servants and orphan father accounted for every Kreutzer, not only to assure Tobias his due but also to plan income and expenditures.
38. StAA, EW 22, Waisenbuch, 1580–1676, 7 May 1592: "Hat nix als armut und elend und vil leüs."
39. Ibid., 16 January 1634.
40. Ibid.: ". . . eß seind vil shulden verhanden un ligt für Gericht daß man noch nit wissen kan, ob dem knaben etwas möge bleiben von seinem vatter."
41. Ibid., 17 December 1590.
42. Ibid., 22 January 1635.
43. StAA, KW 27, Waisenbuch, 1653–1785, 3 October 1679.
44. Ibid., 12 December 1679.
45. Ibid., 17 August 1734.

46. StAA, KW 13, Sammlung der Ratsdekreten, 1572–1790, Decretum in senatum secretioris utrius religionibus, 26 April 1733: "... sowohl gröseren als kleineren milden Stiftungen ... keine Kapitalien mehr in einig fremdes Gericht auszuleihen."
47. Ibid. Decretum in senatum secretioris catholicum, 31 January 1750: "... auf einen in hiesiger Stadt Territorio gelegenen und allhiesiger Jurisdiction unterworfenen hinlänglichen Fundum verzinslichen angelegt...."
48. Ibid. Decretum in senatum secretioris catholicum, 31 July 1788: "... und bleibt dem herren deputirten überlassen, eine anderweite sichere Gelegenheit zu ordnungsmässiger Anlegung der vorhandenen Gelder ausfindig zu machen."
49. Aversion or openness to risk as a defining element of capitalistic behavior has been considered by a number of scholars in a number of contexts. Despite his insistence on genius or charisma as the force for change in social structures and relations, Weber held that risk aversion, achieved through rational strategies, separated the capitalist from the reckless opportunism of his gambling predecessor. In contrast, Schumpeter implied that a kind of risk-readiness characterized the quintessential capitalist, the entrepreneur. An unwillingness to innovate and to entertain the attendant risks marked the manager, the symbol of capitalism in decline. A middle ground between the two seems most reasonable. The ideal capitalist is neither totally open nor totally averse to risk but relies on an ability to calculate the probability of success or failure and shapes his actions accordingly. The limited jurisdiction of Imperial government or the limited protection of private property—institutional factors that were reflected in the 1733 prohibition and might have limited the scope of early modern enterprise—would be part of this calculation. Cf. Marshall, *In Search of the Spirit of Capitalism*, 32; Schumpeter, *Capitalism, Socialism and Democracy*, 132; Weber, *The Protestant Ethic*, 75–76.
50. StAA, Alms, Schuldbuch, 1585–90, 160–80.
51. Ibid., 169.
52. StAA, Alms, Jahresrechnungen.
53. Clasen's estimates of fustian production in the early seventeenth century is a benchmark. Clasen, *Die Augsburger Weber*, passim.
54. StAA, KW 14, Jahresrechnung, 1725.
55. Ibid. The record does not indicate whether these were short-term loans at interest or long-term investments that generated a fixed income but could not be redeemed.
56. Jones, *Charity and Bienfaisance*, 136.
57. StAA, EW 3, Aktenrepertorium.
58. StAA, EW 6, Jahresrechnungen, 1734, 1780; EW 16, Jahresrechnung, 1803.
59. StAA, EW 3, Specificatio, s.a.
60. StAA, KW 12, Jahresrechnungen, 1783–89.
61. Ibid., Jahresrechnungen, 1783–87, 1789.
62. StAA, EW 6, Jahresrechnung, 1780.
63. These groups were organized into three social orders or associations. The first were the *Patrizier*, urban aristocrats who determined their membership by birth (as of 1383) and possessed the exclusive right to hold public office according to the *Constitutio Carolina* of 1548. They formed an association known as the *Herrenstubegesellschaft* that also admitted persons who were not patricians. These formed the second order, known as *Gesellschaft der Mehrer*. Merchants engaged in long-distance trade and frequently numbering the wealthiest citizens

of Augsburg among their ranks constituted the third elite order in Augsburg, the *Kaufleuteschaft*.
64. StAA, KW 13, Sammlung der Ratsdekreten, 1572–1790, Decretum in senatum secretioris catholicum, 23 September 1749.
65. StAA, EW 7, Oeconomie des evangelischen Waisenhauses, 3 August 1780.
66. Ibid.: "... das Waysenhaus jährlich selbst von seinen Capitalien zu setzen müssen ... wie höchst nöthig es ist in allen mögl. dingen zu menagiren."
67. StAA, Alms, Fasc. II, Supplikation umb aufnemmung ihrer 2 groessen Waisen in das evang. Waisen Haus, Anno 1654: "Anlangendt, weil etwan sich begibt, dass die allernegste freundt der Waisen selbst arm, die nachgehendte und weitere freundt aber etwas vermoeglicher seien, ist uf solchen fall, da je die naehere freundt selbst so arm, das sie entweder mit vil khindern beladen, oder selbst im Allmosen weren, derselbigen nit wol mer ufzuetringen, sondern solche arme khinder sollen den jenigen, die is boesser zu ertragen, anzuebevelchen sein, und die freundtschafft diss Falls in allweg auf den vierten gradum der geshwisterigt Khinder ausgerechnet und deme also nachgegangen werden."
68. Ibid., 15 April 1586.
69. StAA, EW 22, Waisenbuch, 1580–1676, 20 July 1586.
70. Since marriage portions usually matched dowries, Jörg's wife probably brought property to the marriage worth 100 fl. Though not a princely sum, 100 fl. is not an unusual dowry among the solidly established petty craftsmen of early modern Augsburg.
71. StAA, EW 22, Waisenbuch, 1580–1676, 18 September 1580.
72. Ibid., 12 December 1580.
73. Ibid., 12 March 1635.
74. StAA, KW 27, Waisenbuch 1663–1785, 31 July 1680.
75. Ibid.: "... weiln Jerg Widenmann zu keinem hantwerckh tauglich hat ihn sein Vöter zu versorgen angenommen."
76. Ibid., 22 November 1690.
77. Ibid.
78. Ibid., 4 August 1703.
79. Ibid., 6 April 1728.
80. StAA, KW 13, Sammlung der Ratsdekreten, 1572–1790, Decretum in senatum secretioris utrius religionis, 17 April 1788.
81. StAA, EW 4, Lehrzettel, 1721.
82. Ibid., Supplikation des Friederich Otts Nürnberger Bott, 6 January 1737.
83. Fassl, *Konfession, Wirtschaft und Politik*, 152.
84. StAA, EW 18, Deputiertensitz im evangelischen Waisenhaus, 17 December 1723.
85. Ibid., 23 February 1723.
86. StAA, EW 22, Waisenbuch, 1580–1676, 17 August 1581.
87. StAA, KW 13, Sammlung der Ratsdekreten, 1572–1790, Decretum in senatum secretioris catholicum, 29 January 1785.
88. Ibid.: "... zumalen es gar nicht schicklich und von die [sic] Stiftung nuzlich seyn will, Gelder aufzuborgen um Passiv Kapitalien und respective Deposita absulößen und andererseits wiederum Capitalien auszuleihen."
89. Thomas Max Safley, *Children at the Edge: Expectation and Experience among the Orphans of Augsburg* (forthcoming). This volume shifts attention from the orphanages to the orphans by using the Waisenbücher—the admissions registers—of the Catholic and Lutheran orphanages as the basis for an examination

of the fortunes and fates of approximately 6,000 orphans and their families.
90. StAA, EW 7, Bericht des Pfarrers J. J. Wasser, 18 July 1793.
91. StAA, EW 18, Deputiertensitz im evangelischen Waisenhaus, 17 December 1723.
92. Ibid., 9 February 1723: "... wegen ihres wol. Verhalten und guten Attestats wird es ihr jedoch ohne Consequenz verwilliget."
93. StAA, EW 22, Waisenbuch, 1580–1676, 22 January 1594.
94. StAA, KW 27, Waisenbuch, 1653–1785, 30 January 1714.
95. StAA, EW 4, Fall Thomas Schmid Backerknecht, s.d. 1760.
96. StAA, EW 22, Waisenbuch, 1580–1676, 4 March 1652.
97. StAA, EW 7, Antwort der Vorsteher auf den Verordneten des heiligen Almosenamts, 27 March 1781.
98. The financial records of both orphanages in the late seventeenth and eighteenth centuries indicate that this was the case. Donors frequently hoped to assist orphans beyond the orphanage and so specified savings as the object of their charity. Therefore, the superintendents were correct when they insisted that these funds did not consist solely of the orphans' property.
99. StAA, EW 7, Antwort der Verordneten..., 9 April 1781.
100. Geremek, *The Poor of Late Medieval France*, passim.
101. StAA, Alm, Fasc. II, Supplikation umb gnedige einnemmung eines armen Waisens in das Waisen Haus, 1629.
102. Ibid.: "... seinen 4 albarn kindern welche jr brot nit gewinnen noch ein bidermann dienen koennen."
103. de Vries, "The Industrial Revolution and the Industrious Revolution." Jan de Vries points to a reallocation of resources that led to an increasing supply of marketed goods and labor and, more importantly, an increasing demand for these commodities. The suggestion that a demand-side revolution preceded the traditionally understood supply-side Industrial Revolution finds circumstantial confirmation in the capital transactions of Augsburg's orphanages.
104. StAA, EW 22, Waisenbuch, 1580–1676, 27 July 1580.
105. This is almost the universal image of the orphanage-poorhouse-workhouse projected by modern scholarship. Though doubtless accurate in many instances, it derives much from Victorian literature and should be avoided as a generalization. The example of Augsburg reveals its limitations.

5

Provisioning Augsburg: Buying and Selling Commodities in an Early Modern City

The same calculation and manipulation that characterized incomes held true for commodities, particularly those for which demand was more or less inelastic, the necessities of life. Essentials included wood for fuel, tallow for light, water for drink, and grain for nourishment.[1] Because Augsburg's orphanages acquired basic commodities—grain, lard, and wood—from the stores of the Alms Office, much of the discussion that follows concentrates on the purchases and practices of that larger administration. Debates concerning the disposition of capital in the Alms Office and the orphanages expose differing concepts of commodities. When purchased for immediate consumption, they were goods subject to prevailing market conditions, especially supply and price, that determined expenditures. Stockpiled against future needs, foodstuffs and other goods became a form of capital that involved speculation concerning market forces, that is, demand and production, that affected price trends and opportunity costs.[2] As they discussed the purpose of commodities, Catholic and Lutheran administrators also revealed differing concepts of economic organization, the ways in which an enterprise or foundation operated within and worked to change given sets of institutional constraints. Their disagreements rested on a common foundation of economic practice and experience, a foundation visible in the city's provisioning policies. On the one hand, magistrates commonly manipulated commodity supplies as a means of altering market conditions. They hoarded and released stocks to guarantee the availability of essential goods at a just price. And indeed, such supply-side practices appear to have been a common feature of early modern statecraft. On the other hand, the administrators of Augsburg's orphanages made use of the aggregate demand of Augsburg's needy population in order to control market forces. They used their purchases to

Confession and Commodities

Catholic and Lutheran alms lords considered the issue of consumables versus capital in their debate over the reform of alms financing in 1724. Noting that one of the city's granaries (*Kornstadel auf dem Kreutz*) was in an extreme state of disrepair and unusable, the Catholic Leopold Ferdinand von Rehlingen proposed selling or renting it.[3] He insisted that the building was no longer needed to store grain and so should not be maintained as a financial loss and liability to the Alms Office. Rehling's Lutheran colleagues shared his concern for the expense created by the facility.[4] They expressed regret that repairs had not been undertaken when the task was smaller and less expensive and that the building had stood empty and useless as a result. Lack of use only raised the costs of maintenance. Despite the expense of keeping the building, however, the Lutheran authorities could not support its sale or rental. They pointed out that the granary served both confessions. It was part of the parity-based structure of poor relief in Augsburg and could not be alienated without the consent of officials of both confessions. Moreover, the granary served an important purpose: it provided an opportunity to stock grain when it was cheap against those times when it was dear. According to the Lutherans, the Alms Office maintained stores of 100 schaff of grain at all times.[5] Rather than sell or rent the building, therefore, they recommended that it be repaired in order to serve its proper purpose, holding grain for Augsburg's needy. In deciding whether to purchase commodities as capital, the administrators balanced future gains in consumption with present expenditures in cash.[6] The discussion over the fate of the granary exposed differing economic perspectives: Catholic adminstrators wished to save; Lutherans were willing to speculate.

Both sides calculated real and opportunity costs carefully. The Lutherans acknowledged the actual expense and loss associated with substantial repairs but insisted that private donations would meet them.[7] Theirs was an understandable position; the Lutheran Orphanage had always benefitted from extensive contributions from Lutheran citizens. Yet, they also recognized the opportunity: savings from stockpiling grain at low prices would recover the costs of maintenance. Catholic authorities emphasized the real costs of repair and discounted the potential for profit. The building could not be kept at little or no expense to the Alms Office.[8] Funds to repair it were not available; public officials could not rely upon private generosity. Neither would grain hoarding offset building maintenance. Catholics and Lutherans alike engaged in cost-benefit analysis without rigorous costing.

As deliberate and calculating as the matter appears to have been, neither side was really open to the arguments of the other. In part, this was a function of long-standing confessional tensions and jealousies. In these reform debates, Rehling argued repeatedly that economic burdens weighed more heavily on the Catholic poor and Catholic organizations, and complained about the Lutherans' stubborn selfishness and lack of public spirit.[9] Given the disproportionate concentration of wealth among Augsburg's Lutherans and the private resources they placed at the disposal of the Lutheran Orphanage, this was probably a justifiable opinion. Confessional differences in this matter exposed different economic orientations as well. Perhaps because of a general lack of resources and the constraints that lack imposed, Catholic authorities focused on present resources and current costs. The material assistance of other Catholic foundations, such as the bread and grain supplied by various Augsburg monasteries, did not shield the Catholic Orphanage completely from the market and its pressures. In any case, Catholic administrators were unwilling either to increase expenditures or to gamble on commodity prices. Their assessment of risk was much more conservative.

The arguments from experience and precedent, mustered by both confessions, further emphasized their differences. The original orphanage building in the Bakers' Alley had been sold in 1697 when its repair and maintenance became too expensive. Lutheran authorities alleged that their experience could serve as a guide for the sale of the granary.[10] Rather than resulting in a savings to the Alms Office, the purchase of a new Lutheran Orphanage, located, paradoxically, in a former Fugger house, had required one and one-quarter times the money needed to keep the original house in operation. The sale of the granary, advocated by the Catholics, would similarly fail to realize any savings because another building would have to be acquired. Speaking in defense of his proposal, Rehling denied the aptness of the comparison.[11] Not the new building but the liens (*Hauszins*) on it created the extra costs. As purchasers, the Lutheran Orphanage and the Alms Office had had to redeem those obligations by paying the principal owed the lien-holders. The granary was not encumbered by the capital of strangers, which Rehling interpreted as being unrelated to the fabric and value of the building itself. The sale would free the Alms Office from financial responsibilities and expenses rather than involve it in new ones. Lutheran thinking on this problem seems distinctly oriented toward the future, that is, inclined to reckon the opportunity costs in long-term utility and gain. The Catholics held resolutely to their concern about current resources. They seem to have viewed the Alms Office as operating on a fixed income that could not be expanded but could only be redistributed.

In 1734 the Alms Office received permission from the Small Council to sell its granary.[12] Whether this marked the outcome of the debate of a decade earlier is not entirely clear. It did not, however, resolve the tensions between current and future consumption of commodities, between stocks and capital.

Both orphanages had their own granaries and storage facilities, located in the lofts under their steeply pitched roofs. How best to exploit this space was a matter intrinsic to the administration of both houses.

As noted, the Lutheran Orphanage listed rents received for its loft (*Kornbodenzins*) in 1734 and 1735 and again in 1778 and 1780.[13] The administrators rented all or part of the available space to generate cash and maximize resources for the house. In August 1780 they reported that the house's storage space, if properly repaired, could contain 150 schaff of grain.[14] They urged that it be set in order and that grain be purchased and stored there. According to the orphan father, the orphanage could make a capital of 1,200 fl. available for the purpose. Considering the poor prospects for the year's harvest, he believed that hoarding grain as a hedge would be a better investment than loaning capital at interest.

A short time thereafter, the Catholic Orphanage leased its three grain lofts to a local brewer named Felix Baur.[15] The annual rent was 85 fl. The Small Council objected to this arrangement, saying that the rental required a public solicitation of bids and that possession had been given to the brewer too quickly and without due process.[16] Interestingly the public solicitation, which followed in March 1784, attracted no interest.[17] There was little demand for granary space in Augsburg at that time. How the orphanage made use of its storage facilities at other points in its history is unknown.

Such records as survive indicate that the orphanages pursued relatively consistent strategies toward commodity purchases. The Catholic Orphanage treated commodities as consumption goods for immediate use. The orphan father and administrators strove to maximize resources by minimizing costs, that is, to supply the most consumption for the least expense in the present. The Lutherans operated somewhat differently. They, too, sought to maximize resources but by generating wealth. They were more willing to assess the probabilities and accept the risks of commodities as capital investments. In this regard, the Lutheran Orphanage seems more attuned to market conditions and more open to mercantile opportunities.

To posit a market orientation among Lutherans that was lacking among Catholics obscures more subtle and important similarities. Catholics dominated the social extremes, constituting the majority of aristocrats and laborers, while Lutherans filled the middle ranks of merchants and craftsmen. Throughout the debates and negotiations over parity, the Lutherans seemed at ease with the risks and rewards of the marketplace. They were more willing to use organizational resources to develop commodity supplies that would allow them to exploit the market for price flexibility and shield them from the market in periods of inflation. Sharp dealing and keen business sense derived in this case less from a sense of calling than from the weight of experience and custom. Neither were Catholics strangers to these same calculations. They too weighed future benefits against present costs; they too factored changing supplies and prices; they too assessed risk on the basis of probable losses and gains. Their reasons for alienating the grain lofts make this very plain. Limited resources and the need for cash rendered speculation in commodity futures risky. Also, connections to other Catholic organizations and foundations limited their direct dependence on local commodity markets. As a result, Catholic administrators were more inclined to a thrift that would limit consumption and, with it, expenditures. The ability to calculate risk and a consciousness of market conditions, experience and knowledge that led to very different assessments of the same economic circumstances, were not given to the elect but required of all.

Market Supply and Market Regulation

Attempts to control prices by manipulating supplies were characteristic of the preindustrial economies of Augsburg and of all early modern cities, economies marked by violent fluctuations in harvests and extreme insecurity of transportation. Crop failures created irregular supplies of most raw materials, from foodstuffs to threads and dyes, and periodic shortages caused price instability. The great expense of transporting bulk goods long distances overland further increased the prices that occasional scarcity drove upward. Indeed, transportation increased the costs of some goods, notably grain, to such an extent that they became uneconomical and even unaffordable during periods of inflation. Consequently, despite the assurances of otherwise acute contemporary observers such as Martin Luther that "there is little or no reserve in the hands of the common man, who lives from year to year on his annual income," stockpiling and hoarding were commonplace at all levels of the early modern economy.[18] Regardless of wealth or confession, all people who possessed any means maintained stocks of commodities as a hedge. Testaments bear eloquent witness to the material insecurities of the age in the stores of foodstuffs and textiles usually maintained in great and small households. Merchants and craftsmen invested much of their working capital in stocks of raw materials and semi-finished or finished goods. What Luther noted as one of the "tricks and evil practices," that some "buy up the entire supply of certain goods or wares in a country or a city in order to have these goods entirely under their own control," was a thing apart.[19] State officials took great pains—what Luther described as "a good and proper Christian foresight for the good of the community and for others"—to insure against famine and revolt by maintaining sufficient stores of basic necessities to provide for their neediest subjects.[20]

The staggering costs of provisioning a city, however, made it impossible to maintain reserves at uniformly high levels. The catastrophic inflation of 1622–23 cost Augsburg 562,835 fl. in grain alone.[21] To make matters worse, revenues from direct and indirect taxes remained stable despite the steady increase in prices from the late sixteenth century.[22] The combination of static income and rising expenses forced the city to shift from income to credit financing in the 1620s and after. Any possibility of a rapid recovery was checked by the events of 1633 to 1635, when Augsburg was repeatedly besieged and occupied, its population was decimated, and its industry was destroyed. The contributions, requisitions, and expenses of this period added to the burden of a decade earlier. To reinvigorate its economy, the city had to raise revenues and reduce expenditures. Thus, commodity reserves were not renewed at the old level, and purchases by the state fell drastically after mid-century.

Yet, the need for reserves of foodstuffs did not disappear with the violence of the Thirty Years' War. The crop failure of 1770–71 caused severe inflation and famine. In response, Augsburg again purchased foodstuffs, from suppliers as far away as Italy and Hungary. Between September 1770 and February 1772, the magistrates claimed expenditures for grain in excess of 1.5 million gulden.[23] The economy remained extraordinarily unstable and given to variations of supply and price. Families and foundations responded by continuing to maintain stockpiles of necessities.

Supplies were precarious and, therefore, expensive due also to Augsburg's lack of a dependent hinterland.[24] To an unusual degree, the movement of commodities depended on political and economic relations with its immediate neighbors. Fishers plied their trade in the streams and pools of the Bishop of Augsburg.[25] Butchers pastured their oxen in the meadows of the Duke of Bavaria. Many of the mills and fields that served Augsburg's industry and filled its marketplaces lay in foreign jurisdictions. Under normal circumstances, the inhabitants of Augsburg relied on the sufferance of their neighbors and on their own enterprise for their basic needs and, in some instances, their very livelihoods. In periods of crisis and tension, access to these resources was frequently impossible. After 1537, when the city declared itself for the new teaching of the Reformation, Catholic polities occasionally closed their borders or seized the goods of Augsburg's citizens. Natural catastrophes, such as the dearth of 1622 or the pestilence of 1628, often caused border closings. During the Thirty Years' War and again during the wars associated with the reign of Louis XIV, Augsburg found itself on military frontiers, occasionally besieged, and therefore unable to attract the commodities needed by its industries and inhabitants. The city's geopolitical situation exacerbated the structural instability of the economy.

That commodities continued to flow through the gates of the city depended on a number of factors. Augsburg's ecclesiastical foundations possessed large rural estates, whose produce found its way into the city's monasteries, granaries, and marketplaces. Church estates played a crucial role in supplying Augsburg's demand for grain.[26] The financial power and entrepreneurial skill of Augsburg's merchants helped them to organize supplies from regions as distant as Italy and Austria, Hungary and Bohemia, England and the Low Countries, or Scandinavia.[27] Political contact, diplomatic finesse, and even intelligence activity allowed Augsburg's leadership to keep borders open and goods flowing.[28] At the best of times, these advantages sufficed to supply so large a city as Augsburg with all that it needed, but the worst of times proved amply that the margin for error was small.

A minute regulation of market activities helped to maintain that margin. Except for individuals or institutions who possessed either rural estates that produced grain or rights in kind that were rendered in grain (*Getreidegilt*), Augsburgers usually purchased their grain at the city's grain market (*Kornschranne*). It exemplified, in a general way, commodity trading in most early modern cities. Magistrates organized market activities in such a way as to maintain adequate supplies and just prices. Indeed, as the indirect manipulation of price through control of supply ended, after the mid-1600s, market regulation became the centerpiece of the city's economic policy.

Magistrates had an arsenal of means to control both price and supply. Direct limits on prices (*Preistaxen*) were always possible. The authorities imposed them repeatedly, one of the more detailed and notable being that of 8 October 1622.[29] Though they enabled the authorities to fix prices exactly, absolute limits occasionally hindered sales altogether. Grain merchants withheld commodities or sold them elsewhere, if the city set local prices too low to make a profit. Far from assuring the availability of affordable commodities, price controls sometimes caused the movement of necessities away from Augsburg's marketplaces.

If it was difficult to transport adequate supplies of essential commodities to Augsburg during periods of inflation, then it was equally difficult, and no less important, to prevent the export of those supplies from the city. Secular and spiritual authorities often sought to ship grain out of Augsburg in order to supply their rural subjects or even themselves. No less frequent were the attempts of bakers, merchants, and millers to ship grain to towns and villages beyond the city's jurisdiction for resale at higher prices. Magistrates regulated such shipments in order to assure adequate provisions for Augsburgers themselves. Two measures stood to hand: a tariff (*Ungelt*) on exports made commodities more expensive outside of the city; a ban on the removal or export (*Ausfuhrverbot*) of specific commodities made that activity illegal.

The prevention of speculation and price gouging was among the foremost duties of early modern magistrates. As Luther's diatribe made clear, to exploit the need of others and profit at their expense was understood by Catholics and Protestants alike to be sinful, if not illegal.[30] Volumes of ordinances and statutes threatened sanctions against the practices of middlemen who purchased in volume to create and profit from artificial scarcity (*Fürkauf, Zwischenhandel*) in every conceivable commodity. The most efficient methods, however, were prophylactic rather than penal.

Forcing transactions to occur in the marketplace, under the magistrate's watchful eye, discouraged the activities of middlemen. Commodity trading typically occurred at set times and places. Market days at Augsburg's grain market were Thursdays and Fridays.[31] Officials raised the market banner at six o'clock in the morning in summer and seven in winter to signal the beginning of sales. Trading continued until four o'clock in the afternoon. The unloading, storage, and loading of grain occurred only in the presence of officials responsible for these activities. The grain measurer (*Kornmesser*), arguably the highest authority at the market, controlled the quality and the measurement of grains that were purchased and sold. Once a transaction was complete, the bags of grain were sewn shut; further sale or resale of their contents was strictly forbidden. Thus the magistrates attempted to regulate every aspect of grain sales: they limited time and place; they identified seller and buyer; they controlled quantity and price; and they sealed the finished deal. These measures offered the best hope of frustrating speculation and guaranteeing local supplies. They also served a fiscal purpose.

Tariffs and duties functioned as a deliberate brake on market activities. Authorities used them to slow and direct the exchange of commodities that were valued for one reason or another. Such indirect taxes also provided the state with considerable revenue.[32] Augsburg's bakers paid a duty on the grains purchased for their wares. To evade this expense, which could not be easily passed on to consumers because of price and weight controls, many resorted to fraudulent assessments or extra-market transactions. Given the pressures of inflation and warfare on public finance, the City Council felt compelled to pursue every possible source of income and raised the tariff on grains. Ironically, the same factors that forced an end to direct provisioning also worked to raise commodity prices.

Though markets for all commodities were closely controlled, the purpose of market regulation indicates the signal difference between foodstuffs and other commodities. The demand for grain, a basic foodstuff, was inelastic. People required grain regardless of economic circumstances, and its loss triggered social as well as economic chaos. At such times, reserves and regulations simultaneously influenced market activities and constituted social assistance. In the grain market, economic and social control were nearly identical.

Caught between rising population and rising prices throughout the sixteenth century, Augsburg established a state Provisions Office (*Proviantamt*). Its officials purchased critical commodities, such as grain, wood, tallow, lard, and textiles, releasing them for sale during periods of dearth.[33] To store these essential goods and so promote price stability, the Provisions Office acquired at least six granaries in the sixteenth century alone, of which the facility "auf dem Kreutz" was one.[34] Increased supplies moderated the inflation caused by scarcity and ensured adequate provisions for the city's residents.

How the Provisions Office organized reserves varied from commodity to commodity. Although it controlled the market for certain commodities, the office preferred to work in conjunction with private enterprise and limited direct intervention to periods of need. Even when buying and selling a limited number of essential goods, its servants ranged among Augsburg's scattered marketplaces and affected all of them through the size of their transactions.

Of all the necessities of life, the most important was certainly grain. No single commodity so captured the imagination of that era. That the poor lived in a near constant state of malnutrition and semi-starvation and that even the rich could plunge quickly to the margin of subsistence explains the ritualistic and symbolic importance of bread specifically and the Rabelaisian approach to food generally.[35] For this reason, organizations, individuals, magistrates, and householders devoted a large proportion of their consciousnesses and of their resources to securing this most fundamental foodstuff.

Individual families collectively hoarded an estimated 10,000 schaff of rye in 1622.[36] Most of this lay in the cellars and attics of the very wealthy, who drew supplies from their own estates as well as from local markets.[37] The Fugger admitted owning 578 schaff of rye, and the family von Rehlingen claimed 300. Even the humble craftsmen and shopkeepers of Augsburg frequently kept one or two schaff in reserve, which could be cooked at home into a porridge or baked by local bakers into bread intended for consumption rather than sale (*Hausbrot*). Not surprisingly, then, bakers and millers also possessed considerable supplies of grain, 447 and 256 schaff of rye respectively in 1622.[38] The city's guilds also maintained grain stores, purchased with contributions from their members. A list compiled in 1595 revealed 12 crafts with total reserves of rye equalling 5,306 schaff, intended to support the members of each guild in time of need.[39] Not only orphanage administrators but also magistrates, craftsmen, and householders understood the connection between price and supply and took steps to anticipate changes and control the consequences.

At the best of times, the Provisions Office maintained stores sufficient to feed the entire city. An inventory from 1595 listed over 45,000 schaff, supposedly enough to sustain a population of 30,000 for a year.[40] By August 1621, in response to the inflation gripping the city, these stores had dwindled to 36,131 schaff of rye and other grains, to which the authorities added a further 13,139 schaff in the course of the year.[41] Under the pressure of hyper-inflation, which forced the authorities to pour commodity reserves into the market to control prices, public stores slipped to the still considerable volume of 23,198 schaff in 1623, an amount worth 270,000 fl. at that time.[42] By 1627, on the eve of a great outbreak of pestilence, they had fallen to 2,202 schaff of grains of all sorts.[43] Again, the crisis conditions of the mid-seventeenth century lessened Augsburg's capacity to stockpile commodities.

Acquiring the supplies that filled Augsburg's public and private granaries and provided for a population as high as 40,000 to 45,000 in the early seventeenth century was a massive undertaking. Most citizens and officials bought their grain locally, in the grain market or from Augsburg's ecclesiastical institutions, but trips to purchase grain in nearby communities, such as Friedberg over the border in Bavaria, were not uncommon.[44] The Provisions Office drew most of its grain supply from within a 50-kilometer radius marked by the Danube to the north and the city of Mindelheim to the southwest.[45] Bavarian peasants produced most of the grain that met Augsburg's demand, a further indication of the close economic and commercial connections between the city and its neighbors.

At need, however, Augsburg and its citizens went further afield. A 1622 purchase of 800 schaff of grain, grown in Upper Austria but stored in Regensburg, reveals the opportunities, complexities, and expenses that confronted the city's merchants and provisions lords (*Proviantherren*) when local sources failed.[46]

Balthasar Lorenz, one of Augsburg's most substantial merchants in the early seventeenth century, apparently discovered the grain and realized its value in the Augsburg market sometime in 1621. Late that year he sent his step-son and a grain expert to Regensburg to determine the quality of the merchandise. While his associates were under way, Lorenz discussed conditions for the purchase and transportation of the grain with Provisions Lords Christoph Rem, Christoph Rehlinger von Haldenberg, and David von Stetten. Ordinarily the Provisions Office did not use middlemen for such transactions, but the pressures on grain prices in local markets caused by poor harvests may have forced it to adopt such unusual measures.

Two contracts eventually emerged. According to the first, Lorenz agreed to deliver 200 schaff of wheat to the city at a unit cost of 27 fl. per schaff. The city would assume all expenses and risks and arrange the necessary tolls and passes required by the Bavarian authorities. Transportation by water would begin as soon as the spring thaw made the Danube navigable. If delivery of the grain proved impossible for any reason, Lorenz would inform the provisions lords, sell the grain immediately, and recoup as much of the expense as possible. The second agreement concerned the sale of 600 schaff of rye at 32 fl. per schaff. In this case, however, Lorenz assumed the risk of loss due to shipwreck on the Danube and the city assumed the risk of loss due to warfare, evidence of the uncertainties associated with travel and transportation in that day. Should Bavaria refuse to allow the grain to pass, Lorenz would not sell it but store it at his own expense.

The purchase proved no less complicated in fact. Numerous delays greeted the transaction along the way. The grain completed the trip up the Danube by September 1622, but did not arrive in Augsburg until October. Measuring and handling such a large quantity of grain were long and costly processes.

For the consignment of 200 schaff of wheat, Lorenz reckoned 7,551 fl. in total expenses. The grain alone cost 5,400 fl. Transportation and accommodation along the way accounted for a further 1,883 fl. Provisions and other fees constituted the balance of 268 fl.

Lorenz's experience demonstrates the difficulty of supplying commodities. Simply finding adequate sources of grain, for example, might lead merchants and officials far from home. Once purchased, that grain had to be measured, loaded, shipped, unloaded, and remeasured. If not immediately transportable because of the season or because of political conditions, it had to be stored. In transit, it had to cross borders and render tariffs, all of which increased the time and expense of the entire process. At any point, truculent noblemen or recalcitrant officials could halt or even seize the shipment. Such emergencies could cause added expense and delay as messengers moved back and forth trying to resolve the deadlock. Under these circumstances, supplies of commodities fluctuated wildly over time, and city officials took further steps to control price and consumption.

The Provisions Office trafficked in other commodities too. Indeed, the provisions lords altered their market activities to fit the particular market forces of different goods.

For example, they exercised near monopoly control over Augsburg's market for fat products. The Provisions Office purchased tallow as well as lard directly from butchers at the state slaughter house (*Stadtmetzg*) and sold them to shopkeepers throughout the city and to marketholders in the Jews' Alley (*Judengasse*), who resold it to consumers.[47] A state agency served as middleman for this commodity and used its position to control supply and price.

Wood, on the other hand, lay in the hands of private enterprise, which undertook harvesting and transporting essential fuel and building material from as far away as Tyrol. But the city maintained a presence in this market too.[48] Augsburg exploited considerable tracts of forest in Swabia and Tyrol and sent officials to these regions annually to oversee the felling of trees for the city's reserves. The steady rise in wood and charcoal prices and the increase in forestry ordinances, beginning in the sixteenth century, speak of the deforestation of Europe and the need for regulating these precious commodities. Augsburg's Provisions Office organized a supply of wood to control local market prices and provide for the poor. Once in Augsburg, wood appeared at three marketplaces, scattered in corners of the city. The southern marketplace, by the Imperial Abbey of Sts. Ulrich and Afra, traded in wood from Tyrol; the eastern marketplace, by the Chapel of St. James, featured woods from Bavaria; the western marketplace, in the Cross Alley (*Kreuzgasse*) behind the Holy Cross Gate (*Heiligerkreuztor*), sold wood from Swabia. Here the agents of the Provisions Office bought and sold large quantities, making them one of Augsburg's largest consumers and suppliers of wood.

Although it maintained textile reserves, the Provisions Office was not so deeply involved in the supply and price of this commodity. The demand for cloth was far more elastic than that for foodstuffs or, arguably, even wood. Moreover, the strength of Augsburg as a center of industrial production and exchange made it the focal point of a market network in textiles extending throughout Upper Swabia, a center where supplies rarely ran short.[49] For this reason, though Augsburg was by no means immune to problems of textile supply and price, it resisted them in linens and fustians more effectively than other cities. The Provisions Office probably entered the public marketplaces for textiles, located in the Stone Alley (*Steingasse*) and at the Fruit Market (*Obstmarkt*), along with Augsburg's many private consumers. Because of the large quantities it purchased, it also dealt directly with major merchants and purchased from the stores held at the Weavers' Hall (*Weberhaus*). Although the Provisions Office did not control textile prices through such practices as dumping reserves, its demand must have encouraged production and attracted sellers. In this case, supply may have followed demand.

Controlling prices by regulating supply had both humanitarian and disciplinary aspects. In fact, humanity and discipline were inseparable elements of the common good (*bonum commune*) of the early modern city. The magistrates bore a moral responsibility for the physical well-being of their subjects, because a minimal existence could no more be separated from spiritual salvation than from social stability. By assuring adequate supplies of necessities, the city fathers also took steps to prevent the violence and upheaval that could be born of misery and despair.

The activities of the Provisions Office make clear how thin the line between discipline and assistance could be. During the inflation of 1622, when the cost of rye had risen to 18 fl. per schaff, the city sold reserves for less than 11 fl.[50] Low prices readily attracted bakers, millers, or merchants with sufficient capital to buy in quantities for eventual resale; the problem of assuring that individual consumers received aid in the form of affordable grain remained despite intervention and regulation.

Unable to control middlemen and speculators, Augsburg's magistrates opted for direct grain distribution. Street captains (*Gassenhauptleute*) compiled lists of poor residents according to such varied indices as local rumor, rental payments, family size, and household capital. Before any grain was distributed, however, the magistrates inquired into the individual circumstances of those households held to be needy. Only after close examination did the authorities permit people to purchase limited quantities of grain at subsidized prices. Efforts to control markets had evolved into ad hoc measures for the relief of poverty.

Despite apparent similarities, however, provisioning and assisting had real differences. The Provisions Office used stockpiles of basic commodities to influence market conditions, dumping the goods at critical moments to alter supplies and lower prices. By providing essential commodities to all consumers at affordable prices, such supply-side policies upheld the social order, that is, they enforced an external discipline. Though the singleminded concentration on availability ameliorated the worst consequences of dearth, still it did nothing to correct it. In particular, it limited an internal discipline that might have enabled individuals to anticipate or escape need. It obviated calculation.

Consumption and Charity

Scholars have long recognized supply as the principal means of shaping and regulating preindustrial markets; more recently, they have claimed that the development of supply alleviated want and increased consumption at the dawn of industrialization.[51] Linking the forces of production and trade to the conditions of supply and price, demand required at least as thorough a knowledge of markets and implied a no less sophisticated understanding of their function. Though it maintained reserves of goods as a defense against inflation, the Alms Office never manipulated supplies to influence market conditions. Rather than releasing goods into the market to alleviate scarcity and lower prices, Augsburg's public charity relied on demand to buy down price and establish long-term commercial relations. Demand also allowed the Alms Office to shape market forces. Incorporating the aggregate need of the city's poorest inhabitants, it regularly purchased large volumes of goods, thus attracting trade and stimulating production. Relatively unexamined, demand seems more germaine to modern economic thinking and behavior.

Until the early eighteenth century, the orphanages received basic commodities, such as lard and grains, wood and hides, clothing and textiles, from the stores of the Alms Office. Transfers of this kind shielded the orphanages somewhat from changing market conditions, freed them to develop sound capital bases, and enabled them to provide, as will be seen, a

TABLE 5.1
Cash and Commodities Distributed by the Alms Office

		1599	1609	1629	1634–35	1655	1665
Cash	(fl:kr)						
	to orphanages	1393:57	1773:32	3684:38	4123:03	4488:46	6594:29
	to chapels	—	1856:59	—	2275:53	—	5297:40
Rye	(in *Schaff*)						
	to orphanages	169	166	236	215	—	133
	to chapels	—	590	—	8	—	613
	value (fl:kr)	676:00	3022:00	2032:23	1941:04	—	3408:50
Lard	(in *Pfund*)						
	to orphanages	1828	2053	3213	1817	2400	2950
	to chapels	—	9911	—	0	—	5606
	value (fl:kr)	200:09	1510:36	564:55	612:07	—	1220:33
Wood	(in *Klafter*)						
	to orphanages	117	43	168	67	222	133
	to chapels	—	228	—	21	—	356
	value (fl:kr)	311:43	806:30	264:44	383:40	—	830:36
Linen	(in *Elle*)						
	to orphanages	769	1105	5719	2823	1824	1760
	to chapels	—	692	—	54	—	1909
	value (fl:kr)	103:32	222:39	821:47	233:11	—	769:45
Calf skins							
	to orphanages	100	92	41	51	252	288
	to chapels	—	8	—	0	—	268
	value (fl:kr)	20:03	56:40	36:52	54:24	—	262:24

surprisingly high standard of care. It encouraged a disregard for economy that led to crisis and reform in the city's organization of poor relief, but it protected to some extent the city's orphanages and the city's orphans from the volatile influence of supply on price.

The Alms Office spent thousands of gulden annually on a variety of commodities[52] (see Table 5.1). In most years, the volume purchased shifted according to a complex calculation involving the size of the needy population, the cost of the commodities, and the perceptions of the magistrates. Accounts give some indication of what goods were considered essential to maintain a minimal existence, those absolute necessities of life. The Alms Office sought to ameliorate the condition of the poor by providing food, warmth, and clothing.[53] They distributed basic foodstuffs, fuel, and textiles to the dependent poor in the Alms House, the Pilgrim House, and the City Orphanage, and to the independent poor from stockpiles kept in the chapels.

The fates of the Alms Office's commodity reserves paralleled those of the

Provisions Office.[54] The lion's share of alms in the late sixteenth and early seventeenth centuries underwrote commodities supplied directly to the independent poor from the city's chapels (see Appendix I, Figure 11). In 1600, replenishing stocks of foodstuffs, clothing, and fuel for the needy was the Alms Office's largest single expense; it consumed 37.1 percent of the entire budget. Owing to the expenses and losses occasioned by warfare, siege, and occupation, the Alms Office gradually ceased to maintain stores of essential goods in the various thirds of the city. As a proportion of total expenditures, commodities declined to 23.5 percent in 1635. Not until the late 1650s did chapel expenditures begin to recover in absolute terms. By the late 1660s, the Alms Office disbursed amounts similar to those of the first decade of the century, that is, 5,000 to 6,000 fl. annually. As a proportion of total spending, however, the chapels had long since yielded pride of place to the city's charitable foundations. The Alms Office never ceased to distribute commodities directly to the poor but gradually shifted emphasis to support via fixed organizations.

In 1522 the Alms Office deliberately removed the needy from the marketplace by prohibiting alms in cash in favor of alms in commodities. From that time until the annexation of the Imperial city, the Alms Office supported the deserving poor with goods and services and not with subsidies.

Large sums of money continued, nonetheless, to be disbursed annually to and through the chapels. Accounts offer only a hint as to the eventual purpose of this money. Every year they recorded a certain amount "to the three chapels in addition to foodstuffs in cash."[55] This money could not constitute expenditures on nourishment, warmth, or clothing, as these items were accounted for elsewhere. Neither could it have been spent on wages or fixed capital; again, these items appeared in categories of their own. The entries imply that the money supported the poor above and beyond direct sustenance. In all probability, cash provided services for the needy: it satisfied a landlord with the rent on a poor family's dwelling; it paid a cobbler to make or repair shoes for some needy person; it compensated a smith or some other craftsman for repairing the tools of a destitute laborer; it provided an apprenticeship to the son or a dowry to the daughter of a widow; it supported a needy scholar with a stipend; it supplied living expenses (Kostgeld) for a needy child in a foster family or in one of the orphanages. Evidence exists for all of these activities, testimony to the many ways of charity in early modern cities.

Of all commodities stored and distributed from the chapels, grain, especially rye, was the most voluminous and expensive. In 1609, the Alms Office acquired 590 schaff for 2,358 fl. (4 fl. per schaff), to store in and distribute from the chapels. The amount of rye fell to a paltry 8 schaff for 139 fl. (17 fl. per schaff) in 1635, but rebounded to 613 schaff for 2,799 fl., when the unit price declined to 5 fl. per schaff in 1665. Other grains, such as milled dinkel, oats, and barley, were purchased too, but these were insignificant in comparison.

The hiatus in rye distribution in 1635 probably resulted from two quite different situations. First, the crisis caused by the siege and occupation of Augsburg in that year created shortages of cash and commodities, making purchases of most goods difficult and expensive. Second, a gradual shift in policy regarding poor relief became visible at about the same time.

The inmates of Augsburg's poorhouses, hospitals, and orphanages began to fare much better than the independent poor. Those poor people who lived outside enclosed organizations were left more to their own devices. Thus, when only 7 schaff of rye, 2 of oats, and 1 of barley were distributed to the independent poor in 1635, the Alms Office provided the dependent poor—those housed in organizations—with 71 schaff of rye, 16 of dinkel, 6 of barley and 5 of oats. The children of the orphanage also fared better; they were fed 98 schaff of rye, 34 of dinkel, and 14 of oats. Given the relative scarcity of such commodities in a city recently conquered and reconquered, the differences in provisioning created even more striking distinctions of capital. All grains in the chapels were valued at only 200 fl. in 1635. By contrast, the Alms Office paid 3,288 fl. for grains for the orphanage and 1,922 fl. for the Alms House.

These material advantages probably endured beyond the crisis years. Beginning in the 1620s and 1630s, under pressure from rising prices, public charity began to shift its commodities from the independent to the dependent poor.

Scholars usually associate Foucault's great enclosure of the poor during the late seventeenth and eighteenth century with a greater desire for security and discipline.[56] Only within walls could the poor be controlled and reformed. Equally compelling, however, was the economy of enclosure. The poor were more easily policed within walls but they were also more inexpensively provisioned. This was not simply a function of economies of scale, as had been argued at the founding of Augsburg's orphanage, but also a matter of efficient distribution of goods and services. Although material constraints limited the effectiveness of enclosure in countries such as France, they seem clearly to have been a part of its inspiration in Augsburg.[57] The redistribution of resources away from vagabonds and other independent poor people, to orphans and the dependent poor, began in a period of economic crisis for Augsburg in which prices for such basic commodities as rye, lard, wood, and cloth rose sharply.

Unit prices for rye reveal just how acute the pressure of rising prices was[58] (see Table 5.2). In the late sixteenth and early seventeenth century, ending only in the aftermath of the great pestilence of 1628, the Alms Office usually purchased commodities at prices below market averages. In 1634, with

TABLE 5.2
Average Price per Schaff of Rye

Year	Alms Office	Hospital
1599	4.0 fl.	5.3 fl.
1609	4.0 fl.	5.3 fl.
1629	8.6 fl.	6.5 fl.
1634	8.4 fl.	23.4 fl.
1636	18.8 fl.	11.4 fl.
1649	15.9 fl.	13.7 fl.
1665	4.6 fl.	3.4 fl.

grains becoming unaffordable, the Alms Office acquired rye for one-third the rate paid by Augsburg's *Spital*. That officials purchased so little suggests that only limited quantities were available. When prices recovered somewhat with the occupation of the city by Imperial forces, in the late 1630s and 1640s, the Alms Office paid prices for rye considerably above the market. The customary relationship only began to recover in the second half of the seventeenth century.

These unusual price differentials have a number of possible explanations, all speculative given the lack of records but all probable under the circumstances. First, supplies held as stock may have helped the city to avoid excess costs during periods of high prices. Annual volumes of rye acquired during the seventeenth century show that the Alms Office took advantage of low or stable prices to buy in large quantities, evidence of a consistent effort to maintain reserves. Relying on those stockpiles purchased at lower prices, it weathered periods of scarcity and inflation, still provided for the poor, but bought less grain at higher prices. Second, the aggregate demand of Augsburg's poor may have helped the Alms Office to force prices below market levels. Buying in large quantities for its needy clientele, it probably negotiated prices somewhat lower than individual consumers paid. Moreover, consistent demand, expressed in regularly large-scale purchases, may have encouraged the administrators to seek out stable commercial relations with suppliers in the form of subcontracting. Third, different sources of supply may have permitted the Alms Office to pay lower prices for goods. Consistent price differentials could have been the result of purchases made outside Augsburg's markets or from suppliers able to sell at lower rates. In short, the administrators may have relied on extensive knowledge of market conditions. Whether by exploiting supply, demand, or information, the Alms Office reduced purchases during periods of inflation and built stocks during periods of deflation, evidence of a determined effort to use market conditions to advantage.

The same held true for other, less costly foodstuffs supplied by the Alms Office. Large quantities of lard were also distributed to the poor. Still popular in Swabia and Bavaria as a spread on bread and as a source of fat in cooking, lard seems to have been a dietary staple in the early modern period, providing not only calories but also a small amount of protein. Though less nourishing than grain, it was easily the most cost effective source of energy available to the poor and was certainly consumed in massive quantities.

In St. Ulrich's third, the least needy of Augsburg's three districts, the Alms Office stored 153 barrels, or 21,449 pfund, of lard with a market value in excess of 2,900 fl.in 1579.[59] By 1609, the Alms Office's entire store of lard had fallen to 64 barrels, or 9,911 pfund, at just over 1,251 fl. The decline continued throughout the period. In 1634, a general shortage of large and small livestock, due to requisitioning and slaughtering by occupying armies, created an abrupt, though temporary, shortage on the open market. The Alms Office purchased no lard for the chapels that year. After the hard times, much smaller quantities of the foodstuff reappeared in stock. By 1665, the chapels once again distributed large quantities of lard, but the dependent poor, at least those in the Catholic and Lutheran orphanages, received proportionally more.

This shift to organizational assistance coincided with rising prices. The average price per pfund of lard rose catastrophically during the 1620s and 1630s, just at the time that the Alms Office reduced the relief it made available to independent poor (see Table 5.3). The enclosure of the poor rested on a foundation of economy.

The same pattern of consumption obtained with lard as with rye: the Alms Office frequently purchased at prices below those paid by other organizations and, presumably, below the market in general. During inflationary periods, such as 1634, it acquired large quantities at surprisingly low cost, and as prices fell it bought smaller amounts at higher prices. The pattern, again, suggests a manipulation of markets by means of aggregate demand and commodity stockpiles, all based on superior knowledge of local and regional supplies and prices.

As noted, the Provisions Office occupied a nearly monopsonistic position in the market for lard, that is, it occupied a position as sole buyer of a commodity offered by several sellers, and thus organized the labor of numerous petty producers. Unlike the Provisions Office, however, the Alms Office did not organize consortia of butchers and other suppliers to meet its demand for lard. Initially, like the merchants and artisans of Augsburg, it looked to the Provisions Office for supplies. Alms Lord Hieronymus Harder noted in his account of 1579 that he acquired 21,445 pfund from Provisions Lord Lucas Ulstett. Later, merchants or factors served as middlemen for large-scale transactions, an undertaking that required considerable knowl-

TABLE 5.3
Average Price per Pfund of Lard

Year	Alms Office	Hospital
1609	7.0 kr.	8.0 kr.
1629	11.0 kr.	9.2 kr.
1634	20.0 kr.	26.6 kr.
1636	30.0 kr.	11.9 kr.
1649	10.0 kr.	8.7 kr.
1665	8.0 kr.	8.1 kr.
1675	4.0 kr.	8.7 kr.

edge of local and regional markets. In 1655, Johann Bonaventura Wanner recorded a number of large purchases from sources in the Augsburg area. The Alms Office paid Philipp Jacob Imhof 64 fl. for 513 pfund of lard, and purchased a further 1,609 pfund at 219 fl. from Jeremia Seitzen, both scions of notable merchant families in Augsburg. The largest supplier of lard, however, was not local. Mates Schneid from the town of Weiding sold 7,640 pfund of lard for 608 fl. in 1655. As a result, the Alms Office paid an average price of 19.2 pfennig, or 1.6 pfennig below market, for lard in 1655.[60] The mere fact that such transactions took place on such a scale, demonstrates the ability of the administrators of charity to use local knowledge and accumulated demand to influence the flow of commodities and to shape markets.

After foodstuffs, fuel constituted the most important material made available to the poor. The Alms Office purchased a wide variety of woods. For example, of the 1,740 klafter (5,220 cubic meters) it purchased in 1579, 226 were spruce and the rest were harder, more expensive birch and beech. A large number of small-scale suppliers were involved in this trade, including 26 individuals who sold 1 to 5 klafter from such villages and towns as Burgadelshausen, Rinental, Binenbach, Eglingen, Amaltingen, Altomünster, and Wissertshausen. As with lard, the volumes of wood acquired by the Alms Office declined steadily over the course of the late sixteenth and seventeenth centuries. In 1609, the office bought nearly 348 klafter (1,044 cubic meters), at a total cost of 987 fl. This amount apparently proved insufficient to meet the needs of the poor because the Alms Office also distributed 268 wood marks (Holzzeichen), worth 116 fl., that year. These entitled the bearer to draw a fixed quantity of wood from the stores of the Provisions Office. During the period of scarcity in 1635, the volume of wood purchased by the Alms Office fell to less than 216 klafter (648 cubic meters), at about 976 fl. By 1665, wood purchases had rebounded to 432 klafter (1,296 cubic meters), at a price of 837 fl, still not the level of the late 1500s. But the proportion of soft wood to hard wood had inverted; that year the Alms Office bought 432 klafter (1,296 cubic meters) of wood, 315 of pine and 117 of birch, beech, and oak. Soft woods were less expensive, enabling charity to make large quantities available for smaller amounts of money. Changes in the average unit cost per klafter of wood, which rose from 1.3 fl. in 1579 to a peak of 3.7 fl in 1635, then retreated to 1.5 fl. in 1665 and 1.7 fl. in 1675, suggest that problems of supply and price influenced the size of purchases.[61] These market forces may have altered the source of supply, too. By the middle of the seventeenth century, the Alms Office received shipments of wood from seven sellers, including two women, who trafficked in wood from sources as distant as the top of the Lech valley in the Alps beyond Füssen.

The Alms Office entered local and regional markets to deal directly with numerous suppliers. Initially, the needs and resources of the Alms Office helped organize local wood supplies and shaped the local marketplace. Individuals transported small quantities of merchandise to the central marketplace for sale. The risk of doing so, which was a function of the time and expense involved in moving bulk commodities overland, was guaranteed to an extent by the certainty of large-scale demand. Because such demand was not forthcoming from individuals, it seems possible that these commodities might not have reached Augsburg at all without the demand of city agencies, such as the Alms Office. As its resources and demand declined, the net effect of the Alms Office on the market for wood seems to have changed. It no longer attracted local suppliers, and it paid a higher price.[62] Perhaps local forests were exhausted; perhaps local supplies were expensive. In any case, only substantial merchants and suppliers could deal in quantities sufficiently large to achieve economies of scale and secure a reasonable profit over long distances.

Of the purchased total in 1579, less than half benefitted the independent poor of Augsburg. Once again, they suffered a gradual erosion of support from the chapels in favor of the dependent poor in enclosed organizations. Not only did they receive less wood, but the independent poor also received cheaper varieties. Though the Alms Office distributed the majority of its supply of wood to the chapels in 1645—207 klafter (621 cubic meters) as opposed to 108 (324 cubic meters) for the institutions—the consignment consisted entirely of pine, the cheapest wood in the inventory. It proved an aberration in any case; by 1655 the city's dependent poor again received more commodities generally.

The Alms Office seldom stockpiled wood. In 1579, however, it retained a surplus of 1,199 klafter (3,597 cubic meters) from the total amount acquired that year. Although prices varied according to kind and supply in the marketplace, the average unit cost of wood purchased by the Alms Office that year was 1 fl. 20 kr. per klafter. Its wood reserves of about 1,200 klafter

(3,600 cubic meters) represented a capital worth roughly 1,600 fl. The only other instance of a surplus in Alms Office accounts occurred in 1655. Of 701 klafter (2,103 cubic meters) of wood only 497 (1,491 cubic meters) were used in the city's charitable foundations or disbursed directly to the poor. A surplus of 204 klafter (612 cubic meters), with an approximate value of 310 fl., was accounted to the working capital of the Alms Office.

The declining supplies of wood purchases and infrequency of reserves suggests two possible conclusions. First, as a commodity supplied to Augsburg's poorer citizens, wood became less important to the city over time. Although the poor required fuel for heating and cooking no less urgently than in the sixteenth century, the Alms Office made less of it available in the eighteenth. With the need for austerity that accompanied Augsburg's economic recovery in the late seventeenth century and its renewed economic difficulties in the eighteenth century, wood became an expendable form of social assistance. Second, the value attached to wood reserves as a form of working capital decreased as well. Generally speaking, the city government and its agencies became more involved in Augsburg's capital market over the course of the early modern period. Evidence from the orphanages and the Alms Office indicates, however, a greater need for liquidity and security of capital in the seventeenth and eighteenth centuries. The requirements of far-flung credit operations, the unusual imperatives of property held in trust, and the pressing imbalance of payments all cried for a cash basis of operations. Whatever the desirability of commodities as a hedge against the future, other forms of capital proved more advantageous.

Food and fuel were arguably the most pressing needs of the poor, and the city spent more public resources for them than for any other of life's necessities. But the needy also required cloth and clothing to maintain a fitting modesty in public and to protect themselves from the elements. Many accounts of early modern poverty testify to the ragged, semi-naked state of the sufferers. To assist them, the Alms Office also purchased large consignments of textiles—as bulk materials or as finished articles—to preserve public decency and clothe the needy. At different times Augsburg offered the poor linen, wool, and blended fabrics as well as calfskins and sheepskins. Availability and price rather than suitability or quality probably determined the selections.

The city's textile industry had been in the hands of cloth merchants since the fifteenth century. Certainly Augsburg harbored weavers, some of them very substantial, who maintained the status of independent craftsmen by possessing their own capital and selling their own products.[63] Organized for export to distant markets and depending on distant sources for raw materials, however, the industry as a whole relied on merchants to provide capital and purchase products. Although the putting-out system (*Verlagssystem*) was illegal in Augsburg and supposedly did not evolve before the second half of the seventeenth century—at least among the city's linen weavers—most of those who operated small (one or two loom) shops fell into some form of credit or market dependency.[64] Merchants could respond to mass demand more efficiently than a cooperative of small craftsmen. Thus, merchants rather than the weavers brought finished textiles to market and supplied the needs of the Alms Office.

The amount and cost of cloth given to the poor rose steadily in this period; textiles assumed an important place in the finances of charity. As was the case with other commodities, most of these textiles went to the dependent poor. The city could conceivably have organized petty producers to supply its needs, as it had with wood, but the Alms Office was not a dominant consumer of cloth. Its demand hardly compared with that of export markets. The Alms Office relied, therefore, on the agency of middlemen for cloth. In 1579, for example, Caspar Ettinger, Lucas Zolling, the heirs of Hans Gienger, and the brothers and sons of Joachim Jenisch supplied the Alms Office with textiles worth 460 fl. Of the 2,751 elle purchased, only 38 were distributed from the chapels.[65] This entire consignment was made up of a coarse fabric called *Rupfen*. No finer linens or woolens made their way into the households of the independent poor; these were reserved for the city's charitable organizations. The City Orphanage received 84 elle of fustian for bedding, 126 elle of linen to serve as underclothing for the children, and 85 elle of *Rupfen* "to sew up the dead" and "for straw sacks," that is, as shrouds and mattresses.[66] The passing of hard times after the middle of the seventeenth century did not end the city's apparent preference for the dependent poor. By 1665, the Alms Office purchased linens and woolens worth 1,067 fl. Though the suppliers changed in this period, the names of Axster, Reichard, and Werewag continued to be reckoned among the *Kaufleuteschaft* of Augsburg. The independent poor received no linens at all, while the inmates of the two orphanages and the Pilgrim House got 1,900 elle.

These disparities between support given to the dependent and the independent poor applied to all other unfinished fabrics and finished clothing. In 1609, for example, the chapels distributed 233 fur hoods, 260 pairs of hose, and 3 pairs of gloves. This compared favorably to the clothing given to children in the City Orphanage: 48 hoods, 36 hose, and 37 pairs of gloves. By 1635, the Alms Office supplied only 88 fur hoods to orphans and 6 to the independent poor. No articles of clothing appear in the 1665 inventory. The movement toward enclosure affected the consumption of all commodities.

The Alms Office made extensive use of hides, too, in the form of calf- and sheepskins that went almost exclusively to orphans. Only in 1609 did the Alms Office distribute calfskins through the chapels, a total of 8 pieces going to the independent poor of St. Ulrich's. By contrast, it purchased 92 in 1609 and 100 a decade earlier for the orphanage. In the early seventeenth century, the Alms Office shifted to sheepskins. It purchased 51 for orphans in 1634, 268 in 1665, and 150 in 1675.

The total cost to the Alms Office in any year never exceeded 140 fl., not expensive relative to other commodities in city stores. But the city occasionally bought them at extraordinarily high prices. The 100 calfskins purchased in 1599 cost the Alms Office 12 kr. each, the average unit price on the market.[67] It was the best the Alms Office ever did. It acquired calfskins at 34 kr. apiece in 1609, at 69 kr. apiece in 1627, and at 64 kr. in 1634. In contrast, the average price paid by the hospital for calfskins hovered at 12 kr. in 1609, rose to 28.5 kr. in 1627, then fell to 15 kr. in 1634. The cause of this disparity can only be guessed. The Alms Office may have acquired hides of much higher quality and, therefore, price. The Hospital possessed meadows to graze the animals that may have been used to provide the skins it needed. By contrast, public charity depended fully on the commodity market.

The demand for commodities encouraged small producers and middlemen to bring their goods to market. By relying on demand, the administrators of charity demonstrated their understanding that supply was itself the result of more complex economic processes and market forces. The organization of production, the availability of transportation, and the calculation of risk—to name but a few factors—determined the cost of goods, and cost was an essential variable in supply. Aggregate demand aligned these components to create optimal market conditions. It enabled the administrators of charity to acquire essential commodities at prices frequently below those paid by comparable organizations. Purchasing in periods of feast to avoid purchasing in periods of famine, they minimized the risks inherent in price volatility and maximized their resources at the same time.

Conclusion

In the eighteenth century, Catholic and Lutheran administrators debated the disposition of fixed capital in the domestic economy of charity. It rapidly became clear, however, that the question whether to repair or replace a granary could not be separated from confessional and material tensions, much less from fundamental economic orientations and affiliations. The Catholics viewed alms as a matter of consumption, in which the transfer of resources from haves to have-naughts bound the latter to an economy of thrift. Augsburg's Lutherans understood charity in terms of production, in which the transfer of resources bound the poor and their governors to a degree of self-sufficiency. The relative value of fixed capital depended upon the function attributed to liquid capital, cash, and commodities.

This debate would never have occurred—the issues would have been incomprehensible—had not the parties been accustomed to thinking of essential goods as commodities, that is, as objects produced for sale in markets and, therefore, "subject to supply-and-demand mechanisms interacting with price."[68] Augsburg's administrators drew on their substantial experience in commodity trading as a matter both of economic policy and of economic activity. They managed supply and demand to influence market conditions, to ensure adequate supplies and stable prices.

In Augsburg, the Alms Office and the orphanages entered the marketplace and dealt directly with merchants, shopkeepers, and craftsmen. Though needy persons consumed little because of their limited means, still the consumption of goods by the poor taken as a group constituted an important economic force. Certainly, a cursory and incomplete survey of goods purchased by the city's public charities indicates the large volume of these transactions. Despite the decline in amounts of commodities purchased on behalf of the poor and despite the turn to enclosure, the Alms Office remained one of Augsburg's most important consumers. Here the object was neither to control prices indirectly, by dumping commodity reserves, nor to limit them directly, by magisterial fiat, but rather to use the weight of aggregate demand to obtain goods and services at economical prices. Charity acted as sole buyer or one of so few buyers—monopsony or oligopsony—in particular commodity markets that its actions could affect prices.

This was not uniformly possible. Just as different commodities were traded in different physical locations in Augsburg, the markets for different commodities were subject to different sets of conditions. These were a function of market forces such as the organization of production. For example, butchering was a local industry dominated by independent craftsmen; by contrast, weaving was an export industry in the hands of merchant entrepreneurs. The Alms Office conformed to these parameters in order to acquire the goods it needed. Even as it shaped commodity markets, it was shaped by them.

Manipulating commodities yielded, therefore, a practical knowledge of markets, the conditions that prevailed in them and the forces that governed them. Administrators understood that prices, and consequently costs, were a function of supply and demand. Though abstract, these factors were knowable and workable; they could be altered to create optimal conditions for buying and selling. As a result, the Alms Office and the orphanages gradually developed strategies of consumption that were consistent with a more systematically capitalistic approach to management.

Notes

1. To this list of essentials Roeck added meat. He might also have included textiles and leather. Roeck, *Bäcker, Brot und Getreide in Augsburg*, 37–65 passim.
2. In periods of inflation, such stockpiles were more valuable than cash reserves. Augsburg's Incomes Officer regularly accounted the cash equivalent of commodity stores as part of the city's ready capital under the heading *Rats-Conto*. The same may well have applied to the capital accounts of the city's orphanages. Cf. Ibid., 39.
3. StAA, EW 4, Generalia, 1665–1767, Bericht des Herrn von Rehlinger Almosenherr katholisches Teils, 6 February 1724.
4. Ibid., Antwort der Almosenherren Augustanae Confessionis, s.d. 1724.
5. One schaff = eight metzen = ca. 215 liters.
6. Cipolla, *Before the Industrial Revolution*, 108.
7. StAA, EW 4, Generalia, 1665–1767, Antwort der Almosenherren Augustanae Confessionis, s.d. 1724.
8. Ibid.
9. Ibid.
10. Ibid.
11. Ibid.
12. StAA, KW 2, Decretum in senatum secretioris utrius religionis, 16 March 1734.
13. StAA, EW 6, Jahresrechnungen, 1745, 1735, 1778, 1780.
14. StAA, EW 7, Oekonomia des evangelischen Waisenhauses betr., 3 August 1780.
15. StAA, KW 13, Sammlung der Ratsdekreten, 1572–1790, Decretum in senatum secretioris catholicum, 13 November 1783.
16. Ibid., Decretum in senatum secretioris catholicum, 15 November 1783.
17. Ibid., Signatum, 6 March 1784.
18. Luther, "Trade and Usury," 263.
19. Ibid., 262.
20. Luther, "Trade and Usury," 263; Cipolla, *Before the Industrial Revolution*, 51–52.
21. Roeck, *Bäcker, Brot und Getreide in Augsburg*, 105–120.
22. Ibid., 110.
23. Bátori, *Die Reichsstadt Augsburg*, 96.
24. Kellenbenz, "Wirtschaftsleben der Blütezeit," 258–301; Enderle, *Konfessionsbildung und Ratsregiment*, passim.
25. Kellenbenz, "Wirtschaftsleben der Blütezeit," 258.
26. Ibid., 259. The role of church granaries in Augsburg's grain market is undisputed, but their relative importance remains a matter of debate. Cf. Roeck, *Bäcker, Brot und Getreide in Augsburg*, 123.
27. Kellenbenz, "Wirtschaftsleben der Blütezeit," 259.
28. Roeck offers evidence of a system of commodity espionage, in which Augsburg sent scouts into the surrounding countryside to locate stocks of essential goods. Roeck, *Bäcker, Brot und Getreide in Augsburg*, 93.
29. Ibid., 121.
30. Luther, "Trade and Usury," passim.
31. Roeck, *Bäcker, Brot und Getreide in Augsburg*, 121–29.
32. Ibid., 121–29. See especially his statistics on grain duties from 1624–48, on 126.
33. Ibid., 37–82, passim.

34. Kellenbenz, "Wirtschaftsleben der Blütezeit," 259.
35. Cf. Burke, *Popular Culture in Early Modern Europe*; Muchembled, *Culture populaire et culture des élites dans la France moderne*; Imhof, *Die verlorenen Welten*; Sabean, *Power in the Blood*; Roeck, *Bäcker, Brot und Getreide in Augsburg*, 9–24, passim.
36. Roeck interpreted this figure, offered by Kellenbenz, as exagerrated. His analysis placed greatest emphasis on public reserves; private stocks did not, in Roeck's estimation, play a large role in provisioning Augsburg. Cf. Kellenbenz, "Wirtschaftsleben der Blütezeit," 259; Roeck, *Bäcker, Brot und Getreide in Augsburg*, 97.
37. Kellenbenz, "Wirtschaftsleben der Blütezeit," 259.
38. Roeck, *Bäcker, Brot und Getreide in Augsburg*, 97.
39. Ibid., 99.
40. Ibid., 96. The actual totals were 45,422 schaff of rye, 306 of dinkel, 223 of wheat, and 296 of oats.
41. Kellenbenz, "Wirtschaftsleben der Blütezeit," 259. Kellenbenz estimated that these supplies would provision the entire population of Augsburg—approximately 40,000 in the early 1620s—for eight months.
42. Roeck, *Bäcker, Brot und Getreide in Augsburg*, 96.
43. Kellenbenz, "Wirtschaftsleben der Blütezeit," 259. When compared to these seventeenth-century statistics, the figure of 100 schaff, alleged by Lutheran magistrates in 1724, reveals the declining importance of provisioning as a policy of state.
44. Ibid., 85.
45. Ibid., 86.
46. The affair was reconstructed by Roeck in *Brot, Bäcker und Getreide*, 91–92.
47. Ibid., 37–38.
48. Ibid., 41–44.
49. Kießling, *Die Stadt und Ihr Land*, 701–41, passim.
50. Roeck, *Bäcker, Brot und Getreide in Augsburg*, 101–05.
51. Among many others, Joel Mokyr has argued forcefully for the primacy of supply. See Mokyr, "Demand vs. Supply," 110. For a more recent, measured dissent, see de Vries, "The Industrial Revolution and the Industrious Revolution," esp. 257.
52. StAA, Alms, Jahresrechnungen. Annual accounts recorded not only moneys received and disbursed but also the amount and value of commodity reserves. These constituted part of the working capital of the Alms Office. The weights offered are the standard ones of that time, used in the accounts themselves. Thus, a *Schaff* is the equivalent of about 205.3 liters in volume. An *Elle* was a unit of measure for length that came in various magnitudes, thus a *Große* and a *Kleine*. For linen, the small elle was usually applied, and it measured 0.587 meter in length. A *Klafter* was a specialized measure of volume for wood, at about 3 cubic meters similar to the modern cord. The *Pfund* measured approximately 0.491 kilogram in weight. See the discussion of Augsburger measures and weights in Elsas, *Umriss einer Geschichte der Preise und Löhne in Deutschland*, 152–54.
53. StAA, Alms, Jahresrechnungen, 1579, 1609, 1635, 1665, 1675.
54. StAA, Alms, Jahresrechnungen, 1600–1675. Changing accounting practices make conclusive statistical analysis impossible. For example, distinctions were not made in every year between expenditures on commodities and cash disbursals in the three chapels. In many years only undifferentiated sums were given. Moreover, certain types of commodities might be accounted under different rubrics.

Thus, from 1635, only foodstuffs appear in the accounts of the chapels. Wood and textiles were entered under common expenditures. Nonetheless, these summary accounts give some indication of the changing scope of Alms Office expenditures and activities.

55. StAA, Alms, Jahresrechnungen, 1579, 1609, 1635, 1665, 1675: "In den 3 Caplen neben den Speiß an pahren gelt...."
56. Cohen, *The Evolution of Women's Asylums since 1500*, 5–6; DeLacy, *Prison Reform in Lancashire*, 70–94; Foucault, *Discipline and Punish*, 141–49; Jones, *The Charitable Imperative*, 8; Rothman, *The Discovery of the Asylum*, 30–56.
57. Jones, *Charity and Bienfaisance*, 4.
58. The benchmark for commodity prices used in this table is based on prices calculated by Elsas, *Umriss einer Geschichte der Preise und Löhne in Deutschland*, I, 593–624, passim. He listed prices in *Denarien* of pfennig; these were translated to gulden at a rate of 210:1.
59. Ibid., 609. The author calculated 20.0 pfennig per pfund as the average price for *Schmalz* in 1579. Accepting this value, Alms Office stores that year would have been worth nearly 2,043 fl. The state agency paid "above" the estimated rate of the *Spital* that year.
60. Cf. Elsas, *Umriss einer Geschichte der Preise und Löhne in Deutschland*, I, 593–624, passim. The author based his tables of commodity prices on the accounts of the Heiliger Geist Spital in Augsburg. His analysis provided a benchmark for the costs of basic goods and services.
61. Elsas offered no data on the average price of wood in late medieval and early modern Augsburg.
62. No reliable statistics exist for wood prices in early modern Augsburg. In his 1572 projection, Stöcklin estimated the cost of 18 klafter of pine at 18 batzen, or 201.6 pfennig per klafter. The Alms Office paid an average price of 392.2 pfennig per klafter in 1579 and 538.2 pfennig per klafter in 1655 for all types of locally grown wood. Without some evidence of prices, however, hypotheses about the market activity of the office are premature.
63. Clasen, *Die Augsburger Weber*, 17–69, passim.
64. Ibid., 330–32. Clasen insists on the absence of the *Verlag* among Augsburg's linen weavers and implies the essential independence—though not the prosperity—of even the most humble of them. In this his argument seems to rely too heavily on the dictates of *Weberordnungen* and the role of wage labor. Whereas wage labor was clearly illegal for Augsburg's linen weavers, other forms of dependency existed and could, in fact, support a modified *Verlagssystem*. Furthermore, the very existence of such regulation suggests that wage labor was not unknown in the city's industry.
65. Though a standard term for the measurement of length in textiles, the elle was anything but a standard measure. It varied according to place and according to the type of textile to be measured. Elsas records the standard elle in Munich as 83.5 cm. In Augsburg, however, two elle existed: the large elle measured 60.6 cm; the small elle (also known as the linen or fustian elle, perhaps a reflection of its particular use) measured 58.7 cm. Elsas, *Umriss einer Geschichte der Preise und Löhne in Deutschland*, I, 146, 154.
66. StAA, Alms, Jahresrechnung, 1579. The terms used were "zum einnehen der todten" and "zue strohseckhen."
67. Ibid.
68. Polanyi, *The Great Transformation*, 73.

6

Charity and Consumption in the Orphanages

Early modern magistrates understood commodities both as capital and as consumables.[1] Augsburg's provisions lords purchased stores of essential goods, especially foodstuffs, as a hedge against scarcity and inflation. In the event of a crisis, such as crop failure, they dumped reserves into the market to increase supplies and lower prices. The alms lords entered Augsburg's marketplaces to acquire an assortment of commodities. Using the aggregate demand of the city's needy population, they bought commodities in bulk to obtain advantageous prices. In these ways, administrators demonstrated their awareness of forces that shaped markets, and they manipulated supply and demand to lower costs and maximize resources.

Whether Johannes Stöcklin, the author of the 1572 proposal to found an orphanage, foresaw the organization as a means of accumulating supplies or concentrating demand in order to influence market prices cannot be readily determined. He did not project unit prices for various commodities that were noticeably lower than those common in the marketplace, as might have been expected were that his intention. By contrast, his analysis of orphanage expenses shows that he clearly understood that centralized charities benefitted from economies of scale, that is, that concentrating the care of needy children under a single roof would reduce various operation and transaction costs.

Augsburg's orphanages played a different, more restricted role in the city's markets and marketplaces than did the provisions and alms offices. The size of the orphanage operations provided assistance for hundreds instead of thousands of needy people and limited the organizations' capacity to manipulate market conditions. The orphanages never purchased quantities as large as those of the higher offices. Although they maintained modest stores of goods, they rarely stockpiled commodities as a hedge against inflation. Also, until the eighteenth century, Augsburg's orphanages received many goods from the Alms Office rather than in the marketplace. They entered markets to acquire many goods and services, but they were shielded from market conditions by participation in the transfer of commodities between state agencies.

Poor relief served as a system for the redistribution of resources in Augsburg. Cash and commodities flowed through the city's marketplaces directly and indirectly into the hands of the poor, a group that might otherwise have been conspicuous by their absence from trade. The orphan fathers purchased many goods and services directly from suppliers. For these, they submitted open accounts every month, which were rendered in full with little more than an occasional exhortation to thrift by the alms lords. But the orphan fathers also received essential commodities, such as grain, wood, tallow, and cloth, in the form of extra-market exchanges from the stores of the Alms Office. This system of accounts and transfers made the orphanages absolutely dependent on the Alms Office and made the Alms Office absolutely vulnerable to it. Consequently, the orphanages were a great drain on city resources. At the end of the Thirty Years' War, for example, as the citizens of Augsburg set about the task of rebuilding a shattered city and economy, they provided their orphanages with nearly 10,400 fl. in state funds. As one magistrate noted at the time, "though in other offices large debts and expenditures exist without the means to meet them, in this case [the Catholic and Lutheran orphanages] there is enough property [mobilia] for both parties."[2] The orphans of Augsburg were much better supported than many other people in Augsburg. Parity and the establishment of two separate but equal organizations, however, did nothing to ease this task. By 1665 Catholic and Lutheran orphanages together consumed more commodities, despite a smaller population of orphans, than their single, biconfessional predecessor and became the most expensive items in the budget of the Alms Office. The authorities responded over the course of the eighteenth century by ending the system of commodity transfers and thrusting the orphanages directly into the marketplace.[3] In 1740, monthly accounts payable yielded to cash subsidies for specific goods. These subsidies were fixed finally in 1788. Only then did the orphan fathers fully assume the burdens of disbursing limited funds and purchasing goods directly. It is another irony of the history of Augsburg's orphanages that they were created in response to changing market conditions but became totally involved in the markets some two hundred years after the fact.

Nonetheless, the orphanages always purchased large quantities of commodities, and the office of orphan father required calculation predicated on an exact knowledge of market forces and conditions. Moreover, operations reflected the same systematic application of this practical knowledge. Unable to reduce prices by influencing supply and demand, the orphan fathers sought price stability instead by means of subcontracting and long-term commercial relations. They then instituted a material regime based on disciplined consumption that emphasized efficiency through standardization and routinization rather than thrift through reduction and abstinence. Capitalistic patterns of consumption, therefore, trace their roots not to the creation of commodity markets but rather to the management of commodities.

ECONOMIES OF SCALE

This management began with the effort to reduce costs and maximize resources. Economies of scale were the heart of the argument in favor of an orphanage. The 1572 proposal listed those goods and services considered essential to support a household of 200 orphans and 8 staff members for one year (see Appendix II). Although its purpose was fiscal, the document spoke as well to the perceptions of the magistrates and the material texture of life in the orphanage to be, the minimum necessary to sustain life, and the optimum necessary to shape it. That balance helped determine the weight attributed to commodities as consumables and as capital.

Stöcklin did not make allowance for direct housekeeping costs. As the building would be purchased by the city and donated to the use of the orphanage, it would require no funding beyond occasional maintenance. The accounts of actual orphanage expenses in the late sixteenth century show this to have been a great oversight because the building needed renovation and repair regularly and the costs were high over the first several decades of the organization's life. Beyond shelter from the elements, light and heat were also essential: the orphanage would consume about 200 pfund (between 94 and 98 kg.) of candles per year and 60 klafter (180 cubic meters) of pine and beech at a cost of 106 fl., 2.5 percent of the total, annual budget.[4] Various housewares would require a further 25 fl. annually[5] (see Table 6.1). It seems certain that the authorities expected these costs to be much less than if the 200 orphans were accommodated in as many private dwellings.[6] Perhaps for this reason, Stöcklin estimated light and fuel needs that were lower than those suggested by Provisions or Alms Office acquisitions.

The regular services of a tailor, a seamstress, and a cobbler imply that the orphanage would supply clothing—probably uniform—for its inhabitants rather than rely on their private property. Stöcklin projected the costs of unfinished cloth and a few specialized articles of clothing at 430 fl. per year, or 13 percent of the total budget. The children would require minimally 800 elle of fine linen to produce blouses and doublets. The same amount of coarser linen would provide for their bedding. Fifteen pieces of ticking were probably intended for the bundles of straw (Börtzen) that served as mattresses. Twenty pieces of fustian would be made into clothing, and

TABLE 6.1
Approximate Calculation of What an Orphanage, in Which 200 Children Might be Supported, Might Cost Yearly

First a pious Christian married couple with a good conscience and no children, who could honestly lead and teach the children to the fear of God, to prayer, as well as to work and all good virtues, their wages might be about	fl. 50
More, six maids who are pious and honest, each fl. 5 per year	fl. 30
Rye 160 schaff at fl. 9	fl. 1440
Dinkel [Kern] as fine flour 20 schaff at fl. 11	fl. 220
White bread each week ca. 30 kr.	fl. 26
Wine, mead, beer in cases of need	fl. 20
Pease 4 schaff about	fl. 20
Millet 3 schaff about	fl. 18
Barley 4 schaff about	fl. 16
Oats 4 schaff as oat flour about	fl. 12
Meat every week 170 pfund for a year	fl. 294
For 5 pigs	fl. 25
Lard every week 25 pfund or 13 centner at fl. 9 per centner	fl. 117
Salt 5 blocks	fl. 9
Candles 200 pfund at 5 kr.	fl. 17
Root vegetables [= turnips, beets, or carrots, T.M.S.] 300 metzen at 4 kr.	fl. 20
White cabbage for	fl. 25
Green cabbage, fruit, and eggs	fl. 20
Grapes, almonds, figs, soap, and elderberry preserves (Holderseltz)	fl. 20
Sachet [Wechholder], flints [Kimel], brooms, scouring sand, tubs, and cookware	fl. 25
Wood 35 klafter pine and 25 klafter beech at 18 and 28 batzen per klafter	fl. 89
Straw bundles 30 schober for	fl. 10
For 10 cows fl. 100 they should live 6 years at fl. 17 each year for hay and straw fl. 100 annual total	fl. 117
Woolen cloth [Nördlinger Loden] 20 at fl. $7\frac{1}{2}$ each piece	fl. 150
Fustian [Barchent] 20 pieces at fl. $2\frac{1}{2}$ each piece	fl. 50
Ticking [Mittler] 15 pieces	fl. 60
To the tailor yearly	fl. 50
To the cobbler for 2 pair of shoes for each child at 8, 10, and 12 kr.	fl. 67
Linen for blouses and doublets 800 elle at 5 kr. per elle	fl. 67
Linen for bedding 800 elle at 4 kr. per elle	fl. 53
For hats and scarves	fl. 50
Quarterly and sewing money	fl. 50
Total yearly	fl. 3237

20 pieces of woolen cloth (*Loden*) into coats and other items of outer wear. Only hats and scarves would be purchased as finished goods. Stöcklin also allowed each orphan two pairs of shoes per year. Calf- and sheepskins would serve as outer garments, such as jerkins, trousers, or leggings, but they also found uses in protective clothing for some trades, such as heavy aprons for smiths. According to a later ordinance in 1638, orphaned boys were "to be clothed in leather and woolen cloth, cloaks of dark blue *Meixner*, hose, shoes, and so forth."[7] Girls wore black woolen aprons over "dresses of red and green cloth all according to need." Leather trousers (*Lederhosen*) continued to be the order of dress for orphan boys everyday of the week with a formal black pair worn to worship on Sundays.[8] Homogeneous dress made of the most durable materials very quickly became characteristic of orphanage life.

The commodities that the provisions and alms offices struggled to acquire and maintain in the largest reserves were those that would absorb the largest share of the orphanage's resources. Foodstuffs alone would require nearly 70 percent of the projected budget, evidence of charity's mission to feed the hungry and of the importance attached to adequate, regular sustenance in a subsistence economy.[9] The children would enjoy a diet that was nourishing. It would be rich in complex carbohydrates supplied by grains and grain products. Animal proteins and fats would be a regular, but modest, feature, with each inhabitant receiving somewhat less than one pfund of meat per week. Fruits and vegetables, mostly in the form of cabbages and turnips, would appear in the menu as well, though neither in great quantities nor with great frequency. Eggs, beans, and dairy products would round out the regular fare. The allowances for diet were intended to sustain life and health at a minimum of expense.

This is not to say that parsimony forebade all festivity. One intriguing entry projected a small expenditure for such "luxuries" as figs, almonds, and grapes. Some allowance would be made for the observance of holidays and other occasions. Stöcklin never indicated how many or how often treats of this sort would be provided or even to whom they would be provided. It was not uncommon for such delicacies to grace only the tables of administrators or other high dignitaries. Whether the orphans enjoyed them or not, however, the founders of the orphanage seem to have been prepared to allow variety in an otherwise regular diet.

Strikingly large sums would be spent on essentials, most notably grains and bread. The city fathers were prepared to pay 53 percent of the total budget, that is, 1,726 fl. annually, for bread, oats, barley, millet, dinkel, and especially rye. Though the orphanage would purchase an unspecified quantity of white bread each week, it would consume far greater amounts of unmilled grains. These might be baked into dark breads or cooked into stews, soups, or gruels.

Large as they bulked in the budget, however, the proposed quantities of grains were none too generous. Assuming a resident population of 208 people in the orphanage and allowing an annual consumption of 160 schaff of rye alone, each adult and child would receive about 6 Metzen (161 liters) of rye per year.[10] If the average monthly requirement of grain per person in an early modern city were 1 metz (27 liters), then Stöcklin prepared to meet only half that need.[11] Even if the calculation included all other types of grain or flour, the total annual grain allowance per person rose to only 7.3 metzen (196 liters), still far short of the estimated average need. Two possible hypotheses suggest themselves: first, Stöcklin pressed for economy without regard for or in ignorance of nutritional needs; second, the projected quantity of grains assumed that children consume less than the average adult. Both were probably true.

Whether stingy or generous, such figures dwarfed those of every other food category. Meat products would be the second largest budgetary item, costing less than one-third the amount annually spent on grains. Lard and meat would be part of the daily fare of the orphanage at a cost of 411 fl., or 12 percent of the annual budget. These comestibles would be augmented by the produce of the orphanage's own livestock; 5 pigs and 10 cows would be kept at a cost of 142 fl. annually. Fruits, vegetables, and eggs would require 65 fl., less than 2 percent of the budget. Drink—estimated at only 20 fl. per year—would be negligible in cost if unspecified in quantity. This is all the more astonishing in light of the fact that beer and wine largely supplanted water in the age before public hygiene, and were an important part of the early modern pharmacopoeia.

THE RISING COST OF ORPHAN CARE

The City Orphanage achieved the foreseen economies of scale in its early years. Annual budgets from the 1570s and 1580s show that the costs of operating a central organization were less than initially forecast and far less than the costs of fostering an equal number of orphans in private homes, owing partly to the fact that food and clothing could be purchased in bulk and shelter could be provided once for all. For example, the City Orphanage spent a mere 947 fl. in 1577, but its expenses rose quickly to 1,546 fl. in 1595 and to 2,248 fl. in 1612.[12] No fiscal mechanism assured that costs would remain low or that funds would be wisely spent. The Alms Office urged but could not compel thrift. By the 1590s, an increased number of orphans drove up the overall costs of maintenance despite economies of scale. As catastrophic inflation gripped Augsburg in the early seventeenth century, the expenses of the orphanage climbed further still. As the costs grew so did the drain on the Alms Office's shrinking resources.

Economies derived in the first place from the scale of the City Orphanage itself. They were not, however, the sole means by which costs would be contained and resources extended. Standardization of attire and diet, implicit assumptions of the 1572 projection, would serve this purpose too. Experience quickly revealed the imponderables of this material regime. Among other factors, orphan demography and price volatility forced administrators to adapt new means to check expenditures.

Monthly accounts give precise information as to the ways in which the orphan fathers met household needs within economic constraints. These records indicate goods and services purchased directly, as opposed to those transferred from city stores. Thus, market activities for 1595, 1680, and 1774—the first two centuries—may be compared, if somewhat crudely.[13]

The demand for goods and services in Augsburg's orphanages was subject, among other things, to the number of orphans and servants in residence. Records indicate that the average number of institutionalized orphans fell, between the sixteenth and the eighteenth centuries, from nearly 300 per month in 1596 to less than 100 in either the Catholic Orphanage or the Lutheran Orphanage between 1680 and 1774 (see Appendix I, Figure 14). Yet, at the same time total expenditures rose (see Appendix I, Figure 15). By 1774, the Lutheran Orphanage paid more to care for 80 children than the City Orphanage had paid to care for 300 in 1595. The average annual cost of supporting and raising a single orphan had risen to nearly 30 fl., triple the expenditure foreseen by Stöcklin in 1572. The question is why.

Monthly expenditures may be grouped by function into four broad categories. Ordinarily orphanages spent money on the orphans, on labor, on the household, and on food. Over the three dates in question, the costs of all four rose steadily despite declining numbers of orphans, clear evidence of the chronic inflation of prices that affected all of Europe during the early modern period.

The costs of caring for the orphans rose sharply between the late sixteenth and late eighteenth centuries, and the Lutheran Orphanage seems to have borne the greater share of this burden (see Appendix I, Figure 16). The cause is hard to isolate; for some reason the Catholic Orphanage simply spent less on its charges.

These expenses included ordinary matters such as bathing, shoeing, clothing, and laundering, as well as extraordinary expenses from sweets and treats, to bleedings and extractions, to tuitions and apprenticeships. Over time, these costs became fewer and simpler. Whereas bathing and laundering were weekly rituals, contracted to independent tradespersons in 1595 and 1612, they became occasional indulgences by 1680 and 1774 that involved external, labor quarterly at most. Though house servants may have assumed some of these chores, which would explain their less frequent mention in the accounts, it is equally possible that the standard of hygiene changed. The cost of clothing and shoes also declined noticeably. In the 1500s, a tailor and cobbler regularly provided for the orphans; their receipts survive and reveal a considerable monthly expense. By the eighteenth century, tailors and cobblers were members of the household staffs, took room and board in the orphanages, and supplied clothing and shoes at a fraction of the earlier costs. The same applies to teachers and seamstresses, those figures from whom the orphans received their earliest educations. In 1577, the City Orphanage paid three German schoolmasters (*Deutscheschulmeister*) and three German schoolmistresses (*Deutscheschulmeisterin*) a basic fee of 6 kr. per student to instruct 33 boys and 16 girls in reading. Seven other boys learned Latin at the Lutheran College of St. Anna. Some evidence even suggests that a few of these orphan students pursued a more advanced course of humanistic studies: two bookbinders billed the City Orphanage for the repair of 12 volumes, including three copies of *Grammatica Graeca* and three copies of *Gnomologias Isocrates*. Like clothing, education was an in-house affair by the late eighteenth century. Services previously contracted from independent masters and mistresses were placed in the hands of a praeceptor and governess, who lived with their charges and taught basic skills for a fixed annual retainer.

One item that drove the cost of childcare upward by 1774 was the rising cost of apprenticeships, about which more later. These expenses increased dramatically, especially for the Lutheran Orphanage, and forced measures designed to limit support for craft training to a fixed sum.

Labor costs, too, rose—for the Lutherans in particular—during the early modern period (see Appendix I, Figure 17). The most notable years are 1612 and 1774, when the orphanage undertook an unusually high number of renovations and repairs. The extremely low figures for 1680 may be explained by the fact that the surviving months run from late August to early January, excluding the summer months that were the peak period for labor in construction and agriculture. The increase in labor costs was, however, more apparent than real. Although the Lutheran Orphanage paid extremely high total wages in 1774, over one-third of its total budget, it employed many more people than at any other time in its history. In 1595, the City Orphanage hired 26 full- and part-time workers, including household staff, contracted craftsmen, and day laborers. The number fell to 20 in 1612 and so marked that year with the highest average wage per worker of any year in the recorded history of the orphanages. By 1774, when total wages were comparable with those of the earlier century, the Lutheran Orphanage managed to employ 75 persons on a permanent or occasional basis, nearly one employee for every orphan. The Catholic Orphanage paid less than one-sixth of its budget to only 37 workers, half of the staff of the Lutheran Orphanage, but for a quarter fewer orphans. This development may be attributed to two causes. First, the permanent staff became increasingly specialized. Second, both orphanages tended to provide the more important or frequently needed services in-house rather than from the marketplace. As noted, tailors, cobblers, teachers, and seamstresses became members of the household. So did physicians and surgeons and possibly even the bathers and launderers. Though sources offer no reasons for the rise of labor, still the likely explanations are economy and discipline. Providing services through in-house staff increased expenses over the short-term but offered administrators greater control over expenses in the long-term. Moreover, wages could be offset through the provision of room and board. Administrators could also exercise greater supervision over an in-house staff. The ordinances of the eighteenth century are no less concerned with the behavior of state employees than with the behavior of state dependents. Measured in wages, labor costs increased in absolute terms but decreased relative to the number of laborers. The orphanages were becoming more labor-intensive.

Over the course of a year, the orphanage employed many craftsmen and laborers. The lists of skills and work required changed little over time but departed starkly from the 1572 projection. Stöcklin had allowed for an in-house staff of only eight persons, supplemented by the services of a cobbler, a tailor, and a seamstress, all at an annual cost of 247 fl., or 7.6 percent of the total budget. This proved conservative. In addition to the regular staff of administrators, teachers, and servants, which quickly exceeded Stöcklin's hopeful estimate, both Catholic and Lutheran orphanages turned to Augsburg's artisanal laborforce for many services. In 1706, for example, the Catholic Orphanage paid wages to glaziers and potters, barbers and bathers, tanners and cobblers, tailors and seamstresses, sweeps and launderers, masons and plasters, coopers and coppersmiths, millers and bakers, herders and day laborers, weavers and dyers, clockmakers and even bell-founders, in short, representatives of nearly every trade an early modern city had to offer.[14] As will be seen, the orphanages not only shaped commodity markets but were considerable organizers of labor.

The cast of laborers appearing in orphanage accounts changed character with the seasons. During the summer, masons, carpenters, and other construction workers made such repairs and alterations as the fabric of the orphanage required. Agricultural laborers harvested hay in the house's fields and tended the house's livestock during the late summer and fall. Butchers slaughtered orphanage livestock in the winter. Day laborers prepared the gardens for planting in the spring.

In addition to these seasonal services, a number of regular and irregular tasks required compensation. A chimneysweep cleared the house's eight chimneys monthly. A fodder-cutter (*Yodschneider*) prepared feed for livestock—cows and pigs—from grain and hay. A glazier repaired tiles on the heating oven in the orphan father's apartment. The occasional or unplanned needs of the orphanage provided opportunities for all sorts of laborers and craftsmen and created all sorts of expenses for the Alms Office.

Like childcare and labor, housekeeping proved more expensive than the original estimates. Stöcklin allowed a meager 25 fl. annually. The real costs were far higher, grew consistently between the late sixteenth and late eighteenth centuries, and affected the Lutheran Orphanage particularly (see Appendix I, Figure 18). Though the cost of housewares declined in general for the Catholic Orphanage between 1680 and 1774, the Lutheran Orphanage paid more than twice its earlier costs. As was the case in any household, the orphanages required housewares and notions constantly. Everything from buttons, thread, and bands for clothing to brooms, ash, and scouring sand (*Fegsand*) for cleaning appeared in the accounts of the orphan fathers. The house purchased paper and ink almost monthly for the use of the governors. On 23 April 1612, the Lutheran Orphanage even paid 2 kr. for a commodity for coloring Easter eggs.[15] Pots, pans, and tableware had to be repaired or replaced at the same rate. These were frequent expenses, part of the normal wear and tear of domestic existence. Such sundries consumed over 10 percent of the Lutheran budget but less than 5 percent of the Catholic (see Appendix I, Figure 18a). In fact, the Catholic Orphanage spent surprisingly little on such mundane but essential items; brooms and soap, for example, almost never appear in its monthly accounts for 1680 and 1774.

This observation awakens the suspicion—shared at the time by Lutheran magistrates—that the Catholic Orphanage may have relied on some kind of organizational connection, perhaps to local monasteries, lay confraternities, or the Cathedral Chapter, to supply certain necessities at no cost. Lacking any similar source of support, the Lutheran Orphanage purchased what it needed in the marketplace. The Lutherans, however, may not have been completely exposed to market forces (see Appendix I, Figures 18b and 18c). Though the Catholic Orphanage spent nothing for cloth, for example, the Lutheran Orphanage spent nothing on tallow. Since the former could no more do without bedding than the latter could forego light, both houses must have exploited some extra-market sources for certain commodities. The city shielded them somewhat from market forces through the agency of its subventions. Donors apparently did the same through contributions in kind. In this respect the Catholic Orphanage enjoyed a relative advantage.

Food accounted for nearly half the monthly expenditures of the City Orphanage in 1595, absorbing even more with the passage of time (see Appendix I, Figure 19). By 1774, the Lutheran Orphanage spent a bit more than 50 percent of its resources on foodstuffs every month, and the Catholic Orphanage devoted an extraordinary 75 percent of its funds to feeding orphans and servants.

Receiving grains and lard from the Alms Office until the late eighteenth century, the orphanages still had to purchase any number of other commodities to provide meals for orphans and servants. In their monthly accounts, the orphan fathers listed the makings of a rudimentary diet.

In 1595, the list was relatively simple. As noted above, the house kept its own dairy herd at this time and did not need to purchase milk products. Likewise, a small amount of meat was produced in house, though not enough to free it from dependence on butchers. Therefore, every month of the year the orphan father purchased beef and veal (*Rind* and *Kalb*). Drink, too, had to be purchased monthly; wine and mead were favored for children and adults alike. Wine was also an essential component of the diet of sick children. Beer appeared not as a regular beverage at house meals but occasionally as a traditional part of the compensation due workers and servants after particularly strenuous labors. The orphans and their keepers ate breads, but the orphanage did not purchase these. Rather, they delivered grain, transferred from the Alms Office, to bakers who had it ground into flour and baked it into bread. Apart from baking charges and occasional gratuities, no money changed hands. Seasonal and occasional foodstuffs rounded out this modest list. Pease or beans and rice or barley were purchased to strengthen a stock or thicken a soup. From late spring to early fall, chicken eggs added protein to the diet. Beginning first in June and lasting until August or September, fresh turnips and cabbage appeared in Augsburg's marketplaces and also in the orphanage's accounts. The orphan father bought pears and plums in August and apples in September, adding appeal to the diet.

By the early seventeenth century, food purchases had changed somewhat, becoming more expensive and more elaborate. Meat, wine, and mead were still the most regular items in the monthly budget. Yet, there were a number of additions. Fish now made occasional appearances in the orphanage. Because quantities were small, rarely more than two pfund (a bit more than a kilogram) in any month, they were probably reserved for the orphan father's table. On holidays, he also enjoyed veal, earlier a staple in the orphanage diet that had been replaced by less expensive fried or roasted meats, possibly sausages (*Bratfleisch*). More beer was drunk by servants and, given the quantities purchased, children in the orphanage. Though most of the bread consumed by orphans still came from the grain supplied by the Alms Office, this was increasingly supplemented by purchases from Augsburg's bakers. Since the demise of the dairy herd in the 1590s, milk had to be purchased, in huge quantities, between 850 and 900 Maß (1,214 and 1,285 liters) monthly.[16]

From the late seventeenth century onward, purchases became more lackluster. Beef and veal, grain and bread, beer and cabbage had become the staple items that appeared in accounts and on the table with striking regularity. Though more limited and disciplined consumption may have been inspired by notions of economy, it hardly served to limit the costs. These spiralled upward throughout the last century of the early modern period.

Most of the food groups that appear in orphanage accounts seem to have shared the tendency to rise in price. Expenditures on meats were sharply higher in 1774 compared to 1680, 1612, or 1595, a fact made even more striking by lower consumption (see Appendix I, Figures 19a and 19b). The same applied to grain-based products, including raw grains, flours, and breads, and fruits and vegetables, most usually apples, pears, and plums along with cabbages and turnips (see Appendix I, Figures 19c and 19d and Figures 19h and 19i). Prices for these groups rose at the same time that volumes fell.

Beer and dairy products constitute two interesting and interrelated exceptions. Expenditures for beer rose between the sixteenth and eighteenth centuries, but so did consumption (see Appendix I, Figures 19e and 19f). Lutherans paid more but drank less. Catholics, however, drank unusually large quantities of beer; it was the standard beverage for servants and orphans alike in 1774. If the Lutheran Orphanage did not rely on beer to quench thirst, then the question remains of what they drank. Wine no longer figured as substantially in their budgets as in the late sixteenth century (see Appendix I, Figure 19g). Though dairy products had been a very prominent feature of the monthly accounts in earlier years, milk, too, was no longer consumed. Lutherans served no dairy products in any form to the orphans; Catholics purchased only a modest quantity of cheese as a collation on Fridays. The drinking habits of both orphanages had apparently changed.

Like childcare, labor, and housekeeping, food cost differentials were distinctly confession-specific. Catholic and Lutheran administrators alike attended the city's markets on Saturdays to buy the week's supply of meat, bread, and beer. The Catholic Orphanage, however, boasted a more generous table. Though housing fewer dependents, it consumed larger quantities of meat, dairy products, and beer as well as nearly equal quantities of grains. The Lutherans outdid their rivals only in the category of fruits and vegetables. The Catholics served fish on Fridays, a thing unknown on any day of the week in the Lutheran house. Again, the possibility arises that the Catholic Orphanage enjoyed direct or indirect support from other Catholic institutions, that is, that it received support in the form of commodities or services from monasteries, confraternities, or the diocese. The Lutherans met most of their needs in the marketplaces of Augsburg. There they paid disproportionately greater sums to maintain their organization, provide for their orphans, and compensate their workers.

THE PURCHASE OF GOODS AND SERVICES

Regardless of confession-specific advantages or disadvantages, Augsburg's orphanages all suffered a steady increase in operating costs. The overall expansion in the monthly accounts was driven by two factors. First, the chronic inflation of the early modern period increased unit costs for most commodities. Larger sums of money purchased smaller quantities of goods. Between 1595 and 1612, for example, the price paid by the City Orphanage for a pfund of beef rose from 9 pf. (*Pfennig*) to 12 pf. By 1680, Catholic and Lutheran orphanages paid 5 kr. or 17.5 pf., and by 1774 the price per pfund of beef had risen to 6.5 kr., or 22.75 pf. For one maß of brown beer the orphanages paid 10 pf. in 1680. Compared to prices paid by the Hospital of the Holy Spirit, the orphanages paid approximately the going rates for most commodities.[17] Second, the orphanages purchased a broader range of commodities directly from the city's marketplaces. An examination of only the earliest accounts indicates that a state orphanage was a far more ambitious and complicated undertaking than its founders realized.[18] As extra-market transfers ended, both orphanages were driven further into the city's marketplaces and exposed to market forces. Simplicity and efficiency were the products of time and experience.

Unlike the Alms Office, which was a much larger organization and could use its size and resources to shape commodity markets, the orphanages never exercised the same control. While buying many goods in substantial quantities, their demand never dominated markets. Except for certain non-perishable goods, such as grain or lard, the orphanages maintained no stores as hedges against sudden scarcity and inflation. Neither, apparently, did the orphan fathers go outside the city's marketplaces, taking advantage of market information to secure goods and services at rates below the market. Yet, they managed to acquire commodities at stable, competitive prices. Beef and milk, for example, cost the orphanage exactly the average market prices; these remained fixed in a period noted for price instability. To accomplish this, the orphanages relied on contracting to establish long-term commercial relationships.

In 1577, a number of craftsmen and shopkeepers regularly served the needs of the orphanage.[19] They exercised an exclusive right to supply the City Orphanage during the fiscal year of 1577 and perhaps beyond. Relationships of this sort signify more than the normal combination of habit and loyalty that frequently grows between consumers and producers. There were many occasional services and purchases of this sort as well, but the shopkeepers (*Krämer*), herbalists (*Kräutler*), and laborers (*Tagwerker*) did not merit a mention by name. Cobblers, tailors, and bakers, on the other hand, provided the orphanage more important goods at greater expense. Accounts, therefore, recorded not only their names but also the exact extent of their dealings. In the fiscal month from mid-April to mid-May, Jacob Bockh baked 803 loaves from 7.5 schaff of flour. According to the same account, Michael Eberhart and his wife fashioned 33 articles of clothing (24 blouses, 8 aprons, and 1 petticoat) from cloth supplied by the Alms Office. Hans Hainrich wove linen dish towels from the homespun created by the orphans themselves. Bernhart Hartmannsberger made 60 ceramic milk mugs, green on the outside and white on the inside. The following month, Michael Frey delivered 73 pair of new shoes and 51 pair of repaired shoes, providing footwear for nearly all the orphans at one time. If not inexpensive, they had the virtue of stability. A blouse with a ruff cost 3 kr.; with a flat collar the price fell to 2 kr. For a pair of new shoes Frey charged 15.5 kr. Prices for all of these items never varied over the period in which a supplier served the orphanage. The evidence suggests that the orphanage contracted for essential goods and services, so achieving through the effective use of market relations what the Alms Office achieved through the manipulation of market conditions.

By 1612 the names had changed but the essential character of orphanage purchasing remained the same.[20] Eustachius Lutz supplied over 800 pfund (370–393 kg.) of beef at 12 pf. the pfund (up from 8 pf. in 1577), as well as smaller amounts of roasting meats and veal every month. Jörg Lotter baked breads. Every month Jörg Mausihler and Joachim Pfefferlin supplied nearly 500 maß (714 liters) of milk for 1 kr. per maß. Thomas Bogner wove homespun, and Caspar Kesseler sewed clothing. Jörg Schreier cobbled shoes for the orphans, charging 20.5 kr. for a new pair, 5 kr. more than in 1577. Again, these craftsmen delivered large consignments of goods at prices that never varied over the year.

Accounts do not permit a more detailed view of the effects of contracting. By 1680, the names of merchants, shopkeepers, and craftsmen had largely disappeared from the accounts. Many services once provided by independent contractors were performed by an expanded in-house staff in the eighteenth century. As noted, the tailor and cobbler joined the praeceptor and seamstress as permanent members of orphanage households. Rather than the usual piece rate for goods or services, they received an annual wage plus room and board. Their duties changed as well to include housekeeping and childrearing responsibilities in addition to the performance of their craft or profession. Whether contracting ceased altogether is uncertain.

Certain calculations in the acquisition of commodities are not entirely clear. The records do not reveal whether the City Orphanage dissolved established relationships in periods of deflation in order to create new, more advantageous one. Neither do they indicate whether the orphan fathers deliberately sought these relationships as a protection against price increases. Contracting did, however, have immediate implications for Augsburg's orphanages and their inhabitants. It was a reasonable means of maintaining a balance between material resources and material needs, between inputs and outputs, in periods of extreme economic instability.

Contracted commodities tended to be uniform. The accounts show a variety of goods that gradually shrank to a few standard items. Repeated purchases of the same goods in very nearly the same quantities were a sign of planning on the part of the orphan fathers. They eased potential problems of supply and cost. In short, standardization offered the same efficiencies and economies in the early modern period as in the modern period. It also created a material regime within the orphanage that was uniform and routine.

CONSUMPTION, STANDARDIZATION, AND DISCIPLINE

Changing patterns of food purchases not only reveal the course of standardization and routinization but also suggest their consequences. As inferred from the projected budget of 1572 and the accounts from later years, the diet of Augsburg's orphans was high in carbohydrates and fats and relatively low in proteins, vitamins, and minerals.[21] Though these records indicated the foodstuffs placed at the disposal of the orphanage, they gave little information about the types of food actually consumed by orphans, and did not compare them to those which they might have received in private households. These records also indicated an increased uniformity and regularity of commodity consumption, rooted in economic considerations, the need to limit costs and maximize resources.

The demand for and consumption of goods cannot be separated from their various uses and the importance attached to them. Based on conformity and custom, they constitute a discipline in themselves. Such considerations digress from the general topic of commodities and commodity markets. Nonetheless, the texture of material life in the orphanage, the feel of which was captured in weekly menus, inculcated orphans with the virtues that went beyond parsimony to efficiency and thrift in the use of goods. It encouraged a step away from *Schlaraffenland*, where every desire was gratified, to a place where appetites and needs were a matter of calculation. A brief reflection on menus in and out of organizations may clarify the notion of charity as a force in the marketplace and commodities as a source of discipline.

The 1572 projection of goods and services for an orphanage corresponded fairly closely to the needs of an artisanal household of the same period. A 1596 estimate of weekly domestic expenses among Augsburg bakers indicated a larger portion of the budget devoted to household expenses than were estimated for an orphanage [22] (see Table 6.2). The author of the baker's estimate listed no expenditures for items such as housewares, light, and heat, but rents consumed over 15 percent of the budget. By contrast, the Alms Office owned the building that would house the orphanage and made it available at no charge. A baker's family devoted a proportionately smaller amount to clothing than would an orphanage, a consequence perhaps of the extraordinary need for shoes and clothing among a large group of growing

TABLE 6.2
Comparison of Expenses for Private and Public Households

COMMODITIES	FAMILY, 1596	ORPHANAGE, 1572	ORPHANAGE, 1595
Grains	23.0%	52.1%	0.7%
Meats	40.0%	13.0%	35.3%
Milk, eggs	4.6%	3.5%*	0.2%
Vegetables	4.6%	2.0%†	11.7%
Wine, beer	—	0.6%	0.2%
Foods (total)	72.2%	71.2%	53.4%
Clothing, shoes	12.3%	22.0%	8.7%
Rent	15.4%	—	—
Light, heat	—	3.5%	3.7%
Housewares	—	0.8%	6.4%
Shelter (total)	15.4%	4.3%	10.1%

* Milk only
† Vegetables and eggs

children. Interestingly, however, the proportions of the "household" budgets expended for foodstuffs were almost equal, albeit with striking differences in diet.

A comparison with the 1595 budget of the City Orphanage indicates that state organizations enjoyed a different set of advantages and disadvantages relative to private households. Housekeeping in the City Orphanage, for example, proved less expensive than in a baker's family but more expensive than planned, owing largely to the unique situation of the building and its inhabitants. The orphanage spent nothing on rent. Neither did fuel constitute an expense; the city provided wood at no charge. The figure listed represented the cost of tallow only. The difference was the unexpectedly high costs of housewares. Clothing, however, proved less expensive for the City Orphanage than for the baker's family and much less expensive than projected in 1572, a probable function of economies of scale. The most interesting point of departure was the expense of food. Here the organization enjoyed the greatest advantage.

The artisanal family spent more money on food, especially on grains and meat. The City Orphanage could lower its costs by purchasing in bulk and by transferring provisions from Alms and Provisions Office stores. The differences may also have stemmed from the desire of orphanage administrators to control costs by consuming less expensive foodstuffs, such as grains. Of interest as well is the relatively small amount of money allotted to drink. For reasons unknown, the author of the bakers' statement deliberately omitted wine and beer. Doubtless many consumers, especially children and servants, usually drank milk or water, but the 1596 estimate misrepresented artisanal preferences just as the 1572 projection underestimated orphanage needs.

The earliest reference to actual meals, contained in an ordinance concerning the governance of orphans, dated 21 January 1638, offered only the most general and simplest of guidelines[23] (see Appendix II). Over the course of a week the orphans were to receive minimal amounts of certain foods. Three times each week, they would eat meat, sauce, noodles, cabbage, oatmeal, beans, barley, plums, rice, and dried fruit. The actual menus were left to the imagination of the cooks and the limits imposed by budget and season. Evening meals had to include soup, roast, bread, and beer. Holidays would be marked by festive meals of soup, meat, bread, pudding, and beer.

The basic foods prescribed for Augsburg's orphans in 1638 did not differ greatly from the foodstuffs proposed in 1572, but the ordinance of 1638 offered a certain flexibility. It set the outer limits of the diet—those foods which had to be eaten over a week's time—but left the actual preparation and combination to the cook's discretion. Economy, nourishment, and entertainment were not mutually exclusive, whatever the importance attached to each. Moreover, holidays and evenings would be more festive with meat, beer, and the occasional sweet. Even in the straitened circumstances of the 1630s, the administrators of Augsburg's orphanage clearly intended to feed their children well.

A change marked the purchase and consumption of foodstuffs by the second half of the seventeenth century. A specification ca. 1660 listed the principal meals of the day, prepared in the Lutheran Orphanage[24] (see Appendix II). Though dietary parameters were comparable, the flexibility and spontaneity of the menu had disappeared. In their place, uniformity and regularity ruled.

On Sundays the orphans received a soup made from a meat stock with noodles (*Spatzenbrühe*) and a rice pudding at noon. If there were no milk, either because it had spoiled or been consumed, beer or sliced apples would replace the pudding. In the evening they ate soup and beef. On Monday the fare varied little. The midday meal was a meat soup accompanied by an oat porridge, and the evening meal featured a dish of thick noodles made from dough and cooked with kraut and turnips (*geschupffte Notteln*). At noon on Tuesdays the children ate soup prepared from the stock used to cook Monday's evening meal and served with "well cooked" lentils. The evening meal was soup and beef, again. On Wednesdays a new dish appeared, a soup (*Brandsuppe*) that incorporated roasted (*gebrante*) semolina to which chunks of rye bread had been added, served with either a fruit sauce or baked plums. That evening the children ate meat soup thickened with barley. This delicacy, accompanied by rye bread spread with lard, was repeated on Thursday. In the evening the children received soup and beef for the third time in five days. The midday meal on Fridays was a meat soup with well-cooked beans or, in winter, Bavarian turnips. That evening the children ate soup with small noodles made from baked dough (*Knöpflen*). At noon on Saturdays the leftovers were added to a soup and served with sauerkraut. The day ended with a noodle made from cooked batter that was either roasted or served in a stock. Noodle stock formed the basic ingredient for the Sunday meal, and the culinary cycle began again.

Lutheran orphans could mark the days of the week by the regular appearance of certain dishes and meals. Although administrators allowed no variety from week to week, exceptions were made on feast and wash days. For holidays, the cook prepared a sweet cake (*Kugelhopf*), provided that dishes involving flour were already planned for the day. The inference is that flour might not be consumed as a treat unless it were also to be used in the meal. For wash days, baked noodles replaced cooked ones. The reason for this is obscure unless the intent were to balance the physical humors of the children by avoiding too much water. A degree of repetitiveness lent itself to the efficiency of a fixed, simple menu. For example, the soup served with beef for supper on Thursday was used to create a stock at noon on Friday. Leftover noodles from Friday evening thickened a soup for the midday meal on Saturday. The stock used to prepare noodles on Saturday night provided the basis for a soup on Sunday. And so it went through the weeks with very little wasted food and even less wasted effort.

Efficiency yielded a diet that may not have been prized for entertainment but possessed undeniable value as nourishment. Immediately apparent in this meal specification is the lack of reference to drink. Its authors simply left the matter implicit; the organization purchased beer and wine in quantity. The meals themselves were simple, with a few simple dishes made from a few basic ingredients. The children consumed grains in the form of noodles and porridges, and what meat they received usually arrived cooked in stocks and soups. Some of these, especially with different forms of noodles, still grace traditional Swabian and Bavarian cuisine. Orphanage fare in fact was composed largely of carbohydrates and fats. Fruits and vegetables rounded out the diet at regular intervals, the former served each Wednesday and occasionally on Sunday, the latter eaten only somewhat more frequently on Tuesdays, Fridays, and Saturdays. As the commodity and budget estimate of 1572 implied and the comparison with a baker's household confirmed, institutional cooking was less expensive but as nourishing as that of most homes.

Though the menus allow an occasional indulgence or extravagance, still it remains unclear who benefitted. Both orphanages regularly purchased spices. These might have been reserved for the orphan father's table, but they conceivably added a bit of zest to the common fare too. In August of 1680,

Sebastian Biberger sold a consignment of spices to the Catholic Orphanage that included pepper, ginger, nutmeg, cinnamon, clove, cream of tartar, almonds, and two types of sugar.[25] These luxuries became increasingly unusual with time.

By the late seventeenth century, the prescribed menus had become still more specific[26] (see Appendix II). The administrators allowed variation, but the variables were specified. For the first time, breakfasts—a simple piece of bread eaten at about eight o'clock in the morning—were listed as part of the daily fare. Contrary to earlier menus in the Lutheran Orphanage, this one also included a piece of bread served to each child at four o'clock as an afternoon snack.

Apart from these innovations, the menus of the late seventeenth century displayed remarkable continuity with their predecessors. The midday and evening meals continued to be the principal ones of each day. Midday meals became more predictable, certain menus occurred not once but several times each week. Evenings usually featured soup and bread. The reason may have been based on folk wisdom and twice-told tales that understood intuitively the dietary advantages of light, easily digestible meals late in the day. They may also have had to do with the lack of storage and preservatives; soups provided the best means to combine varieties of leftover foodstuffs and avoid losses due to waste or spoilage. As with all other menus, which worked from the same basic repertoire of dishes, the emphasis seems to have been on economy and efficiency at the expense of variety and nourishment.

By the early eighteenth century, meals in the Lutheran Orphanage retained their predictability but for the gradual disappearance of bread from the menu[27] (see Appendix II). Although the weekly menu made no further mention of breakfasts or snacks, these probably took place as usual. Midday and evening meals were tersely described and continued along familiar lines. Apart from the variety—not to mention the essential nutrients—afforded by seasonal fruits and vegetables, such as white cabbage, white or Bavarian turnips, and pears, only the sick enjoyed any release from the routine. According to the menu, these alone might have other food, cooked and served "according to the dictates of need." Likewise only the sick received an allowance of beer. The 7 maß (10 liters) allowed them weekly were the only beer drunk by Lutheran orphans except on holidays.

It is impossible to know or even guess why certain foods were served at certain times or, for that matter, why certain types of menus gave way to others over the course of time. Patterns persisted. The meals remained extremely simple and displayed an economy of ingredients, of effort, and therefore of cost. The tendency to organize evening meals in such a way as to take advantage of uneaten or unused foodstuffs continued. The avoidance of waste remained a paramount concern of the administrators.

The Orphanage Ordinance of 1780 provides the most detailed prescriptions of diet and foodstuffs in the Lutheran Orphanage[28] (see Appendix II). A statement of reform that set forth in detail every aspect of orphanage function and discipline, it demonstrated considerable continuity with the past, at least in this matter.

Like earlier menus, the 1780 ordinance listed meals to be served daily to orphans and servants in the house. Unlike that of 1638, however, the latest allowed no flexibility or variation. No aspect of diet could be changed without the advice and consent of the administrators and overseers. The meals set forth thus unalterably fell into the usual pattern. A 1784 menu from the Catholic Orphanage—the only one from that organization that survives—is very similar to those that had become the rule for the Lutheran house: a soup in the morning; meat or meatless meals at midday; bread in the afternoon; soup and bread at night.[29] It was, with almost no exceptions, the fare that had been standard in the orphanages since the early 1600s.

In contrast to those earlier menus, which were presented without elaboration or explanation, the Lutheran ordinance of 1780 went into considerable detail on matters of preparation, hygiene, etiquette, and consumption. Accordingly, it not only set the progression of dishes to be served daily but also instructed governors, cooks, servants, and orphans on all matters relevant to the handling of food. Beyond economy and efficiency, which had always inspired thinking about diet and shaped the consumption of commodities in the orphanages, a discipline based on uniformity, thrift, regularity, and obedience had taken shape by 1780.

An unvarying progression of meals reduced the efforts required of servants by facilitating planning and limiting preparation. For instance, the cook was expected to provide only one hot meal daily (presumably the midday meal), which served as the basis for other meals later in the day or week. The rule also supported minimal culinary and hygenic standards by simplifying cooking to a few basic tasks and reducing scullery work as much as possible. The administrators' required that hot meals be cleanly and well cooked. The copper kettles, in which most foods were cooked, were to be kept clean.[30] Moreover, the principal members of the staff—the teacher (*Praeceptor*) for boys, the governess (*Aufseherin*) for girls, and the sick-maid (*Krankenmagd*) for the infirm—bore the responsibility for inspecting food as it came from the kitchen to ensure that it was in no way lacking, that it was prepared and served according to regulation, and that the children had clean tableware with which to eat it.

At the same time, uniformity simplified the acquisition of commodities and reduced their costs by encouraging administrators to contract for supplies and to purchase in bulk. The ordinance of 1780 prohibited the cook in the Lutheran Orphanage from deviating in the least from the prescribed menu.³¹ This enhanced economies of scale and long-term market relations, both of which assured supplies and reduced costs. Meat, bread, and milk, for example, were purchased once weekly from the same suppliers. It might also have reduced waste by permitting administrators to adjust the purchase of supplies to match more closely the actual pattern of consumption in the house. To simplify preparation and reduce waste, for example, the ordinance specified that the butcher would deliver meats in convenient chunks—one-pfund pieces for children and two-pfund pieces for adults. By the same token, the orphan father was expected to order bread from the baker at such a time that it was neither too old, dry, and weak, nor too fresh, moist, and soft when served. Although there is no clear evidence that such fine tuning actually occurred, its possibility suggests an awareness of planning and a reliance on calculation that characterized the economic activities of both orphanages.

By preventing flexibility, uniformity could have been a double-edged sword. Orphanage accounts are striking for their extreme standardization over time. Types, volumes, and prices of commodities changed little, suggesting that administrators depended on their city regulations, long-term relationships, and open-ended subsidies rather than market conditions to guide their food purchases. A report of 1780 noted that the Lutheran orphan father had since 1772 been purchasing flour from an individual identified only as Holzbaur.³² This had resulted in considerable added expense for the orphanage; whereas the Alms Office paid 34 kr. per schaff of flour, the orphanage paid more than twice as much, 74 kr. The report also focused on the baking of bread. In what may have been a masterpiece of understatement, the administrators admitted that the bread was "not bad but not nearly so good and tasty as bread purchased from a baker."³³ Baking had hitherto been entrusted to the house servant (*Hausknecht*), who confessed that he had trouble sometimes with mixing and kneading, and sometimes with baking, resulting in bread that was "really bad." The authorities suspected that the source of the difficulties had to do less with his incompetence than with the quality of the flour.³⁴ In sum, quality was poor, quantity was small, and costs were high. The report suggested trading with Master Bellman, a baker who charged 32 kr. per schaff of wheat and delivered 76 loaves from each schaff. The limits placed on subsidies in 1788 may be understood, therefore, as an attempt to force the administrators of charity to attend more closely to the markets for basic commodities. Prior to the fiscal reforms of 1788, however, opportunities based on over-supply or competitive pricing were either not recognized or not seized. The administrators preserved at all costs the uniformity that had been intrinsic to the diet of Lutheran orphans since the early seventeenth century.

Standardization and routinization constituted the works of a clock-like discipline. Meals occurred at strictly set times each day, at noon and seven o'clock on weekdays and at eleven and six o'clock on Sundays.[35] In addition, children and staff took a breakfast of bread and soup every day immediately after morning prayers and received a mid-afternoon snack of bread at four o'clock. At these times all children and staff were required to be present and to dine together.

Holiday meals in the form of beer, roast meats, white bread, and the occasional sweet formed the only relief from this strict regime. All children received one-half maß (0.714 liter, nearly the volume of a standard bottle of wine) of a light beer brewed from malted wheat rather than barley (Weißbier), white bread, and roasted meat in the evenings of Easter, Pentecost, the greater and lesser celebrations of the end of the Thirty Years' War (Friedensfeste), Christmas, the Feast of St. Jacob, the Sunday after the Feast of St. Martin, and so forth.[36] Some holidays stood out particularly because of special dishes prepared at no other time.[37] Children and servants must have greeted with special joy a cake on Shrove Tuesday (Faßnacht), a sweet porridge on the Feast of St. James, or a traditional cookie made from apples, nuts, and chestnuts (Lebkuchen) on Christmas. The greatest occasion of all, however, may well have been the children's peace celebration (Kinderfriedensfest), in the summer of each year. On that day of days, the orphans left the city to stroll and picnic on beer, bread and one-eighth maß of wine (Achterle) in the Siebentischlerwald, a forest to the south of Augsburg and still a beloved locale for a Sunday outing. Yet, these rare celebrations served to highlight a diet characterized throughout the year by an unswerving uniformity and a hidebound economy.

Thrift, understood as the avoidance of unnecessary expense and waste, was the reason for uniformity and regularity even as it was the genius inspiring the diet and, indeed, the acquisition of all commodities in the Lutheran Orphanage. Whatever the potential costs of inflexible planning, the entire process of purchasing, cooking, and serving food was organized not only to achieve cost effectiveness for the house but also to teach thrift as a virtue by demonstration and example.

Though careful regulation of the size of portions reinforced the uniformity of diet, it also embodied the distinctions between persons and the virtue of submission. On those days when meat was served, the orphan father and his household received one pfund of beef per person; servants and older orphans who assisted in housekeeping received two-thirds pfund; and younger children received one-third pfund without regard to gender. The orphan mother oversaw the serving of meat to assure that each person, especially the children, got just their alloted share.[38] The same guidelines governed the portions of bread and beer. With the exception of the tailor, who received his daily allotment of one-third loaf (1.5 pfund) of bread all at once because of the unusual circumstance that he resided outside the house, members of the orphanage received bread four times daily: in the morning, at noon, in the afternoon, and in the evening. The orphan father received 6 kr. worth of white bread daily compared to the boys' teacher, who received 1 kr. worth. Children and other servants received so much less that their bread was measured by a jeweler's weight rather than by cash value. The house servant went from table to table asking each person whether they wanted bread and cutting it only for those who wished it.[39] Servants received a six-*Lott* (about 90 gr.) slice and children a portion weighing three lott (about 45 gr.).[40] Again, the point was to prevent waste. Beer, too, was served regularly and generously at the orphan father's table. He received one maß of barley or wheat beer daily as he wished.[41] Only on holidays or after specified tasks did children or servants partake. At those times, the usual shares were observed: servants and older children received one maß, and youngsters got one-half maß each.[42] Meals, then, were a daily exercise in the rigors of hierarchy.

If the shared experiences of a common table bred a sense of communality and familiarity, the marks of privilege served as a constant reminder of distinctions in age, gender, and authority that were intrinsic to a ranked society of orders. Those who were older or more powerful received more or different foods or sat at separate tables. Despite a certain solidarity, born of meals shared with a circle of compatriots, therefore, the physical and dietary lines of demarcation may have militated toward obedience to authority and encouraged submission to one's condition.

The discipline of commodities was woven seamlessly into the fabric of daily life within the orphanages. Their walls marked the line of demarcation between a world of feast and famine and a regime of uniformity and regularity. For administrators these were the key to a planned, cost-effective approach to commodities. Predictable needs encouraged long-term commercial relations. For orphans, regularity and uniformity fettered unrealistic expectations even as they fostered sober habits. The privileges of rank, in the orphanages no less than in society, accustomed them to inequality as part of the natural order; the lack of want that stopped short of surfeit encouraged a calculating attitude toward material goods.

Yet, the rhythm of orphanage routine was not without irregularities. The implicit contradiction between a world accepted as fixed and behavior designed to alter it either escaped the notice of contemporaries or struck them as unavoidable. In this, the orphanages reflected the society of which they were part. The fascination of early modern commentators with rank and hierarchy suggests an awareness that these were by no means permanent. In the closing of its patriciate, the striving of its merchants, and the grumbling of its commoners, Augsburg experienced tensions between stability and mobility, between the fixed status accorded birthright and the fluid change of circumstance. It comes as no surprise, therefore, that the orphanages captured something of the incongruity of their day and reinforced deference to social hierarchy while teaching elements of a capitalistic individualism.

WASTE AS DEVIANCE

Lutheran administrators characterized orphanage discipline as that "so necessary uniformity" not only because it preserved economy but also because it shaped behavior.[43] It would curb expectations and limit appetites. Strict regulations on the size of portions and the avoidance of waste would inculcate a sense of commodities both as consumables and as capital, as things of value beyond their immediate uses. Through distinctions observed in diet the children would learn to recognize and accept as inevitable the distinctions that separated and ranked groups in society according to their access to more or less of the community's goods. If the discipline of commodities was passive, a matter of routine, it had an active element as well that regulated behavior through a series of sanctions to punish violations.

The Orphanage Ordinance of 1780 captured this process nicely. It stated specifically, for instance, that the staff was to prepare and serve, willingly and without greed or jealousy, sufficient food to satisfy the appetites of the children in their charge but not to encourage gluttony.[44] The administrators intended to resolve two problems in this way. First were the governors who misused their authority. The orphan father at the time was infamous for his stingy servings of food. He "withheld bread from his wife so that she was unable to give a poor orphan an extra piece on request and cursed the bread into the throat of the poor children when such a request was referred to him."[45] Perhaps for this reason, too, they placed the bread knife in the hands of the house servant and set specific weights for bread due to each person in the orphanage at each meal. Second were the children who misbehaved. Orphans were to "remain healthy" but not "be raised rapaciously." Again, the administrators admitted freely that servings of bread in the Lutheran Orphanage were "noticeably small but it was preferable to leave them so."[46] They hoped to strike a balance in which the children would be satisfied enough not to steal but not sated by superabundance.

Punitive as well as preventative measures were conceived to prevent theft and gluttony. Interestingly, earlier ordinances never mentioned food as the cause of misbehavior. Although stealing, over-eating, and careless eating were condemned as practices in young and old alike long before the eighteenth century, they never excited the concern of the governors of charity. In 1791, however, whether out of a concern for economy or a more thorough concept of discipline, the Alms Office published a list of house sanctions

(*Hausstrafen*) that dealt extensively with food. They were to be applied by the orphan father in cases of notorious misbehavior, possibly a sign that the less restrictive measures put forth in 1780 had not achieved the desired results.[47] Theft of any sort was to be reported to the highest authorities for immediate adjudication, an indication of the seriousness with which this crime was treated.[48] Although no fixed punishments were mandated, the stolen goods were confiscated, and each case was handled according to the specifics of the incident and the persons involved. This meant that the entire range of orphanage sanctions might be called into play, from warnings to beatings, from imprisonment to expulsion. The schedule of penalties described insatiability as "this damaging vice," and it left punishment to the discretion of the administrators in all cases that were not the result of ill health. Sanctions might range from a warning, to denial of food, to imprisonment in the closet or space set aside as the orphanage's jail (*Hauscarcer*). Similarly, drunkenness was punished severely.[49] When an incident revealed no force of habit or degradation of person, it might be met with a stern lecture on the evils of drink. More stubborn cases merited imprisonment, beatings, or banishment according to the nature of the offense. The other extreme—picky or finicky eaters—faced the possibility of a tongue lashing or a period of little or nothing to eat.[50] Orphans who deliberately ruined the food they were served might be warned, beaten, or imprisoned.[51]

These problems were not limited to the poor. Administrators and servants alike might indulge in drunkenness and gluttony or commit theft and embezzlement to the detriment of the city and its resources. The 1780 ordinance offered servants a fourth meal of soup and bread nightly that the orphans themselves did not receive.[52] Here, too, the concern of the administrators was less dietary than disciplinary. Orphanage servants maintained a black market in orphanage stores, regularly stealing and selling uncooked and leftover foodstuffs from the house's pantries. "In order to prevent the otherwise so common theft and sale of food by the servants," the suspected culprits would be encouraged to eat more.[53] In a regime that neither starved nor satisfied, this extra meal may well have been a mark of distinction much envied by those who did not enjoy it. In other respects, it was a curious acknowledgment of the material circumstances surrounding what would otherwise be treated as a most serious crime.

The commodities of the orphanages of Augsburg were public resources, the conservation of which was pursued and the loss of which was to be avoided. So understood, theft or misappropriation of these goods by the staff of the orphanage was more than simple theft. It was a violation of trust. For this reason, it was listed among the misdeeds set forth by Georg Paul Hörn in his 1761 *Betrugs-Lexikon* (Swindle Lexicon), a copy of which was kept by the administrators of the Alms Office. Hörn listed eight common offenses regularly commited by orphan fathers and mothers in violation of their offices. Among these were the misappropriation of orphanage food and clothing for their own use and profit or the falsification of commodity accounts to claim greater costs than were actually disbursed. Throughout the late seventeenth and eighteenth centuries, both the Lutheran and Catholic orphanages were beset by irregularities in the office of the orphan fathers. Though malfeasance was never directly proven in any single case, two fathers were removed from office for questionable practices. The reforms of the eighteenth century, including the 1780 ordinance, followed the line suggested by Hörn, that such offenses were best prevented and discipline best maintained through the careful appointment of honorable officials and the close inspection and regulation of their activities.[54] As such, the discipline that surrounded all commodities, especially food, in the orphanages, was not limited to the shaping of a hierarchical society, but included the recasting of an authoritarian state. Its intent exceeded accustoming orphans to their place to include quickening officials to the dictates of efficiency.

CONCLUSION

Commodity transactions resulted in the slow accumulation of experience and knowledge that could be applied systematically beyond the arena of economic action. Although an individual or organizational virtue, a disciplined consumption that achieved satisfaction and avoided starvation and immoderation alike originated in markets where institutional constraints, such as production, transportation, and regulation, determined supply and price. The administrators of Augsburg's charity understood full well that commodities subject market conditions could be manipulated to achieve the twin desiderata of limited costs and maximized resources.

The Provisions Office used supply to regulate price. Its agents ranged across Europe to accumulate stockpiles of essential commodities for which demand was inelastic. The magistrates grasped the relationship between the volume of goods in trade and the price of those goods in the marketplace and used it to limit the market's most catastrophic excesses. They sold reserves in times of scarcity and inflation to increase supplies and moderate prices.

The tasks of the Alms Office were related but different. Rather than ensure commodities at affordable prices, the administrators of charity had to care for society's needy. To this end they purchased goods for transfer and redistribution rather than for resale and exchange, relying not on supply to achieve their goal but on market information and cumulative demand. They scoured local and regional markets for necessary commodities and exploited their stature as the single purchasing agent for a large proportion of the Augsburg's entire population. The Alms Office gave Augsburg's poor a stature in the marketplace that they could not have possessed as individuals.

Patterns of acquisition and price differentials indicate that the Alms Office used demand to shape commodity markets, a process made possible by highly sophisticated information on production, supply, and price. The constant need for basic commodities forced its administrators to rely on an awareness of local and regional market conditions to locate supplies, to organize their production and transportation, and ultimately to purchase them at the lowest available rates. By so doing, the Alms Office manipulated market forces to influence the supply and price of commodity in one of Europe's principal economic centers.

As individual organizations, the orphanages lacked the size and resources to affect markets directly in the same manner as the provisions and alms offices. Though able to achieve economies of scale, they were exposed to market conditions in much the same manner as any private household. To acquire large volumes of food, heat, and clothing, as well as other essentials for the care and rearing of children, and to avoid the worst consequences of uncertain supplies and unstable prices, the orphan fathers turned from market conditions to market relations, establishing long-term contracting arrangements with merchants and craftsmen. Such transactions assured regular supplies at market rates even in the most strained circumstances. Like their colleagues and superiors in Augsburg, the orphan fathers used a sophisticated understanding of markets and institutions to achieve particular economic ends. They sought a disciplined approach to market activities, and so influenced the markets themselves.

The practical knowledge, born of capitalistic transactions, extended from the economic to the non-economic sphere. In the course of manipulating and negotiating in markets to purchase goods and services at the lowest possible price, administrators invested commodities with a value beyond their actual utility. Although they never articulated these notions abstractly, the orphan fathers and the alms lords grasped them as a discipline to be exercised in public and to be taught in private. The orphanages exposed children to this disciplinary regime at every turn. Commodities became things of worth to be treated with care and even respect. They were to be used not stingily but sparingly for essential, utilitarian purposes. Wanton destruction or waste was more than a material loss, it was a violation of economic principle elevated to moral imperative. Even as they shaped commodity markets, the orphanages of Augsburg shaped young people thoroughly at home in the market's discipline and thereby prepared them for the harsh realities both of life outside the orphanage and of a world increasingly dominated by market relations.

Notes

1. Changing patterns of consumption and their implications for economic development have recently become the object of historical speculation and research. See, for example, de Vries, "The Industrial Revolution and the Industrious Revolution."
2. StAA, W A1, Notamina, 18. Jhdt, Acta die Abteilung der Fahrnisse im Waisenhaus betreffend, 1649, Relation, 17 July 1649: "... dann wie sonsten in allen Ämtern nur grose Schulden und Ausgaben hiezu aber einige Mittel nicht vorhanden seyn: also seyn dißfalls für beeden Theile mobilia genug da vorhanden...."
3. StAA, W 5, Acta im Sachen den Beitrag des älteren heil. Allmosens an die beiden Waisenhäuser und über deßen Gleichstellung verrichteten Vergleich betr., 1783–95.
4. In Augsburg, merchants distinguished between a *Pfund Schwergewicht* and a *Pfund Leichtgewicht*. The difference was actually minor. The former weighed 490.82 grams and the latter weighed 472.38 grams. The *Klafter* was a special measure of volume for wood, much like the modern cord. It was roughly equivalent to 3 cubic meters. Elsas, *Umriss einer Geschichte der Preise und Löhne in Deutschland*, 154.
5. StAA, W 10, Ain ungefarlicher uberschlag Was ain Waisenhaus Darinnen 200 Kinder Erhalten Mochten werden Jerlich Kosten möcht, 8 April 1572.
6. Roeck, *Bäcker, Brot und Getreide in Augsburg*, 24; Clasen, "Armenfürsorge in Augsburg vor dem Dreißigjährigen Krieg," 105ff.
7. StAA, EW1, Ordnung und Beshaffenheit der Waisenkinder so sich im Waisenhauß befinden allhier in Augspurg, 21 January 1638.

    Von Kleidung.

    1.) Die Knaben werden gekleidt von Leder u. Wüllen tuch, Mändel von einem dunkklen blauen Meixner tuch, Strümpf, Schue.

    2.) Die Mäydlen Brüstlen von shwarzen wüllen tuch, Röck von rothen und grünen tuch alles nach Nothdurfft.

    3.) Alle zwo Wochen wird ihnen geben neu gewashne Leinwad, Hemder, Fatzenet, Krägen, die Better überzogen.

8. StAA, EW 12, Waisenhausordnung, 1780, Articulus XXII, §1–3.
9. Roeck, *Bäcker, Brot und Getreide in Augsburg*, 24–26.
10. 1 schaff = 8 metzen = ca. 215 liters.
11. Roeck, *Bäcker, Brot und Getreide in Ausburg*, 103: "Ein Metzen Brotgetreide monatlich entspricht ziemlich genau dem Durchschnittsbedarf eines Menschen."
12. StAA, W 10, Monatsrechnungen, 1577, 1595, 1612.
13. StAA, W 10, Monatsrechnungen 1595; EW 10, Monatsrechnungen 1612; Alms, Monatsrechnungen 1680, 1774.
14. StAA, KW 13, Jahresrechunung, 1706.
15. StAA, W 10, Monatsrechnung, 12 April–11 May 1612.
16. According to Elsas, the Augsburger *Maß* for beer measured 1.428 liters, a measure that remained constant until the city became part of the Kingdom of Bavaria. Elsas, *Umriss einer Geschichte der Preise und Löhne in Deutschland*, 152.

17. The orphanages paid the same price for beer and approximately 1 kr. more per pfund of beef than did the hospital. These differentials tended to shift somewhat with time. Ibid., 612, 621.
18. StAA, W 10, Monatsrechnungen, 1577, 1612.
19. Ibid., Monatsrechnungen, 1577.
20. Ibid., Monatsrechnungen, 1612.
21. Ibid., Ain ungeferlich Uberschlag Was ain Waisenhauß darinnen 200 Kinder Erhalten Mochten werden Jerlich Kosten Möcht, 1572.
22. StAA, Proviantamt, Bäcker/Getreide, 9 December 1596. The projected domestic expense for an average baker's family in Augsburg is cited in Roeck, *Bäcker, Brot und Getreide in Augsburg*, 27–28:

Ittem ain wochen hauß Zinß	fl. 1
Ain wochen 4 schmaltz	kr. 24 h. 8
Jtem ain wochen drej schlacht täg, vnd auf ein Schlacht tag 12 Rindtfleisch	fl. 1 kr. 32 h. 4
ain wochen 8 Bratfleisch	kr. 24
ain wochen vmb air	kr. 6
ain wochen vmb Ziemes	kr. 6
Jtem ain wochen umb flaisch, in Rieb vnd Kraut	kr. 12
ain wochem vmb Rieb vnd Kraut	kr. 8
Ain wochen vmb Rugges vnd schöns brot dz. ainer mit seim Gesindt braucht, Zue seiner vnderhaltung	fl. 1 kr. 30
Jtem ain wochen, Mann vnd Weib, mit sambt seine kindern mit Re[verenz] zue melden, vmb Schuh und Gewandt an ihren Leib darfür	kr. 48

23. StAA, EW 1, Ordnung und Beshaffenheit der Waisenkinder so sich im Waisenhauß befinden allhier in Augspurg, den 21. Jan. Ao. 1638.
24. Ibid., Specification, s.d. s.a. [ca. 1660].
25. StAA, Alms, Monatsrechnungen, August 1680.
26. StAA, EW 1, Speiß-Ordnung des Evangl. Waÿßenhaüßes, s.d. s.a. [ca. 1690].
27. Ibid., Speißzettel deß Evangel. Waÿsenhaüßes, s.d. s.a. [ca. 1730].
28. StAA, EW 12, Waisenhausordnung, 1780, Articulus XXI, Ordnung wegen der Kost der Domesticken und Kinder. See especially §14.
29. StAA, KWA 16, Samlung aus den katholishen Waisenhauß Ackten über die bedeutendste Gegenstände, 78.
30. StAA, EW 12, Waisenhausordnung, 1780, Articulus XXI, §3. The ordinance revealed indirectly the nature of food preparation. Extensive use of copper kettles for cooking "most foods" implies the prevasive use of soups, stews, and porridges. Even meats were boiled or simmered for the most part. This suggests something of the hygienic problems in the kitchen. The kettles had to be large to provide for 100 or more diners, and the amount of spillage on the floors and counters as well as the task of cleaning were probably considerable. That this was so and that the cook and servants rarely met the expectations of the ad-

ministrators with regard to cleanliness may be inferred from the fact that scrubbing the kettles had to be specifically noted.
31. Ibid., Articulus XXI, §1: "... nur einerley Speise nach dem No. 15 angegebenen Speise Zettel rein u. gut gekocht werden."
32. StAA, EW 7, Bericht der Vorsteher z. hl. Almosen Augustanae Confessionis, 3 August 1780.
33. Ibid.: "Was antrift die Qualität des Brodes, so ist solches, so oft wir es gesehen haben, eben nicht schlecht, doch freylich auch so gut und schmackhaft nicht als das bey becken erkaufte und nach des Hausknechts einenem Geständnis mißräth es manchmal ihm in kneten und zurichten manchmal dem beckun im Ofen und wird also wahrhaftig schlecht...."
34. Ibid.: "... der vermuthlich nach Mullers Gebrauch sogenanntes Mußgetraid dazu abgibt. Auch wird das sogenante Rauhmehl alles hinein gemahlen."
35. StAA, EW 12, Waisenhausordnung, 1780, Articulus XXI, §1.
36. Ibid., Articulus XXI, §10.
37. Ibid., Articulus XXI, §12.
38. Ibid., Articulus XXI, §4. These were measures of edible meat and did not include bone or waste.
39. Ibid., Articulus XXI, §8. Cf. StAA, EW 7, Bericht der Vorsteher z. hl. Almosen Augustanae Confessionis, 3 August 1780. That this task fell to the house servant rather than the orphan father, as established by a ruling in 1750, probably reflected the complex interests of the father and the equally complex realities of the orphanage. The serving of bread was a symbolic act that underscored the orphan father's authority as "father" of orphans. His was the task of providing for them along with the responsibility of disposing of them. Beyond the responsibilities of his office, it was certainly to his advantage to run an efficient and economical house. Yet, given the subsidies provided by the city for basic commodities, the orphan fathers may have been tempted to withhold food, reduce expenditures, and pocket the difference. This sort of graft was the basis of anonymous accusations in the 1720s and 1730s, about which more later.
40. A *Lott* was one thirty-second of a pfund. Because Augsburg maintained two pfund measures, heavy-weight and light-weight, the lott varied from 14.76 gr. light to 15.34 gr. heavy. Elsas, *Unriss einer Geschichte der Preise und Löhne in Deutschland*, 154.
41. StAA, EW 12, Waisenhausordnung, 1780, Articulus XXI, §5.
42. Ibid., Articulus XXI, §10.
43. Ibid., Articulus XXI, §9.
44. Ibid., Articulus XXI, §2: "Soll auch den Waisen die ihnen verordneten Kost jedemal mit gutem Willen ohne Neid u. Geiz gewissenhaft u. im solcher Maaße aufgetragen und zugetheilet werden, daß sie zwar an der einen Seÿte nicht unersättlich gezogen werden, doch aber auch an der andern Seÿte nicht Mangel leiden und hungern dürfen, sondern satt haben und gesund bleiben."
45. StAA, EW 7, Bericht der Vorsteher z. hl. Almosen Augustanae Confessionis, 3 August 1780: "... denn es ist, wie wohl extra judicialiter zu vernehmen gewesen, daß der dermahlige Waisenvater hierinnen gar zu karg und geizig seye, seinem eigenen Weib das Brod verschluße, deswegen sie ausser Stand setzte, einem armen Waisen auf sein Bitten noch ein Stückle weiter zu geben, und wann Bitten der Art an ihm selbst gebracht werden, den armen Kinder das mit Unwillen weiters hergegebene Brod in den Hals hinein fluche."
46. Ibid. "... freylich auffallend klein ist denoch beliebt worden es dabey belassen."

47. StAA, EW 7, Hausstrafen, 10 May 1791.
48. Ibid., Stehlen u. Betrug.
49. Ibid., Völerei u. Trunkenheit.
50. Ibid., Näscherei u. lekerhaftes Wesen: "... gesuchten offt wiederholten Auswahl der täglich vorkommenden Speisen...."
51. Ibid., Muthwilliges Verderben des Brods u. der Speisen.
52. StAA, EW 12, Waisenhausordnung, 1780, Articulus XXI, §9.
53. Ibid.: "... theils um die sonst üblich gewesenen Unterschlief u. Speise-Verkauf bey den dienstbothen vorzubeugen...."
54. StAA, W A1, Die Errichtung, Abtheilung und paritätische Gleichstellung der beiden Waisenhäuser, 1571–1795. Extract copied from Georg Paul Hörn, Betrugs-Lexikon (Koblenz, 1761): "Mittel: daß man gewissenhafte und verständige Leute zu Inspectoren und Pflegern des Waisenhauses setze, welche ordnungsmäßige fleisige Aufsicht über den Waisenvater, dessen Treüe und Redlichkeit man ebenfalls vor seiner Bestellung vergewissert seyn muß und dessen Vorrichtungen führen."

7

Labor and Industry

The relationship between urban poor relief and early modern markets was complex. Charitable organizations influenced markets through transactions that affected supply, demand, and price. Engaged in market activities, these organizations absorbed the rules of economic behavior that prevailed and translated them into a discipline for the needy. Charity, as it influenced the early modern economy, was influenced by it in turn. This was the case in the capital and commodity markets of Augsburg and in the city's labor market as well.

Though never engaged directly in industrial production, the orphanages were always deeply engaged in work and work-related activities. This applied to organized charity in general, although the matter was far from straightforward. The consolidation of the city poor house with a workhouse in 1755 constituted direct attempt to exploit the labor of the poor. The experiment lasted only until 1772. Likewise, the use of day laborers for public works by Augsburg's Construction Office (Bauamt) was likened to charity in its own day.[1] Generally speaking, however, Augsburg did not substitute work for welfare.

Salaries and wages paid to the many officers, servants, and workers of the Alms Office testify to the employed and subcontracted labor required to support the needy (see Appendix I, Figures 8 and 9). As noted above, the orphanage proposal of 1572 foresaw a permanent, full-time staff of eight persons at annual wages of 80 fl., mentioned the services of a cobbler, a tailor, a seamstress, and a praeceptor, and implied the regular services of many others.[2] It made no mention, however, of the many construction workers who renovated and maintained the buildings. Over the years that followed, the city's orphanages emerged as employers on a larger scale than had ever been predicted.

They exercised a profound influence over labor and labor markets through the children who passed through their doors. By providing a consistent structure through which information reached prospective laborers and their masters, these organizations introduced a degree of regularity and order into the otherwise inchoate process of finding work. As places where a supply of workers met the demand for labor, the orphanages became marketplaces in their own right.

THE ORGANIZATION OF ARTISANAL CRAFTS

Augsburg was a great manufacturing center, and to its laborers the city owed not only much of its considerable wealth but also much of its reputation. Of 10,285 taxpayers listed in the tax registers of 1610, 4,586 practiced some kind of artisanal craft.[3] The balance comprised aristocrats, merchants, day laborers, and persons of non-artisanal or unidentifiable occupations. From the fifteenth to the nineteenth centuries artisanal craftsmen, working in small shops, dominated production in Augsburg.

Certainly, large-scale, concentrated manufacturing also existed there throughout the 1700s, first in cotton printing, in which Augsburg held a leading position, then in the production of tobacco products. By the 1770s, the city was home to as many as nine calico manufactories. The owner of the largest mill at that time, Johann Heinrich von Schüle, employed a total of 3,500 persons, 350 of whom labored directly in his mill, and in 1785 produced goods with a gross value over 1,000,000 fl.[4] Although by no means as large or as valuable an industry as textiles, tobacco also achieved an important status as an employer and producer. By the early nineteenth century, over 200 people found employment in tobacco factories that manufactured goods worth 300,000 fl.[5] Though dominated by handicrafts, Augsburg developed into an early center of proto-factory production.

Even on the eve of industrialization, however, these few large concerns did not displace Augsburg's many petty producers.[6] Technically, the factories still relied on handicraft methods and benefitted only from such efficiencies as concentrated production bestowed. The many finishing processes, traditionally executed by different artisans in specialized workshops, were located under a single roof. But improved organization yielded no greater volume of goods. The total production in 1811 of all Augsburg manufactories achieved a value of 1,221,688 fl., a considerable sum in itself, but less impressive when compared, for example, to the 972,000 fl. that flowed from the brewers or the 32,395 fl. pounded out by iron and coppersmiths.[7]

Augsburg's thousands of artisanal masters pursued an astonishing variety of occupations. A survey of 1806 revealed craftsmen and shopkeepers engaged in 118 crafts, up from 71 in 1720.[8] A rough count revealed the same number in 1548 as in 1720. The constitutional reform of 1548 reorganized these individual crafts into some 17 guilds, which fell into six industrial sectors according to the demands they met or the materials they used.[9] Thus, the food, building, clothing, and decorative-arts sectors included those crafts that met demand for certain products. Metal and wood sectors consisted of artisans who used metal or wood as a raw material. Organized in this system of specialized crafts, interlocking guilds, and overlapping sectors, the structure of the artisanal economy in early modern Augsburg appeared straightforward but was, in fact, dauntingly complex.

To begin, the logic of shared methods or materials did not always determine the structure of artisanal production. Crafts that belonged to one sector, by virtue of the demands they met, frequently took their places in another because of the materials they used. Thus, the carpenters (*Zimmerleute*), cabinetmakers (*Schreiner*), book printers (*Buchdrucker*), and bookbinders (*Buchbinder*) were all part of the wood sector, despite the very different goods they produced.

More striking was the example of the Shopkeepers' Guild (*Kramerzunft*). Though formally part of the food sector, they included within their ranks, as their designation suggests, almost anyone engaged in small-scale trade. In the last decades of the eighteenth century, the guild admitted members who pursued at least 46 different crafts and trades.[10] Among these were apothecaries, chemists, and chocolatiers; barometer makers, spectacle makers, and instrument makers; ironmongers, jewelers, and bell founders; map publishers, music publishers, and booksellers. Because almost any trade might take the form of shopkeeping, which required no particular training or qualification, many artisans joined this guild when they saw no prospect of becoming a master or securing a livelihood on their own. This led to a double bind. The representatives of the abandoned guilds complained that the refugees would continue to practice their old crafts under cover of shopkeeping and so form a source of competition outside their guild's jurisdiction. No less fearful and resistant were the shopkeepers themselves, who worried that their growing numbers would increase competition and dilute earnings. The variety and fluidity that characterized Augsburg's shopkeepers rendered the designation uninformative. Nor were the shopkeepers singular in this regard.

Even within more coherent guilds, distinctions of status and function existed. The Bakers' Guild (*Backerzunft*) included 142 members but fewer bake ovens in 1536.[11] In other words, some master bakers depended on the city or their better situated colleagues for access to the fixed capital they themselves did not possess. In 1548, the guild distinguished its members by specialization as well as wealth—the so-called sweet and sour bakers—according to the kinds of dough used and the kinds of products sold. In time, these differences hardened into privileges of association and production. Certain kinds of bakers possessed full rights in the guild (*Vorbäcker*), while their disadvantaged colleagues (*Nachbäcker*) were limited to certain kinds and certain amounts of production. The butchers, who numbered 120 in 1536, in 1548 recognized formally the differences between those who specialized in beef, those who specialized in pork, and those who specialized in roasts and sausages. The Brewers' Guild (*Brauerzunft*) was one of the largest and most prosperous in Augsburg. Among 135 masters, in 1536, were brewers of sweet beers and brewers of sour beers. These specialized branches of the same craft became separate guilds in 1548. Goldsmithing may have been one of the most highly specialized of all crafts. Artisans became masters of specific handling or finishing processes, such as pounding, etching, casting, and drawing. A high degree of fragmentation, therefore, and decentralization characterized many of the city's crafts and trades.

Specialization and subdivision in Augsburg's artisanal economy posed considerable practical problems for the prospective apprentice or journeyman. Simply locating a master who possessed all the qualifications and privileges of his craft could be daunting: No central agency provided information on shops in need of hands. Not until the eighteenth century did Augsburg make use of a work permit or similar artifact to govern employment, like the French *livre de congé* that recorded the bearer's work history. The city lacked a central marketplace for labor, like the *Place de Grève* in early modern Paris, where masters and men might meet. Guild halls could have served this purpose, but records suggest that these associations became involved only after master and man had entered into a working relationship.

To reach that point, most youths, parents, or guardians probably depended on private information, which was limited by the extent of their personal or professional contacts. Johann Dietz described his experience at age fourteen when his father suddenly put the matter before him: "You must go away; now choose today what you want to be."[12] For the young man it was "a time of mental anguish, of mourning and weeping and praying all night long." Because he "dreamed of medicine" Dietz turned to his cousin, Master Schobern, whom he paid 70 thalers for an apprenticeship as a barber surgeon. Because these networks existed outside the public realm, it is impossible to do more than speculate about their efficiency. Without sufficient knowledge of the productive limits or market conditions governing a given master and his craft, apprentices may have entered the workshops of men who were unqualified to teach their craft or whose craft could not provide an adequate livelihood. Journeymen, already initiated in the ways of their craft, faced a different set of constraints. Their own collectives eased the search for work, but the matter might be far more complicated where these were lacking. A foreign journeyman, if unaided by his comrades, had no local knowledge to help him find a position; a local man, knowledgeable about the masters of his craft, still had to negotiate the uncertainties of the market. Many wage laborers eked out a marginal existence by bouncing from one shop to the next. Without some mechanism for supplying labor, the complex structure of Augsburg's artisanal economy worsened the constant struggle to secure and sustain work.

Individual guilds did little to simplify the process. Each had its own set of statutes and internal regulations, which guided every aspect of the production and sale of goods but set only minimal standards for the recruiting, training, and employing of labor. Indeed, the purpose of these was not to promote work but rather to limit the total supply of labor in the craft and so maintain its value.

The Furriers' Ordinance (*Kürschnerordnung*) of Augsburg is a typical case in point.[13] It erected an array of fiscal and administrative barriers to entering the craft. Any person wishing to work as a furrier had to pay steep admission fees as well as meet certain personal and legal qualifications. Candidates had to be of legitimate and honorable birth and possess the right to practice a craft (*Handwerkgerechtigkeit*). Those qualified had to acquire and demonstrate technical competency. This meant an extended period of dependence, first three years as indentured apprentices, then four to six years as wage-earning journeymen. Strict limits on the number of apprentices and journeymen a master could employ simultaneously—never more than one apprentice, three journeymen, and one piece-worker—kept the cohort of new entrants minimal. Piece-rate schedules, which set wages for the working of different types of fur, fixed some of the costs of production and served as an incentive to limit workshop size.

Guild ordinances, like those of the furriers, left relations on the shop floor to the master's discretion. Only the vaguest statute governed the actual training of apprentices: masters were to teach their craft "in an upright and honest manner" (*aufrecht und redlich*) to their apprentices; apprentices were to submit with "the fear of God and due obedience" (*Gottesforcht auch schuldigen Gehorsam*) to the authority of their masters. Beyond a warning not to burden the boys with useless housework and other distractions, the ordinance offered no further guidance. It made no mention of the nature or process of apprenticeship. It did not describe the screening of candidates or masters, assign specific tasks to be attempted and learned, detail the requirements and contingencies of the indenture, or list the rights and responsibilities of the parties. The guild left these and all other aspects of training apprentices in the hands of each master. The affairs of journeymen were treated with similar dispatch. They were in all things subject to their masters: their wages set, their freedom limited, and their obedience required. Guilds regulated production but not employment. How master and man negotiated their respective needs for labor and livelihood—the multitude of transactions that constituted their work relationship—became a matter of interest to the guild only if these negotiations erupted in public discord.

Those who labored with their hands depended on word of mouth to regulate the supply of labor within the craft. Again, the experience of Johann Dietz reveals the risk and uncertainty: "I traveled by post as far as Magdeburg, where the broad streets promised me well paid employment. . . . I found no such employment"; "I had an aunt in Merseburg, the wife of the Secretary of the Revenue, who . . . recommended me to the Grand Duke and Duchess."[14] Dumb luck and personal connections counted for much.

The Furriers' Ordinance suggests that masters located journeymen and secured their services through direct personal contact. Regulations limited their ability to do so, however, by prohibiting any master from bidding the services of a journeymen away from another master without that other's knowledge and consent. How they arranged apprenticeships is completely obscure. Such contacts might have occurred at the guild hall or hostel. A seventeenth-century ordinance noted that a hostel (*Herberg*) housed the furrier apprentices and journeymen of Augsburg, though it may well have existed much earlier.[15] Here was a place where hands could gather to discuss matters of common interest, such as the misadventures of the road, the state of their craft, or the iniquities of their masters. Though such potentially inflammatory talk was usually prohibited, the predilection of working men to seek solace in the solidarity of their comrades made it all but inevitable. It was also a place where masters in need of hands could find a ready supply of qualified labor. Yet, as was the case with the guild itself, the hostel existed to control rather than provide work by regulating the habits of laborers and by forcing them to support themselves. As soon as they accepted work in Augsburg, all journeymen and apprentice furriers had to register there and submit to its discipline. As captured in a detailed ordinance from the seventeenth century, this discipline extended to all aspects of work culture on the shop floor and outside the shop door. The hostel collected funds, to which all journeymen and apprentices had to contribute, for the support of sick or needy comrades. In these and other ways, it extended the masters regime by promoting their interests and reducing their expenses. Viewed as a craft organization, the hostel maintained a ready supply of labor but did not obviously helped laborers to secure or sustain work.

FINDING WORK FOR ORPHANS

Neither the furriers nor any other craft or guild gave much thought to a market for labor. By controlling the population of artisans in any given craft, guilds hoped to restrict both competition for raw materials, which would raise the masters' costs, and the production of finished goods, which would lower prices. Ironically, it was not in any guild's interest to expand the supply of labor or promote its employment. These tasks fell to organizations such as the orphanages.

Direct intervention in the labor market began with out-placement, the selection of a trade and master for an orphan. That often difficult and frustrating process started with an assessment of the child. Age, desire, and means all figured in the arithmetic of the orphanage administrators. In 1721, for example, a directive stated simply that "the youths who were recognized to be sufficiently raised, instructed, and grown and to be suited and have the desire to enter service or a craft should be shown to the deputies, who will make suitable arrangements for their placement."[16] Unfortunately, no surviving document records the exact combination of factors or the weight given to each, and so creates the impression that out-placement was an ad hoc affair, driven as much by externalities, such as the availability of resources or space, as by the condition of the orphan in question. The lack of strict regulations probably offered orphanage administrators freedom and flexibility to negotiate individual apprenticeship contracts. Out of this practice emerged rules of thumb.

Attaining the age of first communion marked a threshhold in the lifecycle of orphans.[17] At that point, and not before, they were considered strong enough physically and spiritually to enter the world of work. By the time they received their first communion, usually between the ages of twelve and fifteen, they were big enough to labor. No less importantly, confirmation and communion marked a point at which they were morally firmed both by their training in the elements of the Christian faith and by the sacrament itself. Thus prepared, they could withstand days of exertion and nights of temptation and become self-sufficient.

The deputies denied or delayed many requests for servants and apprentices for this reason. Master Schlemmer had to wait until Johann Schönfeld, the orphan he wanted as his apprentice, had taken communion.[18] Likewise, master gardener Matheus Seuter had to do without an apprentice until Matheus Braun received the sacrament.[19] Once the orphan had received the sacrament, however, there were no further hindrances to consenting parties. Johannes Berthold became apprentice to master cobbler Johann Christoph Schwalb because he wished to enter this craft and had already taken communion.[20] He was ready to make his way independently in the world.

Simply bringing together masters in need of men and orphans in need of work was far from simple. Because the labor market of Augsburg was decentralized and complex, without the means efficiently to disseminate information or to respond to change, the city's orphanages had to do these things themselves. Deputies and administrators spent a great deal of time recruiting masters or responding to their requests. That the orphanages supplied a ready source of labor, and that masters approached the orphanage to acquire it, proves not only that these organizations mediated labor in Augsburg but that their function was recognized and accepted by the artisans.

Finding masters for orphan apprentices did not always require action by the administrators. Occasionally, they could rely on the boy or his family to make the necessary arrangements or at least provide direction. For example, a lacemaker named Johann Georg Seyfried requested that his nephew and ward, Ulrich Gerner, be made his apprentice.[21] The deputies consented but delayed placement four months until the boy received first communion. This did not mean that the boy left the house or lost his trade. Rather, he enjoyed the benefits of both simultaneously. A list of orphanage students described him as learning a craft and studying Latin and arithmetic—an unusual curriculum for an apprentice lacemaker—in house until his first communion.[22]

Personal preference was also an important but unreckonable element in apprenticeship. The desire (*Lust und Liebe*) to practice a trade had always played a role in out-placement. All children had to work but few were placed against their will. A directive from the Alms Office instructed both Catholic and Lutheran orphanages to place orphans, whenever possible, in a craft or trade according to their preference and ability.[23]

Experience shaped this as all other managerial practices and policies. Orphans placed against their will rarely persisted in workshop or household. When Joseph Tobias Schuester was apprenticed to the turner Leonhard Mayr in 1770, their working relationship lasted only four months.[24] His master returned him to the Catholic Orphanage with the observation that he was unable to learn the trade, and a search began for a master tailor to train the boy. The orphan father reported that Schuester had always objected to the trade of turner and shown a preference for that of tailor. Five years later, Schuester had completed an apprenticeship to the tailor Lorentz Widemann. The father noted his opinion that it was a mistake to push a boy into a craft against his will. Accordingly, when Paul Gottfried Iherot, a master lacemaker, requested an apprentice from the Lutheran Orphanage, he was granted the services of Imanuel Steber because the boy "desired to do so."[25]

Important as willingness was, however, masters and orphans could always change their minds. Sebastian Hoffmann was granted the services of another apprentice from the Lutheran Orphanage after Johann Berthold lost interest and reneged on his agreement to learn lacemaking.[26] Another master reported that his apprentice, an orphan named Paulus Weidenauer, had no further desire to learn his craft.[27] Instead of dissolving the agreement and making new arrangements, the deputies ordered Weidenauer to wait eight days and reconsider his decision to quit his master's service. The seamstress Gertraut Wolhöferin pleaded that an orphan not be taken from her service despite the girl's expressed desire to leave, unless the Lutheran Orphanage replaced her with another.[28] Wolhöferin engaged to teach the fundamentals of sewing in exchange for a quarterly stipend and the orphan's labor. The deputies evidently valued her service to the house because they agreed to replace one disgruntled girl with two, who were willing.

Not only an orphan's condition and inclination but also those of the master or mistress were taken into account. Certainly, employers had to be qualified and honorable, but they also had to be able to train apprentices. For example, the administrators refused Johann Bausch's request that David Wolf be made his apprentice because the master chimneysweep already had three apprentices and because the boy's mother wanted her son placed in a different craft.[29] Generally speaking, such trade law as existed in Augsburg permitted a master craftsman to train only one apprentice at a time and required that he wait one year after an apprentice finished training before engaging another.

By scrutinizing prospective masters as well as prospective apprentices, orphanage administrators contributed to the regulation and mediation of Augsburg's labor market. Suspicion of unacceptable abuse or exploitation might be grounds for refusal of an apprenticeship or service agreement. One instance reveals much about the nature of apprenticeship and its place in a world of work. It deserves to be considered in more detail.

Orphan girls learned the essentials of household service at the hands of a foster mother (*Ziehmutter*), before 1780, when these tasks were given to an in-house governess. The title is misleading in that these women were usually seamstresses, who instructed girls in a sort of apprenticeship but apparently did not assume their care and support more broadly. Thus, girls acquired marketable skills in the same manner as boys, by donating their work in order to observe and imitate. And their mistresses, like the masters of apprentices, took full advantage of that labor in accordance with the dictates of the market.

Maria Sabina Weisin supplemented her income as a seamstress in this way. In a letter to the deputies of the Alms Office, dated July 1726, she sketched her work with the orphans and her troubles with the orphanage, revealing some of the complexities of training orphans and shaping labor.[30] It was a multivalent process that involved constant negotiation and transaction not only between the house and its employee but also between the orphans and their mistress.

Six orphan girls learned housekeeping and sewing from Weisin. The number was fixed.[31] The house paid a quarterly stipend for the instruction of four girls, who worked exclusively on articles of clothing to be worn by orphans. The other two received instruction at no cost "but sewed for me [Weisin]."[32] Her compensation, in their case, was free labor to increase her productivity. Because these terms had endured over a period of years, she and the Lutheran Orphanage found the arrangement mutually advantageous.

Problems arose, however, upon the appointment of a new orphan mother, probably the wife of Johann Sturm. She had taken girls out of the seamstress' service and not replaced them, causing a loss of productivity and income. The reason, according to Weisin, was a rumor, started by one of the girls, that they were forced to sew more clothing than was needed by the Lutheran orphans. If true, Weisin profitted from the labor of these children beyond the limits allowed by the authorities. For her part, the seamstress claimed that the four girls, for whose instruction she was paid, worked one to four hours each week and then only on clothing for the orphanage. The rumor-monger—one of these four—had been dissatisfied with the work regime and unwilling to learn the sewing and cleaning skills required of all girls.

Charge and counter-charge were serious. Weisin stood accused of exploiting the needy in ways that were detrimental to the orphans and to other seamstresses. The practice was similar to a master's employing more journeymen and apprentices in his shop than allowed by guild regulations. Seeking to produce and sell more than a fair share was both a violation of guild authority and a threat to the livelihoods of other masters. Yet, her accuser was guilty too. She gossiped maliciously and avoided work, activities that violated both the accepted standards of servants' behavior, as set forth in the householder literature of that day (*hausväterliche Literatur*), and the statutory conditions of support in the Lutheran Orphanage. Standard works on domestic economy and discipline, such as Coler's *Oeconomia* and Spangenberg's *Haustaffel*, warned specifically against such evils.[33] As early as 1599, house regulations incorporated these admonitions and forbade gossip, slander, and idleness as activities detrimental to legitimate authority, communal life, and moral discipline.[34] Moreover, the ability to work and be self-supporting had always been a prerequisite for admission.[35] In short, the worst that Weisin and the orphan girl could allege of one another was that both had violated the terms of their employment.

Had the matter gone no further, the administrators would probably have punished the tale-bearing orphan and so resolved the dispute. Yet, new evidence of the mistreatment of orphans seemed to confirm the accusation of exploitation and led to a complete rupture between Weisin and the orphanage.

One of Weisin's apprentices, a girl named Regina Köpfin, became ill. Described as "broken out" (*ausschlegig*), her body was covered by purulent, stinking sores. Maladies of this sort were usually the result of insufficient hygiene or unsanitary conditions, neither of which were uncommon in early modern cities. The sight and smell were so unsettling in this case that, although the orphan mother kept Köpfin at home, all the other orphans left Weisin's service. Another girl, Sophia Beirin, developed sores on her throat at about the same time, and the orphan mother refused to place any more children in the seamstress' hands. Although her decision implied some connection between illness and service, she excused it by blaming the girls: "There are none here, and the entire house is full of talentless people, who can do nothing and know nothing."[36]

The seamstress recognized that the orphans' labor rather than their ability was the real issue. By sewing clothing that she could then sell, her girls "also learned to do more subtle work well."[37] The clothing worn by orphans incorporated only the poorest cloth, was of very low quality, and required little skill. If they were to live by the sweat of their brows and the labor of their hands, orphan girls had to master the more sophisticated techniques demanded by consumers. Rather than see such production as a form of exploitation, Weisin treated work for the market as an opportunity that benefitted her girls as well as herself.

The mounting distrust between Weisin and the orphan mother was not limited to the girls and the terms of their labor but extended to other, customary elements of early modern work relations. Weisin reported with distress that she no longer received her usual gratuity, the New Year's coin (*Sylvestergeld*). The Lutheran Orphanage held to the common practice among early modern employers of giving money to each of its servants and workers on New Year's Day. The usual New Year's gratuity was one gulden, a considerable amount for any artisan. Since the troubles began, Weisin had received a local coin (*Landmünz*) of far less value.

More than a loss of cash, the base coinage represented a stinging devaluation of Weisin's work. She understood that her labor on behalf of the orphans "is a good deed rather than a duty but it still does one good or ill when it is recognized or not that it takes much effort to get something into hard heads."[38] What seems a digression from a dispute regarding the uses of orphan labor was, in fact, a fundamental issue of labor discipline. Of central concern to the orphanage was the value of labor understood in market terms; the seamstress insisted that its value be reckoned in moral terms as well. The orphan mother evidently required that the girls in her charge labor only to the extent that they learned essential skills and served the economic needs of the house. Production beyond that point might benefit the seamstress but did not serve the needs of the orphanage and orphans. Although neither the orphan mother nor the other administrators testified to the utility of rewards and penalties as a means of shaping labor, they apparently considered the New Year's coin a suitable method to encourage and acknowledge satisfactory work. Payment and gratuities only followed the acceptable execution of work; their withdrawal signalled work that was not up to specification. Weisin, however, evoked the moral ties binding employer to employee, when she sought to justify the New Year's gift by stating that she "did it [teach the orphans] gladly and [it] is my obligation."[39]

Because she took these girls in charge and taught them the techniques of her trade—a task made at once charitable by their need and difficult by their hard heads—the orphanage was obligated too. For Weisin, a monetary gratuity symbolized the social rather than economic relationship within her labor. That the orphan mother failed to grasp this fact attested, in Weisin's too directly stated opinion, to a lack of experience and comprehension. "In sum there is more understanding in the little finger of the previous orphan mother than in this one's whole body."[40] Here, then, were irreconcilably different notions of labor: on the one hand a commodity of precise value and limited significance; on the other hand an activity joining human beings in terms of mutual dependence and responsibility.

The Rights and Responsibilities of Apprenticeship

Very few written agreements between master craftsmen and orphan apprentices survive. They communicate so little that they awaken the suspicion that certain details were left deliberately obscure. A note concerning the apprenticeship of Johann Christoff Nagel to master baker Johann Sigmund Leyh stated only that training would last three and one-half years and cost 24 fl.[41] It mentioned neither the responsibilities for payment of fees and the boy's care nor the expectations of master and apprentice.

Fortunately, a handful of agreements reveal the issues to be negotiated and resolved before an apprenticeship could begin. The orphan August Gueter apprenticed to master silver engraver Leonhard Jacob Muller in 1721.[42] For artisans, success, if not survival, depended in the first instance on training at the hands of a qualified master in a craft capable of providing a livelihood. This contract apparently fulfilled both prerequisites for Gueter: silverworking flourished in Augsburg in the early eighteenth century, and Muller was a master in the craft. In return for four years of instruction, Master Muller would receive a fee of 40 fl., paid in three installments of 13 fl. 20 kr., one at the beginning of the apprenticeship, one at the end of the second year, and one upon completion of training. Installments protected both parties against a rupture in their relationship, but this agreement failed to specify exactly who the parties were. Though not impossibly large, 40 fl. was a considerable sum for any orphan to possess and raised the possibility of a third, unnamed party who might be willing to meet this obligation.[43] The Lutheran Orphanage would continue to support Gueter by supplying him with clothing and bedding and by paying 30 kr. weekly for his place at the master's table. Apparently, then, Gueter would live in Muller's household but rely on the financial resources of the orphanage; the costs of an apprentice's support were not included in the apprenticeship fee and had to be reckoned against it. Finally, the contract stipulated the behavior expected of apprentice and master. Gueter promised in writing to be industrious and well-behaved. Muller agreed to teach the boy his craft honorably and to engage him as a journeyman for "an appropriate weekly wage" after his training. Gueter remained free, however, to seek wage-labor elsewhere. It was important to bind the apprentice to service as well as to assure his future, in a sense guaranteeing the interests of both parties. Concern focused, then, on these issues: fees and costs, responsibilities and rights, training and employment.

In 1723 the master engraver (*Bildhauer*) Johann Wolfgang Schendell accepted Tobias Printzing as his apprentice.[44] The orphan would serve him for five years and pay 35 fl. as an apprenticeship fee (*Lehrgeld*) and a further 30 fl. for his board. Before Printzing could begin, however, his new master required that he acquire the necessary skills in drawing at his own expense. Understandably, fees and costs drew the particular attention of the administrators. Implicit and of particular interest is the fact that the orphanage approached the master. He agreed to train the orphan and drove an unusually hard bargain, placing nearly all the expense and risk on the boy and the organization.

The expense of such agreements and the powers of the masters forced orphanage administrators to limit their liability in apprenticeships. As noted, the fee for training young men in the craft of their choice was the single greatest expense in childrearing. Likewise, myriad other costs might burden the orphanages. Some restrictions were required that would spare the organizations without spoiling the apprenticeships.

The 1780 Orphanage Ordinance codified the process of out-placement as understood after two hundred years of experience and captured hitherto unstated practical considerations.[45] Orphans who had received their first communion, were clean and healthy, and had demonstrated those virtues required of all wage laborers were to be placed in the craft, trade, or service of their choice. The realities of housekeeping, however, may have played a role as well. Out-placement extended orphanage resources by reducing the costs of support, which passed to the orphan's new master or mistress, and made space available for other needy children. Older boys moved out of the house, reducing the difficulties associated with adolescence. Girls caused worries of a different sort. The ordinance warned administrators to be wary of a prospective maid's suitability, that is, that she have the "habits, ability, and temperament" to ensure that she would earn her bread honorably and conscientiously. Taken together, the regulations suggest—but do not prove—that the condition of the child was uppermost in the minds of orphanage administrators but not necessarily out of regard for the child's well-being alone. Their concerns were political and economic as well as social or psychological. They considered the value of the child's labor, the costs of the child's support, and the child's submission to proper authority.

In all its regulation of the orphans, the 1780 ordinance was inspired by a more explicit insistence on utility. Though it assured orphans of their traditional prerogative to choose their trade or craft, still their choices now were to be guided in useful directions by the administrators. Not only must the crafts of choice correspond to the talents and abilities of the apprentices, but they also must contribute to the "common good" (*Gemeinnutz*).[46] Young women entering service were even more closely fettered; under no circumstances, except with special permission, were they allowed to choose their own position.[47] Earlier pronouncements treated males and females alike and merely directed the administrators to locate suitable employment for any orphan, deemed sufficiently mature to labor.[48] The Lutheran Orphanage now took it upon itself to lead young people to appropriate employment. All employers had to appear at the weekly meeting of the superintendents to arrange the services of an orphan and to permit the authorities to review the situation. Orphans could still seek their own masters and mistresses, but the ordinance assured orphanage administrators a degree of oversight.

The use of the term common good suggests both positive and negative purposes in the out-placement of orphans. It presupposed certain positive standards of behavior for laborers and their masters. By disciplining orphans and monitoring their work relations, the Lutheran Orphanage sought to achieve these standards. Anxiety expressed over the work ethic of orphans in household service and the work persistence of those in artisanal crafts make clear that administrators were no longer willing to risk the consequences of job selections that ended in conflict and unemployment, the frequent result of an inefficient or ineffective transactions in the labor market. At least in the case of servants they articulated a clear concern that these workers demonstrate those qualities that promised steady work. Employers must get their money's worth, or, more broadly expressed, servants must offer satisfaction. This probably applied to the masters of apprentices as well. Apprentices must successfully learn their trade, begin to support themselves, and not linger in dependence on welfare and the orphanage. Ultimately, self-sufficiency served the common good, while dependence damaged it.

Avoiding unnecessary costs to the orphanage was another implication of the administrators' interpretation of the common good. This could be done by regulating the masters themselves or by fixing some of the expenses of apprenticeship.

The required appearance at the weekly superintendents' meetings of masters in search of orphan apprentices or servants created an excellent opportunity to check their qualifications and reputation and to arrange advantageous terms of employment before committing orphans to their service. The 1780 ordinance set explicit standards for the masters (and mistresses) of orphans. They had to demonstrate certain technical proficiencies, "both the talent and the will to teach a poor orphan his craft," and they had to possess a public reputation for moral rectitude, expressed in decorum and integrity.[49] The article implies that the superintendent might refuse to place orphans with employers not known for these qualities.

Regulations limited some of the normal expenses of out-placement. Young men, for example, were forbidden to apprentice to any master who refused to provide room and board in his own household. Similarly prohibited were apprenticeships that required the boy to supply his own bed and bedding. These practices, commonplace before the first half of the eighteenth century as demonstrated by surviving contracts, placed an intolerable burden on orphanage resources, a burden borne in the final instance by younger children still resident in the house. Feeding and furnishing orphans no longer strictly in need of support deprived dependent orphans of their fair share of assistance.[50] The orphanage would continue to provide apprentices and servants with clothing that they had to keep in good order and return every Saturday for mending and laundering. The forced presence of these young people on a regular basis offered administrators an ideal opportunity to monitor their progress and conditions as they left the shelter of the orphanage and entered the world of work. Other necessities, such as the tools of an apprentice's trade, had to be purchased with the orphan's own resources, which remained in the keeping of the orphanage. Even as the administrators sought to limit the financial ties which bound orphans to the orphanage, they assiduously upheld every opportunity for regulation and control.

The ordinance limited apprenticeship fees (Lehrgelder) too.[51] The Alms Office and the Lutheran Orphanage would pay no more than 30 fl. for any apprenticeship regardless of its duration or other considerations. Charges in excess of this limit would have to be met by the orphans themselves or by donations from patrons. In some crafts the masters could expect even less. Weavers and chimneysweeps received only 18 fl. for apprenticing orphans, the same fee paid by sons of masters. Butchers and book printers got no apprenticeship fee at all, which may explain why only a single orphan apprenticed in these crafts. Although the ordinance gives no explanation, this regulation may have been a response to any of a number of conditions. Arbitrary fee schedules corresponded to a pattern of discrimination among various crafts in the Augsburg labor market; unfortunately the evidence of orphan employment supports no firm conclusion regarding their rationality.

The common good, as applied to out-placement, expressed the economic and political utility of work and self-sufficiency. Service and apprenticeship met these goals directly, and the orphanage sought to shape and regulate masters and workers alike to serve the common good. Whether the term also connoted a response to changing market conditions as well as a sensitivity to work relations is difficult to determine. It would certainly not have been in the common good nor in the orphans' interests to place them in employment that neither contributed to the wealth and well being of the city nor yielded an adequate livelihood. Though the ordinance did not explicitly direct orphans into certain crafts or industries, the statistics of outplacement suggest that administrators were and, indeed, had always been conscious of shifting demand for labor and worked to supply it.

THE LABOR MARKET AND ORPHAN APPRENTICES

Before the nineteenth century, Augsburg's orphanages were never schools for factory hands. Though work routines within the walls came to resemble those of a factory in a few respects, especially time discipline, only an insignificant number of orphans entered identifiable, factory-based industries.[52] Most girls found employment in household service; almost all of the boys apprenticed in artisanal crafts.

The pattern of service and apprenticeship reveals both structures and conditions in the labor market. Orphans flowed into the established, traditional crafts in accordance with market conditions and avoided the unregulated trades where change and innovation were at home. Orphans apprenticed to master weavers in large numbers, long after the handloom weaving industry in Augsburg was moribund, and almost never apprenticed in nonguild or factory-based trades that ill fitted the accepted image of artisanal production. However conservative their placement of the orphans in their charge, administrators responded to the constantly shifting demand for labor from the various economic sectors, which was the result of changing demand for the goods and services these trades and crafts provided. The number of apprentices indentured in various trades corresponded roughly to the vitality of those trades as measured by the number of masters practicing them.

All sectors of the artisanal economy of Augsburg, with the exceptions of foods and decorative arts, declined in membership by 50 percent or more between the early seventeenth and the early eighteenth centuries[53] (see Table 7.1). Smaller numbers of masters reflected simultaneously the drastically reduced population of Augsburg and the correspondingly diminished demands for goods and services. That foods and arts were able to resist this development better than other trades probably reflected the relative inelasticity of demand for food and the burgeoning market in luxury goods. All other crafts had to adjust not only to a smaller population of candidates from which to replace each passing generation of masters but also to dramatically altered market conditions. The loss of regional and international markets affected Augsburg's entire artisanal economy directly, but no one sector was hit as hard as clothing. All sectors declined again at the end of the eighteenth and into the nineteenth centuries. Fewer masters practiced their crafts in

TABLE 7.1
Guild Masters in the Artisanal Economy of Early Modern Augsburg

Trades	1610	1720	1788	1806
Food	500–650	470	590	620
Metal	216–502	139	156	144
Art	286–502	404	284	237
Building	259	84	131	97
Wood	444	202	232	199
Clothing	2975	1220	1457	1278

the city. Nonetheless, the number of crafts they represented remained surprisingly large and, indeed, grew larger still, a function of specialization as well as consumption. The decline of dominant export industries, especially textile manufacturing and goldsmithing, contributed to the more even distribution of crafts among Augsburg's artisanal masters at the end of the Old Regime.

The food sector demonstrated considerable long-term stability. According to the 1610 tax assessment, 404 masters engaged in crafts and trades related to foodstuffs (Lebensmitteln), including the shopkeepers (Krämer), peddlars (Hucker), merchants (Kaufleute), bakers (Bäcker), butchers (Metzger), fishers (Fischer), and brewers (Brauer).[54] To these might be added the 96 publicans (Gastwirte). The number of masters in the food trade had shifted little by the eighteenth century. Lists of craft masters indicated 470 in the food trade in 1720, 590 in 1788, and 620 in 1806.[55]

The number of orphans apprenticed in the food sector, however, did not follow this pattern of slow growth. In fact, the food trades seem to have closed their doors to orphans. In the 1580s a single boy apprenticed as a peddlar, and that apprentice may have had nothing to do with food at all. A century later, another orphan boy apprenticed to a miller. Only in the eighteenth century did a few orphans finally penetrate the food trades: three apprenticed to gardeners in the 1720s; another three apprenticed to gardeners and one became a butcher's apprentice in the 1760s. Thus, with the slow growth in the food sector came a noticeable but infinitesimal increase in the number of orphan apprentices in it.

Like the food trades, Augsburg's building sector grew also, though at different times and for different reasons. It experienced particularly rapid expansion in the sixteenth century, in conjunction with the period of Augsburg's commercial and financial preeminence. In 1536, the carpenters counted 203 masters.[56] Though precise numbers are lacking, building must have been one of Augsburg's largest industries, exceeding foods and second only to clothing.

The building sector underwent reorganization as a result of the constitutional reform of 1548. Three omnibus guilds appeared that combined a number of formerly independent crafts. Those engaged or even possibly engaged in the decoration of buildings, such as engravers, painters, goldleaf pounders, glaziers, and saddlers, formed a single guild. Wood-workers, among whom were the carpenters and masons (*Maurer*) as well as cabinet- or trunkmakers (*Kistler*), bowmakers (*Bogner*), gunstock-makers (*Buchsenschifter*), organ-, harmonium-, and instrumentmakers (*Orgel-, Positiv-,* and *Instrumentenmacher*), formed another. Those who produced specialized products, such as coopers (*Schäffler*), wheelwrights (*Wagner*), and turners (*Drechsler*), formed a third guild onto themselves.

According to the tax register of 1610, masters engaged in woodworking of any sort, in production involving stone or glass, and in general construction numbered 660.[57] Of these the woodworkers were the most numerous with 401. By 1720, long after the glory of Augsburg had faded, the number of masters in the building, stone, and earth-working trades—admittedly an imperfect match with the general building trade as understood in the sixteenth and early seventeenth centuries—had fallen to 84.[58] Those engaged in wood- and paperworking numbered 202. During the eighteenth century both of these trades enjoyed renewed growth fueled by the general expansion of Augsburg's economy. In a survey from 1788 the number of construction masters had grown to 131 and the number in woodworking had risen to 232. Both shrank with the contraction of the late eighteenth and early nineteenth centuries. Construction masters fell to 97 and woodworking masters to 199 by 1806, when Augsburg's economic life suffered the consequences of Napoleonic warfare and mediatization.

Again, the placement of apprentices mirrored general economic trends. The building sector, like the food trades, offered few opportunities to orphans. None entered these crafts in the 1580s or the 1620s. Only eight ever apprenticed in it, three as chimneysweeps. More boys found their way into the wood trade; 20 took apprenticeships between the 1620s and the 1720s. Most of these occurred in the 1620s, a period of considerable demographic and economic pressure in orphanage and city alike. Once again, however, the majority of orphan apprentices were found in such humble crafts as brushbinders, bookbinders, sievemakers, turners, and cardmakers. In the food and building sectors, then, orphans gravitated toward marginal crafts that offered less income and status and were more open as a result.

To consider the artisanal economy broadly, in terms of industrial sectors, permits a more efficient consideration of general trends but obscures the often quite different fates of individual crafts. Construction and wood generally experienced steady growth until the late eighteenth century; some crafts within them enjoyed periods of marked prosperity, while others decline precipitously. The rococo taste for decorative architecture and furnishings, for example, helped the painters (*Maler*), who adorned the urban palaces of the elite with elaborate facades, to achieve sustained growth in the last century of the Old Regime.⁵⁹ Between 1720 and 1788 the building trade expanded by 56 percent, led by the painters, who grew by 39 percent, from 23 to 34 masters. At the end of the century, however, when the building sector declined in the aggregate 26 percent, painters managed better, shrinking only 12 percent. As a result of this prosperity, four orphans apprenticed to master painters in the 1720s. Likewise, the furniture-makers (*Schreiner*) and coopers grew more than the woodworking trades generally on the strength of demand for elaborately carved and decorated furniture.⁶⁰ As the total number of woodworking masters grew 15 percent between 1720 and 1788, the number of coopers rose 21 percent, from 33 to 40 masters, and the number of furniture-makers rose 20 percent, from 61 to 73 masters. In the decline that set in thereafter, the entire trade shrank 14 percent by 1806, but furniture-making declined only 7 percent, from 73 to 68 masters. The coopers were less fortunate, sliding 30 percent, from 40 to 28 masters. Only in the 1620s did masters in either craft accept orphan apprentices, seven in a single decade. All of these crafts were sensitive to demand for luxury goods, which came under increased pressure as political conflict flowed into economic crisis at the end of the Old Regime. This had little effect on orphans, perhaps because they tended to find positions more frequently outside of elite crafts.

If the food sector experienced slow growth due to increasing population after 1680, and building was given to sharp fluctuations based on demand for large construction projects, then the metalworking sector followed still another pattern of development. These crafts demonstrated long-term stability, broken only by the crisis of the seventeenth century.

In this case particularly, the number of master craftsmen alone does not necessarily indicate the importance of a craft. At the height of its industrial power, Augsburg was an important center for heavy metalwork, especially for the production of armor and cannon. The fame of certain of its masters, such as the cannonmaker Georg Löffler and the armorers Colman Helmschmied, Hans Lutzenberger, and Anton Pfeffenhauser, and the volume and quality of their products, which may be found today in museums from New York to Madrid, prove that Augsburg in the sixteenth and seventeenth centuries was a center for artillery and armor no less renowned than Milan. In 1536 Augsburg's smiths numbered 341.⁶¹ They included not only the traditional blacksmith but also such specialized crafts as lock-, nail, copper-, knife, and kettle smiths. The reorganization of 1548 added to these any other crafts whose materials were metal. Complex crafts, such as those practiced by gunsmiths, armorers, swordsmiths, spurmakers, and cannon and bell founders, as well as mechanical trades, such as watch-, clock- and toolmakers, joined smiths of every variety in the new metalworking guild. Their number must have reached well over 400. By 1610, the population of metalworking artisans who paid taxes in Augsburg had risen to 502.[62] Though these figures are inconclusive, due both to the lack of accurate statistics and to the changing definition of crafts in the metal sector, they suggest relatively little expansion despite both the growing demand for metal products, particularly weapons and armor, and the almost frantic expansion of Augsburg's economy in the late 1500s.

The crisis of the seventeenth century ended the city's leadership in metalworking. Not only did its foremost exponents die or emigrate, but the total number of metalworking craftsmen shrank to a quarter of its former size. By 1720 only 139 Augsburg masters engaged in these crafts.[63] The vast majority of these were not weaponsmiths or armorers but rather simple locksmiths (26) or metalsmiths (57), engaged in meeting the mundane demands of local markets. The rest included specialized crafts that had not earlier been accounted part of the sector, such as enamellers and polishers. Their numbers varied insignificantly throughout the century, grew with the general expansion of the local economy to 156 by 1788, but shrank again to 144 by 1806. Despite long periods of relative stability, then, the metalworking crafts declined noticeably as an industrial sector of Augsburg's economy.

This observation applies as well to orphan apprentices in the trades. Over the entire period of study, the orphanages channeled a relatively steady stream of boys into metalworking. The majority of them became locksmiths, but they regularly entered other forms of smithing and founding as well. After 1650, the number of apprenticeships fell by roughly half but remained remarkably stable until the end of the eighteenth century.

The city's gold- and silversmiths remained separate from the other metalworkers, forming their own guild and serving a different sector of the artisanal economy. Fine metalworking grew steadily from the early sixteenth until the late eighteenth century. Indeed, as part of the decorative art sector, which included jewellers, carvers, engravers, illustrators, printmakers, portrait and picture painters, clock- and watchmakers, and fine instrumentmakers, gold- and silversmiths contributed substantially to Augsburg's economic renaissance in the late seventeenth century. They used a peerless craftsmanship in precious metals to stimulate commerce and generate capital.[64] Paul von Stetten, in his 1779 memorial on the occasion of the expansion of the civic Academy of Arts, observed that "a large share of the flowering of commerce" rested on the decorative arts.[65] The decorative arts in general and gold- and silversmithing in particular were to Augsburg in the seventeenth and eighteenth centuries what textile manufacturing had been in the fifteenth and sixteenth centuries.

As remarkable as its fame and fortune were in the later period, the demographic expansion of gold- and silver smithing was no less noteworthy.[66] In 1529 gold- and silversmithing in Augsburg employed 56 masters and journeymen. This figure rose to 63 in 1555, 130 in 1573, and 200 in 1594. The last figure included 100 native and 24 foreign journeymen and excluded more than 100 apprentices at home and 300 Augsburg journeymen abroad. By 1615 Augsburg workshops employed 199 masters and 164 journeymen. In less than a century, the fine metal trades had more than quadrupled in size. As siege, epidemic, and famine swept half the population away in the 1630s and 40s, the number of masters decreased correspondingly. By 1635, immediately after the worst period of crisis, the number of masters in the decorative arts stood at 262, of which those in goldsmithing and related, specialized crafts comprised 154.[67] The decline in numbers was neither so great nor so long-lasting as might have been expected. Throughout the early modern period, the fine metalworking crafts constituted 55 to 65 percent of the entire sector. By 1668 the proportion of all masters to those in gold- and silversmithing stood at 308 to 183. In 1701 it had risen to 379 to 224; by 1720 it climbed further to 404 to 268; and in 1734 it reached a peak of 523 to 343.[68] A gradual decline began around mid-century and gained momentum into the early 1800s. The proportion of masters slid from 463 to 268 in 1755 down to 231 to 132 in 1806. Although gold and silver workers proved more resistant to decline, the sector as a whole was in eclipse.

The reasons are not entirely clear. Perhaps, as von Stetten suggested, the masters in those later decades lacked the artistic vision needed to maintain creativity. Perhaps the economic prerequisites for luxury trade were lacking, the victims of concentrated production, mounting competition, and eroding demand.[69] Before the events of the Thirty Years' War closed in on the city, fine metalworking had already embarked on large-scale production. Artisans crafted simpler items for the homes of burghers as well as luxurious, decorative pieces for aristocratic households. These especially required a variety of shaping and finishing techniques that rapidly led to specialization and division of labor within the trade. As a result, the putting-out system emerged in Augsburg gold- and silversmithing during the first half of the seventeenth century. Customers placed orders for large or complex projects with a single merchant or a substantial smith, who served as the entrepreneur-organizer, dividing the work among many, otherwise unconnected, independent workshops. The trade developed a sophisticated but dispersed organization of production in advance of its real period of growth. When growth ended, it may have been unable, by virtue of that organization, to respond to reduced demand or introduce a more efficient structure. By the 1790s, with the population of masters declining, the effects of revolution and war deflected state budgets from conspicuous consumption to military expansion. The decorative arts in Augsburg, which had always depended on the patronage of aristocratic courts to support their luxury production, never recovered.

Despite economic contraction, the performance of orphans within this elite sector remained strong relative to other sectors of the artisanal economy. Indeed, more of Augsburg's orphans were apprenticed in the decorative arts than in any other craft sector except clothing. Perhaps the orphans enjoyed a reputation for a high degree of education and discipline; perhaps the material support of the orphanages made them more cost effective; perhaps the organization of production created conditions for which orphans were better suited. In any case, both orphanages regularly attached boys to master goldsmiths, illustrators, illuminators, and watchmakers. In the 1620s three began work with illustrators, two with watchmakers, one with a diamond cutter, and eight with goldsmiths. By the 1680s the numbers had shifted only slightly. Only four boys became apprentice goldsmiths, but two became portraitists, two became illustrators, and two became illuminators. By 1760, with a decline proceeding in the sector as a whole, three orphans found positions as apprentices: one as an engraver, one as a copper etcher, and one as an illuminator.

Like masters in the decorative arts and unlike masters in food or building, the vast majority of those in Augsburg's clothing sector were organized for export. The clothing trades required larger numbers of laborers, including those drawn from the city's orphanages, to produce for distant markets. Yet, textiles distinguished itself from the arts because it constituted both the largest and the poorest of the city's industrial sector.

As early as 1536, textile manufacturing was already big business that involved a wide range of crafts in an interlocking complex of processes. The weavers (*Weber*) alone numbered 1,451, most of whom were engaged in the production of fustians. Assisting them were many artisans, who specialized in the preparation or finishing processes. These included the carders (*Karter*), who combed the filaments to clean and straighten them for spinning into thread or yard, the spinners themselves, and the yarn-soakers (*Garnsieder*), who soaked the brittle linen thread in order to keep it supple enough for warping and weaving. Raw woven cloth left the weaver's hand and passed to any of a number of other craftsmen such as fullers, bleachers, dyers, shearers, and sizers.

The reorganization of 1548 forced Augsburg's fustian producers into two major guilds. Yarn-soakers, carders, and loom-warpers (*Blättersetzer*) joined the weavers. The cloth-cutters and -sizers (*Tuchscherer* and *Tuchmacher*) entered a guild of their own. Other finishing processes remained outside the administrative and regulatory structure of the guilds and, perhaps for this reason, attracted no orphan apprentices. Bleachers, for example, remained an unorganized and unregulated industry. The dyers, most of whom happened to be black or blue dyers (*Schwarz-* or *Blaufärber*) in Augsburg, formed their own guild much later.

Augsburg's clothing trades included artisans other than those directly engaged in the production of fustian. By 1720 some 32 crafts used textiles, leathers, skins, furs or other materials to create everything from clothing and accessories to saddles and rope. A very few weavers devoted themselves to the production of fine woolen cloth. The woolen weavers (*Lodweber*) maintained their own guild, but their numbers were never significant; 62 in 1536, 40 in 1548, 28 in 1720, and 18 in 1806.[70] Furriers, too, traditionally enjoyed the status of an independent guild.[71] Among the wealthiest and most prominent of Augsburg's craftsmen in the fifteenth and sixteenth centuries, they declined steadily, to the point that they numbered only 12 in 1788.[72] Not unlike their weaver colleagues, they fell victim to a potent combination of new competition, mechanized production, altered supply, and changing demand. Always more numerous and with the passage of time more important were the leather-working crafts, organized with clothing makers into a single guild in 1548. In addition to tanners (*Gerber*), saddlers (*Sattler*), cobblers (*Schuhmacher*), and parchmentmakers (*Pergamentmacher*), this association included tailors, bathers, barbers, and millers among others.[73] It was an interesting combination of crafts that neither shared common materials nor met a coherent set of demands. The motives for creating an omnibus guild remain obscure, but no less so than the rationale for including them in clothing. At the very least, their presence exposes once again the labyrinthine structure of Augsburg's artisanal industry.

In the late sixteenth and early seventeenth centuries, Augsburg's clothing sector, led by the fustian industry, grew extraordinarily. By 1601 the city housed 2,297 masters, operating 3,677 looms and producing more than 400,000 pieces of cloth for export.[74] The weavers were by far the largest guild in Augsburg. In 1612, their numbers reached 3024, of whom 2,199 were independent masters. The high proportion (nearly one-third) of dependent masters, those who lacked the resources to operate their own shops and so were reduced to wage labor for their more substantial brethren, might suggest growing pressure on export markets and straitened circumstances in the industry. The failure of Augsburg's linen weavers to adapt to the demand for new textile blends and the emergence of new markets and competition doomed them to decline before the crisis of the mid-seventeenth century.[75] Nonetheless, they managed to produce 430,636 pieces of linen in 1612.

They could not, however, maintain these extraordinary efforts in the face of crisis and change. The weavers were not only the most numerous but also, and especially, the poorest of all Augsburg's crafts. Though the tax register of 1610 listed a total of 2,040 weavers, 1,143, or slightly more than

56 percent, rendered only the base tax that have-naughts without any taxable property were assessed.[76] More than 93 percent paid taxes of 1 fl. or less. These figures compare most unfavorably with all other crafts, for which 39 percent were have-naughts and less than 78 percent paid 1 fl. or less.[77] They had no resources to withstand an interruption in trade or a decline in demand. Both happened in the 1630s and 40s with disastrous results. By 1653 the number of master linen weavers had fallen to about 500, a decline of 75.5 percent.[78] By comparison, the number of masters in all other crafts fell 47 percent in the same period. The crisis of the seventeenth century destroyed the traditional basis of Augsburg's industry and commerce.

Although the city's economy as a whole gradually recovered and even regained something of its old vigor in the course of the late 1600s and early 1700s, the weavers' craft and the clothing sector never shared this prosperity. The loss of Italian markets, due to the Thirty Years' War and the competition of English and Dutch producers, who specialized in new linen blends, deprived Augsburg of its export trade and largely reduced it to regional production.[79] Though the rise of a new textile specialty in the form of printed cottons provided new opportunities and fueled a modest recovery, the weavers never regained their old preeminence. They retained the dubious distinction of being Augsburg's largest and poorest craft but lost the reputation of being Europe's foremost producers of fustian.

As a group, weavers declined faster than other crafts in the clothing sector[80] (see Table 7.2). Whereas the number of all other masters demonstrated a remarkable stability over the period of crisis, the population of master weavers was decimated. Only toward the end of the eighteenth century, fueled by the demands of the city's printing factories for raw cotton cloth, did they recover slightly. As a proportion of the entire sector, however, the weavers maintained and even improved their position as the larg-

TABLE 7.2
Master Craftsmen in the Clothing Trade of Augsburg

CRAFT	1610	1720	1788	1806
Weaver	2040	468	700	671
	(69%)	(38%)	(48%)	(53%)
Cobbler	—	133	186	174
		(11%)	(13%)	(14%)
Tailor	—	167	226	191
		(14%)	(16%)	(15%)
Others	935	452	345	242
	(31%)	(37%)	(24%)	(19%)
Total	2975	1220	1457	1278

est of its constituent crafts. By contrast, the cobblers and tailors, the other leading clothing crafts, though considerably fewer, were also considerably more stable in both absolute and relative terms. Hence, although weaving shrank markedly in the late eighteenth and nineteenth centuries, marginal crafts, such as furriers, tanners, woolen weavers, and lace- and braidmakers, suffered more. The end of the early modern period marked not so much the fall of the weavers' craft as the fall of the clothing sector in Augsburg.

Weaving, tailoring, and cobbling were traditionally among the more open of crafts and were practiced by the largest number of masters. They offered more opportunities and fewer barriers to orphans, and more orphans received apprenticeships in weaving, tailoring, and cobbling than in any other craft (see Table 7.3). Apprenticeships in weaving, numerous in the late sixteenth century, declined with the industry as a whole. Likewise, the fall of furriers as artisanal aristocrats is reflected in the number of apprentices acquired from the city's orphanages. Orphans learned tailoring more frequently than any other craft; the steady flow of apprentices out of the or-

TABLE 7.3
Orphan Apprentices in the Clothing Trade of Augsburg

CRAFT	1580s	1620s	1650s	1680s	1720s	1760s
Weaver	16	5	1	2	6	6
Tailor	8	9	12	8	11	11
Cobbler	0	1	3	2	2	10
Furrier	3	6	0	0	0	0
Braidmaker	0	1	3	5	2	0
Others	1	7	1	1	2	1
Total	28	29	20	18	23	28

phanages bespeaks the stable number of masters and their need for labor. Shoemaking became a craft of choice for orphans in the late eighteenth century. Because the need for apprentices here as in tailoring, measured by the number of masters and the demand for their goods, did not grow noticeably, orphans must have become either more available or more desirable relative to other pools of candidates in the late 1700s. Once again, the number of apprenticeships reflects the rise and decline of crafts and trades in clothing, as in all other sectors of the artisanal economy.

As the orphanage statistics indicate, the distribution of orphan apprentices followed trends in the economy as a whole (see Table 7.4). Apprenticeships declined in the late eighteenth century even as their distribution across the artisanal economy rose. That more orphans placed in the food,

TABLE 7.4
Orphan Apprentices in the Artisanal Economy of Augsburg

Trade	1580s	1620s	1650s	1680s	1720s	1760s	Total
Food	1	—	—	1	3	4	9
Metal	3	13	4	2	2	1	25
Arts	3	14	4	9	5	3	35
Building	—	—	1	1	5	1	8
Wood	—	13	—	4	3	—	20
Clothing	28	29	20	18	23	28	146

building, and wood sectors, which apparently had been closed to these boys, suggests a widening of opportunity. So, too, do the shifts in apprenticeships from weavers to other crafts, especially cobbling, and from goldsmiths to portraitists, illuminators, and illustrators. In conjunction with the city's economy, the placement of orphans became directed less toward certain crafts and more diffused over the entire range of artisanal industry. The result was a broadened engagement in a completely different sector of the labor market, one marked by different demands. The labor-intensive export crafts, such as fustian weaving and goldsmithing, declined in the late eighteenth century. As the number of apprenticeships fell, the orphanages placed their boys in those crafts oriented toward production for local markets and, therefore, somewhat more resistant to cycles of expansion and contraction. For the same reason, their demand for labor in the form of apprentices was somewhat less volatile. A net loss in the volume of positions available to orphans increased the opportunity costs of their care and may explain the pressure orphanage administrators felt to restrict admissions and expand outplacement in the eighteenth century, a pressure they translated directly into the Orphanage Ordinance of 1780.

The Fates of Augsburg's Orphans

Being apprenticed by the orphan father to master artisans was by no means the fate of all or even, in hard times, of most orphans. Though a detailed discussion is reserved for the forthcoming companion volume, still a brief survey of selected decades is appropriate here.

A noteworthy proportion of orphans were released into the care of parents or relatives[81] (see Table 7.5). In periods of extreme hardship, many families were simply unable to support children and placed them whenever possible in the orphanage; the longer the duration of the crisis, the more likely the children were to remain there permanently. That the proportion of those released to a parent or relative was stable over time suggests that the practice by poor families of using the orphanages to provide for their

TABLE 7.5
Fates of Augsburg's Orphans

	1580s	1620s	1650s	1680s	1720s	1760s
Fate unknown	3	23	12	1	4	2
Deceased	125	190	37	11	46	37
	(51%)	(52%)	(29%)	(12%)	(32%)	(30%)
Released	56	21	20	8	22	21
	(22%)	(6%)	(16%)	(9%)	(15%)	(17%)
Entered church	1	1	3	1	1	0
Institutionalized	6	1	0	0	2	0
Placed in service	18	49	26	31	25	25
	(7%)	(14%)	(21%)	(35%)	(18%)	(20%)
Apprenticed	38	78	29	37	43	40
	(15%)	(22%)	(23%)	(42%)	(30%)	(32%)
Total	247	363	127	89	143	125

young in hard times—a means of extending the domestic economy at need—was constant rather than occasional. For example, Regina Bertholdin requested that her daughter be admitted to the Lutheran Orphanage in 1723 "until completion of training," probably a reference to the acquisition of some skill.[82] This was no case of hardship but rather a simple request to augment the mother's resources for the good of the child. The request was denied, but only because Bertholdin had two children in the orphanage, and the daughter in question was "too old and furthermore a bit simple-minded."[83] Under normal circumstances, then, charitable organizations provided a resource of which the needy made regular, voluntary use.

In-house mortality declined steadily in Augsburg's orphanages. Although catastrophically high during the late sixteenth and early seventeenth centuries, a consequence of crowding in the house and the weakened condition of orphans in times of dearth and pestilence, it fell noticeably as conditions improved after the 1650s.[84] By the eighteenth century, in fact, mortality among orphans compared favorably with that of children in urban societies generally.[85] Orphanages corresponded only inexactly to the charnel houses depicted in Victorian literature and recent scholarship.

As death rates decreased, the number of children placed in service or apprenticeship grew. By the mid-seventeenth century, this was the most common fate of Augsburg's orphans. The orphanages came to serve not as endpoints but as way stations for children without parents and for children with parents temporarily incapable of their support. For young men, the orphanages promoted entry into the world of artisanal labor; for young women, they opened the door to domestic service.

The orphanage chronicler implied in 1585 that young women, unlike the male journeymen who entered the market to learn a craft or trade and support themselves honorably, would always be dependent, either in the orphanage, in their mistresses' households, or in their own homes.[86] "When they behave well and are physically mature, they are married." Servants and especially maids were sheltered from the necessity of providing for themselves; they worked "in return for board and at no cost." What mattered to the administrators of the orphanage was that all had some form of occupation in order to sustain themselves physically without recourse to alms.

Servants occupied a unique place in the economy and society. Outside the administrative structure of the guilds and related associations, they lacked any means of collective representation or action. Rather, servants belonged to the patriarchal community of the household, a membership that conferred its own status and privilege. As domestic dependents and marginal wage earners, they rarely appeared in tax registers. Nonetheless, servants constituted between 10 and 12 percent of the entire population of Augsburg in the seventeenth and eighteenth centuries.[87] In the same period, 15 to 35 percent of Augsburg's orphans took employment in household service. This was understood to be as typical a phase of the lifecycle for young women as apprenticeship was for young men. Perhaps because of their more marginal economic and social circumstances and consequently their reduced probability of marrying, a large number of orphan girls found permanent rather than temporary occupations in household service.

Some parentless young women may have avoided service and established themselves in non-regulated trades. Recall, for example, the apprenticing of Christiana Durschner in 1737 to serve as a die cutter in the cotton-printing factory of Franz Gignoux, one of Augsburg's most substantial industrialists in the early eighteenth century.[88] Recall also the "apprentices" of Mistress Weisin, some of whom may have established themselves as seamstresses in their own right. Non-regulated trades may have offered greater opportunities to female workers. That more orphan women did not labor in factories or in unregulated trades is probably attributable to the moral and economic conservatism of orphanage administrators; a fear of masterless men and women and a faith in traditional work; a conviction that women required the paternal supervision of a household master, and that any worker would fare better in artisanal production.

Given this innate conservatism it is not surprising that the orphans of Augsburg left the orphanages to pursue predictable occupations and ends. Their fates conformed to the expectations of a preindustrial world. Some rejoined their families; some died; most entered service in household or workshop. The changing proportions reveal something of the texture of life within Augsburg's orphanages. More importantly, they shed light on the nature of early modern labor markets, the difficulties intrinsic to them, and the role of the orphanages in mediating the orphans' passages into them.

CONCLUSION

In the labor market of early modern Augsburg few fixed places or permanent structures served to bring masters and men together. No mechanism set the value of labor in accordance the dictates of supply and demand, and then proclaimed that value in such a way as to win it general recognition and acceptance. Insofar as places, structures, or mechanisms existed, they were matters of tradition, reputation, and association, specific to the many crafts and trades that comprised the artisanal economy. Under such circumstances, finding work depended upon local knowledge, a familiarity with the best masters and the going rates. In this fragmented, arcane world, the orphanages served as labor marketplaces, where supplies of workers met the demand for their labor, where orphans were placed in traditional occupations, where artisanal labor relations were articulated. They were organizations created in response to the institutions—the methods of production, the inefficiencies of transportation, the confines of regulation—that governed preindustrial work.

The orphanages of Augsburg negotiated the realities of the economy and society. They were not created to herald a new order; they served to perpetuate the old. They were the handiwork of men who were fundamentally risk-averse. They negotiated and exploited constraints to lower the economic and social costs of providing charity. The administrators of the orphanages responded to the demand for labor not to improve the performance of the economy as a whole or to promote some new organization of production, but rather to provide needy men and women with an independent means of subsistence. To achieve this end, they took advantage of their own knowledge of labor markets, entered into them as suppliers of labor, and shaped them not according to the dictates of an emergent technology but rather according to the dictates of hard-won wisdom. Even as they supported traditional modes and organizations, however, the orphanages of Augsburg helped forge new social relations of production.

Notes

1. Cf. Bátori, *Die Reichsstadt Augsburg*, 27.
2. StAA, W 10, Ain ungefarlicher uberschlag Was ain Waisenhaus Darinnen 200 Kinder Erhalten Mochten werden Jerlich Kosten möcht, 8 April 1572.
3. Clasen, "Arm und Reich in Augsburg vor dem Dreißigjährigen Krieg," 324.
4. Bettger, *Das Handwerk in Augsburg*, 48.

5. Ibid., 49.
6. The artisans certainly did not see it so. The violent uprisings of weavers in 1794 protested what they thought to be the unfair labor practices and insurmountable price competition of factory-produced textiles, especially those manufactured by von Schüle. Cf. Bátori, *Die Reichstadt Augsburg*, 135–37; Clasen, *Streiks und Aufstände der Augsburger Weber im 17. und 18. Jahrhundert*, 231–319.
7. Bettger, *Das Handwerk in Augsburg*, 51.
8. Ibid., 177–82.
9. Ibid., 57.
10. Ibid., 46.
11. H. Kellenbenz, "Wirtschaft der Blütezeit," 261.
12. Dietz, *Master Johann Dietz*, 28–29.
13. StAA, Handwerker Akten, Kürschner, 10, Kürschner Ordnung, Renoviert dato 2 May Anno Domini 1671.
14. Dietz, *Master Johann Dietz*, 94, 183.
15. StAA, Handwerker Akten, Kürschner, 10, Folgende Articul die Khürschner Gesellen und Jungen betreffen mögen durch der ordenlichen Obrigkeit Guetachten Ratificiert unnd Erkandt werden, s.a. s.d.
16. StAA, EW 1, Instruction für den Weysen Vatter und Mutter, 11 May 1721: "... die Jugend in einem, und anderm zimmlicher massen aufferzogen, unterrichtet, und erwachsen, zu Herrn oder Frauen diensten, Item Handtwerckhen zu lernen Lust und Liebe haben auch tauglich zy seyn erkandt werden, Solle es den Herrn Deputierten beyzeiten angezeigt und sie dessen gehorsamlich berichtet werden, damit sie weitere Verordnung mit anderwärtiger Unterbringung Solcher im Weysen-Hauß erzogene Kinder verfüegen und vornehmen können."
17. StAA, EW 12, Waisenhausordnung, 1780, Articulus 15, § 1: "... auch um der von allzu großen Knaben zu besorgenden Unordnungen willen hinfüro keiner der bereits comunciert hat und gesund ist länger mehr im Waisenhaus geduldet werden."
18. StAA, EW 18, Deputiertensitz im evangelischen Waisenhaus, 19 April 1723.
19. Ibid.
20. Ibid.
21. Ibid.
22. StAA, EW 4, Studenten die das Rechnen lernen, 1723.
23. StAA, Alms, Instruction für beide Waisenhäuser, s.d., s.a.: "... lust und lieb haben und tauglich sein mögen...."
24. StAA, KW 28, Waisenbuch, 1653–1785, Joseph Tobias Schuester, 1 October 1761.
25. StAA, EW 18, Deputiertensitz im evangelischen Waisenhaus, 24 April 1723: "lust darzu hat...."
26. Ibid., 23 February 1723.
27. Ibid., 19 April 1723.
28. Ibid., 23 February 1723: "ihr die mägdlein nicht aus der nehet nehmen...."
29. Ibid.
30. StAA, EW 13, Recommendationsschreiben für die Waisenmutter, 12 July 1726.
31. Ibid.: "... wan eine seind draus gstellt worden so hat sie mir wider andre davor geben, das es bey der zahl gebliben...."
32. Ibid.: "aber vor mich zu nehen...."
33. *Gesinde* were constantly admonished to hold their tongues and concentrate on their work. See appropriate chapters in StBA, Th Pr/2123, Cyriacus Spangenberg, *Catechismus: Die Funff Heuptstuck der Christlichen Lehre sampt der Haußtaffel und*

dem Morgen und Abendt Gebet Benedicite und Gratias etc. (Erfurt, 1567); StBA, 4° Ldw/39, Johannes Coler, *Calendarum Perpetuum et Libri Oeconomii* (Wittemberg, 1592).
34. StAA, EW 1, Waisenhausordnung, 17 February 1599. Waisenvater Lymm prescribed readings from the *Schwäz-Capital* and the *Faul-Capital*, both references to the the hortatory genre known as *Teufelliteratur*, as the proper response to these failings in orphan children.
35. This restriction was implicit in references to the support of children only until such time as they could enter service or an apprenticeship and, so, earn their daily bread. It was also apparent in numerous decisions to deny to the orphanage to children with physical or mental disabilities because they could never support themselves and would be a permanent burden. See StAA, EW 1, Waisenhausordnung, 21 January 1638; Alms, Fasc 4, Versorgung armer verlassener Kinder betr., vom Jahr 1548 bis 1778.
36. StAA, EW 13, Recommendationsschreiben für die Waisenmutter, 12 July 1726: "Es sey keine da und ist das ganze haus voler grose ungeschickt menschen die nichts können noch wisen."
37. Ibid.: "damit sie etwas sauber auch lehrnen machen von subtiler arbeit...."
38. Ibid.: "... es ist kain gsatz sondern ein guter wil aber doch thuts einem wol oder weh wan mans erkönt oder nit es hat eins gewis vil mieh bis man in die harten köpf etwas hin ein bringt nu ich thus gehrn und ist meine shuldigkeit...."
39. Ibid.
40. Ibid.: "Suma es ist in der vorigen weisen mutter im kleinen finger mehr verstand als bey der iber al."
41. StAA, EW 18, Deputiertensitz im evangelisches Waisenhaus, 22 April 1739.
42. StAA, EW 4, Lehrvertrag, 3 September 1721.
43. That third party might be a patron, a relative, or the orphanage itself. When Christian Philipp Lindemann apprenticed to the master copper engraver N. Herz, his fee of 180 fl. far exceeded his means. Indeed, it was an astronomical sum by the standards of the day. In the end, his uncle, N. Holeisen, agreed to pay 100 fl., and the Lutheran Orphanage would provide the balance. Ibid., Lehrzettel, s.d., 1721.
44. StAA, EW 18, Deputiertensitz im evangelischen Waisenhaus, 23 February 1723.
45. StAA, EW 12, Waisenhausordnung, 1780, Articulus XV, §1: "Zu Lehrjungen sollen angestellt werden alle Knaben, die ein Handwerk zu erlernen Lust haben, gesund, rein, und zum erstenmal beym H. Abendmal gewesen sind, und sollen, damit andern armen minderjährigen Waisen Weeg, und Zugang ins Waisenhauß nicht versperrt werde, auch um der von allzu großen Knaben zu besorgen Unordnungen willen hinfüro keiner, der bereits comuniciert hat, und gesund ist, länger mehr im Waisenhauß gedultet werden." Cf. Articulus XVI, §1: "Zu Diensten werden solche Waisen-Mägdlen angestellet, die nicht nur bereits comuniciert haben, und im Christenthum hinlänglich unterrichtet, sondern auch gesund, rein, und nicht mehr bleichsichtig [sic], auch von solchen Sitten, Fähigkeit und Gemuths-Gaben sind, daß man zum voraus versichert seyn kann, daß sie ihrer künftigen Herrschaft ihr Stück Brod ehrlich und gewissenhaft abverdienen können."
46. Ibid., Articulus XV, §2: "Handwerker und Professionen mögen sie zwar erlernen, welche sie wollen, doch werden die Herren Vorsteher dran seyn, ihre Inclination in Zeiten auf etwas Gemeinnüziges, ihren Talenten, Leibes, und Seelen-Kräften angemessenes zu richten...."

47. Ibid., Articulus XVI, §2: "Es is keinem Waisen-Mägdlen erlaubt sich selbst um einen Dienst zu sehen, er wäre denn, daß sie dazu besondern Erlaubniß von den Herren Vorsteher erhielte."
48. StAA, EW 1, Instruction für den Weysen Vatter und Mutter, §7, 11 May 1721.
49. StAA, EW 12, Waisenhausordnung, 1780, Articulus XV, §4: "... jedoch muß derselbige den Herrn Vorsteher anständig und als ein rechtschaffener nicht ur, sondern auch als ein seiner Profession wohlerfahrener Mann bekannt seyn, daß er beydes, die Gabe und den Willen haben werde, einem armen Waisen sein Handwerk gründlich und wohl zu lehren."
50. Ibid., Articulus XV, §3: "... weil sie auf solche Weise in Ansehung der Unterhaltung dem Waisenhaus zu beschwerlich fallen, und auch dem annoch kleinern Waisen-Kindern die Portion an Gaben, und Austheilungen verringern."
51. Ibid., Articulus XV, §7.
52. See chapter 6. The various ordinances of Augsburg's orphanages from the late sixteenth century until the late eighteenth century contained detailed, daily agendas for the children. Their days consisted of an unvarying routine of prayer, work, and study, interrupted only briefly for meals and almost never for leisure. These organizations give the lie to the contention that routinized activity was the discovery of the factory age.
53. Statistics as cited in Bettger, *Das Handwerk in Augsburg*, 177-82; Clasen, "Arm und Reich in Augsburg vor dem Dreißigjährigen Krieg," 317; Fassl, "Wirtschaft, Handel und Sozialstruktur 1648-1806," 427. Clasen's statistical categories do not correspond exactly to those of Bettger and Fassl, a function of his reliance on the tax register of 1610 rather than official surveys. Hence, ranges are provided in a few categories to avoid misleadingly high or low numbers.
54. Kellenbenz, "Wirtschaft der Blütezeit," 261.
55. Bettger, *Das Handwerk in Augsburg*, 178; Clasen, "Arm und Reich in Augsburg vor dem Dreißigjährigen Krieg." 317. Comparisons of this sort have only heuristic value because the groupings of various crafts in different trades or sectors changed with the changing purposes of bureaucrats and scholars. Clasen's designation of crafts in the food trades is an attempt to organize the data of a tax register according to the demand each craft met. This, however, bears no necessary resemblance to the organization of guilds undertaken in 1549 or to that of 1720. In the former, the food trades could include, in addition to the obvious crafts of *Metzgern*, *Bäckern*, *Fischern*, and *Brauern*, the less obvious ones of *Kramern*, *Gastwirte*, and even *Kaufleute*. By the eighteenth century, with a clear expansion in the range of consumer tastes and consumer goods, city administrators had to cast their net much more broadly to include *Zuckerbäcker*, *Obster*, *Gärtner*, *Gewürzmüller*, and *Kaffeeschenken*, among many others. Attempts to offer statistical comparisons on the basis of these surveys can give only the most general, nonspecific impressions of economic development and no reliable information whatever on the economic vigor of a particular sector or its place in the labor market.
56. Kellenbenz, "Wirtschaft der Blütezeit," 262.
57. Clasen, "Arm und Reich in Augsburg," 317.
58. Bettger, *Das Handwerk in Augsburg*, 178-81.
59. Ibid., 61.
60. Ibid.
61. Kellenbenz, "Wirtschaft der Blütezeit," 262.
62. Clasen, "Arm und Reich in Augsburg vor dem Dreißigjährigen Krieg," 317.

The figure given is the sum of tax-paying artisans in metalwork (216) and in fine mechanical work (286).
63. Bettger, *Das Handwerk in Augsburg*, 178.
64. Fassl, *Konfession, Wirtschaft und Politik*, 123.
65. Paul von Stetten, "Gedanken über Erweckung des schlafenden Kunsttriebes, des Fleißes und der Gewerbigkeit unter der hiesigen Bürgerschaft" (Denkschrift, 30 March 1779), as cited in Fassl, "Wirtschaft, Handel und Sozialstruktur 1648–1806," 473.
66. Kellenbenz, "Wirtschaft der Blütezeit," 262.
67. Fassl, "Wirtschaft, Handel und Sozialstruktur 1648–1806," 473.
68. Figures as cited in Bettger, *Das Handwerk in Augsburg*, 182; Fassl, "Wirtschaft, Handel und Sozialstruktur 1648–1806," 473.
69. Fassl, "Wirtschaft, Handel und Sozialstruktur 1648–1806," 474.
70. Kellenbenz, "Wirtschaft der Blütezeit," 263; Bettger, *Das Handwerk in Augsburg*, 179.
71. Kellenbenz, "Wirtschaft der Blütezeit," 263.
72. Bettger, *Das Handwerk in Augsburg*, 179.
73. Kellenbenz, "Wirtschaft der Blütezeit," 263.
74. Ibid., 264.
75. Ibid.
76. Clasen, "Arm und Reich in Augsburg vor dem Dreißigjährigen Krieg," 324.
77. Considering that the averages for all crafts included weavers, the percentages for all crafts excluding weavers were lower.
78. Fassl, "Wirtschaft, Handel und Sozialstruktur 1648–1806," 469.
79. Ibid., 475.
80. Bettger, *Das Handwerk in Augsburg*, 179; Clasen, "Arm und Reich in Augsburg vor dem Dreißigjährigen Krieg," 317.
81. StAA, EW 18. Deputiertensitz im evangelischen Waisenhaus, 23 February 1723: "bis zur volliger Unterrichtung."
82. The statistics collected in this table are based on cross-sectional summations for certain decades.
83. Ibid: "gar groß überdas am verstand einige mangel leidet."
84. Lower mortality rates had to do with the restriction against infants as well. According to regulations, any orphan had to be able to walk before he or she could be admitted to either Catholic or Lutheran Orphanage. The ostensible reason was the increased, individual care—and, therefore, the increased costs—associated with the care of infants and toddlers. Because the notoriously high death rates among children in preindustrial societies resulted from infant mortality—the result, in turn, of malnutrition and disease—Augsburg's orphanages housed populations that had passed the period of highest risk and were more likely to survive. The connection between age and mortality among institutionalized children has been noted by other scholars. Cf. Gavitt, *Charity and Children in Renaissance Florence*, 218–25; Hunecke, *Die Findelkinder von Mailand*, 113–26.
85. The most reliable demographic histories reckon gross mortality in early modern cities under normal circumstances, that is, without the effects of epidemic disease or food shortage, at between 35 and 45 percent. See Mols, *Introduction à la démographie historique des villes d'Europe du XIVe au XVIIIe siècle*, II, 455. For children specifically, mortality was greatest after the first year. A conservative figure set mortality for persons between one and twenty years of age at 30

percent. Cf. Isenmann, *Die deutsche Stadt im Spätmittelalter*, 33. In any case, the Augsburg orphanages managed to keep death rates among their inhabitants surprisingly low.
86. StAA, Alms, Schuldbuch, 1585–1590, Waisenhauß betreffende, p. 161. "Also wiert es auch mit den medlen gehalten. So bald sy erstarckhen etlich umbs brot und sonnst verdingt werden auch wann sy sich wolhalten und manbar sein verheirrat."
87. Fassl, *Konfession, Wirtschaft und Politik*, 73.
88. StAA, EW 4, Supplikation des Friedrich Otts Nürnberger Bott, 16 January 737. Ott considered the girl an orphan because her surviving parent abandoned her and deprived her of the means of subsistence ("ubel gefuhrte oeconomie ihres dato in Schwebach befindlichen leiblichen Mutter um alle das ihrige gebracht").

8

Welfare and Work in the Orphanages

Placing orphans in workshops and households, Augsburg's orphanages functioned as a marketplace for labor. Yet, their influence transcended supplying workers for the city's masters and mistresses. The orphanages took a hand in the entire process of shaping work relations: they trained, placed, and maintained orphans in lives of labor. Consider, for example, the service of Ursula Schmiedin.

In March 1632, Orphan Father Jonas Seyboldt placed the thirteen-year-old orphan in the service of Philipp Jacob Imhof.[1] The daughter of a weaver, Ursula had been admitted four years earlier at age nine. Her circumstances were painfully reduced; the orphan father recorded neither personal property nor craft right as her estate or expectation. Indeed, she received no notice whatever until she entered the Imhof household as a nursemaid.

The matter excited some comment and concern on the part of the alms lords because Ursula, though born of Lutheran parents, had been placed in a Catholic household. This undesirable arrangement persisted until July 1632, when the authorities formally requested that she be returned to the orphanage and the keeping of "our religion."[2] Imhof was one of Augsburg's leading Catholic patricians, a man not likely to shy away from a confrontation with Lutherans or to be intimidated by city officials. He refused their request—roughly, as they saw it—and forced the alms lords to seek an order from the City Council.

That a Lutheran child could have been placed in a Catholic home for four months had much to do with the fluid governance of the orphanage in the 1620s and 1630s. At the time of Ursula's admission, in 1628, the orphanage was in Lutheran hands. A year later, in the wake of the Edict of Restitution, the Alms Office and the City Orphanage came under direct Catholic control. The Catholic Seyboldt replaced the Lutheran Heinrich Fischer. Reflecting on these events more than a century later, the Lutheran clergyman Kaspar Krez referred to "times of deplorable affliction," during which the children were deprived of God's Word and so doubly orphaned.[3] They were forced to learn the Canisian catechism; they were forced to observe Catholic ritual; they were forced to convert to the Catholic Church; and they were forced to live with Catholic orphans. The placement of Ursula Schmiedin in the Imhof household can be understood as part of the Catholic effort to encourage the conversion of Lutheran children, an effort that Lutheran authorities strove to check. The coup endured until the summer of 1632, when Swedish forces recaptured the city, expelled the Catholics, and established a Lutheran government. Ursula became a pawn in the bitter political maneuverings of religious parties.

Though confessional tensions marked the dispute between Imhof and the Alms Office, no less central were the rights of a master over the person and labor of a servant. Responding to the complaint, Imhof insisted on his prerogative as the girl's master.[4] Because he had hired her as a maid for his children, her condition was now his affair.

Imhof's claim rested implicitly on two theoretical propositions. First, service was a form of employment, and employers enjoyed certain rights in the labor of their servants. Second, servants were family members of a sort, and heads of households enjoyed certain rights in the persons of their servants. Though neither of these gave unqualified support to the patrician's argument, both could serve to justify the sanctity of master-servant relations.

In early modern Augsburg, no uniform ordinance governed domestic service. Not organized in any form of guild or association, servants belonged individually to the households that employed them, and, for that reason, their situations varied individually. Wages, for example, could not be made uniform because the nature of service, the wealth of the household, and the status of the servant differed from one household to the next.[5] With only 14 days' notice, servant or master could dissolve their working relationship without specifying cause. An Augsburg servant had the right to change masters as often as four times a year. Masters, too, were free to release a servant who became unable to fulfill his or her duties; they were required neither to care for nor to pay the nursing costs of a sick servant. Service in Augsburg has been likened to wage labor rather than more traditional notions of service.[6] It resembled a free contract.

If customary practices minimized the mutual obligations implicit in service in Augsburg, the ties binding servant to master did not entirely disappear. Though the city knew no ordinance like the Bavarian Servants' Ordinance (Gesindeordnung), with its emphasis on obedience and discipline among household servants, the same message was communicated in other ways. A wide range of hortatory literature reinforced the moral ramifications of the master-servant relationship, the child-like status of the latter, and the paternal responsibilities of the former.

In his *Haustaffel*, Cyriacus Spangenberg explored the nature of service.[7] The servant's duty was relatively straightforward: to perform what was required without hesitation. A servant owed his or her master loyalty, industry, and subservience. Tasks were to be executed quickly and gladly; idleness was to be avoided. Indeed, servants were to care for the master's property as if it were their own. In their obedience and modesty, they were to honor the master and mistress as parents. The servant shared those qualities that Spangenberg attributed ideally to a son or daughter, namely, honor, obedience, patience, and gratitude. His charge to householders was similar to that given parents: they should support, instruct, and correct. The master should supply adequate, healthy fare. He should provide work that encouraged skill and discipline. He should punish mildly, only resorting to violence or dismissal when all else failed. The similarities of language indicate that the duties of master and servants were most easily communicated in terms of those obligations binding a father and his children.

Whatever the moral imperatives guiding these relationships, however, their bases were fundamentally different. The ties binding the servant to the master were economic rather than biological. No natural inclination to affection existed. Rather, both sides sought their own advantage. Spangenberg's use of negative constructions in the form of a list of restrictions suggests his awareness of this fact and his wish to curb it. Servants should not be idle; servants should not speak out of turn; servants should not betray their masters. The master should not withhold or reduce earned wages; the master should not withhold food or shelter; the master should not slander reputations; the master should not punish violently; the master should not overwork. Johannes Coler came more directly to the point in his *Oeconomia*. Listing the same essential qualities desirable in masters and servants, he concluded that servants, though essential, were dangerous. "However many servants one keeps, so many thieves has he."[8] For this reason, they should not be paid too much and not at all until their period of service is over. Savings, namely, made servants more independent and less pliable, a bit of paternal wisdom that might have tightened the orphanage's grip on orphan capital. The householder must govern firmly but gently with an unswerving eye on his subjects. In the final analysis, "the household is a monarchy . . . only one rules."[9] The analogy to parents and children, therefore, should not be pushed too far. Its purpose was only to reform and improve a reality that was altogether different. In fact, servants were alien workers in the household, exposed to every form of use and abuse, subject to the will of the master, and bereft of every appeal or protection.

In Augsburg, theory and practice supported the inviolability of this working relationship. Apart from the few customary and moral restrictions on the master, his authority in his household and over his servants was absolute. In challenging this arrangement, the alms lords labored to define both the terms of service and their responsibility for orphan servants.

Imhof cast doubt upon their concerns. He claimed that the orphan father had known of the religious differences between the maidservant and the household. Although these differences had made her presence and service difficult in some ways, Imhof insisted they had not kept him from offering her employment. Neither had he compelled or encouraged Ursula to convert to Catholicism in the four months of her service. She had always known elements of the Catholic religion—knowledge probably acquired in the orphanage itself—and now accepted that faith freely. Because he had not forced her to convert, Imhof expressly refused to hinder her. Ursula was no longer a child and, therefore, was free to choose her religion. She was no longer dependent upon alms and as a result no longer subject to the authorities. The King of Sweden expressly permitted the free observance of both Catholic and Lutheran faiths in Augsburg, so she could worship as she chose. For all of these reasons, the complaint of the alms lords violated natural law, city statute, and royal decree. Imhof argued that, if Ursula were subject to any authority, she was subject to his, an authority all the more weighty in that it had not been abused in a matter of faith.

In their response, the alms lords avoided the rights of the master altogether, perhaps a tacit admission of the strength of these arguments.[10] They emphasized instead the paternal responsibility of the orphanage. Ursula was too young to decide in matters of religion. Moreover, Imhof's request—not theirs—violated civic tradition and ordinance. The orphan father and mother were responsible for the proper religious instruction of the children. This had always been understood as instruction in the religion of the children's parents. Because Ursula had no surviving kin, the administrators of the orphanage exercised that duty by demanding her return in order to protect her Lutheran faith. Although the orphan had been placed in another household and under the nominal authority of another *pater familias*, the orphanage and its administrators retained an interest in and a responsibility for the child. This interest limited the rights of a master in the person or labor of his servant.

Though compelling in the metaphorical context of orphanage as family, still the arguments for the paternal power of the orphan father or the alms lords to dispose of orphans even after they left the house had no basis in law. Not until 1721 were the duties of the (Lutheran) orphan father codified.[11] Prior to that year, the orphanages had relied on experience and tradition to guide them in such matters. Now the authorities pursued a precedent consistent with the tacit separation of confessional communities that guided social relations in early modern Augsburg and would shape the nature of work for one of the city's largest groups of laborers.

That work as well as religion was at stake in the case of Ursula Schmiedin soon became obvious. In his final appeal, Imhof abandoned the topic of paternal authority and focused directly on the issue of household service.[12] He excused any appearance of defiance on his part by his obligation to resist the "feverish" attempts of the alms lords to deprive him of his servant. The customary practice of Augsburg, Imhof argued, forbade the separation of servants from their masters without an express order of the City Council. Only thus would he yield Ursula. Though he made no specific use of the term, still Imhof's argument implicitly used the notion of service as an inviolable contract between master and servant.

On 13 July 1632, the Senate issued the necessary order, making specific mention of Imhof's defiance of the civil authority. Ursula Schmiedin returned to the City Orphanage.[13] In its decree, the council offered no further discussion either of service as one of many forms of work in Augsburg or of the relative merits of the paternal authority of master and magistrate. Yet, it vindicated the responsibility of the authorities to intervene in matters such as religion or work, which concerned the well-being of their dependents.

Schmiedin's experience suggests that the orphanages mediated a part of the city's labor supply in three ways. First, they functioned as clearinghouses for work and workers, that is, they engaged in an extensive program of outplacement. Artisans and householders in and around Augsburg turned to the orphanages in order to meet their demand for labor. Second, the orphanages served as schoolhouses that trained future laborers within their own walls, in the households of burghers, and in the shops of craft masters. The administrators' concern to place orphans extended to their efforts to shape them in such ways that they became stable and persistent in their efforts. Third, the orphanages served as halfway houses that maintained and supported orphans in the world of work. As apprentices and journeymen entered or reentered the workforce, shifted from one shop to another, or tramped in and out of the city, the organizations that fostered them assisted them during the difficult transitions that were every dependent laborer's lot. By placing, training, and maintaining orphans in the artisanal economy, Augsburg's orphanages reduced the transactions costs of labor. They provided a fixed structure for the labor market, a central location to which masters in need of hands or hands in need of work could turn. By arranging work for those in need and helping workers respond to crisis and change, the orphanages also contributed a necessary element of flexibility to the labor market.

The Orphanages as Schools of Labor

When entering one of Augsburg's orphanages, a child entered a world shaped by work. The orphanages understood their task not merely in terms of securing employment for orphans but essentially in terms of preparing these young people for it. The organizations raised, trained, and educated orphans only until such time as they could be placed in service of some kind and made self-supporting. Magistrates constantly stressed the self-sufficiency of the poor as the highest goal of the city's charity. An anonymous account penned in 1585 described the process with evident satisfaction.[14] All orphans received appropriate food, drink, and education from the orphanage. This care, however, lasted no longer than necessary. As soon as boys were big enough and old enough to learn a trade, they apprenticed according to their personal preferences and abilities. The chronicler stated that over 100 young men had completed apprenticeships, become journeymen, and "now earned their daily bread with honor" in the thirteen years since the orphanage opened its doors. Girls, too, were raised with an eye to their eventual employment. Beyond the basic education provided to all children in the orphanage, they learned sewing, spinning, and housekeeping. As soon as any girl grew "sufficiently strong," she was placed in household service.

To promote self-sufficiency, the orphanages strove not so much to provide specific competencies as to inculcate habits of mind and body that might prove their worth under a master's tutelage. The curriculum of an orphanage education assisted this process, but reading, writing, and reckoning, which all orphans learned and which any master might value, were not the essence of charitable pedagogy. Rather, the orphans' daily agenda supplied an orderly, fixed routine that required of all a degree of persistence, stability, and regularity. A chronic indoctrination in time discipline, by which "new labour habits were formed, and a new time discipline imposed," began well before industrialization with "the division of labour; the supervision of labour; fines; bells and clocks; money incentives; preachings and schoolings; the supression of fairs and sports."[15]

Regulations, written for the City Orphanage in 1599 by Orphan Father Hanns Limm, captured the daily routines of the house.[16] Even under Lutheran inspiration and guidance, its unchanging cadence of study, work, and prayer echoed the rhythms of the monastery, an earlier foundry of mind, body, and spirit.

Mornings were a time for study. All children rose at six o'clock and offered prayers of thanks for the new day as they dressed. Thereafter they washed face and hands, answered roll call, and presented themselves for inspection. Person and attire were to be clean and orderly at the beginning of each day. All residents then proceeded to breakfast, which was preceded by prayers, including a special blessing on the magistrates, accompanied by spiritual readings and followed by prayers. Limm's ordinance specified each and every prayer, homily, psalm, and passage for every occasion of every day, a droning litany of gratitude for human generosity and divine grace, submission to one's estate and fate, and obedience to authority. After breakfast on weekdays, the children went to school. The morning agenda changed only on weekends. On Saturdays the children applied themselves to housekeeping in the orphanage. On Sundays the boys attended church at St. Ulrich's in the morning, while the girls did housework.

At noon, the orphans took their principal meal of the day, but not before they had been closely examined in their studies by the praeceptor and had given prayerful thanks for it and all their other blessings. Again, they ate to the sound of a sort of *lectio continuo*. After grace, all proceeded to the afternoon's work.

This portion of the day varied more than the mornings but still held to a regular, weekly schedule. On Monday, Wednesday, and Friday, the boys returned to school while the girls attended instruction in sewing and other domestic skills. By four o'clock, all were back in the orphanage for further examination and inspection. Tuesdays, the girls studied Luther's catechism under the guidance of a local pastor. At the close of their lesson, they prayed for the needy everywhere, mentioning by name those who requested the spiritual assistance of the orphanage in writing. The boys were similarly instructed on Thursdays. Though none were idle, Saturday afternoons were understood to be a time of rest. The girls busied themselves about the house, while the boys studied the disciplinary adages of Erasmus' *Civilitate morum puerilium*. On Sunday afternoons, the girls worshipped at St. Ulrich's while the boys stayed behind to contemplate Cyriacus Spangenberg's synopsized versions of the Gospels and Epistles. Mornings were given to study; afternoons were a time of work.

Evenings, like Sundays, were devoted to prayer and contemplation. All orphans attended late afternoon worship services on Wednesday and Saturday. The evening meal followed, which, like all other meals in the orphanage, was set about by prayers and accompanied by biblical verses or homilies. Each day ended with an in-house service of song and prayer before orphans and servants alike went prayerfully to bed.

Though clear record of a bell to mark the passing of the hours survives only from the eighteenth century, still the orphanages must have relied always on some similar mechanism to lend a uniform motion to each day. Idleness and lateness, not to mention recreation, had little place in the house agenda of 1599. Although the daily routines were by no means machine-like, they were regular and precise. The orphans had to move purposefully from one task or duty to the next, if they were to avoid falling hopelessly behind schedule. Thrice daily inspections made this a risky proposition. Any tardy or lazy child risked public humiliation; offenders' names were posted for the purpose of ridicule and improvement. It is difficult to gauge the effect of uninterrupted, purposeful activity on growing minds and bodies; to posit a lifetime of industry or idleness is to assume the mechanical efficiency of routines or an equally mechanical psychology of the young. It is impossible to know the influence of endless prayers of obedience, humility, and thanks; to insist that they could only invoke blind submission or equally blind rebellion is specious. But the intentions of both are by no means opaque. The adminstrators of the orphanage hoped that a regime of extreme regularity and industry, enforced by moral instruction and disciplinary sanction, would imbue needy children not only with the ability to work but also with the desire to do so.

Over the years, these routines changed little, regardless of confession or ideology. In 1638 the City Orphanage was in Catholic hands, but its daily regimen retained the character developed under Lutheran tutelage.[17] That is, the children still followed a tight schedule intended to school mind, body, and spirit. The days retained their quasi-monastic character. Days and meals began and ended with prayer. Silence, broken only by the reading aloud of some spiritual work, accompanied their daily bread. At midday, 12 selected orphans offered special prayers for grace and guard, "but especially against the plague" (*insonderheit aber vor die Pest*), a dark acknowledgment of the realities of the 1630s. Mornings were given to study and the afternoons to work. Evenings remained a time of contemplation. It was a rhythm that would persist until the coming of the machine.

Some things changed, however. By the seventeenth century, orphanage administrators demonstrated a new awareness of the differing needs of children at different ages. Not all could or should be treated alike. The "older and middling" (*grosern und mitlern*) children rose at five o'clock in order to attend morning worship services, while the younger ones remained in bed until six.[18] Where the administrators made no allowance for relaxation in 1599, it had become a regular part of each day by 1638. After the noon meal, all orphans "had a whole hour of recreation."[19] The middling and younger children were released from all labor again after the evening meal. It seems unlikely that free time was spent in undirected play; probably the children whiled away the hour with some quiet, constructive activity: handwork for the girls and homilies for the boys. Perhaps Catholic administrators recalled that monastic rules usually allowed time for relaxation amid the rigors of prayer, labor, and study. For whatever reason, the new regime acknowledged as fact the notion that children, especially younger ones, could not be compelled to work day in and day out without periodic rest.

Just as the perceived relationship between work and leisure became more nuanced, so did notions of appropriate work. From seven until eleven o'clock and again from one until four o'clock, all children in the City Orphanage went about their given duties. The administrators probably assigned work according to the age and gender of each child, but their ordinances do not record tasks more exactly. Generally speaking, however, work (Arbeit) took on a broader meaning: some went to school; some learned to sew; some engaged in handwork (Wircken). It was all work. The early emphasis on activities distinct or separate from labor had begun to yield in favor of a definition that was all-encompassing.

The tendency to differentiate the needs and abilities of children and to interpret their activities in terms of work persisted into the eighteenth century. The Orphanage Ordinance of 1780 treated the daily "study, work, rest, recreation and expeditions of orphan boys" separately from those of orphan girls and from other matters, such as worship, hygiene, or diet.[20] Although the ordinance's organization suggests a greater appreciation for work as a single, discrete element in an orphan's life, the content makes clear that work was still the central principle that defined and determined everything else. No such regulation survives from the Catholic Orphanage, but the tenor of orphan supervision there indicates the existence of a similar regime.

The days retained a liturgical character made customary by constant usage. Eighteenth-century administrators were apparently unwilling to forego all those aspects of worship which had so occupied the days of orphans in the past. Accordingly, prayer and contemplation continued to set the tone of each meal and every day. All occupants of the Lutheran Orphanage rose early—at five o'clock in the summer or six o'clock in the winter—in order to attend an hour-long, in-house, prayer service. Breakfast and all the meals that followed began and ended with prayer too. Each day closed as it opened with an hour of psalms and hymns. The ordinance no longer specified which prayers were to be offered at specific times and on specific days. Neither did it make any mention of such cloistered practices as silence and readings in the refectory or blessings and prayers for the needy at set times of day. In all probability the verses and texts, which the children repeated every day, were unchanged over two hundred years; after all, the emphasis on gratitude, submission, and obedience as desirable characteristics for needy children endured throughout the period. Simply put, worship, though still important, no longer dominated the thinking of the administrators or the activities of the orphans. It occupied two hours in every day but received bare mention in a 200-page rule. Religious devotions had become a means of supporting those activities that prepared the children for entrance into a market society.

Recreation was also part of that preparation in the Lutheran Orphanage. Daily schedules were less tightly organized by the end of the eighteenth century. For one hour after the midday meal and in the time between evening prayers and bed, the orphans were released from the normal regimen of study, work, and worship. The boys occupied themselves "with respectable games under appropriate supervision" in the courtyard.[21] The girls did not join them but went to their common room, where they were warned "to avoid all mischievousness and exuberance."[22] The normal workday ended at four o'clock, and the two hours that remained until dinner could be used for a variety of activities. Examinations and inspections probably absorbed most of this time, but the 1780 ordinance also referred to expeditions. Groups of boys or girls might, with prior permission and under the necessary supervision, take walks in the late afternoons beyond the orphanage's and, indeed, beyond the city's walls. In fact, they left the orphanage regularly. On holidays—specifically, Christmas Day, New Year's Day, Easter Monday, Pentecost Monday, and St. Michael's Day—orphans might visit their relatives. The orphanage's release policy was limited to a single day with the provisions that visitors must return at the appointed times and that small children must not go unaccompanied. Holidays, as well as Saturdays and alms days, were free days too. Alms days occurred when a donation was distributed among the children; they were released from their labors in order to show due appreciation for the "kindness of strangers."[23] Though by no means free, the orphans of 1780 enjoyed some free time.

Leisure derived its meaning from the work that was the orphans' daily lot. On those days when work ceased, that is, on Saturdays, holidays, or alms days, Lutheran orphans received no recreation period in the afternoon. Alms days were declared holidays to serve as a sort of ritual display that focused and enforced the gratitude of the needy and encouraged more frequent generosity. The recreational periods promoted good health. Boys and girls were to get the necessary and usual amount of exercise; they were not permitted to stand or sit idly. At all times, but especially when the children were not working, their governors and governesses observed them closely to ensure that recreation was not misused. They had to make particularly sure that "all mischief and disorder, especially all contact with the girls [or boys] and with the ill, who have their own places of recreation, be prevented" during play.[24] Leisure served, therefore, both the physical and the moral development of the orphans. It was purposeful, to be productively spent. In the Lutheran Orphanage, recreation was both an essential element of discipline and a logical extension of work.

Despite a modicum of flexibility in the orphans' activities, work and discipline were still the undisputed order of the day in the Lutheran Orphanage of 1780. Boys started to work at eight o'clock and continued until noon. After the midday meal and recreation hour, they returned to their several occupations again from three until four o'clock. Beyond a certain minimal instruction by the orphanage praeceptor, orphan boys now pursued activities suited to their individual abilities. Some attended Latin or German schools outside the orphanage. Those better suited to heavy physical labor assisted the orphanage servants around the house. Orphan girls followed a very different curriculum. The older ones, those who had received their first communion, were allowed to join the boys under the tutelage of the praeceptor. Thus, they learned elements of reading, writing, arithmetic, and Christian (Lutheran) doctrine.

Instruction continued only so long as the administrators deemed it necessary; the Lutheran Orphanage no longer educated its younger girls outside the walls. From age six to age ten, they learned from their governess to sew and knit. From age ten until such time as they left the house to enter service, all girls practiced other domestic chores, such as tending fires, dusting rooms, washing floors, and making beds. As such, they received a practical education in the skills required of a household servant. Certain boys also learned marketable skills before leaving the orphanage and entering a wider world. Those who expected to apprentice to a master tailor spent their last year in a practicum, assisting the house tailor (*Hausschneider*). The youngest and weakest boys occupied themselves with spinning. This is the only definite reference to factory-like work performed in any of Augsburg's orphanages. Those children instructed to spin were expected to produce no less than 100 threads (*Faden*) daily. The ordinance makes no mention, however, of the ultimate purpose of this production. Whether the thread was used in the house itself, donated to some other charity, or sold on the open market cannot be determined from any protocol or account. Whether the orphans actually worked for some form of profit remains uncertain. Certain, however, is the fact that they were accustomed to the rhythms of labor, even as they had been exposed to the discipline of time, from the moment they entered the orphanage until the day they left it. All of this occurred within the walls, but few documents record the activity.

The 1780 ordinance described the duties of the Lutheran governess and revealed some elements of the domestic craft regimen.[25] Above all, this woman taught by her own example of piety, respect, obedience, and submissiveness. Character more than skill determined a governess' suitability for office, because the office consisted primarily in the constant supervision of the girls. Instilling godliness, industry, order, and cleanliness, and preventing sin, sloth, wantonness, and disrespect were her paramount tasks.[26] Only after these issues were treated in considerable detail did the ordinance turn to the practical matter of craft. The governess had to instruct each girl thoroughly in sewing and knitting. Young people who were slow to learn were to be guided gently and patiently. Special mention was reserved for the orphans' posture and the teacher's pet. Girls should avoid a bent or crooked posture and be constantly instructed to work upright and erect. A crooked spirit required similar correction: favoritism of any sort was to be strictly avoided. Sewing in the orphanage may have been a part of any girl's training for household service, but it was also an opportunity for moral correction and improvement. Discipline preceded skill.

The same principle applied to the house tailor. When orphan boys received their introduction to the craft by assisting him, they observed an artisan hired to be submissive. The 1780 ordinance reduced the duties of the orphanage tailor to behaving like a servant rather than like a master.[27] He was to observe all regulations, be honest and faithful, avoid contact with females, conserve his materials, steal nothing from the house, avoid complaining about conditions, demand neither payment nor gifts from orphans or staff, refer all problems to the administrators, and attend to the boys in his charge. In short, he was to comport himself in a manner that was "Christian, industrious, and loyal."[28] Like all other elements in the rearing of orphans, crafts in the Lutheran Orphanage emphasized moral discipline rather than artisanal technique. Skill and the relations that it forged had to be learned outside the walls.

Though the children rarely passed the gates of the Lutheran Orphanage unattended after 1780, they frequently sallied into a wider world in earlier decades. They ran errands and received instruction outside the walls. The lessons learned casually while under way to and from school and church in markets, streets, and shops must have provided a raucous, combative counterpoint to the formal instruction of the house.

The dispute with Maria Sabina Weisin, as detailed above, demonstrates that orphans experienced far more of the rough and tumble of workshop relations at large in the world of labor than confined in the discipline of the house. They came to know elements of exploitation and resistance in employer-employee relations by observing and participating. Some may have labored under abusive or unhealthy circumstances far different from those of the paternalistic house. They learned that workers protected their interests at the expense of their masters and mistresses. For these reasons, perhaps, the administrators determined in 1780 to limit exposure of this sort.

At the close of the Old Regime in Augsburg, the basic education of Lutheran orphans—whether reading, writing, and arithmetic or basic techniques of handicrafts—occurred within the orphanage. As in 1572, when the city's magistrates resolved to abandon the fostering of parentless children in favor of caring for them in a central orphanage, the reasons for in-house training inextricably combined disciplinary concerns with fiscal imperatives.

The orphans traditionally had scattered across the city to receive their education from private schoolmasters and seamstresses. This practice posed difficulties for the orphanage administrators. The treatment of children and the quality of learning must have varied from person to person and place to place. The house's experience with the seamstress Weisin was probably not the only instance in its history of practices detrimental to the health and character of the orphans and contradictory to the economy and discipline of the orphanage. Given the state of early modern administration, however, it was virtually impossible to police employees of the institution, so long as they worked outside the walls and away from the administrators' watchful eyes.

As they debated the ordinance of 1780, administrators and magistrates recognized and prized the greater efficiency of a central school within the orphanage itself.[29] The wish for both lower costs and greater control compelled them to hire a praeceptor and a governess to instruct and monitor the boys and girls around the clock.

The duties of these new appointees became all-encompassing when they moved inside the orphanage. Formal teaching was, in fact, the least demanding or time-consuming aspect of their new duties: the praeceptor was to provide no less than six hours of instruction on every day designated a school day; the governess had to teach all orphan girls to sew and knit and to see to it that their work was thorough and neat. General supervision of the children, however, required much more time and energy. Praeceptor and governess got out of bed before the children to make sure that all rose, washed, dressed, and presented themselves for inspection promptly when the morning bell rang. They joined them in their devotions, their meals, and their recreation. They were responsible for all work performed by the orphans in the house, and they accompanied them to church or on excursions through the city and in the countryside. In short, the praeceptor and governess could never leave their orphans unattended.

In most respects, the positions of these two servants were similar. Though subject to the orphan father and mother, the praeceptor and governess enjoyed pay and privileges above those of the other house servants, due in no small measure to the nature of their skills and the importance of their tasks. The governess, however, shouldered a wider range of duties in the house because of the gender-specific division of housekeeping tasks. Thus, she mended clothing for all the orphanage's residents, supervised the serving of meals to the girls, and assisted them and the female servants in heating and cleaning the entire building. By contrast the praeceptor had no specific duties apart from the education of all children and the supervision of the boys.

The ordinance of 1780 recognized types of behavior that were specific to boys or girls and so posed challenges to their supervisors. The ordinance enjoined the governess to promote good posture and avoid favoritism. In the case of boy orphans, however, a broader range of behavior needed policing.

For example, the praeceptor had to pay particular attention to the boys' use of the toilets. He had to see to it that they always used the facility alone and never took too long doing so. Administrators intended to frustrate certain kinds of unsavory horseplay that must have proven problematic in the past. The praeceptor was charged more strictly than the governess with the supervision of recreation. He had to prevent all boisterous and disorderly activities; the boys could never even leave his sight during their leisure periods. Table manners were also a concern. The praeceptor labored to prevent sloppiness and waste, problems not mentioned among the girls. It seems that attaining moral behavior among boys posed greater difficulties for the orphanage staff.

The ordinance urged praeceptor and governess to imbue their charges with the "fear of God, industry in their work, and the observance of good order," by example as well as by instruction and supervision.[30] The qualities that determined the choice of a praeceptor and a governess were exactly those that the orphanage sought to instill in its children. Praeceptor and governess had to be persons "of sufficient age and unimpeachable character."[31] Not only were they to raise the children to "piety, industry, order, and cleanliness as well as other good habits and Christian virtues," and to prevent "useless, much less sinful and shameful" behavior, but they were also to embody these qualities and ideals themselves.[32] Both were enjoined to execute the orders of their superiors promptly and "joyfully"; their reliability and willingness were paramount considerations. Neither were encouraged to develop familiar relations with the orphans or with other servants. They were to keep themselves to themselves. Though responsible for the children's behavior in the widest possible sense, their authority was limited absolutely to matters of instruction. The praeceptor and governess were expected to observe and supervise all aspects of life for the orphans but were allowed to remonstrate or punish only violations of classroom or workroom discipline. They depended on the orphan father or his superiors in the Alms Office for the resolution of any other problems, thus rendering them both obedient and subservient. Basic skills were the least of the lessons they offered; more important was the model of servile comportment.

Under the 1780 ordinance, both instructors effectively became dependent servants of the orphanage rather than independent sub-contractors. The praeceptor and governess earned fixed salaries of 52 fl. and 16 fl. per year respectively—a stunning differential considering the similarities of their work— instead of the customary fee of 1 fl. 12 kr. per student.[33] Administrators were less concerned with reducing expenses than with controlling them and making them predictable. Since 1770, the costs of educating and training orphans had fluctuated, growing from 49 fl. in 1771 to 71 fl. in 1775, before sliding back to 62 fl. in 1778.[34] The orphanage needed a fixed expense that would not change with the population of orphans or the ambitions of their teachers. This the new regime of 1780 provided.

The administrators of organizational charity sought to erect an efficient system to support and discipline the poor; the mission could not be and never was understood apart from its cost. They strove to control minutely the motions and motives of orphans and servants and to control the expense of doing so at the same time.

The praeceptor's salary as instructor and overseer was probably considerably less than might have been earned as a teacher of private students. Perhaps as an inducement to attract more qualified candidates, the administrators permitted him to supplement his income in this way for as many as two hours each day. The rest of his time, however, had to be devoted to the orphan boys in his care. Such opportunities were denied the governess, who was forbidden to work outside the house and had to direct all her energy and attention to her charges. The earnings of both servants derived almost exclusively from their constant care of the children; their privacy was reduced to a small wooden cell built into each dormitory.[35] The orphanage even provided such basic needs as medicine, clothing, food, and drink from its own stores. So, a wider world with its freedom and opportunity, which had been prescribed to a large extent by the city's shops and marketplaces, gradually closed to orphans and servants alike.

It is small wonder that the administrators found few persons interested in working under these new conditions. As they noted, those women who were suited to be governesses in the orphanage were unwilling to serve, and those who were willing to serve were unsuited. In the end they offered the position to Felicitas Eisenmayerin, a twenty-three-year-old orphan who had already worked in the house as a children's maid. She seemed to be no one's first choice; they promoted her "in spite of her own weaknesses," a cryptic reference both to a scandalous interlude with a servant named Reinhard and to her inability to sew a stitch. Eisenmayerin had to swear henceforth to avoid all contact with men as a condition of employment. She also had to learn her new craft, the costs of which would be deducted from her salary. Whatever her disadvantages, however, Eisenmayerin offered distinct advantages to the orphanage. As an adminstrator put it: "She would be of no further use in the new regulation and for that reason would be discharged completely, but because of her expressed love for the orphanage, good humor, familiarity in the house, but especially because of her native ability to turn her hand to any task, [she is] to be named seamstress and governess of the girls."[36] What mattered in the end was not her moral or technical shortcomings but rather her work discipline, that is, her willingness, pliability, and reliability—characteristics amply proven by her years of service in the house.

Hiring a praeceptor proved no simpler. Again, the new conditions of employment were a stumbling block. The former praeceptor was unequal to the new, disciplinary tasks of his office and was pensioned off. What was worse, the orphanage staff offered no prospect who could be groomed for the job. Even among Augsburg's schoolmasters, the best candidates were unwilling and the willing were not the best. These circumstances forced the administrators to seek further afield. "Thus, one chooses a house praeceptor with good references and credentials from Weiher in Württemberg, Johann Jakob Breymair."[37] Willingness and reliability were no less important than competence, with Breymair as with Eisenmayerin.

For these paragons of virtue to achieve their greatest effect, all other influences had to be carefully controlled. The ordinance of 1780 sharpened orphanage discipline, the ways orphans were trained and molded into workers and burghers. A list of the rights and responsibilities of each resident provided an exact program for all house offices and a formal benchmark to measure their execution. A precise chain of command and competence linked orphans, servants, and officers to a series of higher authorities that extended beyond the walls, subjecting all activities to a close observation and binding the orphanage to the city. So armed, orphanage administrators turned the lenses of their scrutiny from the quantity to the quality of work. Constant supervision replaced constant activity. The days were no longer quite so tightly regimented. All residents in the house, however, whether children or adults, were watched in every waking or sleeping moment, and their behavior was measured against explicit norms. Attention to the manner of work—its tone and texture—would open a door on the character of the worker, and his or her character would provide the key to the habit of work.

Regulated behavior required a regulated environment. Henceforth servants and orphans would be sheltered from the world and spared distractions from and contradictions to the orphanage's regime of paternal authority and influence. This is worth emphasizing: contacts were limited and regulated not to protect society from the needy but to protect the needy from society. Seen this way, the prophylactic quality of social discipline, even in the extreme form of a great enclosure, warded off the mainstream rather than the marginal. It shielded orphans from the deleterious effects of laboring society even as it sought to mould them into self-sufficient laborers.

The Orphanages as Halfway Houses of Labor

The training and support that a child received while in the orphanage forged an enduring relationship between individual and organization, a web of reciprocal rights and responsibilities that bound the two in the outside world. The orphans worked to support themselves and relied on the orphanages for help in need. The orphanages policed the behavior of their wards, both while they lived within the houses and after they were grown and on their own, and they provided material and moral support for apprentices, journeymen, and servants already in the work force, ostensibly to ensure their persistence at work. By maintaining labor, the orphanages mediated Augsburg's labor market.

For many orphans, the world of work must have been a forbidding and difficult place. Successfully arranging an apprenticeship could be a difficult, frustrating experience. Michel Braun was dismissed by his first master, the weaver Jerg Beham, because he lacked the motor skills to practice the craft.[38] The orphanage immediately located another master weaver, Jerg Neher, under whose direction the boy completed his training. Hanns Hoffschneider, the son of a weaver and an orphan of Augsburg since 1579, was apprenticed to a blind craftsman named Hanns Mair in 1591.[39] The boy remained in place little more than two years before he left to seek a new craft and master. Without commenting, the orphanage helped its charge to make a new beginning. Perhaps the fact that Hanns possessed property valued at 44 fl. made a degree of inconstancy affordable, if not conscionable. Two months after joining the workshop of master weaver Abraham Ott, Hoffschneider was dismissed from service because of a suppurating skin ailment.[40] The orphanage came to his aid again, this time admitting him to the Pilgrim House to convalesce. The last entry noted that Hanns was killed in the Hungarian wars. Guiding and assisting needy young people as they reentered urban society demanded resourcefulness, as well as resources, on the part of the authorities.

For these and most other orphans, the orphanage did little more than facilitate their careers by acting as an intermediary with magistrates or masters and by disbursing or augmenting the young person's own property. The implications of this assistance for the persistance of dependent children as independent adults, citizens, and laborers is worthy of consideration. This kind of maintenance might be described in a limited sense as material or administrative, but it had a psychological dimension too. Accompanied and assisted by the orphanages, orphans must have felt somewhat more confident seeking employment, just as employers must have felt more confident hiring them.

Indeed, the orphanages of Augsburg stood behind their orphans throughout their adult lives[41] (see Table 8.1). In the period of apprenticeship, while a young man was indentured to a master craftsmen to learn his trade, or the first six months to two years of household service, after which a young woman could demand her marriage portion (*Aussteuer*) and cut her formal ties to the house, orphans relied on the assistance of the organization to resolve problems in their working relationships with their masters and

TABLE 8.1
Persistent Reliance of Orphans on Orphanages

	1580s	1620s	1650s	1680s	1720s	1760s
Placed out of house	56	127	55	68	68	65
1 petition before training completed	15	24	5	7	6	11
2+ petitions before training completed	2	13	1	2	2	2
Training completed	38	14	7	36	48	63
1 petition after training completed	27	6	5	23	26	31
2+ petitions after training completed	9	5	1	12	22	31

mistresses. Even after orphans became independent wage-earners, they continued to rely on the orphanages to provide material assistance in times of need.

In the crisis decades of the 1620s and 1650s, for example, higher proportions of apprentices and servants failed to complete their initial phase of employment. This is consistent with periods of high mortality or economic uncertainty, and was certainly reflected in the higher instance of orphans petitioning the orphanage before their training was complete. The living needed help finding new situations; the dead had to be recorded and buried. Though no documents report the fact, many young people may have found employment as wage-laborers.

Apart from the difficult period between 1620 and 1660, however, a large and increasing proportion of orphans placed in training or employment apparently demonstrated an acceptable degree of stability. Apprentices completed their training and became journeymen; servants worked in a single household for the period of time required to receive their property. Despite the apparent improvement in their stability, however, these newly trained and employed laborers petitioned the orphanages with increasing frequency over the course of their working lives.

Most of these requests for material assistance were occasioned by the fact that the organizations retained administrative control of the orphans' savings and property (see Table 8.2). The preservation and manipulation of orphan capital had been a responsibility of the orphanage since 1572. Over the course of the eighteenth century, however, orphan journeymen and servants became more reliant on the orphanages to provide for them from their own resources and from those of the organizations themselves. Whether this was

TABLE 8.2
Type of Assistance Requested by Out-Placed Orphans

	1580s	1620s	1650s	1680s	1720s	1760s
Administrative	32	18	5	3	10	10
Material	15	6	7	36	45	62
Employment	4	15	1	8	2	8

an expression of an increased degree of economic uncertainty or of organizational supervision is difficult to determine. Nonetheless, adult orphans, many of whom had lived outside the orphanages for years, returned again and again for a helping hand.

The earliest references to the maintenance of orphans outside of the orphanage prescribed the supervision and oversight of young apprentices and servants. Once young people left the house for the first time, the orphanage administrators were to check their progress by periodically questioning their masters and mistresses.[42] The reasons were, at least in part, economic. Orphans were expected to apply themselves to their work in such a way that the money spent on apprenticeships would not be wasted. Moreover, their behavior was to exhibit a "good, honorable manner," one that proved that the care and rearing they received in the orphanage had not been in vain. The regulations of the orphanage presupposed a long-term relationship among organization, master, and orphan, in which only the orphan's qualities and characteristics as a worker were at stake.

This did not always come to pass. In many cases, no evidence suggests an interlocutory role for the orphanage between master and servant. The administrators simply arranged employment and let things take their course. Katharina Engellerin, the daughter of Augsburg locksmith Hanns Engeller, entered the orphanage in 1580 and was placed in service, "for a fitting annual wage," to the wife of an Augsburg merchant, Jacob Hoser, in 1588.[43] Likewise, in 1586 the orphanage placed Samuel Furst in service to Jonas Wickert, a weaver of some substance.[44] Samuel would wash and soak linen thread and would accompany his master's children to school. In return, Wickert agreed to provide the boy with food, drink, and clothing, and to teach him the craft. Like many others, these orphans simply disappeared from the organization's purview after they left the house.

Orphan apprentices, journeymen, and servants frequently approached the orphanage with requests for material support of various kinds. In most instances this involved nothing more than a few articles of clothing or bedding, with which the orphanage traditionally furnished its dependents. Isaac Meixner, an apprentice cobbler, asked the deputies for a new shirt and jacket.[45]

He got his wish, "because he had behaved well to date." Whether the clothing constituted an act of largesse by the orphanage or a debit against the boy's savings is unclear. In the case of Johann Balthas Kieffer, however, there is no doubt. When he asked for a new shirt and money to pay certain guild fees, he received 3 fl. and a shirt from his own property, with a warning that no more could be had until he completed his apprenticeship.[46] That the orphans themselves could bear the costs in no way guaranteed that their petitions would always be granted. Abraham Westermayer, who was no apprentice but a master painter, requested 10 fl. for a new suit. The deputies granted only 7 fl. 30 kr.[47] Anna Catherina Anheckerin convinced the deputies to provide her with bedding worth 10 fl., but that amount of material support was unusual and, again, had to be paid from her own property.[48] Rendering minor fees or providing adequate clothing were ways the orphanage ensured that orphans remained employed and cut a proper figure.

By 1780 the Lutheran Orphanage had established formal procedures for meeting such eventualities. As noted, out-placed orphans were entitled to receive clean clothing every Saturday from the house, at which time they surrendered any that needed laundering or mending. Apprentices might exercise this privilege for the entire period of their training; servants had to provide their own clothing after two years.[49] They could request additional clothing or advances from their property only by attending the weekly meeting of the deputies, providing an opportunity for oversight as well as a control on expenditures.[50] As practice made clear, the fate of these requests depended frequently on the authorities' assessment of the petitioner's comportment as well as need. A note regarding good behavior usually accompanied assistance.

The connection between assistance and behavior was not, however, perfectly consistent. Although ready to punish violations directly, administrators usually preferred to reward good, submissive behavior by granting extra considerations. A tendency to encourage conformity and the hope of eventual improvement could lead the authorities to support miscreants. Euphrosina Binzin's guardians appeared before the deputies in 1723 to request assistance for their ward, when her pregnancy made household service impossible.[51] Though the young woman had no matrimonial prospects, still the orphanage came to her aid. Doubtless deprecating the actions of both this and many other orphans, the administrators had to act in the interest of their self-sufficiency and the organization's stated goal. Failure to do so would surely have forced Binzin into a marginal life of beggary, criminality, and dependence.

To shape young people into pliant, hard-working laborers, the 1780 Orphanage Ordinance discussed in detail the kind of behavior required of apprentices and servants. Certainly they had always been expected to be industrious, obedient, and loyal, but these guidelines went considerably further, demanding a complete identification with the masters' interests.

Falsify, neglect, and omit nothing, neither large nor small, no matter how unimportant it may seem, never bark [sic] back but accept discipline, display every respect to their masters and the masters' wives, also be mannerly, polite, and modest to the journeymen and indeed to everyone, in short to conduct and behave themselves as befits a Christian orphan and honor-loving young person. They should promote the use and advantage of their masters, hinder and prevent their damage and loss, to that end complete the assigned work with unfettered zeal and industry, apply all their strength to learn their craft and profession thoroughly; when they are sent out to work, not inflate its value and worth and hold something back from that sum any more than from the gratuity given them—under pain of severe punishment [for disobedience].[52]

Because they were raised and supported by public charity, the orphans bore a particular responsibility to reject bad company, to engage in proper behavior, and to undertake nothing without the master's knowledge and consent. In short, as orphans they were expected to display exemplary comportment and avoid the boisterous "drinking, gaming, dancing, and other youthful excesses as well as all taverns and public places."[53] The isolation that marked their training in the orphanage was meant to continue in the workshops. They were cut off from the sociability that constituted much of the work culture of wage laborers.

The maintenance of apprentices offered by the orphanages served the interests of the masters. It created opportunities to discipline laboring men and women. Moreover, it deferred or reduced the fixed costs of labor.

For all of these reasons, petitions for material assistance were often brought by the employers themselves on behalf of their employees. A master lacemaker, Jacob Oberbach, requested that Johann Bock, "who was training with him and behaves well and honorably," receive clothing and linen from the Lutheran Orphanage "because of the indigence of his mother."[54] Their agreement stipulated that the orphanage pay the usual fees and the mother supply her son's clothing during his training. On the strength of the master's recommendaton, the deputies agreed to furnish one pair of new shoes, one pair of new stockings, and a fresh set of linen every year until Bock completed his indenture. Another lacemaker, Johann Daniel Mertz, appeared on behalf of his servant, an orphan named Catharina Falchin.[55] She needed new clothing, for which her master had already loaned her 6 fl.[56] His request that she be given an advance of 15 fl. from her savings was approved with the condition that he forgive half her debt to him. The deputies probably feared that Falchin's meager resources might find their way into her master's pocket.

Sickness or accident might render apprentice or servant unable to work, burdening the masters with unexpected expenses and lost productivity. As with such necessities as clothing, the orphanage reduced transactions costs by assuming the care of its own and relieving masters of the responsibility. Should illness or injury make an apprentice useless, his master could return him to the orphanage, where he would be admitted at no cost to the infirmary (*Krankenstube*).[57] This was undoubtedly a service to the orphan, who might otherwise languish without care in his master's household or in a craft hostel. But it was also a tremendous service to the employer, who was spared an extra mouth to feed and might immediately apply for a healthy replacement.

Caring for sick, injured, or disabled apprentices and servants in the orphanages was fairly common practice. In 1723, Catholic and Lutheran administrators drew up lists of orphans whose prospects for employment and self-sufficiency were limited and who had become chronic burdens to their respective institutions.[58] The Catholic Orphanage housed 14 severely handicapped orphans, ranging in age from eleven to fifty-four, all of whom had spent most of their lives within those walls. The Lutheran Orphanage was no different, sheltering 20 diseased or deformed persons from ages eleven to seventy-one. In both houses, the chronically ill, physically deformed, and mentally disturbed constituted 20 to 25 percent of the total dependent population. Most of these had been placed in service or apprenticeship at least once; some had worked for several masters. The results were always the same. A twenty-four year old woman, Sabina Prinzingin, had lived in the Lutheran Orphanage eleven years and was "a simpleton who has been released from service and returned to the house often because of her clumsiness."[59] She contributed to the orphanage as she could by sewing and cleaning. Johann Georg Stegherr was sixteen years of age and had lived in the Catholic Orphanage since he was seven. The record described him as "lying sick with fever and otherwise is lame in arm and foot and for that reason has been sent back by one artisan after another."[60] Georg Bock, at twenty-three years of age a seven-year resident of the Lutheran Orphanage, had "been sent home by craftsmen because of his constant ailments and the fistulous damage on one of his hands."[61] Jonas Paul Kling had been an apprentice painter, but his master terminated their relationship and returned him to the Lutheran Orphanage because of a damaged, probably twisted foot and a declining capacity for work.[62] At twenty years of age, ten of which he had spent in the organization, he could do little more than join his fellows, all of whom made themselves useful by lending the house-tailor a hand.

At the proper time, the administrators made every effort to place their charges, regardless of inability or infirmity, in some kind or work. The hard realities of labor before the machine, however, doomed those without sufficient strength of mind and body to perpetual or periodic unemployment. Some masters and mistresses were prepared to hire disabled or deformed orphans, but they used any pretext to sever the working relationship and "send the orphan home."

Committed to the maintenance of these young people, the orphanages accepted them, cared for them, and sought new work for them. At this point, as at others, the maintenance of laboring men and women was a service to the employers. It relieved or deferred costs that the masters themselves would have had to bear. Such "services" probably gave orphan laborers a competitive advantage over others, but they also carried unforeseen consequences for the houses.

The experience of these older, disabled orphans captured the ambiguity of the orphanages' intervention in the labor markets. Pledged to support the often conflicting interests of the employers of labor and of the laborers themselves, they frequently abandoned their own purposes and provided services beyond those set forth in their regulations or financed in their budgets. Augsburg's orphanages cared for the parentless children of deceased citizens in such a way as to prepare them for lives of labor and self-sufficiency, and so ensure that they not become dependent on the charity of others and a burden to society. To this end, the magistrates charged orphanage administrators to accept only those qualified orphans who were physically and mentally able to work. All others were to be shunted to some other organization, charged with the care of the disabled. Lack of resources or alternatives and the inability to distinguish clearly the causes of need usually forced even theoretically specialized facilities to maintain a diverse population of needy people: young and old, sick and healthy, indigent and marginal, honorable and dishonorable. The reality of social welfare frustrated specialization and dictated omnicompetence.

Employers and employees, predictably, attempted to exploit the provision of health care through the orphanage infirmary for their own ends: orphans who wished to avoid work feigned illness; masters who wished to save the costs of room and board demanded assistance.[63] To control costs to the orphanage and keep feckless or disabled workers away from impressionable orphans, administrators recommended that servants and apprentices receive no further medical care in the orphanages. Should they be injured or become sick, these orphans would be placed in the Pilgrim House. Costs would be borne by the orphanage cashier and, in extreme cases, the affected person's savings. The City Council approved the measure on 3 July 1790; whether it accomplished its purpose is unknown.[64]

The 1780 Ordinance had to establish a series of checks and inspections by which deviant behavior might be exposed and corrected. Much of this was not new, having been house practice since the beginning of the eighteenth century at least, but its codification gave new weight to the supervision and correction of orphans after they left the orphanage. The deputies were charged directly with the oversight of orphans in the workplace. The ordinance specified that they send the praeceptor or the house servant to each and every orphan's master to inquire "after their apprentice's industry, loyalty and conduct" every six months.[65] Similar questions were put to the masters and mistresses of household servants. Neither had the masters to wait for these semiannual visits; they could bring any problem directly to the deputies, and, indeed, were charged to do so in every case without delay.

One of the complaints voiced most frequently by administrators, craftsmen, and householders was that servants and apprentices abandoned their work without cause and without notice. Lack of persistence was, to judge by the records of the orphanages themselves, a common problem that deprived employers of labor, damaged the reputation of the orphanage, and prejudiced the employability of all orphans. The Police Ordinance of 1559 captured the seriousness of this "crime" in the eyes of masters and magistrates by imposing stern penalties, including banishment and blacklisting, on those who committed it. By contrast, instances in which orphans fled their employment in the eighteenth century gave rise only to perplexed tongue clicking and head shaking. The world of work apparently had become less harsh, at least for orphans. Orphanage administrators could do little more than seek to locate the absconding young people and to find them new positions.

Many orphans bounced from one master to another, often from one craft to another, before developing an enduring work relationship and completing an apprenticeship. After all, the boys were to be apprenticed in crafts not only for which they were suitable but also to which they had some inclination. Locating a craft that met these requirements might involve some—but not too much—trial and error. Eustachius Weber, for example, was originally apprenticed to master tailor Ulrich Glöggle but ran away after a couple of months because "he had a greater desire for the baker's craft."[66] The orphan father promptly apprenticed the boy to Balthasar Schuester, who agreed to teach baking to the willing apprentice at no charge. In 1672, the authorities noted that Eustachius had died in Rome, probably on the road as a soldier or a pilgrim.

If circumstances conspired to prevent some people from locating or keeping work, character got in the way of others. Even when discipline and correction appeared necessary, the orphanage could prove a patient support to the young. Paulus Mair, the son of a carpenter, entered the City Orphanage in 1594 at the age of twelve.[67] Beyond the right to practice a craft in Augsburg, Paulus possessed only debts. Apprenticed to master weaver Philip Gaisfues at age sixteen, Paulus immediately fled his position, sold the clothing off his body, and took to life on the streets of Augsburg.[68] Taken in charge again by the orphanage administrators, he was deloused, clothed, and apprenticed anew. Still, he refused to learn a trade, preferring a masterless, vagabond existence. The orphanage reluctantly decided he was incorrigible and released him into the care of his older brother Hanns, a book merchant (*Buchhandler*), who undertook to teach the boy his trade and took him to Vienna on business. Carol Kaisser served as apprentice to no less than four master weavers between 1617 and 1623, before he foresook Augsburg in the company of other "wicked boys."[69] So long as he remained in the city, however, the orphanage sheltered him within its walls, placed him with unsuspecting masters, and hoped he would improve. Jeremias Gürtler tested their patience and resolve even further.[70] Not only did the boy refuse to learn one craft after another, he also stole from the orphanage and was punished by the street watch (*Gassenknecht*) for his crime. Still, the orphan father never turned him out of the house.

Neither were young women necessarily more stable. The administrators placed Maria Sedelmairin five times in two years.[71] The first master, Leonhard Widemann, described her as "a lazy thing"; she fled the second after eight days; she developed a growth and was released by the third. Only the fourth and fifth situations lasted more than a month. To judge from these few cases, orphanage administrators were prepared to go to considerable lengths and to tolerate considerable expense in order to find work for orphans and make them self-sufficient. More often than not, their persistence was rewarded with success. Most orphans seem to have conformed, formally at least, to the expectations of their governors by settling into some honorable trade.

Official tolerance was not, however, without limits, and the administrators could treat unrepentant youth harshly. Instability and lack of persistence, for example, deprived masters of their rights in the labor of their apprentices and violated the legal agreement entered into by the orphanage on behalf of the orphan. Moreover, they gave evidence of character that did not bode well for an orphan's productive, self-sufficient future. Rebelliousness of this sort, while far from the norm, was not uncommon.

Georg Heuffl entered the Catholic Orphanage at age eleven in 1658.[72] One year later, he fled the house and settled in Bavaria in the household of a village priest. After a period of time, Heuffl returned to Augsburg and sought readmission to the orphanage. This the authorities refused, and returned the boy to his mother "as an example to others." When the braid- and lacemaker Meister Kraus complained to the administrators of the Lutheran Orphanage that his apprentice, Matheus Eberhart, had fled his authority and willfully damaged the tools of his trade, the deputies did not hesitate to order that the truant be arrested and beaten.[73] Understood to be subversive by nature, resistance to legitimate authority provoked strong responses at nearly every level.

One of the most spectacularly enterprising of these hard cases was Hans Gsell.[74] The son of a weaver, he entered the City Orphanage in 1618 with nothing but sharp wits and few scruples. His intellectual gifts may be inferred from his enrollment in the St. Anna Collegium, a place usually reserved for the university-bound sons of elite families. His lack of ethics became clear as he repeatedly defied authority, escaped the orphanage, and swindled his way across southern Germany. In 1621, he abandoned the life of the mind and headed for the city of Ulm. The orphanage retrieved him at considerable expense and promptly apprenticed the truant to goldsmith Balduino Trentwed. Gsell served neither long nor well. He deserted his master and stole 50 fl. worth of silver from him. Caught in the neighboring village of Pfersee, where he had fenced the metal to a Jewish merchant for 8 fl., Gsell was punished and returned to the orphanage, from which he escaped once again. Officials in the Goldsmiths' Guild reported in 1623 that they had received a communication from colleagues in the city of Nuremberg, that Gsell had appeared in the nearby town of Wörth, where he passed himself off as the son of an Augsburg smith. He had been lodged out of pity but, after a few months, had "borrowed" 9 *Taler* (roughly equivalent to 54 fl.) from a local baker and skipped once again. Another period of silence ended in 1624 with a note that Gsell had written from Ulm to ask that the orphanage provide a certificate to identify him as a farrier. The administrators refused this extraordinary request and washed their hands of the young man. Gsell took to the road once more and was last reported in Munich.

The unusual mobility of this orphan reflects certain realities: early modern society possessed strata that were permanently on the move; it was relatively easy even for inexperienced people to travel far.[75] The ready handout, the night's shelter, and the occasional job were common knowledge in each community. These things—to say nothing of the unusual latitude of the magistrates—made it easy for orphans to slip the traces of poor relief and hard for orphanages to keep track of their wandering charges.

Gsell's story is unusual insofar as most orphans did not so readily or determinedly resort to crime or abandon familiar surroundings. Nonetheless, it represents an entire class of orphans, who steadfastly refused the moral and material regime of organized charity. It also captures the patience of the orphanage administrators, who followed the careers of their orphans, assisted them at need, and gave up only when all means had proven futile.

Rather than a stick, a carrot worked wonders in some cases. Friderich Wagner entered the orphanage at age eight, the orphaned son of a day laborer who had never earned the right to practice a craft or trade in Augsburg.[76] Hard times and a hard life had left their marks on the boy. The orphan father wrote, "He is a wicked, unpunishable boy; only time will tell what discipline will bring." After nine years in the house, he was placed in service to a local merchant, Abraham Mayr, who took the boy, "so long as he submits to direction."[77] The situation was apparently to Friderich's liking because within several months he was sent to Württemberg on his master's business and served as his factor there. The closing note in the entry expressed clearly the administrators' relief: "He has a good opportunity, praise God."[78] Here was an orphan who might yet make good.

By 1780, however, tolerance seems to have failed to induce the desired degree of persistence, and the administrators fastened on sterner, less forgiving measures. Orphan apprentices who fled their masters' service immediately lost all claim to benefits from the orphanage.[79] They became instant outcasts, a most dangerous situation in an age when master-less men were not only unemployed but also highly suspect.[80] This did not mean that apprentices and servants had no recourse but to endure harsh or unjust treatment. In such circumstances, they could turn to the deputies or to their confessor (*Beichtvater*) for aid or counsel, but had to submit to their disposition of the case.[81] Very few appeals of this sort survive. The orphans must have realized what the 1780 ordinance made clear under all circumstances: the administrators upheld the interests of the masters.

Despite the impositions of a regime that favored the forces of authority and discouraged self-determination, if not self-sufficiency, increasing numbers of orphans completed their initial phases of employment over the course of the eighteenth century. Beyond apprenticeship, the maintenance that the orphanages offered laboring men and women entered a distinctly new phase. Those orphans who became journeymen or servants were no longer indentured and dependent as they had been in the orphanages or in their masters' workshops and households. Nominally, at least, they now controlled their own fates. Except in the most unusual circumstances, the orphanages did not seek employment for journeymen or servants who had not proven themselves to be stable, persistent workers. Neither did they offer material assistance, except in cases of the utmost need. While continuing to administer the savings and other property of adult orphans living outside the house, the orphanages were far less willing to intervene in the affairs of independent wage earners and did so far less frequently.

As orphans were released finally into the world of work, Augsburg's orphanages provided one last measure of assistance, which symbolized the orphans' new status as self-sufficient wage-laborers. New journeymen required suitable clothing, money for the road, and the tools of their trade. Household servants needed clothing and linen suitable to their station. Requests for these things, the journeyman's suit (*Gesellenkleid*) and the marriage portion (*Aussteuer*) or settlement (*Ausfertigung*), were granted as a matter of course at the weekly meetings of the deputies.[82]

The journeyman's suit could be an expensive item. For example, it cost 14 fl. to dress journeyman weaver Johann Polier.[83] Costs notwithstanding, it served the interests of orphanage, master, and journeyman alike that the orphans were fully equipped as well as fully prepared to engage in wage labor. The necessities had to be furnished, but at the lowest possible expense. As in so many other things, the 1780 Ordinance listed explicitly the items constituting suit and settlement and so limited their cost. Upon proof of completion of an apprenticeship, the administrators outfitted the orphan with a vest and jacket of blue linen, trousers of black leather, a new hat, black stockings, new shoes, three shirts, three handkerchiefs, a red woolen vest, four scarves, and a pair of gloves.[84] To maintain this dashing figure, the new journeyman also received 44 fl. for provisions and accommodations wherever his wanderings took him. Were clothing and cash not enough, were the master to attest to the need for tools or other goods, the administrators could draw on the journeyman's own property. Household servants were somewhat less well accoutered. After two years of service, an orphan maid received a hooded cape and dress of loden, a camisole, a scarf, a pair of stockings, a pair of shoes, three blouses, and three handkerchieves.[85] The ordinance made no mention of a cash payment; this and other eventualities had to be met from the servant's savings. Thus, orphans entered the world of work neatly and modestly attired, projecting an appearance that corresponded to the ideal of morality, subservience, and industry.

With suit and settlement the claims of orphans upon orphanages supposedly ended. Once employed, these young people theoretically ceased to be a source of concern and, not incidentally, expense.[86] The orphanages continued, however, to administer any property still held as capital. Orphans could seek to draw on these resources at need, but the administrators retained the authority to determine how much could be spent. In case orphans wished to marry or become masters in foreign parts, they had to approach the authorities concerning the necessary certificates of personal status. For adult orphans, journeymen, and servants alike, the orphanages frequently offered what might be called administrative assistance. They supplied them with the documents and certificates that were essential for full participation in early modern society. These could be withheld for cause. Orphans were on their own, self-supporting, but still curiously subordinate.

Jörg Lauterer entered the Augsburg orphanage in 1612 and was apprenticed to the master gunsmith Jörg Albrecht three years later.[87] He completed his training in 1618 and left Augsburg, after four years of wage labor in various workshops, with the note that "he has wandered and has behaved himself well to date." In 1625 Lauterer wrote to the orphan father from Rothenburg ob der Tauber, where he had worked for eighteen months and married his master's daughter, requesting certification of legitimate birth and apprenticeship (*Geburtsbrief* and *Lehrbrief*), as well as the balance of his property. He evidently planned to settle there and open his own shop as a master gunsmith, all of which required papers and resources. For Lauterer and many other orphans, the orphanages acted as intermediaries to the state, by providing proof of status and achievement essential to self-sufficiency.

In fact, maintenance by the orphanages continued as a lifelong opportunity for Augsburg's orphans. Certainly, older journeymen and servants were no longer as dependent on the organizations that had assisted them as children. Their experience gave them a toughness, resilience, and resource that younger people lacked. Yet, as wage-laborers, they rarely had secure livelihoods and were the likely victims of natural and human catastrophes of every sort. Inflation and famine struck the margins of society first. Even the turning of the lifecycle could tumble them into need. A marriage, a birth, or a death might leave laboring orphans with nowhere to turn but to the orphanages, on whose material, moral, and administrative support and supervision they continued to rely.

In a few cases, the orphanages tried to find employment for journeymen or servants in need. Jacob Rößle was apprenticed from the Augsburg orphanage to master watchmaker Caspar Pfaff in 1630.[88] The agreement between them stipulated that Pfaff would employ Rößle as a wage-laborer as soon as his training was complete. This he apparently did, until 1635, when the master released him for lack of work. These were hard times in the city, and the orphanage could not locate a new situation for their unemployed orphan. Before he found a new master, Rößle became sick and died in the orphanage. Household servants seem to have relied on the orphanage as a kind of employment service somewhat more frequently than craftsmen. Sabina Mairin entered the orphanage at age nineteen in 1626, and within one year was placed in service to master weaver Jacob Metzger.[89] She remained in the Metzger household until 1629, but for one brief period of convalescence in the orphanage. The orphan father found a new position for her in the service of another weaver, which lasted until 1635. In that year, she entered her third position, in the household of Otto Christoph Bodenburger, and passed out of the orphanage record.

Hanns Schweigger was typical of needy orphan laborers and their enduring relationship to the orphanages.[90] He entered the City Orphanage in 1608 at age ten, and apprenticed to Conrad Hirsch, a master gunsmith, in 1615. Apprenticeship completed in 1618, Schweigger worked as a journeyman, attracting no attention from the authorities until he moved to Nuremberg in 1623. Less than three months later, he returned to Augsburg in ill health and entered the Pilgrim House. The orphanage paid the costs of his care, though he had long been self-supporting, and even gave him 4 fl. as soon as he was on his feet again. Finding work as a locksmith, Schweigger paid back the 4 fl., though he was under no obligation to do so, and left the city in 1626.

The orphanage assisted another journeyman in a similar manner. Hanns Seidler completed his apprenticeship as a wool weaver in 1621 and, after four years as a wage laborer in various shops, resolved to try his fortune elsewhere.[91] He receive 6 fl. for the road and left Augsburg in 1625. Three years later, the orphan father received a letter from Seidler, who claimed he had been robbed by highwaymen near Nördlingen. Without further ado, the orphanage gave him 2 fl. to support him until he found employment.

In both cases, the orphanage gave alms to needy workmen. By their actions, the administrators acknowledged more than the simple duty of every Christian to succour the poor. These were orphans, former dependents of the house. The provision of assistance, even after years of independence, marked an enduring bond between individual and organization. Moreover, they were orphans, who had successfully acquired a trade and made their way in the world of work. Failure to respond to their need would almost surely have condemned them to destitution and beggary, the very things the orphanages existed to prevent. Dedication to self-sufficiency bound them to their long-term maintenance.

Conclusion

The orphanages of Augsburg could contradict the will and interdict the authority of masters in their own workshops and households. Heinrich Beck lodged a complaint of mistreatment against his master, the cobbler Peter Mangeldt.[92] The alms lords found in Beck's favor, forcing Mangeldt to repay half the apprenticeship fee he had received and apprenticing the boy to a new master. They intervened in this manner infrequently. Defending the interests of laboring men and women by directly attacking those of their employers would certainly have limited the capacity of the orphanages to influence the city's labor force and give shape to the labor market. Masters would have avoided employing orphans or violated orphanage regulations where these became too costly or intrusive. They did neither, but employed ever larger proportions of Augsburg's orphan population, in an ever broader range of crafts and trades. The number of orphans employed in the city remained small relative to the total population of workers; nevertheless, the orphanages exercised a qualitative influence on labor and labor markets that exceeded the number of orphan laborers and promoted the interests and utility of Augsburg's masters.

Generally speaking, the orphanages deferred the costs and risks of employing labor by training orphans to work as part of a daily routine, placing orphans in the workforce as apprentices of craft masters, and maintaining orphans in the workforce as independent wage-laborers. In all of these efforts, the organizations acted to reduce transaction costs in the labor market.

The degree to which the orphanages instilled habits of body and mind cannot be determined exactly, though the growing proportion of out-placed orphans who completed their initial training as apprentices and servants and became independent wage-laborers suggests that it was not entirely ineffective. Masters, however, may well have recognized and come to insist on the benefits of a consistent discipline. Apprenticeship contracts between orphans and masters gave both parties the added security of an organizational guarantor.

In placing orphans, the orphanages paid all the necessary fees and provided substantial material support in the form of clothing, bedding, and care. Limits were imposed only in 1780. The masters' labor costs were reduced, thus giving orphans a sort of competitive advantage over other young people in the labor market. Moreover, the orphanages provided fixed organizations, to which masters and hands might appeal in defense of their interests. If laborers were unwilling or unable to work, the orphanages supplied new servants and disciplined the old. If masters exploited or abused their hands, the orphanage sought new employment and occasionally disciplined the masters. As a result, the costs and risks of non-payment and non-compliance were reduced somewhat for employees but more substantially for employers.

Training, placing, and maintaining orphans, the orphanages of Augsburg helped to develop part of the city's labor supply. They became a permanent feature of the otherwise decentralized labor market. The orphanages were structures through which information was transmitted and conflicts were resolved. They inculcated a basic labor discipline, assigned value to different forms of labor, and responded to shifting demand with an ever-ready supply. In short, the orphanages provided a physical, tangible locus for those processes that constituted labor markets themselves.

As schoolhouses, clearinghouses, and halfway houses, the orphanages mobilized the human resources of Augsburg's needy inhabitants in ways quite similar to the mobilization of their capital resources and their aggregate demand. Far from segregating the poor within walls, they prepared orphan children for a life of labor, located employment for them, and invested capital and authority to keep them at it. The orphanages invested the human resources of the poor in the city's labor markets. By pursuing these ends consistently under changing circumstances—a process of involution—they helped to create a massive system of social and economic discipline, extending throughout the entire city, that promoted the utility of masters and the order of their society by enforcing the efficiency of self-support.

Notes

1. StAA, EW 22, Waisenbuch, 1580–1676, Ursula Schmiedin, 27 July 1628.
2. StAA, W A7, Streitsache des Philipp Jacob Imhofs wegen eines Dienstmädchens, s.d., 1632; Supplikation der Almosenherren wegen Ursula Schmiedin, 1 July 1632.
3. StAA, W A1, Notamina 18. Jhdt, Extractus eines Jubiläumspredigt des Kaspar Krez, 8 November 1750: "jämmerliche transaals Zeiten. . . ."
4. StAA, W A7, Streitsache des Philipp Jacob Imhof wegen eines Diesntmädchens, s.d., 1632, Erklarung des Philipp Jacob Imhofs, 3 July 1632.
5. Fassl, *Konfession, Wirtschaft und Politik*, 72. Consequently, a 1791 attempt to regulate servants' wages failed.
6. Ibid., 73.
7. StBA, 4°ThPr 821, M. Cyriacus Spangenberg, *Catechismus: Die Funff Heuptstuck der Christlichen Lehre Sampt der Haßtaffel und dem Morgen und Abendt Gebet Benedicite und Gratias etc. Ausgelegt durch M. Cyriacum Spangenberg* (Erfurt, 1567). See especially *Predigten* 9 and 10, "Wie sich Herrn und Frawen gegen ihr Gesinde halten sollen" and "Wie sich das Gesinde halten sol (gegen ihren Herren u. Frawen)."
8. StBA, 4°Ldw/39, M. Johannus Colerus, *Calendarum Perpetuum, er Libri Oeconomici: Das ist ein sietswerender Calendar darzu sehr nutzliche und notige Hausbücher* (Wittemberg, 1592), 10.
9. Ibid., 4.
10. StAA, W A7, Streitsache des Philipp Jacob Imhofs wegen eines Dienstmädchens, s.d., 1632, Gegenerklärung der Almosenherren, 8 July 1632.
11. StAA, EW 1, Instruction für den Weysen Vatter und Mueter, s.d. 1721.
12. StAA, W A7, Streitsache des Philipp Jacob Imhofs wegen eines Dienstmädchens, s.d., 1632, Finalerklarung und Supplikation des Philipp Jacob Imhofs, 10 July 1632.
13. Ibid., 13 July 1632.
14. StAA, Alms, Schuldbuch, 1585–1590, Waisenhauß betreffennde, 161–62: "Sollichen kindern geshieht durch den Waisen Vater Muter und Zuchmaister Ir geburliche Wartt mit Essen und trinckhen der Shuel lernunng und dem gebet die medlen auch mit Neen Spinen und Haußhaltung. So bald dann nun die Knaben so groß erwachsen das Sy ain hanndwerckh lernen kinden So werden Sy zu dem selben darzue Sy tauglich und lust haben gethon und das leeren gelt Von Inen betzalt. Deren Jn 14 Jaren her ob 100 ausgelernet Und gewanndert seyen Und sich nun selbst mit ehren ernoren. Also wiert es auch mit dem medlen gehalten. So bald Sy erstarckhen etlich Umbs brot Und sonnst Verdingt werden auch wann Sy sich Wolhalten und Manbar sein Verheirrat Und Jnen Jr aigenthumb waß Sy Jns hauß gebracht Und sich Jm hauß durch Erbfal Jrer Freundt oder Verstorbne Waisen kinder gebessert Zum Heirratgut Aber auß dem h. Allmusen sonst nichts geben."
15. Thompson, *Customs in Common*, 394 as reprinted from "Time, Work Discipline and Industrial Capitalism," *Past and Present* 38 (1967).
16. StAA, EW 1, Ordnung in dem Waisenhauß wie es mit den Kindern gehalten wird auf alle tag wie auch andere ding im Waisenhauß durch das ganze Jahr, 17 February 1599.
17. StAA, EW 1, Ordnung und Beshaffenheit der Waisenkinder so sich im Waisenhauß befinden allhier in Augsburg, 21 January 1638.

18. The ordinance does not specify whether these hours were annual or seasonal, that is, intended to apply only at particular times of the year.
19. StAA, EW 1, Ordnung und Beshaffenheit der Waisenkinder so sich im Waisenhauß befinden allhier in Augsburg, 21 January 1638. "Darnach habe sie eine ganze Stunde Recreation."
20. StAA, EW 12, Waisenhausordnung, 1780, Articulus XVIII.
21. Ibid.: "unter der gehörigen Aufsicht mit allerley anständigen Spielen...."
22. Ibid., Articulus XIX: "allen Muthwillen und ausgelassenes Wesen sorgfältig zu vermeiden."
23. Boswell, *The Kindness of Strangers*, passim. The finely turned phrase is oddly inept for relief organizations whose premise was that wealthy and poor were not strangers but rather members of a single community.
24. Ibid., Articulus V: "... auch aller Muthwillen und Unordnung besonders aller Umgang mit den Mägden und mit den Kräzigen, welche beiden ihren eigenen Recreations-Platz haben, verhütet werden."
25. Ibid.
26. Ibid.: "... zur Gottesfurcht, zum Lernen ihrer Lectionen, zum Fleiß, Ordnung, und Reinlichkeit, wie auch zu guter Sitten und anderen Christlichen Tugenden angewöhnen...."
27. Ibid., Articulus XII.
28. Ibid.: "überhaupt sich Christlich, fleißig, und treue zu halten."
29. StAA, EW 7, Bericht die Notturfte des evangelischen Waisenhauses betr., 3 August 1780.
30. StAA, EW 12, Waisenhausordnung, 1780, Articulus V: "... die Knaben wie zu förderst zu einer wahren Furcht Gottes, also auch zum Fleiß in der Arbeit, zumal im Spinnen zu Stille, und wohlanständigen Sitten zu Beobachtung guter Ordnung, und nöthiger Reinlichkeit bey Tische, besonders das Brot und Speise nicht sundlicher Weise herumgeworfen, verschleppt, vertauscht oder wohl gar verkauft werden, und auf den Tafeln liegen bleiben, mit Ernst und Liebe anzugewöhnen."
31. Ibid., Articulus VI: "eine Persohn von gestandenem Alter und ohnbescholtenem Lebenswandel...."
32. Ibid.: "... zur Gottesfurcht, zum Lernen ihrer Lectionen, zum Fleiß, Ordnung, und Reinlichkeit, wie auch zu guter Sitten und andern Christlichen Tugenden angewöhnen, in der Stube sowohl als in der Schlafkammer Stille und Ordnung erhalten, kein unnuzes, viel weniger sundliches und schändliches Geschwäz, Klätschereyen, Lästerungen, Verläumdungen, Lügen, und Spottereyen dulden, viel weniger sich selbst dergleichen ergeben oder herauslocken lassen."
33. StAA, EW 7, Bericht der Notturfte des evangelischen Waisenhauses betr., 3 August 1780.
34. Ibid.

Schul- und Näh-Quartal-Geld

1770	48 fl. 20 kr.
1771	49 fl.
1772	63 fl. 20 kr
1773	63 fl. 20 kr.
1774	69 fl. 30 kr.
1775	71 fl.
1776	71 fl. 30 kr.
1777	67 fl. 30 kr.
1778	62 fl.
1779	63 fl. 30 kr.
Summa	629 fl.

35. Ibid.: "einen eigenen kleinen bretteren Unterschlag sowohl in der Buben Stube als in der Buben Kammer...."
36. Ibid. The position of girls' maid had been abolished: "... bey der neuen Einrichtung ohnedem doch nimmer brauchbar und daher gänzl. zu dimittiren gewesen wäre, wegen ihrer geäußerten Liebe für das Waisenhaus, guter Humeurs, bekantshaft in demselben, vorzüglich aber wegen der ihr bey wohnenden Fähigkeit jeden guten Unterricht anzunehmen zur Näherin und Aufseherin über die Mägdlein zu ernennen."
37. StAA, EW 7, Bericht der Verordneten zum heiligen Almosen augustanae confessionis, September 1780.
38. StAA, EW 22, Waisenbuch, 1580–1676, Effersina u. Michel Braun, 2 July 1596: "ist der geschicht halben darvon kommen...."
39. Ibid. Matheus and Hanns Hoffschneider, 2 November 1579.
40. Ibid.: "... alle weil er aller reidig unnd kretzig worden ist und hat im ein grosse faulkait zue geschlagen ... ist besser ob der Pilgerhaus ligen...."
41. StAA, EW 22, Waisenbuch, 1580–1676; KW 27, Waisenbuch, 1653–1785. Statistics were tabulated from those orphans who left their orphanages in the given decades.
42. StAA, EW 1, Instruction für den Weysen Vatter und Mutter, §8, 11 May 1721: "Wann dann fürs achte die Kinder also wohl erzogen, zu Diensten oder Handtwerckhen gethan seyn, Sollen sie auch ihres verhalten in obacht genommen und gesehen werden, daß sie in gutem erbarn Wandel verharren, und ihre Aufferziehung im Weysen Hauß wohl angelegt zu seyn, bey ihnen ersheine, und so viel die Lehrnung bey Handwerckhern betrifft, daß das Geld nicht vergeblich, für sie ausgegeben werde, an ihnen nichts zu verabsaumen, zu welchem Ende beyde respective Vatter und Mutter monthl. bey denen samtl. dieser Weysen Kinder Herrshafften und Meistern die behörige Nachfrag ihres Verhaltens thun, und in Übelverhaltungsfall solche den Herrn Deputierten anziegen, auch die Mägdlein, da sie entweder ihres Dienst entlassen, oder sie selbsten dieselbe aufgeben und andere annehmen wolten, shultig sein sollen."
43. StAA, EW 22, Waisenbuch, 1580–1676, Katharina Engellerin, 2 October 1580.
44. Ibid., Samuel Furst, 19 January 1581: "... zue dem Jonas Wickert weber will bei jm Spüllen und sein Kind in die Schul führen will jn mit Speiß, Tranck und Kleider versorgen und sein Handwerk lernen."
45. StAA, EW 18, Deputiertensitz im evangelischen Waisenhaus, 23 February 1723: "weil er sich bißher wolgehalten hat...."
46. Ibid., 19 April 1723.
47. Ibid.
48. Ibid., 24 September 1723.
49. StAA, EW 12, Waisenhausordnung, 1780, Articulus XV, §8; Articulus XVI, §4.
50. Ibid., Articulus XV, §12.
51. StAA, EW 18, Deputiertensitz im evangelischen Waisenhaus, 19 April 1723.
52. StAA, EW 12, Waisenhausordnung, 1780, Articulus XV, § 10: "... nichts weder grosses noch kleines, wie gering es auch wäre, veruntreuen, verwahrlosen und versaumen, nicht wiederbellen sondern Zucht annehmen, ihren Lehrmeister und desen Frauen allen Respect erweisen, auch gegen die Gesellen, wie überhaupt gegen jedermann manierlich, höflich und bescheiden seyn, kurz sich also conduisieren und betragen wie es einem christlichen Waisen und ehrliebendem jungen Menschen zustehet. Sie sollen ihres Lehrmeisters Nuzen und Vortheil

fördern und suchen, dessen Schaden und Nachtheil aber hindern und wenden daher die aufgetragene Arbeit mit unverdroßenen Eyffer und fleiß verrichten, ihre Handthierung und Profession grundtlich zu erlernen, alle Kräften anstrengen, wen sie mit Arbeit ausgeschickt werden, den Lohn und Werth desselben nicht eingemächtig erhöhen und davon so wenig als von dem ihnen etwa geschänkten Trinkgeld bey Verwendung schweren Ahndung zuruckbehalten." Cf. Articulus XVI, § 1: "... auch von solchen Sitten, Fähigkeit und Gemuthsgaben sind, daß sie ihrer kunftigen Herrschaft ihr Stuck Brod ehrlich und gewissenhaft abverdienen können."

53. Ibid.: "... alles Trinken, Spielen, Tanzen, und andere jugendliche Ausschweifungen, sondern auch überhaupt alle Wirthshäuser und öffentliche Pläze gänzlich vermeiden...."
54. StAA, EW 18. Deputiertensitz im evangelischen Waisenhaus, 23 February 1723: "... der bey jhm in der Lehr ist und sich wol und ehrlich hält ... wegen durfftigkeit seiner mutter...."
55. Ibid., 24 September 1723.
56. Transactions of this sort cast a critical light on the supposed familial status of domestic servants in early modern households. Falchin—and many of her peers, in all probability—labored in the cash nexus of the urban markets for labor and commodities.
57. StAA, EW 12, Waisenhausordnung, 1780, Articulus XV, § 13: "... so hat er in der Krankenstube des Waisenhauses seine Aufnahme und unentgeldliche Verpflegung zu gewarten."
58. StAA, EW 13, Verzeichnus bresthaffter Kinder, 7 July 1723.
59. Ibid.: "... ein simple persohn, ist wegen ihrer ungeshicklichkeit shon öffters auß den diensten haimb geschickt worden...."
60. Ibid.: "... ligt kranckh am fieber ist sonst am armb und S. V. fuß lahm, deßwegen ein und andern Handwerkheren zuruck gesandt worden...."
61. Ibid.: "... wegen seiner beständigen unpäßlichkeit und fistulierten shäden an der hand von handwerkeren haimb geshickt worden...."
62. Ibid.: "... ist shadhaff an S. V. Füssen, deßwegen und auß abgang der Capacität von der Mahler Kunst haimb geshickt worden...."
63. StAA, EW 7, Neue Einrichtungen des evangelischen Waisenhauses, s.d., 1790.
64. StAA, EW 7, Ratsdekretum, 3 July 1790.
65. StAA, EW 12, Waisenhausordnung, 1780, Articulus XV. § 9: "nach ihrer Lehrknaben Fleiß, Treue, und Conduite...."
66. StAA, KW 28, Waisenbuch, 1653–1785, Eustachius and Maria Weber, 16 February 1656: "ist davon gelaufen—hat besseren lust zum Bäckerhandwerk."
67. StAA, EW 22, Waisenbuch, 1580–1676, Paulus Mair, 6 July 1594.
68. Ibid.: "... dem nach er kain guet thon will had das hes ab dem laib verkauft und on worden ist wider im waissen haus geklaidt und aus dem leisen geseibert worden wider verdingt aber bald wider in der statt umbgangen fieren ist der halben seinem brueder Hanns Mair Buchhendler haim geschaft worden er sol im selber versorgen ist also von im aufgenommen worden will im jm Österreich gen Wien fieren."
69. Ibid., Carol Kaisser, 8 November 1606: "ist er mit mehr anderen hailoßen buben weck zogen...."
70. Ibid., Jeremias Gürtler, 10 September 1610.
71. Ibid., Maria Sedlemairin, 10 November 1605.
72. StAA, KW 28, Waisenbuch, 1653–1785, Georg Heufflen, 23 September 1658:

"den 24. Julii 1659 ... ohn alle ursach auß dem Wayßenhaus in daß Bayrlandt undt sich etlich dag bey einem dorf priester ufgehalten hernach aber widerumb alher kommen undt alda im Wayßenhaus einstellen wollen ist ehr mit angenommen sondern seiner mueter anderer zum exempel an heimbs gewiesen worden."
73. StAA, EW 18, Deputiertensitz im evang. Waisenhaus, 24 September 1723: "... wegen daß derselbe wegganagen und bittet demselben sonderlich wegen des erbrochenen Zettels und veränderten Zahl ... seinem meritum nach ... mit gebührenden tractament blohnet werden."
74. StAA, EW 22, Waisenbuch, 1580–1676, Hanns Gsell, 21 April 1617.
75. Hufton, *The Poor of Eighteenth-Century France*, 69–106.
76. StAA, EW 22, Waisenbuch, 1580–1676, Friderich Wagner, 28 September 1620: "Er ist ein böser unsträflicher bube, was zucht an jhm ergeben wirdt, gibt zeit."
77. Ibid.: "so ferr er sich lesst abrichten...."
78. Ibid.: "hat gute gelegenhait Gott lob."
79. StAA, EW 12, Waisenhausordnung, 1780, Articulus XV, § 11. Cf. Articulus XVI, § 6.
80. Beier, *Masterless Men*, passim.
81. StAA, EW 12, Waisenhausordnung, 1780, Articulus XV, § 13: "Eben so darf er auch seine gegründete Klagen wider ein zu hartes Tractament seines Meisters entweder vor dem Sitz, oder vor seinem Hr. Beichtvater, an den er unter allen Herren Vorsteher zu erst gewiesen ist, bescheidentlich vorbringen, und der Hoffnung leben, daß man sich seiner aufs Beste annemen werde."
82. Surviving protocols record large numbers of these petitions at every meeting of the deputies. The entries are usually terse: Matheus Eberhardt requested and received a "gesellen Kleid" on 19 April 1723.
83. StAA, EW 18, Deputiertensitz im evangelischen Waisenhaus, 17 December 1723.
84. StAA, EW 12, Waisenhausordnung, 1780, Articulus XV, § 14.
85. Ibid., Articulus XVI, § 4.
86. Ibid., Articulus XV, § 14: "Von der Zeit an höret aber auch aller Genuß vons Waisenhauß gänzlich auf und muß er auch als Geselle, er mag gleich hier oder in der Fremde in Arbeit stehen, die Herrn Vorsteher geziemend bitten, oder bitten lassen, wen er von seinem Sparhafen etwas nöthig hätte, auch deren jederweiligen Gutbefinden er anheimstellen, ob und wie viel sie ihm verabfolgen lassen wollen."
87. StAA, EW 22, Waisenbuch, 1580–1676, Jörg Lauterer, 5 January 1612: "ist er gewandert, hat sich biß hero wol gehalten...."
88. Ibid., Jacob Rößle, 29 March 1623.
89. Ibid., Sabina Mairin, 24 March 1626.
90. Ibid., Hanns Schweigger, 2 May 1608.
91. Ibid., Hanns Seidler, 16 November 1610.
92. Ibid., Heinrich Beck, 12 December 1616: "den Maister wegen daß er den Buben so hart gehalten verklagt...."

Conclusion: Toward a New Organizational History

The history of Augsburg's orphanages presents the paradox of a story without a story. Into the nineteenth century these organizations clung with remarkable tenacity to purposes set in 1572, that is, "to erect and furnish a house for the poor, fatherless and motherless orphans that have been supported from the common alms sack so miserably and at great cost in order that they might be reared in the true fear of God, propriety, and honor."[1] Here briefly were the dictates of efficiency—reduced inputs and expenses through economies of scale, and improved outcomes and behavior through rigorous training—that dominated the logic and activities of these organizations into the modern era. This continuity of purpose and practice in Augsburg created a history remarkable for its evenness and lack of change.

Yet, innovation occurred as the orphanages sought to provide acceptable care at the lowest cost under greatly changing circumstances. They adapted to market forces and confessional tensions without ever abandoning their ultimate ends or means. The introduction of parity as a modus vivendi for Catholics and Lutherans after the Thirty Years' War created new institutional constraints that sharpened their need for efficiency. Thus, crisis and discord constituted moments of historical clarity that revealed the essential continuities of the orphanages.

CHARITY AND CAPITAL

Charity has been described and too often understood as "outside the logic of the system," that is, as alien to any economy that set the value of goods and services according to supply and demand.[2] This notion makes little sense in an agrarian society where the availability of foodstuffs directly or indirectly set prices for most goods and services and determined, as a result, the fortunes of entire populations. Periodic crop failures, such as those of 1571–72 and 1771–72, produced effects well beyond the agricultural sector: they reduced demand for manufactured goods; they increased the number of unemployed laborers; they propelled disproportionately large parts of the population into need. Neither does it conform easily to an economy characterized by simultaneous surpluses and shortages of labor, by the paradox of too many able and too few qualified workers.[3] Guild-imposed strictures on employment increased the number of marginally employed artisans and decreased the volume of manufactured goods. Taken together, the inefficient production of foodstuffs and the inefficient utilization of labor created chronic imbalances between resources and population. Transferring wealth to provide bread and work for sometimes large portions of the population under these circumstances required efficiency, a requirement the administrators of charity met in the marketplace. As a result, charity not only responded to market forces but also became a force in itself. Constantly reckoning costs and benefits to their organizations and dependents, the administrators of charity participated and intervened in the city's markets. The orphanages engaged in a far-flung system of capital transactions, made large-scale commodity purchases, and helped to shape the urban workforce. Their activities supplied workers for shops and households, altered the demand for goods and services, and maximized the resources of Augsburg by mobilizing the poor and their property.

Charity is traditionally considered an activity apart from the mainstream of life, just as the poor are usually understood as marginal to or completely outside of society, and this distance seems to have increased as relief was rationalized and its recipients scrutinized in the early modern period. So conceived, this centuries-long process finds its last act and logical conclusion in the immurement of the poor. The daily rough and tumble of the orphanages' market transactions demonstrate, however, that the economic influence of charity could extend far beyond the walls of organizations and that their capitalistic practices served to integrate the poor and their relief into the landscape of urban society and the texture of urban experience.

To provision the poor efficiently and to maintain that activity over time required the organization and redistribution of capital, commodities, and labor, a notable intervention in the markets for each.[4] Calculation marked these transactions as the orphanages sought goods and services at the lowest prices within the constraints set by market imperfections and their own resources. To achieve efficiency, administrators pursued their material advantage in a flexible, adaptive manner by striving constantly both to maximize resources and to minimize risks. The role of land in their domestic economies serves as an apt allegory for this activity. Due to the land-poverty that shaped the entire city's economy, the orphanages never relied on landed capital for their support. Rather, they exploited land in accordance with its relative costs and turned to diverse sources of income in a never-ending effort to maintain charity efficiently. In so doing, the administrators of the orphanages demonstrated all the elements of an unsystematic, empirical capitalism. To generate capital they calculated costs and benefits, pursued economies of scale and expenditure, expanded income and resources, and controlled costs and externalities. In the end, circumstances revealed the utility of a wide and shifting array of subventions from the state, donations from patrons, and earnings from capital as the basic resources of the orphanages.

Following a consistent strategy of diversity, the orphanages served as bankers to the region, the city, and its burghers. They accepted the donations of individuals and organizations as investments on which regular interest was paid, and they provided capital in the form of annuities and credit to rich and poor alike. More important still, the orphanages managed the property of their orphans long after the children became self-supporting adults, thus allowing these assets to circulate as capital and so enforcing the virtues of thrift and gain on the owners. Diversity in this case permitted a degree of flexibility and independence. The orphanages shifted their reliance on these various sources of income in response to changing social, political, and economic realities and thereby avoided the chronic shortage of funds that haunted states and doomed so many social organizations in the eighteenth century.

Independence, however, should not be construed as autarky; the orphanages remained completely integrated into the markets and marketplaces of Augsburg. As they entered the market for capital to augment resources won from more traditional sources, the orphanages also entered the marketplaces to acquire food for the hungry and clothing for the naked. The Alms Office, the orphanages, and all of the city's charities constituted an aggregate consumer that purchased goods and services on behalf of the poor. They concentrated and directed the demand of this segment of the urban population, projected it into the market with a force that these people would have lacked individually, and attracted suppliers who might otherwise have been absent from the marketplaces. Stockpiling and contracting helped to ameliorate the worst effects of market instability and price volatility. Within their walls, they provided a material regime that was bountiful compared to the norm of that time. A discipline that emphasized the avoidance of waste and excess alike accompanied this plenty. Asceticism, therefore, was inseparable from the regular, uniform provision of commodities; discipline and demand together broke the traditional cycle of feast and famine. The result was a moderation of consumption and a manipulation of markets.

Traditionally, historiography recognizes supply as the stick used by early modern magistrates to regulate markets. States dumped strategic reserves of commodities to control prices and maintain order. The orphanages were suppliers, too, but of labor. While not providing hoards of workers for public projects or setting captive hands to profitable tasks, nonetheless, they trained, placed, and maintained a steady stream of craftsmen in the artisanal economy of Augsburg. The orphanages offered no technical training beyond the rudiments of those tasks performed regularily in-house, but their daily routines and regimens emphasized obedience, persistence, and industry, qualities ideally suited to subordinate positions in the workshop, household, or proto-factory. Those orphans mature enough to learn a trade were placed in domestic service or craft apprenticeship. The pattern of this activity reflected quite accurately the changing demand for labor and the changing scope of the city's economy, from foreign to local production and from mass to luxury trades. Involvement in the lives of laborers or in the labor market did not cease with placement; the orphanages provided a structure for the mediation of work disputes and the maintenance of work relations. Masters turned to Augsburg's orphanages to obtain apprentices, to discipline unruly workers, and to avoid certain labor costs. Hands returned to the orphanage for material assistance and moral support. The orphanages defined the economic value and social relations of production at the same time that they provided a location where the demand for workers could find a ready supply. They were at once market and marketplace for labor.

Efficiency was the hallmark of administration and discipline in Augsburg's orphanages; to achieve it alms lords and orphan fathers entered the city's capital, commodity, and labor markets and acted in capitalistic ways. The orphanages never engaged in production or exchange for profit. Insofar as their methods reveal an emergent capitalism, it was a fiscal capitalism that sought to mobilize resources in order to provide a service and assure its maintenance. This was the strategy throughout the early modern period, one that demanded creativity on the part of their administrators. Their tactics were an empirically acquired, non-systematic set of practices to which they clung despite the vicissitudes of chance and circumstance. In short, the need for efficiency constituted an element in the genius that inspired and spurred the rise of modern capitalism.

Parity and Capital

To care for needy children at the lowest possible cost had always been the charge of the orphanages, a charge they strove to fulfill despite changing economic conditions. In the period from 1572 to 1806 they confronted catastrophic inflation and economic collapse. Harrowing as these were, none transformed charity so completely as did the Treaty of Westphalia in 1648. The principle of parity between Catholics and Lutherans and its corollary of separate but equal confessional organizations formed a new institutional constraint that directly contradicted the established imperative of efficiency. Parity reduced the capital potentially available for each orphanage. It dictated the organizational and market relations open to each. It politicized the domestic economies of each. Without abandoning their pursuit of efficiency, their engagement in the city's markets, or their reliance on certain managerial techniques, Catholics and Lutherans adapted to the restrictions and opportunities imposed by the new order.

Mandated by Augsburg's politics and political economy, parity became the benchmark for a division of power and a redistribution of resources that proved disruptive of the once simple notion of efficiency. Henceforth, not only the movement of prices and of populations, but also the constant, contentious imperative of equality dictated the fates of orphans and the fortunes of the orphanages. The inexorable demands of the economy and the iron law of parity forced the introduction and establishment of such notions as equity and entitlements, ultimately transforming charity into welfare.

The design and discipline of both orphanages emerged from this process. Parity dictated organizational equality vis-à-vis the state. The relationship of the orphanages to Augsburg's society and economy, however, could not be ruled in this manner. For one thing, parity implied an absolute separation of each from the other and of Catholic from Lutheran. Although this may have been observed more often in the breach—at least, their contacts were frequent if not always friendly—it changed the nature of their material support and the quality of their charity. Parity limited the resources available to either house. Now the orphanages could depend only on their own confessional communities, a division that placed the Catholic Orphanage at a distinct disadvantage. Furthermore, parity limited the capacity of each house to respond to economic change. Regardless of circumstances, any increase or decrease in the resources available to one would be accompanied by the demand for equal treatment of the other. Both orphanages clung to tried-and-true managerial techniques to assess advantage, maximize resources, minimize risk, and utilize markets. But a dissonant note had been introduced, and the rhythms of administration and assistance changed.

Consider the issue of support from private burghers. Lutherans gave frequently and generously to their orphanage; Catholics were unable to do so. As a result, the Catholic Orphanage sought closer ties to other Catholic organizations. Lacking institutional backing on this level, the Lutheran house cast its lot with the city's Lutheran merchants and entrepreneurs and, ultimately, with its emerging factory industries. This, in turn, may have altered the experiences of orphans within the walls and their fates without.

The economic regimes of each orphanage changed under the influence of parity. Confession-specific patterns of consumption emerged almost immediately after the creation of Catholic and Lutheran orphanages. These were accompanied by confession-specific attitudes toward commodities. Catholic administrators treated goods as consumables to be saved and used. Their Lutheran counterparts inclined rather toward an understanding of goods as capital, the object of investment and accumulation. Although both parties saw the end in terms of the maintenance of their organizations, they differed in the preferred means to accomplish it.

As parity limited the financial support available for indentures, it may have shaped the choice of trades open to orphans. The orphanages enjoyed different connections to Augsburg's labor market by virtue of the distribution of Catholic and Lutheran populations. Lutherans tended to predominate in the ranks of merchants, professionals, and independent masters, while Catholics concentrated in the lower ranks of dependent masters and wage-laborers. As a consequence, each confession's orphans passed via apprenticeship and service into distinct levels: Lutherans enjoyed broader opportunities across a wider spectrum of the economy; Catholics were limited to the less exalted or rewarding crafts.

The interaction of economy and parity had something to do as well with the reform undertaken in the late eighteenth century. The massive Orphanage Ordinance of 1780, written for the Lutheran Orphanage but adapted later to the Catholic Orphanage as well, sought to capture in a set of coherent, enlightened regulations the ethical and economic realities that had governed these organizations since the middle of the previous century. It sketched in minute detail the duties of every person in the orphanage, their relationship to one another, and their dependence upon superior authority. Set in writing, these rights and responsibilities codified the hitherto implicit institutional ramifications of parity. The ordinance also extended into the orphanage proper that material regime born in the marketplace. It described every article of clothing, every scrap of food, every piece of wood, and every bit of candle and set in place regulations for their proper use. It laid out thoroughly every aspect of the orphans' education and catechization, including complete prescriptions to guide comportment in the orphanage and beyond it.

Here were the bourgeois virtues of thrift and frugality, industry and persistence, regularity and reliability, obedience and deference that signaled a rethinking of old values. The material regime, shorn of all excess and waste, gave rise to a moral order embodied by the orphanage itself. Clothing, food, light, and fuel were held to a level made sufficient by ceaseless admonitions to careful husbandry and endless sanctions against extravagance and complaint. The traditional context of such mundane activities as eating, dressing, and socializing yielded, in theory, to a regularity and uniformity that were both old and new. Though expressed in terms reminiscent of the medieval cowl and cloister, this *habitus* served well the needs of an emerging social and economic order. Constant productive activity during a tightly scheduled day accustomed orphans to routines that could be ruled more efficiently only by machines. The social relations of production—the constant give and take between masters and hands and the ribald, roistering world of wage laborers and journeymen—would have to be learned outside the orphanage and would therefore seem all the more alien. A daily litany of thanksgiving underscored the complete prohibition of any activity not specifically approved by superior authority. Taken together these routines constituted a paternal regime of submission, in which any act of resistance or rebellion appeared dangerously deviant. In and of themselves these virtues were age old; thrift, industry, regularity, and obedience had been overt desiderata in the orphanage since the sixteenth century. Indeed, they were preached as ideals of domestic life much earlier. The moral order of the orphanages was a synthesis of Christian ethics and market experience. Given the interplay between efficiency and parity, however, such values took on a new immediacy and importance. These were not merely bourgeois virtues but rather market virtues. The training in them reflected the orphanage's engagement in the markets of Augsburg and constituted an emerging system of values in which capital, goods, and labor were shorn of their cultural and social significance and vested instead with tradable economic value. The second volume of this study will address the fates of Augsburg's orphans and the degree to which they carried these bourgeois virtues and capitalist values beyond the walls and into society. The orphans of Augsburg were encouraged to see their persons and their property as commodities. From traditional charity grew a capitalistic discipline.

SOME THOUGHTS ON WEBER: CHARITY, PARITY, AND CAPITAL

This study did not begin as an examination of the connection between the ethics of what Weber and, following him, much of modern sociology calls ascetic Protestantism and the emergence of a spirit of modern capitalism. Nonetheless, both the notion of efficiency as part of the mentality of modern capitalism and the confessional comparison of capitalistic practices that emerge from the history of Augsburg's orphanages encourage a brief reflection on the Weber thesis.

Often misinterpreted, this issue must be approached with some care.[5] Weber addressed but a single element in the emergence of modern capitalism. With other scholars of his day, particularly Werner Sombart, he recognized an entire complex of preconditions for the modern economic system. These included the separation of business and household capital, the use of rational bookkeeping and accounting, the creation of a formally free labor force, the adoption of rational laws and administration, the development of industrial processes and technology, and finally, the appearance of a spirit of modern capitalism.[6] Never intending to associate the Reformation with the rise of capitalism, Weber concerned himself only with the relationship between ascetic Protestantism and the capitalistic spirit. He located the former most ideally in the teachings of John Calvin and some of his disciples, who offered both a system of ethics based on diligence, asceticism, and industry, and a sanction to enforce it through the doctrine of predestination. Weber understood both system and sanction as values governing the actions of entrepreneurs and conformance to that system.[7] That he identified Protestant asceticism with the spirit of capitalism had to do with his particular interpretation of Calvinist theology and his reliance on ideal typical sociological methods. Though diligence, asceticism, and industry were not values unique to Calvinism, according to Weber only Calvinism contained the sanction that could translate the ideal into the real and so make the ethos a basis of daily life.[8] Moreover, these were the very values that emerged when he reduced the mentality of a modern capitalist to an ideal type, that is, systematically focused it on its single most important aspect, the maximization of profit.[9] Thus, the sanctioned ethics of Calvinism were precisely those intrinsic to the modern capitalistic spirit. The emergence of the former gave rise to the latter.

Many problems exist, not least of which is the circularity of Weber's argument, that is, that he defined his conclusion in terms of his premise, the spirit of capitalism in terms of ascetic Protestantism.[10] As a result, at least two objections emerge. Modern capitalism is assumed to have arisen where the ethos of Calvinism held sway, thus ignoring early modern Catholic states that rationalized their economies. And, the modern capitalist is idealized and distorted to appear at once more rational and more saintly than was the case in a more various, frequently tawdry reality. Be that as it may, the much debated Weber thesis has still not been subjected to rigorous proof. Nor is it the purpose of this study to do so. Augsburg's Catholic and Lutheran orphanages offer, nonetheless, insights into the complex problem of the emergence of capitalism, its practices, and its values.

Weber understood the essential, the ideal-typical, spirit of modern capitalism in terms of diligence, asceticism, and industry—which he summarized as bourgeois rationality—practiced daily and exercised singularly to maximize capital.[11] These values were everywhere present in the administration of Augsburg's orphanages and the discipline of their charges. Although they did not work for profit, administrators seized every possible advantage or gain, avoided every possible waste or loss, and labored ceaselessly to maintain the services of their organizations. Not all measured up to this figure of the model administrator, but the exceptions are exceedingly rare in the documentation and provoked swift censure from their superiors. Nor was it otherwise with the orphans. Every aspect of their daily routine admonished them to the same virtues. Whether such a regimen proved effective, the ethos recognized by Weber was at work.

This ethos, present in both Catholic and Lutheran orphanages, cannot, however, be adduced from the precepts and sanctions of an ascetic Protestantism that was native to neither. Rather, the need for efficiency inspired diligence, asceticism, and industry in both alike. To this end, administrators were expected to maximize resources, and orphans were advised to avoid waste. For this sake, all members of both organizations were measured against ideals of persistence and exertion. The alternatives, somewhat overstated in terms of disorder, expense, and starvation, were their own penalty. Efficiency, therefore, provided the values and implied the sanctions.

The question remains as well whether rationalization, that is, the regular application of these values to one's calling, served merely to maintain a given standard of life or whether they promoted accumulation and growth, that is, maximization as a duty and end in itself. Weber recognized that traditionalism existed even in the presence of capitalistic organizations and practices, and he pointed to the *Verleger* as an example of the early entrepreneur engaged in capitalistic enterprise but lacking the capitalistic spirit.[12] Though he might amass huge fortunes, this entrepreneur banked on high-risk venture and speculation and squandered the proceeds in extravagant consumption. The capitalist Weber sought was a risk-minimizer as well as a profit-maximizer.[13] The orphanage administrators consistently demonstrated some of these qualities, but their reasons conform less clearly to the Weberian model. Though they did not engage in traditionalism, still it seems unlikely, given the nature of their organization, that they sought to maximize capital as an end in itself. Rather, they maximized resources and other factors in each orphanage's economy. State support, first in the form accounts receivable, later in the form of regular subventions, guaranteed basic consumption. Such maximization served, therefore, not to sustain a given standard of living but rather to maintain a stable organization. It assured the orphanages against the vagaries of economics, politics, and religion; it guaranteed survival beyond the span of a single life or generation. Early modern capitalism might best be likened to practices in a spot market: short-term transactions to achieve the greatest gain. A managed, fiscal capitalism sought to sustain organizational growth without personal profit-taking. In this case, capitalistic practices and values did not constitute rationality as understood by Sombart and Weber but contained elements of it. For the orphanages of Augsburg, however, that rationality derived less from the tenets of ascetic Protestantism than from the pursuit of efficiency and the rigors of institutional constraint that shape economic organizations.

CONCLUSION

Organizational charity, at least as captured in the orphanages of Augsburg, was a medium for capitalism rather than a bulwark against it or a tool of it. This is not as surprising as it might seem. Augsburg was a major commercial and industrial center that had long been dominated by the early practitioners of commercial capitalism, the same group that supplied the Alms Office with its administrators. It stands to reason that these hard-headed individuals sought to administer their organizations in ways familiar and sensible to themselves and that, therefore, the transactions by which they translated charitable imperatives into social realities should be marked by the same flexible approach to changing circumstances and the same calculated search for advantage that characterized the trading of mercantile concerns. Though the orphanages were not given to the pursuit of profits or the production of goods; though they were, in fact, non-capitalistic organizations, still they were successful capitalistic experiments. Through their daily, monthly, and yearly transactions they captured and transmitted their concern for efficiency, and the capitalistic practices and values associated with it, outward to the city's markets and inward to the city's orphans.

Charity, therefore, was an economic activity that found its proper place in the market. This fact the peoples of late medieval and early modern Europe never entirely forgot, whatever the moral imperatives of a selfless *caritas*. Though not a commodity in the strict sense, it was the object of an economic transaction, an exchange of money, goods, or services for returns both material and immaterial, from personal sanctity and status to public welfare and order. The orphanages of Augsburg and the entire apparatus of the Alms Office stood in the center of a vast system in which resources of every sort circulated. Charity was subject to strict, market-like regulation. The various alms ordinances of the sixteenth and seventeenth centuries specified where charity might occur, what charity might be given, when charity might be offered, and by whom it might be received. From market-like conditions evolved a market-like sensibility. Donors of charity exhibited a tight-fisted generosity that carefully weighed costs and benefits. During a period of financial crisis, troubled by accusations of fraud and mismanagement on the part of Lutheran Orphanage administrators, an anonymous magistrate exclaimed in evident despair that the house might lose its credibility.[14] Essential benefactors would withdraw "because they would see that which they do for the good of the house or the children wasted or consumed by others." Thus, charity in early modern Augsburg expressed a calculation presupposing limited resources and necessitating fixed purposes. Both selfish and selfless, it reflected a market orientation that was common to the entire city.

Modern historians have missed an important point. Their studies have never assessed the economic nature of charity, either as an activity in itself or as an activity conditioned by material realities. Rather, the more traditional analyses tend to rely on guidelines and regulations that set the structure of poor relief but rarely measure such prescriptions against their actual function. The current vogue seeks to capture the perception of poverty with records that are usually marked by a relative lack of reliable historiographical detail and a tone of barely cloaked official hostility.[15] Charity becomes either a beneficent means of preserving paternalistic social relations or a sinister and sometimes brutal method of exploiting the masses.

None of these perspectives, in fact, are without merit. They remain, however, exercises in motives shorn of any basis in experience. By ignoring or discounting the importance of efficiency and the means by which it was achieved, they have distorted early modern charity. By failing to see charity in material terms, that is, as an activity which assisted and shaped the poor economically through the transfer of resources, this literature has robbed the history of poor relief of its significance for a post-modern world. The value of close economic studies of early modern organizations, apart from the fact that they fill a void in the historiography, is that they avoid these flaws. They demonstrate how traditional, state-sponsored organizations became the agents as well as the objects of change, how established charity served as herald and handmaiden of emerging capitalist society.

The orphanages propagated a moral order that reflected their own capitalistic practices and interests; they did so by steadily pursuing efficiency, by persistently calculating and innovating to generate capital and shape markets. Their methods and purposes changed little, but shifting circumstances—the push and pull of economy and parity—gave them a new content. Involution of this sort poses a conundrum for German institutions and organizations, the puzzle of change through continuity. The scholarly interpretation of *Heimat* tends to emphasize forms of organization and behavior that are traditional, experiential, and organic.[16] Having a much larger population and more than its share of "movers and doers," Augsburg does not conform exactly to the definition of such a parochial, provincial community. Even the smaller home towns, however, housed within their inward-looking communities people whose eyes were lifted above the walls. The smaller Imperial cities of southern Germany demonstrate this point aptly. Moreover, even the largest city sought to promote local interests by the self-conscious suppression and exclusion of all that was alien. In short, even the largest metropolis had something of the home town at heart. Augsburg's orphanages contained elements of this in that they never abandoned established, familiar structures and terminologies. Theirs is a tale of hard-won wisdom gained through experience in the markets and marketplaces and refined over centuries of application. The consistent pursuit of efficiency despite economic crises and institutional change presents an image of stasis and conservatism. As it occurred in Augsburg's orphanages, however, involution permitted an element of calculation, experimentation, and generation in the way these organizations adjusted to gradually changing conditions and turned in upon themselves to become something quite different. The orphanages created something new without abandoning their traditional goal, function, and structure. As a result, traditional, precapitalistic charity became a bearer of modern capitalism. Far from being "outside the logic of the system," the orphanages of Augsburg were intrinsic to it.

Notes

1. StAA, Alms, Jahresrechnungen, 1570-79, Waisenhaus, 1572: "... für die armen, vatter- und muetterlosen Waisen, so in gemainen Allmuesenseckhl ellendigelich mit shwerem Cossten erzogen worden, ein aigen Haus auf- und anzurichten, damit dieselbigen in wahrer forcht Gottes, Zucht und aller erbarkhait auferzogen mögen werden...."
2. Stigler, *The Theory of Price*, 5, as quoted in Cipolla, *Before the Industrial Revolution*, 20. Stigler's observation characterized the historiography of charity all too well. Most historians have been content to see it as a product of economic change, responding belatedly and half-heartedly to crisis and transformation, but have yet to evaluate it as an economic agent of considerable potency.
3. Werner Sombart, *Der moderne Kapitalismus*, I, 788.
4. Cipolla, *Before the Industrial Revolution*, 18. A list of surveys indicates that the proportion of poor people in early modern cities varied from 5 to 20 percent.
5. See the masterly discussion in Marshall, *In Search of the Spirit of Capitalism*.
6. Weber, *The General Economic History*, passim.
7. Marshall, *In Search of the Spirit of Capitalism*, 64-65.
8. Weber, *The Protestant Ethic and the Spirit of Capitalism*, 110-12, 117-18.
9. Marshall, *In Search of the Spirit of Capitalism*, 51-52.
10. Ibid., 119-23.
11. Weber, *The Protestant Ethic*, 56-58, 155f. The term bourgeois rationality appears in Marshall, *In Search of the Spirit of Capitalism*, 44.
12. Weber, *The General Economic History*, 354f; *The Protestant Ethic*, 58f.
13. Weber, *The Protestant Ethic*, 194-98.
14. StAA, EW 13, 13 February 1726. Marginal comment on a letter from Lutheran Orphan Father Johann Christoph Sturm to officials of the Alms Office: "Wolte Got man thät sein alles vor eine gewissen sach halten würde auch mehr seegen ins hauß kommen wegen der vielen Kränzel und schmausereyen aber bleibt mancher gutthäter aus weilen er sehen muß, daß dasjenige so er dem haus oder Kinder gutes thun will, con andern weggefressen ... oder verspielt wird."
15. Just about the only convincing exception to this rule to date is the magisterial work of K.D.M. Snell. It makes telling use of the examination records of English parish relief. Very few scholars have matched Snell's good fortune in sources that contain a wealth of information or persistence in making them reveal it. See Snell, *Annals of the Labouring Poor*.
16. Mack Walker's masterful study of the German home towns provides the fullest discussion of this notion. See Walker, *German Home Towns*, 11-142.

Appendix I

FIGURE 1
Value (fl.) of Types of Alms Office Income, 1600–80

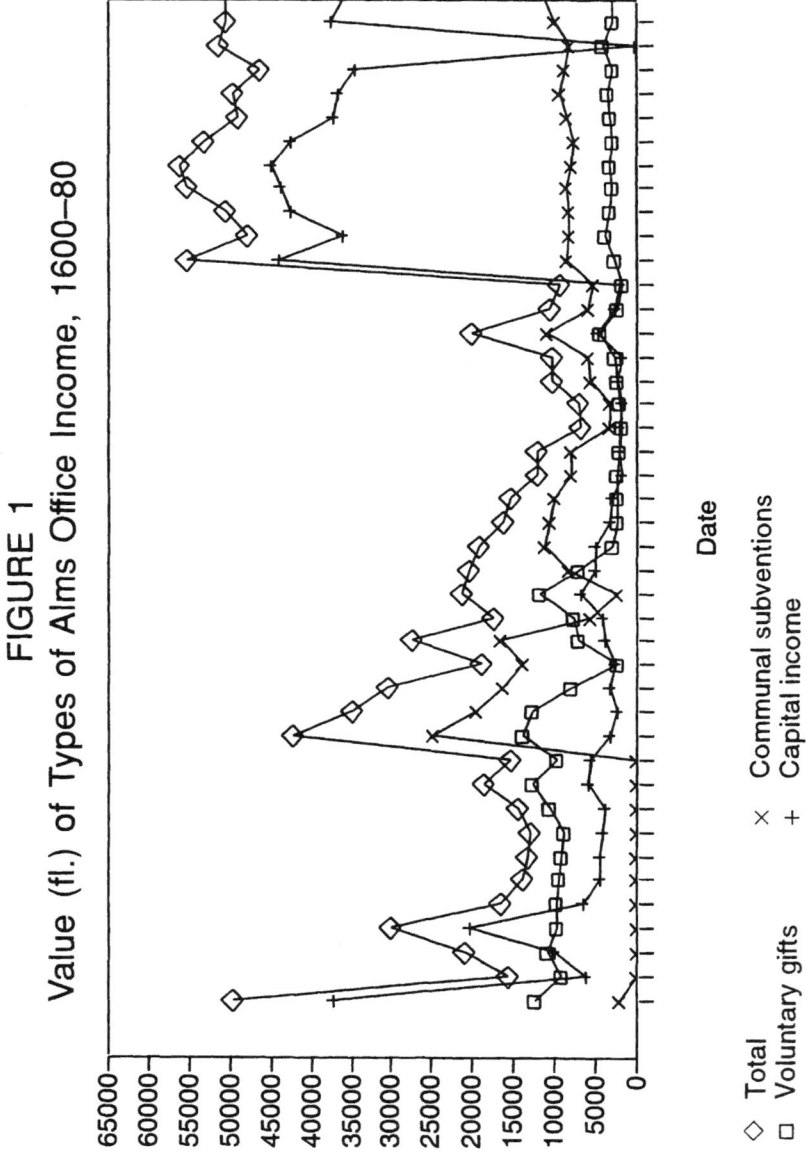

FIGURE 2
Value (fl.) of Collections by Alms Office, 1600–80

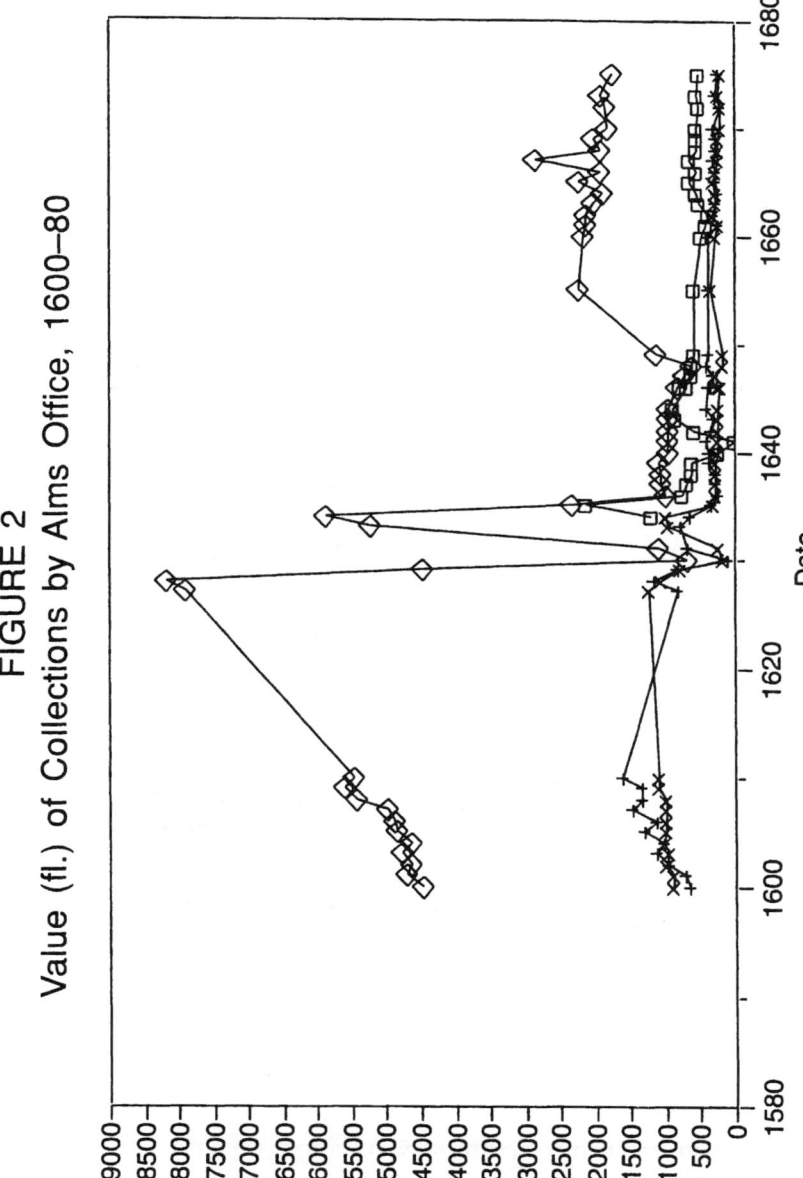

◇ Church collections   □ Citizens' collections   × Bapt./marr./bur. collections   + Collection boxes

294　APPENDIX I

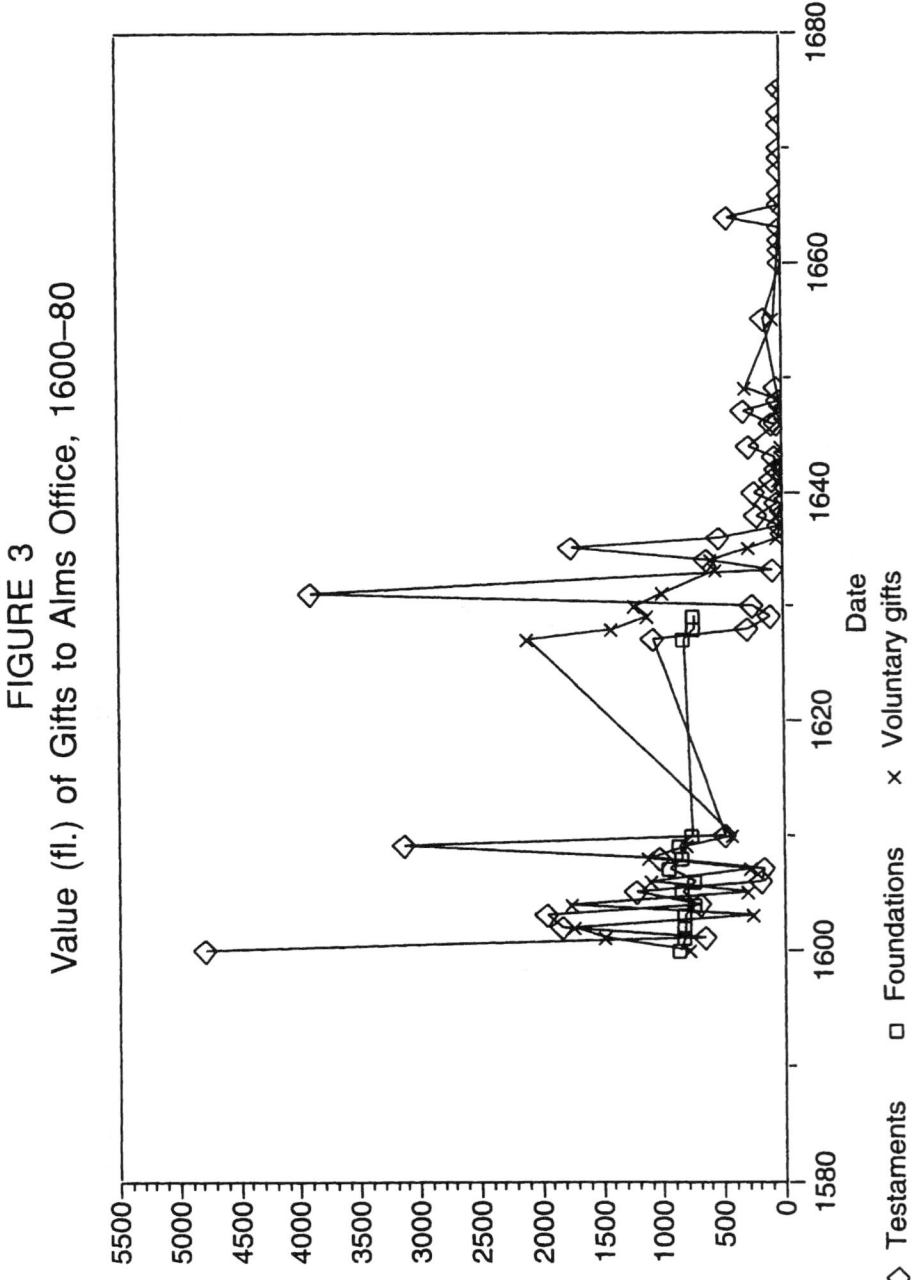

FIGURE 3
Value (fl.) of Gifts to Alms Office, 1600–80

FIGURE 4
Interest Income (fl.) of Alms Office, 1600–80

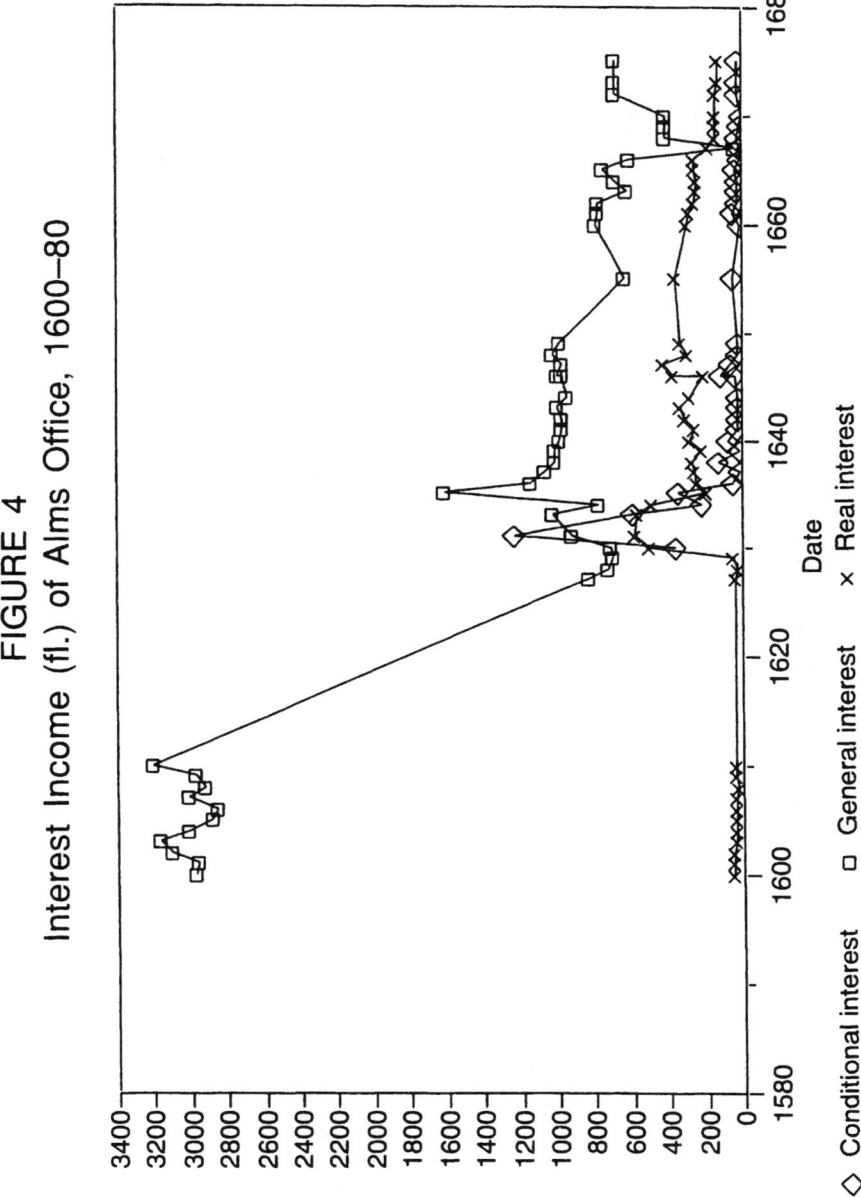

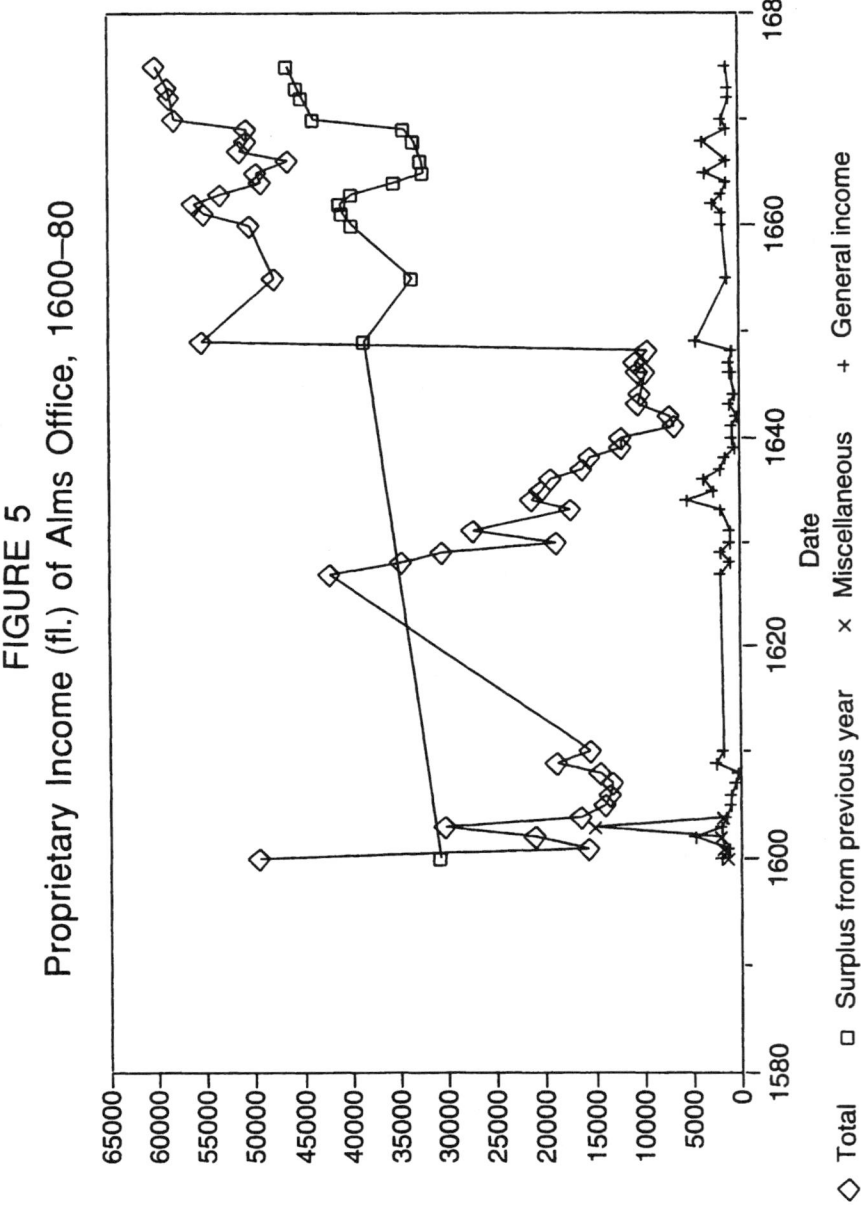

FIGURE 5
Proprietary Income (fl.) of Alms Office, 1600–80

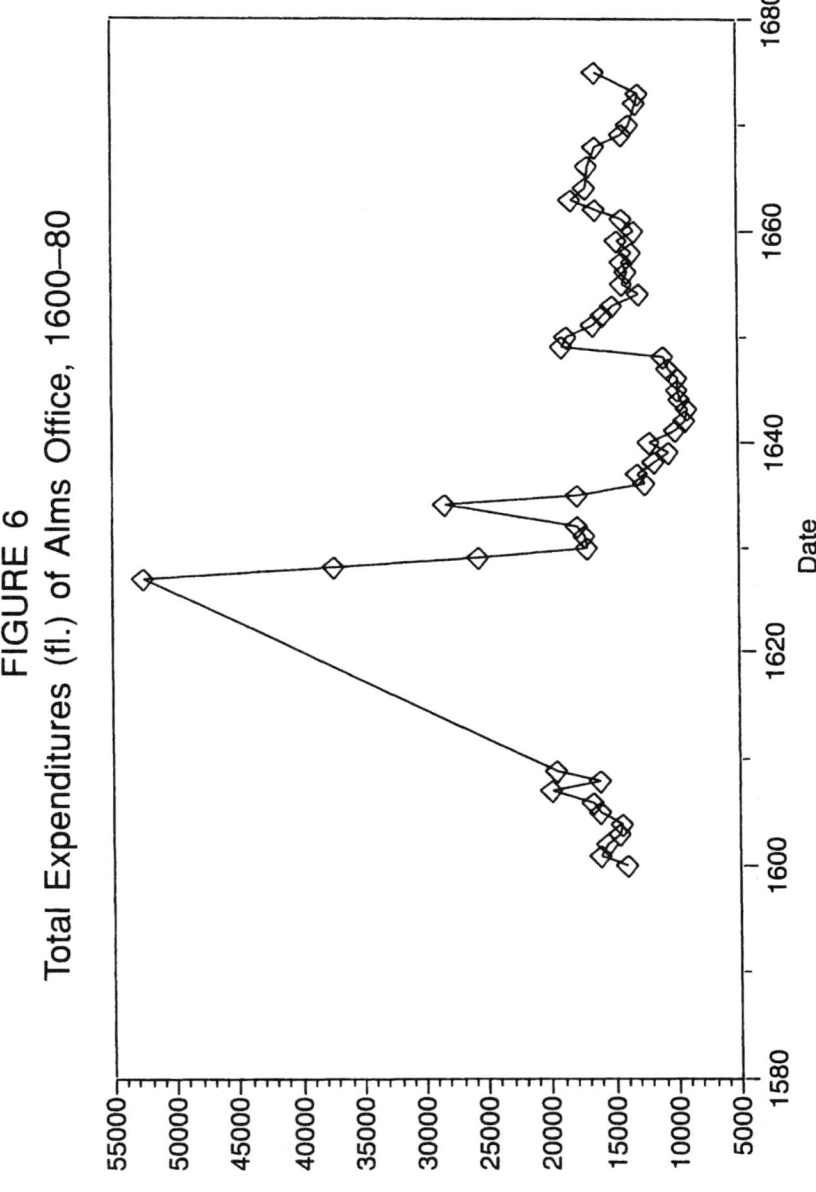

FIGURE 6
Total Expenditures (fl.) of Alms Office, 1600–80

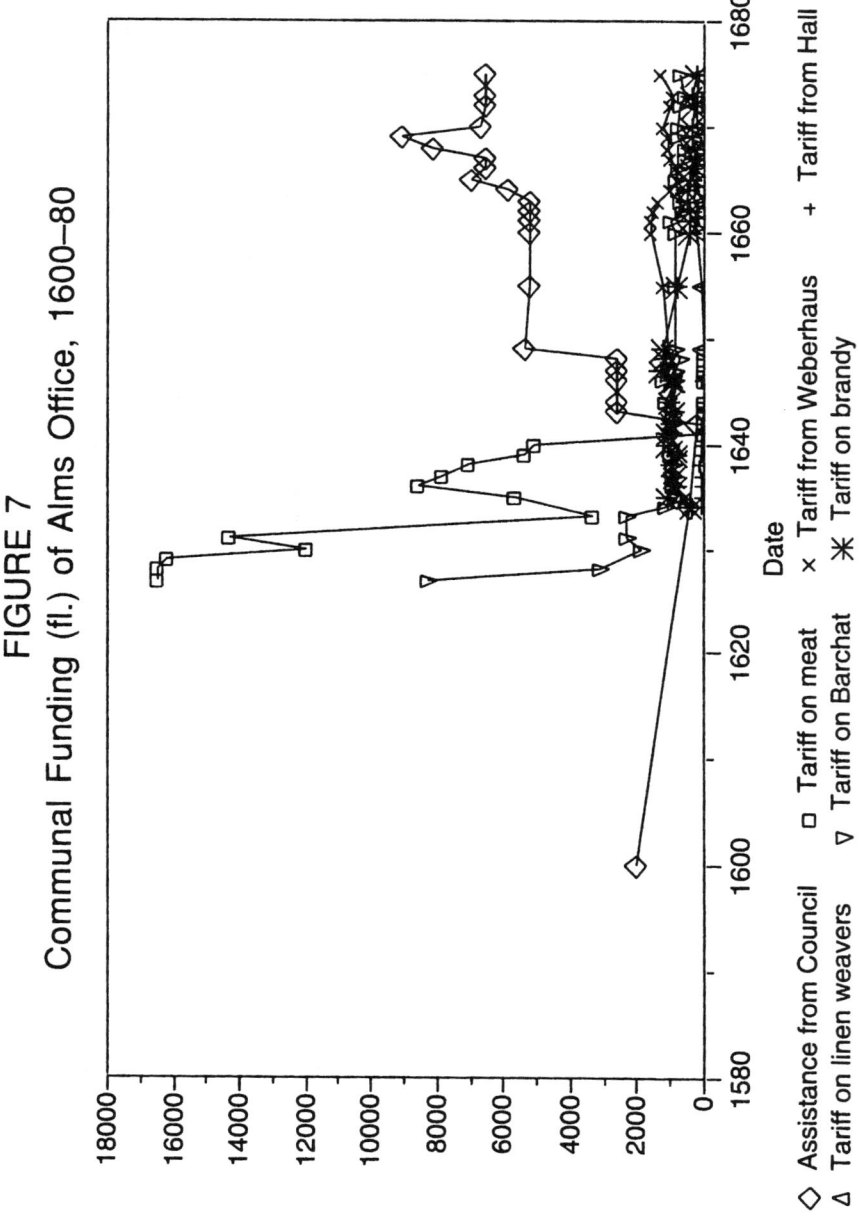

FIGURE 7
Communal Funding (fl.) of Alms Office, 1600–80

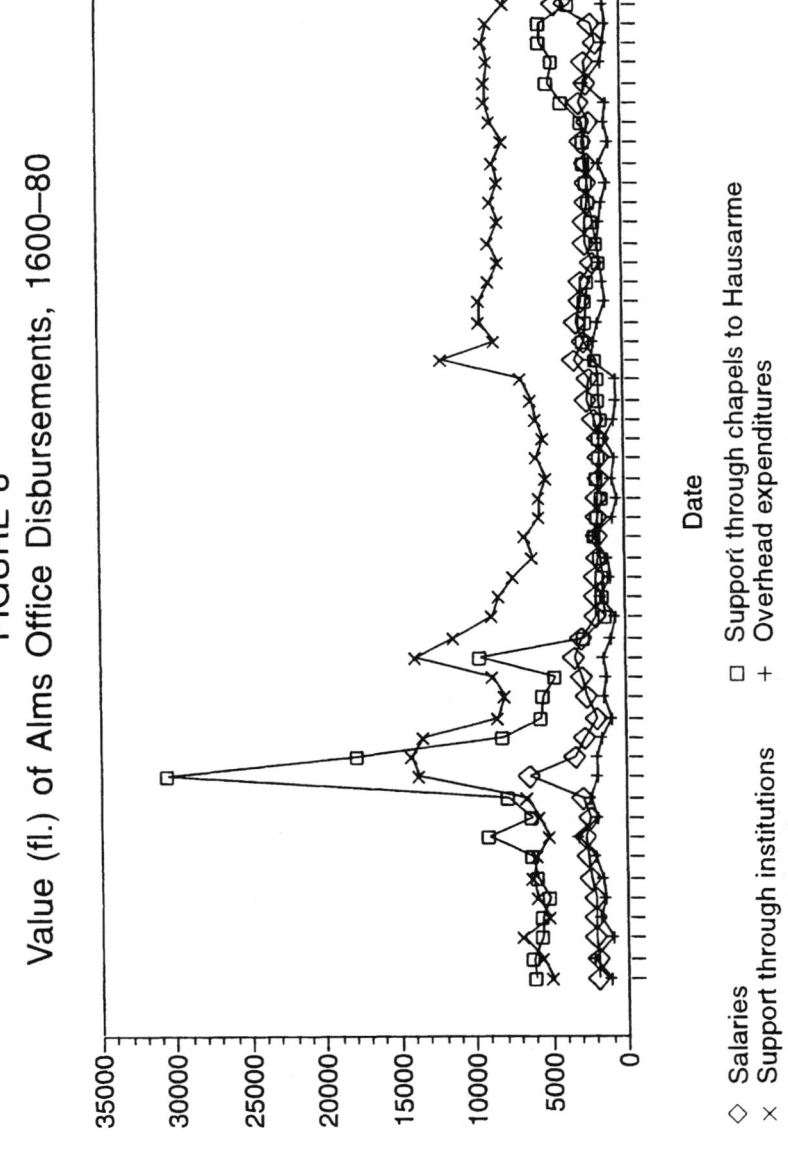

FIGURE 8
Value (fl.) of Alms Office Disbursements, 1600–80

◇ Salaries   □ Support through chapels to Hausarme
× Support through institutions   + Overhead expenditures

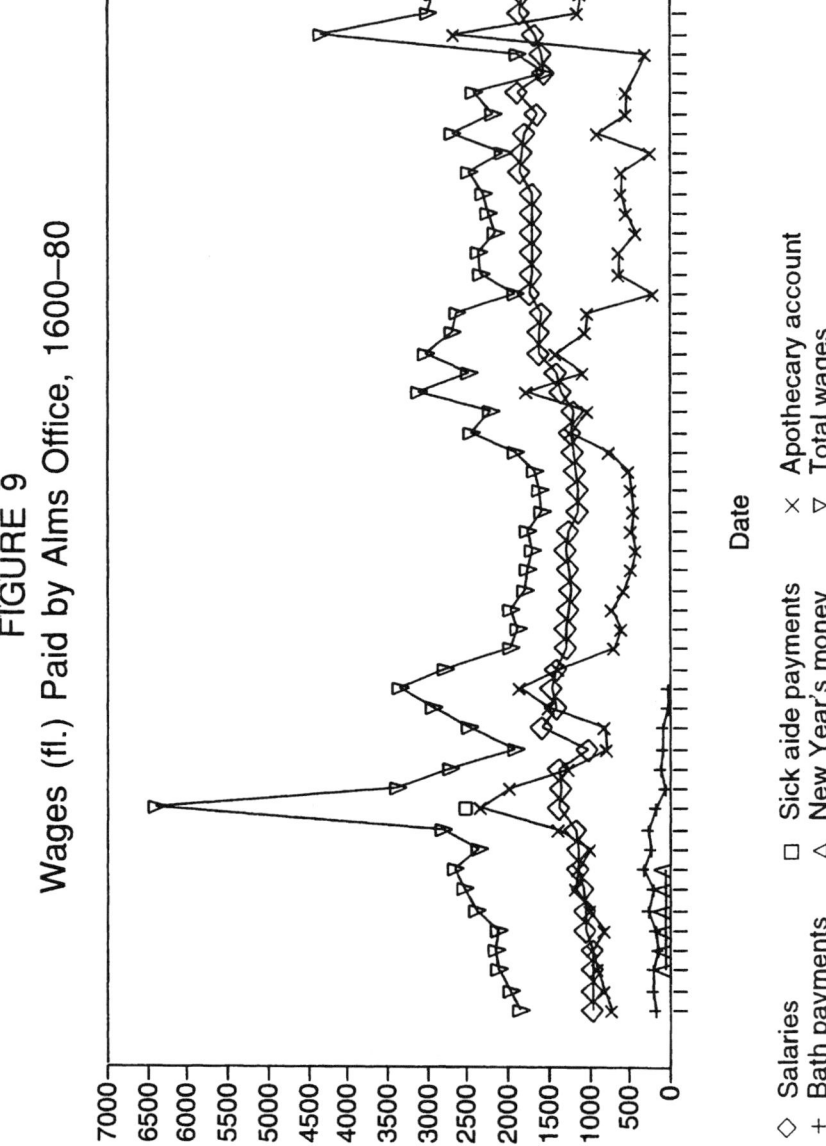

FIGURE 9
Wages (fl.) Paid by Alms Office, 1600–80

Appendix I 301

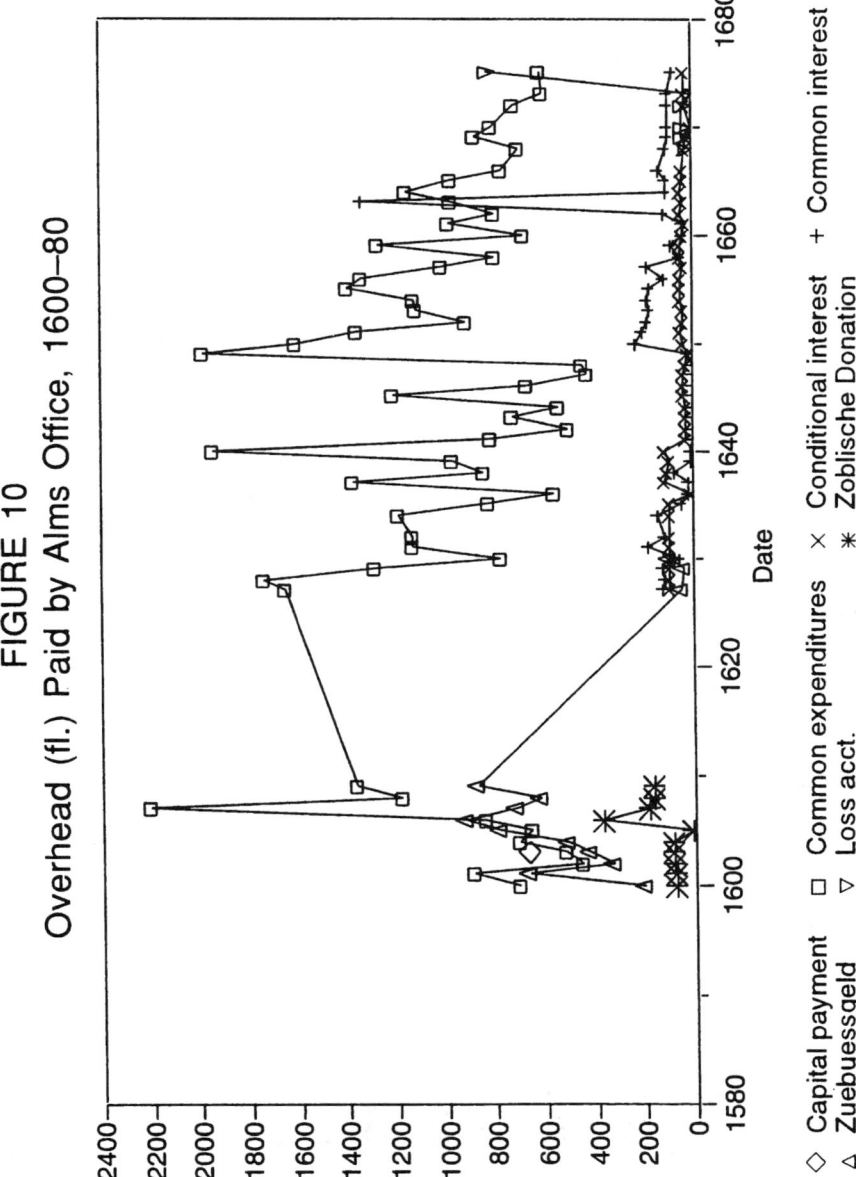

FIGURE 10
Overhead (fl.) Paid by Alms Office, 1600–80

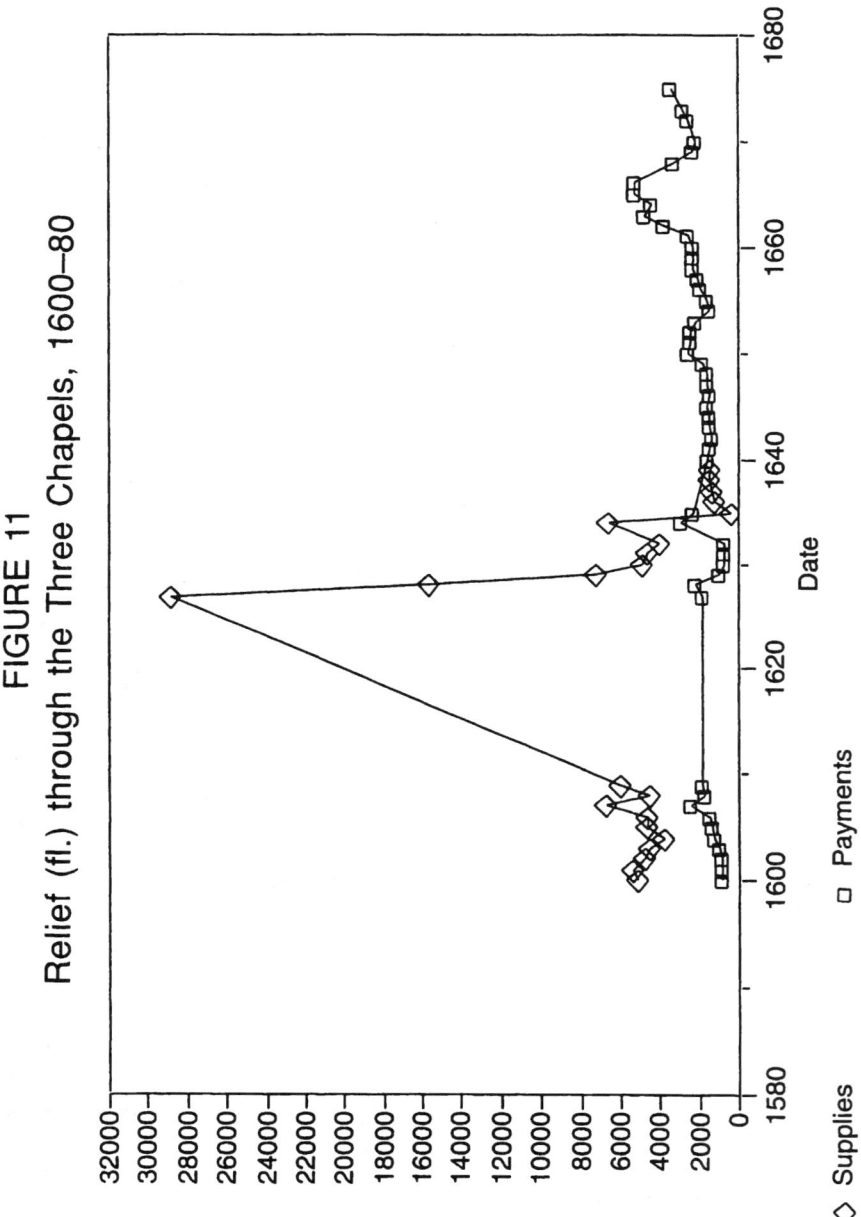

FIGURE 11
Relief (fl.) through the Three Chapels, 1600–80

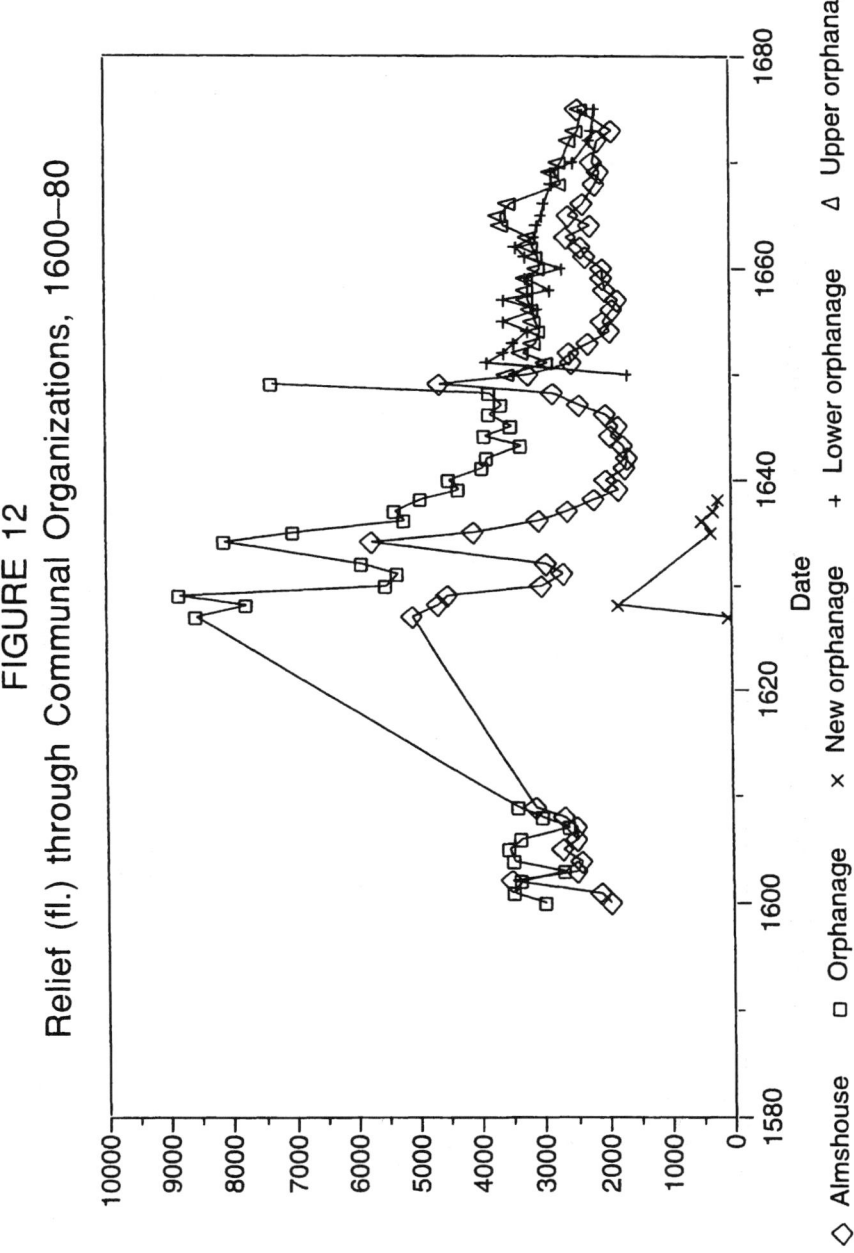

FIGURE 12
Relief (fl.) through Communal Organizations, 1600–80

◇ Almshouse □ Orphanage × New orphanage + Lower orphanage △ Upper orphanage

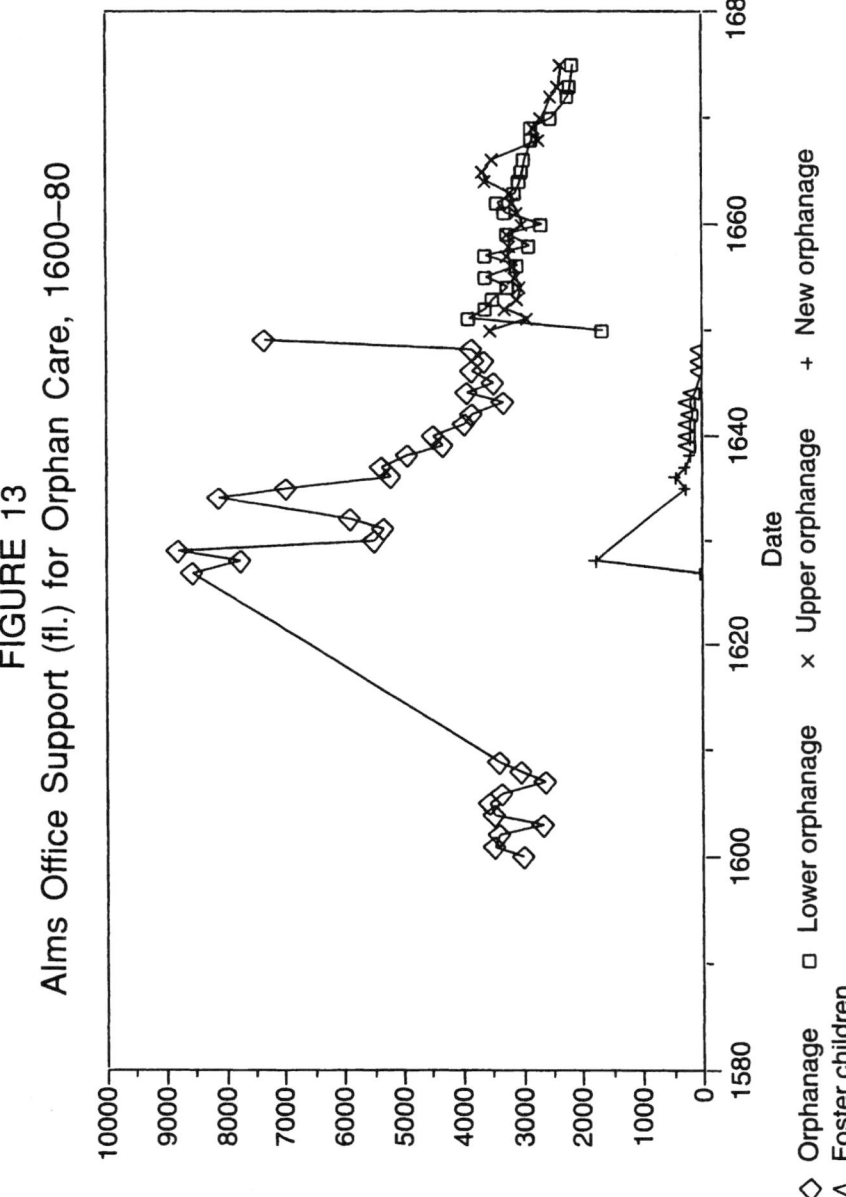

FIGURE 13
Alms Office Support (fl.) for Orphan Care, 1600–80

Appendix I 305

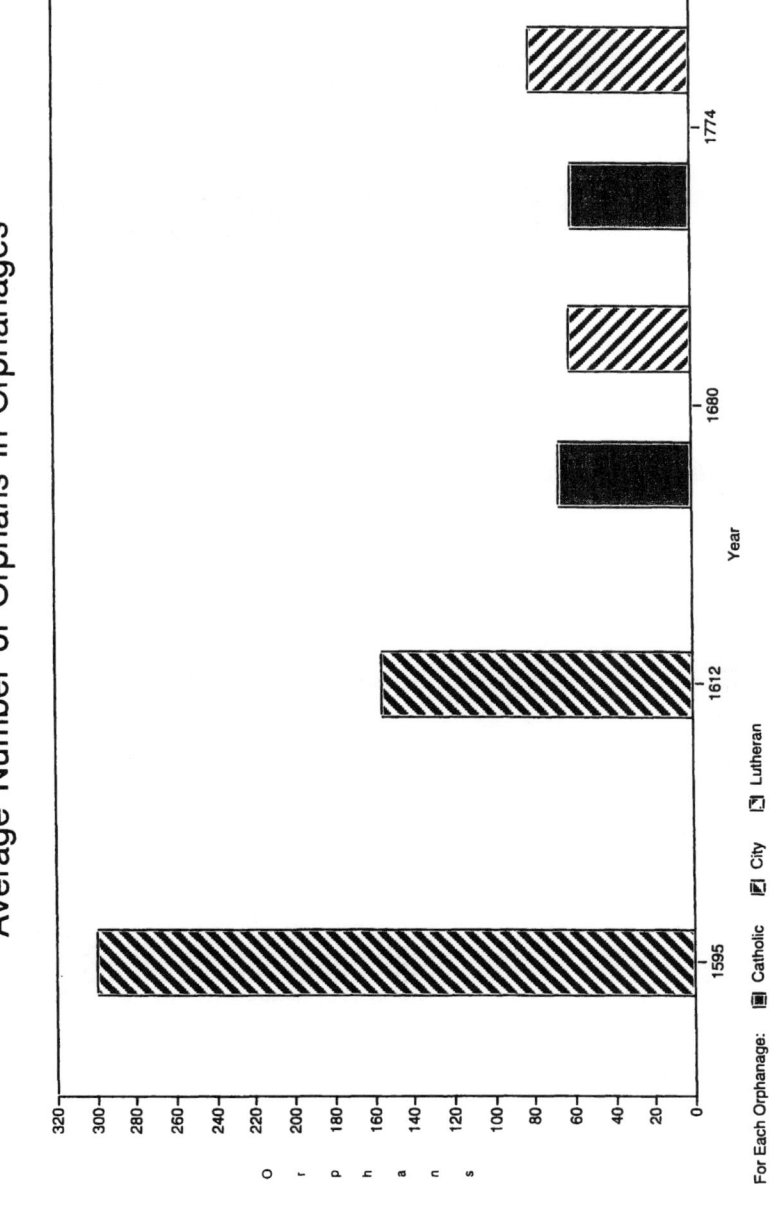

FIGURE 14
Average Number of Orphans in Orphanages

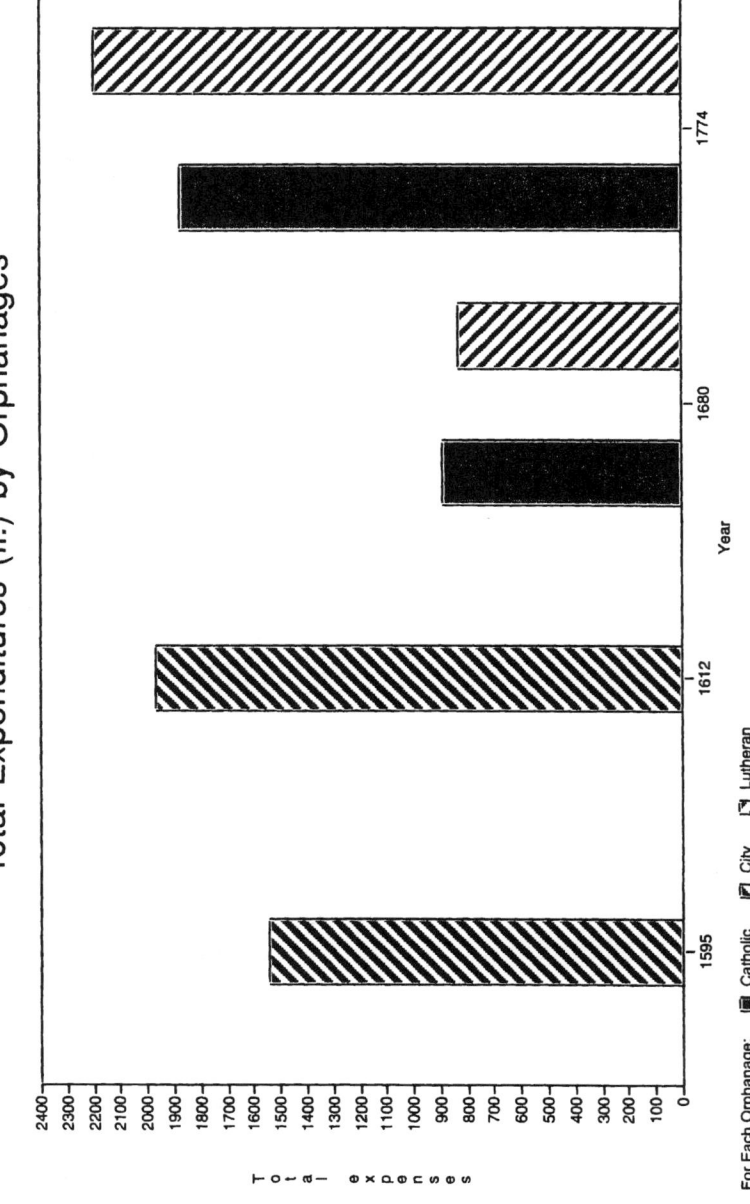

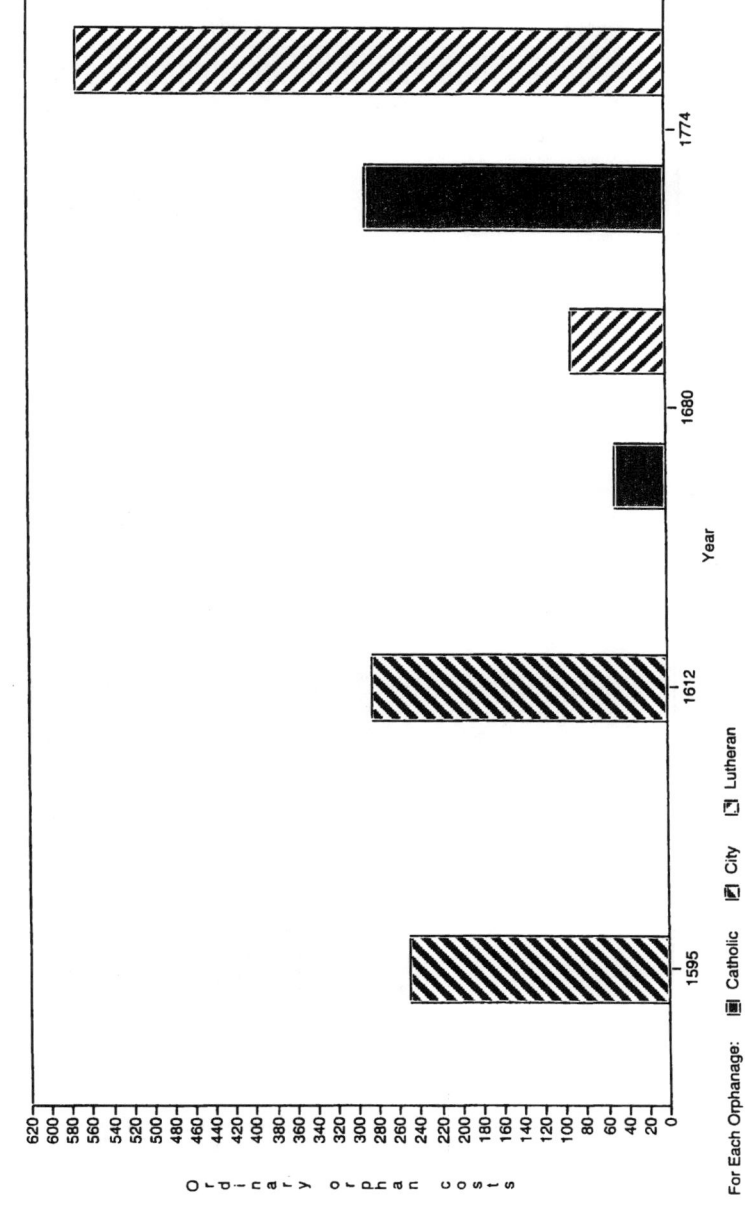

FIGURE 16
Total Ordinary Costs (fl.) of Orphan Care

APPENDIX I

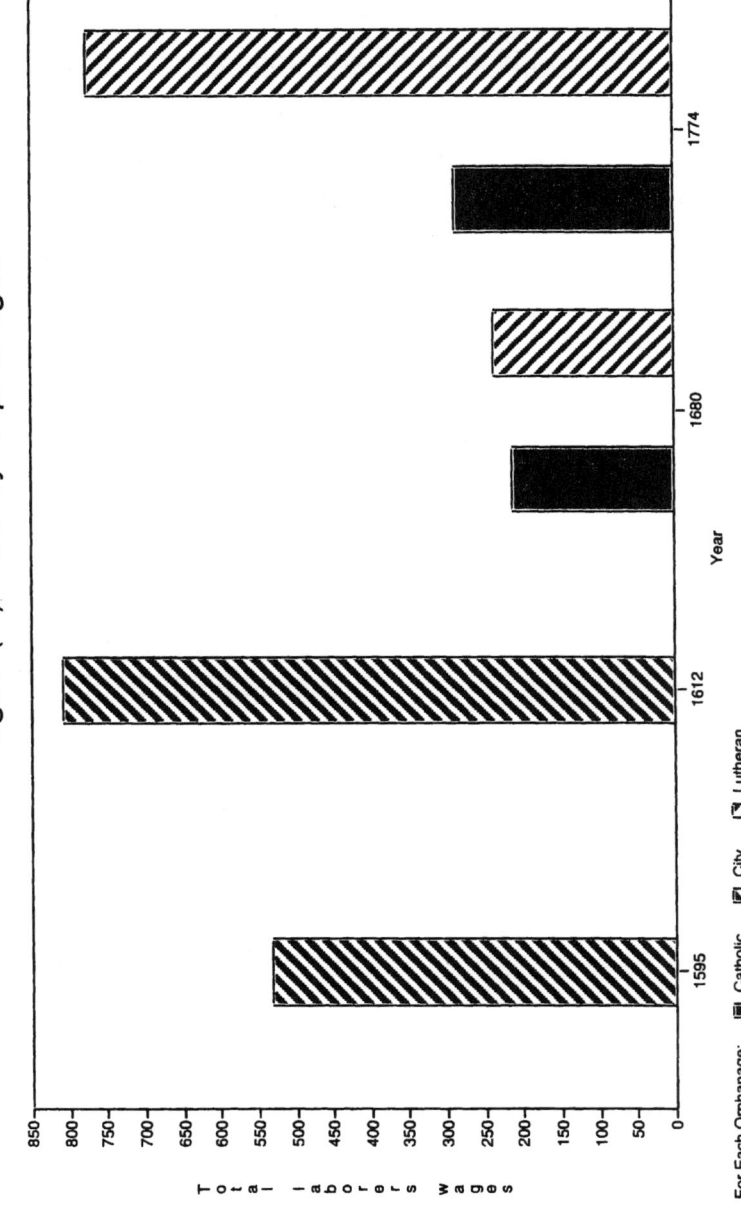

FIGURE 17
Total Wages (fl.) Paid by Orphanages

Appendix I

FIGURE 18
Total Housewares Expenditures (fl.) by Orphanages

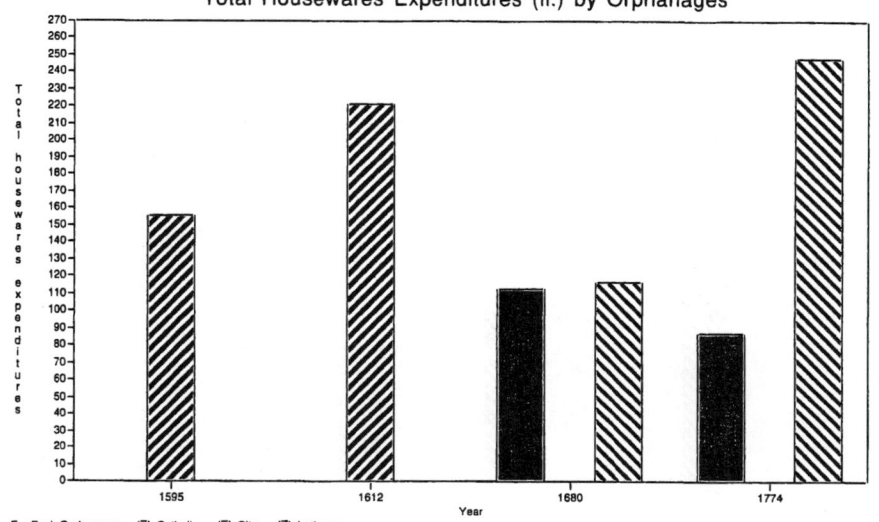

For Each Orphanage: ■ Catholic ▨ City ▧ Lutheran

FIGURE 18a
Expenditures (fl.) on Sundries

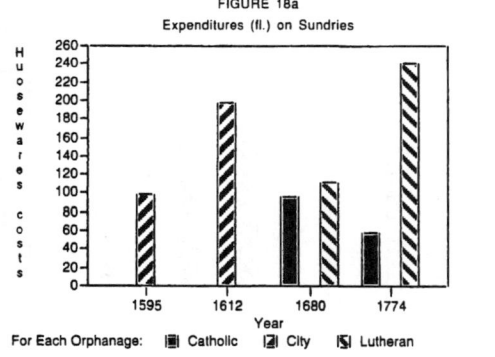

For Each Orphanage: ■ Catholic ▨ City ▧ Lutheran

FIGURE 18b
Expenditures (fl.) on Tallow

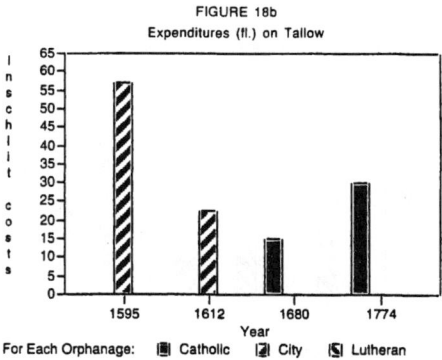

For Each Orphanage: ■ Catholic ▨ City ▧ Lutheran

FIGURE 18c
Expenditures (fl.) on Cloth

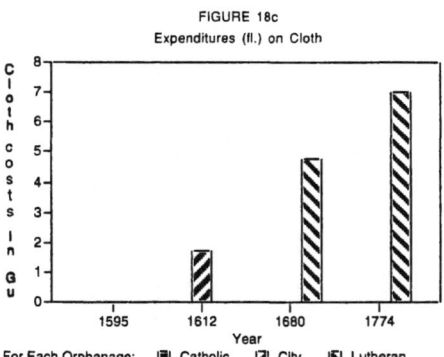

For Each Orphanage: ■ Catholic ▨ City ▧ Lutheran

FIGURE 19
Total Expenditures (fl.) on Food by Orphanages

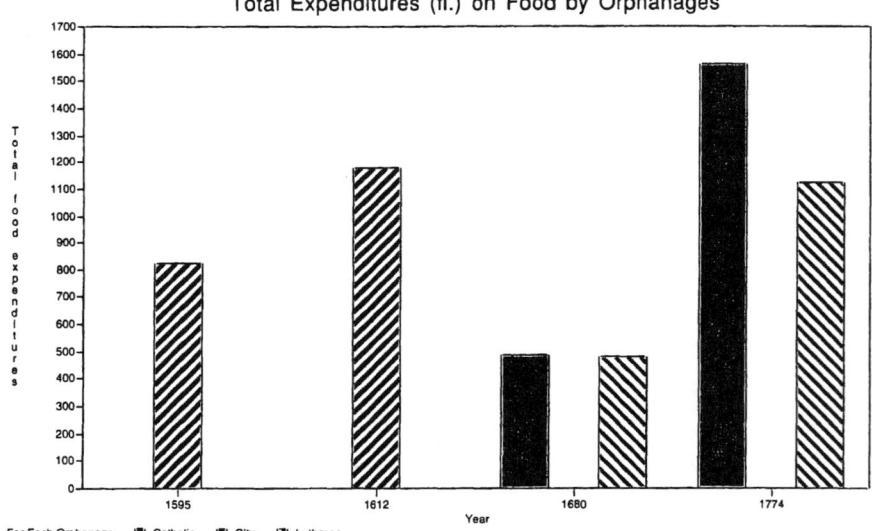

FIGURE 19a
Expenditures (fl.) on Meats

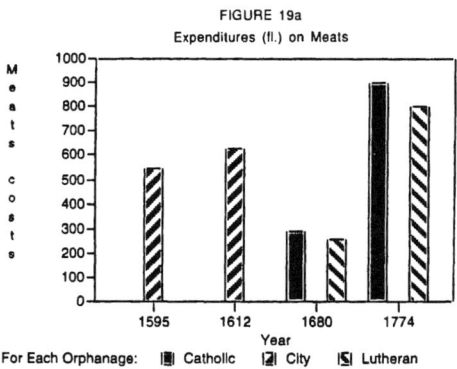

FIGURE 19b
Monthly Consumption (*Pfund*) of Meats

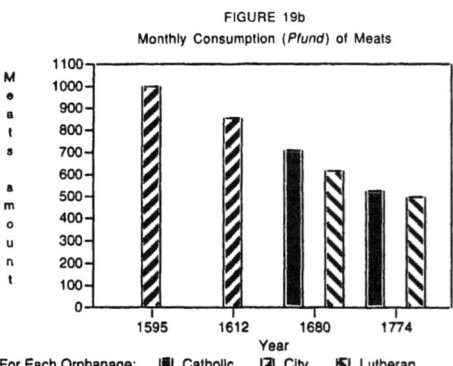

FIGURE 19c
Expenditures (fl.) on Grains

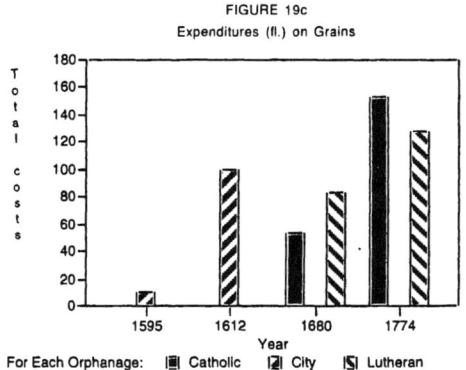

FIGURE 19d
Month Consumption (*Schaff*) of Grains

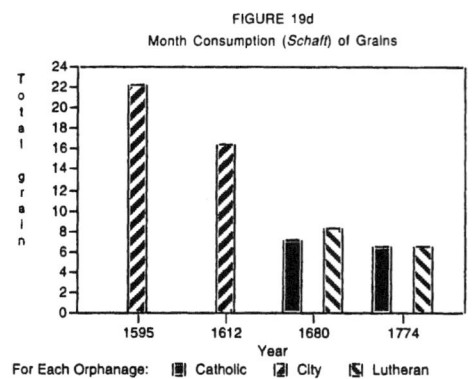

Appendix I

FIGURE 19e
Expenditures (fl.) on Beer

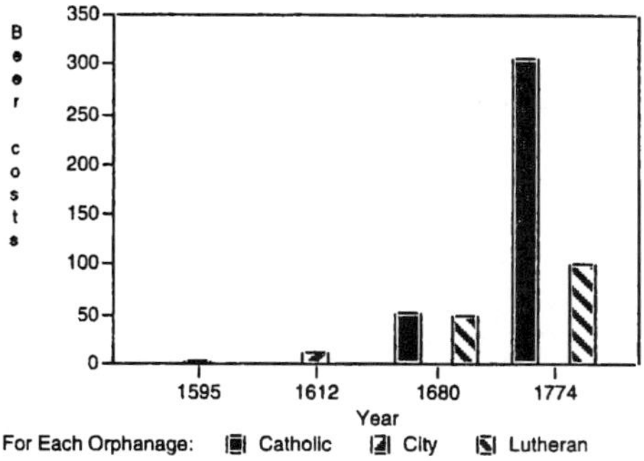

FIGURE 19f
Monthly Consumption (Maß) of Beer

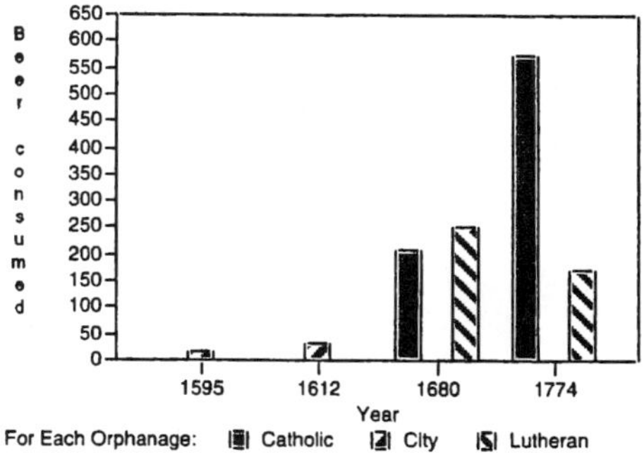

FIGURE 19g
Expenditures (fl.) on Dairy Products

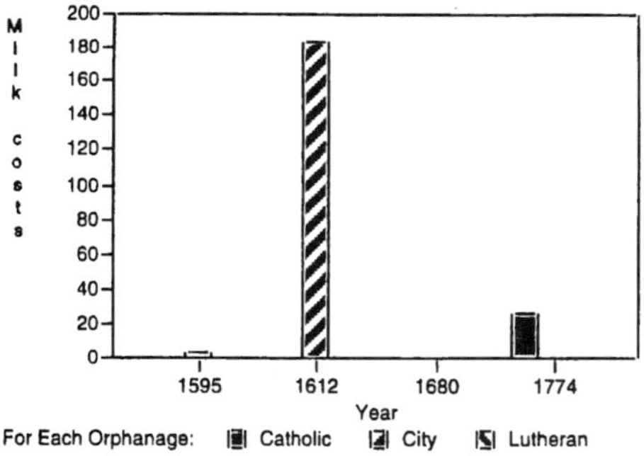

FIGURE 19h
Expenditures (fl.) on Garden Produce

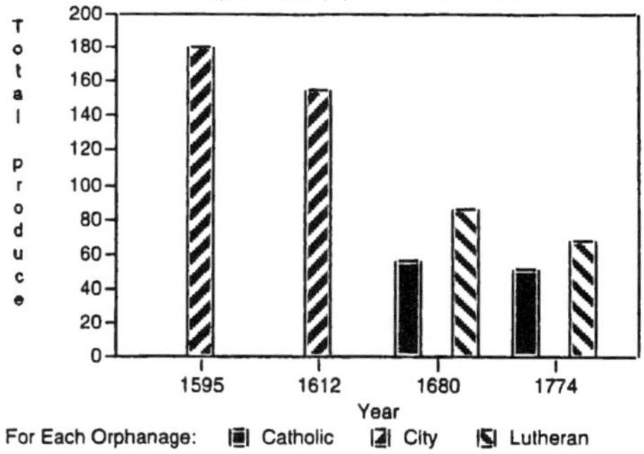

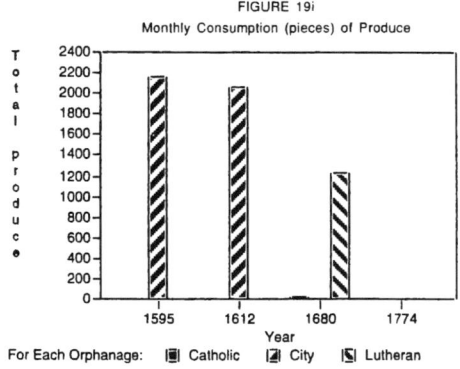

FIGURE 19i
Monthly Consumption (pieces) of Produce

Appendix II

ORPHANAGE PROPOSAL OF 1572
Ain ungefarlicher uberschlag Was ain Waisenhaus
Darinnen 200 Kinder Erhalten Mochten werden
Jerlich Kosten möcht.

Erstlich ain Gottseelig Christenlich par Eevolck, die ain gut gewissen unnd kaine Kinder hetten, weliche die Kinder zu der Forcht Gottes, dem gepett, auch zur Arbaitt und allen gueten thugeten trewlich underwisen unnd keerten, dero besoldung möcht sein ungefar	fl.	50
Mer 6 megt die from und trew Jeder fl. 5 Jars	fl.	30
Rogken 160 Schaff zu fl. 9	fl.	1440
Keren zu shönem meel 20 Schaff zu fl. 11	fl.	220
Weiß brott alle wochen ungefar 30 kr.	fl.	26
Wein, met, bier Im fall der Not	fl.	20
Erbis [= Erbse, T.M.S.] 4 Schaff umb	fl.	20
Hirsch [= Hirse, T.M.S.] 3 Schaff umb	fl.	18
Gersten 4 Schaff umb	fl.	16
Haber 4 Schaff zu Habermeel umb	fl.	12
Flesch alle wochen 170 £ ain Jar	fl.	294
Umb 5 Schwein	fl.	25.
Schmalz alle wochen, 25 £ cl. 13 zu fl. 9 den cl.	fl.	117
Salz 5 Scheiben	fl.	9
Liechter 200 £ zu 5 kr.	fl.	17
Rueben 300 Metzen zu 4 kr.	fl.	20
Weißkrautt umb	fl.	25
Grienkrautt, ops, unnd aÿr	fl.	20
Weinp[eeren], Mandl, Feigen, Saiffen, und Holderseltz	fl.	20
Wechholder, Kimel, Bösen, Fegsand, Scheffler, und Kuchgeschir	fl.	25
Holtz 35 Klaffter thenne und 25 Klaffter buche zu 18 und 28 patzen die Klaffter	fl.	89
Bortzen 30 Schober umb	fl.	10
Umb 10 Kue fl. 100 die mögen 6 Jar weren, Jst ain fl. 17 umb hew und stro fl. 100. Suma Jerlich	fl.	117
Nörlinger Loden 20 zu fl. 7½ ain Stuck	fl.	150
Barchant 20 Stuck ain St. zu fl. 2½	fl.	50
Zwilch [= Zwillich, T.M.S.] oder Mittler 15 St.	fl.	60
Dem Schneider Jerlich	fl.	50
Dem Schuester ÿeden Kind 2 par Schuech zu 8, 10, und 12 kr.	fl.	67
Leinwat zu Hemeder und Goller 800 Elen ain Eln 5 kr.	fl.	67
Leinwat zu Leilacher 800 Eln zu 4 kr.	fl.	53
Umb Huet unnd Schleplen	fl.	50
Cottember unnd Neegelt	fl.	50
Summa Jerlich	fl.	3237

Appendix II

WEEKLY MENU OF THE CITY ORPHANAGE, 1638
Speiß-Ordnung

1. Auf jeden tag haben sie ihre gewiße Speiß, als wochentlich 3. mal Fleisch, Mues, Knöpflen, Kraut, Gsodhaber, Erbis, Gersten, Zwetschgen, Reiß, dirr Obß und nach beshaffenheit der Zeit.
2. Jnsonderheit aber an hohen Festtägen als zu Weÿnachten, Ostern, Pfingsten, Kirchweÿ haben sie zu Mittag Suppen und Fleisch, ein Reiß in der Milch, ein Semel $\frac{1}{4}$ oder $\frac{1}{2}$ Maß bier, welche communiciren.
3. Zu nacht ein Suppen und ein bratens, ein Semel und jedem $\frac{1}{2}$ Maß bier.

WEEKLY MENU OF THE LUTHERAN ORPHANAGE, CA. 1660

An Sontags Mittags.	Ein Suppe von der Spatzen-brühe und Milch-Reiß: aber im abgang der Milch, bier oder Apffelshnitz. Abendts. Suppen und Rindfleish.
Montags Mittags.	Ein Fleisch-Suppen und Gsotthaber. Abendts. Geschupffte Nottlen.
Dienstag Mittags.	Die Nottelbrüh zur Suppen, und Linßen wohl eingekocht. Abendt. Suppen u. Rindfleisch.
Mittwoch Mittags.	Ein brändte Suppe und ein Schön-Muß oder Zwetschgengeröst und Roggenbrodt darinn geschnitten. Abendts. Gersten in der Fleisch-brühe kocht.
Donnerstag Mittag.	Ein brente Suppe und ein Roggen geschmalten brodt. Abendts. Suppen und Rindfleisch.
Freÿtag Mittags.	Fleisch-Suppe und wohl eingekochte Erbßen oder zur Winters-Zeit baÿrische Rüben. Abendts. Knöpfflen von breet sambt der Suppen.
Sonabend Mittag.	Knöpfflen-Suppen u. Sauer Kraut. Abendts. Spatzen jn der Brüh oder geröst.
NB.	Fällt ein feürtag, wann mann vonn meehl speist, so macht mann ein Kogelhopffen. Mit der Kraütelwahr ist bißweilen auch eine abwexlung geschehen.
NB.	Zur Waschzeit seind vor alle jm hauß becken-notteln gemacht worden.

Weekly Menu from the Lutheran Orphanage, ca. 1690
Speiß-Ordnung des Evangl. Waißenhauses

	Morgens	Mittags	Nachmittags	Abends	
Sonntags		Fleisch-Suppe Rindfleisch 1 Stückl. brod	um 4 Uhr 1 Stück brod	Fleisch-Suppe Gogelhopff	Alternatim Reiß-Suppe 1 Stk. brod.
Montags	um 8 Uhr 1 Stückl. brod	Erbßen-Suppe geschupffte Nudl.	ut supra	Fleisch-Suppe 1 Stk. brod.	
Dienstags	ut supra	wie am Sonntag aber ohne bier	ut supra	Reiß-Suppe 1 Stk brod.	olim Gersten Suppe.
Mittwochs	ut supra	Linsen-Suppe geröste Spatzen alternat. Brüh-Spatzen 1 Stk. brod	ut supra	Fleisch-Suppe 1 Stk. brod.	
Donnerstags	ut supra	wie am Sonntag mit 1 Quärtl. bier	ut supra	Groos-Suppe 1 Stk. brod.	
Freytags	ut supra	Fleisch-Suppe Mehl-Knöpffen 1 Stk. brod olim ordin. Saur-Kraut	ut supra	gebrännte Sup. 1 Stk brod	alternat. Schnitz-Röster 1 Stk. brod.
Sonnabends	ut supra	Knöpffl. Suppe brät-Knöpffle. 1 Stk. brod.	ut supra	aufgekochte Suppe 1 Stk. brod.	

Weekly Menu from the Lutheran Orphanage, ca. 1730
Speißzettel deß Evangel. Wayßenhauses.

	Mittags.	Abends.
Sonntags	Suppen und Fleisch.	Reiß, bisweil ein gogelhopff.
Montags	Wassersuppen u. Linsen.	gshupffte oder gshnittene Nudel.
Dienstags	Suppen und Fleisch.	Gersten.
Mittwochs	Suppen und Erbiß.	Spatzen.
Donnerstags	Suppen und Fleisch.	Reiß, Schnitz, oder Zwetschgen.
Freytags	Gsotthaber.	Suppe u. brätene Knöpfflen.
Sonnabends	Sauerkraut u. Suppen.	Schmaltz u. brod, oder Suppen.

Appendix II

WEEKLY MENU FROM THE LUTHERAN ORPHANAGE, CA. 1780

So viel endlich die tägl. ordentl. Kost der Kinder u. Dienstbothen betrifft, so soll dieselbige in nachfolgenden bestehen.

a. Sontag.	Mittag, Fleisch u. Zugemüß, oder Reis.
	Abends geschnittene Nudeln.
b. Montag.	Mittags. Becken-Nudeln, u. Erbsen-Suppe.
	Abends eine Suppe.
c. Dienstag.	Mittag. Fleisch u. Zugemüß.
	Abends eine Gersten Suppe.
d. Mittwoch.	Mittag geschupfte Nudeln u. Linsen-Suppe.
	Abends eine Fleischsuppe.
e. Donnerstag.	Mittag. Fleisch u. Saurkraut.
	Abends eine Grooß Suppe.
f. Freÿtag.	Mittag. Backen-Nudeln und Suppen.
	Abends eine gebrännte Suppe.
g. Sams-Tag.	Mittag. Mehl-Knöpfeln.
	Abends eine aufgekochte Suppe.

Bibliography

ABBREVIATIONS

Alms	Reichsstadt Akten, Almosenamt
BHStA	Bayerisches Hauptstaatsarchiv
EW	Reichsstadt Akten, Almosenamt, Evangelisches Waisenhaus
EWA	Evangelisches Wesensarchiv
Geschichte	Gottlieb, Gunther, Wolfram Baer, Josef Becker, Josef Bellot, Karl Filser, Pankraz Fried, Wolfgang Reinhard, and Bernhard Schimmelpfennig (eds.), *Geschichte der Stadt Augsburg von der Römerzeit bis zur Gegenwart*, Stuttgart, 1984.
KW	Reichsstadt Akten, Almosenamt, Katholisches Waisenhaus
KWA	Katholisches Wesensarchiv
Lexikon	Baer, Wolfram, et al. (eds.), *Augsburger Stadtlexikon*, Augsburg, 1985.
StAA	Stadtarchiv Augsburg
StBA	Stadtbibliothek Augsburg
W	Reichsstadt Akten, Almosenamt, Waisenhäuser
ZHVS	*Zeitschrift des historischen Vereins für Schwaben*

UNPUBLISHED SOURCES

Bayrisches Hauptstaatsarchiv München
  Reichstadt Literalien, B 2a/X.H./67
Stadtarchiv Augsburg, Reichsstadt Akten, Almosenamt
  Evangelisches Waisenhaus, 1–23
  Katholisches Waisenhaus, 1–29
  Waisenhäuser, 1–10
Stadtarchiv Augsburg, Reichsstadt Akten, Evangelisches Wesensarchiv
  Akten, 314
  Akten, 1525
Stadtarchiv Augsburg, Reichsstadt Akten, Katholisches Wesensarchiv
  D1
  D2
  E18
  E20
  E21
  E29
  F55
  G17
  J14
  J20
  K16
  L155
  WkW4

PUBLISHED SOURCES AND LITERATURE

Abel, Alves A. "The Christian Social Organism and Social Welfare: The Case of Vives, Calvin, and Loyola," *Sixteenth Century Journal* 20 (1989), 3–22.

Abel, Wilhelm. *Massenarmut und Hungerkrisen im vorindustriellen Europa: Versuch einer Synopsis*, Hamburg, 1974.

———. *Massenarmut und Hungerkrisen im vorindustriellen Deutschland*, Göttingen, 1986.

Abu-Lughod, Janet L. *Before European Hegemony: The World System, A.D. 1250–1350*, Oxford, 1989.

Adler, Max. *Fabrik und Zuchthaus: Eine sozialhistorische Untersuchung*, Leipzig, 1924.

Alvarez, Santaló and León Carlos. *Marginación y mentalidad en Andalucía Occidental: Expósitos en Sevilla (1613–1910)*, Seville, 1980.

Andrew, Donna T. *Philanthropy and Police: London Charity in the Eighteenth Century*, Princeton, 1989.

Appleby, Joyce Oldham. *Economic Thought and Ideology in Seventeenth-Century England*, Princeton, 1978.

Ariés, Philippe. *Centuries of Childhood*, New York, 1962.

Arkell, Thomas. "The Incidence of Poverty in England in the Later Seventeenth Century," *Social History* 12 (1987), 23–47.

Armengaud, André. *La famille et l'enfant en France et en Angleterre du XVIe au XVIIIe siècle: Aspects demographiques*, Paris, 1975.

Arnold, K. *Kinder und Gesellschaft in Mittelalter und Renaissance: Beiträge und Texte zur Geschichte der Kindheit*, Paderborn, 1980.

———. "Mentalität und Erziehung—Geschlechtsspezifische Arbeitsteilung und Geschlechtersphäre als Gegenstand der Sozialisation im Mittelalter," in Frantisek Graus (ed.), *Mentalitäten im Mittelalter: Methodische und inhaltliche Probleme* (Sigmaringen, 1987), pp. 257–88.

Baer, Wolfram. "Die Entwicklung der Stadtverfassung, 1276–1368," in *Geschichte*, pp. 146–50.

———. "Das Stadtrecht vom Jahre 1156," in *Geschichte*, pp. 132–35.

———. "Der Weg zur königlichen Bürgerstadt," in *Geschichte*, pp. 135–40.

Baer, Wolfram, and Hans Joachim Heckler (eds.), *Die Jesuiten und ihre Schule St. Salvator in Augsburg, 1582*, Augsburg, 1982.

Baier, Helmut. "Die evangelische Kirche zwischen Pietismus, Orthodoxie und Auflkärung," in *Geschichte*, pp. 518–29.

Bakhtin, Mikhail. *Rabelais and His World*, Bloomington, 1984.

Bakker, Lothar. "Die Anfänge der Zivilsiedlung Augusta Vindelicum," in *Geschichte*, pp. 34–41.

———. "Das wirtschaftliche Leben im römischen Augsburg," in *Geschichte*, pp. 62–73.

Barbour, Violet. *Capitalism in Amsterdam in the Seventeenth Century*, Baltimore, 1950.

Barge, Hermann. "Die älteste evangelische Armenordnungen," *Historisches Vierteljahreschrift* 11 (1908), 193–225.

Bärlehner, Franz Xavier. *Die Entwicklung der karitativen Wohlfahrtspflege in Bayern*, Nuremberg, 1927.

Bátori, Ingrid. *Die Reichsstadt Augsburg im 18. Jahrhundert: Verfassung, Finanzen und Reformversuche*, Göttingen, 1969.

———. "Reichsstädtisches Regiment, Finanzen und bürgerliche Opposition," in *Geschichte*, pp. 457–68.

Bátori, Ingrid (ed.). *Städtische Gesellschaft und Reformation*, Stuttgart, 1980.

Bátori, Ingrid, and Erdmann Weyrauch. *Die bürgerliche Elite der Stadt Kitzingen: Studien*

sur Sozial- und Wirtschaftsgeschichte einer landesherrlichen Stadt im 16. Jahrhundert, Stuttgart, 1982.
Bechtold, K. D., Zunftbürgerschaft und Patriziat: Studien zur Sozialgeschichte der Stadt Konstanz im 14. und 15. Jahrhundert, Sigmaringen, 1981.
Becker, Marvin. "Aspects of Lay Piety in Renaissance Florence," in Charles Trinkaus and Heiko Oberman (eds.), The Pursuit of Holiness in Late Medieval and Renaissance Religion, Leiden, 1974, pp. 177–99.
Behlmer, George K. Child Abuse and Moral Reform in England, 1870–1908, Stanford, 1982.
Beier, A. L. Masterless Men: The Vagrancy Problem in England, 1560–1640, London, 1985.
Bellot, Josef. "Humanismus—Bildungswesen—Buchdruck und Verlagsgeschichte," in Geschichte, pp. 343–57.
———. "Politische Ereignisse und Festlichkeiten," in Geschichte, pp. 451–57.
Benscheidt, Anja R. Kleinbürgerliche Besitz: Nürtinger Handwerkerinventare von 1660 bis 1840, Münster, 1985.
Berger, W. Das Sankt-Georg-Hospital zu Hamburg: Die Wirtschaftsführung eines Großhaushalts, Hamburg, 1972.
Berweck, W. Das Heilig-Geist-Spital zu Villingen im Schwarzwald von der Gründung bis zum Beginn des 17. Jahrhunderts: Verfassung und Verwaltung, Villingen, 1963.
Bettger, Roland. Das Handwerk in Augsburg beim Übergang der Stadt an das Königreich Bayern: Städtisches Gewerbe unter dem Einfluß politischer Veränderungen, Augsburg, 1979.
Bierbrauer, Volker. "Alamannische Besiedlung Augsburgs und seines näheren Umlandes," in Geschichte, pp. 87–100.
Billot, Claudine. "Les enfants abandonnés à Chartres à la fin du moyen âge," Annales de démographie historique (1975), 167–86.
Bisle, Max. Die öffentliche Armenpflege der Reichsstadt Augsburg mit Berücksichtigung der einschlägigen Verhältnisse in anderen Reichsstädten Suddeutschland: Ein Beitrag zur christlichen Kulturgeschichte, Paderborn, 1904.
Blaufuss, Dietrich. "Das Verhältnis der Konfessionen in Augsburg 1555 bis 1648: Versuch eines Überblicks," Jahrbuch des Vereins für Augsburger Bistumsgeschichte 10 (1976), 27–56.
———. Reichsstadt und Pietismus: Philipp Jacob Spener und Gottlieb Spizel aus Augsburg, Neustadt/Aisch, 1977.
Blendinger, Friedrich. "Versuch einer Bestimmung der Mittelschicht in der Reichsstadt Augsburg vom Ende der 14. bis zum Anfang des 18. Jahrhundert," in Erich Maschke and Jürgen Sydow (eds.), Städtische Mittelschichten, Stuttgart, 1972, pp. 32–78.
———. "Die Zunfterhebung von 1368," in Geschichte, pp. 150–53.
Blockmans, W. P., and W. Prevenier. "Poverty in Flanders and Brabant from the Fourteenth to the Mid-sixteenth Century: Sources and Problems," Acta Historiae Neelandicae 10 (1978), 20–57.
Bog, Ingomar. "Reichsverfassung und reichsstädtische Gesellschaft: Sozial-geschichtliche Forschungen über reichsständische Rezidenten in den freien Städten, insbesondere Nürnberg," Jahrbuch für fränkische Landesforschung 18 (1958), 325–39.
———. "Über Arme und Armenfürsorge in Oberdeutschland und in der Eidgenossenschaft im 15. und 16. Jahrhundert," Jahrbuch für fränkische Landesforschung 34/35 (1974/75), 983–1001.
Bosl, Karl (ed.). Frühformen der Gesellschaft im mittelalterlichen Europa, Munich, 1964.
———. "Potens und Pauper: Begriffsgeschichtliche Studien zur gesellschaftlichen

Differenzierung im frühen Mittelalter und zum 'Pauperismus' des Hochmittelalters," in Karl Bosl (ed.), *Frühformen der Gesellschaft im mittelalterlichen Europa*, Munich, 1964, pp. 106–34.

———. *Die wirtschaftliche und gesellschaftliche Entwicklung des Augsburger Bürgertums vom 10. bis zum 14. Jahrhundert*, Munich, 1969.

———. "Die 'familia' als Grundstruktur der mittelalterlichen Gesellschaft," *Zeitschrift für bayerische Landesgeschichte* 38 (1795), 403–24.

———. "Über soziale Mobilität in der mittelalterlichen 'Gesellschaft': Dienst, Freiheit, Freizügigkeit als Motive sozialen Aufstiegs," *Vierteljahrsschrift für Sozial- und Wirtschaftsgeschichte* 67 (1980), 306–32.

Boswell, John. *The Kindness of Strangers: The Abandonment of Children in Western Europe from Late Antiquity to the Renaissance*, New York, 1988.

Brady, Thomas A., Jr. *Ruling Class, Regime and Reformation at Strasbourg, 1520–1555*, Leiden, 1978.

———. *Protestant Politics: Jacob Sturm (1489–1553) and the German Reformation*, Atlantic Highlands, N.J., 1995.

Bramley, Glen. "The Inner City Labour Market," in Colin Jones (ed.), *Urban Deprivation and the Inner City*, London, 1979, pp. 63–91.

Branca, Lodovico. "Pauperismo, assistenza, e controllo sociale a Firenze (1621–1632): Materiali e ricerche," *Archivio storico italiano* 141 (1983), 421–62.

Braudel, Fernand. *Civilization and Capitalism, 15th–18th Centuries*, 3 vols., New York, 1982.

Braun, Karl. "Das Zucht- und Arbeitshaus in Ravensburg, 1725–1808: Ein Wegbereiter moderner Anstalten," *Zeitschrift für württembergische Landesgeschichte* 10 (1951), 158–65.

Brunner, Otto. "Das 'ganze Haus' und die alteuropäische 'Ökonomik,'" in Otto Brunner, *Neue Wege der Verfassungs- und Sozialgeschichte*, Göttingen, 1968, pp. 103–27.

———. *Neue Wege der Verfassungs- und Sozialgeschichte*, Göttingen, 1968.

Bückling, Gerhard. *Die Rechtsstellung der unehelichen Kinder im Mittelalter und in der heutigen Reformbewegung*, Breslau, 1920.

Burke, Peter. *Popular Culture in Early Modern Europe*, London, 1978.

Büttel, Maria. *Die Armenpflege zu Frankfurt/Main mit besonderer Berücksichtigung der Kinderpflege im 18. Jahrhundert bis zum Eintritt der neuen Armenordnung im Jahre 1883*, Frankfurt/Main, 1913.

Campbell, J. K. *Honour, Family and Patronage: A Study of Institutions and Moral Values in a Greek Mountain Community*, Oxford, 1964.

Cappelletto, Giovanna. "Infanzia abbandonata e ruoli di mediazione sociale nella Verona del Settecento," *Quaderni storici* 52 (1983), 421–43.

Cavallo, Sandra. "Conceptions of Poverty and Poor-relief in the Second Half of the Eighteenth Century," in Stuart Woolf (ed.), *Domestic Strategies: Work and Family in France and Italy, 1600–1800*, Cambridge, Eng., 1991, pp. 148–200.

Chamoux, Antoinette. "L'enfance abandonnés à Reims à la fin du XVIIIe siècle," *Annales de demographie historique* (1973), 263–301.

Chandler, Alfred Dupont. *The Visible Hand: The Managerial Revolution in American Business*, Cambridge, Mass., 1977.

Chatellier, Louis. *Tradition chrétienne et renouveau catholique dans l'ancien diocèse de Strasbourg, 1650–1770*, Paris, 1981.

Chrisman, Miriam Usher. "Urban Poor Relief in the Sixteenth Century: The Case of Strasbourg," in Miriam Usher Chrisman and Otto Gründler (eds.), *Social Groups and Religious Ideas in the Sixteenth Century*, Kalamazoo, 1978, pp. 59–67, 169–71.

Chrisman, Miriam Usher, and Otto Gründler (eds.). *Social Groups and Religious Ideas in the Sixteenth Century*, Kalamazoo, 1978.
Cipolla, Carlo. *Before the Industrial Revolution: European Society and Economy, 1000–1700*, New York, 1976.
Clark, Elaine. "City Orphans and Custody Laws in Medieval England," *American Journal of Legal History* 34 (1990), 168–87.
Clasen, Claus-Peter. *Die Augsburger Steuerbücher um 1600*, Augsburg, 1976.
———. *Die Augsburger Weber: Leistungen und Krisen des Textilgewerbes um 1600*, Augsburg, 1981.
———. "Arm und Reich in Augsburg vor dem Dreißigjährigen Krieg," in *Geschichte*, pp. 312–36.
———. "Armenfürsorge im 16. Jahrhundert," in *Geschichte*, pp. 337–43.
———. "Armenfürsorge in Augsburg vor dem Dreißigjährigen Kriege," ZHVS (1984), 65–115.
———. *Streiks und Aufstände der Augsburger Weber im 17. und 18. Jahrhundert*, Augsburg, 1993.
Cohen, Sherrill. *The Evolution of Women's Asylums since 1500: From Refuges for Ex-Prostitutes to Shelters for Battered Women*, Oxford, 1992.
Cohn, Samuel. *Death and Property in Siena, 1205–1800: Strategies for the Afterlife*, Baltimore, 1988.
Coler, Johannes. *Calendarum Perpetuum et Libri Oeconomii: Das ist ein stetswerender Calendar darzu sehr nutzliche und notige Hausbücher*, Wittemberg, 1592.
Corsini, Carlo. "Materiali per lo studio della famiglia in Toscana ne secoli XVII–XIX: gli esposti," *Quaderni storici* 33 (1976), 998–1052.
———. "L'enfant trouvé: note de démographie différentielle," *Annales de démographie historique* (1983), 95–102.
Coulton, Jeremy. *Neighborhood and Society: A London Suburb in the Seventeenth Century*, Cambridge, Eng., 1987.
Cressy, D. R. (ed.). *The Prison: Studies in Institutional Organization and Change*, New York, 1961.
Cunningham, Carole. "Christ's Hospital: Infant and Child Mortality in the Sixteenth Century," *Local Population Studies* 18 (1977), 37–40.
Cunningham, Philis, and Catherine Lucas. *Charity Costumes*, London, 1978.
Danckert, W. *Unehrliche Leute: Die verfemte Berufe*, Bern, 1963.
Davis, Natalie Zemon. "Poor Relief, Humanism and Heresy: The Case of Lyon," *Studies in Medieval and Renaissance History* 5 (1968), 217–75.
Davis, Ralph. *The Rise of the Atlantic Economies*, Ithaca, 1973.
DeLacy, Margaret. *Prison Reform in Lancashire, 1700–1850: A Study in Local Administration*, Stanford, 1986.
de la Roncière, Charles. "Pauvres et pauvreté à Florence au XIV e siècle," in Michel Mollat (ed.), *Études sur l'histoire de la pauvreté (Moyen Age–XVIe siècle)*, Paris, 1974, pp. 661–745.
Delasselle, Claude. "Les enfants abandonnés à Paris au XVIIIe siècle," *Annales: Economie, Société, Civilisation* 30 (1975), 187–218.
deMause, Lloyd. *The History of Childhood*, New York, 1974.
de Roover, Raymond. *Money, Banking and Credit in Medieval Bruges*, Cambridge, Mass., 1948.
de Vries, Jan. *The Dutch Rural Economy in the Golden Age, 1500–1700*, New Haven, 1974.
———. *The Economy of Europe in an Age of Crisis*, Cambridge, Eng., 1976.

———. *European Urbanization, 1500–1800*, Cambridge, Mass., 1984.

———. "The Industrial Revolution and the Industrious Revolution," *The Journal of Economic History* 54 (1994), 249–70.

Dey, Wilhelm. *Die Entstehung und Entwicklung der Augsburger Textilindustrie unter besonderer Berücksichtigung der weltwirtschaftlichen Beziehungen, 1648–1914*, Munich, 1948.

Deyon, Pierre, *Amiens, capitale provinciale*, Paris, 1969.

———. "A propos du paupérisme au milieu du XVIIe siècle—peinture et charité chrétienne," *Annales: Economie, Société, Civilisation* 22 (1967), 137–53.

Dietz, Johann. *Master Johann Dietz, Surgeon in the Army of the Great Elector and Barber to the Royal Court: From the Old Manuscript in the Royal Library of Berlin*, London, 1923.

Dinges, Martin. "Materielle Kultur und Alltag: Die Unterschichten in Bordeaux im 16. und 17. Jahrhundert," *Francia* 15 (1987), 257–79.

———. *Stadtarmut in Bordeaux, 1525–1675: Alltag—Politik—Mentalitäten*, Bonn, 1988.

———. "Attitudes à l'egard de la pauvreté aux VXIe et VXIIe siècles à Bordeaux," *Histoire, Économie et Société* 10 (1991), 360–74.

Dirlmeier, Ulf. *Untersuchungen zu Einkommensverhältnissen und Lebenshaltungskosten in oberdeutschen Städten des Spätmittelalters (Mitte 14. bis Anfang 16. Jahrhundert)*, Heidelberg, 1978.

Dirr, Pius. "Augsburger Textilindustrie im 18. Jahrhundert," *ZHVS* 37 (1911), 1–106.

Dobb, Maurice. *Studies in the Development of Capitalism*, New York, 1947.

Dollinger, Phillipe. "Die deutschen Städte im Mittelalter: Die sozialen Gruppierungen," in Heinz Stoob (ed.), *Altstädtisches Bürgertum*, Vol. II, Darmstadt, 1978, pp. 269–300.

Donzelot, Jacques. *The Policing of Families*, New York, 1979.

Dorwart, Rainhold August. *The Prussian Welfare State before 1740*, Cambridge, Mass., 1971.

Dotterweich, Volker. "Die Mediatisierung der Reichsstadt," in *Geschichte*, pp. 541–47.

Dotterweich, Volker, Karl Filser, Pankraz Fried, Gunther Gottlieb, Wolfgang Haberl, and Gerhard Weber (eds.). *Geschichte der Stadt Kempten*, Kempten, 1989.

Dreher, Alfons. *Geschichte der Reichsstadt Ravensburg und ihrer Landschaft von den Anfängen bis zur Mediatisierung, 1802*, 2 vols., Weißenhorn, 1972.

Dulman, Richard van (ed.). *Kultur der einfachen Leute: Bayerisches Volksleben vom 16. bis zum 19. Jahrhundert*, Munich, 1983.

Ehrle, Franz. *Beiträge zur Reform der Armenpflege*, Freiburg/Br., 1881.

———. "Die Armenordnungen von Nürnberg (1522) und von Ypern (1525)," *Historisches Jahrbuch* 9 (1888), 450–79.

Eisenstadt, S. N. (ed.). *Max Weber on Charisma and Institution Building*, Chicago, 1968.

Eitel, Peter. *Die oberschwäbischen Reichsstädte im Zeitalter der Zunftherrschaft: Untersuchungen zu ihrer politischen und sozialen Struktur unter besonderer Berücksichtigung der Städte Lindau, Memmingen, Ravensburg und Überlingen*, Stuttgart, 1970.

———. "Die politische, soziale und wirtschaftliche Stellung des Zunftbürgertums in den oberdeutschen Reichsstädten am Ausgang des Mittelalters," in Erich Maschke und Jürgen Sydow (eds.), *Städtische Mittelschichten*, Stuttgart, 1972, pp. 79–93.

Ellermeyer, J. "'Schichtung' und 'Sozialstruktur' in spätmittelalterlichen Städten," *Geschichte und Gesellschaft* 6 (1980), 125–49.

Elsas, M. I. *Umriß einer Geschichte der Preise und Löhne in Deutschland vom ausgehenden Mittelalter bis zum Beginn des neunzehnten Jahrhunderts*, 2 vols., Leiden, 1949.

Enderle, Wilfried. *Konfessionsbildung und Ratsregiment in der katholischen Reichsstadt Überlingen (1500–1618): im Kontext der Reformationsgeschichte der oberschwäbischen Reichsstädte*, Stuttgart, 1990.

Endres, Rudolf. "Das Armenproblem im Zeitalter des Absolutismus," *Jahrbuch für fränkische Landesforschung* 34/35 (1974/75), 1003–20.

Ernst, V. "Das Biberacher Spital bis zur Reformation," *Württembergische Vierteljahrshefte für Landesgeschichte* 6 (1987), 1–112.

Fairchilds, Cissie. *Poverty and Charity in Aix-en-Provence, 1640–1789*, Baltimore, 1976.

Fassl, Peter. "Wirtschaft, Handel und Sozialstruktur, 1648–1806," in *Geschichte*, pp. 468–80.

———. *Konfession, Wirtschaft und Politik: Von der Reichsstadt zur Industriestadt: Augsburg, 1750–1850*, Sigmaringen, 1988.

Feilzer, H. *Jugend in der mittelalterlichen Ständegesellschaft: Ein Beitrag zum Problem der Generationen*, Vienna, 1971.

Feuchtwanger, Ludwig. "Geschichte der sozialen Politik und des Armenwesens im Zeitalter der Reformation," *Jahrbuch für Gesetzgebung, Verwaltung und Volkswirtschaft* 32 (1908), 167–201; 33 (1909), 191–228.

Fideler, Paul A. "Christian Humanism and Poor Law in Early Modern England," *Societas* 4 (1974), 269–85.

Finzsch, Norbert. *Obrigkeit und Unterschichten: Zur Geschichte der rheinischen Unterschichten gegen Ende des 18. Jahrhunderts und zu Beginn des 19. Jahrhunderts*, Stuttgart, 1990.

Fischer, Thomas. *Städtische Armut und Armenfürsorge im 15. und 16. Jahrhundert: Sozialgeschichtliche Untersuchungen am Beispiel der Städte Basel, Freiburg i. Br. und Straßburg*, Göttingen, 1979.

Fischer, Wolfram. *Armut in der Geschichte: Erscheinungsformen und Lösungsversuche der 'Sozialen Frage' in Europa seit dem Mittelalter*, Göttingen, 1982.

Fissel, Mary E. *Patients, Power, and the Poor in Eighteenth-Century Bristol*, Cambridge, Eng., 1991.

Flynn, Maureen. *Sacred Charity: Confraternities and Social Welfare in Spain, 1400–1700*, Ithaca, 1989.

Forrest, Allen. *The French Revolution and the Poor*, Oxford, 1981.

Forster, Robert, and Orest Ranum (eds.). *Deviants and the Abandoned in French Society*, Baltimore, 1978.

Förstl, Johann N. *Das Almosen: Eine Untersuchung über Grundsätze der Armenfürsorgung im Mittelalter und Gegenwart*, Paderborn, 1909.

Foucault, Michel. *Madness and Civilization*, London, 1967.

———. *Discipline and Punish: The Birth of the Prison*, London, 1977.

François, Etienne. "Das System der Parität," in *Geschichte*, pp. 514–19.

———. *Die unsichtbare Grenze: Protestanten und Katholiken in Augsburg, 1648–1806*, Sigmaringen, 1991.

Fried, Pankraz. "Augsburg in nachstaufischer Zeit (1276–1368)," in *Geschichte*, pp. 145–46.

———. "Augsburg unter den Staufern (1132–1268)," in *Geschichte*, pp. 127–32.

Friedrichs, Christopher R. *Urban Society in an Age of War: Nördlingen, 1580–1720*, Princeton, 1979.

Frölich, Sigrid. *Die soziale Sicherung bei Zünften und Gesellenverbänden*, Berlin, 1976.

Fuchs, Rachel Ginnis. *Abandoned Children: Foundlings and Child Welfare in Nineteenth-Century France*, Albany, N.Y., 1984.

Fugger und Glött, Albert Graf v. "Augsburg, geprägt von seinen Stiftungen," in Rolf Haner, Jürgen Rossberg, and Winfrid Frhr. von Pölnitz-Egloffstein (eds.), *Lebensbilder deutscher Stiftungen*, Vol. 5, Tubingen, 1986, pp. 93-102.

Fuhl, Beate. "Randgruppenpolitik des schwäbischen Kreises im 18. Jahrhundert: Das Zucht- und Arbeitshaus zu Buchloe," ZHVS 81 (1988), 63-115.

Garrioch, David. *Neighborhood and Community in Paris, 1740-1790*, Cambridge, Eng., 1986.

Gavitt, Philip. *Charity and Children in Renaissance Florence: The Ospedale degli Innocenti, 1410-1536*, Ann Arbor, 1990.

Geertz, Clifford. *Agricultural Involution: The Process of Ecological Change in Indonesia*, Berkeley, 1963.

———. *Peddlers and Princes: Social Development and Economic Change in Two Indonesian Towns*, Chicago, 1963.

Geffcken, Peter. *Soziale Schichtung in Augsburg, 1396 bis 1521: Beitrag zu einer Strukturanalyze Augsburgs im Spätmittelalter*, Munich, 1983.

Geremek, Bronislaw. *The Margins of Society in Late Medieval Paris*, Cambridge, Eng., 1987.

———. *Geschichte der Armut*, Munich, 1988.

———. *The Poor in Late Medieval France*, Cambridge, Eng., 1989.

Goffman, Erving. *Asylums: Essays on the Social Situation of Mental Patients and Other Inmates*, New York, 1961.

Goldthwaite, Richard. *Private Wealth in Renaissance Florence: A Study of Four Families*, Princeton, 1968.

———. *The Building of Renaissance Florence: An Economic and Social History*, Baltimore, 1980.

Goody, Jack. *The Development of the Family and Marriage in Europe*, Cambridge, Eng., 1983.

Goody, Jack, Joan Thirsk, and E. P. Thompson (eds.). *Family and Inheritance: Rural Society in Western Europe, 1200-1800*, Cambridge, Eng., 1976.

Gottlieb, Gunther. "Bevölkerung und Sozialordnung," in *Geschichte*, pp. 60-62.

Gottlieb, Gunther, Wolfram Baer, Josef Becker, Josef Bellot, Karl Filser, Pankraz Fried, Wolfgang Reinhard, and Bernhard Schimmelpfennig (eds.). *Geschichte der Stadt Augsburg von der Römerzeit bis zur Gegenwart*, Stuttgart, 1984.

Graus, Frantisek. "Randgruppen der städtischen Gesellschaft im Spätmittelalter," *Zeitschrift für historische Forschung* 8 (1981), 385-437.

Graus, Frantisek (ed.). *Mentalitäten im Mittelalter: Methodische und inhaltliche Probleme*, Sigmaringen, 1987.

Greif, L. *Beiträge zur Geschichte der deutschen Schulen Augsburgs*, Augsburg, 1921.

Greiff, B. "Tagebuch des Lucas Rem aus den Jahren, 1494-1541: Ein Beitrag zur Handelsgeschichte der Stadt Augsburg," *Jahresbericht des historischen Vereins für Schwaben und Neuburg* 27 (1861), 1-110.

Greiner, J. "Geschichte des Ulmer Spitals im Mittelalter," *Württembergische Vierteljahrshefte für Landesgeschichte* 16 (1907), 78-156.

Greyerz, Kaspar von (ed.). *Religion and Society in Early Modern Europe, 1500-1800*, London, 1984.

Griessinger, Andreas. *Das symbolische Kapital der Ehre: Streikbewegungen und kollektives Bewußtsein deutscher Handwerker im 18. Jahrhundert*, Frankfurt/Main, 1981.

Grimm, Harold J. "Luther's Contribution to Sixteenth-Century Organization of Poor Relief," *Archiv für Reformationsgeschichte* 61 (1970), 222-34.

Gutton, Jean-Pierre. *La Société et les pauvres: L'example de la généralité de Lyon, 1534-1789*, Paris, 1971.

———. *L'État et la mendicité dans la première moitié du XVIIIe siècle: Auvergne, Beaujolais, Forez, Lyonnais*, Lyon, 1973.
———. *La Société et les pauvres en Europe (XVIe–XVIIIe siècles)*, Paris, 1974.
Haase, Carl (ed.). *Die Stadt im Mittelalter*, 3 vols., Darmstadt, 1976/78/84.
Hackler, Otto. *Soziale Eigentümlichkeiten der Konfessionen in Deutschland*, Bückeburg, 1936.
Haertel, Volker. "Die Augsburger Weberunruhen 1784 und 1794 und die Struktur der Weberschaft Ende des 18. Jahrhunderts," *ZHVS* 64/65 (1971), 121–268.
Hartung, Julius. "Die direkten Steuer und die Vermögensentwicklung in Augsburg von der Mitte des 16. bis zum 18. Jahrhundert," *Jahrbuch für Gesetzgebung, Verwaltung und Volkswirtschaft* 22 (1898), 1256–97.
———. "Die Augsburger Vermögenssteuer und die Entwicklung der Besitzverhältnisse im 16. Jahrhundert," *Jahrbuch für Gesetzgebung, Verwaltung und Volkswirtschaft* 19 (1895), 867–83.
Hartung, Wolfgang. "Gesellschaftliche Randgruppen im Spätmittelalter: Phänomen und Begriff," in Bernhard Kirchgässner und Fritz Reuter (eds.), *Städtische Randgruppen und Minderheiten*, Sigmaringen, 1986, pp. 49–114.
Hausmann, Karl Eduard. *Die Armenpflege in der Helvetik*, Basel, 1969.
Haverkamp, Alfred (ed.). *Haus und Familia in der spätmittelalterlichen Stadt*, Cologne, 1984.
Hay, Douglas, Peter Linebaugh, John G. Rule, E. P. Thompson, and Cal Winslow. *Albion's Fatal Tree: Crime and Society in Eighteenth-Century England*, New York, 1975.
Head, Anne-Lise, and Brigitte Schnegg (eds.). *Armut in der Schweiz, 17.–20. Jahrhundert*, Zurich, 1989.
Heckel, Martin. "Die Parität im Heiligen Römischen Reiche deutscher Nation," *Zeitschrift der Savigny-Stiftung für Rechtsgeschichte, Kanonistische Abteilung* 49 (1963), 261–420.
Heilbroner, Robert L. *The Worldly Philosophers: The Lives, Times, and Ideas of the Great Economic Thinkers*, New York, 1953.
———. *The Making of Economic Society*, Englewood Cliffs, 1985.
———. *The Nature and Logic of Capitalism*, New York, 1985.
Heimann, Heinz-Dieter. "Küche, Kinder, Kirche in der Überwindung der Krise des Spätmittelalters," in Alfred Haverkamp (ed.), *Haus und Familia in der spätmittelalterlichen Stadt*, Cologne, 1984, pp. 338–57.
Heimpel, C. *Die Entwicklung der Einnahmen und Ausgaben des Heiliggeistspitals zu Biberach an der Riß von 1500 bis 1630*, Stuttgart, 1966.
Herlihy, David, and Christiane Klapisch-Zuber. *Les toscans et leurs familles*, Paris, 1978.
Hermann, H. *Die Stellung unehelicher Kinder nach kanonischem Recht*, Amsterdam, 1971.
Herre, Franz. *Das Augsburger Bürgertum im Zeitalter der Aufklärung*, Augsburg, 1952.
Hessel, August. *Das öffentliche Armenwesen in Augsburg und den später eingemeindeten Vororten, 1800–1870*, Munich, 1921.
Himmelfarb, Gertrude. *The Idea of Poverty: England in the Early Industrial Age*, London, 1984.
Hirschman, Albert O. *The Passions and the Interests: Political Arguments for Capitalism before Its Triumph*, Princeton, 1977.
Hohenberg, Paul, and Lynn Lees. *The Making of Urban Europe, 1000–1950*, Cambridge, Mass., 1985.
Holzapfel, P. Heribert. *Die Anfänge der Montes Pietatis*, Munich, 1903.

Hoppit, Julian. *Risk and Failure in English Business*, Cambridge, Eng., 1987.
Hörberg, Norbert, and Karl Schnith. "Das Geistesleben," in *Geschichte*, pp. 213–20.
Hörmann, Ludwig. "Zur Geschichte des Heilig-Geist-Spitals in Augsburg," *ZHVS* 6 (1879), 145–76.
Hornstein, W. *Jugend in ihrer Zeit: Geschichte und Lebensformen des jungen Menschen in der europäischen Welt*, Hamburg, 1966.
Hsia, R. Po-chia. *Society and Religion in Münster, 1535–1618*, New Haven, 1984.
———. *Social Discipline in the Reformation: Central Europe, 1550–1750*, London, 1989.
Huberti, Irmgard. *Das Armenwesen in der Stadt Trier vom Ausgang der kurfürstlichen Zeit bis zum Ende der französischen Herrschaft (1768–1814)*, Berlin, 1935.
Hufton, Olwen. *The Poor of Eighteenth-Century France, 1750–1789*, Oxford, 1974.
Hunecke, Volker. "Überlegungen zur Geschichte der Armut in vorindustriellen Europa," *Geschichte und Gesellschaft* 9 (1983), 396–418.
———. *Die Findelkinder von Mailand: Kindsaussetzung und aussetzende Eltern vom 17. bis zum 19. Jahrhundert*, Stuttgart, 1987.
Hutchison, Terence. *Before Adam Smith: The Emergence of Political Economy, 1662–1776*, Oxford, 1988.
Ignatieff, Michael. *A Just Measure of Pain: The Penitentiary in the Industrial Revolution, 1750–1850*, Harmondsworth, 1978.
Imhof, Arthur E. *Einführung in die historische Demographie*, Munich, 1977.
———. "Die Funktion des Krankenhauses in der Stadt des 18. Jahrhunderts," *Zeitschrift für Stadtgeschichte, Stadtsoziologie und Denkmalpflege* 4 (1977), 215–41.
———. *Die verlorenen Welten: Über die Alltagsbewältigung unserer Vorfahren und warum wir uns heute so schwer damit Tun*, Munich, 1984.
Imhof, Arthur, E. (ed.). *Historische Demographie als Sozialgeschichte: Giesen und Umgebung vom 17. zum 19. Jahrhundert*, 2 vols., Darmstadt, 1975.
Immenkötter, Herbert. "Kirche zwischen Reformation und Parität," in *Geschichte*, pp. 391–413.
Irsigler, Franz. "Divites und pauperes in der Vita Meinwerci," *Vierteljahrsschrift für Sozial- und Wirtschaftsgeschichte* 57 (1970), 449–99.
Isenmann, Eberhard. *Die deutsche Stadt im Spätmittelalter*, Stuttgart, 1988.
Jaher, Frederic C. (ed.). *The Rich, the Well-born, and the Powerful: Elites and Upper Classes in History*, Urbana, Ill., 1973, pp. 64–109.
Jahn, Joachim. "Die Augsburger Sozialstruktur im 15. Jahrhundert," in *Geschichte*, pp. 187–93.
Jesse, Horst. *Die Geschichte der evangelischen Kirche in Augsburg*, Pfaffenhofen/Ilm, 1983.
Jetter, Dieter. *Geschichte des Hospitals*, Vol. I, Wiesbaden, 1966.
———. *Grundzüge der Hospitalgeschichte*, Darmstadt, 1973.
Joachimsohn, Paul. "Augsburger Schulmeister und Augsburger Schulwesen in vier Jahrhunderten," *ZHVS* 23 (1896), 177–247.
Jones, Colin. *Charity and Bienfaisance: The Treatment of the Poor in the Montpellier Region, 1740–1815*, Cambridge, Eng., 1982.
———. *The Charitable Imperative: Hospitals and Nursing in Ancien Régime and Revolutionary France*, London, 1989.
Jones, Colin (ed.). *Urban Deprivation and the Inner City*, London, 1979.
Jordan, William K. *Philanthropy in England, 1480–1660*, London, 1959.
Jünginger, Fritz. *Geschichte der Reichsstadt Kaufbeuren im 17. und 18. Jahrhundert*, Neustadt/Aisch, 1965.

Jütte, Robert. "Poor Relief and Social Discipline in Early Modern Europe," *European Studies Review* 11 (1981), 25–52.

———. *Obrigkeitliche Armenfürsorge in deutschen Reichsstädten der frühen Neuzeit: Städtisches Armenwesen in Frankfurt am Main und Köln*, Cologne, 1984.

———. *Abbild und soziale Wirklichkeit des Bettler- und Gaunertums zu Begin der Neuzeit: Sozial-, mentalitäts- und sprachgeschichtliche Studien zur Liber vagatorum (1510)*, Cologne, 1988.

———. "Diets in Welfare Institutions and in Outdoor Poor Relief in Early Modern Western Europe," *Ethnologia Europaea* 16 (1988), 117–35.

———. *Poverty and Deviance in Early Modern Europe*, Cambridge, Eng., 1994.

Kaplan, Steven Laurence. *Provisioning Paris: Merchants and Millers in the Grain and Flour Trade during the Eighteenth Century*, Ithaca, 1984.

Kaplow, Jeffrey. *The Names of Kings: The Parisian Laboring Poor in the Eighteenth Century*, New York, 1972.

Katz, Michael. *In the Shadow of the Poor House: A Social History of Welfare in America*, New York, 1986.

Katzinger, Willibald. "Das Bürgerspital," *Historisches Jahrbuch der Stadt Linz* (1977), 11–102.

———. "Zum Problem der Armut in den Städten Österreichs vom Spätmittelalter bis ins 18. Jahrhundert," in Thomas Riis (ed.), *Aspects of Poverty in Early Modern Europe*, Vol. II, Odense, 1986, pp. 31–47.

Kellenbenz, Hermann. *Deutsche Wirtschaftsgeschichte*, 2 vols., Munich, 1977/81.

———. "Die Gesellschaft in den mitteleuropäischen Städten im 16. Jahrhundert: Tendenzen der Differenzierung," in W. Rausch (ed.), *Die Stadt an der Schwelle der Neuzeit*, Linz, 1980, pp. 1–20.

———. "Wirtschaftsleben der Blütezeit," in *Geschichte*, pp. 258–301.

Kießling, Rolf. *Bürgerliche Gesellschaft und Kirche in Augsburg im Spätmittelalter*, Augsburg, 1971.

———. "Augsburg zwischen Mittelalter und Neuzeit," in *Geschichte*, pp. 241–52.

———. "Augsburgs Wirtschaft in 14. und 15. Jahrhundert," in *Geschichte*, pp. 171–81.

———. "Bürgertum und Kirche im Spätmittelalter," in *Geschichte*, pp. 208–13.

———. *Die Stadt und ihr Land: Umlandpolitik, Bürgerbesitz und Wirtschaftsgefüge in Ostschwaben vom 14. bis ins 16. Jahrhundert*, Cologne, 1989.

Kingdon, Robert M. "Social Welfare in Calvin's Geneva," *American Historical Review* 76 (1971), 50–70.

Kintner, Philip. "Die Teuerung von 1571/72 in Memmingen," *Memminger Geschichtsblätter* (1987/88), 27–75.

Kirchgässner, Bernard. *Wirtschaft und Bevölkerung der Reichsstadt Eßlingen im Spätmittelalter: Nach den Steuerbüchern 1360–1460*, Eßlingen, 1964.

———. "Probleme quantitativer Erfassung städtischer Unterschichten im Spätmittelalter, besonders in den Reichsstädten Konstanz und Eßlingen," in Erich Maschke und Jürgen Sydow (eds.), *Gesellschaftliche Unterschichten in den südwestdeutschen Städten*, Stuttgart, 1967, pp. 75–89.

Kirchgässner, Bernard, and Fritz Reuter (eds.). *Städtische Randgruppen und Minderheiten*, Sigmaringen, 1986.

Kirshner, Julius. *Pursuing Honor While Avoiding Sin: The Monte delle Doti of Florence*, Milan, 1978.

Kirshner, Julius, and Anthony Molho. "The Dowry Fund and the Marriage Market in Early Quattrocento Florence," *Journal of Modern History* 50 (1978), 403–48.

Klapisch-Zuber, Christiane. "L'enfance en Toscane an debut XVe siècle," *Annales de demographie historique* (1973), 99–122.

———. "Parents de sang, parents de lait: La mise en nourrice à Florence, 1300–1500," *Annales de demographie historique* (1983), 33–64.

Knodel, John. *Demographic Behavior in the Past: A Study of Fourteen German Village Populations in the Eighteenth and Nineteenth Centuries*, Cambridge, Eng., 1988.

Knodel, John, and Etienne van de Walle. "Breast Feeding, Fertility and Infant Mortality: An Analysis of Some Early German Data," *Population Studies* 21 (1967), 109–31.

Köberlin, Karl. *Geschichte des humanistischen Gymnasiums bei St. Anna in Augsburg von 1531 bis 1931*, Augsburg, 1931.

Köbler, Gerhard. "Das Familienrecht in der spätmittelalterlichen Stadt," in Alfred Haverkamp (ed.), *Haus und Familia in der spätmittelalterlichen Stadt*, Cologne, 1984, pp. 136–60.

Kopitzsch, Franklin (ed.). *Aufklärung, Absolutismus und Bürgertum in Deutschland*, Munich, 1976.

Kraus, Jürgen. *Das Militärwesen der Reichsstadt Augsburg, 1548–1806: Vergleichende Untersuchungen über städtische Militäreinrichtungen in Deutschland vom 16.–18. Jahrhundert*, Augsburg, 1980.

Kreuzer, Georg. "Augsburg als Bischofsstadt under den Saliern und Lothar III. (1024–1133)," in *Geschichte*, pp. 121–27.

———. "Augsburg in fränkischer und ottonischer Zeit (ca. 550–1024): Bischof Ulrich von Augsburg," in *Geschichte*, pp. 115–21.

Küther, Carsten. *Menschen auf der Straße: Vagierende Unterschichten in Bayern, Franken und Schwaben in der zweiten Hälfte des 18. Jahrhunderts*, Göttingen, 1983.

Kuznets, Simon Smith. *Population, Capital and Growth: Selected Essays by Simon Kuznets*, New York, 1973.

Lamprecht, Karl. "Zur Sozialstatistik der deutschen Stadt im Mittelalter," *Archiv für soziale Gesetzgebung und Statistik* 1 (1888), 485–532.

Lane, Frederic C. "Venetian Bankers, 1496–1533: A Study in the Early Stages of Deposit Banking," *Journal of Political Economy* 45 (1937), 187–206.

Laslett, Peter. *The World We Have Lost*, New York, 1965.

Lebrun, François. "Naissances illégitimes et abandons d'enfants en Anjou au XVIIIe siècle," *Annales: Economie, Société, Civilisation* 27 (1972), 1183–89.

———. *La vie conjugale sous l'Ancien Régime*, Paris, 1975.

Lengle, Peter. "Handel und Gewerbe bis zum Ende des 13. Jahrhunderts," in *Geschichte*, pp. 166–71.

———. "Spitäler, Stiftungen und Bruderschaften," in *Geschichte*, pp. 202–08.

———. "Findelhaus," in *Lexikon*, p. 108.

———. "Waisenhäuser," in *Lexikon*, p. 399.

Lenk, Leonhard. *Augsburger Bürgertum im Späthumanismus und Frühbarock, 1580–1700*, Augsburg, 1968.

Letzing, Heinrich. *Augsburger Handwerksgeschichte: Kleines Archivalien- und Bücherverzeichnis*, Augsburg, 1992.

Liebhart, Wilhelm. "Stifte, Klöster und Konvente in Augsburg," in *Geschichte*, pp. 193–202.

Lindberg, Carter. "There Should Be No Beggars among Christians: Karlstadt, Luther and the Origins of Protestant Poor Relief," *Church History* 46 (1977), 313–34.

———. *Beyond Charity: Reformation Initiatives for the Poor*, Minneapolis, 1993.

Lindemann, Mary. "Love for Hire: The Regulation of the Wet-Nursing Business in Eighteenth-Century Hamburg," *Journal of Family History* 6 (1981), 379–95.

———. *Patriots and Paupers: Hamburg, 1712–1830*, Oxford, 1990.
Lindgren, Uta. "Europas Armut," *Saeculum* 28 (1977), 396–418.
———. *Bedürftigkeit, Armut, Not: Studien zur spätmittelalterlichen Sozialgeschichte Barcelonas*, Münster, 1980.
Linebaugh, Peter. *The London Hanged: Crime and Civil Society in the Eighteenth Century*, Cambridge, Eng., 1992.
Lis, Catharina, and Hugo Soly. *Poverty and Capitalism in Pre-industrial Europe*, Hassocks, Sussex, 1979.
Little, Lester K. *Religious Poverty and the Profit Economy in Medieval Europe*, Ithaca, 1978.
Lutz, Heinrich. "Augsburg und seine politische Umwelt, 1490–1555," in *Geschichte*, pp. 413–33.
Lutz, Heinrich (ed.). *Zur Geschichte der Toleranz und Religionsfreiheit*, Darmstadt, 1977.
Marshall, Gordon. *Presbyteries and Profits: Calvinism and the Development of Capitalism in Scotland, 1560–1707*, Oxford, 1980.
———. *In Search of the Spirit of Capitalism: An Essay on Max Weber's Protestant Ethic Thesis*, New York, 1982.
Martin, J., and August Nitschke (eds.). *Zur Sozialgeschichte der Kindheit*, Freiburg, 1986.
Martz, Linda. *Poverty and Welfare in Habsburg Spain: The Example of Toledo*, Cambridge, Eng., 1983.
Marx, Karl. *Capital*, 3 vols., London, 1976.
Maschke, Erich. "Verfassung und soziale Kräfte in der deutschen Stadt des späten Mittelalters, vornehmlich in Oberdeutschland," *Vierteljahrschrift für Sozial- und Wirtschaftsgeschichte* 46 (1959), 289–349, 433–76.
———. "Die Unterschichten der mittelalterlichen Städte Deutschlands," in Erich Maschke and Jürgen Sydow (eds.), *Gesellschaftliche Unterschichten in den südwestdeutschen Städten*, Stuttgart, 1967, pp. 1–74.
———. "Mittelschichten in deutschen Städten des Mittelalters," in Erich Maschke and Jürgen Sydow (eds.), *Städtische Mittelschichten*, Stuttgart, 1972, pp. 1–31.
———. *Die Familie in der deutschen Stadt des späten Mittelalters*, Heidelberg, 1980.
———. *Städte und Menschen*, Wiesbaden, 1980.
Maschke, Erich, and Jürgen Sydow (eds.). *Gesellschaftliche Unterschichten in den südwestdeutschen Städten*, Stuttgart, 1967.
———. *Städtische Mittelschichten*, Stuttgart, 1972.
Mayr, Anton. *Die großen Augsburger Vermögen in der Zeit von 1618 bis 1717*, Augsburg, 1931.
McClure, Ruth K. *Coram's Children: The London Foundling Hospital in the Eighteenth Century*, New Haven, 1981.
McKee, Elsie. *John Calvin on the Diaconate and Liturgical Almsgiving*, Geneva, 1984.
Meckseper, C., and E. Schraut (eds.). *Mentalität und Alltag im Spätmittelalter*, Göttingen, 1985.
Medick, Hans, and David W. Sabean (eds.). *Interest and Emotion in Family and Kinship Studies: A Critique of Social History and Anthropology*, Cambridge, Eng., 1984.
Melosi, Dario, and Massimo Pavarini. *The Prison and the Factory: Origins of the Penitentiary System*, London, 1981.
Mennel, Erich. "Die Geschichte des katholischen Waisenhauses in Augsburg in reichsstädtischer Zeit," in Erwin Reiber (ed.), *Katholisches Waisenhaus Augsburg, Ursprung—Wege—Schicksale*, Augsburg, 1973, pp. 28–48.

Menning, Carol Bresnahan. "The Monte's 'monte': The Early Supporters of Florence's Monte di Pietà," *Sixteenth Century Journal* 23 (1992), 303–18.

———. *The Monte di Pietà of Florence: Charity and the State in Late Renaissance Italy*, Ithaca, 1993.

Merzbacher, F. "Das Spital im kanonischen Recht bis zum Tridentinum," *Archiv für katholisches Kirchenrecht* 148 (1979), 72–92.

Meuller, Reinhold. "Charitable Institutions, the Jewish Community, and Venetian Society: A Discussion of the Recent Volume by Brian Pullan," *Studi Veneziani* 14 (1972), 37–81.

Meyer, Jean. "Pauvreté et assistance dans les villes bretonnes de l'ancien régime," *Actes du 97e congrès national des sociétés savantes*, Paris, 1977, Vol. I, 445–60.

Mitterauer, Michael. "Probleme der Stratifikation in mittelalterlichen Gesellschaftssystemen," *Geschichte und Gesellschaft* 3 (1977), 13–43.

———. *Ledige Mütter: Zur Geschichte illegitimer Geburten in Europa*, Munich, 1983.

———. "Familie und Arbeitsorganisation in städtischen Gesellschaften des späten Mittelalters und der frühen Neuzeit," in Alfred Haverkamp (ed.), *Haus und Familie in der spätmittelalterlichen Stadt*, Cologne, 1984, pp. 1–36.

———. *Sozialgeschichte der Jugend*, Frankfurt/M, 1986.

Mitterauer, Michael, and Reinhard Sieder. *The European Family: Patriarchy to Partnership from the Middle Ages to the Present*, Chicago, 1982.

Mollat, Michel (ed.). *Études zur l'histoire de la pauvreté (Moyen Age-XVIe siècle)*, 2 vols., Paris, 1974.

———. *The Poor in the Middle Ages: An Essay in Social History*, New Haven, 1986.

Möller, Helmut. *Die kleinbürgerliche Familie im 18. Jahrhundert: Verhalten und Gruppenkultur*, Berlin, 1969.

Mols, R. *Introduction à la démographie historique des villes d'Europe du XIVe au XVIIIe siècle*, 3 vols., Louvain, 1954/56.

Mommsen, Hans, and Winfried Schulze (eds.). *Vom Elend der Handarbeit: Probleme historischer Unterschichtenforschung*, Stuttgart, 1981.

Monachino, Vincenzo. *La carità cristiana in Roma*, Bologna, 1968.

Moritz, Werner. *Die bürgerlichen Fürsorgeanstalten der Reichsstadt Frankfurt am Main im späten Mittelalter*, Frankfurt/Main, 1981.

Mörke, Olaf. "Der gewollte Weg in Richtung 'Untertan': Ökonomische und politische Eliten in Braunschweig, Lüneburg und Göttingen vom 15. bis ins 17. Jahrhundert," in Heinz Schilling and Herman Diedericks (eds.), *Bürgerliche Eliten in den Niederlanden und in Nordwestdeutschland: Studien zur Sozialgeschichte des europäischen Bürgertums im Mittelalter und in der Neuzeit*, Cologne, 1985, pp. 111–33.

Mörke, Olaf, and Katarina Sieh. "Gesellschaftliche Führungsgruppen," in *Geschichte*, pp. 301–12.

Muchembled, Robert. *Culture populaire et culture des élites dans la France moderne*, Paris, 1978.

Muller, Konrad (ed.). *Instrumenta Pacis Westphalicae: Die Westphalische Friedensverträge*, Bern, 1975.

Mummenhoff, Ernst. "Das Findel- und Waisenhaus zu Nürnberg, orts-, kultur- und wirtschaftsgeschichtlich," *Mitteilungen des Vereins für Geschichte der Stadt Nürnberg* 21 (1915), 57–336; 22 (1918), 1–146.

Münch, Paul. *Ordnung, Fleiß und Sparsamkeit: Texte und Dokumente zur Entstehung der "bürgerliche Tugenden,"* Munich, 1984.

———. *Lebensformen in der frühen Neuzeit, 1500 bis 1800*, Berlin, 1992.

Mundy, John. "Charity and Social Work in Toulouse, 1100–1250," *Traditio* 22 (1966), 203–87.

Nagel, Adalbert. *Armut im Barock: Die Bettler und Vaganten in Oberschwaben*, Weingarten, 1987.
Naujoks, Eberhard. "Vorstufen der Parität in der Verfassungsgeschichte der schwäbischen Reichsstädte, 1555–1648: Das Beispiel Augsburg," in Jürgen Sydow (ed.), *Bürgerschaft und Kirche*, Sigmaringen, 1980, pp. 38–66.
Newman-Brown, W. "The Receipt of Poor Relief and Family Structure: Aldenham, Herfordshire, 1630–1690," in Richard M. Smith (ed.), *Land, Kinship and Life-Cycle*, Cambridge, Eng., 1984, pp. 405–22.
Nitschke, August. "Die Stellung des Kindes in der Familie im Spätmittelalter und in der Renaissance," in Alfred Haverkamp (ed.), *Haus und Familie in der spätmittelalterlichen Stadt*, Cologne, 1984, pp. 214–43.
Noppel, E. *Die katholischen Waisenhäuser Deutschlands*, Freiburg i. Br., 1915.
Norberg, Kathryn. *Rich and Poor in Grenoble, 1600–1814*, Berkeley, 1985.
Norris, Geoff. "Defining Urban Deprivation," in Colin Jones (ed.), *Urban Deprivation and the Inner City*, London, 1979, pp. 17–31.
North, Douglass C. *Structure and Change in Economic History*, New York, 1981.
———. *Institutions, Institutional Change and Economic Performance*, Cambridge, Eng., 1990.
Nuglisch, A. "Die Entwicklung des Reichtums in Konstanz, 1338–1550," *Jahrbuch für Nationalökonomie und Statistik* 87 (1907), 365–71.
Nussbaum, Frederick S. *A History of the Economic Institutions of Modern Europe*, New York, 1933.
Obermeier, Anita. "Findel- und Waisenkinder: Zur Geschichte des Sozialfürsorge in der Reichsstadt Augsburg," *ZHVS* 83 (1990), 129–62.
Oestreich, Brigitta (ed.). *Strukturprobleme der frühen Neuzeit*, Berlin, 1980.
Oestreich, Gerhard. "Strukturprobleme des europäischen Absolutismus," *Vierteljahrschrift für Sozial- und Wirtschaftsgeschichte* 55 (1968), 329–47.
———. *Geist und Gestalt des frühmodernen Staates: Ausgewählte Aufsätze*, Berlin, 1969.
———. "Policey und Prudentia civilis in der barocken Gesellschaft von Stadt und Staat," in Brigitta Oestreich (ed.), *Strukturprobleme der frühen Neuzeit*, Berlin, 1980, pp. 367–79.
Origo, Iris. *The Merchant of Prato: Francesco di Marco Datini, 1335–1410*, New York, 1957.
Oxley, Geoffrey. *Poor Relief in England and Wales, 1601–1834*, London, 1974.
Pavan, Elisabeth. "Police des moeurs, société et politique à Venise à la fin du moyen âge," *Revue historique* 264 (1980), 241–88.
Penrose, Edith Tilton. *A Theory of the Growth of the Firm*, Oxford, 1959.
Pfaud, Robert. *Das Bürgerhaus in Augsburg*, Tübingen, 1976.
Pinchbeck, Ivy. *Women Workers and the Industrial Revolution, 1750–1850*, London, 1930.
Pischl, Felix. "Die erste Armenordnungen der Reformationszeit," *Deutsche Geschichtsblätter* 17 (1916), 317–29.
Pitz, Ernst. "Wirtschaftliche und soziale Probleme der gewerblichen Entwicklung im 15./16. Jahrhundert nach hansisch-niederdeutschen Quellen," in Carl Haase (ed.), *Die Stadt des Mittelalters*, Darmstadt, 1984, Vol. 3, pp. 137–77.
Polanyi, Karl. *The Great Transformation*, New York, 1957.
Pollard, Sidney. *The Genesis of Modern Management*, Cambridge, Mass., 1965.
Prochaska, Frank. "Charitable Motives," *Times Literary Supplement* 4804 (1995), 27.
Press, Volker, Eugen Reinhard, and Hansmartin Schwarzmaier (eds.). *Barock am Oberrhein*, Karlsruhe, 1985.
Preußer, Norbert. *Not macht erfinderisch: Überlebensstrategien der Armenbevölkerung in Deutschland zeit 1807*, Munich, 1989.

Provence, Sally, and Rose Lipton. *Infants in Institutions*, New York, 1962.
Pullan, Brian. *Rich and Poor in Renaissance Venice: The Social Institutions of a Catholic State, to 1620*, Cambridge, Mass., 1971.
———. "Catholics and the Poor in Early Modern Europe," *Transactions of the Royal Historical Society*, 5th series, 26 (1976), 15–34.
———. "Support and Redeem: Charity and Poor Relief in Italian Cities from the Fourteenth to the Seventeenth Century," *Continuity and Change* 3 (1988), 177–208.
Radlkofer, M. "Einleitung und Notizen zu 'Die Teuerung zu Augsburg in den Jahren 1570 und 1571' in Versen beschrieben von Barnabas Holzmann, Maler und Bürger zu Augsburg," *ZHVS* 19 (1892), 45–87.
Rajkay, Barbara. "Die Bevölkerungsentwicklung von 1500 bis 1648," in *Geschichte*, pp. 252–58.
Ransel, David L. "Abandoned Children in Imperial Russia: Village Fosterage," *Bulletin of the History of Medicine* 50 (1976), 501–10.
Ransel, David L. (ed.). *The Family in Imperial Russia: New Lines of Historical Research*, Urbana, Ill., 1978.
Rappaport, Steve. *World within Worlds: Structures of Life in Sixteenth-Century London*, Cambridge, Eng., 1989.
Ratzinger, Georg. *Geschichte der kirchlichen Armenpflege*, Freiburg/Br., 1884.
Rausch, W. (ed.). *Die Stadt an der Schwelle der Neuzeit*, Linz, 1980.
Rauter, Konrad. *Vom Waisenhaus zum Kinderheim: 400 Jahre evangelischer Waisenerziehung in Augsburg*, Augsburg, 1972.
Reiber, Erwin (ed.). *Katholisches Waisenhaus Augsburg, Ursprung—Wege—Schicksale*, Augsburg, 1973.
Reicke, S. *Das deutsche Spital und sein Recht im Mittelalter*, Stuttgart, 1932.
Riebartsch, Joachim. *Augsburger Handelsgesellschaften des 15. und 16. Jahrhunderts: Eine vergleichende Darstellung ihres Eigenkapitals und ihrer Verfassung*, Cologne, 1987.
Riis, Thomas (ed.). *Aspects of Poverty in Early Modern Europe*, 3 vols., Stuttgart, etc., 1981–90.
Ritter, Gerhard A. *Social Welfare in Germany and Britain: Origins and Development*, Leamington Spa, 1986.
Robins, Joseph. *The Lost Children: A Study of Charity Children in Ireland, 1700–1900*, Dublin, 1980.
Roche, Daniel. *The People of Paris: An Essay in Popular Culture in the Eighteenth Century*, Berkeley, 1987.
Roeck, Bernd. "'Arme' in Augsburg zu Beginn des Dreißigjährigen Krieges," *Zeitschrift für bayerische Landesgeschichte* 46 (1983), 515–58.
———. "Wirtschaftliche und soziale Voraussetzungen der Augsburger Baukunst zur Zeit des Elias Holl," *Architectura* 14 (1984), 119–38.
———. *Elias Holl: Architekt eine europäischen Stadt*, Regensburg, 1985.
———. "Geistiges Leben, 1650–1800," in *Geschichte*, pp. 480–90.
———. *Bäcker, Brot und Getreide in Augsburg: Zur Geschichte des Bäckerhandwerks und zur Versorgungspolitik der Reichsstadt im Zeitalter des Dreißigjährigen Krieges*, Sigmaringen, 1987.
———. *Eine Stadt in Krieg und Frieden: Studien zur Geschichte der Reichsstadt Augsburg zwischen Kalenderstreit und Parität*, 2 vols., Göttingen, 1989.
Romon, Christian. "Le monde des pauvres à Paris au XVIIIe siècle," *Annales: Economie, Société, Civilization* 37 (1982), 729–63.
Roper, Lydal. "Going to Church and Street: Weddings in Reformation Augsburg," *Past and Present* 106 (1985), 62–101.

———. *The Holy Household: Women and Morals in Reformation Augsburg*, Oxford, 1989.
Rosa, M. "Chiesa, idee sui poveri e assistenza in Italia dal Cinque al Settecento," *Societá e Storia* 10 (1980), 775–806.
Rothman, David J. *The Discovery of the Asylum: Social Order and Disorder in the New Republic*, Boston, 1971.
Rückert, G.. "Die Pflege der Volkswohlfahrt im ehemaligen Herrschaftsgebiet des Domkapitels Augsburg," *ZHVS*, 50 (1932), 29–50.
Rummel, Peter. "Fürstbischöfliches Hof und katholisches kirchliches Leben," in *Geschichte*, pp. 530–41.
———. "Katholisches Leben in der Reichsstadt Augsburg, 1650–1806," *Jahrbuch des Vereins für Augsburger Bistumsgeschichte* 18 (1984), 9–161.
Rüth, Fritz (ed.). *Lebensbilder deutscher Stiftungen*, Vol. 3, Tübingen, 1974.
Sabean, David W. *Power in the Blood: Popular Culture and Village Discourse in Early Modern Germany*, Cambridge, Eng., 1984.
———. *Property, Production, and Family in Neckarshausen, 1700–1870*, Cambridge, Eng., 1990.
Sablayrolles, Elisabeth. *L'enfance abandonnée à Strasbourg au XVIIIe siècle et la fondation de la Maison des enfants trouvés*, Strasbourg, 1976.
Sachße, Christoph, and Florian Tennstedt. *Geschichte der Armenfürsorge in Deutschland: Vom Spätmittelalter bis zum Ersten Weltkrieg*, Stuttgart, 1980.
Sachße, Christoph, and Florian Tennstedt (eds.). *Bettler, Gauner und Proleten: Armut und Armenfürsorge in der deutschen Geschichte: Ein Bild-Lesebuch*, Reinbek, 1983.
———. *Soziale Sicherheit und soziale Disziplinierung: Beiträge zu einer historischen Theorie der Sozialpolitik*, Frankfurt/Main, 1986.
Safley, Thomas Max, and Leonard N. Rosenband (eds.). *The Workplace before the Factory: Artisans and Proletarians, 1500–1800*, Ithaca, N.Y., 1993.
Sage, Walter. "Frühes Christentum und Kirchen aus der Zeit des Übergangs," in *Geschichte*, pp. 100–12.
Scherner, K. O. "Das Recht der Armen und Bettler im Ancien régime," *Zeitschrift der Savigny-Stiftung für Rechtsgeschichte, Germanistische Abteilung* 96 (1979), 55–99.
Scherpner, Hans. *Theorie der Fürsorge*, Göttingen, 1962.
Schiller, Lotte. *Das gegenseitige Verhältnis der Konfessionen in Augsburg im Zeitalter der Gegenreformation*, Munich, 1933.
Schilling, Heinz. "Die Konfessionalisierung im Reich: Religiöser und gesellschaftlicher Wandel im Deutschland zwischen 1555 und 1630," *Historische Zeitschrift* 246 (1988), 1–45.
———. *Konfessionskonflikt und Staatsbildung: Eine Fallstudie über das Verhältnis von religiösem und sozialem Wandel in der Frühneuzeit am Beispiel der Grafschaft Lippe*, Gütersloh, 1981.
Schilling, Heinz (ed.). *Die reformierte Konfessionalisierung in Deutschland: Das Problem der "Zweiten Reformation,"* Gütersloh, 1986.
Schilling, Heinz, and Herman Diedericks (eds.). *Bürgerliche Eliten in den Niederlanden und in Nordwestdeutschland: Studien zur Sozialgeschichte des europäischen Bürgertums im Mittelalter und in der Neuzeit*, Cologne, 1985.
Schimmelpfennig, Bernhard. "Religiöses Leben im späten Mittelalter," in *Geschichte*, pp. 220–25.
Schmelzeisen, Gustaf Klemens. *Polizeiordnungen und Privatrecht*, Munster, 1955.
Schmidt, Rolf. "Das Stadtbuch von 1276," in *Geschichte*, pp. 140–45.
Schneider, Robert. *Public Life in Toulouse, 1463–1789: From Municipal Republic to Cosmopolitan City*, Ithaca, 1989.

Schnith, Karl. "Die Reichsstadt Augsburg im Spätmittelalter (1368–1493)," in *Geschichte*, pp. 153–66.
Schnyder, Werner. "Soziale Schichtung und Grundlagen der Vermögensbildung in den spätmittelalterlichen Städten der Eidgenossenschaft," in Heinz Stoob (ed.), *Altständisches Bürgertum*, Darmstadt, 1978, Vol. 2, 425–44.
Schofield, Roger, and John Walter (eds.). *Famine, Disease and the Social Order in Early Modern Society*, Cambridge, Eng., 1989.
Schreiber, Aloys. "Die Entwicklung der Augsburger Bevölkerung vom Ende des 14. Jahrhunderts bis zum Beginn des 19. Jahrhunderts," *Archiv für Hygiene* 123 (1939/40), 90–177.
Schremmer, Eckart. "Handel und Gewerbe zur Zeit des Merkantilismus," in Max Spindler (ed.). *Handbuch der bayerischen Geschichte*, Vol. 4, Munich, 1974/75, pp. 1100–07.
Schröder, Detlev. *Stadt Augsburg*, Munich, 1975.
Schubert, Ernst. "Gauner, Dirnen und Gelichter in deutschen Städten des Mittelalters," in C. Meckseper and E. Schraut (eds.), *Mentalität und Alltag im Spätmittelalter*, Göttingen, 1985, pp. 97–128.
———. "Soziale Randgruppen und Bevölkerungsentwicklung im Mittelalter," *Saeculum* 39 (1989), 294–339.
Schulze, Winfried. "Augsburg, 1555–1648: Eine Stadt im Heiligen Römischen Reich," in *Geschichte*, pp. 433–47.
———. "Die ständische Gesellschaft des 16./17. Jahrhunderts als Problem von Statik und Dynamik," in Winfried Schulze (ed.), *Ständische Gesellschaft und soziale Mobilität*, Munich, 1988, pp. 1–17.
Schulze, Winfried (ed.). *Ständische Gesellschaft und soziale Mobilität*, Munich, 1988.
Schumpeter, Joseph A. "The Instability of Capitalism," *Economic Journal* 38 (1928), 361–86.
———. *History of Economic Analysis*, Oxford, 1954.
———. *Capitalism, Socialism and Democracy*, New York, 1975.
———. *The Theory of Economic Development*, New Brunswick, 1983.
———. *Essays: On Entrepreneurs, Innovations, Business Cycles, and the Evolution of Capitalism*, New Brunswick, 1989.
Schuster, Peter. *Das Frauenhaus: Städtische Bordelle in Deutschland, 1350 bis 1600*, Paderborn, 1992.
Schwartz, Robert M. *Policing the Poor in Eighteenth-Century France*, Chapel Hill, 1988.
Screech, Michael A. *The Rabelaisian Marriage*, London, 1958.
Seida und Landensberg, F. Eugen Freiherr v. *Historisch-statistische Beschreibung aller Kirchen-, Schul-, Erziehungs- und Wohltätigkeits-anstalten in Augsburg*, 2 vols., Augsburg, 1812.
Shahar, Shulamith. *Childhood in the Middle Ages*, London, 1990.
Sherwood, Joan. *Poverty in Eighteenth-Century Spain: The Women and Children of the Inclusa*, Toronto, 1988.
Sieber, Karl-Heinz. "Die Entwicklung der Augsburger Gesellschaft bis zum Jahre 1368," in *Geschichte*, pp. 181–87.
Sieh-Burens, Katarina. *Oligarchie, Konfession und Politik im 16. Jahrhundert: Zur sozialen Verflechtung der Augsburger Bürgermeister und Stadtpfleger, 1518–1618*, Munich, 1986.
Sievers, Kai Detlev. *Leben in Armut: Zeugnisse der Armutskultur aus Lübeck und Schleswig-Holstein vom Mittelalter bis ins 20. Jahrhundert*, Heide, 1991.
Simon-Muscheid, Katharina. "Die Kleidung städtischer Unterschichten zwischen

Projektionen und Realität im Spätmittelalter and in der frühen Neuzeit," *Saeculum* 44 (1993), 47–64.

Slack, Paul. *Poverty and Policy in Tudor and Stuart England*, London, 1988.

Smith, Richard M. (ed.). *Land, Kinship, and Life-Cycle*, Cambridge, Eng., 1984.

Snell, K. D. M. *Annals of the Labouring Poor: Social Change and Agrarian England, 1660–1900*, Cambridge, Eng., 1985.

Soliday, Gerald. *A Community in Conflict: Frankfurt Society in the Seventeenth and Early Eighteenth Centuries*, Hanover, N. H., 1974.

Sombart, Werner. *Das moderne Kapitalismus: Historisch-systematische Darstellung des gesamteuropäischen Wirtschaftslebens von seinen Anfängen bis zur Gegenwart*, 3 vols., Leipzig, 1902/27.

Sonenscher, Michael. *Work and Wages: Natural Law, Politics and the Eighteenth-Century French Trades*, Cambridge, Eng., 1989.

Sothmann, Marlene. *Das Armen-, Arbeits-, Zucht- und Werkhaus in Nürnberg bis 1806*, Nuremberg, 1970.

Spangenberg, Cyriacus. *Catechismus: Die Funff Heuptstuck der Christlichen Lehre sampt der Haußtaffel und dem Morgen und Abendt Gebet Benedicite und Gratias etc. Ausgelegt durch M. Cyriacus Spangenberg*, Erfurt, 1567.

Spierenburg, Pieter (ed.). *The Emergence of Carceral Institutions: Prisons, Galleys and Lunatic Asylums, 1550–1900*, Rotterdam, 1984.

Spindler, Max (ed.). *Handbuch der bayerischen Geschichte: Franken, Schwaben, Oberpfalz bis zum Ausgang des 18. Jahrhunderts*, Munich, 1971.

Spree, Reinhard. *Soziale Ungleichheit vor Krankeit und Tod: Zur Sozialgeschichte des Gesundheitsbereichs im Deutschen Kaiserreich*, Göttingen, 1981.

Stahnke, Joachim. *Skizzen zur Geschichte des russischen Findelhauswesens: Erläutert am St. Petersburger Erziehungshaus*, Pattensen, 1983.

Stark, Theodore. "Die christliche Wohltätigkeit im Mittelalter und in der Reformationszeit in den ostschwäbischen Reichsstädten," Diss., Erlangen, 1926.

Steinbickler, Carl. *Poor-Relief in the Sixteenth Century*, Washington, 1937.

Stetten, Paul v., d. Ä. *Geschichte der Heiligen Römischen Reichs Freyen Stadt Augsburg: Aus bewährten Jahrbüchern und tüchtigen Urkunden gezogen*, 2 vols., Augsburg, 1743/58.

Steuer, Peter. *Die Außenverflechtung der Augsburger Oligarchie von 1500–1620*, Augsburg, 1988.

Steynitz, Jesko v. *Mittelalterliche Hospitäler der Orden und der Städte als Einrichtungen der sozialen Sicherung*, Berlin, 1970.

Stier, Bernhard. *Fürsorge und Disziplinierung im Zeitalter des Absolutismus: Das Pforzheimer Zucht- und Waisenhaus und die badische Sozialpolitik im 18. Jahrhundert*, Sigmaringen, 1988.

Stone, Lawrence. *The Family, Sex and Marriage in England, 1500–1800*, New York, 1977.

Strieder, Jakob. *Studien zur Geschichte kapitalistischer Organizationsformen*, Munich, 1914.

———. *Zur Genesis des modernen Kapitalismus: Forschungen zur Entstehung der großen bürgerlichen Kapitalvermögen am Ausgange des Mittelalters und zu Beginn der Neuzeit, zunächst in Augsburg*, Munich, 1935.

———. *Das reiche Augsburg*, Munich, 1938.

Stoob, Heinz (ed.). *Altständisches Bürgertum*, 3 vols., Darmstadt, 1978/89.

Strang, H. *Erscheinungsformen der Sozialhilfebedürftigkeit: Beitrag zur Geschichte, Theorie und empirischen Analyse der Armut*, Stuttgart, 1970.

Stürmer, Michael (ed.). *Herbst des alten Handwerks: Zur Sozialgeschichte des 18. Jahrhunderts*, Munich, 1979.
Supple, B. E. *Commercial Crisis and Change in England, 1600–1642: A Study in the Instability of a Mercantile Economy*, Cambridge, Eng., 1959.
Sussman, George D. *Selling Mother's Milk: The Wet-Nursing Business in France, 1715–1914*, Urbana, Ill., 1982.
Sydow, Jürgen (ed.). *Bürgerschaft und Kirche*, Sigmaringen, 1980.
Tawney, Richard Henry. "A History of Capitalism," *Economic History Review*, 2nd series, 2 (1950), 307–16.
———. *Religion and the Rise Capitalism*, Gloucester, Mass., 1962.
Teuteberg, Hans, J. and Günter Wiegelmann. *Der Wandel der Nahrungsgewohnheiten unter dem Einfluß der Industrialisierung*, Göttingen, 1972.
Thomas, Keith. "Work and Leisure in Pre-industrial Society," *Past and Present* 29 (1964), 50–62.
Thompson, Edward P. *The Making of the English Working Class*, New York, 1964.
———. "Time, Work Discipline and Industrial Capitalism," *Past & Present* 38 (1967), 56–97.
———. "The Moral Economy of the English Crowd in the Eighteenth Century," *Past & Present* 50 (1971), 76–136.
Thompson, John, and Grace Goldin. *The Hospital: A Social and Architectural History*, New Haven, 1975.
Tierney, Brian. *Medieval Poor Law: A Sketch of Canonical Theory and Its Application in England*, Berkeley, 1959.
Tilly, Charles. *The Contentious French*, Cambridge, Mass., 1986.
Todd, Emmanuel. *The Explanation of Ideology: Family Structures and Social Systems*, Oxford, 1985.
Trenard, Louis. "Pauvreté, charité, assistance à Lille, 1708–1790," *Actes du 97e congrès des sociétés savantes*, Paris, 1977, Vol. I, 473–98.
Trexler, Richard C. "Charity and the Defense of Urban Elites in the Italian Communes," in Frederic C. Jaher (ed.). *The Rich, the Well-born, and the Powerful: Elites and Upper Classes in History*, Urbana, Ill., 1973, pp. 64–109.
———. "The Foundlings of Florence, 1395–1455," *History of Childhood Quarterly* 1 (1973), 259–84.
———. "In Search of Father: The Experience of Abandonment in the Recollections of Giovanni de Pagolo Morelli," *History of Childhood Quarterly* 2 (1975), 225–51.
———. *Public Life in Renaissance Florence*, New York, 1980.
Trinkaus, Charles, and Heiko Oberman (eds.). *The Pursuit of Holiness in Late Medieval and Renaissance Religion*, Leiden, 1974.
Uhlhorn, Gerhard. *Die christliche Liebestätigkeit in der alten Kirche*, 3 vols., Stuttgart, 1882/90.
Ulbricht, Otto. "The Debate about Foundling Hospitals in Enlightenment Germany: Infanticide, Illegitimacy, and Infant Mortality Rates," *Central European History* 18 (1985), 211–56.
Usher, Abbott Payson. *The Early History of Deposit Banking in Mediterranean Europe*, New York, 1967.
Viguerie, Jean de. *L'Institution des enfants: L'Education en France, XVIe–XVIIIe siécles*, Paris, 1978.
Vogel, Hermann. *Die Exekution der die Reichsstadt Augsburg betreffenden Bestimmungen des Westfälischen Friedens*, Augsburg, 1890.

———. *Der Kampf auf dem Westfälischen Friedenskongreß um die Einführung der Parität in der Stadt Augsburg*, Munich, 1900.
Vogler, Günther. "Probleme der Klassenbildung in der Feudalgesellschaft: Betrachtungen über die Entwicklung des Bürgertums in Mittel- und West-Europa vom 11. bis zum 18. Jahrhundert," *Zeitschrift für Geschichtswissenschaft* (1973), 1182-208.
Vovelle, Michel. *Piété baroque et déchristianisation en Provence aux XVIIIe siécle*, Paris, 1973.
Walker, Mack. *German Home Towns: Community, State, and General Estate, 1648-1871*, Ithaca, 1971.
Wallace, Peter G. *Communities and Conflict in Early Modern Colmar: 1575-1730*, Atlantic Highlands, N. J., 1995.
Wallerstein, Immanuel. *The World System*, 2 vols., New York, 1974/80.
Walter, John. "The Social Economy of Dearth in Early Modern England," in Roger Schofield and John Walter (eds.). *Famine, Disease and the Social Order in Early Modern Society*, Cambridge, Eng., 1989, pp. 75-128.
Wandel, Lee Palmer. *Always Among Us: Images of the Poor in Zwingli's Zurich*, Cambridge, Eng., 1990.
Warmbrunn, Paul. *Zwei Konfessionen in einer Stadt: Das Zusammenleben von Katholiken und Protestanten in der paritätischen Reichsstädten Augsburg, Biberach, Ravensburg und Dinkelsbühl von 1548 bis 1648*, Wiesbaden, 1983.
Weber, Max. *The General Economic History*, London, 1923.
———. *Theory of Social and Economic Organization*, New York, 1947.
———. *The Protestant Ethic and the Spirit of Capitalism*, New York, 1971.
———. *Economy and Society: An Outline of Interpretive Sociology*, 2 vols., Berkeley, 1978.
Weber, Wolfgang. "Bevölkerung—Gesellschaft und Wirtschaft—Wohlfahrtspolitik und Stadtfinanz," in Volker Dotterweich et al. (eds.), *Geschichte der Stadt Kempten*, Kempten, 1989, pp. 222-40.
Weidenbacher, Josef. *Die Fuggerei in Augsburg*, Augsburg, 1926.
Weigand, Rudolf. "Die Ehe- und Familienrecht in der mittelalterlichen Stadt," in Alfred Haverkamp (ed.). *Haus und Familie in der spätmittelalterlichen Stadt*, Cologne, 1984, pp. 161-94.
Weisbrod, Bernd. "Wohltätigkeit und 'symbolische Gewalt' in der Frühindustrialisierung: Städtische Armut und Armenpolitik in Wuppertal," in Hans Mommsen and Winfried Schulze (eds.). *Vom Elend der Handarbeit: Probleme historischer Unterschichtenforschung* (Stuttgart, 1981), pp. 334-57.
———. "How to Become a Good Foundling in Early Victorian London," *Social History* 10 (1985), 193-209.
Weissman, Ronald. *Ritual Brotherhood in Renaissance Florence*, New York, 1982.
Wellschmied, K. *Die Hospitäler der Stadt Göttingen*, Göttingen, 1963.
Werner, Anton. *Die örtlichen Stiftungen für die Zwecke des Unterrichts und der Wohltätigkeit in der Stadt Augsburg*, Augsburg, 1899.
Weyrauch, Erdmann. "Über soziale Schichtung," in Ingrid Bátori (ed.), *Städtische Gesellschaft und Reformation*. Stuttgart, 1980, pp. 5-57.
Whaley, Joachim. *Religious Toleration and Social Change in Hamburg, 1529-1816*, Cambridge, 1985.
Winckelmann, Otto. "Die Armenordnungen von Nürnberg (1522), Kitzingen (1523), Regensburg (1523) und Ypern," *Archiv für Reformationsgeschichte* 10 (1912/1913), 1-18.

Bibliography

———. *Das Fürsorge der Stadt Straßburg vor und nach der Reformation bis zum Ausgang des 16. Jahrhunderts*, Leipzig, 1922.
Woolf, Stuart. *The Poor in Western Europe in the Eighteenth and Nineteenth Centuries*, London, 1986.
Woolf, Stuart (ed.). *Domestic Strategies: Work and Family in France and Italy, 1600–1800*, Cambridge, Eng., 1991.
Wrightson, Keith, and David Levine. *Poverty and Piety in an English Village: Terling, 1525–1700*, New York, 1979.
Wunder, Gerd. "Unterschichten der Reichsstadt Hall: Methoden und Probleme ihrer Erforschung," in Erich Maschke and Jürgen Sydow (eds.). *Gesellschaftliche Unterschichten in den südwestdeutschen Städten*, Stuttgart, 1967, pp. 101–18.
———. "Die soziale Struktur der Handwerkerschaft in unseren alten Städten," in Erich Maschke and Jürgen Sydow (eds.). *Städtische Mittelschichten*, Stuttgart, 1972, pp. 120–34.
———. *Die Bürger Von Hall: Sozialgeschichte einer Reichsstadt, 1216–1802*, Sigmaringen, 1980.
Wunder, Heide. "Probleme der Stratifikation in mittelalterlichen Gesellschaftssystemen," *Geschichte und Gesellschaft* 4 (1978), 542–50.
Wüst, Wolfgang. "Bettler und Vaganten als Herausforderung für die Staatsraison im Hochstift und der Reichsstadt Augsburg," *Jahrbuch des Vereins für Augsburger Bistumsgeschichte* 21 (1987), 240–79.
———. "Bürgertum, Handel, wirtschaftliche und politische Außenbeziehungen der Reichsstadt," in Volker Dotterweich et al. (eds.), *Geschichte der Stadt Kempten*, Kempten, 1989, pp. 202–22.
Zeeden, Ernst Walter. *Die Entstehung der Konfession: Grundlagen und Formen der Konfessionsbildung im Zeitalter der Glaubenskämpfe*, Munich, 1965.
———. *Konfessionsbildung: Studien zur Reformation, Gegenreformation und katholisches Reform*, Stuttgart, 1985.
Zeller, Bernhard. *Das Heilig-Geist-Spital zu Lindau im Bodensee von seinen Anfängen bis zum Ausgang des 16. Jahrhunderts*, Lindau/Bodensee, 1952.
———. "Die schwäbischen Spitäler," *Zeitschrift für württembergische Landesgeschichte* 13 (1954), 71–89.
Zink, Burkhard. *Bourkard Zink et sa chronique*, 1868.
Zorn, Wolfgang. *Handels- und Industriegeschichte Bayerisch-Schwabens, 1648–1870: Wirtschafts-, Sozial- und Kulturgeschichte des schwäbischen Unternehmertums*, Augsburg, 1961.
———. *Augsburg, Geschichte einer deutschen Stadt*, Augsburg, 1972.
———. "Geschichte der Augsburger Waisenhäuser," in Fritz Rüth (ed.), *Lebensbilder deutscher Stiftungen*, Vol. 3, Tübingen, 1974, pp. 339–49.

Index

Abbey of Sts. Ulrich and Afra, 2, 23, 28, 117, 162, 226
Academy of Arts, 228
accounting, 11. See also practices, managerial
adaptability, 79–80, 113, 143, 145
Albrecht, Jörg, 270
Almosenstiftung, 30
Alms House, 34, 83
alms lords, 1, 4–7, 35; as capitalists, 132–33; as pater familias, 246; attitude toward commodities, 152–55; authority over orphan father, 2; responsibility for orphans in service, 245–46
Alms Office, 30 178, 203, 217, 243–47, 281; administration of granaries by, 152–55; as consumer, 84; as employer, 209–10; authority, 34–35; as capitalistic organization, 286–89; capital in 124–25; capital transactions by, 117–18; cash distributed by, 165; commodities as capital in, 151; commodities stored by 151, 164; commodities distributed by, 165–73, 193; commodities distributed to orphanages, 187–89; confessionalization of, 38–39, 85–97; credit transactions, 81–83; decline of donations to, 82–83; economic independence of, 79, 80; effects of crisis on, 41–42; effects of Edict of Restitution on, 40; expenditures by, 95; founding of, 19; land owned by, 58; operating expenses of, 86; parity in 45–49; regulation of out-placement, 216; relationship to orphanages, 5, 36; sanctions, 201–2; subventions, 83, 89, 96
Alms Ordinance: of 1459, 33; of 1522, 19, 33–34; of 1563, 35; motives, 7
alms servants, 34, 120

alms-giving. See charity
Altomünster, 109
Amaltingen, 169
Amman, Johann Paulus, 63–66, 69
Anheckerin, Anna Catharina, 262
annuities, 81, 119
apprentice: failure of, 259; finding positions, 212, 213; lack of persistence, 266–69; rights and responsibilities of, 220–24; success of, 260; training of, 213. See also apprenticeship
apprenticeship: accident or illness during, 266–69; costs of, 184; fees, 3; limits on stipends, 123, 136–37, 139; rising costs of, 136; support during, 259
asceticism, 281
Asylum, 6
Augsburg: Bishop of, 37, 61, 62, 156; building boom, 32; Cathedral Chapter of, 117–18, 126; crafts in, 210–14; Diocese of, 23, 131; economic collapse, 47–49; economic growth, 26–27; economic recovery, 44, 49–51; epidemic, 40; fiscal crisis, 105–6; geographic location, 20; grain stores in, 156; granaries, 152–53; hinterland, 60–63; industrial sectors, 210–14; industrialization, 210; landed capital in, 61–63; manufacturing in, 210–14; mediatization of, 45, 105–6; population growth, 27, 31–32; Religious Peace of, 38; siege of, 40; textile industry in, 171–72
Augsburg Confession, 37
Augsburg Interim, 37
Augusta Vindelicum, 20
Augustinian Canons, 28
Ausfertigung, 138
Aussteuer, 138

341

Austria, 140, 157
Axster, 172

Babenhausen, 63
Bakers' Guild, 211-12
Baur, Felix, 154
Baur, Michael, 127
Bausch, Johann, 217
Bavaria, 131, 140, 160, 168; as source of wood, 162; Augsburg's location on border of, 23; Duke of, 156; Kingdom of, 45; political relations with, 27, 37
Bavarian Servants' Ordinance, 244
Beck, Heinrich, 272
Beckhin, Susanna, 137-38
Beham, Jerg, 259
Beirin, Sophia, 218
Berthold, Johann, 215, 216
Bertholdin, Regina, 235
Betrugs-Lexikon, 202-3
Biberger, Sebastian, 196
Binenbach, 169
Binzin, Euphrosina, 262
Blintheim, 62
Bobingen, 62
Bock, Georg, 264
Bock, Johann, 263
Bodenburger, Otto Christoph, 271
Bogner, Thomas, 191
Bohemia, 157
Bohm, Andreas, 130
Böshin, Regina, 122
Braun, Matheus, 215
Braun, Michael, 259
Braunin, Theresia, 122
Brewers' Guild, 212
Breymair, Jakob, 258
budgeting, 11. See also practices, managerial
building sector, 225; orphans employed in, 225-26, 234
bureaucratization, 80
Burgadelshausen, 169
Burgau, 37

Calendar Conflict, 38, 39
Calvin, John, 285
capital, 173, 209; accumulation of, 31; active, 129-30; Alms Office, 41, 81-83; City Orphanage, 2; concentration of, 41-42, 49-51; confession-specific attitudes toward, 72-74; conformity encouraged by, 140-41; definition of, 11; fixed, 119; liquid, 143-44; orphans', 260-61; passive, 129-30; rewards and punishments, 140-41; sources of, 119-20; source of self-sufficiency, 138; source of solidarity, 143; transactions, 138
capitalism, 20, 113, 133, 145; early modern, 287; emergence of, 255; empirical, 9, 60, 79 80, 145, 280; existence of, 12; fiscal, 287; preconditions of, 285; spirit of, 285. See also Weber, Max; Weber Thesis
capitalist, 59; characteristics of, 123-24, 148n. 49, 237, 287; donors of charity, 33
Caspar, Franz Xavier, 140
Catholic Church, 26, 40
Catholic Orphanage: capital of, 126-32; commodities, 163-64; consumption, 184-87; disabled orphans in, 264-65; land, 66-72; mediatization, 106; parity, 48-49; relationship to Catholic foundations, 117-18, 185, 283; rents, 154; subventions, 87-97
centralization, 3, 7, 80
Chapel of St. James, 162
chapels, 35
charity: as cultural rite, 8; as market force, 280; as medium of capitalism, 287-89; as personal exchange, 29; confession-specific attitudes toward, 87, 92-93, 101-2, 173; economic nature of, 288; historical changes in, 7, 26, 33; institutionalized, 6; Marxist interpretation of, 10; motives, 7-8; nature of, 82; relationships to capitalism, 10, 20, 209-10, 279-80; social meaning, 8; utilitarianism in, 46-47
Charles V, Holy Roman Emperor, 37
children's moneys, 90, 98-99, 129, 130. See also property, orphan's
Church of the Holy Cross, 28, 101

Citizens' Confederation for the Bearing of Lights, 101
City Council, 1, 2, 3; authority over alms, 34; concern over fraud, 89; constitutional changes in 1548, 37; effects of Edict of Restitution, 40; fiscal policies, 44; investigation into orphanage budgets, 95; regulation of capital market, 123, 129; regulation of orphan care, 265; sale of state granaries, 153 54; subventions, 80, 86
City Orphanage, 2, 243; apprenticeship stipends, 134–35; budget of 1595, 193; capital, 124–25; clothing provided orphans, 172; commodities from Alms Office, 163–64; confessionalization, 39–40; consumption in, 183–87; contracting, 190–92; costs, 85, 183–84; costs of childcare, 184; costs of education, 185; costs of foodstuffs, 187–90; daily routines in, 248–50; diet, 194; differentiation of orphans, 250–51; division in 1649, 9; Edict of Restitution, 40; founding of, 1–2; hides provided, 172–73; income, 98–99; inspection of orphans, 249–50; labor, 185–87; land, 66–71; number of orphans, 184
Civilitate morum puerilium, 249
Cloister of St. Clara on the Horbruck, 34. See also Foundling Home
Closterholz, monastery of, 126
clothing: for orphans, 137; projected costs of, 180–82
clothing sector, 224; orphans employed in, 230–34
Coler Johannes, 218, 245
collections. See donations
College of St. Anna, Lutheran, 46, 185, 268
College of St. Salvador, Jesuit, 38
Colmar, 45
commodities, 151–74; as capital, 154–55, 173–74; speculation in, 157–58; theft of, 202; transactions in, 203
commodity market, 209
common good, 222, 224
communalization, 3, 7

confessionalization, 9, 37–39, 87, 94, 141–42, 244; economic strategies, 153–55; market orientations, 154
Constance, Lake, 20
Constitutio Carolina, 37, 56n. 11, 210–12, 226, 230
Construction Office, 209
consumption, 178–204; confession-specific patterns, 189, 283; costs of, 189–92
contracting, 11, 59, 167, 190–92, 281
costing, 12, 59, 152
cotton printing, 210
Counting House, 94
crafts, 210–14, 224
credit, 59. See also capital
Crisis of the Seventeenth Century, 40–42

dairy products, 188
Danube River, 160–1
David Linck, Hans Langnauer, Melchior Linck and Associates, 66
debt, 81. See also capital
decorative arts sector, 224; orphans employed in, 230, 234
demand, 167, 204, 209; aggregate, 151, 173–74, 178; economic function of, 151; manipulation by Alms Office, 163–73; orphanage use of, 281
Diettrichin, Maria, 122
Dietz, Johann, 212, 214
Dinkelscherben, 117–18
discipline, 103, 208; confessionalization of, 283; effect on market, 209; from capitalistic practices, 133, 180; labor, 6, 7, 218, 219; maintenance as means of, 262–66; of capital, 139–44; of consumption, 192, 200–01, 281; of state through markets, 97; prophylactic quality of, 258; punishments, 201–3, 204, 250; social, 7, 10, 83; time, 224, 248
domestic service: regulation of, 244–45. See also Bavarian Servants' Ordinance
donations, 11, 33, 79, 80–84; as capital, 2, 280–81; as income, 113, 118, 123–34, 144–45, 152; changing

levels of, 98–105; effects of parity on, 86–89
Dotenpfennige, 119–20, 147n. 28
dowry, 123, 137–38
drunkenness, 202
Durschner, Christian, 137, 236

earnings, 81–84, 113, 123–24, 144–45; as capital, 281; changing levels of 98–105; effects of parity on, 86–89. *See also* interest
Eberhardt, Michael, 190
Eberhart, Matheus, 267
Eberth, Ignatius, 136
economic strategies: confession specific, 90–91
economies of scale, 59, 166, 180, 198, 279–80; effect of parity on, 85
economy: market, 58, 65; moral, 58
Edict of Restitution, 39–40, 85
efficiency, 195–201, 273, 288; effect of parity on, 282; goal of poor relief, 50; source of capitalism, 286
egalitarianism, 135
Eglingen, 169
Eisenmayerin, Felicitas, 257
elders, 88, 97. *See also* alms lords
empiricism, 12
Engeller, Hanns, 261
Engellerin, Katharina, 261
endowment, 11; capital, 2; historical change in, 126
England, 157
Ensisheim, 135
entrepreneur, 12, 59, 229. *See also* capitalist
Erasmus, Desiderius, 249
Ettingen, Count of, 101
Ettinger, Caspar, 172
export: regulation of, 157

Falchin, Catharina, 263
Ferdinand, Holy Roman Emperor, 39
Fischer, Heinrich, 39, 40, 243
Fischer, Matheus, 135–36
flexibility. *See* adaptability
food sector, 224; orphans employed in, 225, 234
foodstuffs: patterns of consumption, 192–93; projected costs in orphanage, 181–83; real costs in orphanage, 187–89
foster home, 1, 2
fostering, 3
foundation, 79; bazaar-like array of, 31; charitable, 29–30, 38, 58, 81–83; decline of support for, 87; ecclesiastical, 58, 131; economic activities of, 151
Foucault, Michel, 7, 10, 166
Foundling Home, 5, 15n. 20, 34, 82, 106
Frey, Michael, 191
Friedberg, 160
Friedens-Executions-Receß, 42
Fugger, 27, 38, 63, 140, 153, 159; Anton Joseph, 46–47; Marquand, Count, 100
Furriers' Guild, 213–14
Furst, Samuel, 261
Füssen, 170
fustian, 27, 172, 180–82, 231

Gadner, Caspar Balthus, 72, 88–89, 100
Gaisfues, Hanns, 267
Gaisfues, Philip, 266–67
Garb, 130
Gassenhauptleute, 163
Gassenknecht, 267
Gauting, 20
Gerner, Ulrich, 216
Getreidegilt, 157
Gienger, Hans, 172
gifts, 80. *See also* donations
Gignoux, Franz, 137, 236
Glöggle, Ulrich, 266
gluttony, 201, 202
goldsmithing, 212, 228–29; putting-out system in, 229
Goldsmiths' Guild, 268
Gottberate, 30
governess, 197
Graf, Franz, 119
grain, 151; acquisition of, 160–61; marketplace, 157–58; price of, 166–67; projected cost in orphanage, 181–83; stores of, 156–61
great enclosure, 7
Greiff, Gerhard, 130, 131
Groß, Tobias, 118, 146n. 24

Gsell, Hans, 225–26
Gueter, August, 220
guild: regulation, 6, 213–14
Gürtler, Jeremias, 267

Hainrich, Hanns, 191
Haldenberg, Christoph Rehlinger von, 160
Handwerksgerechtigkeit, 213
Harder, Hieronymus, 168
Hartmannsberger, Bernhart, 191
Haustafel, 218, 245
hausväterliche Literatur, 218
Heimat, 289
Helena Streissin Business, 124
Herrenstube, 34
hides: provided as poor relief, 172–73
Hieber, Anton, 138
Hillerbrand, Johann Georg, 131
Hindenmayr, Matthäus, 128
Hirn, Konrad and Afra, 34
Hirsch, Conrad, 271
Hofel, 127
Hoffmann, Sebastian, 216
Hoffschneider, Hans, 259
Holl, Jonas, 122
Holy Roman Empire, 23, 31
Holzhäuser, 38
Hörn, Paul, 202–3
Hoser, Jacob, 261
hospital, 6, 28–29, 58, 134, 166, 190
hostel, 214
household: comparative expenses, 192–94
housewares: projected cost in orphanage, 180–81; real cost in orphanages, 187
Hungary, 140, 156, 157
Hungerin, Anna Maria, 137

ideal type, 286
ideology, 59
Iherot, Paul Gottfried, 216
Ilsung, Johann Christoph Ignatz Maria, 115
Imhof, Hieronymus, 62
Imhof, Philipp Jacob, 169, 243–47
immigration, 31, 44; consequences for confessionalization, 45–46
Income Office, 84, 130

indoctrination, 6. See also discipline
infirmary, 264–65
inflation, 1, 87, 125, 167; of 1571–52, 1, 8, 19, 35; of 1622–23, 40, 88, 156, 162; of 1770–71, 44
inheritance, 121–22
institution, 17n. 42
interest, 11, 81–83. See also earnings
investment, 120. See also endowment
involution, 273
Italy, 156, 157
itio in partes, 42

James Suburb, 23, 26
journeymen: dependence on masters, 213; finding employment, 212–13; maintenance of, 269–72

Kaisser, Carol, 267
Kammer, Leonhart, 144
Kaufbeuren, 45
Kaufleutestube, 34, 142, 172
Kempten, 131
Kesseler, Caspar, 191
Kieffer, Johann Baltas, 262
Kinderfriedensfest, 199
Kipper- und Wipperzeit. See inflation of 1622–23
Klauck Foundation, 106
Kling, Jonas Paul, 264
Köpfin, Regina, 218
Kornmesser, 158
Kraus, 267
Krez, Kaspar, 244

labor, 6, 20; independence of, 60; subcontracted, 209
labor market, 209–37, 247; information in, 214; regulation of, 213
Lady Suburb, 26
Laire, Peter, 128, 143
land: confessionalization of, 72–74; role in economic strategies, 62, 63–66; uses by orphanages, 66–71; value, 73–74
Langenmantel, 28, 142; Bernhard Valentin, 94; Johann Georg Anton, 114–16
lard, 151, 161; account, 102; stores of, 168; price of 168–69

Lauterer, Jörg, 270
Lech Quarter, 23
Lech River, 20, 170
Lechhausen, 122
legacies, 80–81, 98. See also donations; testaments
leisure, 251, 252
Leonberger Accord, 40
leprosarium, 29
Leschin, Maria, 122
Leschin, Sybilla, 122
Leschin, Veronika, 122
Leyh, Johann Sigmund, 220
lien, 153
Limm, Hanns, 39, 122, 248
Lindau, 20, 131
Lindemann, Christian Philipp, 137
linens: projected cost in orphanage, 180–82
Lipp, Jacob, 138
Lippin, Anna Barbara, 138
liturgy: donations for, 39
livre de congé, 212
Lorenz, 143–44
Lorenz, Balthasar, 160
Louis XIV, King of France, 156
Low Countries, 157
Luther, Martin, 155, 158
Luther Catechism, 249
Lutheran Beneficent Foundation, 106–7
Lutheran Orphanage, 63; apprenticeship stipends, 136–37; capital transactions, 125, 127–28, 130–32; commodities from Alms Office, 163–64; costs of consumption, 184–87; diet, 194–201, 207; disabled orphans, 264–65; income, 97–105; labor relations, 217–20; land, 66, 72; mediatization, 106–7; new building, 153; parity, 48–49; relationship to Lutheran merchants, 128, 283; rents, 154; subventions, 87–97. See also Ordinance of 1780
Lutz, Eustachius, 191
luxuries, 181–82

maintenance: of orphan apprentices, 261–65, 269–72

Mair, Hanns, 259
Mair, Paulus, 268
Mairin, Sabina, 271
manager, 59
Mangeldt, Peter, 272
Manlich Company, 66
market, 1; confession-specific involvement in, 154–55; effects of charity on, 174; effects on charity, 209; effects on orphanages, 58; for capital, 11, 12, 114, 116, 118, 129, 138, 142; for commodities, 12; for labor, 12; imperfections, 19; mentality, 97; regulation of, 155–56
marketplace, 1, 11, 13; confession-specific engagement in, 154–55; location, 23
Martin Zobel Foundation, 124
Marx, Karl, 10
master: finding hands, 212, 213; obligations, 245; recruitment of, 215, 216; relationship to hands, 6; relationship to orphanage, 209–10; rights and responsibilities, 220–24
Mausihler, Jörg, 68, 191
Mayr, Abraham, 269
Mayr, Leonhart, 216
meat: consumption in orphanages, 188; projected cost in orphanage, 183; real cost in orphanages, 188–89
Meixner, Isaac, 261–62
Memmingen, 20, 131
merchant, 62–63
Merseberg, 214
Mertz, Johann Daniel, 263
metal sector, 225; orphans employed in, 227, 234
Metzger, Jacob, 271
Meuting, 27
Michel, Johann Christoph, 130
middlemen, 158; regulation of, 160–63; use of, 168
Miller, Lienhart, 135
mobility: of apprentices, 268
monthly moneys, 89, 102
Muller, Leonhard Jacob, 220
Mullerin, Maria Margaretha Barbara, 140
Münch, Christian von, 63
Munich, 20, 138, 268

Nachbäcker, 211
Nagel, Johann Christoph, 220
Need House, 34
Neher, Jerg, 259
Neuhoferin, Sabina, 131
New Orphanage, 85
Newmayr, Hans Jerg, 122
Nördlingen, 121, 272
North, Douglass, 17n. 42
Nuremberg, 134, 135, 271; Alms Ordinance of 1380, 30–31

Oberbach, Jacob, 263
Oeconomia, 218, 245
Oestreich, Gerhard, 7, 16n. 27
opportunity costs, 151, 152
Ordinance of 1780: apprentices' clothing, 262; daily routines, 251–58; diet, 197–201; discipline, 255–56, 258; education, 254–55; efficiency, 255, 257; excursions, 254; governess, 253–54, 255, 256–58; house tailor, 253, 254; instruction, 253; journeyman's suit, 270; masters' interests, 262–63, 269; out-placement, 221–24; praeceptor, 253, 255–58; recreation, 251–52; regulation of orphans in the workplace, 265–66; release policy, 252; settlement, 270; visitors, 252; work, 252–53
organization, 287
orphans: definition of, 5; education of, 3; employment of, 224; fates of, 234–37; number of, 36, 39; out-placement of, 214–20; property of, 103–4, 118–19, 120–23, 141–42
orphan father, 234, 243; as capitalist, 132–33, 204, 287; as manager, 2, 3, 12; as purchaser, 179; authority, 2, 3, 255, 256; diet of, 195; duties of, 5, 86, 89, 118–19, 133; malfeasance by 88, 92–93, 114; social origins of, 5
orphan mother, 217–20; 255
orphanage: as capitalistic organization, 286–89; as clearinghouse for labor, 247, 273–74; as consumer, 178–79; as employer, 209; as family, 246; as halfway house for labor, 247, 258 272, 273; as industrial schools, 224; as intermediary between masters and hands, 259–61, 265; as marketplace for labor, 210, 215, 247, 273, 282; as schoolhouse for labor, 247, 248–58, 273; as source of labor, 215; capital transactions, 113–23; capitalistic nature of, 75; consumption in, 36; education, 248; effect on labor discipline, 273; effect on labor markets, 209; effect on labor supply, 275; effect on transaction costs of labor, 247; engagement in work process, 209; estimated cost of, 2; founding of, 1; in labor market, 265; jail in, 202; land, 58, 60; *lectio continuo* in, 249; leisure in, 250–51; maintenance of labor, 282; mediation of labor, 282; proposal of 1572, 178, 180–83, 192–95, 209–10; regulation of labor market, 217; relationship to orphans, 258, 263–65; sale in 1697, 153; staff, 36; work in, 250–51
Oswaldt, Hanns, 39
Ott, Abraham, 259
Ott, Melchior, 127

parity, 9, 19, 282–85; confession-specific interpretations of, 92, 93; consequences for City Orphanage, 42, 43; debate in Alms Office, 88–97; division of political power, 42; division of property, 43–44; effect on Alms Office, 488–49; effect on capital, 116, 118; effect on commodities, 152–55; effect on economy, 43–44, 289; effect on income, 84–97; effect on orphanages, 48–49; effect on property, 71–75; institution of, 2; renewal in 1788, 49, 95–97
pater familias, 240
paternalism, 138, 284–85
Pawn Shop, 128
Peace of Westphalia, 42–44
persistence, 222
Peuttinger, Christoph, 101
Pfaff, Caspar, 271
Pfaffenhofen, 20

Pfefferlin, Jochim, 68
Pfleger, 115
Pfrund, 30, 119, 146n. 24
Pilgerhaus, 5, 34. See also Pilgrim House
Pilgrim House, 265, 271
Place de grève, 212
Police Ordinance: of Augsburg, 26, 33; of Württemberg, 26; of 1559, 266
Polier, Johann, 137, 270
poor: as cultural object, 8; deserving, 34; honorable, 89; number of, 27–28, 34, 35–36, 45–46
Poor House, 46, 209
poor relief, 3, 9, 13; as system of redistribution, 179; characteristics of, 3; historical changes in, 82; relationship to market, 85, 142, 209. See also charity
poverty, 8–10, 29, 33
practices: capitalistic, 11–13, 50–51, 58–60, 68–71, 107, 132, 142, 203–4, 280, 288–89; managerial, 11, 74, 83, 132, 145–46, 167, 190, 203–4, 280–81. See also accounting; budgeting; contracting; costing; supervising
praeceptor, 197, 209
Predigthaus at St. Ulrich's, Lutheran, 249–50
price, 209; changes in, 151; regulation of, 155–59, 162
Price Revolution, 20. See also inflation
Printzing, Tobias, 221
Prinzingin, Sabina, 264
Probst, Hans Georg, 136
production, 60; artisanal, 6, 210; industrial, 209; mode, 11; protoindustrial, 27; social relations of, 6, 139, 213–14, 284; specialization, 212
profit, 280
proletarianization, 31
proletariat, 10
property: movable, 71; orphans' 2, 133–38; radical distribution of, 20, 27–28, 32–33, 41–42, 44–45, 49–51; real, 58, 71; restoration to Lutheran Church, 42–43
Protestantism: relationship to capitalism, 285
proto-factory, 210
provisions lords, 160
Provisions Office, 35, 178, 203; distributor of commodities, 193; purchaser of commodities, 159–63, 168
public works, 209
purchase account, 89
putting-out system, 171

Rad, Christoph von, 130
rationality, 286
rationalization, 287
Rauner, Johann Thomas, 131
Reformation, 3, 36–37, 61–62, 156; registration, 3, 5
Rehlingen, 159; Leopold Ferdinand von, 72, 88–90, 92, 101, 152–53; Maria Josepha Antonia von, 115–16
Rehlinger, 27, 117; Leonhart, 81
Reichard, 172
Reichsstadtvogt, 115
Reischle, Jacob, 136
Rem, Lucas, 27, 160
rent, 61, 64, 72, 115, 127–28
Renz, Ferdinand, 130
Rinental, 169
Roeck, Bernd, 39, 41, 45
Rößle, Jacob, 271
Rothenburg ob der Tauber, 270
routine, 281
routinization, 6, 197–99. See also discipline
Rupfen, 172

Salzburg, 20
sanitaria, 28–29
Scandinavia, 157
Schaumann, Hieronymus, 140
Schaumännin, Theresia, 122–23
Schäzler, Johann Lorenz Freiherr von, 107
Schendell, Johann Wolfgang, 221
Schillerin, Wallburga, 140
Schlaraffenland, 192
Schlemmer, 215
Schmalkaldic War, 37
Schmid, Thomas, 140
Schmiedin, Ursula, 243

Schneid, Mates, 169
Schnurbein, Balthasar von, 62
Schönfeld, Johann, 215
Schuester, 143
Schuester, Balthasar, 206
Schuester, Joseph, 127
Schuester, Joseph Tobias, 216
Schuester, Tobias, 120–22
Schüle, Johann Heinrich von, 210
Schumpeter, Joseph A., 148n. 49
Schwab, 127
Schwalb, Johann Christoph, 215
Schweigger, Hanns, 271–72
Sedelmairin, Maria, 267
Seelgeräte, 30
Seelhaus, 30
Seidler, Hanns, 272
Seitz, Bartholome, 135–36
Seitz, Jeremias, 109
self-sufficiency, 7, 8, 222, 223; of Alms Office, 107; of orphanages, 69–71; of orphans, 123, 137–38, 237, 248, 265, 269, 272
Sembler, Johann Franz, 127
Senate, 247. See also City Council
servants: domestic, 243–47
service: domestic, 267. See also servants
Seuter, Matheus, 215
Seybold, Jonas, 243
Seyfrid, Anna Catharina, 116–17
Seyfried, Johann Georg, 216
shelter, 180–81
Shopkeepers' Guild, 211
Siebentischlerwald, 199
Sigmaringen, Count of, 135
sobriety, 200
society: hierarchical, 26–27, 32, 44–45, 145, 200
Sombart, Werner, 15n. 17, 285, 287
Sozialdisziplinierung. See discipline, social
Spangenburg, Cyriacus, 218, 248–49
specialization, 6, 265
Stadtmetzg, 32, 161
standardization, 184; as response to rising costs, 192; as source of discipline, 192–201
Steber, Imanuel, 210
Stegherr, Johann Georg, 264
Stenglin, Lucas, 46, 130

Stetten: David von, 160; Paul von, 62, 105, 228
Stöcklin, Hanns, 2, 39, 178, 180, 182–84
stockpiles. See stores
stockpiling, 281
stores, 151–52; by private families, 159; economic function of, 167
Straßvogtei, 61
Sturm, Johann, 218
subsidies. See subvention
subvention, 2, 11, 36, 113, 118, 123–24, 144–45, 280; as consequence of crisis, 41; changing levels of, 98–105; confession-specific disparities, 48; effects of parity on, 79, 83–84, 86–89; reforms in, 48–49
Sulzer, Wolfgang Jakob, 128
superintendent, 222–23
supervising, 4
supervision: of orphans, 255–58
supply, 163, 167, 209
Swabia, 23, 161, 168
Sylvestergeld, 219

tallow, 151, 161
tariffs, 157, 158
taxes: indirect, 83–84
technology: machine, 59
testaments, 155, 159. See also legacies
Teufelliteratur, 239n. 34
textiles: as commodity, 171; as poor relief, 171; distributed by Alms Office, 172; marketplace, 162; stores of, 172
theft, 202
Thirty Years' War, 38–42, 156, 179
thrift, 59, 199
training, 3, 6
transactions, 209
Treaty of Westphalia, 282
Trentwed, Balduino, 268
Tyrol, 161

Ulm, 23, 131, 268
Ulrich, Bishop of Augsburg, 28
Ulstett, Lucas, 168
uniformity, 197–98
Upper City, 26
utility, 222

values: capitalistic, 12; related to charity, 82
Venice, 136
Vetter, Hans, 135
Via Claudia Augusta, 23
virtues: bourgeois, 284–85
Vogel, 143
Vogel, Jörg, 134–35, 137
Vogel, Thomas, 134–35
Vogelmair, Hans, 135
Vorbäcker, 211
Vorsteher, 139. See also superintendent

wages, 209
Wagner, Friderich, 268
Walter, 130
Wangner, Barthlme, 135
Wanner, Johann Bonaventura, 169
war, 88; of the League of Augsburg, 87, 109n. 20; of the Spanish Succession, 47, 73, 88
Wasser, Johann Jakob, 139
waste, 210–3
weaving, 231–33. See also textiles
Weber, Eustachius, 266
Weber, Max, 17n. 42, 29, 148n. 49, 285–87
Weber Thesis, 285–87
weekly assistance, 84
Weidenauer, Paulus, 216
Weiding, 169
Weisin, Maria Sabina, 217–20, 236, 254
welfare, 82

Welser, 27; Lorenz Sigmund, 131; Maria, 62
Wenzer, Hartmann Lorenz, 140
Werewag, 172
Wertach River, 20
Westermayer, Abraham, 262
Wickert, Jonas, 261
Widenmann: Hans Jerg, 136; Leonhard, 267; Lorentz, 216
Widholz, Daniel Philipp, 128
Winterholer, Bernhard, 140
Wissertshausen, 169
Wolf, David, 217
Wolfegg, Countess of, 101
Wolhöferin, Gertraut, 216–17
Wöllenburg, Count of, 101
wood, 151; 161–62; distribution of, 169; marketplaces for, 162; prices of, 169–70; purchases of, 169; stores of, 169
wood account, 102
wood sector, 211; orphans employed in, 226, 234
woolen weavers' account, 89
work ethic, 3, 46
Workhouse, 6, 46, 209
Württemberg, 209

Ziehmutter, 217
Zink, Burkhard, 27
Zobel, Anna Regina, 130
Zolling, Lucas, 172
Zusam River, 63

STUDIES IN CENTRAL EUROPEAN HISTORIES

FORTHCOMING
FALL 1999

*Before the Enemy is Within Our Walls. Catholic Workers in Cologne. 1885-1912:
A Social, Cultural and Political History*
Raymond Chien Sun

*On the Verge of War: International Relations and the Jülich-Kleve
Succession Crises (1609-1614)*
Alison Deborah Anderson

Priest and Parish in Vienna. 1780 to 1880
William David Bowman

Fertility, Wealth, and Politics in Three Southwest German Villages 1650-1900
Ernest Benz

*The Cross and the Ballot:
Catholic Political Parties in Germany, Switzerland, Austria, Belgium and
the Netherlands. 1785-1985*
Ellen Lovell Evans

PUBLISHED

*Communal Reformation: The Quest
for Salvation in Sixteenth-Century Germany*
Peter Blickle

*Protestant Politics: Jacob Sturm (1489-1553)
and the German Reformation*
Thomas A. Brady

*Military System and Social Life in
Old Regime Prussia, 1713-1807: The
Beginnings of the Social Militarization
of Prusso-German Society*
Otto Büsch

*Karl Lamprecht:
A German Academic Life (1856-1915)*
Roger Chickering

*Conflicting Visions of Reform: German Lay
Propaganda Pamphlets, 1519-1530*
Miriam Usher Christian

*Migration and Urbanization
in the Ruhr Valley, 1821-1914*
James H. Jackson

*Revolution from the Right:
Politics, Class, and the
Rise of Nazism in Saxony,
1919-1933*
Benjamin Lapp

*German Encounters with Modernity:
Novels of Imperial Berlin*
Katherine Roper

*Charity and Economy in the Orphanages of
Early Modern Augsburg*
Thomas Max Safley

*Alfred von Tirpit and
German Right-Wing Politics,
1914-1930*
Raffael Scheck

*German Villages in Crisis: Rural Life in
Hesse-Kassel and the Thirty Year's War
1580-1730*
John Theibault

*Communities and Conflict in
Early Modern Colmar: 1575-1730*
Peter G. Wallace